D0918620

EQUALITY
OF
EDUCATIONAL
OPPORTUNITY

EQUALITY
OF
EDUCATIONAL
OPPORTUNITY

A Handbook for Research
Edited, with an Introduction, by
LaMar P. Miller
and
Edmund W. Gordon

AMS Press, Inc.
New York

370.1934
M648e

Copyright © 1974 AMS Press, Inc.

All rights reserved. Published in the United States of America by AMS Press, Inc., 56 East 13th Street, New York, New York 10003

Library of Congress Cataloging in Publication Data

Miller, LaMar P   comp.
    Equality of educational opportunity.

    1. Educational equalization—United States—
Addresses, essays, lectures. 2. Handicapped
children—Education—United States—Addresses, essays,
lectures. I. Gordon, Edmund W., joint comp.
II. Title.
LA210.M54   370.19'34   73-9244
ISBN 0-404-10535-1

Manufactured in the United States of America

table of contents

V. NEW PERSPECTIVES FOR RESEARCH

chapter 13: future problems and research

acknowledgments

Acknowledgement is made to the authors and publishers below who have granted permission to reprint material and who reserve all rights in the articles appearing in this anthology.

Carlson, "Equalizing Educational Opportunity," *Review of Educational Research*, Volume 42, Number 4, Fall, 1972, pp. 453-475.

Carroll, "Basic and Applied Research in Education," *Harvard Educational Review*, Volume 38, Spring, 1968, pp. 263-276. Copyright © by President and Fellows of Harvard College.

Cohen, "Politics and Research," *Review of Educational Research*, Volume 40, Number 2, pp. 213-238.

Coleman, "The Concept of Equality of Educational Opportunity," *Harvard Educational Review*, Volume 38, Winter, 1968, pp. 7-22. Copyright © 1968 by President and Fellows of Harvard College.

Deutsch, Platt, and Senghaas, "Conditions Favoring Major Advances in Social Science," *Science*, Volume 171, February 5, 1971, pp. 450-459.

Dreger and Miller, Excerpts from "Comparative Psychological Studies of Negroes and Whites in the United States: 1959-1965," *Psychological Bulletin Monograph Supplement*, Volume 70, Number 3, Part 2, September 1968, pp. 19-24 and pp. 37-39.

Epps, "Correlates of Academic Achievement among Northern and Southern Urban Negro Students," *Journal of Social Issues*, Volume 25, Number 3, pp. 55-70.

Frank, "Evaluation of Educational Programs," *Young Children*, 1969, National Association for the Education of Young Children, Washington, D. C.

Friedenberg, "Social Consequences of Educational Measurement," *Proceedings of the 1969 Invitational Conference on Testing Problems*, 1970, Educational Testing Service, New York, New York.

Gordon, "Compensatory Education," *IRCD Bulletin*, Volume VI, Number 5, December, 1970, pp. 1-5.

Gordon, "Equalizing Educational Opportunity in the Public School," *IRCD Bulletin*, Volume III, Number 5, pp. 1-4.

Gordon, "Significant Trends in the Education of the Disadvantaged," *ERIC-IRCD Urban Disadvantaged Series*, Number 17, August, 1970, Eric Information Retrieval Center on the Disadvantaged, Teachers College, Columbia University, New York, New York 10027.

Gordon, "Toward Defining Equality of Educational Opportunity," from *On Equality of Educational Opportunity*, edited by Frederick Mostellar and Daniel P. Moynihan, Copyright © 1972 Random House, Inc.

Gowin and Millman, "Research Methodology — A Point of View," *Review of Educational Research*, Volume 39, Number 5, December, 1969, pp. 553-560.

Jensen, O'Kane, Graybeal, and Friedrichs, "Evaluating Compensatory Education," *Education in Urban Society*, Volume 4, Number 2, February, 1972, pp. 211-233.

Katz, "Review of Evidence Relating to the Effects of Desegregation on the Intellectual Performance of Negroes," *American Psychologist*, 1964, Volume 19, Number 6, pp. 381-399.

Mercer, "Sociocultural Factors in Labeling Mental Retardates," *Peabody Journal of Education*, Volume 48, April, 1971, pp. 188-203.

St. John, "Desegregation and Minority Group Performance," *Review of Educational Research*, Volume 40, Number 1, pp. 111-133.

Shulman, "Reconstruction of Educational Research," *Review of Educational Research*, Volume 40, Number 3, pp. 371-396.

Teaching and Learning Research Corporation, "The Purpose, Design Interpretation, and Policy Determination of Evaluation Research," from *Utilizing Information from Evaluation, Research, and Survey Data Concerning Compensatory Education*, 1971, New York, pp. 153-157.

Wax and Wax, "Indian Communities and Project Head Start," Report for the U. S. Office of Economic Opportunity, Contract OEO-520, September 15, 1965.

Weikart, "Comparative Study of Three Preschool Curricula," paper presented at the biennial meeting of the Society for Research in Child Development, Santa Monica, California, March, 1969.

introduction

This handbook is an outgrowth of a manual prepared for the U.S. Office of Education's Office of Equal Educational Opportunity which was designed to provide an orientation for people working in the field. Its content is embedded in two historical frameworks. The first is the history of American education in which the basic underlying premise is that education is a means of achieving equality in our society. The other is the development of educational research in the United States which was founded on a deep conviction that we could find solutions to complex problems through scientific inquiry.

The 1954 Supreme Court decision, Brown vs. The Board of Education, highlighted the importance of equality of opportunity in education and gave legal recognition to the concept. This monumental decision affecting the education of millions of children raised a variety of related issues which have been contaminated by political questions related to public policy as well as by emotional attitudes which color such considerations. For this reason research has been unable to yield clear-cut answers to prematurely posed and intricate questions. Whatever else it may be, equality of educational opportunity is an intriguing, important, and complex phenomenon. Like other concepts which affect education, it attracts scientific attention because it is intriguing, and it merits careful research because it is important. Finally, the assumption warrants our attention as educators because of more than 300 years of subjugation of black and other minority citizens in the American experience.

Whereas a number of people had been concerned with the issue of inequality in the schools prior to 1954, the Supreme Court decision resulted in legislation, compensatory education programs, direct action efforts to bring about desegregation, and at least one major research effort. Legislation includes the enactment of the Civil Rights Act, the Elementary and Secondary Education Act in 1965, and the Emergency School Aid Act of 1972. The most important research effort was the publication in 1966 of the Coleman Report. Each of these events in one way or another was based on the notion that schools, given the resources, could do much more to offer all Americans equal educational opportunity. As a result we have spent millions of dollars on educational research and accumulated a large body of literature.

Except for the Coleman Report, however, the literature on equal educational opportunity has been largely polemic and includes few investigations that can be considered good research. Some studies were obviously influenced by the work of Coleman but few inquiries focused directly on equality of opportunity. On the other hand, researchers from a wide variety of disciplines have conducted investigations which indirectly concentrate on problems which have significance for equal educational opportunity. Psychologists studied the motivation and aspirations of individuals; anthropologists surveyed traits dealing with culture; sociologists investigated the middle class, the lower class, minorities and institutions; and the linguists studied the non-verbal, the non-communicative or those learning English as a second language. In the meantime, educators explored the dropout, the underachiever and the disadvantaged. Since researchers were often locked into specific disciplines, only a few individuals looked at the problem from a multi-faceted point of view. As a consequence, the task of unraveling the many factors involved and of subjecting them to systematic inquiry has left us with many voids in the research literature on equal educational opportunity.

As public concern with finding solutions to the many problems involved in schooling increases, the demand for research on equal educational opportunity mounts. Individuals trained in this area, however, are in short supply. Thus in keeping with the original purpose, the handbook is intended to serve as an introduction and resource for readers whose previous experience and preparation have not included systematic training in evaluation and research. Since the handbook brings together major efforts by noted investigators whose work is related either directly or indirectly to equality of educational opportunity, it will serve as a reference work, as a tool in formulating new investigations, and as an aid for administrators in school districts across the country. Others should also find the book useful – the professor of education who teaches courses relating to the disadvantaged; the student preparing to work in a wide variety of fields or to do research; and the citizen who is interested in what affects children and their education.

ORGANIZATION AND FORMAT

Since the book is intended to serve a wide audience, we chose a traditional organization and format. To most successfully benefit our readers we decided that Part I would provide some notion of the meaning of equality of educational opportunity. Indeed the need for introducing the handbook by defining and assessing equal educational opportunity took on added significance in view of the discussion precipitated by Jencks in his book *Inequality* and the resulting controversy over the distinction made between the concepts of equality of opportunity and equality of results. The fact that the assumption has been brought into question suggests that, in spite of our previous acceptance of the notion, various interested parties and groups see equality of educational opportunity in different ways. James Coleman, in his article, "The Concept of Equality of Educational Opportunity," uses an evolutionary perspective in order to show how the meaning of equal educational opportunity has changed over the past century and a half. Whereas the responsibility for providing equal educational opportunity resided within the individual family unit, Coleman feels that today and in the future, educational institutions are obligated to take on this responsibility. Some of the ways in which educational institutions might begin to create equality of opportunity are discussed by Edmund Gordon in his article, "Toward Defining Equality of Educational Opportunity." It is Gordon's major premise that if the schools are going to be responsible for providing equal opportunities for all learners, they must compensate for the unequal learning achievements and patterns children bring to the classroom. The core of compensatory education would be individualized learning experiences based on each child's unique learning characteristics.

Part II, a discussion of the implications of research and evaluation, is important as a result of the national thrust of large scale programs of social action in education, and the controversy that has surrounded evaluation efforts. The objectives of program evaluation in education have changed radically since the establishment of the educational improvement programs in the early 1960's. Moreover, there has been a change in thinking from the more traditional method of looking at schools in terms of the quality of the school plant, the facilities and the credentials of professional personnel to a reliance on measuring the performance of the children who attend the schools. Thus we are faced with the issue of testing and its relationship to political, social and ideological questions. Edgar Friedenberg discusses, "The Social Consequences of Educational Measurement." He suggests that in America we have been under an illusion of objectivity insofar as tests are concerned because biases useful in maintaining our status structure and our institutions are successfully hidden beneath several levels of abstraction. He maintains that most individuals are unlikely to recognize the biases inherent in the practice of basing judgments that may determine the life and even the death of a youngster. David Cohen in his article, "Politics and Research: Evaluation of Social Action Programs in Education," suggests that educational improvement programs such as Headstart and Follow-through, differ from traditional objectives of educational evaluation since they are social action programs directed at millions of children, created by Congress and administered by Federal agencies rather than programs that are more narrow in scope, conceived by school personnel and administered by institutions closer to home. He explores these differences by suggesting major new evaluation problems. He attempts to delineate the political character of new programs, to define the major obstacles, to evaluate and to suggest some new elements of a strategy which might improve the evaluation of social action programs.

Part III provides an overview of research which in our judgment is essential for those who need a background for examining the concept of educational equality. John B. Carroll discusses differences and interactions between applied and basic research in his article, "Basic and Applied Research in Education: Definitions, Distinctions, and Implications." It is his conclusion that there is a strong need for both types of research in education, and that recent government funding policies giving support to applied research ought to be modified in the direction of providing a better balance. Kenneth Carlson in his article, "Equalizing Educational Opportunity," reviews evidence of the financial inequities, both between and within schools, and expresses the view that economic inequality is at the root of unequal educational opportunities. Carlson argues that equalizing opportunity in education means compensating for the disadvantages of a poor home environment. It is his conviction that federal support ought to be given to a variety of programs designed to offset and possibly prevent the inequalities disadvantaged children suffer as a result of their poverty environment.

In "Significant Trends in the Education of the Disadvantaged," Edmund Gordon presents an extensive review of the literature on the education of the disadvantaged minority group pupil. He critically reviews studies dealing with population characteristics of minority students as well as research which describes and evaluates compensatory education programs. In addition, areas in which further investigation is needed are pointed out. Nancy St. John provides an exhaustive review of empirical evidence relating school desegregation to the academic performance of black children in her article, "Desegregation and Minority Group Performance." In surveying "pre-Coleman, Coleman, and post-Coleman" research on desegregation, she notes that most of the findings show that students usually perform better (and certainly no worse) in integrated schools. However, because of political problems involved in conducting research in this area, virtually all of the studies done suffer from a lack of adequate experimental controls. A great many of the investigations have failed to control for school quality and family background. While such methodological problems prevent us from accepting any definite conclusions about the effect of school desegregation on minority group achievement, St. John points out that perfectly controlled research in this area is extremely difficult to do because we are dealing with "real life" as opposed to laboratory situations.

The heart of the book is Part IV, "Exemplary Evaluation and Research Studies." We have categorized the investigations included in this chapter as status, experimental, survey, evaluative,, comparative and descriptive. Under status studies, we have included Edmund Gordon's summary of the Coleman Report. This is a vitally important article because as Dr. Gordon suggests, "it points to the findings generated by the Coleman data which most reviewers feel would stand the test of reanalyzing or reinvestigation should the study be replicated or its data subjected to further analysis." In addition, we have included a summary of the U.S. Commission on Civil Rights Report, "Racial Isolation in the Public Schools." The handbook would be incomplete without the inclusion of this history making report which included among its major findings the contention that racial isolation in the public schools, whatever its origin, inflicts harm upon Negro students and that it is intense and is growing worse.

As we expected the task of finding experimental investigation was more difficult. Irwin Katz, however, has put together a series of excellent studies in his, "Review of Evidence Relating to the Effects of Desegregation on the Intellectual Performance of Negroes." These studies suggest very strongly that motivation does affect intellectual test performance. Similarly, Deutsch and Solomon in their article, "Patterns of Perceptual, Language and Intellective Performance in Children of Low Socioeconomic Status,," have written about the intervention enrichment program conducted by New York University's Institute for Developmental Studies in the Harlem Schools in New York City. This cognitively oriented program was aimed at assessing the interrelationship of effects of intervention programs. Under survey studies, we included LaMar Miller's, "Integration and Ethnic Studies in Elementary and Secondary Schools," which cites evidence that there is a close relationship between the physical integration of students and the integration of the curriculum. "Correlates of Academic Achievement Among Northern and Southern Urban Negro Students," by Edgar Epps, reports the results of a survey of high school students attending city schools in a large northern city and in a large southern city in order to identify some personality factors which are predictive of the Negro students capacity to utilize his intellectual potential to achieve academically.

Under evaluative research studies, David Weikart reports on the "Ypsilanti Pre-School Curriculum Demonstration Project," which was established to docu- ment and evaluate three curricula thought to have remedial potential for the disadvantaged. Philip K. Jensen et. al. have assessed the impact of a long range compensatory education program in Newark, New Jersey in their article, "Evaluating Compensatory Education."

Under comparative studies, Jane Mercer in her article, "Sociocultural Factors in Labeling Mental Retardates," explores the hypothesis that the high rate of examination of persons from lower social economic status and/or ethnic minorities to the status of mental retardates is related to an interaction between socio cultural factors and the clinical referral and labeling process which makes persons from these backgrounds more vulnerable to the labeling process than persons from the Anglo-middle class majority. We have also included excerpts from Dreger and Miller's "Comparative Psychological Studies of Negroes and Whites in the United States: 1959-1965." Two descriptive studies are included. One describing "The College Readiness Program for Third World Students in the College of San Mateo, California," by Carol Lopate, and the other describing, "Indian Communities and Project Headstart," by Murray and Rosalie Wax. We make no claim that those studies included in Part IV of the handbook are the most important or the only investigations dealing with equal educational opportunity. However, they are illustrative of the variety of research conducted to date around problems related to equality of educational opportunity.

Part V, "New Perspectives for Research," is self-explanatory. Looking at past research is obviously not enough. If the book is to serve its purpose, it ought to provide new directions, describe conditions which favor advances, and suggest how research might be reconstructed to lead to the kind of equality of education that benefits all Americans.

Moreover, our experience in the development of the book and in taking a broad look at related research suggests that there is a need to encourage more researchers to conduct investigations that will focus more directly on the concept of equality. We believe it is possible through a determined effort to find solutions to some of the heretofore unresolved problems. In essence, we hope that better research will affect the actions of those involved in attempts to provide equal educational opportunity in such a way that their efforts will not be misguided as they sometimes have been in the past and that the results will be more clearly and constructively discernible. Finally, we believe that the time has come for us to balance areas of moral and technical evaluation in education. Even the casual observer of the educational scene knows that steps need to be taken in the public interest to protect minorities from the impact of inequitable and traumatic social policy that result from spurious interpretations of research. While responsible scholarship must be protected so must the interest of the millions of minority children in our schools.

ACKNOWLEDGMENTS

A number of individuals at Teachers College, Columbia University contributed to the development of the handbook. Members of the staff of the National Center for Research in Equal Educational Opportunity contributed to the collecting of articles in various ways. To these individuals we are grateful. We are particularly indebted to Effie Bynum, Jean Barabas and Chester Thomas who shared the task of bringing together the original manual. Reneé Woloshin contributed much more than can ordinarily be expected of a graduate assistant. The tedious job of checking references, obtaining permissions from authors and publishers, and in keeping track of the immense amount of detail was undertaken with professional skill. To her we express our sincere appreciation. At New York University Rosie Caraballo carried much of the load in retyping many marked up pages of manuscript and in checking and proof reading the galleys and pages. And finally, to the many authors and publishers who granted us permission to use their works, we extend grateful acknowledgments.

—LaMar P. Miller
Edmund W. Gordon

I.
DEFINING
AND
ASSESSING
EQUAL
EDUCATIONAL
OPPORTUNITY

chapter 1
the meaning of equal educational opportunity

THE CONCEPT OF EQUALITY OF
EDUCATIONAL OPPORTUNITY

James Coleman

The concept of "equality of educational opportunity" as held by members of society has had a varied past. It has changed radically in recent years, and is likely to undergo further change in the future. This lack of stability in the concept leads to several questions. What has it meant in the past, what does it mean now, and what will it mean in the future? Whose obligation is it to provide such equality? Is the concept a fundamentally sound one, or does it have inherent contradictions or conflicts with social organization? But first of all, and above all, what is and has been meant in society by the idea of equality of educational opportunity?

To answer this question, it is necessary to consider how the child's position in society has been conceived in different historical periods. In pre-industrial Europe, the child's horizons were largely limited by his family. His station in life was likely to be the same as his father's. If his father was a serf, he would likely live his own life as a serf; if his father was a shoemaker, he would likely become a shoemaker. But even this immobility was not the crux of the matter; he was a part of the family production enterprise and would likely remain within this enterprise throughout his life. The extended family, as the basic unit of social organization, had complete authority over the child, and complete responsibility for him. This responsibility ordinarily did not end when the child became an adult because he remained a part of the same economic unit and carried on this tradition of responsibility into the next generation. Despite some mobility out of the family, the general pattern was family continuity through a patriarchal kinship system.

There are two elements of critical importance here. First, the family carried responsibility for its members' welfare from cradle to grave. It was a "welfare society," with each extended family serving as a welfare organization for its own members. Thus it was to the family's interest to see that its members became productive. Conversely, a family took relatively small interest in whether someone in *another* family became productive or not — merely because the mobility of productive labor between family economic units was relatively low. If the son of a neighbor was allowed to become a ne'er-do-well, it had little real effect on families other than his own.

The second important element is that the family, as a unit of economic production, provided an appropriate context in which the child could learn the things he needed to know. The craftsman's shop or the farmer's fields were appropriate training grounds for sons, and the household was an appropriate training ground for daughters.

In this kind of society, the concept of equality of educational opportunity had no relevance at all. The child and adult were embedded within the extended family, and the child's education or training was merely whatever seemed necessary to maintain the family's productivity. The fixed stations in life which most families occupied precluded any idea of "opportunity" and, even less, equality of opportunity.

With the industrial revolution, changes occurred in both the family's function as a self-perpetuating economic unit and as a training ground. As economic organization developed outside the household, children began to be occupationally mobile outside their families. As families lost their economic production activities, they also began to lose their welfare functions, and the poor or ill or incapacitated became more nearly a community responsibility. Thus the training which a child received came to be of interest to all in the community, either as his potential employers or as his potential economic supports if he became dependent. During this stage of development in eighteenth-century England, for instance, communities had laws preventing immigration from another community because of the potential economic burden of immigrants.

Further, as men came to employ their own labor outside the family in the new factories, their families became less useful as economic training grounds for their children. These changes paved the way for public education. Families needed a context within which their children could learn some general skills which would be useful for gaining work outside the family; and men of influence in the community began to be interested in the potential productivity of other men's children.

It was in the early nineteenth century that public education began to appear in Europe and America. Before that time, private education had grown with the expansion of the mercantile class. This class had both the need and resources to have its children educated outside the home, either for professional occupations or for occupations in the developing world of commerce. But the idea of general educational opportunity for all children arose only in the nineteenth century.

The emergence of public, tax-supported education was not solely a function of the stage of industrial development. It was also a function of the class structure in the society. In the United States, without a strong traditional class structure, universal education in publicly-supported free schools became widespread in the early nineteenth century; in England, the "voluntary schools," run and organized by churches with some instances of state support, were not supplemented by a state-supported system until the Education Act of 1870. Even more, the character of educational opportunity reflected the class structure. In the United States, the public schools quickly became the common school, attended by representatives of all classes; these schools provided a common educational experience for most American children — excluding only those upper-class children in private schools, those poor who went to no schools, and Indians and Southern Negroes who were without schools. In England, however, this class system directly manifested itself through the schools. The state-supported, or "board schools" as they were called, became the schools of the laboring lower classes with a sharply different curriculum from those voluntary schools which served the middle and upper classes. The division was so sharp that two government departments, the Education Department and the Science and Art Department, administered external examinations, the first for the products of the board schools, and the second for the products of the voluntary schools as they progressed into secondary education. It was only the latter curricula and examinations that provided admission to higher education.

What is most striking is the duration of influence of such a dual structure. Even today in England, a century later (and in different forms in most European countries), there exists a dual structure of public secondary education with only one of the branches providing the curriculum for college admission. In England, this branch includes the remaining voluntary schools which, though retaining their individual identities, have become part of the state-supported system.

This comparison of England and the United States shows clearly the impact of the class structure in society upon the concept of educational opportunity in that society. In nineteenth-century England, the idea of *equality* of educational opportunity was hardly considered; the system was designed to provide *differentiated* educational opportunity appropriate to one's station in life. In the United States as well, the absence of educational opportunity for Negroes in the South arose from the caste and feudal structure of the largely rural society. The idea of differentiated educational opportunity, implicit in the Education Act of 1870 in England, seems to derive from dual needs: the needs arising from industrialization for a basic education for the labor force, and the interests of parents in having one's own child receive a good education. The middle classes could meet both these needs by providing a free system for the children of laboring classes, and a tuition system (which soon came to be supplemented by state grants) for their own. The long survival of this differentiated system depended not only on the historical fact that the voluntary schools existed before a public system came into existence but on the fact that it allows both of these needs to be met: the community's collective need for a trained labor force, and the middle-class individual's interest in a better education for his own child. It served a third need as well: that of maintaining the existing social order — a system of stratification that was a step removed from a feudal system of fixed estates, but designed to prevent a wholesale challenge by the children of the working class to the positions held for children of the middle classes.

The similarity of this system to that which existed in the South to provide differential opportunity to Negroes and whites is striking, just as is the similarity of class structures in the second half of nineteenth-century England to the white-Negro caste structure of the southern United States in the first half of the twentieth century.

In the United States, nearly from the beginning, the concept of educational opportunity had a special meaning which focused on equality. This meaning included the following elements:

1. Providing a *free* education up to a given level which constituted the principal entry point to the labor force.

2. Providing a *common curriculum* for all children, regardless of background.

3. Partly by design and partly because of low population density, providing that children from diverse backgrounds attend the *same school*.

4. Providing equality within a given *locality*, since local taxes provided the source of support for schools.

This conception of equality of opportunity is still held by many persons; but there are some assumptions in it which are not obvious. First, it implicitly assumes that the existence of free schools eliminates economic sources of inequality of opportunity. Free schools, however, do not mean that the cost of a child's education become reduced to zero for families at all economic levels. When free education was introduced, many families could not afford to allow the child to attend school beyond an early age. His labor was necessary to the family — whether in rural or urban areas. Even after the passage of child labor laws, this remained true on the farm. These economic sources of inequality of opportunity have become small indeed (up through secondary education); but at one time they were a major source of inequality. In some countries they remain so; and certainly for higher education they remain so.

Apart from the economic needs of the family, problems inherent in the social structure raised even more fundamental questions about equality of educational opportunity. Continued school attendance prevented a boy from being trained in his father's trade. Thus, in taking advantage of "equal educational opportunity," the son of a craftsman or small tradesman would lose the opportunity to enter those occupations he would most likely fill. The family inheritance of occupation at all social levels was still strong enough, and the age of entry into the labor force was still early enough, that secondary education interfered with opportunity for working-class children; while it opened up opportunities at higher social levels, it closed them at lower ones.

Since residue of this social structure remains in present American society, the dilemma cannot be totally ignored. The idea of a common educational experience implies that this experience has only the effect of widening the range of opportunity, never the effect of excluding opportunities. But clearly this is never precisely true so long as this experience prevents a child from pursuing certain occupational paths. This question still arises with the differentiated secondary curriculum: an academic program in high school has the effect not only of keeping open the opportunities which arise through continued education, but also of closing off opportunities which a vocational program keeps open.

A second assumption implied by this concept of equality of opportunity is that opportunity lies in *exposure* to a given curriculum. The amount of opportunity is then measured in terms of the level of curriculum to which the child is exposed. The higher the curriculum made available to a given set of children, the greater their opportunity.

The most interesting point about this assumption is the relatively passive role of the school and community, relative to the child's role. The school's obligation is to "provide an opportunity" by being available, within easy geographic access of the child, free of cost (beyond the value of the child's time), and with a curriculum that would not exclude him from higher education. The obligation to "use the opportunity" is on the child or the family, so that his role is defined as the active one: the responsibility for achievement rests with him. Despite the fact that the school's role was the relatively passive one and the child's or family's role the active one, the use of this social service soon came to be no longer a choice of the parent or child, but that of the state. Since compulsory attendance laws appeared in the nineteenth century, the age of required attendance has been periodically moved upward.

This concept of equality of educational opportunity is one that has been implicit in most educational practice throughout most of the period of public education in the nineteenth and twentieth centuries. However, there have been several challenges to it; serious questions have been raised by new conditions in public education. The first of these in the United States was a challenge to assumption two, the common curriculum. This challenge first occurred in the early years of the twentieth century with the expansion of secondary education. Until the report of the committee of the National Education Association, issued in 1918, the standard curriculum in secondary schools was primarily a classical one appropriate for college entrance. The greater influx of noncollege-bound adolescents into the high school made it necessary that this curriculum be changed into one more appropriate to the new majority. This is not to say that the curriculum changed immediately in the schools, nor that all schools changed equally, but rather that the seven "cardinal principles" of the N.E.A. report became a powerful influence in the movement toward a less academically rigid curriculum. The introduction of the new nonclassical curriculum was seldom if ever couched in terms of a conflict between those for whom high school was college preparation, and those for whom it was terminal education; nevertheless, that was the case. The "inequality" was seen as the use of a curriculum that served a minority and was not designed to fit the needs of the majority; and the shift of curriculum was intended to fit the curriculum to the needs of the new majority in the schools.

In many schools, this shift took the form of *diversifying* the curriculum, rather than supplanting one by another; the college-preparatory curriculum remained though watered down. Thus the kind of equality of opportunity that emerged from the newly-designed secondary school curriculum was radically different from the elementary-school concept that had emerged earlier. The idea inherent in the new secondary school curriculum appears to have been to take as given the diverse occupational paths into which adolescents will go after secondary school, and to say (implicitly): there is greater equality of educational opportunity for a boy who is not going to attend college if he has a specially-designed curriculum than if he must take a curriculum designed for college entrance.

There is only one difficulty with this definition: it takes as *given* what should be problematic — that a given boy is going into a given post-secondary occupational or educational path. It is one thing to take as given that approximately 70 per cent of an entering high school freshman class will not attend college; but to assign a *particular child* to a curriculum designed for that 70 per cent closes off for that child the opportunity to attend college. Yet to assign all children to a curriculum designed for the 30 per cent who will attend college creates inequality for those who, at the end of high school, fall among the 70 per cent who do not attend college. This is a true dilemma, and one which no educational system has fully solved. It is more general than the college/noncollege dichotomy, for there is a wide variety of different paths that adolescents take on the completion of secondary school. In England, for example, a student planning to attend a university must specialize in the arts or the sciences in the later years of secondary school. Similar specialization occurs in the German gymnasium; and this is wholly within the group planning to attend university. Even greater specialization can be found among noncollege curricula, especially in the vocational, technical, and commercial high schools.

The distinguishing characteristic of this concept of equality of educational opportunity is that it accepts as given the child's expected future. While the concept discussed earlier left the child's future wholly open, this concept of differentiated curricula uses the expected future to match child and curriculum. It should be noted that the first and simpler concept is easier to apply in elementary schools where fundamental tools of reading and arithmetic are being learned by all children; it is only in secondary school that the problem of diverse futures arises. It should also be noted that the dilemma is directly due to the social structure itself: if there were a virtual absence of social mobility with everyone occupying a fixed estate in life, then such curricula that take the future as given would provide equality of opportunity relative to that structure. It is only because of the high degree of occupational mobility between generations — that is, the greater degree of equality of *occupational* opportunity — that the dilemma arises.

The first stage in the evolution of the concept of equality of educational opportunity was the notion that all children must be exposed to the same curriculum in the same school. A second stage in the evolution of the concept assumed that different children would have different occupational futures and that equality of opportunity required providing different curricula for each type of student. The third and fourth stages in this evolution came as a result of challenges to the basic idea of equality of educational opportunity from opposing directions. The third stage can be seen at least as far back as 1896 when the Supreme Court upheld the southern states' notion of "separate but equal" facilities. This stage ended in 1954 when the Supreme Court ruled that legal separation by race inherently constitutes inequality of opportunity. By adopting the "separate but equal" doctrine, the southern states rejected assumption three of the original concept, the assumption that equality depended on the opportunity to attend the same school. This rejection was, however, consistent with the overall logic of the original concept since attendance at the same school was an inherent part of that logic. The underlying idea was that opportunity resided in exposure to a curriculum; the community's responsibility was to provide that exposure, the child's to take advantage of it.

It was the pervasiveness of this underlying idea which created the difficulty for the Supreme Court. For it was evident that even when identical facilities and identical teacher salaries existed for racially separate schools, "equality of educational opportunity" in some sense did not exist. This had also long been evident to Englishmen as well, in a different context, for with the simultaneous existence of the "common school" and the "voluntary school," no one was under the illusion that full equality of educational opportunity existed. But the source of this inequality remained an unarticulated feeling. In the decision of the Supreme Court, this unarticulated feeling began to take more precise form. The essence of it was that the *effects* of such separate schools were, or were likely to be, different. Thus a concept of equality of opportunity which focused on *effects* of schooling began to take form. The actual decision of the Court was in fact a confusion of two unrelated premises: this new concept, which looked at results of schooling, and the legal premise that the use of race as a basis for school assignment violates fundamental freedoms. But what is important for the evolution of the concept of equality of opportunity is that a new and different assumption was introduced, the assumption that equality of opportunity depends in some fashion upon effects of schooling. I believe the decision would have been more soundly based had it not depended on the effects of schooling, but only on the violation of freedom; but by introducing the question of effects of schooling, the Court brought into the open the implicit goals of equality of educational opportunity – that is, goals having to do with the *results* of school – to which the original concept was somewhat awkwardly directed.

That these goals were in fact behind the concept can be verified by a simple mental experiment. Suppose the early schools had operated for only one hour a week and had been attended by children of all social classes. This would have met the explicit assumptions of the early concept of equality of opportunity since the school is free, with a common curriculum, and attended by all children in the locality. But it obviously would not have been accepted, even at that time, as providing equality of opportunity, because its effects would have been so minimal. The additional educational resources provided by middle- and upper-class families, whether in the home, by tutoring, or in private supplementary schools, would have created severe inequalities in results.

Thus the dependence of the concept upon results or effects of schooling, which had remained hidden until 1954, came partially into the open with the Supreme Court decision. Yet this was not the end, for it created more problems than it solved. It might allow one to assess gross inequalities, such as that created by dual school systems in the South, or by a system like that in the mental experiment I just described. But it allows nothing beyond that. Even more confounding, because the decision did not use effects of schooling as a criterion of inequality but only as justification for a criterion of racial integration, integration itself emerged as the basis for still a new concept of equality of educational opportunity. Thus the idea of effects of schooling as an element in the concept was introduced but immediately overshadowed by another, the criterion of racial integration.

The next stage in the evolution of this concept was, in my judgment, the Office of Education Survey of Equality of Educational Opportunity. This survey was carried out under a mandate in the Civil Rights Act of 1964 to the Commissioner of Education to assess the "lack of equality of educational opportunity" among racial and other groups in the United States. The evolution of this concept, and the conceptual disarray which this evolution had created, made the very definition of the task exceedingly difficult. The original concept could be examined by determining the degree to which all children in a locality had access to the same schools and the same curriculum, free of charge. The existence of diverse secondary curricula appropriate to different futures could be assessed relatively easily. But the very assignment of a child to a specific curriculum implies acceptance of the concept of equality which takes futures as given. And the introduction of the new interpretations, equality as measured by results of schooling and equality defined by racial integration, confounded the issue even further.

As a consequence, in planning the survey it was obvious that no single concept of equality of educational opportunity existed and that the survey must give information relevant to a variety of concepts. The basis on which this was done can be seen by reproducing a portion of an internal memorandum that determined the design of the survey:

> The point of second importance in design [second to the point of discovering the intent of Congress, which was taken to be that the survey was not for the purpose of locating willful discrimination, but to determine educational inequality without regard to intention of those in

authority] follows from the first and concerns the definition of inequality. One type of inequality may be defined in terms of differences of the community's input to the school, such as per-pupil expenditure, school plants, libraries, quality of teachers, and other similar quantities.

A second type of inequality may be defined in terms of the racial composition of the school, following the Supreme Court's decision that segregated schooling is inherently unequal. By the former definition, the question of inequality through segregation is excluded, while by the latter, there is inequality of education within a school system so long as the schools within the system have different racial composition.

A third type of inequality would include various intangible characteristics of the school as well as the factors directly traceable to the community inputs to the school. These intangibles are such things as teacher morale, teachers' expectations of students, level of interest of the student body in learning, or others. Any of these factors may affect the impact of the school upon a given student within it. Yet such a definition gives no suggestion of where to stop, or just how relevant these factors might be for school quality.

Consequently, a fourth type of inequality may be defined in terms of consequences of the school for individuals with equal backgrounds and abilities. In this definition, equality of educational opportunity is equality of results, given the same individual input. With such a definition, inequality might come about from differences in the school inputs and/or racial composition and/or from more intangible things as described above.

Such a definition obviously would require that two steps be taken in the determination of inequality. First, it is necessary to determine the effect of these various factors upon educational results (conceiving of results quite broadly, including not only achievement but attitudes toward learning, self-image, and perhaps other variables). This provides various measures of the school's quality in terms of its effect upon its students. Second, it is necessary to take these measures of quality, once determined, and determine the differential exposure of Negroes (or other groups) and whites to schools of high and low quality.

A fifth type of inequality may be defined in terms of consequences of the school for individuals of unequal backgrounds and abilities. In this definition, equality of educational opportunity is equality of results given *different* individual inputs. The most striking examples of inequality here would be children from households in which a language other than English, such as Spanish or Navaho, is spoken. Other examples would be low-achieving children from homes in which there is a poverty of verbal expression or an absence of experiences which lead to conceptual facility.

Such a definition taken in the extreme would imply that educational equality is reached only when the results of schooling (achievement and attitudes) are the same for racial and religious minorities as for the dominant group.

The basis for the design of the survey is indicated by another segment of this memoranudm:

> Thus, the study will focus its principal effort on the fourth definition, but will also provide information relevant to all five possible definitions. This insures the pluralism which is obviously necessary with respect to a definition of inequality. The major justification for this focus is that the results of this approach can best be translated into policy which will improve education's effects. The results of the first two approaches (tangible inputs to the school, and segregation) can certainly be translated into policy, but there is no good evidence that these policies will improve education's effects; and while policies to implement the fifth would certainly improve education's effects, it seems hardly possible that the study could provide information that would direct such policies.
>
> Altogether, it has become evident that it is not our role to define what constitutes equality for policy-making purposes. Such a definition will be an outcome of the interplay of a variety of interests, and will certainly differ from time to time as these interests differ. It should be our role to cast light on the state of inequality defined in the variety of ways which appear reasonable at this time.

The survey, then, was conceived as a pluralistic instrument, given the variety of concepts of equality of opportunity in education. Yet I suggest that despite the avowed intention of not adjudicating between these different ideas, the survey has brought a new stage in the evolution of the concept. For the definitions of equality which the survey was designed to serve split sharply into two groups. The first three definitions concerned input resources: first, those brought to the school by the actions of the school administration (facilities, curriculum, teachers); second, those brought to the school by the other students, in the educational backgrounds which their presence contributed to the school; and third, the intangible characteristics such as "morale" that result from the interaction of all these factors. The fourth and fifth definitions were concerned with the effects of schooling. Thus the five definitions were divided into three concerned with inputs to school and two concerned with effects of schooling. When the Report emerged, it did not give five different measures of equality, one for each of these definitions; but it did focus sharply on this dichotomy, giving in Chapter Two information on inequalities of input relevant to definitions one and two, and in Chapter Three information on inequalities of results relevant to definitions four and five, and also in Chapter Three information on the relation of input to results again relevant to definitions four and five.

Although not central to our discussion here, it is interesting to note that this examination of the relation of school inputs to effects on achievement showed that those input characteristics of schools that are most alike for Negroes and whites have least effect on their achievement. The magnitudes of differences between schools attended by Negroes and those attended by whites were as follows: least, facilities and curriculum; next, teacher quality; and greatest, educational backgrounds of fellow students. The order of importance of these inputs on the achievement of Negro students is precisely the same: facilities and curriculum least, teacher quality next, and backgrounds of fellow students, most.

By making the dichotomy between inputs and results explicit, and by focusing attention not only on inputs but on results, the Report brought into the open what had been underlying all the concepts of equality of educational opportunity but had remained largely hidden: that the concept implied *effective* equality of opportunity, that is, equality in those elements that are effective for learning. The reason this had remained half-hidden, obscured by definitions that involve inputs is, I suspect, because educational research has been until recently unprepared to demonstrate what elements are effective. The controversy that has surrounded the Report indicates that measurement of effects is still subject to sharp disagreement; but the crucial point is that *effects* of inputs have come to constitute the basis for assessment of school quality (and thus equality of opportunity) in place of using certain inputs by definition as measures of quality (e.g., small classes are better than large, higher-paid teachers are better than lower-paid ones, by definition).

It would be fortunate indeed if the matter could be left to rest there — if merely by using effects of school rather than inputs as the basis for the concept, the problem were solved. But that is not the case at all. The conflict between definitions four and five given above shows this. The conflict can be illustrated by resorting again to the mental experiment discussed earlier — providing a standard education of one hour per week, under identical conditions, for all children. By definition four, controlling all background differences of the children, results for Negroes and whites would be equal, and thus by this definition equality of opportunity would exist. But because such minimal schooling would have minimal effect, those children from educationally strong families would enjoy educational opportunity far surpassing that of others. And because such educationally strong backgrounds are found more often among whites than among Negroes, there would be very large overall Negro-white achievement differences — and thus inequality of opportunity by definition five.

It is clear from this hypothetical experiment that the problem of what constitutes equality of opportunity is not solved. The problem will become even clearer by showing graphs with some of the results of the Office of Education Survey. The highest line in Figure 1 shows the achievement in verbal skills by whites in the urban Northeast at grades 1, 3, 6, 9, and 12. The second line shows the achievement at each of these grades by whites in the rural Southeast. The third shows the achievement of Negroes in the urban Northeast. The fourth shows the achievement of Negroes in the rural Southeast.

When compared to the whites in the urban Northeast, each of the other three groups shows a different pattern. The comparison with whites in the rural

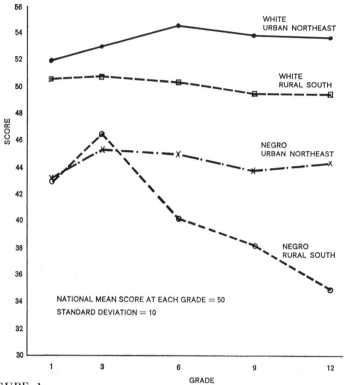

FIGURE 1

Patterns of Achievement in Verbal Skills at Various Grade Levels by Race and Region

South shows the two groups beginning near the same point in the first grade, and diverging over the years of school. The comparison with Negroes in the urban Northeast shows the two groups beginning farther apart at the first grade and remaining about the same distance apart. The comparison with Negroes in the rural South shows the two groups beginning far apart and moving much farther apart over the years of school.

Which of these, if any, shows equality of educational opportunity between regional and racial groups? Which shows greatest inequality of opportunity? I think the second question is easier to answer than the first. The last comparison showing both initial difference and the greatest increase in difference over grades 1 through 12 appears to be the best candidate for the greatest inequality. The first comparison, with whites in the rural South, also seems to show inequality of opportunity, because of the increasing difference over the twelve years. But what about the second comparison, with an approximately constant difference between Negroes and whites in the urban Northeast? Is this equality of opportunity? I suggest not. It means, in effect, only that the period of school has left the average Negro at about the same level of achievement relative to whites as he began — in this case, achieving higher than about 15 per cent of the whites, lower than about 85 per cent of the whites. It may well be that in the absence of school those lines of achievement would have diverged due to differences in home environments; or perhaps they would have remained an equal distance apart, as they are in this graph (though at lower levels of achievement for both groups, in the absence of school). If it were the former, we could say that school, by keeping the lines parallel, has been a force toward the equalization of opportunity. But in the absence of such knowledge, we cannot say even that.

What would full equality of educational opportunity look like in such graphs? One might persuasively argue that it should show a convergence, so that even though two population groups begin school with different levels of skills on the average, the average of the group that begins lower moves up to coincide with that of the group that begins higher. Parenthetically, I should note that this does *not* imply that all students' achievement comes to be identical, but only that the *averages* for two population groups that begin at different levels come to be identical. The diversity of individual scores could be as great as, or greater than, the diversity at grade 1.

Yet there are serious questions about this definition of equality of opportunity. It implies that over the period of school there are no other influences, such as the family environment, which affect achievement over the twelve years of school, even though these influences may differ greatly for the two population groups. Concretely, it implies that white family environments, predominantly middle class, and Negro family environments, predominantly lower class, will produce no effects on achievement that would keep these averages apart. Such an assumption seems highly unrealistic, especially in view of the general importance of family background for achievement.

However, if such possibilities are acknowledged, then how far can they go before there is inequality of educational opportunity? Constant difference over school? Increasing differences? The unanswerability of such questions begins to give a sense of a new stage in the evolution of the concept of equality of educational opportunity. These questions concern the *relative intensity* of two sets of influences: those which are alike for the two groups, principally in school, and those which are different, principally in the home or neighborhood. If the school's influences are not only alike for the two groups, but very strong relative to the divergent influences, then the two groups will move together. If school influences are very weak, then the two groups will move apart. Or more generally, the relative intensity of the convergent school influences and the divergent out-of-school influences determines the effectiveness of the educational system in providing equality of educational opportunity. In this perspective, complete equality of opportunity can be reached only if all the divergent out-of-school influences vanish, a condition that would arise only in the advent of boarding schools; given the existing divergent influences, equality of opportunity can only be approached and never fully reached. The concept becomes one of degree of proximity to equality of opportunity. This proximity is determined, then, not merely by the *equality* of educational inputs, but by the *intensity* of the school's influences relative to the external divergent influences. That is, equality of output is not so much determined by equality of the resource inputs, but by the power of these resources in bringing about achievement.

Here, then, is where the concept of equality of educational opportunity presently stands. We have observed an evolution which might have been anticipated a century and a half ago when the first such concepts arose, yet one which is very different from the concept as it first developed. This difference is sharpened if we examine a further implication of the current concept as I have described it. In describing the original concept, I indicated that the role of the community and the educational institution was relatively passive; they were expected to provide a set of free public resources. The responsibility for profitable use of those resources lay with the child and his family. But the evolution of the concept has reversed these roles. The implication of the most recent concept, as I have described it, is that the responsibility to create achievement lies with the educational institution, not the child. The difference in achievement at grade 12 between the average Negro and the average white is, in effect, the degree of inequality of opportunity, and the reduction of that inequality is a responsibility of the school. This shift in responsibility follows logically from the change in the concept of equality of educational opportunity from school resource inputs to effects of schooling. When that change occurred, as it has in the past few years, the school's responsibility shifted from increasing and distributing equally *its* "quality" to increasing the quality of its *students'* achievements. This is a notable shift, and one which should have strong consequences for the practice of education in future years.

TOWARD DEFINING EQUALITY OF EDUCATIONAL OPPORTUNITY

Edmund W. Gordon

One of the traditional roles of education in the U.S.A. has been to broaden opportunities for productive, influential, and rewarding participation in the affairs of the society by developing those skills and entry credentials necessary for economic survival and social satisfaction. The idea of education for all grew gradually. In this country we extended this opportunity to more and more of our people, by a steady increase in the quantity of educational experiences available and the quality of the educational product. While the quantity of available educational experiences has grown, there also has been a marked increase in the quality of the skills and competencies demanded of those who would achieve much. Similarly, the individual's goals are higher. He wants to be productive in the sense that the society sees his effort as resulting in a valued product; influential in the sense that his participation is viewed as having some influence on outcomes; and rewarded for his effort both materially *and* psychologically.

Increased perception of this role of education makes us want to equalize access to basic education of high quality. Spurred on by the civil rights movement of the 1950's and 60's, equal opportunity in education has become an issue of crucial national concern. By many, it is regarded as the base for all the rights, privileges, and responsibilities of membership in this modern democratic society.

Our country's desire to equalize educational opportunities is in part a product of advances in the organization and development of human societies during the past six centuries. In earlier periods when neither the need nor the resources for wide access to education existed, the ideal of universal equalization of education opportunities also did not exist, certainly not in the public policy sphere. The concept itself and the concern for its implementation could not have emerged as an important issue, even now, if we had not earlier developed an awareness of the universality of educability. Human societies have always considered educable those categories of persons thought to be needed in the maintenance of the social order. Consequently, as the human resource requirements of social orders have changed, concepts of educability have changed. Educability in human subjects has been defined less by the actual potentials of persons and more by the level of society's demand for people capable of certain levels of function. In more simplistic and exclusive social systems most people were considered uneducable and effort was not "wasted" on their formal training. As long ago as the early Christian period and as recently as the early nineteenth century, it was only the religious and political nobility who were thought to be capable and worthy of academic learning. The social order was maintained by the machinations of these elite groups and the simple and routine gaming, farming and crafting skills of illiterate masses.

Under the triple pressures of the reformation in religion, mechanization in industry, and institutionalization in commerce, categories of persons thought to be capable of academic learning were greatly expanded. Opportunities for active participation in religious activities and rituals made reading and writing more widely usable and saleable skills. Similarly, the emergence of collective machine production in shops and the expansion of commerce and trade through institutions made necessary the broader distribution of these skills. The combined impact was a greatly increased societal need for computational and communicative skills in larger numbers of people. As a corollary, previously illiterate people were drawn into the small body of literates and the mass of "uneducables" was reduced.

In the United States, where religious freedom and diversity became wide-spread, where democracy in government became the ideal, and where industrialization and economic expansion advanced most rapidly, more and more literate persons were required. In mid-nineteenth century U.S.A., society's view of who could be educated quickly expanded to include all people in this country except for slaves. With the end of slavery and the incorporation of ex-slaves into the industrial labor force, ex-slaves gradually came to be regarded as educable. Through the exercise of briefly held political power, together with uneducated poor whites, they literally forced increased access to public education as a vehicle for their education. These indigenous poor were later joined by waves of immigrants who also saw the public school as their major route to economic and social salvation. In the metropolitan areas of the period, the school also became the major vocational training resource that prepared semiskilled and commercial workers for rapidly expanding industries. Although the school did not succeed in educating all of these new candidates, the once narrowly defined concept of educability was now nearly universal in its inclusiveness.

Our conception of education has also changed over the years. In Thomas Jefferson's view the school was expected to provide the technical skills and basic knowledge necessary for work and economic survival. It was from newspapers, journals, and books and from participation in politics that people were to be really educated. In reviewing Jefferson's position on education, Cremin (1965) has concluded that it never occurred to Jefferson that schooling would become the chief educational influence on the young. However, changes in the number and variety of persons served by the school, changes in the functioning of the society and changes in the nature of the skills and competencies required by the social order have also changed the nature of education.

By the middle of the nineteenth century in this country, public schools serving the upper classes had developed curriculums basic to a liberal education. In this period the secondary school was quite selective and was designed to prepare a relatively few young people for entrance into college where most of them would pursue studies leading to one of the professions. While this trend continued through the latter half of that century, the first half of the twentieth century was marked by a high degree of proliferation in the development of technical and vocational training programs. Preparation in the liberal arts was considered a luxury and was thought by some to be relatively useless. It was the Jeffersonian concept of utilitarian education which prevailed. And it was this utilitarian education which came to be the mode in the growing acceptance of universal educability. "Everyone can and should be taught to do useful work and to hold a job" was the prevalent view.

The wide acceptance of this view contributed to the salvaging of education for Negroes following the betrayal of the Reconstruction Period and its leadership. In the great debate symbolized by verbal conflict between Booker T. Washington and William E.B. DuBois, the real struggle was between those who stood for the narrow but practical training of the hands of Negro and poor children so that they could work and those represented by DuBois who believed in the broad and somewhat less immediately practical education of the mind through the liberal arts and sciences. Those favoring the training of the hands won that debate. Educational facilities for Negroes and other poor people slowly expanded under the banner of technical and vocational training. This may have been a victory for expanded access to education, but the neglected concern for the "liberating" study of the arts and sciences made this a victory from which true equality in education has yet to recover. We will return to this point concerning the function of liberal arts and sciences in education later in this paper. At the moment our concern is with the protean nature of educability and education.

In this country the battle for equality of educational opportunity was first waged to establish public responsibility for the education of children in states where public education did not exist. This was followed by the struggle for adequate educational facilities and diverse educational programs. The twentieth century was one-third spent before the struggle for equal though separate schools was engaged. By mid-century it was legally determined that in our society separate schools are intrinsically unequal. However, even before the 1954 Supreme Court school desegregation decision was promulgated, it was becoming clear that racially-mixed school systems do not automatically insure education of high quality. This observation was supported by data on minority-group children from schools in the North where varying degrees and patterns of ethnic mix were extant. Although the performance of minority-group children in some of those schools was superior to that of such children in segregated systems in the South, differences in achievement and in the characteristics of their schools were notable.

The early 1960's brought campaigns for education of high quality provided in ethnically integrated school settings. Some school systems responded with plans for the redistribution of school populations in efforts to achieve a higher degree of ethnic balance. Some of these, along with other schools, introduced special enrichment and remedial programs intended to compensate for or correct deficiencies in the preparation of the children or the quality of the schools. Neither these efforts at achieving integrated education nor at developing compensatory education resulted in success. Ethnic balance and educational programs of high quality proved impossible to achieve instantaneously. Confronted with the failure to obtain ethnic integration and high quality in education, and given the recalcitrant presence of segregation in schools North, South and West, the goals for many minority-grouped parents shifted. In the late 1960's the demand is made for education of high quality, where possible, on an ethnically integrated basis. However, where segregation exists (and it does exist for the great majority of ethnic minorities in this country) the demand increases for control of those schools, serving such children, by groups indigenous to the cultures and communities in which they live. Hence the demand for "black schools run by black people."

Alongside this growing acceptance and promotion of ethnic separation, there continues to be concern for ethnic integration in education and compensatory education as complementary strategies in the equalization of educational opportunity. The introduction of the concept "compensatory education" grew out of the recognition that learners who did not begin from the same point may not have comparable opportunities for achievement when provided with equal and similar educational experiences. To make the opportunity equal, it is argued, it may be necessary to make education something more than equal. It may be necessary to compensate for the handicaps if we are to provide education of equal quality. It may be necessary to change the educational method and create new models in order to meet the learning need and style of the youngster who comes to school out of a different background of experiences.

Out of this concern for equalizing educational opportunity, some thoughtful persons have begun to think about what the criterion is to be. This became a problem of critical importance when Congress placed on the Office of Education the responsibility for determining the status of equal opportunity for education in the U.S.A. James Coleman, the principal investigator for that study, used equality of educational achievement as his criterion. Coleman argued that it is one of the functions of the school to make academic achievement independent of the social background of its pupils. This view holds that the adequate school experience should enable groups of youngsters from different backgrounds to reach the same levels of academic achievement. When the schools do not compensate for the variations in the background experiences of their pupils, they are failing to provide equal educational opportunity. This position assumes general comparability of potential for learning and has not been advanced as applicable in cases of actual intellectual incompetence.

There have been several attempts at defining equality of educational opportunity or at suggesting criteria for assessing its degree. Havighurst (1944) has advanced a position based upon a match between measured intelligence and length of guaranteed educational experience. "We might speak of equality of educational opportunity if all children and young people exceeding a given level of intellectual ability were enabled to attend schools and colleges up to some specified level." Following this position, if all youth with IQ's higher than 100 were assured of a high school education up to the age of 18 and all young people with IQ's over 110 were able to attend college for four years, "we could say that equality of educational opportunity existed to a considerable degree."

Equal education does not mean the same education, according to Tumin (1965), but it does mean

> equal concern . . . that each child shall become the most and the best that he can become . . . equal pleasure expressed by the teacher with equal vigor at every child's attempt to become something more than he was, or equal distress expressed with an equal amount of feeling at his being

unable to become something more than he was . . . and equal *rewards* for all children, in terms of time, attention, and any symbol the school hands out which stands for its judgement of worthiness . . . Equal rewards mean . . . the elimination of competitive grades . . . One simply takes the child and teaches him for a given period of time what one thinks it is important to teach. When he learns that, he then goes on to the next thing . . . The maintenance of the highest standards in public education is achieved by getting out of children the most that each child has in him. Any other notion of high standard fails to take into account the different capacities for development and growth of large numbers of children. Equality of education . . . is the only device that I know of for the maintenance of high standards, as against the false measure that relies on the achievements of the elite minority of the school.

Tyler (1967) argued that since children come to school with different abilities the criterion should be that the learning process continue even though one child's rate may exceed another's. He feels that children do not have equal educational opportunity until the meaningfulness, the stimulation and the conditions for learning are equal among the various children in the school. One measure of equality is that every child is learning. Tyler holds the teacher responsible for insuring that some learning takes place as long as the child remains in school. Negatively, equal educational opportunity is not provided simply by having materials there and time available for learning. Rather, the child himself must perceive the opportunities, feel confident that he can do something with them, and find them within his ability to carry on. Furthermore, according to Tyler, learning should promote a broader range of choice rather than continually narrowing the youngster so that after several years of education he has only one possible direction that he can go.

Lesser and Stodolsky (1967) have advanced a view of the equality of educational opportunity which is based in part on Lesser's finding of differential patterns of intellective function distributed by ethnic group identification. These investigators argue that equal opportunity is provided if the school makes maximum use of the distinctive pattern of ability the child possesses. The school would be held responsible for providing differential education experiences designed to build upon the special abilities the child brings to the learning experience. Thus, if adequate achievement is demonstrated in that special abilities area, the school can be judged to have provided an equal opportunity to learn.

Kenneth Clark (1965) has advanced a more simplistic view. He feels that it is possible to identify certain essential features of good education. Education which includes the best expressions of those features should be made available to all children alike. Clark argues that if just that goal were achieved, we would have moved a long way toward providing equal educational opportunity. He rejects as destructive the search for deficiencies and special characteristics in

Negro children. Rather, his focus is on the deficiencies and special negative characteristics in the schools and the teachers who inhabit them. For Clark, equalizing opportunity involves the removal of the burdens of poor teaching, negative teacher attitudes, and inadequate educational resources from the shoulder of minority-group children.

All of these views have definite merit, and the adoption of any one or combination would significantly improve the quality of educational opportunities. Each view, however, has critical limitations. The mechanical approach advanced by Havighurst is probably the least complicated to implement. Since the schools already have IQ measures on all children above the sixth grade, it would only require that educational resources be made available to insure specified years in school or college for every child in each designated IQ range. The major problems involved would be financial and logistic, if it were not for the fact that the number of those who share this implied confidence in IQ tests is rapidly decreasing. The facts that these scores often misrepresent the functional capacities of the persons studied and that it is the functional capacities of the very groups who are the target of our concern in equalizing educational opportunities that these tests underestimate, make the Havighurst position unacceptable. It would not insure equality of opportunity except in a very limited sense. Everybody with the same IQ would be treated the same. However, it has been demonstrated that IQ is greatly influenced by social and school experience (Klineberg). The school and its society would then be providing education in relation to its success in providing previous education. If it did not provide good and adequate early education, it would be freed of responsibility for providing education at a later stage of development. This is the situation with which we are currently confronted and one which is strongly associated with inequality in educational opportunity. The Havighurst position simply insures a certain period of schooling for those whom the school now succeeds in educating.

The Tyler position places a greater responsibility on the school and teacher insisting that some learning occur as long as the child continues in school. However, this position allows for too little from the school and the child. If the school's function is simply to insure that the child learns at his own rate and functions in his own way, whose estimate of the child's potential shall be used? Whose definition of the child's functional level shall be accepted? This laissez-faire approach to education lends itself to gross underestimation of the potential of youngsters from backgrounds unfamiliar or unappealing to the teacher and the school. Like the Havighurst position, the Tyler position places too great a reliance on inadequate measures of intellectual potential. There are, nonetheless, excellent features in the Tyler position. His concern that the learning experience be meaningful for the learner, that the stimulation be effective and that the conditions be appropriate are important and lead to the kind of individual consideration which may be necessary to the equalization of opportunity. Similarly, his concern that learning should promote a continuing broader range of choice is directed at a key problem in democratic education. The acceptance of the Tyler model would do much to improve education and to broaden education opportunities. Unfortunately, it too does not form a basis for equalizing educational opportunity.

For current developments in individually prescribed instruction applied in public school settings see: Bolvin, S. and Lindvall, C. M. "Individually Prescribed Instruction: One Approach to the Problem of Individual Differences." Pittsburgh, Pa.: Learning Research and Development Center, University of Pittsburgh, 1965; Braddock, C. "Computer Fits Teaching to Individual Student." *Southern Educational Report,* January-February 1968; Esebensen, T. "Individualizing the Instructional Program." Duluth, Minn.: Duluth Public Schools, 1966; and Flanagan, J. C. "Project Plan: A Program of Individualized Planning and Individualized Instruction." Washington, D.C.: Project ARISTOTLE, Symposium, December 1967.

In his effort at identifying equal education, Tumin also takes a laissez-faire approach in which individualization is stressed. He adds a concern with getting the most from each child, and avoids judging individual achievement on group norms. Competition is deemphasized. Teacher concern and reward are stressed. Despite the very humane elements in the Tumin position, he does not take into account the possibility of underestimation of potential or the fact of performance requirements in the real world against which achievement must be measured. He rejects sameness in educational method but accepts a common approach, sameness in reward or pattern of reinforcement. Like Tyler's position, Tumin's approach should improve education but will hardly equalize opportunity.

The Lesser-Stodolsky view of differential patterns among ethnic groups may lead some educators to as limited a definition of potential as those positions advanced by Havighurst and Tumin. Further, this position could lure many people into a racial-ethnic group determined view of behavioral characteristics and developmental expectations. Educators have too often assumed that because certain patterns occur in high frequency in certain groups, intrinsic or genetic factors are the best or sole explanation. Insufficient attention has been given to the facts that the racial or ethnic groupings utilized are by no means pure, to the wide variation in functioning within these identified groups, or to the overlap in quality and character of function between the several groups studied. Nonetheless, we have used these factors and evidence from psychological performance and achievement data to assign individuals and groups to certain categories of educational service and anticipated achievement. Our determination of these assignments has been based upon stereotypes of status rather than analyzed educational need. There remain questions as to whether these differences in the characteristics of children are genetically determined, are peculiar to certain groups due to their cultural history, or are simply environmentally determined characteristics commonly encountered. No matter how these questions are answered, however, the data showing how children with these characteristics function could be used to prescribe the kinds of educational experiences necessary to improve development and learning. The possibility that certain characteristics may be intrinsic to the learner and that these characteristics are different from those of other learners leads to no clear conclusion relative to the modifiability of the characteristics. It is quite possible, even likely, that humans from different family stocks vary with respect to behavioral characteristics just as they do with respect to physical characteristics. It may also be true that certain behavioral characteristics are of greater value in the mastery of certain tasks. What is not known is the extent to which specific characteristics can be adapted or utilized under varied conditions. Questions related to the genetic basis of characteristics are important to our understanding of origin but are considerably less crucial to our understanding of mechanisms for change.

Happily, the Lesser-Stodolsky position has not been used to advance the case for genetically determined patterns of functioning. To the contrary, Lesser and Stodolsky proposed education which would maximize achievement in areas of special ability. For example, Lesser found that children from oriental backgrounds tend to show good performance on tasks requiring mastery of spatial relationships; thus he would argue that the schools should be trying to build upon this special ability and possibly produce more architects or draftsmen among these youngsters. It would be even more appropriate if following models from Special Education, the differential characteristics identified by Lesser-Stodolsky were used as a basis for optimizing total intellectual functioning. For example, the special spatial abilities of certain children could be used in the design of individualized learning experiences through which reading, writing, compositional skills are developed and humanities and science concepts are communicated.

Clearly, some children come to the school situation with a pattern of strengths and weaknesses and styles that may be somewhat atypical to the pupil ability patterns the school is most accustomed to working with. This may mean that the school is now more greatly challenged to design learning experiences that build upon these particular patterns. Opportunity is enhanced when we build upon these patterns in the formal learning experience. We move toward equalization of opportunity when these special patterns become guideposts around which learning experiences are designed to achieve common standards as well as unique achievements.

The Clark position would be more acceptable if we knew that all children learned in much the same manner, and if we had achieved a higher level of pedagogical competence. It is dangerous to settle for the best we currently practice when that practice is so often unsuccessful even with large numbers of children. In addition the Clark definition is only concerned with alleged input and takes no cognizance of output. He says that we have some good schools in this country, "let's make all of our schools good schools." Now, we embrace this as an idea since everybody favors good schools, but if one is concerned about equalizing educational opportunity and compensating for the background variations that youngsters bring to school, then simply taking the best available model may not be enough.

Let us return to the purpose of education in a democratic society. If that purpose is to broaden opportunities for meaningful participation in the mainstream of society through the development of necessary skills and credentials, then educational opportunity is unequal unless it serves that purpose for all learners. At any point in the history of a society, the minimum educational goals are defined by the prerequisites for meaningful participation or for economic, social and political survival. The educational experience can and should enable many persons to go far beyond the development of such survival skills but it cannot be considered to have provided equality of opportunity unless it enables nearly all to reach the survival or participation level. These survival or participation skills (Gordon and Wilkerson, 1966) likely to be required in the emerging period include:

1. *Mastery of basic communication skills:* While physical strength and manual skill represented man's basic tool of survival in years past, it is increasingly clear that communication skills have emerged as the survival tool of the future. Education for all in our society must be built upon the mastery of basic skills in symbolic representation and utilization. Such skills include speech, reading, writing, and arithmetic computation.

2. *Problem solving:* A second tool of survival, somewhat less critical than the basic skills, is skill in the movement from anxiety, confusion, and disorder to problem formulation. This involves competence in problem identification and problem solving.

3. *The management of knowledge:* Knowledge of the physical, biological and social sciences is so vast as to preclude complete content mastery by any single person. Knowledge of the dimensions of these fields, mastery of their principles, skill in the creation or discovery of order or pattern in their data, and competence in the management and utilization of this knowledge are urgently needed survival tools.

4. *Employment, leisure and continuing education:* Theobald sees the world of the future as one where achievement through physical work will no longer be a prime requirement in society. Utilization of leisure will emerge as a central problem. Rapidly changing technology is destroying the lifetime career in a single vocation. Today's children may as adults often change not only jobs but kinds of work and will be required to make quick adaptation to radically different work situations. The demand will be for trainability and continuing education throughout one's life span in the labor force. However, if some of the projections hold true many of today's young people as adults will live in a society which no longer rewards physical work. The new society may reward instead, self-expression through art, through interaction with nature, through social interchange and through symbolization and ideation as art forms. Creative self-expression may become important for vocational utilization as well as for aesthetic purposes.

5. *Self-management:* The achievement of goals such as these will involve the schools in activities more explicitly directed at personal, social and character development. It may require a more adequate understanding of self and others than is usually achieved. It may mean that we give greater attention to the use and control of one's self in interpersonal relations. It may make essential, wider adaptations to multi-ethnic and multi-cultural societies. It may give added urgency to conflict resolution through avenues of non-violence and the development of appreciative and respectful relationships with the world of nature, of man-made objects, of ideas and of values.

With education defining its concerns in such broad terms it seems obvious that the school must speak to the academic, emotional and social developmental needs of pupils. Some children will be better at some of these learnings than at others. Differential levels of achievement will certainly result. But these differences need not be solely determined by cultural, economic or ethnic origins. Rather, achievement should reflect variations in the quality of intellect found in all groups and variations in the adequacy of the learning experiences to which they are exposed. Democratically administered educational programs combined with enlightened educational practices should insure that basic competencies are universally achieved.

Equality of educational opportunity would mean the achievement of at least these basic competencies in all pupils save the 3% to 5% who are truly mentally defective. To make the opportunity equal, the school would have to develop and use whatever methods, materials or procedures are required by the special style, special ability or special background the child may bring. That the school may not yet know what and how to do this is a part of the problem. That it accept the challenge to pose the question and actively pursue solutions is the issue at hand.

Equal educational opportunity demands that, where what children bring to the school is unequal, what the school puts in must be unequal and individualized to insure that what the school produces is at least equal at the basic levels of achievement. Equalization of educational opportunity in a democracy requires parity in achievement at a baseline corresponding to the level required for social satisfaction and democratic participation. It also demands opportunity and freedom to vary with respect to achievement ceilings. It is in the reconciliation of these sometimes conflicting requirements that equality of opportunity is tested. At some points in the development of a society it may be necessary to favor universality to the disadvantage of uniqueness. At other times universality may need to be sacrificed in the interest of unique achievement. If preferential position is continually given to one, equality of opportunity is precluded. However, the more optimistic among us claim that this country can well afford to allocate the necessary resources to give greater priority to health, to education, and to welfare to more nearly insure equal opportunity for basic educational achievement without limiting the freedom of individuals to rise above that baseline. For those of us who are critical of the current priorities at this time in the history of our nation, the vastness of these resources indicates that the conflict simply need not exist.

REFERENCES

Clark, Kenneth B., *Dark Ghetto.* New York, N.Y.: Harper and Row, 1965.

Coleman, James S., "The Concept of Equality of Educational Opportunity," *Harvard Educational Review*, Vol. 38, No. 1, pp. 7-22. Winter 1968.

Cremin, Lawrence A., *The Genius of American Education*, Pittsburgh, Pa.: University of Pittsburgh Press, 1965.

Gordon, Edmund W. and Wilkerson, Doxey A., *Compensatory Education for the Disadvantaged*, New York, N.Y.: College Entrance Examination Board, 1966.

Harrington, Michael, *The Other America*, New York, N.Y.: Macmillan, 1962.

Stodolsky, Susan S., and Lesser, Gerald S., *Learning Patterns in the Disadvantaged*, presented at the Conference on Bio-Social Factors in the Development and Learning of Disadvantaged Children, commissioned under U.S. Office of Education contract, Syracuse, N.Y.: April, 1967.

Theobald, Robert, *Free Men and Free Markets*, New York, N.Y.: Crown Publishing, Inc., 1963.

Tumin, Melvin, *The Meaning of Equality in Education*, Presented at the Third Annual Conference of the National Committee for Support of Public Schools, Washington, D.C.: April, 1965.

Tyler, Ralph W., personal correspondence, October 9, 1967.

Warner, William, Havighurst, Robert, and Loeb, Martin, *Who Shall Be Educated*, New York, N.Y.: Harper and Brothers, 1944.

II.
IMPLICATIONS
OF
RESEARCH
AND
EVALUATION

chapter 2
the functions of research

SOCIAL CONSEQUENCES OF
EDUCATIONAL MEASUREMENT

Edgar Z. Friedenberg

Though its manifold unplanned consequences are probably more important, educational measurement has two generally recognized functions. In a society as hung up on competitive achievement as ours, testing emphasizes the assessment of individual competence. Then it assigns test scores, and with them the persons who made them, to ideologically acceptable social categories. The second of these functions is much the more important of the two, since individual competence is not generally esteemed in our society; nor is it, over the long haul, demonstrably and consistently the major factor determining relative success. It does, of course, become crucial for every individual on certain occasions; but educational testing is not very helpful in assigning particular individuals to particular social roles because the norms on the basis of which their scores might have been interpreted have been grossly contaminated by the factors that have been operating in the meanwhile to keep competence from obstructing the social process.

Preoccupation with individual test scores, though understandable in the individuals being tested, today I believe serves chiefly the ideological function of convincing the young that the American social system recognizes the rewards individual competitive achievement. This has induced them to cooperate in the testing program because they expect it to serve as the gateway to opportunity, based on a precise assessment of their individual merits. But, for the managers of the social system it has a contrary function. Testing is their means of stocking their various manpower pools with compatible varieties matched in predacity and adaptive characteristics so that they will not be troubled later by conflict or random variation. Greater precision and subtlety, in the interests of a just appraisal, scarcely concern them.

Paradoxically, as the ideological impact of testing on students declines, the real rewards for successful test performance may increase. As higher-status, more sophisticated incumbents reject the social system the schools serve, and the concept of success that prevails within it, they will be replaced by lower-status youth who are still hungry for the rewards it offers, and willing to agree that they *are* rewards. It may well be that the ends of social mobility and equality of opportunity are best served by a system of rewards so sickening that the successful are ultimately forced to hasten, tight-lipped and intoxicated, from the arena to make way for those who press upon their heels. Certainly, our educators are fortunate in having still available a pool of some twenty million black people most of whom, having been denied access to these rewards, remain more firmly convinced of their value than their oppressors are. It is understandable that beleaguered college presidents find the angry demands of blacks less threatening and humiliating than the derision of radical whites who treat them like a bad joke that has run on too long.

It is frustrating, therefore, that just when blacks are desperately needed as the last available, large, and untapped pool of candidates for socialization into the American middle class, a serious question should have been raised as to whether they are as capable, on the average, of making it. The issue raised by Jensen(2) in the *Harvard Educational Review* last winter was perceived as a threat by liberals from the moment his article went into galleys.

Jensen's argument, to be sure, is not really very startling. The chromosome being what it is, there are certainly clusters of genetic characteristics that come to be socially defined as racial; and it is surely plausible that certain of these characteristics should be related to cognitive functioning. The proposition is rendered more plausible, moreover, by the fact that ideological inhibition has impeded scrutiny of this possibility by American social scientists. Kurt Vonnegut Jr. is not really being funny when he observes in *Slaughterhouse-Five*(6):

> I think about my education sometimes. I went to the University of Chicago for a while after the Second World War. I was a student in the Department of Anthropology. At that time, they were teaching that there was absolutely no difference between anybody. They may be teaching that still.

They may indeed, but if they are, Jensen is not the only scholar to think they might be wrong. Thus, Gerald Lesser and Susan S. Stodolsky(5), found consistent differences in patterns of mental ability among Chinese, Jewish, Negro, and Puerto Rican first graders in New York that were quite independent of social class. Their findings that Jewish children ranked significantly better than all the other ethnic groups in verbal ability, though as damaging, in view of the prevailing social stereotype, to the Jewish image as anything Jensen has to say about Negroes, caused neither astonishment nor consternation.

Where Jensen is on weakest ground — and ground onto which Lesser and Stodolsky were never tempted to precede him — is in his inference that the differences he cites are not merely ethnic but genetic in origin. In a society as permeated by discriminatory practice and perception as ours, this is hardly an empirically testable proposition, since the possible effects of racism penetrate every situation — certainly in the form of health and nutritional factors, they penetrate the womb — and color every parameter that might be observed. In our society, being black works the way Abe Martin said being poor did, 40 years ago: It ain't a crime, but it might as well be. The experience of stigmatization is simply so pervasive that even attempts as conscientious as those Jensen makes to factor-out its effects remain unconvincing — especially when all he has to work with are data gathered for other purposes than to test his hypotheses and hence incapable of being well-controlled for his purpose. I was hung up, for example, by his citation of evidence that Amerindian children, though more disadvantaged than black children on all citable environmental indices, still do significantly better in school until I realized that this was a classic example of empiricists' folly; and of exactly the kind psychometricians should beware: assuming that what you can assesss on some scale, if you repeatedly get consistent results, must somehow be critical even if it isn't exactly relevant. For the Indian children on whom such comparisons are based are precisely those who still live in communities that, though squalid and poor, retain some supportive sense of a tribal tradition that, in our society, is romanticized now rather than denigrated. To be denigrated, you have to be a "nigra;" the difference is qualitative, and there is no use mucking about with scales to measure it.

Neither Jensen nor his opponents can escape the ethnocentrism implicit in their respective positions by the purifying rituals of science, for those rituals are themselves central to their common ideological position. Both start with the assumption that our society, with its dominant values, is the given — the reality with which one must come to terms — and that those who do not accept its terms or meet its demands have no just basis for demands upon it. Within this context, Jensen is, of course, threatening because he infers that blacks are systematically less able, on the average, to meet those demands than whites; and that efforts to compensate for this difference by education could not be wholly successful, even if racial discrimination could be eliminated. Since both informal observation, like Jonathan Kozol's(3) and James Herndon's(1) and formal studies like Elenor Leacock's(4) and the Bundy report suggest that racial discrimination could only be eliminated from our urban school systems by genocide, the policy implications of Jensen's work seem rather remote. But if success, as society defines it, is what black people want — and most doubtless do — this is bad news, though hardly tragic. Jensen specifically insists that his conclusions cannot justifiably be applied, pejoratively or otherwise, to the cognitive possibilities of any individual. Most people, regardless of ethnic differences, have far more potential ability of every kind than they ever get to use; wherever the mean may be there is room to stand erect under almost any part of the curve. Only a very bad, or disingenuously racist, statistician would infer from his argument that any particular black student would be incompetent to meet the demands of the educational system, though one might quite properly conclude from it that those demands, if consistently inappropriate to the cognitive style most comfortable for black students, do indeed constitute a form of de facto discrimination. But a much more relevant question arises concerning the nature of those demands.

If I read Jensen correctly, he implies that in any large random group of blacks one would be likely to find fewer persons than among a comparable group of whites — and for purely ethnic reasons, leaving aside the question of opportunity — capable of developing the abilities of, say, Robert McNamara, or John McCone, or John Gardner, or Roger Heyns — to name four men whose excellence and consistent devotion to rational cognition undistracted by excessive passion or subjectivity have become a matter of public record and have brought them international distinction and groovy positions of public trust, if that is quite the right phrase for a director of the Central Intelligence Agency or the World Bank. This may be true; I fear it is. There may *never* be a black man with the kind of mind needed to produce a report like that of the McCone Commission on the disorders in Watts a few years ago. But a more fundamental question, surely, is whether and to what degree a person, white or black, must possess such a mind in order to live in this society with a reasonable guarantee against insult and prospect of satisfaction. Must one master the technique of affect-free cognition in order to succeed? Must one succeed in order to retain any shred of self-esteem? Must success be defined as the power to dominate and manipulate the life-styles of others, masked in the rhetoric of pluralism and equality of opportunity? Poverty, burtality, and exclusion are hard to bear; and no race can be so different — or so irrational — as to choose them. Jensen, however, suggests that there may be groups of human beings who cannot become quite like the dominant class in America, even if their lives, or more precisely their life-chances, depend on it.

If this is true, the process of educational measurement cannot have much relevance to their aspirations. Educational measurement is an inherently conservative function, since it depends on the application of established norms to the selection of candidates for positions within the existing social structure on terms and for purposes set by that structure. It cannot usually muster either the imagination or the sponsorship needed to search out and legitimate new conceptions of excellence which might threaten the hegemony of existing elites. Educational measurement is at present wholly committed to the assumption that legitimate forms of learning are rational and cognitive and that such learning is the proper goal of academic process. This is an ideological, not a technical, difficulty. It is perfectly possible to detect and appraise, in critical though not scalar terms, poetic skill, humane sensitivity, breadth and subtlety of human compassion and the like. Educational Testing Service has, in the past, already done some of this in experimental revisions of testing programs in the humanities and in personality assessment, while the analysis of profiles of student activists prepared by the American Council of Education is very useful to college admissions officers in defining criteria by which potential militants among candidates for admission might be identified. Like chemical and biological warfare in relation to public health, this is merely humanism in reverse and a classic example of our commitment to ethical neutrality combined with devoted service to old customers and the power structure. But it is enough to prove that the technology of testing could serve humane goals in a more humane society.

But a more humane society might have little use for large-scale educational measurement because such a society would perforce be less competitive and universalistic and more generous and genuinely pluralistic than ours. I must stress that the reason is ideological, not technical. Educational measurement is technically capable of as great or greater service in helping people find out what kinds of knowledge, or what kind of job, or what college, or even what life would suit them best as it is in serving the competitive ends of society. For a people already ankle-deep in moonshit and happy ever after in the marketplace, even those computer-arranged courtships may be a form of salvation, or at least no joke. But society is not about to buy such a diagnostic use of testing on anything like the scale that it buys a competitive use because under its current ideology, only competitive testing can assign subjects to ideologically defensible categories for social action.

The major premise of the American system of social morality is that every individual should have an equal opportunity to compete for the prizes offered. The less frequently stated, but probably more crucial minor premise is that, if he does, he has no other legitimate basis for complaint. The contest may be destructive or banal, the prizes worthless, and the victory empty or pyrrhic; but to complain of these things is to be a bad sport and perhaps even an elitist, and such complaints are not honored in our system. It is most important, however, that every contest be objectively judged, as impersonally as possible, with no favoritism, nepotism, or any other kind of ism. To make this objectivity evident, access to preferred categories should, wherever possible, be granted on the basis of scaled scores that a machine can handle.

This is a very important dynamic in maintaining the American illusion of objectivity, since it permits the biases useful in maintaining our status structure and our institutions to be hidden beneath several levels of abstraction. Beneficiaries of the system, like middle-class college-bound students and their parents, or even its naive victims, like the more old-fashioned students in "general" or "commercial" tracks, may assume that there is no bias in the tests since there can be none in the scoring. Educators and more sophisticated students and parents, including a growing number of those of lower status, are aware of the problem of bias in the tests themselves, and may demand a "culture-free" test or the use of different norms in grading "disadvantaged" groups or the suspension of the testing program itself. But even they are unlikely to recognize the bias inherent in the very practice of basing judgments that may determine the entire life of a youngster — and, in view of our selective service policy, his death as well — on the display of a narrow range of cognitive behavior, quite apart from any question about the content of the test items. And virtually none recognize the value judgment involved in the monstrous, though familiar, decision that the welfare of any human being in a society with the means to nurture all its members should depend on any test score at all.

The widespread use of educational measurement, in short, reinforces our commitment to universalism, and our conviction that equality is the core of justice and that, moreover, equality is to be assessed by quantitative measurement in presumably scalar units. The value of this set of assumptions in the process of domestic counter-insurgency can hardly be overestimated. Every high school principal, college admissions officer, selections board for fellowship, or employment recruiter lives under continual menace from losers ready to accuse him of favoritism and the impediment of an egalitarian ideology which prevents him from making effectively the obvious rejoinder that favoritism, in the sense of allowing himself to be guided by his human and subjective perception of the needs and qualities of others, is a part of his professional responsibility. Partly for this reason, the use of testing has proliferated far beyond any expectation that the data it yields are needed to make any rational decision. They are needed, rather, to justify decisions for which no data were needed and to get administrators off the hook for having made them by showing that, however insensitive, uptight, and uncritical they might have been, and however willing to serve a corrupt master in a dubious cause, they are fair and impartial and play by the rules and have really nothing to answer for.

Fundamentally, the reason Jensen is so disturbing to liberals is, I believe, because his analysis threatens this basic stabilizing function of educational measurement and, with it, universalism itself. For if he is right, no amount of fairness and psychometric ingenuity can afford equality of treatment. Instead, one must choose between fairness and justice, and if a commitment to justice is to be preserved and finally implemented, the educational system must manage, against the pressure of so-called backlash, the difficult political decision to be generous and, as they say in the South, "partial." There is no reason to suppose that we find ourselves on this earth for the purpose of performing well on tasks involving abstract cognition or, indeed, for any purpose at all except our own. Educational measurement can serve those who want help in making an estimate that is more precise than one they could make themselves of what purposes might be realistic for them in view of their actual characteristics and the actual scenes they might make. It can also help them in legitimating their demands that they be permitted to make those scenes against possible social opposition; Educational Testing Service could, for example, provide SAT and Achievement Test scores in support of applications for college admission by high school dropouts, pushouts, and troublemakers who have poor recommendations and possibly no degree. It can do all this and more quite as proficiently as it can continue to assist in the grand process of channeling by which our society meets its manpower needs, sustains its status system, and brings peace of a kind to Southeast Asia. What it cannot do is get that society to authorize this process and pay for it.

REFERENCES

(1) Herndon, James. *The way it spozed to be.* New York: Simon and Shuster, 1968.
(2) Jensen, Arthur R. How much can we boost I.Q. and scholastic achievement? *Harvard Educational Review*, Winter, 1969.
(3) Kozol, Jonathan. *Death at an early age.* Boston: Houghton Mifflin Co., 1967.
(4) Leacock, Eleanor. *Teaching and learning in city schools.* New York: Basic Books, 1969.
(5) Lesser, Gerald and Stodolsky, Susan S. Learning patterns in the disadvantaged. *Harvard Educational Review*, Fall, 1967.
(6) Vonnegut, Kurt Jr. *Slaughterhouse-Five.* New York: Delacorte Press, 1969. P. 7.

POLITICS AND RESEARCH: EVALUATION OF SOCIAL ACTION PROGRAMS IN EDUCATION

David K. Cohen

Although program evaluation is no novelty in education, its objects have changed radically. The national thrust against poverty and discrimination introduced a new phenomenon with which evaluators must deal: large-scale programs of social action in education. In addition to generating much activity in city schools, these programs produced considerable confusion whenever efforts were made to find out whether they were "working." The sources of the confusion are not hard to identify. Prior to 1964, the objects of evaluation in education consisted almost exclusively of small programs concerned with such things as curriculum development or teacher training: they generally occurred in a single school or school district, they sought to produce educational change on a limited scale, and they typically involved modest budgets and small research staffs.

This all began to change in the mid-1960's, when the federal government and some states established broad educational improvement programs. The programs — such as Project Headstart, Title I of the 1965 ESEA, and Project Follow-Through — differ from the traditional objects of educational evaluation in several important respects: 1. they are social action programs, and as such are not focused narrowly on teachers' in-service training or on a science curriculum, but aim broadly at improving education for the disadvantaged; 2. the new programs are directed not at a school or a school district, but at millions of children, in thousands of schools in hundreds of school jurisdictions in all the states; 3. they are not conceived and executed by a teacher, principal, a superintendent, or a researcher — they were created by the Congress and are administered by federal agencies far from the school districts which actually design and conduct the individual projects.

Simply to recite these differences is to suggest major new evaluation problems. How does one know when a program which reaches more than eight million children "works"? How does one even decide what "working" means in the context of such large-scale social action ventures? Difficulties also arise from efforts to apply the inherited stock-in trade evaluation techniques to the new phenomena. If the programs seek broad social change, is it sensible to evaluate them mainly in terms of achievement? If they are national action programs, should evaluation be decentralized?

This paper is an effort to explore these and other questions about evaluating large-scale social action programs. It has three major parts. First, I delineate the political character of the new programs, in order to distinguish them from the traditional objects of educational evaluation. Second, to illustrate this point and define the major obstacles to evaluation, I review some evaluations of the new programs. Finally, I suggest some elements of a strategy which might improve the evaluation of social action programs.

POLITICS AND EVALUATION

There is one sense in which any educational evaluation ought to be regarded as political. Evaluation is a mechanism with which the character of an educational enterprise can be explored and expressed. These enterprises are managed by people, and they take place in institutions; therefore, any judgment on their nature or results has at least a potential political impact — it can contribute to changing power relationships. This is true whether the evaluation concerns a small curriculum reform program in a rural school (if the program is judged ineffective the director might lose influence or be demoted), or a teacher training program in a university(if it is judged a success its sponsors might get greater authority). Evaluation, as some recent commentators have pointed out, produces information which is at least potentially relevant to decision-making (Stufflebeam, 1967; Guba, 1968). Decision-making, of course, is a euphemism for the allocation of resources — money, position, authority, etc. Thus, to the extent that information is an instrument, basis, or excuse for changing power relationships within or among institutions, evaluation is a political activity.

These political aspects of evaluation are not peculiar to social action programs. They do, however, assume more obvious importance as an educational program grows in size and number of jurisdictions covered: the bigger it is, the greater the likelihood for the overt appearance of political competition.

There is another sense in which evaluation is political, for some programs explicitly aim to redistribute resources or power; although this includes such things as school consolidation, social action programs are the best recent example. They were established by a political institution (the Congress) as part of an effort to change the operating priorities of state and local governments and thus to change not only the balance of power within American education but also the relative status of economic and racial groups within the society. One important feature of the new social action programs, then, is their political origin; another is their embodiment of social and political priorities which reach beyond the schools; a third is that their success would have many far-reaching political consequences.

One political dimension of evaluation is universal, for it involves the uses of information in changing power relationships; the other is peculiar only to those programs in which education is used to rearrange the body politic. Although one can never ignore the former dimension, *its salience in any given situation is directly proportional to the overt political stakes involved;* they are small in curriculum reform in a suburban high school, somewhat larger in a state-wide effort to consolidate schools, and very great in the case of national efforts to eliminate poverty. The power at stake in the first effort is small, and its importance slight. In the social action programs, however, the political importance of information is raised to a high level by the broader political character of the programs themselves.

This should be no surprise. Information assumes political importance within local school jurisdictions, but political competition *among* school jurisdictions usually involves higher stakes — and the social action programs promote competition among levels of government. These programs are almost always sponsored by state or federal government, with at least the implicit or partial intent of setting new priorities for state and local governments. In this situation evaluation becomes a political instrument, a means to determine whether the new priorities are being met and to assess the differential effectiveness of jurisdictions or schools in meeting them. As a result, evaluation is affected by the prior character of intergovernmental relations. State resistance to federal involvement, for example, pre-dates recent efforts to evaluate and assess federal social action programs. The history colors the evaluation issue and the state response reflects the prior pattern of relations, for evaluation is correctly seen as an effort to assert federal priorities. Evaluation also can affect patterns of intergovernmental relations for it can help consolidate new authority for the superordinate government. In general, however, evaluation seems to reflect the established pattern of intergovernmental relations.

Of course, not all the novelties in evaluating large-scale social action programs are political. There are serious logistical difficulties — the programs are bigger than anything ever evaluated in education, which poses unique problems — and there is no dearth of methodological issues. These mostly center around making satisfactory comparisons between "treated" subjects and some criterion presumed to measure an otherwise comparable condition of non-treatment. These are difficult in any program with multiple criterion variables, and when the program is spread over the entire country the problems multiply enormously. But difficult though these issues may be, they are in all formal respects the same, irrespective of the size, age, aim, or outcome of the program in question. The large-scale programs do not differ in some formal property of the control-comparison problem, but only in its size. The bigger and more complicated the programs, the bigger the associated methodological headaches. What distinguishes the new programs are not the formal problems of knowing their effects, but the character of their aims and their organization. These are essentially political.

The politics of social action programs produce two sorts of evaluation problem. Some are conceptual — the programs' nature and aims have not been well understood or adequately expressed in evaluation design. Others are practical — the interested parties do not agree on the ordering of priorities which the programs embody. As a result of the first, evaluation is misconceived; as a result of the second, evaluation becomes a focus for expressing conflicting political interests.

CONCEPTUAL PROBLEMS

The central conceptual difficulty can be simply summarized: while the new programs seek to bring about political and social change, evaluators generally approach them as though they were standard efforts to produce educational change. This results in no small part from ambiguity of the programs — since they are political endeavors in education, the program content and much of the surrounding rhetoric is educational. It also occurs because evaluation researchers identify professionally and intellectually with their disciplines of origin (mostly education and psychology), and thus would rather not study politics. They prefer education and psychology; since that is what they know, what their colleagues understand, and — if done well — what will bring them distinction and prestige (Dentler, 1969).

But whatever the sources of the incongruence, it produces inappropriate evaluation. The aims and character of the programs are misconceived, and as a result evaluation design and execution are of limited value. Title I of ESEA (U. S. Congress, 1965a) is a good example with which to begin.

In the four years ESEA has been in existence, the federal government completed several special evaluation studies, undertaken either by the Office of the Secretary of HEW or the Office of Education.(1) They concentrated mainly on one question — has the program improved achievement over what otherwise might have been expected? The answer in each case was almost entirely negative, and not surprisingly, this led many to conclude that the Title I program was not "working." This, in turn, raised or supported doubts about the efficacy of the legislation or the utility of compensatory education. Yet such inferences are sensible only if two crucial assumptions are accepted: (a) children's achievement test scores are a sufficient criterion of the program's aims — the consequences intended by the government — to stand as an adequate summary measure of its success; and (b) the Title I program is sufficiently coherent and unified to warrant the application of *any* summary criterion of success, be it achievement or something else. Both assumptions merit inspection.

It does not seem unreasonable to assume that improving the achievement of disadvantaged children is a crucial aim of the Title I program. Much of the program's rhetoric suggests that it seeks to reduce the high probability of school failure associated with poverty. Many educators and laymen regard achievement test scores as a suitable measure of school success, on the theory that children with higher achievement will have higher grades, happier teachers, more positive attitudes toward school, and therefore a better chance of remaining and succeeding.

There are, however, two difficulties with this view. One is that achievement scores are not an adequate summary of the legislation's diverse aims. The other is that hardly anyone cares about the test scores themselves — they are regarded as a suitable measure of program success only because they are believed to stand for other things.

The second point can easily be illustrated. Aside from a few intellectuals who think that schooling is a good thing in itself, people think test scores are important because they are thought to signify more knowledge, which will lead to more years in school, better job opportunities, more money, and more of the ensuing social and economic status Americans seem to enjoy. Poor people, they reason, have little money, undesirable jobs (if any) and, by definition, the lowest social and economic status presently available. The poor also have less education than most of thier countrymen. On the popular assumptions just described, it is easy to argue that "poverty can be eliminated" by increasing the efficiency of education for the poor.

Although much abbreviated, this chain of reasoning is not a bad statement of the reasons why improved achievement is an aim of Title I. Improved schooling was a major anti-poverty strategy, and higher school achievement simply a proxy for one of the program's main aims — improving adults' social and economic status. The principal problem this raises for evaluation is that the criterion of program effectiveness is actually only a surrogate for the true criterion. This would pose no difficulty if reliable estimates of the causal relationship between schoolchildren's achievement and their later social and economic status existed. Unfortunately, no information of this sort seems to be available. There is one major study relating years of school completed and occupational status; it shows that once inherited status is controlled, years of school completed are moderately related to adult occupational status (Blau and Duncan, 1968). Other studies reveal no direct relationship between intelligence and occupational status, but they do show that the education-occupation relationship is much weaker for Negroes than whites (Duncan, 1968). The first of these findings should not encourage advocates of improved achievement, and the second is hardly encouraging to those who perceive blacks as a major target group for anti-poverty programs.

There are studies which show that more intelligent people stay in school longer (Duncan, 1968), but it is hardly clear a priori that raising achievement for disadvantaged children will keep them in school, nor is it self-evident that keeping poor children in school longer will get them better jobs.(2) It is, for example, not difficult to imagine that the more intelligent children who stay in school longer do so because they also have learned different behavior patterns, which include greater tolerance for delayed gratification, more docility, less overt aggression, and greater persistence. Several compensatory programs are premised on these notions, rather than the achievement-production idea. Without any direct evidence on the consequence of either approach, however, it is difficult to find a rational basis for choice.

This does not mean that compensatory education programs founded on either view are a mistake — absent any data, one could hardly take that position. It does suggest, however, that using achievement — or any other form of school behavior — as a proxy for the actual long-range purpose of compensatory education is probably ill-founded. The chief difficulty with this variety of agnosticism, of course, is that the only alternative is evaluation studies whose duration would make them of interest only to the next generation. What is more, they would be extremely expensive. The current proportion of program budgets devoted to evaluation indicates that the probability of undertaking such studies is nil.

Even if this scientific embarrassment were put aside, there is the other major difficulty with using achievement as an evaluation criterion. Schoolmen must be expected to assume that the greater application of their efforts will improve students' later lives, but there is no evidence that the Congress subscribed to that view by passing Title I of the 1965 ESEA. Although the title did contain an unprecedented mandate for program evaluation — and even specified success in school as a criterion — this is scant evidence that the sole program aim was school achievement. The mandate for evaluation — like many Congressional authorizations — lacked any enabling mechanism: responsibility for carrying out the evaluation was specifically delegated to the state and local education authorities who operated the programs. It was not hard to see, in 1965, that this was equivalent to abandoning much hope of useful program evaluation.

The main point, however, is that the purposes of the legislation were much more complex: most of them could be satisfied without any evidence about children's achievement. Certainly this was true for aid to parochial school students, and it most likely was also true for many of the poorer school districts: for them (as for many of the congressmen who voted for the act) more money was good in itself. Moreover, the Congress is typically of two minds on the matter of program evaluation in education — it subscribes to efficiency, but it does not believe in Federal control of the schools. National evaluations are regarded as a major step toward Federal control by many people, including some members of Congress.

Although the purposes of the Congress may be too complicated to be summarized in studies of test scores, they are not by that token mysterious. The relevant Committee hearings and debates suggest that the legislative intent included several elements other than those already mentioned.(3) One involved the rising political conflict over city schools in the early 1960's; many legislators felt that spreading money on troubled waters might bring peace. Another concerned an older effort to provide federal financial assistance for public education: the motives for this were mainly political and ideological, and were not intimately tied to achievement. A third involved the larger cities; although not poor when compared to the national average expenditure, they were increasingly hard-pressed to maintain educational services which were competitive with other districts in their areas as property values declined, population changed, and costs and taxes rose. Educators and other municipal officials were among the warmest friends of the new aid scheme, because it promised to relieve some of the pressure on their revenues.

Indeed, many purposes of the legislation — and the Congress's implicit attitude toward evaluation — can be summarized in the form which it gave to fund apportionment. Title I is a formula grant, in which the amount of money flowing to any educational agency is a function of how many poor children it has, not of how well it educates them. In a sense, Title I is the educational equivalent of a rivers and harbors bill. There is no provision for withdrawing funds for non-performance, nor is there much suggestion of such intent in the original committee hearings or floor debates. Given the formula grant system, neither the Federal funding agency or the states have much political room to maneuver, even if they have the results of superb evaluation in hand. Without the authority to manipulate funds, achievement evaluation results could only be used to coax and cajole localities: the one major implicit purpose of program evaluation — more rational resource allocation — is seriously weakened by the Title I formula grant system.

It is, therefore, difficult to conclude that improving schools' production of poor children's achievement was the legislation's major purpose. The legislative intent embraced many other elements: improving educational services in school districts with many poor children, providing fiscal relief for the central cities and parochial schools, reducing discontent and conflict about race and poverty, and establishing the principal of federal responsibility for local school problems. The fact that these were embodied in a single piece of legislation contributed heavily to its passage, but it also meant that the resulting program was not single-purpose or homogeneous. If any supposition is in order, it is precisely the opposite. Title I is typical of reform legislation in a large and diverse society with a federal political system: it reflected various interests, decentralized power, and for these reasons a variety of programatic and political priorities.

Additional References: Bateman, 1969; Campbell, 1969; Campbell and Stanley, 1966; Dyer, in press; Evans, 1969; Hyman and Wright, 1966; Marris and Rein 1967; McDill, McDill and Spreche, 1969; Rivlin, 1969; Rivlin and Wholey, 1967; Rothenberg, 1969; Swartz, 1961; Weiss and Rein, 1969; Wholey, 1969 a and b; Williams and Evans, 1969.

CONSEQUENCES FOR EVALUATION

Misconceptions about program aims result in omissions in evaluations and in distortions of the relationship among various aspects of evaluation. The first problem is mainly confined to program delivery. For Title I, for example, there are several criteria of program success which appear never to have been scrutinized. One involves impact of Title I on the fiscal position of the parochial schools: as nearly as I can tell, this purpose of the Act has never been explored.(4) Another involves the impact of Title I upon the fiscal situation of the central cities and their position vis-a-vis adjacent districts. Although the redistributive intent of the title was clear, there is little evidence of much effort to find out whether it has had this effect. With the exception of one internal Office of Education paper — which showed that Title I had reduced the per pupil expenditure disparity between eleven central cities and their suburbs by about half — this subject appears to have received no attention.(5) A third involves the quality of education in target as compared with non-target schools. Thus far no data have been collected which would permit an assessment of Title I's effectiveness in reducing intra-district school resource disparities, although this was one of the most patent purposes of the Act. There has been an extended effort, covering 465 school districts (Project 465) to gather information on resource delivery to Title I target schools. This might turn up interesting data on differences in Title I services among schools, districts, or regions, but comparison with schools which do not receive Title I aid is not provided. Since Title I seeks to provide better-than-equal education for the disadvantaged, measuring its impact upon resource disparities between Title I and non-Title I schools within districts would be crucial. This is recognized in the Office of Education regulations governing the Title, which provide that Title I funds must add to existing fiscal and resource equality between Title I and non-Title I schools.(6) Important as this purpose of the legislation is, only a few federal audits have been conducted; for the most part, states satisfy the federal requirements simply by passing on data provided by the local education agencies, most of which are so general they are useless.

Such things do not result simply from administrative lapses. Evidence on whether Title I provides better-than-equal schooling would permit a clear judgment on the extent to which Federal priorities were being met. But the legislation allocates money to jurisdictions on a strict formula, and it delegates the responsibility for monitoring performance to those same jurisdictions: this reflects both the decentralization of power in the national school system and the sense of the Congress that it should remain just so. An important source of inadequate program delivery studies is inadequate Federal power or will to impose its priorities on states and localities; the priorities are enunciated in the statute, but the responsibility for determining whether they are being met is left with the states and localities.

The distribution of power is not the sole source of such problems in evaluating program delivery; the sheer size and heterogeneity of the society, and the unfamiliarity of the problems are also important. Project Headstart is illustrative. This program was not initially established within the existing framework of education. It existed mostly outside the system of public schools; its clients were below the age of compulsory education, and its local operating agencies often were independent of the official school agencies. Since the program came into existence, several million dollars have been spent on evaluation, and not a little of it on studies of program delivery. Yet it is still impossible to obtain systematic information on this subject. Several annual national evaluations and U. S. Census studies of program delivery are unpublished. But even if these studies had all been long since committed to print, they would only allow comparisons within the Headstart program. They would provide no basis for comparing how the services delivered to children under this program compare with those available to more advantaged children. That is no easy question to answer, but it is hardly trivial: without an estimate of this program's efficacy in delivering services to children, its efficacy as an anti-poverty program could hardly be evaluated.

There have been some recent efforts to remedy the relative absence of information on Title I program delivery, through an extensive management information program under development in 21 states. Data are to be collected from a sample of schools which receive Federal aid under several programs; it is estimated that the universe of schools and districts from which the sample will be drawn includes roughly 90% of all public school students in those states. Extensive information on teachers, on district and school attributes, and funding will be collected from self-administered questionnaires. Principals and teachers will provide information on school and classroom characteristics and programs, including compensatory efforts. In elementary schools the teachers will provide information on student background, but in secondary schools these data may be taken from the students themselves. Some effort also will be made to measure the extent of individual student's exposure to programs. In addition, common testing (using the same instruments in all schools) is planned, beginning with grades four and eleven. If this ambitious effort becomes operational in anything approaching the time planned, in a few years extensive data will be available with which to assess program delivery for Title I.

In summary, then, an underlying purpose of social action programs is to deliver more resources to the poor, whether they are districts, schools, children, or states. It is therefore essential to know how much more and for whom. It is important both because citizens should know the extent to which official intentions have been realized, and because without much knowledge on that score, it is hard to decide what more should be done. Satisfying these evaluative needs implies measurement that is both historical (keyed to the target population before the program began) and comparative (keyed to the non-target population).(7)

Studies of program delivery also serve a building-block function with respect to evaluating program outcomes. Whatever criterion of program effect one might imagine, it could not intelligibly be evaluated in the absence of data which describe the character of the program. Improved health, for example, is a possible outcome of the health care components of Title I and Headstart: one could not usefully collect evidence on changes in students' health without evidence on the character and intensity of the care they received from the program. And if one were interested in the impact of health care on school performance, it would be necessary to add some measure of students' achievement, classroom behavior, or attitudes. In the case of achievement outcomes, of course, evaluators commonly try to associate information about the type and intensity of academic programs with students' scores on some later test.

Despite the logical simplicity of these relationships, it is not easy to find large-scale social action programs in which outcome evaluation is linked to appropriate program delivery data. Without any direct evidence on program delivery, the only "input" which can be evaluated is inclusion in a program. But an acquaintance with national social action ventures leads quickly to the conclusion that an important aspect of such endeavors is the "non-treatment project." There is no reason to believe that mere inclusion necessarily leads to change either in the substance of education or in the level of resources. This phenomenon takes many forms: it may consist of teachers or specialists who never see the target children; it may involve supplies and materials never unpacked, or educational goods and services which reach students other than those for whom they were intended; in still other cases it may consist of using program monies to pay for goods and services already in use. Whatever the specific form the non-treatment project takes, however, recognizing it requires extensive program delivery data. In a decentralized educational system the probability of such occurrences must be fairly high, and the obstacles to discovering them are considerable.

Even if the non-treatment project problem could be ignored, inadequate evidence on program delivery has other consequences for the evaluation of program outcomes. One of them is illustrated by the following excerpt from one Office of Education study of pre- and post-test scores in 33 big-city Title I programs (Piccariello, undated, p. 4):

> For the total 189 observations [each observation was one classroom in a Title I program], there were 108 significant changes (exceed 2 s.e.). Of these 58 were gains and 50 were losses. In 81 cases the change did not appear to be significant.
>
> As the data in Appendix D show, success and failure seem to be random outcomes, determined neither clearly nor consistently by the factors of program design, city or state, area or grade level.

When one reads Appendix D, however, he finds that the categorization by program design rests exclusively on one-paragraph program descriptions of the sort often furnished by the local project directors in grant applications. This makes it difficult to grasp the meaning of the study's conclusions. Perhaps success and failure were random with respect to program content, but given the evidence at hand it is just as sensible to argue that program content is unrelated to project descriptions, and that some underlying pattern of causation exists.(8) Without evidence on program delivery, it is not easy to see what can be learned from evaluations of this sort.

There is, however, an important counter-argument on this point. The recent Westinghouse evaluation of Project Headstart, for example, took as its chief independent variable *inclusion in Headstart projects*. The premise for this was that the government has a legitimate interest in determining whether a program produces the expected results. On this view, arguments about program delivery are irrelevant, since from the sponsoring agency's perspective, inclusion in the program is of overriding interest. (See Evans, 1969.)

There certainly is no question that in principle over-all program evaluation is justified. But the principle need not lead to a single summary evaluation in practice. Judgments about a program's over-all impact can just as well be derived from an evaluation which distinguishes program types or differentiates program delivery as from one which ignores them. From this perspective, rather than reporting whether the "average" Headstart project raised achievement, it would be more meaningful to identify the several program types and determine whether each improved achievement.

This may seem sensible, but it is not easy to put into practice. How does one collect data on program types or distinguish program characteristics? Assume a hypothetical program in which the outcome variable is school achievement. The first step would be to drop all projects whose purpose is not to improve achievement. But if one reads any compilation of project aims in Title I, he finds that only a minority aim only to improve achievement. Another minority aims to improve something else, and a majority aim to do both, or more. Given this heterogeneity of aims and the non-treatment project problem, one could not proceed on the basis of project descriptions — the stated purpose of improving achievement would have to be validated by looking at programs.

The second step would be to distinguish the main approaches (the program types), from all those which actually sought to raise achievement. The main purpose of the evaluation is to distinguish the relative effectiveness of several approaches to this goal.

But if the logic seems clear, the procedure does not. To empirically distinguish the class of projects aimed at raising achievement one must first know what it is about schooling that affects achievement. Only on the basis of such information would it be possible to sort out those projects whose execution was consistent with their aims from those which were not. But when the new programs were established very little was known on this point: prior compensatory education efforts were few, far between, and mostly failures. The legislation was not the fruit of systematic experimentation and program development, but the expression of a paroxysm of concern. Although a good deal has been learned in the last four or five years, researchers are still a good way from an inventory of techniques known to improve school achievement. The only way one can tell if a project is of the sort which improves achievement, then, is not to inspect the treatment, but to inspect the results.

This creates an awkward situation. If there is no empirical typology of compensatory or remedial programs, what basis is there for distinguishing among programs? What basis is there for deciding which program characteristics to measure — if one does not know what improves achievement, how does one select the program attributes to measure? Some choice is essential, for evaluations cannot measure everything.

These questions focus attention on one important attribute of the new programs. To the extent that they seek to affect some outcome of schooling, such as attitudes or achievement, they represent a sort of muddling-through — an attempt at research and development on a national scale. This is not a comment on the legislative intent, but simply a description of existing knowledge. If program managers and evaluators do not know what strategies will affect school outcomes, it is not sensible to carry out over-all, one-shot evaluations of entire national programs: the results of strategies which improved achievement might be canceled out by the effects of those which did not. If the point is to find what "works," the emphasis should be on defining distinct strategies, trying them out, and evaluating the results. The highest priority should be maximum definition and differentiation among particular approaches. Program managers and evaluators must therefore devise educational treatments based on relatively little prior research and experience, carry them out under natural conditions, evaluate the results, and compare them with those from other similarly developed programs. Insofar as school outcomes are the object of evaluation, the work must take place in the context of program development and comparative evaluation. This requirement raises a host of new problems related to the intentional manipulation of school programs and organization within the American polity.

EXPERIMENTAL APPROACHES

The problem, then, is not only to identify what the programs deliver, but also to systematically experiment with strategies for affecting school outcomes. This idea has been growing in the Federal bureaucracy as experience with the social action programs reveals that the system of natural experiments (every local project does what it likes on the theory that good results would arise, be identified, and disseminated) has not worked. The movement toward experimentation presumes that the most efficient way to proceed is systematic trial and discard, discovering and replicating effective strategies.

Under what conditions might social action programs assume a partly experimental character? For Title I this would not be easy, because the legislation did not envisage it. It is a major operating program, and several of its purposes have nothing to do with achievement. Activities in Washington designed to carry out systematic research and development would generate considerable opposition among recipient state and local educational agencies, and in the Congress. Experimentation requires a good deal of bureaucratic and political control, and there is little evidence of that. The Office of Education, for example, does not require that the same tests be used in all Title I projects — indeed, it does not require that *any* tests be used. The Title I program's managers have neither the power nor the inclination to assign educational strategies to local educational agencies. Even if they did, the legislation would be at cross-purposes with such efforts. It aims to improve resource delivery — to ease the fiscal hardships of city and parochial schools, and to equalize educational resource disparities. Although the formula grant system is quite consistent with these aims, it is not consistent with experimentation. The two aims imply different administrative arrangements, reporting systems, and patterns of Federal-state-local relations. The experimental approach requires a degree of control over school program which seems incompatible with the other purposes of Title I.

The question is whether other programs offer a better prospect for experimentation in compensatory education. In mid-1968, the White House Task Force on Child Development recommended that Federal education programs adopt a policy of "planned variation"; the Task Force report argued that no learning from efforts to improve education was occurring with existing programs, and that it would result only from systematic efforts to try out different strategies of school and community conditions (White House Task Force, 1968).

The Task Force report focused its attention on Project Follow-Through. Follow-Through was originally intended to extend Headstart services from preschool to the primary grades, but severe first year budgetary constraints had greatly reduced its scope. Largely for this reason, the program seemed a natural candidate for experimentation. The Task Force (1968) recommended that Federal officials select a variety of educational strategies and develop evaluation plans using common measures of school outcomes in all cases.

> The administration should explicitly provide budget and personnel allowances for a Follow-Through staff to stimulate and develop projects consistent with these plans. . . .
> The Office of Education should select all new Follow-Through projects in accordance with these plans for major variation and evaluation.

After three years, can the effort be termed a success? Since the program is still under development it would be unwise to deal with the strategies or their impact upon achievement. My concern is only with the quality of the evaluation scheme and the discussion is meant to be illustrative; the evaluation design may change, but the underlying problems are not likely to evaporate.

The Follow-Through program of experimentation is designed to determine which educational strategies improve achievement over what might otherwise be expected, and what the relative efficiency of the strategies is. The program began with little knowledge about the determinants of academic achievement, and as a consequence, equating schools and programs becomes much more difficult. Assume, for example, that all the Follow-Through projects sought to change student achievement by changing teachers' classroom behavior, but no two projects used the same treatment or attacked the same dimension of behavior. Suppose further that in half the projects achievement gains for students resulted. How could one be sure that the gains derived from the Follow-Through strategies, and not from selection or other teacher attributes than those manipulated by the program? The obvious answer is to measure teacher attributes and use the data to "control" the differences. But, since the program begins with little knowledge of what it is about teachers and teaching that affects achievement, evaluators must either measure *all* the teacher attributes which might affect achievement or closely approximate an experimental design. The first alternative is logically impossible, for the phenomena are literally unknown. The second alternative poses no logical problems; it requires only that the Federal experimenter have extensive control over the assignment of subjects (schools, school systems, and teachers) to treatment. The problems it raises are administrative and political.

The Follow-Through program has not been able to surmount them. Neither the districts nor the schools appear to have been selected in a manner consistent with experimental design. The districts were nominated by state officials; those nominated could accept or decline, and those who accepted could pretty much choose the strategy they desired from several alternatives. There was, then, room for self-selection. In addition, the purveyors of the strategies — the consultants who conceived, designed, and implemented or trained others to implement the strategies — seem also to have been recruited exclusively by self-selection. The usual ways of dealing with selection problems (never entirely satisfactory) seem even less helpful here. Although experimental and non-experimental schools could be compared to see if they differed in any important respects, the relevance of this procedure is unclear when little is known about what those "important respects" (vis-à-vis improving education for disadvantaged children) happen to be.

The weight of the evaluation strategy seems to fall on comparison or control groups. The present plan calls for selecting a sample of treatment and control classrooms, carrying out classroom observation, measuring teachers' background and attitudes, and using variables derived from these measurements in multivariate analyses of student achievement. Most of the instruments are still under development. But since there is neither a compulsion nor an incentive for principals in non-Follow-Through schools to participate as controls, how representative will the control classrooms be? What is more, these control or comparison groups cannot serve as much of a check on selectivity among the participants. Many of the comparison schools are in the same districts which selected themselves into the program and chose particular treatments; even those that are not are bound to be somewhat selected, because of the voluntary character of participation. Even if no "significant differences" are found between experimental and control schools, this would only prove that selected experimental schools are not very different from selected control schools.

There also may be some confounding of Follow-Through with related programs. Follow-Through operates in schools which are likely to receive other federal (and perhaps state and local) aid to improve education for disadvantaged children. Students will have the benefit of more than one compensatory program, either directly or through generally improved services and program in their school. There is little evidence at the moment of any effort to deal with this potential source of confounding.

In addition to selection, there are problems related to sample size. The design assumes that classrooms are the unit of analysis; this is appropriate, since they are the unit of treatment. Almost all measurements of program impact are classroom aggregates — i.e., they measure a classroom's teacher, its climate, its teaching strategy, etc. But it seems that relatively few classrooms will be selected from each project for evaluation (the 1969-70 plans call for an average of almost five per project, distributed over grades K-2.) Since there are only a few classrooms per grade per project, it appears that in the larger projects there might be a dozen experimental units (classrooms) per grade. That is a very small number, especially when it is reasonable to expect some variation among classrooms on such things as teacher and student attributes, classroom styles, etc. In fact, since only six or eight of the strategies that are being tried involve large numbers of projects, the remaining strategies (more than half the total) probably will not have sufficient cases for much of an evaluation.

There has been some effort to deal with this problem by expanding the student achievement testing to cover almost all classrooms in Follow-Through. This has not, however, been paralleled by expanded measurement of what actually is done in classrooms, a procedure which is helpful only on the assumption that there is no significant variation among classrooms within projects or strategies on variables related to the treatment or the effect. If this is true, of course, then measuring *anything* about the content, staff, or style of the classroom is superfluous — one need only designate whether or not it is an experimental or control unit. Despite the evaluators' view that this approach is warranted, the inclusion of some classrooms for which the only independent variable is a dummy (treatment-nontreatment) variable seems dubious. This will inflate the case base and therefore produce more statistical "confidence" in the results, but it may so sharply reduce the non-statistical confidence that the exercise will be useless. The evaluators argue that given the fixed sum for evaluation, they cannot extend measurement of classroom content.

Sample size problems are compounded because the evaluation is longitudinal. Since there is inter-classroom mobility in promotion (all classes are not passed on from teacher to teacher *en bloc*), following children for more than one year will sharply reduce the number of subjects for which two- or three-year treatment and effect measures can be computed. Add to this the rather high inter-school pupil mobility which seems to be characteristic of slum schools, and nightmarish anxieties about sample attrition result. Although nothing is certain at this point, there will be considerable obstacles to tracing program effects over time.

A fourth problem relates to student background measures. Apparently these data are being collected only for a relatively small sample of families. The evaluators are not sure that it will be large enough to allow consideration of both project impact and family background variables at once, but budget constraints preclude expanding the sample.

There are a few additional difficulties that merit mention, though they do not arise from the evaluation strategy, but from the nature of social action programs. There are reports of "leakage" of treatments from Follow-Through to comparison schools in some communities; there also seem to have been shifts in program goals in some projects, and apparently there has been conflict in definition of aims between the Follow-Through administration and some projects. In fact, there appears to be an element of non-comparability emerging among the strategies. Some involve very broad approaches, whose aims center around such things as parent involvement in or control of schools; others are more narrowly-defined and research-based strategies for improving cognitive growth. As long as traditional evaluation questions are asked (did treatment produce different results than an otherwise comparable non-treatment?), this poses no problem, but comparing treatments is close to the heart of Follow-Through. It is difficult to see how such comparative questions can be answered when the programs are so diverse. The general change programs, for example, appear to be hostile to the idea of evaluations based on achievement. They seem to be moving toward establishing other outcomes — "structural change" in schools, for example — as the program aim of primary concern. This heterogeneity of aims may well restrict the scope of comparative analysis for Follow-Through.

The common element in all these difficulties is that the Office of Education is largely powerless to remedy them. Random assignment of schools to treatments and securing proper control groups are the most obvious cases; lack of funds to generate adequate samples of experimental classrooms or parents are other manifestations of the same phenomenon. Although there is no doubt that some problems could have been eased by improved management, no amount of forethought or efficiency can produce money or power where there is none. Nor is it easy to see how the Office of Education could effectively compel project sponsors not to change some aspects of their strategies or not to alter their motion of program aims.

The experience thus far with Follow-Throuugh suggests, then, that the serious obstacles to experimentation are political: first, power in the educational system is almost completely decentralized (at least from a national perspective), and federal experimentation must conform to this pattern; second, the resources allocated to eliminating educational disadvantage are small when compared to other federal priorities, which indicates the government's relatively low political investment in such efforts. Consequently, federal efforts to experiment begin with a grave deficit in the political and fiscal resources required to mount them, and there is little likelihood of much new money or more power with which to redress this imbalance. These difficulties are not peculiar to evaluation: they result from the same conditions which make it difficult to mount and operate effective reform programs. The barriers to evaluation are simply another manifestation of the obstacles to federally-initiated reform when most power is local and when reform is a relatively low national priority.

Several dimensions of social action program evaluation emerge from this analysis. My purpose here is not to provide a final typology of evaluation activities, but simply to suggest the salient elements. First among these is the identification of program aims; this ordinarily will involve the recognition of diversity, obscurity, and conflict within programs, and greater attention to program delivery. Evaluators of social action programs often complain that the programs lack any clear and concise statement of aims, a condition which they deplore because it muddles up evaluations. Their response generally has been to bemoan the imprecision and fuzzy-mindedness of the politicians and administrators who establish the programs, and then to choose a summary measure of program accomplishment which satisfies their more precise approach. I propose to stand this on its head and question the intellectually fuzzy single-mindedness of much educational evaluation. It generally has not grasped the diverse and conflicting nature of social action programs, and therefore produces unrealistically constrained views of program aims.

The second element is clarity about the social and political framework of measurement. In traditional evaluation the ideal standard of comparison (the control group or pre-measure) is one that is just like the treatment group in all respects except the treatment. But in social action programs the really important standard of comparison is the non-treatment group — what one is really interested in is how much improvement the program produces *relative to those who do not need it*. As a result the evaluation of social action programs is essentially comparative and historical, despite its often quantitative character: it seeks to determine whether a target population has changed, relative both to the same population before the program began and to the non-target population.

Finally, the evaluation of social action programs in education is political. Evaluation is a technique for measuring the satisfaction of public priorities; to evaluate a social action program is to establish an information system in which the main questions involve the allocation of power, status, and other public goods. There is conflict within the educational system concerning which priorities should be satisfied, and it is transmitted, willy-nilly, to evaluation. This puzzles and irritates many researchers; they regard it as extrinsic and an unnecessary bother. While this attitude is understandable; it is mistaken. The evaluation of social action programs is nothing if not an effort to measure social and political change. That is a difficult task under any circumstances, but it is impossible when the activity is not seen for what it is.

SUGGESTIONS FOR AN EVALUATION STRATEGY

What might be the elements of a more suitable evaluation strategy? The answer depends not only on what one thinks should be done, but on certain external political constraints. There is, for example, good reason to believe that federal education aid will be shifted into the framework of revenue sharing or block grants in the near future, and this is unlikely to strengthen the government's position as a social or educational experimenter. The only apparent alternative is continuing with roughly the present balance of power in education as categorical aid slowly increases the federal share of local expenditures. This seems unlikely to improve the government's position in the evaluation of large-scale social action programs. In addition, there seems to be a growing division over the criteria of program success. Researchers are increasingly aware that little evidence connects the typical criteria of program success (high achievement and good deportment), with their presumed adult consequences (better job, higher income, etc.). More important, in the cities — particularly in the Negro community — there is rising opposition to the view that achievement and good behavior are legitimate criteria of success. Instead, political legitimacy — in the form of parent involvement or community control — is advanced as a proper aim for school change programs. It is ironic that the recent interest in assessing schools' efficiency — which gained much of its impetus from black discontent with white-dominated ghetto schools — now meets with rising opposition in the Negro community as blacks seek control over ghetto education. Nonetheless, this opposition is likely to increase, and the evaluation of social action programs in city schools is sure to be affected.

There is, then, little reason to expect much relaxation of the political constraints on social action program evaluation. This suggests two principles which might guide future evaluation: experiment only when the substantive issues of policy are considerable and reasonably well-defined; reorient evaluation of the non-experimental operating programs to a broad system of measuring status and change in schools and schooling.

The first principle requires distinctions among potential experiments in terms of the political constraints they imply. One would like to know, for example, which pre-school and primary programs increase cognitive growth for disadvantaged children; whether giving parents money to educate their children (as opposed to giving it to schools) would improve the children's education; whether students' college entrance would suffer if high school curriculum and attendance requirements were sharply reduced or eliminated; whether school decentralization would improve achievement; or whether it would raise it as much as doubling expenditures.

These are among the most important issues in American education, but they are not equally difficult when it comes to arranging experiments to determine the answers. In most cases, large scale experimentation would be impossible. Experiments with decentralization, tuition, vouchers, doubling per-pupil expenditures, and radical changes in secondary education have two salient attributes in common: to have meaning they would have to be carried out in the existing schools, and few schools would be likely to oblige. If experimentation occurs on such issues it would be limited — a tentative exploration of new ideas involving small numbers of students and schools. While this is highly desirable, it is not the same thing as mounting an experimental social action program in education.

This may not be the case with one issue, however — increasing cognitive growth for disadvantaged children. It already is the object of several social action programs and would not be a radical political departure. As a result of prior efforts, enough may be known to permit comparative experimental studies of different strategies for changing early intelligence. Several alternative approaches can be identified: rigid classroom drill, parent training, individual tutoring at early ages, and language training. Relatively little is known about the processes underlying these approaches, but there may be enough practical experience to support systematic comparative study. Since all the strategies have a common object, researchers probably could agree on common criterion measures. Since cognitive growth is widely believed to be crucial, investment in comparative studies seems worthwhile. But if such studies were undertaken, they should determine whether the treatment effect itself (higher IQ) is only a proxy for other things learned during the experiment, such as academic persistence, good behavior, and whether cognitive change produces any change on other measures of educational success, such as grades or years of school completed.

In effect, the chances for success of experimental approaches to social action will be directly related to a program's political independence, its specificity of aim, and its fiscal strength. The less it resembles the sort of broad-aim social action programs discussed in this paper, the more appropriate is an experimental approach and the more the "evaluation" looks like pure research. Of course, the further one moves down this continuum the less the program's impact is, and the less relevant the appelation "social action." Early childhood programs may be the only contemporary case in which the possibility of large-scale experimentation does not imply political triviality.

The second principle suggested above implies that the central purpose of evaluating most social action programs is the broad measurement of change. Evaluation is a comparative and historical enterprise, which can best be carried out as part of a general effort to measure educational status and change. The aims of social action programs are diverse, and their purpose is to shift the position of specified target populations relative to the rest of the society; their evaluation cannot be accomplished by isolated studies of particular aims with inappropriate standards of comparison. Evaluating broad social action programs requires comparably broad systems of social measurement.

A measurement system of this sort would be a census or system of social indicators of schools and schooling (not education). It would cover three realms: student, personnel, program, and fiscal inputs to schools; several outcomes of schooling, including achievement; temporal, geographic, political demographic variation in both categories. If data of this sort were collected on a regular and recurring basis, they would serve the main evaluation needs for such operating programs as Title I. They would, for example, allow measurement of fiscal and resource delivery and of their variations over time, region, community, and school type. They would permit measurement of differences in school outcomes, as well as their changes over time. If the measurement of school outcomes were common over all schools, their variations could be associated with variations in other school attributes, including those of students, school resources, and the content and character of federal programs. Finally, if the measurement of outcomes and resources were particular to individual students, many of these comparisons could be extended from schools to individuals.

One advantage of such a measurement system would be its greater congruence with the structure and aims of large-scale multi-purpose programs. Another is that it would be more likely to provide data which could be useful in governmental decision-making — which, after all, is what evaluation is for. Most evaluation research in programs such as Title I is decentralized, non-recurring, and unrelated to either program planning or budgeting; as a result of the first attribute it is not comparable from year to year; and as a result of the third it is politically and administratively irrelevant. Since the main governmental decisions about education involve allocating money and setting standards for goods, services, and performance, evaluation should provide comparable, continuing, and cumulative information in these areas. That would only be possible under a regular census of schools and schooling.

This is not to say there would be no deficiencies; there would be several, all of which are pretty well given in the nature of a census. By definition a census measures stasis, it quantifies how things stand. If done well, it can reveal a good deal about the interconnection of social structure; if it recurs, it can throw much light on how things change. But no census can reveal much about change other than its patterns—probing its causes and dynamics requires rather a different research orientation. And no census can produce qualitative data, especially on such complicated organizations as schools. There is, however, no reason why qualitative evaluation could not be systematically related to a census. Such evidence is much more useful when it recurs, and is connected with the results of quantitative studies. The same is true of research on the political dynamics and consequences of social action programs. Although valuable in itself, its worth would be substantially increased by relating it to other evidence on the same program.

The central problem, however, is experimentation. Using a census as the central evaluation device for large-scale multi-purpose programs assumes that systematic experimentation is very nearly impossible within the large operating programs and can best be carred on by clearly distinguishing census from experimental functions. It would be foolish to ignore experimentation—it should be increased—but it would be illusory to try to carry it out within programs which have other purposes. A clear view of the importance of both activities is unlikely to emerge until they have been distinguished conceptually and pulled apart administratively.

These suggestions are sketchy, and they leave some important issues open. Chief among them are the institutional and political arrangements required to mount both an effective census of schools and schooling and a long-term effort in experimentation.(9) Nonetheless, my suggestions do express a *strategy* of evaluation, something absent in most large-scale educational evaluation efforts. The strategy assumes that government has two distinct needs, which thus far have been confounded in the evaluation of large-scale action programs. One is to measure status and change in the distribution of educational resources and outcomes; the other is to explore the impact and effectiveness of novel approaches to schooling. If the first were undertaken on a regular basis the resulting time-series data would provide much greater insight into the actual distribution of education in America. It would thus build an information base for more informed decisions about allocation of resources, at both the state and Federal level. If the second effort were undertaken on a serious basis, it should be possible to learn more systematically from research and development. Perhaps the best way to distinguish this strategy from existing efforts is this: were the present approach to evaluating social action programs brought to perfection, it would not be adequate — it would not tell us what we need to know about the programs.

Second, my suggestions assume that the evaluation of social action programs is a political enterprise. This underlies the idea of separating experimentation from large-scale operating programs. It also underlies the notion of a census of schools and schooling, which would almost compel attention to the proper standards of comparison and would emphasize the importance of change. In addition, only a broad system of measurement can capture the political variety which social action programs embody. Perhaps most important, measuring the impact of social change programs in this way is not tied to a particular program or pattern of Federal aid.

Finally, such a strategy could be implemented within the existing political constraints. That is not a scientific argument, but that is the real point: evaluating social action programs is only secondarily a scientific enterprise. First and foremost it is an effort to gain politically significant information on the consequences of political acts. To confuse the technology of measurement with the real nature and broad purposes of evaluation will be fatal. It can only produce increasing quantities of information in answer to unimportant questions.

NOTES

(1) The National evaluations of Title I are little more than annual reports based on the state evaluation reports, which are little more than compilations of LEA reports. This is not to say that the reports are useless — but simply that they are not evaluations. The Office of the HEW Secretary was responsible for a study by Tempo, 1968. Also see Piccariello, undated.

(2) By "achievement," I mean measures of reading or general verbal ability; I do not include therein more specialized measures of achievements such as math, social studies, science, or driver education.

(3) A good general treatment is Bailey and Mosher, 1968. See also: U. S. Congress, 1965b; U. S. House Education and Labor Committee, 1965a and b; U. S. Senate Appropriations Committee, 1965; and U. S. Senate Labor and Public Welfare Committee, 1965.

(4) The most recent report of the National Advisory Council on the Education of Disadvantaged Children (1969) contains a brief section on this issue. It does not deal with program impact, but with private-parochial school relations.

(5) Jackson, P. B. (1969). Hartman (undated) concluded that the aims of Title I are so vague as to make the act little more than a general (i.e., non-categorical) vehicle for redistributing educational revenues.

(6) The requirement is found in U. S. Dept. of Health, Education, and Welfare (1968). There also is a special memorandum (Howe, 1968) covering this issue.

(7) Not all the purposes of social action programs are so neat or abstract, nor can they all be evaluated by counting dollars, teachers, or special programs. One of the aims of large-scale social action programs is to produce peace, or at least to reduce conflict. Whether or not they serve these ends is well worth investigating.

Similarly, little is known about the ways in which educational institutions change. This has been highlighted by the ability of many big-city school systems to absorb large amounts of activity and money designated to change them, and emerge apparently unchanged. If any question about the efficacy of social action programs is crucial, it is how such efforts at change succeed or fail. The requirement here may not be quantitative research, but political and social analysis, which follows the political and administrative history of social change programs. It may be possible to learn as much about the sources of programs' success from studying the politics of their intent and execution as from analyzing the quantitative relationships between program components and some summary measure of target group performance. Although such studies would be inapplicable in traditional educational evaluation, they are crucial in the evaluation of social action programs. These programs represent an effort to rearrange political relationships, and the sources of variation in their success are therefore bound to have as much to do with political and administrative matters as with how efficiently program inputs are translated into outcomes.

(8) Actually, the evaluation found that gains were more common among classrooms which had low scores on the pre-tests and that losses were more common among those classrooms which had higher pre-tests. The most economical hypothesis, then, is a regression effect (Picariello, undated).

(9) Creating the capacity for experimentation would involve a few major decisions. One probably would be to separate the activity from the Office of Education, retaining its connection with HEW at the Assistant Secretary level. Another would be to create greater institutional capacity for support and evaluation in the private (or quasipublic) sector; at the moment, this important resource is not well enough developed to bear the load. A third would be to so arrange its management that the decisions about what experiments to fund resulted from systematic and sustained interaction between the political governors of such an institution, its scientific staffers and constituents, and the educational practitioners. Without this, it would probably do interesting but politically unimportant work.

Creating the capacity for a census or system of schooling indicators involves different issues. Here there is good reason for it to be part of USOE. The question is where, and what capacity would be required; though these require more detailed work than is possible here, a bit of speculation is possible. There is some reason to think, for example, that the new 21 state management information system might be a good base from which to begin. There already is an ongoing program, it seems to have promise conceptually, and there seems to be a good state-Federal relationship.

BIBLIOGRAPHY

Bailey, S. and Mosher, E. ESEA: *The Office of Education Administers a Law.* Syracuse, N.Y.: Syracuse Univ. Press, 1968.

Blau, P. and Duncan, O. *The American Occupational Structure.* New York: Wiley, 1968.

Dentler, R. ,*The Phenomenology of the Evaluation Researcher.* Paper presented to the Conference on Evaluating Social Action Programs, American Academy of Arts and Sciences, May 1969. New York: Center for Urban Education, 105 Madison Avenue. (Typewritten.)

Duncan, O. *Socioeconomic Background and Occupational Achievement.* Ann Arbor: Univ. of Mich. Press, 1968.

Guba, E. Development, Diffusion, and Evaluation. *Knowledge Production and Utilization in Educational Administration.* (Edited by Terry Eidell and Joanne Kitchel.) Eugene, Ore.: Univ. Council for Educational Administration and Center for the Study of Educational Administration, 1968. Chapter 3, pp. 37-63.

Hartman, R. *Evaluation in Multi-Purpose Grant-in-Aid Programs.* Washington, D.C.: The Brookings Institution, undated. (Typewritten.)

Howe, Harold (Commissioner). *Special memorandum.* Washington, D.C.: U. S. Dept. of Health, Education, and Welfare, Office of Education, June 14, 1968.

Jackson, P. B. *Trends in Elementary and Secondary Education Expenditures: Central City and Suburban Comparisons, 1965-1968.* Washington, D.C.: U. S. Dept. of Health, Education, and Welfare, Office of Education, Office of Program Planning and Evaluation, 1969. (Mimeo.)

National Advisory Council on the Education of Disadvantaged Children. *Title I ESEA: A Review and a Forward Look.* Washington, D.C.: the Council, 1969.

Piccariello, H. *Evaluation of Title I.* Paper presented to the Dept. of Health, Education, and Welfare, Office of Education, Washington, D.C., undated. (Typewritten.)

Stufflebeam, D. The Use and Abuse of Evaluation in Title III. *Theory into Practice 6:* 126-33; 1967.

Tempo, G. *Survey and Analysis of Title I Funding for Compensatory Education.* Washington, D.C.: U. S. Dept. of Health, Education, and Welfare, Office of the Secretary, 1968.

U. S. Congress, Eighty-nine, First Session. Title I. *Elementary and Secondary Education Act of 1965* Public Law 89-10. U. S. Statutes at Large, 89th Congress, First Session. 1965a.

U. S. Congress, Eighty-nine, First Session. House Report No. 143. *Report of the Committee on Education and Labor, on the Elementary and Secondary Education Act of 1965.* 1965b.

U. S. Department of Health, Education, and Welfare. *Criteria for Applications Grants to Local Educational Agencies Under Title I, ESEA.* Washington, D.C.: the Department, 1968.

U. S. Department of Health, Education, and Welfare. *Summary Report of 1968 White House Task Force on Child Development.* Washington, D.C., USGPO, 1968.

U. S. House Education and Labor Committee. *Hearings before General Subcommittee on Education, Eighty-Ninth Congress, First Session, on Aid to Elementary and Secondary Education. 1965a.*

U. S. House Education and Labor Committee. *Hearings before General Subcommittee on Education, Eighty-Ninth Congress, First Session, on the Elementary and Secondary School Act Formulas. 1965b.*

U. S. Senate Appropriations Committee. *Hearings before Subcommittee on Departments of Labor and HEW Appropriations for 1966, Departments of Labor and HEW Supplemental Appropriations for 1966, Eighty-Ninth Congress, First Session.* 1965.

U. S. Senate Labor and Public Welfare Committee. *Hearings before Subcommittee on Education, Eighty-Ninth Congress, First Session, on the Elementary and Secondary Education Act of 1965.* 1965.

ADDITIONAL REFERENCES

Aldrich, Nelson (Issues Editor). *The Urban Review* 2, No. 6 and No. 7; 1968.

Bateman, W. *An Experimental Approach to Program Analysis: Stepchild in the Social Sciences.* Paper presented to the Operations Research Society of America, Denver, Colo., June 1969. Washington, D.C.: The Urban Institute, 1969.

Campbell, D. Reforms as Experiments. *American Psychologist* 24: 409-29; 1969.

Campbell, D. and Stanley, J. *Experimental and Quasi-Experimental Designs for Research.* Chicago: Rand McNally, 1966.

Dyer, H. Some Thoughts About Future Studies. Draft manuscript for *Equal Educational Opportunity.* (Edited by D. Moynihan and F. Mosteller.) New York: Random House, in press.

Evans, J. *Evaluating Social Action Programs.* Washington, D.C.: Office of Economic Opportunity, 1969. (Typewritten.)

Hyman, H. and Wright, C. Evaluating Social Action Programs. *The Uses of Sociology.* (Edited by Paul Lazarsfeld, William Sewall, and Harold Wilensky.) New York: Basic Books, 1966. Chapter 27, pp. 741-82.

Marris, P. and Rein, M. *Dilemmas of Social Reform.* Atherton, N.Y.: Atherton Press, 1967.

McDill, E.; McDill, M.; and Sprehe, T. *An Analysis of Evaluation of Selected Compensatory Education Programs.* Presented to the American Academy of Arts and Sciences Conference, May 1969. Baltimore, Md.: Johns Hopkins Univ., 1969. (Typewritten.)

Rivlin, A. *PPBS in HEW: Some Lessons from Experience.* Paper prepared for the Joint Economic Committee, Mar. 1969. Washington, D.C.: The Brookings Institution, 1969. (Typewritten.)

Rivlin, A. and Wholey, J. *Education of Disadvantaged Children.* Paper presented to the Symposium on Operations Analysis of Education, Nov.

1967. Washington, D.C.: The Brookings Institution, 1967. (Typewritten.)

Rothenberg, J. *Cost Benefit Analysis: A Methodological Exposition.* Paper presented to the American Academy of Arts and Sciences Conference, May 1969. Cambridge: Mass. Institute of Technology, 1969. (Typewritten.)

Swartz, R. Experimentation in Social Research. *Journal of Legal Education* 13: 401-10; 1961.

Weiss, R. and Rein, M. *Evaluation of Broad-Aim Social Programs.* Paper presented to the American Academy of Arts and Sciences Conference, May 1969. Roxbury, Mass.: Harvard Medical School, 1969. (Typewritten.)

Wholey, J. *Federal Evaluation Practices.* Washington, D.C.: The Urban Institute, 1969a. (Typewritten.)

Wholey, I. Program Evaluation in the Department of Health, Education, and Welfare. *Federal Program Evaluation Practices.* Appendix I. Washington, D.C.: The Urban Institute, 1969b.

Williams, W. and Evans, J. The Politics of Evaluation: The Case of Headstart. *Annals* 385: 118-32; 1969.

chapter 3
evaluative research

THE PURPOSE, DESIGN INTERPRETATION, POLICY DETER-
MINATION OF EVALUATION RESEARCH

Teaching and Learning Research Corporation

One would have to be very naive to assume that, because we know the limited utility of survey techniques in answering substantive evaluative research questions, we will see an immediate retreat from this kind of research and an embracing of other techniques. The practical, administrative, and political situations demand that we have status information and as much substantive knowledge as we can cheaply and quickly come by. We turn then to the questions of what are the uses of national assessment survey data and how can these techniques be better used.

E. A. Suchman has proposed five categories of criteria according to which success or failure of a program may be evaluated. These are: Effort; Perform-ance; Adequacy of Performance; Efficiency; and Process.

Effort has as its criterion of success the quantity and quality of activity that takes place. In the assessment of Title I programs we want to know "what was done," "what services were performed," "who was served by whom," "how much," "how often" and a variety of other questions designed to describe the extent and nature of the program. These questions can be answered through survey techniques. They can be more reliably answered through second party observer or interview techniques than through self-report survey questionnaires.

Performance has as its criterion the result of effort — the impact or effect of the activity which has been determined to have occurred. If objectives are clear and an adequate criterion measure has been applied, data referable to that measure can be collected through survey techniques. Again, accuracy and reliability can be enhanced through the utilization of second party observer-interviewers, assuming that measurement of criterion mastery has been objective. Some recent experiences in pupil progress assessment related to new efforts at accountability suggest that the pressure to have pupils show significant gains in test scores has resulted in inappropriate measurement procedures and data manipulation.

Adequacy of Performance refers to the degree to which effective performance is adequate to the total amount of need. In this category, a Title I assessment effort would be concerned with the number of children in need of special services and the degrees to which they failed to meet specified criteria. Data referable to number and degrees of need can be collected utilizing survey techniques. It would also be necessary to obtain outcome data referable to the target population number and degree of need categories established. Survey techniques can be applied here, but it is important to note that, as the reporting procedures become more complex, accuracy and cooperation are likely to go down. The initial 1965 Head Start assessment looked excellent on paper, but depended too heavily on the cooperation and competence of practitioners in the field who not only lacked skill but were also lacking in commitment to the evaluation reporting tasks.

Efficiency is concerned with how good the treatment is when compared to other strategies, is there a better way, easier way, or cheaper way. Efficiency is concerned with determining if there are alternatives which can produce the same results or more for less of any of the input variables. Here we get into planned variation or the study of natural variation in the population of programs. The latter can be managed utilizing survey techniques. The former usually requires on-the-spot intervention. However, in surveys of naturally occurring program variation it is particularly important to *know* whether what is reported as different actually is different — whether the elements alleged to be present or absent actually are, and to what extent they reach the children for whom they are designed. In comparison studies like these, the validity of the treatment report becomes crucial — is the program what is claims to be and has it been appropriately applied to the target population. *National assessments have not been very successful in answering questions of efficiency.*

Process as a category of criteria according to which a program may be evaluated is concerned with *explanation* — how and why a program works or does not work for whom, when and where. Some might argue that this is not an evaluation question but a research question. We have earlier taken the position that the ultimate questions in any evaluation cannot be distinguished from those of research. To quote Suchman, "making sense of the evaluative findings is the basic reason for adding a concern with process to the evaluation study." Without it one is left with descriptive results, no matter how sophisticated the statistical or graphic presentation. The analysis of process requires 1. the objective and systematic specification of the elements and operations of the treatment variable or variables; 2. the objective and systematic specification of the characteristics and functions of the population with special attention given to the nature of the relevant independent subject variables and dependent subject variables; 3. the objective and systematic specification of the situational context in which the treatment occurs; and 4. the objective and systematic specification of anticipated as well as unanticipated outcomes. In dealing with this process category of criteria, we are well beyond the sphere of survey techniques. It is to be recalled that it was on the shoals of process analysis that the Coleman Report floundered. He was wise enough, however, not to attempt to deal with process in that national survey, but this absence none-the-less limited the interpretations which can be drawn from his findings.

Following the Suchman classification it appears that survey techniques as utilized in the Elementary Education survey can be used to determine aspects of the status of effort and performance. As we move to questions of adequacy, efficiency and process, dependence on the survey becomes progressively inadequate. Given the problem of mandated national assessment, the Office of Education may want to give consideration to combinations of effort. For example, the Elementary Education Survey could be used to determine: 1. program characteristics (number, kind, location, magnitude, staffing patterns, elements of program, program objectives, etc.); 2. population characteristics (including nature and degree of need); 3. budget characteristics; 4. situational characteristics (economic, political, social, geographic, demographic, etc.); 5. opinion measures of impact; and 6. criterion measures of impact.

These data could be used to indicate various aspects of status and appropriate analysis could reflect some elements of performance or impact. If the attributes under each of the five categories are sufficiently delineated, some simple relationships could be determined. All of this is, of course, based on the assumption of accurate data and general respondent cooperation. To support this assumption and to, thus, strengthen the inferences which could be drawn from the survey data, the major variables could be defined and standard criterion measures established. In addition, field teams could be utilized to conduct site visits for the purpose of parallel data collection on a randomly selected sample of programs. If the site visit locations were designated after the status data were reported and the data from the two sources were congruent, there would be provided greater confidence in the total data pool.

In a similar manner, if several small carefully designed and controlled performance, adequacy of performance, efficiency and process studies were conducted, the data from these small studies could be compared to the data from the survey as could be the findings. Where the national assessment data and findings closely correspond to those of these controlled studies, confidence in the survey data and findings would be enhanced. In fact, the findings from the efficiency and process studies could contribute to better understanding the findings from the other studies and thus provide a more appropriate basis for policy determination and new program design.

The evaluative research problems and issues which have been discussed in this section and in Section I are deserving of serious attention. However, an exclusive focus on technical problems of evaluation can be illusionary, particularly in this field. Suchman calls attention to an important issue. He has written:

> To some extent evaluative research may offer a bridge between "pure" and "applied" research. Evaluation may be viewed as a field test of the validity of cause-effect hypotheses in basic science whether these be in the field of biology (i.e., medicine) or sociology (i.e., social work). Action programs in any professional field should be based upon the best available scientific knowledge and theory of that field. As such, evaluations of the success or failure of these programs are intimately tied into the proof or disproof of such knowledge. Since such a knowledge base is the foundation of any action program, the evaluative research worker who approaches his task in the spirit of testing some theoretical proposition rather than a set of administrative practices will in the long run make the most significant contribution to program development.

Now it is infinitely easier for the evaluative research worker to be concerned with testing some theoretical proposition if the program to be evaluated has been developed out of some theoretical grounding. It is to the shame of so many workers in this field that Title I and other compensatory education efforts tend to be sets of administrative devices or practices. There is little to indicate in the mass of these programs that they have been conceived out of any system or organized thought about the nature of development and learning. Even for those programs which have been based on more carefully developed models, the adoption of the model generally reflects the acceptance of a trend or an investigator's reputation and not the examination of alternative theoretical constructs as the basis of the decision. This condition would not be so serious were it not for the fact that we know so little about the educational rehabilitation and habilitation of the disadvantaged.

Let us return for a moment to the studies of compensatory education. Our major findings and conclusions may sound encouraging but on close examination there is no major new finding reported there. From the many studies reviewed, we are able to draw only very general and tentative conclusions. Analysis of the items in the Matrix provides us with not a single identifiable specific treatment or program for any known educational disability. We are unable to specify the nature of the need of any particular category of child and consequently unable to specify a treatment. This is the state of affairs after more than five years of effort and more than 10 billion dollars spent in those efforts. Improving evaluation techniques is not going to solve the problem of ideationally sterile programming.

Some planners have argued for more money   concentrated in fewer locations as a strategy for solving the problems of this field. It is certainly true that there are very few locations where it can be said that funds adequate to the task have been provided. Looked at nationally we are probably spending about 2 billion dollars per year for special educational programs for the disadvantaged. When Cohen estimated the cost of the necessary effort almost 3 years ago, he gave a figure of 10 billion dollars annually. Gordon and Jablonsky were also asked at that time by the Civil Rights Commission to design a program and estimate its cost. The Gordon and Jablonsky estimate was 50 billion additional dollars annually or twice as much as was being spent by the entire public education establishment in 1968, and five times the Cohen estimate. Either of these figures would represent a massive transfusion. Either would represent an essential ingredient for optimal educational development for the people of this country, but even funds of this magnitude will not provide conditions sufficient to the tasks. Before large additional sums are invested, a strategy must be developed.

A strategic attack upon a problem is programatic. The nature of the problem is determined, several tactics are developed to deal with the manifold nature of the problem. Tactics are ordered and sequenced. Priorities are established. Resources are deployed in relation to differential and sequential need. Political and social situational factors are taken into account and planned for. When these and other preparations have been tended to, one is better prepared to begin spending money and may have a program or strategy worthy of the evaluative research effort necessary to answer some of the crucial questions in this field. A recent experience in one of our major cities is illustrative of the insufficiency of adequate funding. Ten million dollars annually were allocated to one of the authors of this report to conduct experimental programs in thirteen elementary schools. Some of the steps enumerated were undertaken but most were not. The program was less than three months old when it became clear that social and political problems related to the teachers union and certain elements in the communities to be served were making aspects of the program impossible to implement. New functions had been prescribed for teachers but teachers had not been trained to perform them (they also had not been convinced that they could and should perform them). The program required changed relations and procedures in the bureaucracy, but the bureaucrats were not ready for change. Different program elements had been prescribed for different schools, as if we were unaware that pupil needs varied within schools and that program elements should be specific to pupils and not to the school buildings to which they are assigned. The fact is that after 30 million dollars and three years of frustrated effort, while there has been some improvement in these schools and in the achievement of the pupils, it is impossible to find 30 million dollars worth of change or new developments in this field.

More important than simply adding money is the need to allocate new and more money for specific kinds of efforts under specified conditions. For example, instead of a national assessment or the simple concentration of funds in particular locations, new monies could be assigned to well-conceived programs having adequate theoretical foundations and coupled with adequate process-oriented evaluation. In these cases program and evaluation funds would be concentrated but quality of program and evaluation would not be left to chance. Under these circumstances random assignment of pupils to treatment and comparison groups could be assured; program elements could be specifically designed in relation to pupil needs, systematically varied for studies of efficiency, and systematically analyzed for studies of process. It will not be until we take the problems of programming and the problems of evaluation seriously and allocate the necessary thought, time, and money that the important questions and issues will be served by evaluative research.

EVALUATION OF EDUCATIONAL PROGRAMS

Lawrence K. Frank

Increasing numbers of education projects and experimental programs, especially for young children, create an insistent demand for evaluation to discover how useful and effective they may be. Intensive efforts are therefore being made to apply and amplify accepted methods and techniques and to devise new ways of "quantifying" achievement by a group of children in order to decide whether a program is worth continuing.

If we were candid we would acknowledge that the assignment of numerical values to scale what individual children do is a pseudoquantitative assessment which we assume is statistically reliable and valid for the group if they display the expected range of variation. Counting and frequency are then accepted as the criteria for the results and a variety of analyses are produced by treating each of these assessments as a significant variable, the aggregate being used to establish norms and correlations with the measures of dispersion around a central tendency.

Unless we are focusing only on cognitive achievements, reading, writing and arithmetic and increasing verbal capacity, it is clear that a program for young children and its evaluation should embrace a wide range of dimensions and appropriate procedures to foster development of the child as a growing, developing and learning organism-personality. This more comprehensive concern for the "whole" child is necessary if any program is to provide what he may need in order to progress and become capable of living effectively as an organism and learn to perform what is required of him as a personality and member of a social order.

But such a comprehensive attempt to establish base lines for a variety of different dimensions presents a number of difficulties, especially the problem of how to deal with a variety of different observations on a single child, some of which — like bodily and physiological dimensions — can be accurately measured, while the others are capable of only scaling and assessment by the use of many different techniques. These are then expressed in terms or units which differ from the others and cannot be aggregated as homogeneous.

The measurements made by physicists, chemists and some biologists are usually in terms of homogeneous units of agreed upon magnitudes which can be treated statistically as the more or less invariant propeties of what they have measured.

By contrast most of the observations and assessments made on human subjects are, of necessity, heterogeneous and represent not invariant properties but the often individuated expressions and performances that differ not only in magnitude but express genuine and intractable differences. Moreover the human subject not only varies from individual to individual but he is subject to almost continual variability. His performances, which appear similar, nevertheless may differ markedly from one time to another. This quality again contrasts with the invariant properties recorded by the natural sciences.

The study of human beings therefore must be approached and carried on in terms of "open systems," as Bertalanffy pointed out some years ago, in which there are continual inputs and outputs and, as noted earlier, an almost unceasing internal variability.(1) In an open system like a human being, what and how a subject perceives and interprets events and situations, including carefully devised stimulation and systematic instruction, will be modified, distorted and interpreted largely according to the previous experiences of that subject.

VARIABILITY IN RESULTS

Moreover, the same process operating in an individual can and does often produce different products. Also a dissimilar process may produce almost equivalent products, as we must recognize in biology, physiology and human psychology. Examples of this are to be found in the process of fertilization and gestation in mammals which produce a great variety of different offspring, what might be called multiproductivity; and the production of truly similar outcomes by different processes, as shown by physiological disturbances and dysfunctions produced by very different impacts and intakes, what Bertalanffy has called the Principle of Equivalents.

Obviously in any serious attempt at evaluating programs undertaken to benefit children, the so-called culturally deprived or others, some base lines should be established at or before the project begins. To be comprehensive this base line should record the child's previous experiences, the vicissitudes to which he has been subject and some assessment of his family and home life including recognition of any siblings, younger or older and the neighborhood and housing from which he comes. These records should be made at the time of admitting individual children to the program.

But the crucial records for evaluation should provide at the beginning of the project a comprehensive set of measurements, whenever possible, or estimates and assessments and whatever other data can be obtained for each individual child. These should include whatever somatic observations that can be made such as height, weight, various physiological functions and capacities to the extent that these can be obtained. Then would come the various motor capacities and performances including manual skills and whatever other activities might be appropriate. These plus any other observations would comprise a sector dealing with the child as an organism and would, of course, include his nutritional condition and any specific deficiency or nutritional disorders.

TESTING THE SENSES

Of special importance would be the measurements or tests of his various sensory acuities, visual auditory, tactile, and perhaps taste and smell if likely to be important in assessing the child. Also some evaluation would be desirable of his kinesthetic awareness and of the flexibility or rigidity of the ligaments in the upper and lower legs. It is sometimes useful to see if a child can maintain a stable, erect posture with his eyes closed without too much swaying and can also touch his eyes, his nose and his ears when his eyes are closed.

A number of standardized neurological tests would also be desirable to indicate the integrity of his nervous system, such as a knee jerk, elbow and ankle reflexes and the Babinski reflexes. Such measurements, when made by trained examiners will be useful in assessing the strengths and weaknesses which, when disclosed, will indicate where remedial treatment and special training will be desirable, if not necessary, for his future development.

Other needed observations on a child will come from tests and measurements of his cognitive capacities and performances. His ability to speak, to listen and interpret language and to communicate by language will disclose his mental and intellectual stage of development and indicate whether he is, for his age, normal, advanced, or retarded and what specific lacks he may show in performing what is required by different tests. Here also should be tested his ability to recognize and discriminate colors. In using these standardized tests it is important to remember that chronological age upon which most of them are based is not a wholly valid criterion for comparing one child to others, because each child grows, develops and matures at his or her own individualized rate of progress. Accordingly, a group of children of similar chronological age may not be a homogeneous sample since some will be slower in attaining the capacities which are assumed to be normal for a given age group.

Also highly important are the different cognitive styles which individual children exhibit in their preferences for learning and their ability to master various tasks. Thus some children learn and have a strong preference for visual experiences, others for auditory experiences and later for reading, and then there are those who prefer and learn through tactile or haptic contacts, finding it more congenial to handle, grasp, manipulate and feel objects, textures, shapes and sizes and weights.

However difficult and baffling, some efforts must be made for systematic observation and recording of the individual personality make-up, emotional and impulsive reactivity, for repression or overt display of feelings, for autonomy and spontaneity or rigidity and restraint in whatever he says or does. For these there are a variety of descriptions and labels expressive of different concepts and assumptions about human nature and personality development, so that the choice of what is to be noted and recorded will depend largely upon those who are directing the program and observations and focusing on selected displays of overt behavior and emotional reaction.

The terms for observing and recording children's behavior in group situations are often ambiguous and subject to conflicting interpretations. Thus the term "aggressive" may be used to designate outgoing energetic activities and approaches to others or may be used for hostile feelings and impulses, most of which have been developed from previous experiences in which the child has learned to react.

It may be appropriate to discover, as far as possible, the individual child's image of himself which he has built up from what he has been told about his self and behavior by others, especially by parents, siblings and playmates. This image of himself is not some esoteric mystery. It is composed of the symbols by which the child gives meanings to the words *I*, *me*, *my*, and *mine*, in terms of which most of his contacts and interpersonal relations with others are carried on. It may require intensive observations to discover what each child means by these terms and what image of himself he has created for his own personal orientation and guidance. Again it should be recognized that many children have a negative and unacceptable image of themselves, derived from their experiences, how they have been treated and how their varied activities and behavior have been labeled by parents and other adults.

Closely associated with and expressive of the image of the self is the child's acceptance of socialization which requires him to recognize and to respect the property and also the personal integrity of others. This comes only with learning self-disciplined conduct, with the capacity to inhibit impulses and provocations to violate these inviolabilities of things and persons upon which social order is dependent. As reported in much research, many young children have not learned self-disciplined conduct or, to use a contemporary phrase, they have not developed the "ego strengths" required for peaceful social living and are frequently at the mercy of their uninhibited impulses, their desire for immediate pleasure with an almost complete insensitivity to the rights and feelings of others.

THERAPEUTIC EDUCATION

This lack calls for what may be termed a "therapeutic education" which helps the individual child in a group to escape from his anti-social and self-defeating behavior and to learn how to live and play and enjoy associations with others. In view of the wide-spread disorder and demoralization, especially in our large cities, emphasis upon programs for young children which seem to be concerned only with cognitive developments, speech training and preparation for formal schooling, may be viewed as ignoring or neglecting the crucial task of helping the young child to learn what is personally and essentially necessary for his future life career. Such programs rarely help the child to attain an identity, as the "I" who thinks, speaks, acts and feels as a unique personality. Nor do they recognize how the child continually talks to himself in his inner speech as he tries to establish his life space and to guard his private world.

Obviously, observations and recording in the personality sector will be difficult but may be, even if somewhat diffuse and imprecise, crucial for evaluating these new educational programs.

FAMILY INTERVIEWS

Supplementing the observations of the child in the program will be recorded interviews with parents who wish to enroll their child in the program, from visits to the home and from all other available sources including confidential information furnished by various agencies, public and private. These records may be supplemented by the use of widely accepted classifications of families, each with their ethnic-cultural backgrounds, former residence in rural or city life, educational attainment of the father and the mother, employment and earnings of father and mother and the customary ratings for socioeconomic status, religious affiliation and perhaps frequency of church attendance, housing and neighborhood conditions, plus whatever can be discovered about the martial state, alcoholism, drug addiction, and so on.

While some of the above items may be given a rating for comparison with other families, most of this information will be useful to supplement the records on individual children and to help interpret a child's present conditions and capacities and his potentialities for the future.

The purpose of these comprehensive observations and recordings is to provide, as indicated above, a base line at the entrance of the child to the program and to show where and how he may be in need of special attention and treatment.

The various measurements, ratings and assessments made for all of the children can be aggregated to show the relative position of each individual child in that group for each specific observation. This may be attained by any number of different methods. It will be helpful to calculate the individual child's percentile rank order in the group for each recorded dimension. His percentile rank order will then clearly show where he stands for each dimension within the group, whether in the upper or lower percentile or in between.

But it must be emphasized that this method is not to show averages or central tendencies or other statistical measures for the whole group. The purpose is to delineate the position or rank order for each child in the group, for each separate dimension. It will be difficult or impossible to handle and interpret such an array of different data by familiar methods or statistical techniques designed primarily for evaluating a group or sample of subjects. To convey these multi-dimensionalities for an individual child, the percentile ranks that he exhibits may be graphically presented on polar coordinates.

A polar coordinate is a graphic device showing a circle with 360 radii which can be divided into a number of segments each of which is allocated to the major classes of recordings and dimensions. Within each such segment an individual radius can be assigned for showing the rank order from 0 to 100 percentiles for each selected dimension as describer earlier. Then on each radius the individual child's rank order for each dimension will be marked on the appropriate radius in terms of his percentile rank for that dimension, preparing a separate polar coordinate for each child's records.

When these several points are connected by a line they will present the shape of an amoeba-like diagram clearly showing any discrepancies, imbalance, handicaps and impairments as well as any favorable or superior rank orders for that individual child. By scanning these graphic models it will be possible to visualize the status and conditions, the strengths and weaknesses in the context of the whole child in so far as he has been observed and recorded. Further, study will reveal what he may need for normal development of a unique organismic personality.

Polar graphs seem to be more illuminating than other forms of graphic presentations, such as the familiar profile which shows a succession of different dimensions difficult to recognize and interpret as representing the child's incongruities and discrepancies. Moreover the profile is usually expressed in a number of different units which are not easily compared or contrasted.

Other graphic presentations such as diagrams for factor analysis, the circumplex and similar graphic charts are used primarily for presenting statistical calculations and relationships for a sample. The familiar two-dimensional charts showing two dimensions as plotted on the simple or logarithmic grids showing dimensions on the abscissa and ordinates likewise may be useful for presenting limited data but may become confusing for more than two or three dimensions. Biologists and pediatricians have devised special graphic methods, such as the Wetzel Grid, to evaluate the status and development of individual children but these have not been found to be reliable indicators or valid assessments.

COMPREHENSIVE MEASUREMENT

Polar coordinates may be especially useful for presenting a comprehensive inventory or assessment of an individual child's status and condition and should be made at the beginning, at repeated intervals, and at the conclusion of the program, as a way of evaluating a project and discovering what and how the individual child in the group has changed.

Prescribed methods for research design focus upon statistical evaluations of the whole group, using averages and central tendencies, norms and various kinds of correlations to show whether the program has been effective. These procedures ignore significant improvements shown by individual children even though the group as a whole may not exhibit what is considered to be appropriate and justifiable gains. If a program has not achieved statistically significant results it may be considered a failure, since it is assumed that the group is made up of more or less homogeneous units whose failure to show anticipated benefits must be ascribed to the methods and techniques of the program. Conversely, significant losses by a single child, despite gains by the group, are not available for study.

This approach therefore appears to be more concerned with the operation of a program as if it were a determinate process rather than focusing on the individual children and what gains or benefits some of the group may have attained even though the whole group may not exhibit the expected results. Apparently the methods and assumptions that have been developed for laboratory experiments under closely controlled conditions and using as far as possible homogeneous subjects have been taken over and applied to educational programs dealing with highly individualized organism-personalities who exhibit not only a wide range of inter-individual variation but also a high degree of internal and behavioral variability. The usual neglect of the latter is frequent among psychologists who assume that they can replicate the findings on human subjects despite their changes over time and the often marked alterations in their and other subjects' physiological states at a later date.

In conclusion, therefore, it may be urged that for the evaluation of programs for young children, and indeed for a wide range of similar problems involving multi-dimensional complexes, graphic symbols and especially polar coordinates be utilized, as offering promising approaches to problems that are not now capable of resolution by familiar and long accepted methods and techniques.

When we approach organized complexities such as organisms, personalities, cultural groups and social orders and a variety of human organizations such as institutions, we should advance beyond many of the now accepted procedures. Instead of relying upon analysis and the fractionation of wholes into seemingly discrete variables, to seek linear cause and effect or stimulus and response or a variety of statistically derived correlations, we might more appropriately view the operation of these organized complexities in terms of closely coupled and entrained processes and the many different kinds of "feed backs" for the operation of these complexes.(2)

As Warren Weaver remarked some years ago:

These new problems, and the future of the world depends on many of them, require science to make a third great advance, an advance that must be even greater than the nineteenth century conquest of problems of simplicity or the twentieth century victory over problems of disorganized complexity. Science must, over the next fifty years, learn to deal with these problems of organized complexity.(3)

NOTES

(1) Bertalanffy, Ludwig. Theory of open systems in physical biology. *Science* III, p. 27. 1950. Also see *Yearbooks of The Society for General Systems Research,* 1950-1967.

(2) A tentative statement of processes which might be assumed and studied has been given in the writer's chapter, "Human Development — An Emerging Discipline" which appeared in *Modern Perspectives in Child Development* edited by A. Solnit and S. A. Provence, New York: International Universities Press, 1962.

(3) Weaver, Warren, Science and complexity. *American Scientist,* Autumn Issue, 1948, 36, 4, p. 536.

THE EVALUATION OF EDUCATIONAL PROGRAMS

Sidney C. Eboch
Daniel L. Stufflebeam

Evaluation is a word that has a long history in education and has had many meanings at many levels of popularity and acceptance over the years. During the past few years, the term evaluation has come to prominence again, especially in connection with federal legislation. It might be worthwhile before beginning our discussion to recall some of the past meanings or frames of reference which we have had for the term evaluation.

Perhaps the most common meaning of the term evaluation has been in the area of tests and measurements. When people in education used the word evaluation in this sense, they usually meant the administration of achievement tests or the development of teacher-made tests and the whole series of processes relating to selecting, administering, scoring and interpreting standardized tests. A second meaning attached to evaluation emphasizes the use of expert judgment. In the absence of some type of mathematical standard or some generally accepted social norm, we have reverted to taking the judgments of some persons deemed to be expert in the particular field, because of their past experience or specialized knowledge in that field. In this sense evaluation has meant expert judgment. A third meaning for the word evaluation is closely related to what we might call experimental testing. In this context, evaluation has meant the establishment of some sophisticated research procedure, usually involving relatively precise statistical techniques, with the intention of achieving an end product which "proves" or "disproves" a given fact.

Clearly each of these definitions has different strengths for particular situations within education. However, each in its way has its limitations. In the extremely varied and diffuse settings existing in education, none of the terms — nor all of them together — has seemed sufficient to adequately attack the problem of evaluating the complex situations in education. This presentation sets forth one approach to developing a comprehensive definition of evaluation which hopefully can encompass (with greater precision than "horseback judgment") almost all of the educational situations we seek to evaluate. Therefore we begin with this broad definition of the word evaluation.

Evaluation is the process of providing information for decision-making. Obviously the two key terms here are information and decision-making. We will deal with each of these in more detail. However it is important to note here that the word "process" also is a key term in the definition. For evaluation, as we are describing it, is not seen as an event which has some obvious and specific starting point and a single terminal point when everything is solved. Although we will discuss four different types of basic evaluation for which there *are* logical beginning and termination points, evaluation itself is viewed as continuing process. Let's look now to some further definition of our key terms "information" and "decision-making."

The process of evaluation is viewed as an activity which involves several specific steps. However, the key relationship to be noted is that an evaluation specialist is working with someone who can be classed as a decision-maker. It is the function of the evaluation specialist to assist the decision-maker in reaching the best possible decision he can make at the moment. It becomes important therefore to realize that decisions may be of many types, although the final decision may be considered merely a "go" or "no go" choice. There are several basic decision situations in which such a choice must be made. In analyzing the possible types of decisions, four general types are particularly relevant. These we define as planning decisions, structuring decisions, implementing decisions and recycling decisions.

Planning decisions can be classified as those related to the determination of major changes which may be needed in the educational program. One way of viewing these may be to think of them as decisions regarding what objectives are primary in the educational situation. At first glance it may seem illogical to think that evaluation should be involved at all if no objectives have been determined. In the real world, we know, that many times there are felt needs which cannot be articulated with precision. There are also those nagging little feelings that something may be wrong or that some new direction is needed and yet these feelings cannot be specified. The decision-maker is intuitively conscious of some disparity between intentions and achievements. However, he is unable to make the appropriate decision in planning any major changes which may be needed without additional information of a qualitative nature which can help him best select his basic objectives.

Structuring decisions relate to the choice of means by which the decision-maker can most effectively achieve the ends or objectives which are known to him. In the decision situation we have labeled "structuring," the decision-maker has some clear goal or objective in mind and his problem is to determine what means, what resources, what mechanisms could or should be applied towards the achievement of the goals or purposes he has chosen. Again the decision-maker needs the best information he can obtain to make his choice of the means which are to be applied to achieve the objectives.

Implementing decisions are those which relate to carrying through the action plan which is known to the decision-maker. At this point, the decision-maker has some conception of the objectives. He has made a preliminary determination of the means by which those objectives should be achieved. The question now before the decision-maker is: What are the actual operational arrangements which would best utilize the resources allocated towards the achievement of objectives? Once again qualitative information regarding the strengths, weaknesses, resources and needs are required.

The fourth basic type of decision situation we have called recycling. In the recycling decision situation, the program or project has been in operation and has completed at least one full phase or cycle of the intended action. The choices facing the decision-maker are: (a) to continue, (b) to discontinue, or (c) to modify the program or project as it has been operating. Again, the decision-maker needs the best information available to know whether in fact the product (the actual achievement of the project) meets the objectives or criteria initially established for the program.

Thus with these four terms: planning, structuring, implementing and recycling, we have a way of classifying the four major decision areas which are faced by most educators in seeking evaluation services of any type. It is important however to realize that of all these decision situations may have originated from one of two gross frames of reference. These two basic frames of reference we call Neo-mobilistic or Homeostatic. By frame of reference we mean that the decision-maker may have been starting from a viewpoint or a basic assumption of strikingly different types.

The decision-maker approaching his problems from a *homeostatic* point of view would be primarily interested in maintaining the status quo. This is not to infer that the status quo is negative or conservative. It merely is recognizing the fact that the decision-maker is relatively satisfied with the general circumstances which exist and his primary aim is to maintain this situation at its highest level of efficiency or achievement. The decision-maker approaching his problems from the *neomobilistic* point of view is viewing the situation as desiring some significant change. He is either deliberately seeking some novel or innovative aspect in the programs or operations he wants to evaluate or he is seeking to *create* a situation which will be, although ambiguous, very opportunistic. From this point of view he seeks to gain new and different advantages within his operations which have not been achieved beforehand or perhaps are not even recognized at the moment.

Having elaborated the general types of decisions as one set of key terms in evaluation, let us turn to a further definition of the "information" which is required for the decision-making situations described. The evaluation specialist who will provide the information for the decision-maker can classify the information to be accumulated as one of four types: context, input, process or product. Context information is that data which describes with some accuracy the total setting of the educational situation, and perhaps more specifically, the program or project goals or objectives which are either unclear or unspecified. Input information is that data which describes those resources which are available or required to achieve objectives or goals which have been specified. Process information is that which describes the procedures or methods which might most efficiently utilize the resources which can be applied to the program or project under consideration. Finally, product information is that data which measures the results of the program or project under consideration. This describes the actual results of the program or project about which a decision must be made.

The evaluation specialist in obtaining the information necessary for the various decision situations and in developing relevant and useful information of each and all of the four basic types described will perform four basic activities. The evaluation specialist will (a) *collect* information, (b) will *organize* the information, (c) will *analyze* the information and (d) will finally *report* the information to the decision-maker.

It is important for the evaluation specialist to recognize the frame of reference which the decision-maker may hold. The evaluation specialist can consider the information being sought as being of two gross types: contingency or congruency. These terms relate to those frames of reference which the decision-maker may hold. Information being developed which could be classified as congruency type information is directed toward the realities of the situation, in parallel with the intentions or expectations of the educational organization. If the information to be collected is better classified as the contingency type, the evaluation specialist will then be directing his attention and shaping his basic activities to monitor information of varied and changing types throughout the entire study.

At this point we can summarize and compare the terms relevant to each of the two key persons or groups involved in any evaluation situation in education. The decision-maker is concerned with four general types of decision-making situations: planning, or the determination of objectives; structuring, or the allocation of resources; implementing, or the determination of procedures; recycling, or the modification, continuation, or elimination decisions. As we have said, all of these decisions may be initiated either from a Neo-mobilistic viewpoint of planned change, or from the Homeostatic viewpoint of maintaining a desired situation at its most efficient state.

The evaluation specialist is concerned with the development of information from the four settings described: context information or the general situation to be described; input information or the analysis of alternative resources which may be required; process information or the desirable alternative procedures which may be available; or product information, the assessment of actual achievements as compared with initial goals. Again the evaluation specialist will want to match his viewpoint or his basic assumptions to those of the decision-maker. The evaluator will be seeking his information from either (a) the viewpoint of describing alternatives which could achieve congruency between original intentions and realities or (b) from a contingency viewpoint which recognizes and describes the varied changing circumstnaces which may provide new values the decision-maker could select as improvements.

What has occurred in the recognition of a need for evaluation as a process which is relatively standard for all such situations? First, there is a felt or recognized need for some type of decision. This need may be very ill-defined or it may be very precise, but out of that need the decision-maker must clarify — either with his colleagues or with the evaluation specialist — criteria which are paramount to any solution for the decision. Beyond this, the decision-maker must again define a minimum range of acceptable alternatives. Obviously, some alternatives will not be acceptable regardless of their effectiveness.

Having described in some fashion the need and defined — at least at a minimum level — the criteria and some of the alternatives, the problem for the decision-maker is obtaining the information on which his choices can be made. It is posited that the evaluation specialist can, more objectively, more systematic-ally, and with possibly greater expertise, collect, organize, analyze and report the needed information to the decision-maker.

As the evaluation specialist completes these functions, he presents the information as *weighted alternatives* from which the decision-maker can choose. By weighted alternatives we mean that several acceptable choices will probably be available for any decision. Each of the possible alternatives will have several comparable characteristics. In turn, each alternative will not have a uniform value for any specific characteristic. Therefore, alternatives are considered weighted through the assignment of some value for each of the characteristics related to each of the specific alternatives. Thus the decision will be the selection of that alternative which provides the maximum values associated to the most essential characteristics of the alternative. The final choice, of course, must be made not by the evaluation specialist but by the decision-maker.

Thus we have two major activities which any evaluation activity must pursue: one, the *focusing* activities which must be completed with the decision-maker; secondly, the evaluation must be *administered*. The evaluation team may be personnel associated either with the evaluation specialist or with the educational organization or perhaps a team combing members from both groups. In the administration of that evaluation activity the four key functions of the evaluation team are to collect, to organize, to analyze and to report the information.

Here we see the cycle which occurs and the interrelationship between the client or agency requesting the evaluation and the evaluation specialists. The evaluation specialist and the chief representative of the client must work closely and cooperatively at the beginning in *focusing* the evaluation problem. Once basic agreements have been reached in this focusing situation the evaluation team can go into action and complete the cycle of collecting, organizing, analyzing and reporting the information. With the reporting of the information to the client, the work of the evaluation specialist is in a sense completed.

The report is made available for judgment by the client or agency. That judgment activity will result in a decision. That decision will take one of two paths. Implementation of the program or that part of the program which has been evaluated *or,* the decision may be to join with the evaluation specialist again and focus on a new phase of the project or operation for a new and different type of evaluation activity. Again we would emphasize the key beginning point is the *focusing* activity in which the client and the evaluation specialist work cooperatively. It should also be recognized that the objective of the evaluation specialist is *not* to make the decision, but to provide the best available information and a range of alternatives for the judgment and decision of the client or agency.

As indicated the key beginning point is what we have defined as focusing. In focusing, the decision-maker and the evaluation specialist must cooperatively define four major areas: 1. The situation to be served, 2. The system which is to be evaluated, 3. The evaluation specifications which are feasible, desirable and acceptable to both, and 4. Some definition of the decision alternatives which are acceptable and desirable.

Each of these four key elements requires a high degree of rapport and honest, open, and positive continuing dialogue. Many of the potential difficulties which can arise in the course of an evaluation activity can be eliminated or at least reduced if some clear and common understanding can be achieved during the focusing activity. It is critical at this point that the evaluation specialist recognize the difficulties which the decision-maker may have in articulating the information desired by the evaluation specialist. It is important for the evaluation specialist to be willing to continue the discussion, to rephrase questions, and to accept the language and terminology of the client or agency being served.

The first key understanding must be a relatively clear description of the decision situation. In attempting to define the decision situation there are seven key questions which will help to delineate the background of the problem, the framework and the ultimate goals of the decision-maker. The first question is the matter of the antecdents to the decision need. This question may be answered by a very generalized description of how the need or the problem or the question first arose. How, when, and under what circumstances was the client first made aware of the problem? The second item of importance is to attempt to formulate the decision need in some question form. If the need can be stated as a question, the goal of the evaluation activity is more approachable. With the formulation of the question what are the possible alternative solutions which the decision-maker has or recognizes? This list of known alternatives may be incomplete; some may actually be irrelevant, but it is important to identify those alternatives which would seem to be recognized and acceptable.

The third point to be determined is the ultimate confirmation authority. Many times the client or agency dealing directly with the evaluation specialist will be seeking information on which to base a decision but the decision will actually be made by some other person or group. For example, the superintendent of the school district may be initiating the evaluation activity, but the ultimate decision will be confirmed or implemented or approved by the School Board. The fourth focusing type activity is the identification of those persons within the educational setting who have actual operational authority and responsibility. Again, the person meeting with the evaluation specialist may bear the responsibility for initiating the evaluation activity, but the actual project or program to be evaluated will be under the direction of one or more other persons who may not be present and active at the initial meetings. It should be clear what persons will be actually managing the project or program which is to be evaluated.

Next is the question of the time requirement when the decision must be made. This is not a terminal date for the evaluation activity, but it does determine when the reporting of information must be completed by the evaluation team. Some clear understanding should be achieved at this point so that sufficient lead-time will be available for the ultimate confirmation authority to read and evaluate the report and to make the judgment and final decision. The final two questions relate to the criteria and the decision rules which will be pertinent to the alternative solutions which will be presented in the evaluation report. These two questions may indeed be difficult to draw from the representative of the agency requesting the evaluation. There obviously will be some key criteria and rules for selecting from the alternatives which are presented. These criteria or rules may be guarded and veiled not only from the view of the public but possibly from the evaluator. The client may not wish to reveal this information in order not to prejudice or point the evaluator either directly or inadvertently to a single choice. Of necessity, the evaluator should be well grounded psychologically and skilled as an interviewer if he is to obtain sensitive information such as this. Yet he must obtain it or estimate it with sufficient accuracy that the information being reported will be relevant and have adequate scope to be of real use in choosing from the various alternatives presented.

One method of summarizing and reviewing the problem of focusing on the situation is to organize these seven key questions in a time framework. There is some information which will bring the evaluation specialist up-to-date on the situation as best known and expressed by the client. These three key questions relate to the antecedents of the problem, a statement of the problem in a question form, and some known alternatives which are recognized by the client. This information should be immediately available and is really background information on the total situation. Immediate information needs include the three key questions relating to operational authority for the program or project to be evaluated and the criteria and decision rules which will be applied to the alternatives suggested by the evaluation report. This information has perhaps not been fully considered by the client and will need to be derived before the evaluation specialist can proceed with any real hope of satisfying the true needs of the client. The terminal type questions are those which are most distant in time and relate to the dates on which the work must be completed and to the person or group who will make the final decision. Although these matters may not seem immediately pertinent, this knowledge would be useful and critical in determining other aspects of the evaluation effort.

The next step in focusing on the situation is to define the system which is to be evaluated. The evaluation specialist will want to obtain some definition of the boundaries of the system or sub-system within the educational agency or organization seeking evaluation assistance. Secondly, the major elements or parts of the system to be evaluated need to be identified by the decision-maker. Third, the evaluation specialist will attempt to elicit the critical characteristics recognized by the decision-maker for each element within the system. Finally, knowing the boundaries, the elements and the characteristics of the elements, a generalized model of the system to be evaluated should be developed.

To summarize the definition of the system, it might be expected that in a decision situation the actual system to be evaluated would be initially grossly defined. Thus the earlier questions in the focusing activity will merely sort from the total educational environment that sub-system which is to be evaluated in this particular activity. Having identified the system, it is then necessary to identify those critical elements which comprise the system or represent the totality of the system being investigated. Many of these may be already known by the decision-maker. Some might be identified only after successful questioning by the evaluation specialist. Once all of the known elements of the system are identified, it then becomes important to identify the characteristics of the elements and the relationship which exists between them. Here, the evaluation specialist must again take the descriptions provided by the decision-maker but pursue the questions regarding these characteristics and relationships to a depth that some relatively complete description of the existing system can be made. Finally, as a basis for other activities and in exploring some of the possible alternatives which may eventually be considered, a representational model of the system could be developed. This might indicate those characteristics and relationships which are fixed, but it might also include other possible alternatives in the arrangement or in the operations of the actual system to be evaluated.

THE DESIGN OF AN EVALUATION STUDY

At this point it becomes necessary to develop the details of the evaluation specifications. The first question of course is to determine both the authority and responsibility for the design and implementation of the evaluation study. It is possible that authority and responsibility may be separated. The *authority* for design and implementation is in the hands of the evaluation specialist but the *responsibility* for the design and implementation may be allocated to staff members of the organization requesting the study. It is also conceivable that the evaluation specialist may be requested to design the study and he assumes full authority and responsibility for that. However, the design once completed is then turned over to a local project staff for implementation. Regardless of the arrangements which are determined, it should be *very* clear to *all* parties concerned, who shall do what in terms of the design and implementation of the evaluation study.

Secondly, the resources for this design and implementation must be either committed by the client agency or provided for in some manner. It may be that some resources can only be secured outside the client agency itself. Regardless of the arrangements, it should be clear to both parties exactly what resources and how those resources will be provided for the development of the evaluation study.

Third, the decision-maker must indicate more details about the report requirements. In one of our major prior steps we indicated the need to provide a deadline date for the report and to indicate the ultimate confirmation authority. In indicating report requirements at this point, the decision-maker and the evaluation specialist must reach an agreement upon exactly what types of reports should be made to what audiences, at what time, and containing what substance or content. It is possible that although some single confirmation authority will make the decision at some future point in time, the materials developed by the evaluation study may be useful to various publics related to the client agency.

Finally, in the design of the evaluation study, it is important that both the decision-maker and the evaluation specialist define the policies, the operating guidelines and the constraints which will be operative in conducting the actual study. Since such a study almost inevitably means the intervention by some evaluation personnel into the on-going operations of the client agency, the evaluation specialist should understand clearly the policies of the institution which might directly affect such matters as the collection of data, the release of data, or the demands which may be required upon personnel with full-time assignments. Operating guidelines would indicate those activities required in the evaluation study which would be permissible to the client agency and would be acceptable to the professional standards of the evaluation specialist. Finally it is inevitable that certain constraints upon both policies and operations of the evaluation specialist may be required because of the public nature of many of the educational agencies with which the evaluation specialist will be working. In addition, the evaluation specialist may need to specify constraints upon the client agency in the treatment of the data and reports which are to be provided and in the use of the name of the evaluation specialist in any information releases provided to the public or the organizational staff itself.

Thus we see the focus on evaluation specifications really is aimed at developing a study which can provide the report which is needed. On one side, there is the matter of determining the authority, the resources, and the responsibility related to design and implementation. The leadership here will be primarily from the decision-maker. In the area of developing policies, guidelines and constraints, open and positive cooperative action in decision-making is required between the evaluation specialist and the client agency. These six specifications are all related to the design and implementation of the study. Design and implementation is further directed toward the report requirements which have been indicated in the focusing operation.

Having now defined the operational arena for the evaluation study itself, it is necessary for the evaluation specialist and the decision-maker to consider the most desirable and feasible approach to the study. By this time it should be clear to the client agency that the evaluation specialist will not attempt to make the final decision. His job is to provide a range of alternatives for decision-making. By this time the decision-maker should recognize also that certain alternatives are acceptable at least for consideration. It should also be obvious to both parties that no study can encompass all the possible alternatives. From decisions made in previous steps of the focusing activity, we have certain criteria which will be critical in the selection of any alternative. Therefore the sequence of actions are 1. to identify sources of alternatives, 2. to assemble a variety of alternatives, 3. to select a feasible number which might appear appropriate for investigation, and 4. to develop an information matrix by which the criteria can be applied to each of the possible alternatives. It is from such an information matrix that the evaluation study can then proceed in the most efficient manner to explore the "best bets" or alternatives for consideration.

To summarize, the initial objective is the development of possible alternative solutions to the problem being investigated, to assemble those alternatives an investigation should be made of many sources. One might turn to *theory* related to the problem being investigated or to *authorities* in the field who have well-developed positions on the problem. *Research data* or prior studies may exist related to the problem. Certain types of *development activities* may have been completed in the past, or be in progress at the moment, based on possible alternatives. And so the list of possible sources goes on. From these various sources an assemblage should be made of the suggested alternatives derived from the various sources. The number of alternatives from each source may vary and obviously more alternatives will be available than can be attempted in any evaluation study commonly conducted within the usual educational setting.

From the assembled alternatives, the evaluation specialist and the decision-maker should agree upon those possible alternatives which would *appear* to be the most feasible and desirable as solutions to the problem being evaluated. These alternatives should then be matched against the criteria developed in prior steps and a judgment based upon these criteria should be made regarding the value of each of the possible alternatives. What would be obtained then would be a *composite rating* of each possible alternative for each of the criteria specified in the prior focusing steps. At this point, the evaluation study may be directed to consider all of the selected alternatives along with the current operating procedures or perhaps it may be directed to implement and evaluate merely one of the alternative actions developed through this procedure.

THE FUNCTONS OF THE EVALUATION TEAM

Now, we turn to the four major functions of the Evaluation Team: Collection, Organization, Analysis, and Reporting of information. At the heart of the evaluation activity we will look at many specific factors in performing each major function.

The first task then is Information Collection. First, the information items which are required must be specified. These items are derived directly from the criteria by using the decision alternatives matrix which we discussed as the final step in focusing the evaluation. An example of an information item is an I.Q. score. Second, the source of each information item should be specified. Such sources are of two kinds: information which has already been collected; and that which remains to be collected. For our I.Q. score example, we might designate a school's cumulative record file as the source of information. Third, we must identify the sample for which data will be collected. In our example, this might be a random sample of 100 sophomores in the public schools of Waterloo, Iowa. Fourth, an instrument, such as the Otis Intelligence Test, should be specified. Depending upon the information item one has in mind, an appropriate data collection instrument may not exist. If so, a plan should be projected for constructing the needed instrument.

The fifth step is to specify the methods for data collection. Will this be the standard administration of a full length test? If only group data is required, will random samples of test items be administered to random sub-samples of subjects so that time can be conserved? How will a clerk draw a random sample from the files? Etc. Clearly, methods of collecting information may vary widely depending upon the information required, the sources of the information, the instruments to be used, etc. Sixth, the conditions under which information is to be collected must be specified. Will trained observers be employed? Will testing be performed in regular classrooms or a large group room? Will a clerk draw a pre-defined sample of records from a file? Will the timing of a test administration be controlled by announcement over the school's intercom? How will different test forms be randomly assigned to subjects? Etc. Finally, a master schedule should be drawn up for the collection of information. Minimally, this schedule should interrelate sources of information, instruments, and time. In two respects, this schedule is helpful for improving the initial scheme for information collection. First, it prevents us from administering too many instruments to the same persons within a limited time span. Second, it helps us to combine similar instruments which are to be administered to the same persons and, thus achieve parsimony in our instruments. Obviously, the schedule of information collection is a valuable device for assigning personnel and resources to the collection process and for maintaining effective communication among the evaluation team members and between the team and those in the system who will be involved in the collection process.

We now move to the second step in the evaluation procedure, that of *information organization.* The first task in organizing information is to lay the framework which will relate the collection system we have just described to the report requirements which have been prescribed earlier in the focusing operation with the decision-maker. You will recall that we indicated that there may be several reports and several types of reports required for the final decision. While some confirmation authority will make the final decision, there are elements of information developed through the evaluation procedure which could be used in reports to other audiences, such as personnel who may operate a new or revised program or public groups who need to be informed of the achievements or the changes in the school system. In any event, in organizing the information it is important to think through quite clearly the various information items to be collected and relate each of these to the reports which are required. In doing this job, the evaluator may become aware of information which *should* be collected but has not been planned. Another value in performing this job of information organization at this time is to indicate the collection of too much or too many types of information for minor types of reports which may be required.

The second major job of information organization is to develop a storage and retrieval system for that information which is to be collected. This information storage and retrieval system is needed not merely to relate that data collected to the specific needs of the various reports which must finally be made; the coding system and the storage-retrieval system also functions as a control mechanism which enables you to place and recall information in such a way that it can be used in developing *new* types of data and relationships which have not been perceived in the initial planning.

Obviously, codes must be established for each *source* of information and each of the *samples* must be identified as well as the *instruments* and the various *items* in each of the instruments.

Further, one needs to plan input schedules which will insure that the information being collected is constantly monitored and tabulated, so the total project does not get behind schedule. In the various types of evaluation studies under consideration, it is possible to accumulate massive amounts of data which are not tabulated or organized during the course of the study. It is quite easy for an evaluation team to feel adequate progress is being made merely because the information is pouring into the evaluation staff offices. This false feeling of security becomes an enormous problem as the study begins to reach its closing phases and reports must be written and the collected data has not been monitored and tabulated upon its receipt.

Finally, some policy decisions must be made regarding under what conditions data can be withdrawn from the system and at what points in time. One can think of particular types of data of a personal nature which should not be released to persons or organizations associated with the institution requesting the evaluation study. Other circumstances suggest that even members of the evaluation staff should not have unrestrained access to portions of the data without maintaining some records of where the material has been taken. These retrieval constraints are merely a control factor to assure that all of the relevant data is available when necessary and it is available only to those persons authorized to receive such data. The data may be incomplete or in an uninterpreted form which should not be made public or released without some processing by the evaluation team.

Plans must also be made for the information *analysis.* You will recall one of the early elements of the focusing operation was developing a statement of the problem in question form. That problem statement or question now becomes relevant and extremely useful in planning the analysis of the information to be collected. Within even the most simple question or problem statement, there will be several key terms. The first step therefore is to identify those key terms or elements of the problem statement. Secondly, in the focusing operation certain criteria statements were made related to the general problem. It now becomes important to take each of the criteria statements and relate them to the various elements of the problem statement. Some criteria may relate to several elements of the problem, while other criteria will relate to only one of the elements in the problem. Such criteria statements related to the problem elements help us to determine which information will be most important in providing a more precise and useful report regarding the alternatives for decision-making.

Next we have seen in the prior activity related to information collection that we have specified certain items which must be collected. It now becomes useful to relate each of the information items identified to the various criteria which will help us to make the appropriate decision regarding each of the problem elements. The matching of information items to specific criteria will reveal of course where adequate and valid information is available. It may be apparent that some *additional* information items are required. As the next step in information analysis, it becomes important to assign personnel on the evaluation staff to monitor the collection of certain information and to concentrate their activities upon certain of the criteria required by the decision-maker. This assignment of personnel to specific parts of the study means that no elements of data or no major criteria will remain unreviewed. At the end of the study, selected personnel will be prepared to draft portions of the analysis required in the final report.

Fifth in the information analysis activities, it is useful to schedule the preparation of summaries and reviews of information collected during the course of the study. In certain types of evaluation studies this interim summary and review is critical. This is especially so in the evaluation studies we have referred to as the process type. The interim summaries and review not only assure that the study is proceeding at an appropriate pace, but may also provide information useful in correcting difficulties which would arise if these reviews were not conducted. Certainly such summaries and reviews are critical in the types of studies we have considered as contingency studies or those decision-making situations we have described as Neo-mobilistic. In these particular types of evaluation the interim summaries and reviews are extremely critical in redirecting or concentrating upon elements which are constantly changing.

A sixth consideration in information analysis is the development of some means to check errors as the information is being collected. This error check not only relates to such simple matters as achieving accuracy in mathematical tabulation and calculation; it also means being alert to such matters as cross-checking data received in one part of the study with data received from perhaps another source or perhaps at another time during the course of the study. One should view this matter of checking for errors not merely in the negative sense of correcting mistakes but recognize it also as a good opportunity to develop new insights on the interrelationship of information being collected which may not have been evident or planned in the original design of the study.

Seventh, in the design of the study, the evaluation team should develop some type of a *warning report* mechanism which would systematically be circulated to those persons collecting the information. Such a warning report might indicate either time delays which are presenting difficulties, or the recurrence of failure to collect certain types of information, or slight deviations in procedures which can creep into a repetitive type of activity. Further a warning report system should keep each person on the staff aware of what is occurring in the entire operation. In a very complex study or a very diffuse operation, it is possible that persons working in one area of the evaluation study may be inadvertently creating problems for other team operations *or* gaining important insights into work being conducted at some other time and place by other personnel. This type of communication can help to eliminate some of the difficulties which can arise in analyzing the information at the close of the study. It may also provide opportunities to develop a new and different type of information of great value in the final report.

Our final major operation in designing and implementing the study is the *reporting of information*. To a decision-maker this may seem like a simple problem of turning in a document to the person requesting the study. The success and the worth of the entire evaluation may rest on the effectiveness as well as the accuracy of the communication between the evaluation team and the client-agency. The first task is to specify the audience or audiences to receive the report. Such specifications would include not only the number of persons involved, but the types of persons, their positions, and their relationships to the decision and its implementation. While the school board may make the final decision, there may need to be reports to such groups as the administrative staff, the general school faculty, or a group of professional employees who will implement a new activity or whose positions may be modified by the decision. The numbers and types of audiences indicated should be known in order for the evaluator to properly prepare and direct his reports.

Secondly, schedules should be prepared for the delivery of each of the required reports to the various audiences. It may be important to sequence the reports for the maximum effectiveness in achieving acceptance of any final decision made. Continuing our prior example, perhaps the first report should be made to the administrative and executive staff of the educational institution requiring the evaluation. Depending on the results of that reporting procedure, the next group may be the faculty or the program personnel directly related to the program or operation being evaluated. From these two reports, the administration may then wish to modify the report to be made to the school board. After the report to the school board, a public meeting may require still a fourth report. The sequence of reporting as indicated here may determine not only the *nature* of the decision but the *effectiveness* of the implementation of the decision or the *acceptance* of the decision which eventually must be made.

A third task is to specify the formats for the reports and meetings. The size of the group, the group's relationship to the report, and the actions which are anticipated or required from the group may determine the format and the nature of the reporting procedure. We tend to think of reports being printed in some single document. Printed documents usually are required. However, the format of the report could vary. Continuing our example, the report to the administrative staff may very well consist of a complete printed document supplied to the administration and an additional set of summary statements which are available to each member of the administrative staff. This summary may be reviewed at a meeting of the administrative staff with the head of the evaluation team who would present and interpret that summary. In the second situation, if we assume it is a large school district and the total faculty is to be involved in at least hearing the report, the report may be prepared in the form of photographic slides or overhead transparencies. The presentation may be made by some member of the administrative staff through an audio-visual presentation to the large group. Perhaps plans should be made to have a questionnaire prepared in advance with sufficient copies to be circulated among the faculty so that they may express their opinions or reactions to the report as it is presented at the large group meeting. An additional type of meeting format may include the acceptance of questions from the floor and open discussion. Such a meeting format may require the presence of the evaluation specialist or team who conducted the study.

Our fourth task in reporting information is to specify the *means* for the production and presentation of the reports. The responsibility for this production effort and the costs involved should be clarified prior to the beginning of the study. Most evaluation specialist may be prepared to provide a printed report either in mimeograph format or in some more sophisticated printing procedure. The various audio-visual formats, public meetings, and even the different levels of printing possibilities need to be considered. Some consideration may be needed to *translate* data which may be printed in a conventional research type figure or tabular presentation. It may need to be modified or redesigned for presentation in photographic slide form or as an overhead transparency. Complex diagrams, charts, and tables may be enhanced by the use of colors or specific types of graphic techniques which are more readable and understandable to the less sophisticated audience receiving one of the report formats indicated above.

The time has now come for the evaluation study to be put into action. We must consider the actual operational administration of the study about to take place. You will recall the evaluation specialist has spent considerable time in what we have described as the focusing operation. We have just reviewed the four major functions to be performed by the evaluation study: Collection; organization; analysis; and reporting of information. The final task is to consider the total operational plan for the evaluation study. First the evaluation specialist will need to summarize the time schedule. Various decisions have been made during the focusing operation involving the four key steps, so that some specific terminal dates are known. Due dates for most activities have now been determined. These need to be placed in a time framework. Perhaps one could even consider the charting of the total activity in something similar to a PERT network. Second, some specific plan is needed for the staff and the resource requirements which have been indicated by all of the decisions made. Third, certain policy requirements have been set forth by both the decision-maker and the evaluation specialist. It is critical at this point that the head of the evaluation team specify those policy requirements in writing and communicate them to the evaluation team in such a manner that they will be met during the course of the evaluation.

Fourth, it is now possible to look at the entire study being planned and to make some estimate of the possible value and potential effectiveness of the total design. This requires a highly objective and rigorous assessment of the total evaluation study. If some potential weaknesses are clear, these must either be corrected by redesign at this point or a clear understanding of these potential weaknesses must be communicated to the decision-maker.

Fifth, the evaluation specialist should indicate some means for up-dating, correcting, or modifying in some fashion, the total evaluation design. Some alternative plans or procedures should be available to prevent the project which has been designed with the best intentions and available knowledge from some unforseen difficulties in its actual operation. This is merely being sensible in terms of protecting the investment of time, energy, and money which will be spent. Finally, the toughest, most critical problem of all must be faced. This is providing the budget. With the thorough type of planning which has been indicated in all the prior steps, a relatively accurate budget should be feasible. Whether in fact these funds do exist, can be provided, and will be available, must now be determined. Plans must be made for the provision of funds on an appropriate and continuing schedule for the completion of the study.

We have finally reached the end of our presentation and it becomes important to consider all of the many specifications that we have provided in the prior steps and return again to our initial point. The purpose of proposing the generalized framework for evaluation which has been given here is to enable us to attack the multiple and varied problems of evaluation in education which have not been completely or effectively achieved through prior definitions or interpretations of the word evaluation. The system we have described today has been called the CIPP Model. This acronym is derived from the four general types of evaluation we have discussed. These four types of evaluation have been developed and described in this fashion because they seem to cover the major generalized types of problems which we face in education.

We are constantly faced with the problem of relating the ends and the means which we have available. These are the realities of the world. At the same time, we attempt to relate our intentions and our achievements. As one considers the relationship of these realities of ends and means and our hopes of intentions and achievements, four key words which we frequently use come into focus.

When we seek to express our intentions in relationship with the ends, we speak of *goals*. When we attempt to identify our intentions in relationship to the means which are available, we speak of *designing* some program or operation. When we attempt to relate these same means which are available to the achievements which are our dreams, we speak of the *procedures* by which the means are applied. Finally, when we attempt to associate those things which we have sought to achieve against the ends which we have predicated, we speak of *outcomes*. It is this cycle of goals, designs, procedures and outcomes which we replicate in virtually every type of educational activity. In the presentation on evaluation as we have described it, we have defined a specific type of evaluation which attempts to approach each of the four separate problems mentioned. In attempting to assess goals, we have spoken of *context evaluation*. In attempting to evaluate designs, we have spoken of *input evaluation*. In attempting to evaluate procedures, we have spoken of *process evaluation*. And in attempting to evaluate outcomes, we have spoken of *product evaluation*.

And in conducting each of these four types of evaluation, we have said there are six major elements to the evaluation process. First, the focusing activity which is the initial consultation between the evaluation specialist and the decision-maker. Next, the four key steps in every type of evaluation: the collection, organization, analysis, and reporting of information to the decision-maker. Finally, we have spoken of the general administration of any type of evaluation study.

The value and effectiveness of the CIPP Model can only be determined as it is applied in various contexts, on various problems, and in various situations. Hopefully, it is more practical and realistically oriented than experimental testing, and at the same time it is more systematic and productive than informal and ill-planned investigations. Perhaps it is a step forward in relating theory and practice and opening up to systematic inquiry the practical problems of better decision-making in educational situations.

III.

A
REVIEW
OF
THE
LITERATURE

chapter 4
research methodology and strategies

BASIC AND APPLIED RESEARCH IN EDUCATION: DEFINITIONS, DISTINCTIONS, AND IMPLICATIONS

John B. Carroll

At a time when questions are being raised with particular poignancy about the value of basic research in the social and behavioral sciences,(1) it seems useful to try to clarify some of the issues as they pertain to research in education. After a period of about ten years during which Federal support of educational research increased markedly — a period in which there was a relative lack of concern as to whether the research being supported was "basic" or "applied," as a result of which a considerable amount of research of a fairly "basic" character was supported — recent Congressional actions and corresponding policy decisions in the Bureau of Research of the U. S. Office of Education(2) have tended to put much more weight on the support of "applied" research which would be directed toward the solution of immediately practical problems in education. This state of affairs appears to reflect considerable confusion about the role of basic research in education and what this research may be expected to achieve. This paper will argue not only that it is possible and useful to distinguish between basic and applied research, but also there is a continuing need for both of these types of research in education. Since funding agencies already give strong support to applied research, an argument in its favor will not be developed. Thus, while recognizing the importance and desirability of applied research, we shall focus attention on the arguments for basic research.

Education is not the only field in which this question has been raised. A spate of articles and editorials in *Science* on basic *versus* applied research is a sign that the issue is one of great concern to scientists in general, particularly where it involves the relative amounts of monetary support given to the two types of research. Many scientists feel that basic science is nowadays being by-passed in favor of large "mission-oriented" programs of applied science such as the man-on-the-moon effort. Some (e.g., Weinberg, 1961) have phrased the issue in terms of an opposition between "little science" — the activities of isolated scientists in their laboratories — and "big science" — the efforts of large, well-funded teams of workers toiling in special-purpose research organizations. Yet Kidd (1959) finds it difficult to arrive at "operational criteria" by which basic and applied science activities can be distinguished. He avers that it may be easy enough to *describe* the differences between clear cases of each, in terms of the nature of the activities or possibly in terms of the motivations of the scientists involved, but that one cannot apply any rigorous and well-established criteria to decide whether any given research project is of a basic or of an applied character. Thus, he contends that statistics compiled by government organizations on the relative amounts of support given to basic and to applied research are inherently meaningless. As a possible criterion, he suggests that an activity is "basic science" to the extent that it has a high probability of yielding a "new scientific finding." But such a criterion is itself problematical: an eminently practical new invention, arising from "applied science" activity, may often represent "new knowledge." A recent article by Reagan (1967) suggests abandoning, for practical political purposes, any distinction between basic and applied science, preserving only a distinction between "research" and "development." Unfortunately, such a step could have the effect of inhibiting or jeopardizing support for promising basic research whose direct relevance to a specific practical goal or mission cannot immediately be demonstrated, because politicians could always claim they are still supporting "research" even if all the research is mission-oriented.

There have been few attempts to define basic research in education or to specify its role. Clark (1963) puts forth a number of general arguments for basic research, mostly revolving around the claim that such research will have broad applications in improving the educational process, in introducing new educational technology, and in establishing new curricula. Ausubel (1953), on the other hand, believes that educational research should restrict itself to "applied science" — testing out the application of "extrapolated basic science" to its own practitioners. But now that the support of basic research in education is a "political" issue, it is critical to consider what possible role basic science activities may have in educational research and to what extent they merit fiscal support either from the government or from private sources. Before we can do so, however, it is necessary to re-examine some of the issues raised by Kidd, Reagan, and others in the context of a broader view of the nature of scientific inquiry and the sources of its motivation.

THE GOALS OF SCIENTIFIC INQUIRY

There has been much confusion in the literature about the goals of scientific inquiry. Although it may be difficult to consider the motives of individual scientists in pursing their work, it remains true that science does have goals and that such goals imply motives to achieve those goals. Indeed, the very notion of inquiry contains the notion of questions needing answers. What some writers have failed to recognize, however, is that motives can be structured in a hierarchy — some goals being more ultimate and others more proximate — and that some of the proximate motives in the hierarchy can be "functionally autonomous," to use Gordon Allport's (1937) phrase. That is to say, from a psychological standpoint, some goals may operate as ends in themselves, without reference to the extent to which they may actually serve still other, more remote goals.

Roughly speaking, the usual goals of scientific inquiry can be arranged in such a hierarchy. The ultimate goal, and the basis of society's general support for science, is usually said to be the solution of utilitarian, practical problems.(4) Ideally, these goals ought to be well defined, e.g., the building of safer automobiles, the reduction of air pollution, or the elimination of cancer; or in the field of education, the overcoming of handicaps due to mental retardation or due to "social disadvantage," the nourishment of creativity in gifted children, the facilitation of the learning of foreign languages, etc.

Many scientific research projects are immediately in contact with such well-defined practical problems. But in order to feed necessary basic knowledge into such activities, science can be said to have a more general utilitarian aim — utilitarian in the best Benthamist sense — to produce knowledge and understanding of all natural phenomena that are likely to be relevant to human concerns. This general utilitarian aim is ordinarily conceived to be characteristic of basic science — and indeed of all scientific and scholarly activities. That it can also be regarded as a "functionally autonomous" motive as illustrated by Seaborg's (1963) claim that the "motivating force [for basic research] is not utilitarian goals, but a search for deeper understanding of the universe and of the phenomena within it."

Some scientists also claim that a basic motive for science is a kind of "curiosity." From the standpoint of the individual scientist, according to Teller (1963), pure research "is a game, is play, led by curiosity, by taste, style, judgment, intangibles." The implication is that the scientist is often motivated not by any ultimate utilitarian aim, not even by some duty to produce new knowledge, but merely by the fun and challenge of unanswered questions (like mountains that must be climbed "just because they're there"). This too — this love of intellectual challenge — is a form of autonomous motive, one that is quite legitimate psychologically as the source of persistent creative effort.(5) As a matter of fact, the public at large may be said to possess curiosity about many questions whose relevance to any utilitarian ends is at best remote. Why does the public support the efforts of linguists endeavoring to decipher Mayan hiero-glyphic writing? I can think of no tangible reason other than societal curiosity, except perhaps for the light the results might throw on the nature of human writing systems or on the character of Mayan society. Yet we have little hesitation in supporting this and similar scholarly work with foundation grants, fellowships, and the like. We may equally well support work aimed to satisfy our curiosity about interesting, albeit possibly useless, scientific questions like the nesting habits of the dodo.

Thus, we can exhibit a hierarchy of motives, each imperceptibly merging into the next, as follows: Curiosity; Better general, undefined, well-defined understanding of natural phenomena, of utilitarian aims, of practical goals.

The questions asked in science can arise from either or both of two sources: 1. our lack of understanding of some given set of phenomena; 2. our inability to achieve some practical goal. Basic science receives its justification both from the fact that better understanding of natural phenomena is a legitimate autonomous motive and from the fact that such understanding has the potential of serving utilitarian aims even though it is not usually possible to define those aims. Applied science derives its justification, obviously, from its orientation towards the achievement of well-defined practical goals. Basic and applied science can thus be roughly distinguished by the types of questions to which they are addressed. Of course, it is frequently the case that applied science must address itself to basic science questions, answers to which are needed to facilitate progress towards the achievement of a practical end. And as Pfaffmann (1965) has pointed out, ". . . often practical problems [and the superficial solutions one finds for them] are symptoms of [and engender] deeper problems that require more basic study and research." But there is no reason why an applied-science research project cannot be broken down into those tasks that are of a basic-science nature and those that are more concerned with testing basic-science knowledge in its application to a specific practical goal.(6)

Although I do not believe that motivation can be wholly ruled out of any attempt to distinguish basic from applied science — precisely because (as I have tried to show above) science starts from questions which are themselves motivating — it is nevertheless possible to decide, on a fairly objective basis, whether a given scientific task is more immediately addressed to the better understanding of phenomena or to the achievement of a specific practical goal. Any well-designed scientific inquiry contains a series of explicit problems, defined variables, and stated procedures. I would venture the guess that a group of experienced and knowledgeable scientists, upon examination of the design of a scientific investigation, could reach a high degree of agreement on the extent to which it is of a basic or an applied character. It would not be necessary for them to hire a psychologist or a psychiatrist to inquire into the inner motives of the scientist; the motives of the scientist should be manifest in his statement of hypotheses, procedures, and expected results.

Some writers on basic and applied research have attempted to distinguish them with reference to the different reward systems that appear to apply to them. Storer (1964), for example, writes: "Basic research is that which is carried out by a scientist who hopes that his findings will be primarily of interest to his scientific colleagues, while applied research is intended to produce findings which will be of greater interest to the investigator's employer or to the lay public." But Storer's remarks seem simply to point out that there are different ways in which the scientist can, if he chooses, confirm whether his work has the outcomes he himself hopes for it. The basic scientist looks to his scientific colleagues, generally, for affirmation that his work is sound, reasonable, and contributory to the advance of knowledge; the applied scientist gets his signals from his sponsors, who can be expected to reward him in material ways when his discoveries result in useful applications. There will be many scientists, however, for whom these particular reward systems will have little appeal. Fundamentally, the reward system for the scientist or even for a team of scientists is inherent in scientific activity itself. That is, in basic science, effort will be continued until the investigators are rewarded with answers to their questions, while in applied science, efforts will persist until the desired practical ends are achieved.

Public acclaim or disapproval is no criterion either. Both basic and applied scientists will continue their work — as they should, if they are otherwise justified — despite lack of public support.

THE DIMENSION OF "RELEVANCE"

Much has been said about the evaluation of research in terms of its "relevance" to utilitarian ends. Most frequently, this question is raised about "basic" research: Is this research even conceivably relevant to *any* kind of utilitarian end? From the point of view expressed here, this question is thoroughly inappropriate for at least three reasons: 1. The better understanding of phenomena is a legitimate end in itself which can be justified, if necessary, on the ground of the general experience that at least *some* scientific activity addressed solely to fundamental questions has "paid off" in unexpected practical applications. 2. The potential applications of many basic-science researches cannot always immediately be anticipated, even when they do in fact result eventually in practical applications. (The long-delayed application of the discovery of penicillin is a classic case in point.) Often a given scientific finding needs to be further investigated or supplemented before a practical application can be perceived. 3. One can never predict whether a given scientific investigation will be "successful" even in its own terms. We are perhaps unaware of the tremendous amount of scientific activity that is "unsuccessful" in the sense that it fails to yield any new knowledge; further, sometimes a negative result (e.g., the failure to confirm a hypothesis or the failure to find a solution to a problem) is a distinct contribution to knowledge because it informs the scientific community that the hypothesis or methodology tried is apparently of no avail. Thus we should not try to evaluate the relevance of a given scientific investigation in terms of its results. Even in the case of "applied science" investigations, the use of this criterion would not be appropriate, for many such studies fail to achieve practical solutions although they are nonetheless clearly so *directed*. To assess relevance, we must concentrate on evaluating the *process* of scientific investigation — the framing of questions and hypotheses, the research design, the analysis of findings, and so on — and not the results.

In this light, basic-science investigation is *inherently* relevant (at least to the undefined utilitarian aims mentioned above) when it is addressed to questions that the investigator — if he is well-trained and knowledgeable in his field — feels are reasonable and useful to answer, and when in the judgment of his fellow scientists it is properly designed to answer those questions. However, there are a number of cases in the history of science where a lone investigator successfully showed that apparently unreasonable questions were in fact worth pursuing.

We should point out, too, that except for rare cases, a scientist pursues questions *within a fairly well-defined area* — one for which it is possible to specify in a general way the kinds of practical applications that can be foreseen. Relevance is therefore specificable in general terms, even for the purest of basic research; and it is on this basis that the public can justify the support of basic research even when specific applications are not immediately foreseen. If society cannot find any area of relevance for an *area* of research, the case might be different. But one must be careful even here: in Galileo's time, society rejected large areas of science, and for a long period the Soviet government rejected work in Mendelian genetics. More recently, the practical relevance of learning theory has been debated, even by learning theorists.

SOME FURTHER, BUT ROUGHER, DISTINCTIONS

If basic and applied research can be distinguished in terms of the nature of the work, the kinds of questions investigated, the procedures, and the like, it will be useful to expand on some of these points. No one of them, however, can be used as a sole criterion.

With respect to the questions asked, basic research tends to differ from applied research in the fact that it is more concerned with "understanding" and the attainment of knowledge about fundamental variables and their relationships; the prediction of socially important phenomena is of secondary concern, arising solely out of the laws and relationships discovered; and control of phenomena is often of only incidental interest except to verify a finding. Applied research, however, is generally concerned with the control of socially significant phenomena, or if control is difficult or impossible, at least their prediction. It is interested in the "understanding" of phenomena in terms of laws and relationships as a basis for prediction and control. Generally it starts with facts and propositions already established in basic science and proceeds to test them in particular situations and/or in particular combinations such that extrapolation from basic science is risky.

Correlated with this difference is the fact that basic science, in order to gain a better understanding of the workings of phenomena, is more often concerned with detailed, fundamental processes, such as chemical reaction mechanisms, nerve impulses, or isolated learnings; applied research, on the other hand, is more often concerned with gross, higher-order macro-processes like wine fermentation, social attitudes, or scholastic achievements, because these are the phenomena one wants to predict or control. In the behavioral sciences, we say that basic research has often to do with a "molecular" level of behavior, while applied research has to do with a "molar" level of behavior. For example, basic research in learning is concerned with the precise combinations of stimulus and response variables that produce certain effects, whereas applied research might be concerned with the effects, say, of massive doses of positive reward, which for certain groups of school learners might *on the average* produce significantly beneficial effects. The applied researcher would not necessarily worry about why positive reward works, or why it does not always work for all students, whereas the basic research scientist — if he is worth his salt — will push for understanding of the total dynamics of the phenomena he is studying. (As soon as the applied researcher starts worrying about deeper questions, he becomes a basic scientist.)

In its concern for processes on a "molecular" level, basic research relies to a greater extent on models of functional relationship that involve relatively small error components, while applied research tends to use models that are more probabilistic and error-laden. It is not an accident that statistical procedures were first developed in applied fields of research like certain branches of economics, agriculture, and psychological testing, even though these procedures are, of course, extensively used in basic research even in theoretical physics.

Basic research is more often conducted in the laboratory, or in highly controlled situations, in order to observe the effects of particular variables independently of other possibly relevant variables. Applied research tends to be done in situations that are identical to, or closely similar to, those in which one wants to apply the findings. On the other hand, some basic research is done in live field situations. In fact, in education there are many arguments for doing certain types of research in such situations. But discussion of this point would take us too far afield.

Basic research is more concerned with the development of theory and of all-embracing models for the explanation of phenomena, while applied research either takes for granted previously established theory and extrapolates from it, or avoids theoretical problems altogether. In any case, basic science stands in a relation of logical priority to applied science. Applied science usually relies heavily upon findings in basic science. It is less often the case that basic science takes off from a finding of applied science; in the instance where this occurs, the purpose usually is to explore the deeper rationale of the finding. Although the essential priority of basic science is not as clearcut in the behavioral and social sciences as it is in the natural sciences, much is to be gained, I think, by following the model of the natural sciences in giving emphasis to basic research at points where applied research cannot make progress alone.

BASIC EDUCATIONAL RESEARCH

It is thus doubtful, in educational research, that we can move ahead to effective educational engineering without an adequate base in fundamental research in mathematics, computer science, genetics, physiology, psychology, sociology, anthropology, and other relevant disciplines. Particularly where applied research seems to be yielding diminishing dividends, we must turn to basic research on the phenomena in which we are interested. I would propose that such research be called *basic educational research*, and that it be thought of as a part of basic science.

It can be easily demonstrated that many of the most fruitful developments in applied educational technology would have been well-nigh impossible without an adequate foundation in basic research. At the same time, some of these same developments have now reached a point of decreasing returns such that they need a new infusion of results from basic research. A good example is the history of so-called programed instruction.

Let us consider what has happened in this field since the publication of B. F. Skinner's well-known article, "The Science of Learning and the Art of Teaching" (1954). It was basic research, of an extensive and profound character, that led Skinner to conclude that certain propositions about "reinforcement" (roughly, the reward of responses) and the temporal relationships between stimuli, responses, and reinforcements could be "applied" in a special way to the conduct of instruction. Skinner felt that he needed to make no apologies for proposing to apply results of research with rats and pigeons to teaching human beings. It took Skinner and others about five years of "applied" research, however, to develop instructional materials that would incorporate the principles he had arrived at from animal research. Many of the "programed" courses that resulted from this development phase seemed to be eminently successful, at least under certain conditions. But others, *apparently* using the same principles as the successful ones, were not as effective.

Many investigators who tried to develop programed courses realized that some of Skinner's principles had not been adequately tested in their application to human learning, and began to investigate them more thoroughly. From the studies that have been conducted over the last ten years, reviewed by such writers as Morrill (1961) and Holland (1965), it can be concluded that many of Skinner's original propositions — deriving from his basic research — were not sufficiently precise to guide the development of programed instruction unfailingly.

At the present juncture, therefore, our ideas as to exactly how programed instruction ought to be developed are confused. It is apparent that we must return to some quite basic research and theorizing in order to bring the various apparently conflicting results of applied research into line. Without the necessary basic research into the detailed processes of perception, learning, and forgetting that underlie programed instruction, further "engineering" development will make little headway.

One can cite other instances in which basic research on psychological processes is needed to guide developmental efforts in education. Levin, Gibson, and their associates (Levin, 1966) at Cornell University have recognized such a need in the field of reading and have devoted several years of a concentrated effort to investigating fundamental processes in reading and learning to read. Some of Levin's research draws heavily upon recent findings and formulations in linguistics. Although results of many of the studies have no immediate application, they promise to contribute towards a new theory of the reading process that will guide the development of practical materials and procedures for the teaching of reading. In another field, Guilford's (1966, 1967) twenty-year program of research on individual differences in cognitive abilities can be regarded as basic educational research that may have far-reaching implications for the design of curricula. In view of the burgeoning of interest in the teaching of creativity, his explorations of the dimensions of "divergent production" are being watched with interest by applied researchers. Basic research investigations into the nature of creativity have also been conducted by Getzels and Jackson (1962), with close relations to the more applied-science work of Torrance (1962). A good deal of this research has been supported by funds from the U.,S. Office of Education.

Of course, it may be observed that there is already much basic-research activity in psychology and other behavioral sciences carried on outside the field of education as such. Should educational agencies continue to support basic research in educational psychology when the needs are being fairly well met by support from noneducational sources? I believe they should, on the ground that the mission of educational agencies can have a beneficial effect on directing the attention of basic researchers to the problem areas of education, which in turn will lead them to select basic research problems that will have an appreciable probability of "pay-off" in educational development — not necessarily immediately, but ultimately, after basic scientific development has run its natural course. The history of research in such areas as programmed instruction and reading shows that the applied researchers have posed problems for basic research that might have never been posed purely in the context of basic science as such. As has been the case in the natural sciences, applied problems can have a rejuvenating effect on the development of basic science.

Applied research, development, and dissemination programs have a well-recognized place in education. It has been my purpose to argue that basic educational research can be clearly distinguished from applied research, and that it has an equally vital role to play. If the U. S. Office of Education and other funding agencies are to carry out their responsibilities to education, they must support basic educational research in a due proportion. Just what this proportion should be, monetarily, is a complex question involving the availability of research facilities and of qualified researchers, the relative expense of basic and of applied research, the total funding available, and other factors. The answer would probably turn out to be somewhere between 15 and 25 per cent. This figure would include the support not only of basic-research programs themselves, but also of the training of basic-research workers in undergraduate and graduate degree programs that would be distinct from, even though possibly allied with, research operations. A clear mandate for basic research should be given to the universities, either as a part of Research and Development Center programs (which ought not to be constrained within narrow problem areas) or in the form of grants for specific projects. Significant amounts of funds would also be made available to public and private research institutions (both nonprofit and profit-making), including Regional Educational Laboratories if they are appropriately staffed, where concentrated and prolonged efforts could be undertaken.

The establishment and steady pursuit, on the part of funding agencies, of a clear policy that would give adequate recognition to basic educational research would be of enormous benefit to education as well as to the discipline of educational research.

NOTES

1. House of Representatives, *The Use of Social Research in Federal Domestic Programs.* Parts I-IV. A staff study for the Research and Technical Programs Subcommittee of the Committee on Government Operations (Washington: U. S. Government Printing Office, 1967).

2. A leading critic of governmental educational research programs has been Lee J. Cronbach (1966), who states that the U. S. Office of Education Bureau of Research "has thrown its forces heavily on the side of 'practical products' and dissemination." "While the USOE is a passive patron of basic research," he continues, "it has done nothing to formulate and sell to Congress a policy that will promote the healthy development or basic investigation." Further, he points out that the Office "declines to support a research and development center unless it includes a dissemination program from the outset," a fact to which I can personally testify. Nevertheless, there are signs of at least a slight change in USOE policy. In an interview (Robinson, 1966), Richard L. Bright, the Assistant Commissioner for Research in the USOE, voiced his hope that an effective program for "more really *basic* research" could be instituted in the near future.

3. Indeed, if anything, one might be tempted to argue against the policy of strong support for applied research on the grounds that there are some respects in which its merits are debatable — for example, its tendency towards lack of generalizability

4. But, as Professor Israel Scheffler has pointed out to me, perhaps even utilitarian, practical goals may be construed only as instrumental to achieving intrinsically valuable cultural goals such as the attainment of knowledge for its

own sake. Thus we would have not a hierarchy but a circular network of goals.

5. See the studies of Rossman (1931) and Roe (1952) for evidence on the role of intrinsic motivation in the creative work of inventors and scientists. In Roe's study, indications of humanitarian motives were found only in some social scientists, and very rarely in natural scientists.

6. For the purpose of this paper, we must rule out the definition of "applied" which is implied by Revelle's (1965) remark that "because the astronomical and earth sciences do not deal with universals, but only with physical laws acting in particular situations, the physicist tends to think of them as applied rather than fundamental sciences." Even if we believe that all phenomena can be explained, reductionistically, by appeal to a small number of physical laws, there is still a place for "basic science" in determining the way in which these physical laws manifest themselves or interact at the higher levels of physical organization represented by biological cells, nervous systems, or social groups. We also must rule out the definition that one might derive from McLane's (1965) statement that "25 years ago symbolic logic was the 'purest' branch of mathematics; today it is heavily applied, as in computers." The fact that a science *has* applications or has *been* applied does not make it an applied science, nor does it exclude the possibility that one can do basic science in such a field. Otherwise we would have to say that theoretical physics, because it spawned the atom bomb, it is an applied science!

REFERENCES

Allport, G. W., *Personality*, New York: Holt, Rinehart & Winston, 1937.

Ausubel, D. P., The nature of educational research. *Educational Theory*, 1953, 3, 314-320.

Clark, D. L., Educational research: A national perspective. In J. A. Culbertson and S. P. Hencley (Eds.), *Educational research: New perspectives*. Danville, Illinois: Interstate, 1963, pp. 7-18.

Cronbach, L. J., The role of the university in improving education. *Phi Delta Kappan*, 1966, 47, (10), 539-545.

Getzels, J. W. and Jackson, P. W., *Creativity and intelligence: Explorations with gifted students.* New York: Wiley, 1962.

Guilford, J. P., Potentiality for creativity and its measurement. In Anne Anatasi (Ed.), *Testing problems in perspective.* Washington: American Council on education, 1966, pp. 429-435.

Guilford, J. P., *The nature of intelligence.* New York: McGraw-Hill, 1967.

Holland, J. G., Research on programing variables. In R. Glaser, (Ed.), *Teaching machines and programed learning, II: Data and directions.* Washington: Department of Audiovisual Instruction, National Education Association, 1965, pp. 66-117.

Kidd, C. V., Basic research — description versus definition, *Science*, 1959, 129, 368-371.

Levin, H., Reading research: What, why and for whom? *Elementary English*, 1966 (Feb.), 138-147.

McLane, S., In *Basic research and national goals.* Report to the House Committee on Science and Astronautics by the National Academy of Science Washington: U. S. Government Printing Office, 1965, p. 196.

Morrill, C. S., Teaching Machines: A review. *Psychol. Bull.*, 1961, 58, 363-375.

Pfaffmann, C., Behavioral sciences. *American Psychologist*, 1965, 20, 667-686.

Reagan, M. D., Basic and applied research: A meaningful distinction? *Science*, 1967, 155, 1383-1386.

Revelle, R., In *Basic research and national goals.* Report to the House Committee on Science and Astronautics by the National Academy of Science Washington: U. S. Government Printing Office, 1965, p. 239.

Robinson, Donald W., The USOE and research in education, an interview with Richard Louis Bright. *Phi Delta Kappan*, 1966, 48 (1), 2-5.

Roe, Anne. *The making of a scientist.* New York: Dodd, Mead, 1952.

Rossman, J., *The psychology of the inventor.* Washington: Inventors Publishing Company, 1931.

Seaborg, G. T., In *Federal research and development programs.* Hearing before the House Select Committee on Government Research, 88th Congress, 1st Session. Washington: U. S. Government Printing Office, 1963, p. 66.

Skinner, B. F., The science of learning and the art of teaching. *Harvard Educational Review*, 1954, 24, 86-97.

Storer, N. W., *Basic versus applied research: The conflict between means and ends in science.* Cambridge, Mass.: Harvard Univer. Press, 1964.

Teller, E., in *Government and science.* Hearings before the Subcommittee on Science, Research, and Development of the House Committee on Science and Astronautics, 88th Congress, 1st Session. Washington: U. S. Government Printing Office, 1963, p. 115.

Torrance, E. P., *Guiding creative talent.* Englewood Cliffs, N.J.: Prentice-Hall, 1962.

Weinberg, A. M., Impact of large-scale science on the United States. *Science*, 1961, 134, 161-164.

RESEARCH METHODOLOGY – A POINT OF VIEW

D. Bob Gowin
Jason Millman

In the practical sense of doing, research is a matter of techniques. An event occurs or is made to happen by the researcher and some record of the event occurs or is made. Careful study of the record generates factual statements serviceable as evidence for inferences leading to generalizations, explanations, interpretations, predictions and decisions. Research technique is the process of converting events into records and records into factual statements (including tables, charts and other ways of showing relationships).

In the theoretical sense of reasoning, research is a matter of using concepts, conceptual systems, constructs, models, theories, etc. An event can be studied effectively if the researcher generates a *telling question*. Such questions require key concepts or generative ideas which lead and guide the inquiry. Facts without concepts are blind and concepts without facts are empty (apologies to Kant). Research brings together conceptual systems and techniques. Appraisal of research is methodology (Kaplan, 1964).

Gage (1964) identified three aspects of the research paradigm: the *substantive*, the *methodological*, and the *logistical*. See Gowan and Strzepek (1969) for a criticism of Gage's article and for a further development of some of the ideas in this paper. Substantive means the basic concerns of the research; this category is further analyzed by Gage into concepts, variables, and the ways in which phenomena are selected, abstracted, and focused by the research workers. We call this area the *context for inquiry*. Expanding Gage's category permits a more complete consideration of what must necessarily be thought about within the research paradigm.

Gage's second category is the methodological, in which he included ways of measuring variables and of collecting and analyzing data. We prefer to call this category *methods of work* because we reserve the term methodology for the study of methods.

Logistical, Gage's third category, means the host of concerns with men and money, organization and administration, etc., that are necessary in planning, executing, interpreting, communicating, applying, and improving research. We do not discuss this important category here.

Two other components of the research paradigm appear to be important. One of these we call *products*, what the research produces. The outcomes of research are usually thought to be limited to published discussions of the research results. By using the broader category, products, a larger number of aspects of research outcomes can be analyzed. The fourth component is *values*. Explicit treatment of the many ways that consideration of value enters into research is especially important in a field as saturated with values as education is. The tug between values and knowledge-claims is particularly fruitful for analysis. We believe that consideration of research within this larger view of methodology is necessary for significant improvement in educational research.

CONTEXT FOR INQUIRY

The *context for inquiry* includes the scene and phenomena of interest, telling questions and principles of evidence, key concepts and conceptual systems, basic assumptions and presuppositions.

By the scene we mean that most inclusive frame of reference in which the phenomena of interest can stand out clearly; the scene is the background for the foreground phenomena. Any research is an abstraction and selection from an infinite variety of possible things one might study. For example, sociologists Harp and Richer identify social interaction as the most inclusive sociological domain. When they turn to educational research they note a quality which colors the scene: "The pervasive character of an ideology of equal opportunity and the continuing role assigned to education as an avenue of mobility in American society could not help but influence the direction and character of sociological research in this area."

It is our belief that the analysis of the scene in any research area will reveal some pervasive quality which helps determine the direction and import of research, and that the identification of this pervasive quality is useful in assessing the logic of the moves back and forth between scene and knowledge (Dewey, 1930).

Emerging from the background scene are the foreground phenomena of interest. The phenomena of interest are simply the more specific researchable domains within a larger scene. In the case of sociology of education they are identified by Harp and Richer as social organizations, collectivities and institutions.

Phenomena of interest are approached in two different ways, ways which appear to correspond to the origin of the inquiry. When "enquiry has its origin in conceptual structure . . . we are able to formulate a telling question" (Schwab, 1962, p. 12). A fool can ask more questions than seven wise men can answer, but a *telling question* is one which "tells" on the phenomena and facilitates inquiry. Telling questions help convert what is puzzling about a situation into something that can be thought about intelligently. There is a close relationship between the telling questions and the key concepts, generative ideas, and conceptual systems. Growing out of the scene of American race relationships is a phenomenon of interest, Negro education of the south. The conceptual model of "conflict − unintention − accommodation" relates to the telling question: In history, are the unintended consequences of man's willful actions as significant as the changes resulting from the "force of intention"?

Inquiry may also have its origin, as John Dewey believed, in problematic situations. Still other writers suggest that inquiry may be brought about by a puzzling observation, by access to a new source of data, subjects, instruments or techniques of study, or by existence of "previously unexamined phenomena."

Most of the phenomena of interest in educational research appear to originate from such ordinary situations and to be approached with questions that are not very telling. An example of such a question is, "What are the faculty and student subcultures and their associated norms?"

Once a question, telling or not, is formulated, the generalized phenomena of interest can be converted into a specific aspect of that phenomenon which will count as evidence. Any question remains ambiguous until the sort of thing which would count as an answer is agreed upon.

There is a crucial connection between concepts and facts. Facts may be given three distinct but related meanings. Fact One is an event which occurs (either being made to occur by the researcher or merely happening). This event must leave a record in order to be chosen for study. Researchers can spend much time profitably thinking about techniques for making records of events. The record is Fact Two. A good device for recording events generates an index to the phenomena of interest. Fact Three is a factual statement, typically in verbal or mathematical form. Factual statements are based on records of events occurring in the phenomena of interest. Since concepts can be related to facts in all three senses (the events, the record, and the statement), it is important for purposes of test, analysis, and criticism to be clear about which level of fact one is dealing with.

One may commit a Type I or II error in relating concepts to data: one may become too specific and lose important evidence; or one may become too loose and include so much that it is impossible to make a legitimate discrimination. Precision and clarity in a conceptual system are commendable, but care must be taken that the legitimate complexity and richness of the phenomena of interest are not lost. The enormous complexity of educational phenomena is a condition of work in education.

How shall *concept* be defined? For all of its frequent use in educational writing, little has been done to clarify its conflicting meanings. In general there is a tension in meanings between the psychological (studies in concept formation) and the logical (concept as a class, as a construct, as a carrier of meaning). A child possesses the concept of "liquidity" when he correctly identifies milk, oil, honey, water as liquids; he sees what is common in events which are quite different. Thus, there are three elements tied together in the meaning of concept; the stability of response, the linguistic sign, and the commonality in different events. We stipulate the following definition of *concept*: a concept is a sign which points to a commonality in events and which permits the concept user to make relatively stable responses to those varied events. The signs which are vehicles for the concept are largely linguistic and conventional. The commonality in events may range from simple similarities to regularities to law-like invariance.

Conceptual structures are logically organized sets of concepts. Conceptual structures serve many roles depending on the phase of the research. They help the researcher formulate the telling question, identify index phenomena through the principle of evidence, formulate knowledge-claims, and interpret products. To identify a conceptual structure is to understand the power and limitation of inquiries that take place under its guidance (Schwab, 1964).

When these elements in the context for inquiry are analyzed, it is possible to expose the basic assumptions and presuppositions of the inquiry. An assumption is what is taken for granted to establish meaningful communication. What is taken for granted in one study may become an object of inquiry in another study, but the second study will necessarily require another set of assumptions.

When Beach, for example, looks at the context for historical research in education he finds a number of assumptions and presuppositions. One of these is the assumption that education is something done to people rather than something they seek and gain on their own. Beach wonders whether historians can escape to some extent the myopia which make historians both distinctively and unimaginatively professional.

We do not want to argue these issues but rather to point out that any set of knowledge-claims rests upon assumptions and presuppositions. Analysis of these elements is basic philosophical work.

METHODS OF WORK

A *method* is a procedural commitment, a collection of techniques or ways of doing things that may be generalized or made common to a variety of situations. Method involves regular steps, planned sequences, ordered phases, and related stages of inquiry. Research methods are of many kinds: experimental, empirical, historical, pedagogical, comparative, conceptual. Techniques of work are the many different specific ways of working. A criticism of research methods in a given work involves the logic of the moves from the occurrence of the event to the record of the event, to the specific tasks of inquiry.

Questions of the validity of methods of work include: Is the prose of other men which remains to be read representative of either the author or some group with whom he is associated? Should mentalistic goals be salvaged from behavioristic criticism? Do participant-observers in the classroom lose objectivity as they become emotionally involved? Do the tools of measurement of situational differences seem to be measuring the wrong variables? Is a series of univariate analyses of several dependent criterion variables inappropriate?

PRODUCTS

If we ask about the *products* which research generates, instead of merely about its findings, we have a broader base of analysis. The typical products are conclusions and decisions (Cronbach and Suppes, 1969) or, more specifically, facts, generalizations, concepts, theories, explanations, predictions, and interpretations. In addition, an inquiry may produce a new question, a new area of uncertainty, a puzzling observation, and a new set of terms. A product may be simply propositional, as most works are, or more tangible such as a set of instructional materials. A product is what the investigator has when the work is finished that he did not have when he began.

Complete analysis of inquiry demands as careful scrutiny of the product of the research as of the context for inquiry and methods of work. An analysis of products includes not only identifying the product or products (e.g., whether explanation or description, fact or concept) but also involves applying criteria of excellence appropriate to the several, specific products. If the products are tangible, such criteria include durability, cost, and effectiveness. Consistency, simplicity, and explanatory power are criteria by which theories, for example, are judged.

VALUES

Values are created at all phases of disciplined inquiry. Values constitute both a separate category and an aspect of each of the other three categories. As a separate category the value questions concern the identification of values, the relation between intrinsic and instrumental values, and the identification of within-the-field values and outside-the-field values. As an aspect of each of the other three categories, the value questions emerge from the specific tasks of inquiry.

In general, values are deliberated interests, justified likings. To identify values, expressions of likings, desires, interests, etc. must be located — not always an easy task. When such expressions show conflict, a principle of decision must be invoked.

The most critical value judgment concerns the significance of the entire research effort. "So what?" questions typically have two answers. One claim is that there was *intrinsic value* in performing the research. Doing research does have intrinsic value; satisfying curiosity is curiously satisfying. The other claim is that there was *instrumental value* in the research products. The outcomes of research are thought to be good for something else: reaching a decision, solving a problem, improving a practice, or stimulating further inquiry.

We believe it is very important for workers to search for and examine the intrinsic values in their field. These values are in much need of explicit recognition and justification. The chief reason for becoming explicit about these intrinsic, within-the-field values is that unless the field has some claim to intrinsic value it may become extinct because the instrumental values it serves may be served by other means. When history, for example, is justified only by its instrumental value in creating patriotic citizens, it lays itself open to abandonment when other means are found equal or superior to achieving love of country. When psychology is justified only on grounds that it helps students understand themselves better, it may be replaced by the guidance counselor or psychotherapeutic encounter groups.

Each of the other three categories has value considerations. In the *context for inquiry* perhaps the most fundamental value orientation of the scene and phenomena of interest is "What knowledge is of most worth? Telling questions and conceptual systems have value in the guidance of inquiry. Other recognized values of conceptual structures are these: clarity of meaning, coherence of ideas, accuracy and precision of reference, power of reasoning.

Values found in *methods of work* include the following familiar list: reliability, systematic procedure, repeatability and replication, technical competence, efficiency, economy, and intersubjectivity.

For *products* other values appear. Research outcomes may have commercial value, aesthetic value, moral value, pedagogical value. These are examples of instrumental values. Within the pattern of inquiry, however, the research product is valued which provides a clear explanation of something which has been puzzling; so is a warranted generalization which helps to connect elements in educational experience which had heretofore been seen as separate. A well-argued prediction is valued since it helps decison-making in the present. Perhaps the value of knowing the truth transcends all others.

What is the value of our point of view toward educational research? We noted the increasing diversity in the way educational phenomena are viewed. The point of view outlined here is a way to bring together in some comprehensible fashion these different approaches to research. Many pleas have been made for interdisciplinary research, but few means have been found to communicate accurately and well between fields. A common set of terms and distinctions is needed to facilitate discussion about inquiry in different areas. We think that our point of view is a step in that direction and we hope that others will challenge and change it and contribute toward a more adequate view. We see improvement in three major areas.

First, a point of view will help in the guidance of research practice because it will help to develop thorough-going and intelligent criticism. We have in mind here the careful analysis of both successful and unsuccessful research practice in much the same way as any practice, such as farming or painting, may be improved as a consequence of ferreting out the conditions of success and failure in each particular case.

Second, a point of view will help in the guidance of research policy based upon an analysis of priorities, and what is important and why. This goal is facilitated by the broader framework for criticism of research proposals and research products. If criticism of research proposals were customarily set in the framework suggested here, the merits of proposals would be more validly assessed.

Third, a fully-developed point of view will be a research theory, i.e., a philosophy of educational research. Some philosophical view of science lies behind or is explicit in every research effort. If it is assumed that distinctive phenomena require distinctive approaches, then one must determine what is distinctive about educational phenomena. The distinctions necessary to solve problems in the conduct of physical inquiry may actually blur or distort the distinctions necessary to solve problems in another context, such as educational inquiry. To the extent that this point of view is correct, the need for a special philosophy of educational research is clear. The categories of such a research theory include the context for inquiry, the methods of work, the products, and the values adumbrated in this essay. The source of meaningful content would come from continued critical analysis of completed studies. More work of this kind would go a long way toward satisfying a critical need for a theory of educational inquiry.

BIBLIOGRAPHY

Beach; Harp and Richer, *Review of Educational Research*, Volume 39, No. 5, December, 1969.

Cronbach, Lee J. and Suppes, Patrick (editors), *Research for Tomorrow's Schools: Disciplined Inquiry for Education.* New York: Macmillan, 1969.

Dewey, John. Qualitative Thought. *On Experience, Nature, and Freedom.* (Edited by R. J. Bernstein.) New York: The Liberal Arts Press, 1960. Chapter 8, pp. 176-99.

Gage, N. L. This Side of Paradigms: The State of Research on Teaching English. *Research Design and the Teaching of English: Proceedings of the San Francisco Conference, 1963.* Chicago: National Council for Teachers of English, 1964. Pp. 22-31.

Gowin, D. B. and Strzepek, J. The Far Side of Paradigms: Conditions for Knowledge Making in English Education. *The English Record.* Binghamton: New York State English Council, Fall 1969.

Kaplan, Abraham. *The Conduct of Inquiry.* San Francisco: Chandler, 1964.

Schwab, J. J. Structure of the Disciplines: Meanings and Significances. *The Structure of Knowledge and the Curriculum.* (Edited by G. W. Ford and Lawrence Pugno.) Chicago: Rand McNally, 1964 Pp. 1-50.

chapter 5
research literature on compensatory education

EQUALIZING EDUCATIONAL OPPORTUNITY

Kenneth Carlson

In four years, the United States will celebrate the 200th anniversary of the Declaration of Independence. The celebration will signify that we as a nation still subscribe to the principles enunciated in the Declaration. The first principle stated therein is that "all Men are created equal," with equality being defined as the unalienable right to life, liberty, and the pursuit of happiness. The celebration should be marked by an air of embarrassment.

In fifteen years, the United States will celebrate the 200th anniversary of the Constitution. The 14th Amendment to that document says that no state "shall deny to any person within its jurisdiction the equal protection of the laws." Unless considerable change takes place between now and 1987, we shall assemble for the ceremonies in acute discomfort.

Education directly determines life, liberty, and happiness and education is a government function. But schooling does not promote equality; it perpetuates inequality. It is the Great Sieve, and the openings are labeled "economic and ethnic origin." For those who were born well, schooling is opportunity; for the rest, it is circumscription. We still profess what our ancestors dreamed, but the Revolution only achieved the domestication of oppression.

> ... when the denial of equality of opportunity to major segments of the population and the shallowness of many prevailing notions of equality are weighed against America's declared ideals, the conclusion can only be that the [American] experiment has been a tragic failure (Greenbaum, 1971, p. 501).

FINANCIAL INEQUALITY

There is a school district in Texas which spends $5334 each year on each student. There is another district which spends $264 (New York Times, December 25, 1971, p. 16; Coons, Clune, & Sugarman, 1971). The difference is 2000 per cent. The dollar disparities between the children of the rich and the children of the poor are not usually this great, but they do have a disheartening consistency. There is the urban expenditure and there is the suburban expenditure. New York City spends $1031 per pupil and Scarsdale spends $1626; Boston spends $655 and Newton spends $842 (Wicker, 1970, p. E13); Newark spends $940 and Millburn spends $1192 (New Jersey Education Association, 1971, p. 23). No wonder James Conant was once moved to write that "the contrast in money available to schools in a wealthy suburb and to the schools in a large city jolts one's notion of the meaning of equality of opportunity (Conant, 1961, pp. 2-3)."

There are also rural-suburban and even suburban-suburban differences. Thus, in Los Angeles County, Beverly Hills can spend $1232 per pupil while Baldwin Park spends $577 (Greenbaum, 1971, p. 508). And finally, there are the inequalities between states, where New York spends an average of $1370 per pupil and Mississippi spends $521 (Maeroff, 1971, p. E7).

All of the foregoing differences are due to two factors: wealth and effort. Since the school tax is a property tax, the town with a lot of highly valued property — commercial, industrial, or residential — has a plentiful resource on which to draw for support of its schools. The property value per pupil in Newark is $20,338, whereas in Millburn it is $92,856 (New Jersey Education Association, 1971, p. 23). In Baldwin Park there is $3706 in property value per child, but the value in Beverly Hills is $50,885 — a ratio of 1 to 13 (Greenbaum, 1971, p. 508).

Effort is the extent to which a town actually draws on this taxable resource. The tax rate in Newark is $3.69; in Millburn it is $1.43 (New Jersey Education Association, 1971, p. 23). Similarly, the tax rate in Baldwin Park is $5.48, compared to $2.38 in Beverly Hills (Greenbaum, 1971, p. 512).

What all of this shows — and it is typical for the nation as a whole — is that poor communities spend less money per pupil but they make a greater effort to support education than do rich communities. As the California Supreme Court pointed out in the Serrano case, "affluent districts can have their cake and eat it too; they can provide a high quality education for their children while paying lower taxes. Poor districts, by contrast, have no cake at all (Greenbaum, 1971, p. 514)." The same can be said for states. It should be borne in mind that taxes hurt the poor more than the rich, because the poor are already at a subsistence standard of living. Moreover, the property tax is especially regressive because it is not based on ability to pay.

A further refinement is in order at this point. There are intra-district disparities in the amount of money spent on students. The children in the wealthier neighborhoods of a school district have more spent on their education than do the children in the poorer neighborhoods. Sexton (1964) has provided a detailed description of this situation as it obtained in the Detroit school system. Even within a school, the students in the higher tracks or ability groupings have more spent on them than do the students in the lower tracks. The higher ability students get more materials, more highly paid teachers, and so forth. Since the students in the higher tracks tend to be from higher social class families (Rothstein, 1971; Schaefer, Olexa, & Polk, 1970) the relationships between how much the family has and how much public money the child gets continues to persist. In 1967, Federal Judge Skelly Wright in Washington, D.C., ruled that tracking was in violation of the 14th Amendment guarantee of equal protection under the law (Hobson v. Hansen, 1967, pp. 401, 437).

MONEY DOES MATTER

There are many people who acknowledge indisputable financial inequalities but who then go on to say that money really doesn't matter. The one thing almost all of these people have in common is money. Some of these people even spend a lot of their money to send their children to private schools. Their actions give the lie to their words.

One method by which the educational value of money can be demonstrated is that employed by Guthrie and his colleagues in their analyses of the extensive data available on the schools in Michigan (Guthrie, et al., 1971). The Guthrie team examined the relationships among the following variables: socioeconomic status, school services, academic performance, and success in later life. Their first set of findings confirms what has already been established in this paper, namely, that those who got, get. To put it pedantically, there is a high positive correlation between a public school student's socioeconomic status and the amount of public money spent on his education. On this issue, Guthrie, et al., (1971) conclude that

> to be an elementary school child of lower socioeconomic status is to experience an extraordinary probability of discriminatory treatment. High-quality school services are provided to children from wealthy homes. Poor-quality school services are provided to children from poor homes [p. 55].

The second set of findings reveals another strong correlation: that between school service components and student performance as measured by standardized aptitude and subject-matter achievement tests. All of the components are affected by the availability of money, and consequently they exist to a more favorable degree in rich schools than in poor ones. Among the components are: student-teacher ratios; in-service training of teachers; the number of classes and courses taught by a teacher; job satisfaction for teachers; released time for department chairmen; the services of a school nurse and psychologist; supplementary teaching materials; library books; newer, less crowded buildings, with better illuminated halls and rooms and more sound dampening characteristics; summer school programs; and special services for students with special needs. All of these components correlate positively with pupil performance, although some may in reality only be proxy measures of others that are more directly significant. For example, a teacher's verbal ability may be an index of her general intelligence and imagination in the teaching task. At any rate, the highest correlations are those that have to do with teacher characteristics, particularly verbal ability, teaching experience, job satisfaction, and amount and type of academic preparation. Thus, there is strong evidence that schools, and especially teachers, do make a difference, and teacher quality is to some extent at least an identifiable, a cultivatable, and, most important, a purchasable commodity.

The last set of positive correlations that the authors derive has to do with the connection between school performance and success in later life. Here it should be noted that success has a social as well as a personal dimension, so that society too is a beneficiary of improved education for the individual. The better educated person is a more informed and active participant in the political process and is less likely to engage in criminal activity (or is less likely to be caught at it).

NEW FORMS OF SCHOOL FINANCING

Given the educational potency of money, what can be done to insure a more equitable disbursement of public education funds? Obviously, local financing of education has to be done away with. This is rapidly coming to pass. State courts in California, Minnesota, and New Jersey, and the Federal district court in Texas have already found local financing of education to be in violation of the equal protection clause of the 14th Amendment, as it applies to both students and taxpayers. A Supreme Court ruling on the Texas case is expected by the spring. The outcome is almost guaranteed, not just because of the pressure of mounting lower court consensus, but also due to thrusts from the legislative and executive branches of government. In Hawaii, of course, the schools have always been state financed. The Maryland state government has assumed responsibility for school construction costs, and in North Carolina most of the teacher salary bill is now picked up by the state (New York Times, September 2, 1971, p. 32). Gubernatorial advisory commissions in New York and New Jersey have within this year recommended that these states take over almost the entire cost of school financing. Governor William Milliken of Michigan is attempting to move his state in the same direction (Wise, 1971). At the Federal level, the Advisory Commission on Intergovernmental Relations has recommended that the states assume "substantially all" of the responsibility for financing the schools (Wise, 1971) and the President's Commission on School Finance just brought forth the same recommendation (Herbers, 1972(a), pp. 1, 9). Most of the recommendations for a state takeover also contain proposals for more equitable tax policies, e.g., a uniform state property tax and greater reliance on income taxes and sales taxes.

So the tide is running, and the question now is whether the tide can or should be stopped at the state line. The Supreme Court will eventually have to address itself to this issue, since the arguments for state financing of education are even better arguments for federal financing. As Albert Shanker (1971) has asked, "if inequality is unconstitutional within a state, need we wait much longer before the doctrine applies *between* states as well (p. E 11)?" In a society as mobile as that of the United States, it is as patently ridiculous to confine equality of opportunity within state lines as within municipal boundaries. Furthermore, "there is no justification for relying purely on state and local taxes to finance education in a nation in which the poor states have about half the per capita income of the rich ones (Calkins, 1971, p. 31)."

Federal financing of local schools may well contradict the 10th Amendment, which reserves to the states the power to educate; however, in recent years the Supreme Court has consistently chosen the individual rights of the 14th Amendment over the states' rights of the 10th Amendment. So while federal school financing may break new ground, it does so in a well-trampled field.

Here again the Court will be mindful of contemporary opinion in coming to its decision. Senator George McGovern has indicated in a campaign letter that he would like to see the Federal government assume a greater share of the costs of education, although how much greater was not specified. Governor Milton Shapp (1971, p. 31) of Pennsylvania has proposed the creation of a National Education Trust Fund, which could eventually handle all the costs of public education. Senator Hubert Humphrey (as quoted in Home News, 1972, p. 1) has just echoed the Shapp proposal, with the recommendation that the trust fund be used to finance at least one-third of the nation's education costs. To date, the most significant support for major federal involvement in school financing has come from a majority of the President's own Commission on School Finance. John Fischer (as quoted in Herbers, 1972b), speaking for that majority, said: "If we really mean it when we say that every American child — rather than every Californian or every Arkansan — is entitled to equal educational opportunity, we must be prepared to use federal means to bring about such equality [p. E 3]."

WHITHER LOCAL CONTROL?

The prospect of state or federal financing raises anew the old fear that central funding will result in central control. The power of the purse is undeniably a first-order power, and they who possess it cannot be expected to relinquish all control of the uses to which their appropriations are put. Indeed, we should demand that they devise and enforce minimal standards as a means of protecting students. It is worth noting that such standards were never applied to the Ocean Hill-Brownsville experimental program in local control until after the experiment had terminated, at which time it was discovered that the reading scores for children in the district were lower than before the experiment began and worse than those of other ghetto schools in New York City (Ravitch, 1972). The application of standards throughout the course of the experiment might have prevented or reversed this trend.

The argument that uniform standards will lead inexorably to deadening homogenization is currently being undermined by the structural and instructional diversity which is finally surfacing in public school systems, e.g., the New York City system. The point is that stifling uniformity is not inevitable, and it can be reversed. The crucial task is to determine how much uniformity is desirable. In the case of educational expenditures, there is now a lamentable lack of uniformity.

Those who have ordered or who advocate state financing of the schools have been careful not to foreclose local control. The California Supreme Court (Greenbaum, 1971), in the Serrano case, said that "no matter how the state decides to finance its system of public education, it can still leave decision-making power in the hands of local districts (p. 524)." In his New Jersey decision, Judge Theodore Botter (Robinson v. State of New Jersey, 1972) wrote that "beyond common essentials, educational goals should be adjusted to community needs (pp. 63-64)." The President's Commission on School Finance (as quoted in Herbers, 1972a) asserted that "local boards of education should be given wide latitude, within general state guidelines, to use resources provided by the state in ways that best meet their needs and demands (p. E 3)." The same sentiments can be invoked for federal financing.

Ironically, those who oppose centralized financing tend to assume that local control presently exists and has only to be preserved. For many school systems, however, local control is a chimera.

> The shortage of funds in some districts actually minimizes local discretion in programming and in the ability to compete for the services of good teachers. School boards in poor districts cannot opt to institute special services when their budgets do not include adequate funds even for essentials. In this sense local control is illusory. It is control for the wealthy, not for the poor (Robinson v. State of New Jersey, 1972, p. 64).

There have been several attempts to develop school financing plans which combine a central input for equalization purposes and a local input to assure a degree of local discretion. Existing state and federal aid formulas are mostly local input, and the "aid" is parceled out in such a way that it actually widens the financial gap between have and have-not school districts (Guthrie, et al.; Meranto, 1970; Schwebel, 1968; Wise & Manley-Casimir, 1971). The newer schemes seek to eliminate this farce. Among the most recent of these have been the Fleischmann Commission report in New York State and the report of the

Governor's Tax Policy Committee (the Sears Report) in New Jersey. The most influential plan has probably been that worked out by John Coons, William Clune, and Stephen Sugarman (1971) which appears in their book, *Private Wealth and Public Education*. The authors advance the concept of "power equalization." Under this plan, the state (or conceivably the federal government) would establish maximum and minimum levels of spending per pupil. Within these limits, a local district can decide how much it wants to spend, and this decision will trigger a pre-set property tax rate. For rich school districts, the revenue generated by this tax rate will be more than is needed to meet the per pupil expenditures. The surplus will therefore be turned over to the state (or, again, the federal government). The revenue resulting from the same tax rate in a poor district will not be sufficient to satisfy the desired per pupil expenditure, and the difference will be supplied by the state (or federal government). In this way, per pupil expenditure will continue to be a product of local decision and effort, but localities will be equalized in their revenue raising capability. The Citizens Group named by the California State Board of Education to work out a means of compliance with the Serrano ruling has just adopted the power equalizing plan (Wicker, 1972b, p. E 11).

COMPENSATORY EDUCATION

What should remain in mind is that the essential objective is not to equalize expenditures but to equalize opportunity. At this time in United States history, given the fact that the rich have their private advantages augmented with public money, equalizing the distribution of this money is a straightforward way to equalize opportunity. But we should not stop there. Equal opportunity can be still more effectively promoted through the expansion of compensatory programs for the disadvantaged. Dwight Allen (as quoted in Nathan, 1971) has stated the case rather succinctly: "equality is a racist notion when you start with a dual society that is systematically discriminatory on a racial basis (p. 53)." Allen's remark should be extended to include socioeconomic status as well as race. In fact, Patricia Sexton (1964) may yet prove to have been prophetic in a comment she made eight years ago.

> In the long run it may turn out that the educational problems of low-income whites are more stubborn and resistant to treatment than those of Negroes. The Negro community is becoming aware of its rights and particularly its right to equal educational opportunity [p. 17].

Perhaps it would be well at this point to present the issue in simplified schematic form as follows:

Educational Opportunity Today

	Home Environment	*School Environment*
Rich	XXXXXXXXXXXXXXXX	XXXXXXXXXXXXXXXX
Poor	XXXXXX	XXXXXX

This represents the present condition of education opportunity in the United States. Those who propose the mere equalization of per pupil expenditures would, at best, only succeeed in converting this picture to the following.

Educational Opportunity After
Expenditure Equalization

	Home Environment	*School Environment*
Rich	XXXXXXXXXXXXXXXX	XXXXXXXXXXXXXXXX
Poor	XXXXXX	XXXXXXXXXXXXXXXX

The poor child would still be left in a non-competitive position due to the relative disadvantagement of his home environment.

Of what does that disadvantagement consist? Quite often it consists of hunger, malnourishment, and sickness. It may consist of brain damage from having eaten peeling paint or because of vitamin or protein deficiency as early as the prenatal period. In the latter respect, it has been said that "deprived children start life at a disadvantage, social handicaps having already been converted to organic defects even at birth (Schwebel, 1968, p. 154)." Educational disadvantagement in the home could result from the absence of a parent or from the inattentiveness of economically harried parents. It may simply mean parents of limited verbal fluency and conversational range due to the restricted opportunities of their own childhood. It could also mean the lack of a quiet place to study, or of books, or of variegated experiences.

> There is no mystery about it: the child who is familiar with books, ideas, conversation — the ways and means of the intellectual life — before he begins consciously to think, has a marked advantage. He is at home in the House of Intellect just as the stableboy is at home among horses or the child of actors on the stage [Barzun, 1959, p. 142].

To equalize opportunity means to offset these disadvantages. Much more appropriately, it means to prevent them. In a provocative paper presented at the American Sociological Association convention last summer, it was contended that the best way to eradicate the ravages of poverty and guarantee equal opportunity is income equalization. Van Til and Van Til (1971) suggested that society be structured so that "the richest he controls a disposable income no more than three times greater than the poorest he (p. 16)." This is the most adequate solution to the problem which this writer has encountered, but politically it is pie in the sky.

A preventive strategy which is politically acceptable is simple vitamin and protein supplementation for undernourished women during pregnancy and lactation. It has been shown that this can increase the intelligence of the children born to these women (Harrell, Woodyyard, & Gates, 1955; Birch & Gussow, 1970). In general, high quality medical care should be easily available to the poor at all times.

A strategy which borders between prevention and compensation is infant education. The Infant Education Center Project in Milwaukee randomly assigned into two groups the new-born children of forty mothers whose I.Q.s were less than 70. The control group was given no special treatment. Each child in the experimental group was well-fed and bathed and stimulated. In addition, the mothers of these children were instructed in homemaking and baby care. In time, the experimental group children attained an average I.Q. of 125, whereas the average I.Q. for the control group children was 95 (The New Republic, 1971; Time, 1972a). Needless to say, this study and the *in utero* studies previously mentioned cast doubt on the intelligence theories of Jensen, Eysenck, Herrnstein, Shockley and others. Infant education is the logical precursor to Headstart programs, and both can be accomplished through a national system of day care centers. Such a system would also provide jobs and careers for many of the poor. However, the most compelling reason for it is so there would no longer have to be a "control group."

This brings us to the compensatory efforts which can be undertaken by the regular public schools. As long as schools are so clearly identifiable along social class lines, money can be allocated to a school according to the socioeconomic status of its students. The lower the socioeconomic status, the more money the school would receive — quite the reverse of what now occurs. Guthrie and his colleagues (1971) believe that public support of education can best be based on the needs of individual schools. This would be a perfectly logical procedure. ". . . the educational system should not distribute its benefits in meager amounts to those of meager abilities, anymore than the health system should lavish its energies on the healthy. Justice demands precisely the opposite (Green, 1971, p. 12)." The additional money which would acrrue to poor schools under this system could be used for such demonstrably salutary purposes as expanding and upgrading the professional staff and the other school service components referred to earlier. The money could even be used for projects of such seemingly limited promise as summer schools. (One study arrived at the conclusion that 80 per cent of the achievement difference between black and white students was due to differential growth over the summer vacation) (Center for Education Policy Research, 1970).

Determining financial support on a school-by-school basis is not a satisfactory arrangement where schools have heterogeneous student populations. In these cases, rich students would be likely to receive as much educational service as poor students. The only answer here is to apportion money on the basis of individual student needs. This practice already has a history in the weighting formulas for academic categories of students — e.g., kindergarten, vocational, secondary — and for categories of the handicapped — e.g., mentally retarded, blind, and so on. Until such time as careful diagnosis and re-diagnosis allow the needs of other students to be better known, it will be necessary to use the gross category of socioeconomic status.(1) There would have to be safeguards, of course, to insure that the extra money allotted for lower socioeconomic status students was not diverted elsewhere. One very specific proposal in this regard is that poor families receive special stipends just to keep their working-age children in school (Solomon, 1971).

I am not prepared to say what the dollar amounts or ratios should be for different social class categories of students. I doubt that anyone can suggest these figures with any confidence. This should not cause alarm, for who would presume to say with authority what the figures should be for the academic and handicapped categories of students? Human wisdom simply does not reach this far, and yet figures, however imperfect, do get arrived at. In New York City, the More Effective Schools program was spending an additional $430 per student. An economist, Dennis J. Dugan (1969) has estimated the educational value that different kinds of parents bring to children, and concluded that an additional $1300 a year should be spent on the education of nonwhite students to match the parental services that white students receive. Bemused looks are in order.

The notion of parental services is itself a valid one. Children do learn from their parents. What and how much the children learn is a function of the parents' own level of education. Some educators have therefore urged that education programs be developed for poorly educated parents (Tanner & Tanner, 1971). In this way these parents will become more concerned and helpful with their children's education. In a sense, then, parent education would be compensatory for the parents and a prophylactic for their children. Whether the regular public school is the best agency to conduct parent education has been questioned. ". . . as a practical matter, if the schools failed the parents as children, it is doubtful that schools will now be able to help the parents teach their children to learn (Dimond, 1971, p. 391)." There are other agencies which may be more congenial to parents whose memories of school are bitter. The United Auto Workers has had success in upgrading the reading skills of its less literate members. Community organizations, including churches, could be publicly subsidized to undertake efforts of this sort. Understandably, financial incentives will have to be offered to parents if recruiting programs are to yield any kind of results.

There are people who believe that compensatory education is tantamount to pouring money down a rathole. The cause-effect relationship they perceive is not that of poverty breeding ignorance, but of ignorance producing poverty. They contend that the primary consideration is one of innate inferiority, and that, intellectually, some groups have just not been too well endowed genetically. Thus, to offer compensatory education is to deny reality and to fight a losing battle. The first reply to these people is to cite the successes which compensatory programs have had even though the funding has generally been parsimonious. There is also a way in which these people's very contentions can be used to allay any hidden fears they may have for their own children's competitive headstart. If compensatory education is merely intended to correct for disadvantaged home environments, then rich children, who are presumed to be genetically superior, will still have this superiority as a competitive edge on poor children. To return to the diagram of a while ago, the compensatory education picture would look like this:

Educational Opportunity With
Compensatory Education

	Genetic Endowment	Home Environment	School Environment
Rich	XXXXXXXXXXXX	XXXXXXXXXXXX	XXXXXXXXXXX
Poor	XXXX	XXXXXXXXX	XXXXXXXXXXXXXXXX

If the people who espouse the genetic position are at all fair-minded, they will have to at least allow poor kids the limited equalization of compensatory education.

INTEGRATION

Social class segregation within schools and among schools is itself a denial of equal opportunity, regardless of the funds and facilities involved. The simple premise here is that students learn from each other. Among the things they learn are attitudes toward school. Students whose home environments do not predispose them toward formal education – generally lower class students – can yet acquire academic motivation from classmates who have it. They are deprived of these classmates, however, by such devices as tracking and the neighborhood school and the school system whose boundaries are coterminous with those of the municipality. The deprivation is mutual, for there are many things of value that the upper class student can learn from the lower class student (Riessman, 1962, pp. 73, 80). Furthermore, the school has been aptly idealized as the marketplace for ideas, the arena in which a robust exchange of beliefs takes place. Homogeneity hardly augurs well for the attainment of this ideal. It would be more amusing if it were less appalling to watch students in a ghettoized society being taught the values of cultural pluralism while they learn about other groups by reading books. Unfortunately, schools seem intent on having students learn about other people as they learn about everything else – on a secondhand basis. The Board of Regents of New York State (The New York Times, 1972b), in a statement supporting school bussing, have expressed the matter well.

> . . . in a multiracial society, a person cannot be considered educated if he remains unexposed on a personal basis to the cultural richness and the individual diversity of his neighbors. It is just as serious to deny a white child the opportunity to know children of other colors as it is for minority children to be denied contact with whites (p. 20).

James Coleman (as quoted in Rosenthal, 1970) director of the most elaborate research yet undertaken on the effects of integrated education, insists that

> school integration . . . is the most consistent mechanism for improving the quality of education of disadvantaged children. Integration alone reduces the existing gap between black and white children by 30 per cent. All the other school factors together don't add up to nearly that much (pp. 1, 26).

Coleman has been faulted for the appropriateness of the statistical methods by which he processed his data (Bowles & Levin, 1968). The dispute with Coleman, then, revolves around the question of which is the more effective mechanism for improving learning — better school services or integration. However, it need not be an either/or proposition, since both sides agree that both approaches have value. (Coleman has written the foreword to the Coons, Clune, and Sugarman book, *Private Wealth and Public Education*, which argues for financial equalization rather than integration.) In fact, equalizing educational expenditures and integrating schools should prove to be reciprocally reinforcing processes. As money becomes available to poor students, rich parents will be less reluctant to have their children integrated with these students. And integration itself assures more equal distribution of education funds.

Coleman can be forgiven for so often speaking of blacks and the disadvantaged as being synonymous, for it remains a shameful reality that "the racially isolated school is one which is also isolated on the basis of economic status (New York State Department of Education, 1969, p. 4)." It is also true that school integration is almost always thought of in terms of race and not social class. But racial integration alone, as long overdue as that is with America's pretensions, does not guarantee social class integration of the schools. It may only succeed in bringing together blacks and whites from different but equally poor neighborhoods of the city. That would be a truncated victory for both groups. As Charles Silberman (1970) explains, "the benefits of integration come almost entirely from the fact that integrated schools tend to be middle class. Placing black students in lower class white schools does not help their achievement at all (p. 74)."

Lest one be concerned that there may not be enough middle class schools to absorb poor blacks *and* poor whites, one should know that the social class structure of the United States is no longer pyramidal; now, in fact, there is a big bulge in the middle. The problem is in finding ways for those on the bottom to penetrate the hard underbelly. One way has been Project Concern, a voluntary program in Connecticut in which randomly selected students from the black ghettos of four cities are bussed to schools in twenty-six suburbs. The bussed students gain 1.2 years worth of reading skills in a four-month period, while the control groups back in the ghettos fall farther behind the national averages. The estimate is that the bussed students have a three times better chance of achieving well in reading and arithmetic than the control groups. Coleman had found that such programs do not depress the educational achievement of the advantaged students, and the Project Concern experiences bears him out (Time, 1971b; Margolis, 1971, p. E 10).

As commendable as Project Concern is, there is a serious flaw to voluntary programs which was made evident by a case in New Jersey. A voluntary program there brought first- and second-graders from Newark to the schools of suburban Verona. The students did significantly better in reading, mathematics, and listening achievement than their peers who continued in the Newark schools (Zdep, 1970). Sadly and incredibly, public opposition in Verona forced the termination of the program. Again, the educational achievement of the advantaged students had not been depressed, so it is difficult to fathom the fears that must have seized the good people of Verona. Maybe it was the fact that the program involved twenty-six little children — a veritable invasion!(2)

The Verona tragedy demonstrated the extreme vulnerability of voluntary programs to community hysteria. Mandatory programs, which are usually ordered by the courts or by state education commissioners, have been restricted to integration within already existing school districts. Even so, similarly positive results have been reported for these programs as for the voluntary programs (Coleman, 1966; Newsweek, 1972). The problem is that the white middle class flight from urban centers has meant that city school districts are rapidly running out of people to integrate with.

It was this situation which led to the federal district court directive that the school system of Richmond, Virginia, be merged with the school systems of the surrounding counties of Chesterfield and Henrico. The reasoning behind the directive was that if segregated schools are in violation of the Constitution, so also are segregated school systems. As the presiding judge, Robert Merhige (as quoted in Wicker, 1972a) wisely reflected:

> ... school authorities may not constitutionally arrange an attendance zone system which serves only to reproduce in school facilities the prevalent pattern of housing segregation.
> ... To do so is only to endorse with official approval the product of private racism (p. 41).

Just as the city's geographic borders, viewed as limits upon pupil assignment, do not correspond to any real physical obstacles, so also are they unrelated to any marked practical or administrative necessities of school operation. The boundaries of Richmond are less than eternal monuments to a city planner's vision (Franklin, 1972, pp. 1, 19).

What Merhige did could have been done by the Virginia state legislature, and done more democratically. In the interest of economy, states have ordered the regionalization of many school districts over the years. In the past twenty years, the number of American school districts has been reduced from over 100,000 to only 17,000 (Hechinger, 1971, p. E-1). Is it too much to expect a state to compel consolidation in the interest of equal rights? The answer, regrettably, is that it is. Legislators (and members of the executive branch) are too politically vulnerable to make a habit of putting principle before popularity, especially with an issue as emotional as that of integration. The best hope for principled action lies with the long-tenured and life-tenured judges of the courts — a melancholy commentary on representative government.

The Merhige ruling was also based on the concept of *de jure* segregation — the fact that the schools of Virginia had a history of legislated segregation. Without this history, the situation in Virginia would presumably have been constitutional. Frankly, the distinction is difficult to appreciate. To quote from Justice Warren's majority opinion in the Brown v. Board of Education of Topeka:

> To separate [black students] from others of similar age and qualifications solely because of their race generates a feeling of inferiority as to their status in the community that may affect their hearts and minds in a way unlikely ever to be undone. Separate educational facilities are inherently unequal.

The important consideration, therefore, is the *effect* of segregation, not the cause. If segregation is unconstitutional because it is inherently unequal, then the causes of that segregation in the public schools would appear to be beside the point, or of secondary importance at best. Federal Judge Stephen Roth has declared that "if racial segregation in our public schools is an evil, then it should make no difference whether we classify it *de jure* or *de facto*. Our objective, legally, should be to remedy a condition which we believe needs correction (Time, 1971a, pp. 23-24)."

Cases now pending in Texas seek to broaden the Supreme Court's definition of segregation to include Chicanos as well as blacks. Hopefully, this will bring the Court a step closer to recognizing and acting against social class segregation in the schools.

To return to the issue of *de facto* segregation. It is encouraging to realize that the constitutionality of this is becoming an academic issue. Recent court suits have established the probability that all segregation in America is of a *de jure* nature. As Judge Roth (Time, 1971a) ruled concerning school segregation in Detroit:

> Governmental actions and inaction at all levels — federal, state, and local — have combined with those of private organizations, such as loaning institutions and real estate associations and brokerage firms, to establish and maintain the pattern of residential segregation (pp. 23-24).

Judge Roth ordered for metropolitan Detroit the kind of school consolidation which Judge Merhige ordered for the Richmond area. Similar findings of *de jure* segregation have appeared in court rulings in Denver, Las Vegas, Los Angeles, Pasadena, and Pontiac. As for social class segregation of a *de jure* nature, the California Supreme Court (as quoted in Greenbaum, 1971), while concerning itself in the Serrano case more with school financing than segregation, did say that:

> we find the case unusual in the extent to which governmental action is the cause of the wealth classifications. . . . such patterns are shaped and hardened by zoning ordinances and other governmental land-use controls which promote economic exclusivity (p. 517).

Two misgivings loom large at this point. First, that the creation of new school districts to eliminate segregation may lead to the continual re-creation of districts as ethnic and social class balances shift. Second, that integration might produce such heterogeneous classroom populations that nothing will occur but wasteful confusion.

The first concern assumes the prevalence of a situation that, on the contrary, will have been markedly reduced by integration, namely, the existence of ethnic and social class enclaves to which the frightened can flee. To paraphrase Joe Louis, those who would avoid the problems of the poor and would avoid poor children themselves may still run, but they'll have trouble hiding. To be sure, there will still be parents who will try to escape by burying their heads out in the exurbs or by resorting to very parochial private schools or very private parochial schools. They are to be pitied, for the loss will be to their children. And if there are too many of them, a national commitment to integration could overtake them in time, anyway. This predicament will insure greater population stability in school districts. It would also be well to begin viewing school districts more in population than geographic terms. This would provide increased flexibility in making minor readjustments in district compositions as they become necessary. In an age of computers, the specific readjustments should not be difficult to determine. They can be timed for natural breaks in students' careers, e.g., the transition from elementary school to junior high school to minimize disorientation.

The anxiety about a defeatingly heterogeneous classroom population is really misplaced. It should be focused on the conditions which obstruct success for heterogeneous classes. Among these are large class sizes, self-contained classrooms, one adult per class, uniform curricula and materials — in short, all the things that prevent individualized instruction. Integration and its concomitant heterogeneity can compel the abandonment of these outworn educational practices. Smaller classes, nongraded classes, departmentalization, team teaching, paraprofessionals, a wide array of materials, schools without walls are some of the advances that might accrue to a school system because of integration. It has been reported that the integration plan in Mobile, Alabama, was made more acceptable to the public by the school superintendent's decision to use it as an opportunity to introduce other reforms such as individualized instruction (Time, 1971b).

BUSSING

Integration means bussing. To endorse integration while rejecting bussing is to say that the goal is worthwhile but the only effective means is unacceptable. This is where President Nixon (1972) ended up when he said that "desegregation must go forward until the goal of genuinely equal educational opportunity is achieved," at the same time that he proposed legislation which would "call an immediate halt to all new bussing orders by Federal courts (p. 72)." It was left to a Southern governor, Reubin Askew of Florida, to draw the issue incisively and courageously.

> I don't like bussing, but we've got to break the cycle of black poverty. We can't afford to isolate and not utilize 12 percent of our people. No large corporation would do it [as quoted in Nordheimer, 1972, p. 56]. The way to end bussing is to seek the broader *community* desegregation which will make it unnecessary.... In the meantime, we must decide which is worse — *temporary* hardship and inconvenience, or *continuing* inequality and injustice [Askew, 1972, p. 5].

Askew is clearly an exception to the pessimism about elected officials that was registered earlier in this paper. The only gratuitous word in his statement is the word black in the first sentence.

Most Americans still indicate a determination to have it both ways, however. The latest poll taken by the National Opinion Research Center shows that 75 percent of white Americans support school integration (Greeley & Sheatsley, 1971). The latest Gallup poll, taken more recently, puts the figure at 66 percent (Newsweek, 1972). 79 percent of the Floridians, black and white, who voted on the integration referendum on March 14 voted in support of integrated education (Time, 1972c). The Gallup poll and the Florida vote also measured attitudes toward bussing. The former revealed that 69 percent of white Americans are opposed to bussing. The latter indicated that 74 percent of the voting Floridians oppose bussing.

The most pertinent comment on poll results was that made by Andrew Greeley and Paul Sheatsley (1971) of the National Opinion Research Center. "... attitudes are not necessarily predictive of behavior ... but one can see them as a sign of progress and as creating an environment for effective social reform (p. 19)." Where there are conflicting signs, however, political leaders have to decide which of the signs is progressive and which reactionary. Or they have to decide which of the signs has greater electoral significance. Richard Nixon, Hubert Humphrey, and Nelson Rockefeller — all politically desperate and dangerous men — made their decisions on the second basis, and on that basis they undoubtedly chose correctly. In so doing, however, they did not act as leaders but as craven lackeys of popular fears and prejudice. The opportunity to appeal to the decent instincts of Americans, which are reflected in the polls, was let pass for the sake of cheap political gain.

The hubbub over bussing might suggest to a foreigner just arrived in America for the first time that yellow buses are lethal instruments, and too much exposure to them can cause cancer. He would then have to reconcile this impression with the fact that about 40 percent of American students are bussed, with only about 3 percent being bussed for purposes of integration (Time, 1971b; Newsweek, 1972; Hesburgh, 1971, p. 47). In Charlotte, North Carolina, the city which last April produced the Supreme Court ruling that bussing was an acceptable tool with which to accomplish court-ordered integration, the number of bussed students only rose from a previous total of 46,076 to 46,849 (Lewis, 1972, p. 31). Even in the Richmond area, where Judge Merhige's consolidation directive is to take effect, 68,000 students are already being bussed and consolidation will only increase this number by 10,000 (Time, 1972b). Many students who walk to school spend more time getting there than students who are bussed. The hazards they encounter along the way are as great as the dire perils which are supposed to confront students on buses.

It would be well at this point to consider the attitudes of blacks toward bussing. The Gallup poll and the Florida referendum indicate that most blacks are not opposed to bussing. Added to this is the fact that the leaders of the Southern Christian Leadership Conference, the NAACP, the National Urban Coalition, the National Council of Negro Women, the A. Philip Randolph Institute, and the Urban League requested a meeting to dissuade Nixon from his anti-bussing position (Herbers, 1972c, p. 45). The National Black Political Convention has generally been reported as having opposed bussing. However Richard Hatcher (1972), one of the convention leaders and mayor of the host city, Gary, Indiana, has challenged the reportage on the convention. He cites the following convention resolution as evidence that the convention did not take a hard stand against bussing.

> Let us further resolve that this convention oppose bussing in instances where it serves as an instrument of destruction of quality education in

black communities and that this convention support bussing in cases where it serves the end of equal education for black people (p. 34).

Still, among blacks there is considerable and growing opposition to bussing. One source has estimated that as much as 40 percent of the black vote in the Florida referendum was opposed to bussing (Time, 1972c). Unlike the white opposition to bussing, the black opposition is more forthrightly a disavowal of integration itself. Roy Innis of the Congress of Racial Equality rejects the "subtle implication that blacks cannot learn unless in the presence of whites (Newsweek, 1972, p. 21)." William Raspberry (as quoted in Kilpatrick, 1972), the black columnist, elaborates on this.

> . . . let us end the humiliation of chasing after rich white children. And it is humiliating. For one thing, it says to black children that there is something inherently wrong with them, something that can be cured only by the presence of white children. Some of us don't believe that. Some of us believe that given adequate resources, financial and other- wise, black children can learn, no matter what color their seatmates happen to be [p. 4].

Raspberry could easily find a lot of whites who would be eager to provide those adequate resources as a means of forestalling integration. Nixon himself is rather stingy in this regard, offering to equalize educational opportunity with only 2.5 billion dollars of previously appropriated or requested money.

Other blacks also say that Coleman is wrong, and they aim to prove it by strengthening the self-images of black students through projects such as New- ark's African Free School. They can refer to a three-year study of integration in the Evanston, Illinois, schools to show that integration was damaging to the self-esteem of black eighth-grade boys (Newsweek, 1972). They, and white separatists as well, can point to the study of 700 high schools done by the Syracuse University Research Corporation which found that classroom disrup- tion was positively related to integreation (Time, 1971b).

There is an ironic counterpoint to this last study, which was done two years ago. The Coleman data of six years ago show that integrated schooling leads to substantial improvement in racial attitudes among students (Katz, 1971). The five-year-old report of the U. S. Commission on Civil Rights, *Racial Isolation in the Public Schools*, points out that integration is most likely to be favored by adults, black and white, who grew up in integrated situations (Meranto, 1970). Apparently, the effect of integrated schooling on students' racial attitudes is a good deal more positive when there are not a lot of adults and politicians around to poison the atmosphere. Given such an atmosphere, the present disruption in high schools is not surprising. One can hope that it will turn out to be but a brief transition to genuine integration. Continued separation will only intensify the hate and distrust and fear that exist on both sides, and that puts all of us in a perilous state mentally and morally.

Since I so strongly support bussing as a necessary means to a desired end, it behooves me to give a further demonstration of its logistical feasibility, regardless of the current political climate. How expensive and burdensome bussing will be depends on how many get bussed how far. This brings up the relevant unit for integration. As Judges Merhige and Roth have directed, this should be the metropolitan region, i.e., the central city and its suburbs. This unit is large enough to cover a wide spectrum of ethnic groups and all social classes, without being so large as to be impractical. Out of such a unit, several representative school districts could be created, most likely by simply dividing the area into so many pie-shaped wedges. Theodore Lowi (1969), a political scientist at the University of Chicago, has plotted such school districts for metropolitan Chicago in a way that limits the one-way commuting distance to less than twenty miles and the time to about thirty to forty minutes. These figures are higher than they need be, since Lowi does not think in terms of cross-bussing, which he should because the benefits of integration do not redound to one party alone. If the districts can be kept this compact for metropolitan Chicago, most other urban areas should be able to do still better. And that would mean that kids would not be getting bussed all over kingdom come, as George Wallace likes to put it.

For a city which borders on the state line, it may be necessary to create an interstate school district. A recent map in the New York Times showed the racial patterns for Bergen County, New Jersey, which is immediately west and northwest of Manhattan. The map was startingly monochromatic. Had the map shown income patterns, the single color might have been green, for Bergen County is not a depressed area. Thus, parts of Bergen County and Manhattan could be merged into a single ethnically and economically integrated school district. A precedent for this kind of interstate operation already exists, and interestingly enough it has to do with transportation. I am, of course, referring to the Port of New York Authority. It would obviously be a better way for the kids in Bergen County to learn about blacks and Puerto Ricans than to go field-tripping into Manhattan to see *Purlie* or a revival of *West Side Story*.

No matter how carefully planned the integrated districts are, some parents are still going to object to the length of the bus ride. They will say that it makes their children's school day unreasonably protracted. Since the duration of the bus ride will be difficult to shorten, the only answer is to shorten the length of time kids spend in school. This should raise no greater hue and cry than it has where schools have gone on split sessions because of overcrowding. It may also be possible to conduct some learning activities on the bus. After all, Adelphi University has even managed to do this with commuting businessmen on the Long Island Railroad.

A ploy to which opponents of bussing still resort is to say that we should wait until residential integration makes school redistricting unnecessary. Since residential integration is darting uphill like molasses in January — it may even be darting downhill — this position certainly seems disingenuous. It also ignores the fact that school integration will remove a major inducement to residential segregation, of both a racial and class nature. Finally, it overlooks the practical reality that children accept integration better than adults. Thus, it is not a chicken-or-the-egg conundrum: priority should be given to school integration.(3)

A final consideration relative to bussing and integration. The abolition of the neighborhood school necessitates a redefinition of community control. The community should now be the school itself — parents, students, and staff. To be sure, there will be standards imposed from some remote central source, but hopefully these will be minimal and wise. The rest will be left to the collective judgment of the three parties most directly involved in the school. For all of these parties, this will mean more power and responsibility and opportunity than they have heretofore known. For all of them, it will also mean more education.

CONCLUSION

There is no better way to end this paper than with a statement from someone who has fought the battle long and well. In this case that someone is Theodore Hesburgh (1971), chairman of the U. S. Commission on Civil Rights.

> If we are to emerge from our present state of inequality, it will not be by insisting on minimum compliance with minimum laws. Generosity, magnanimity and human understanding will alone allow us to transcend, in our day, our dismal history of racial inequality.

NOTES

(1.) Another category could be established for race, since in a white-dominated, racist society blacks are constantly confronted with situations that are fraught with psychological — even physical — damage. However, to put a price tag on this plight could mock it or exacerbate it or both. What else is there to say, except that reader responses are welcomed?

(2.) There are reports that some of the Veronans who most vociferously opposed the program are teachers in the Newark schools. If the residents of Newark know these reports to be true, it can only have injected more venim into the relationship between them and the suburbanites who teach their children.

(3.) This is not intended to de-emphasize the fight for residential integration. There are some promising developments in that direction, among which are the new HUD guidelines which bar the concentration of public housing in inner cities and George Romney's promotion of housing allowances for the poor (Kraft, 1972). There have also been several successful court challenges to restrictive zoning ordinances. Finally, Senator Abraham Ribicoff is pushing a bill which would prevent any federal installation from moving to a community which refused to provide land for workers' housing (Davidoff, Davidoff, & Gold, 1971). Similar bills could be introduced in state legislatures.

REFERENCES

Askew, R. Temporary hardship or continuing injustice? *Integrated Education*, 1972, 10, 5.

Barzun, J. *The house of intellect.* New York: Harper and Row, 1959.

Birch, H. G., & Gussow, J. D. *Disadvantaged children.* New York: Harcourt, Brace & World, 1970.

Bowles, S. S., & Levin, H. M. The determinants of scholastic achievement: An appraisal of some recent findings. *Journal of Human Resources*, 1968, 3.

Brown v. Board of Education of Topeka. United States supreme court reports. 98 L ed 880.

Bussing: An American dilemma. *Newsweek*, 1972, March 13.

Bussing issue boils over. *Time*, 1972, February 28.

Calkins, H. Financing education in the 70s. *Today's Education*, 1971, February, p. 31.

Center for Education Policy Research. *Preliminary report to the Carnegie foundation.* Cambridge, Massachusetts: CEPR, 1970.

Coleman, J. S., et al. *Equality of educational opportunity.* Washington, D.C.: U. S. Government Printing Office, 1966.

Conant, J. B. *Slums and suburbs.* New York: McGraw-Hill, 1961.

Coons, J. E., Clune, W. H. III, & Sugarman, S. D. Private wealth and public education. Cambridge: Harvard University Press, 1971.

Davidoff, L., Davidoff, P., & Gold, N. The suburbs have to open their gates. *The New York Times Magazine*, 1971, November 7.

Dimond, P. R. Toward a children's defense fund. *Harvard Educational Review*, 1971, 41, 391.

Dugan, D. J. The impact of parental and educational investments upon student achievement. *Proceedings of the American Statistical Association, Social Statistics Section*, 1969.

Franklin, B. A. U. S. judge orders schools merged in Richmond area. *The New York Times*, 1972, January 11.

Greeley, A. M., & Sheatsley, P. B. Attitudes toward racial integration. *Scientific American*, 1971, 225, 14-19.

Green, T. F. Two theories of equal opportunity. Paper delivered at The Philosophy of Education Society, Dallas, April 6, 1971.

Greenbaum, W. N. Serrano v. Priest: Implications for educational equality. *Harvard Educational Review*, 1971, 41, 521.

Guthrie, J. W., et al. *Schools and inequality.* Cambridge: The MIT Press, 1971.

Harrell, R. F., Woodyyard, E., & Gates, A. I. *The effects of mothers diets on the intelligence of offspring.* New York: Bureau of Publications, Columbia Teachers College, 1955.

Hechinger, F. M. Some old friends are dropping by the wayside. *The New York Times*, 1971, September 5.

Herbers, J. School financing by states urged in federal study. *The New York Times*, March 7, 1972. (a)

Herbers, J. School financing: A new way to foot the bill. *The New York Times*, March 12, 1972. (b)

Herbers, J. Rights leaders ask Nixon to see them on bussing decision. *The New York Times*, March 14, 1972. (c)

Hesburgh, T. M. It's the end of the bus ride that matters. *The New York Times*, 1971, September 15.

Hobson v. Hansen. (D.D.C., 1967) 269 F. Supp.

Home News, New Brunswick, N.J. HHH, McGovern blast Nixon, 1972, March 21.

Katz, M. B. The present movement in educational reform. *Harvard Educational Review*, 1971, 41, 350.

Kilpatrick, J. J. Humiliating integration. *Home News, New Brunswick, N.J.*, 1972, February 12.

Kraft, J. The coming apart of fortress suburbia. *The New York Times*, 1972, January 31.

Lewis, A. Constitutional crisis: I. *The New York Times*, 1972, March 25.

Lowi, T. J. *The end of liberalism*. New York: W. W. Norton, 1969.

Maeroff, G. I. School districts: Why they are inherently unequal. *The New York Times*, 1971, September 15.

Margolis, R. J. Bussing: You got some nice things here, too. *The New York Times*, 1971, October 24.

Meranto, P. *School politics in the metropolis*, Columbus, Ohio: Charles E. Merrill Publishing Company, 1970.

Nathan, R. S. Messiah of the ed schools. *Change*, 1971, October.

New Jersey Education Association, *Basic statistical data of New Jersey school districts*. Trenton: 1971.

New York State Department of Education: Summary of report: *Racial and social class isolation in the schools*. Albany: 1969.

New Republic, The. Headstart plus. 1971, September 11, p. 10.

Newsweek. Bussing: An American dilemma. 1972, March 13, pp. 20, 21, 23.

New York Times, The. Equal rights to learn. September 2, 1971. (a)

New York Times, The. Tale of two schools. December 25, 1971. (b)

New York Times, The. Hatcher reviews parley of blacks. March 16, 1972. (a)

New York Times, The. Parts of Regents' statement and dissents. March 25, 1972. (b)

Nixon, R. M. Statement on education and bussing. *The New York Times*, 1972, March 17, p. 56.

Nordheimer, J. Florida's supersquare – a man to watch. *The New York Times Magazine*, 1972, March 5.

Ravitch, D. Community control revisited. *Commentary*, 1972, 52, p. 74.

Riessman, F. *The culturally deprived child.* New York: Harper and Row, 1962.

Robinson v. State of New Jersey. Superior Court of New Jersey, L-18704-69, 1972.

Rosenthal, J. School expert calls integration vital aid. *The New York Times,* 1970, March 9.

Rothstein, R. Down the up staircase: Tracking in schools. *This Magazine Is About Schools,* 1971, 5, pp. 103-140.

Schaefer, W. E., Olexa, C., & Polk, K. Programmed for social class: Teaching in high school. *Transaction,* 1970, October, pp. 39-46.

Schwebel, M. *Who can be educated?* New York: Grove Press, 1968.

Sexton, P. C. *Education and income.* New York: Viking Press, 1964.

Shanker, A. Where we stand. *The New York Times,* 1971, October 10.

Shapp, M. J. An education trust fund. *The New York Times,* 1971, October 30.

Silberman, C. *Crisis in the classroom.* New York: Random House, 1970.

Solomon, L. C. Stop trying to make equal education. *National Review,* 1971, October 8, pp. 1107-1108.

Tanner, D., & Tanner, L. N. Parent education and cultural inheritance. *School and Society,* 1971, pp. 21-24.

Time. Attack on defacto. October 11, 1971, pp. 23-24. (a)

Time. The agony of bussing moves north. November 15, 1971, pp. 57, 60, 63. (b)

Time. Nurturing intelligence. January 3, 1972, pp. 56-57. (a)

Time. Rebussing issue boils over. February 28, 1972, p. 14. (b)

Time. Retreat from integration. March 27, 1972, pp. 14, 21. (c)

Van Til, S. B., & Van Til, J. The lower class and the future of inequality. Paper presented at the meetings of the American Sociological Association, Denver, August 1971.

Wicker, T. Resurrecting the Riles report. *The New York Times,* 1970, November 8.

Wicker, T. Cataclysm in Richmond. *The New York Times,* January 13, 1972. (a)

Wicker, T. Equalizing the schools. *The New York Times,* March 12, 1972. (b)

Wise, A. E. The California doctrine. *The Saturday Review,* 1971, November 20, p. 83.

Wise, A. E., & Manley-Casimir, M. E. *Law, freedom, equality – and schooling.* Washington: Association for Supervision and Curriculum Development, 1971.

Zdep, S. M. Evaluation of the Verona plan for sharing educational opportunity. *Research at ETS: Projects and Publications.* Princeton, N.J.: Educational Testing Service, 1970.

SIGNIFICANT TRENDS IN THE EDUCATION OF THE DISADVANTAGED

Edmund W. Gordon

In the past ten years, research related to the education of the disadvantaged has covered a wide variety of approaches and issues. However, most of the work can be classified under two broad categories: 1. the study of population characteristics, and 2. the description and evaluation of programs and practices. In the first category, investigators have focused on eliciting deficits in the conditions or behaviors of the target population — the ways the groups studied differ from alleged "normal" populations. In the second category, which is only now beginning to build a body of theoretical and descriptive material, investigators have attempted to describe what goes on in the schools and to relate such variables as school structure, teaching methods, or a myriad of special services, to student achievement. While the first type of study has been conducted largely by educational psychologists, specialists in testing and measurement, and developmental psychologists, the second has been the product of anthropologists, sociologists, social psychologists and, on a more informal level, of teachers who have worked in the school system. Studies in the former group precede those in the latter and have tended to place responsibility for failure on the children and their background. Although studies in the latter group grew out of the same philosophy and were developed with the goal of designing compensatory experiences for identified deficiencies, newer research in this group has begun to emphasize the role of the educational experience in producing the observed dysfunctions in performance.

POPULATION CHARACTERISTICS

Studies within this category can be further divided between investigations of performance and life conditions. The largest body of research concerns what is called intellectual performance. Most studies in this area have concentrated on I.Q. test results and consistently support the hypothesis that high economic, ethnic or social status is associated with average or high I.Q. scores, while the reverse — low economic, ethnic or social status — is associated with low I.Q. scores relative to the other group.(1)

A by-product of descriptions of the relationship between SES and/or ethnic group and intellectual performance has been the attempt to interpret results with speculations as to causes. On the one extreme, investigators have seen their work as supporting genetic determinants of intelligence;(2) at the other end of the spectrum, researchers have viewed their findings as support for environmental determinants of intelligence.(3) However, the majority of investigators now interpret the data as reflecting a complex and continuous interaction between hereditary and environmental forces.(4)

In contrast to the huge body of statistics and analyses concerning intellectual status as judged by standardized tests, only limited effort has been directed at differences in cognitive style. There has been some attempt to factor-analyze standardized tests,(5) and one substantial investigation deals with differential strengths and deficits in the intellectual functioning of different ethnic groups.(6)

Another area of considerable research is that of the plasticity of intellectual development. This work has been conducted by both those investigators who would support the dominance of genetic determinants of intelligence and those who adhere to the importance of environmental factors in determining the quality of intellectual functioning.(7) Building upon Binet's early concern with the trainability of intellectual functioning and Montessori's efforts to modify intellectual performance in children with subnormal performance levels, investigators have worked with all but the most gifted children.(8) There is only one major longitudinal study which attempts to relate intellectual development to differences in environmental conditions: this investigation traces the development of a sample of twins reared in dramatically different environments over a period of 25 years, and shows significant variations in their level of intellectual functioning.(9)

Short-term studies dealing with the plasticity of the intellect have led to mixed findings. Some reports show intervention to be associated with no significant change in intellect as measured by intelligence test scores.(10) Others have shown only modest change, and many of these results have been interpreted as reflecting a normal fluctuation in intellectual function from one test period to another.(11) On the other hand, some studies have demonstrated significant increases when pre- and post-treatment scores are compared.(12) Unfortunately, these improvements have not yet been tested in large populations, and no follow-up studies have been made after a long enough time period to justify the conclusion of permanent change.

However uncertain these data may be, there remains among many researchers the conviction that intelligence is largely a trainable function. A number of studies have attempted to relate trainability to age.(13) One of the more pessimistic positions is that, due to the lack of powerful and positive environments, the processes underlying intellectual functioning rapidly lose their plasticity after three years of age.(14) More optimistic reports show typical I.Q. gains of ten points with adolescents; however, such gains are still only half as much as can be generated with younger subjects.(15) Studies of such programs as Harlem Prep and Upward Bound support the hypothesis that big changes in achievement, if not in intellectual functioning, can be effected in adolescence.(16)

In general, the data lead one to conclude that, as measured by standardized tests, significant changes in the quality of intellectual function are more likely to occur to the extent that there are powerful positive changes in environmental interactions, and that the changes occur early in the life of the individual. The fact that malleability may decrease with age, however, may not reflect a recalcitrant character of intellectual functioning. Rather, what may be operating is the tendency to rely on earlier patterns of stimulus processing in the absence of exposure to powerful and different environmental input. It has been suggested, for example, that the decreasing malleability of intellectual functioning among the urban disadvantaged may be the result of prevailing school practices, which do not provide new positive inputs and which may even reinforce previous maladaptive patterns of functioning.(17)

As measured by grades, standardized tests, and high school attrition, there is an abundance of data showing that disadvantaged populations do not do as well academically as do more advantaged populations. Their lower achievement and higher dropout rates have been related to such environmental factors as low income (resulting from limited education and occupational level of parents);(18) health and nutritional deficits;(19) childrearing patterns which do not prepare the children for school;(20) cultural differences between disadvantaged students and their teachers;(21) and racial isolation and discrimination as well as other school-related variables.(22)

Demographic studies have fallen into several categories. The more traditional type has concentrated simply on economic, employment and educational levels of the family as they relate to the children's school performance.(23) A newer type attempts to go beyond a strictly economic kind of data and, centering its interest around what has become known as the "culture of poverty," examines various aspects of family disorganization such as consensual marriage, out-of-wedlock children, divorce rates, broken homes, and matriarchal or female-dominated households.(24) One or more of these configurations are then related to children's performance in school. However, the concept of the "culture of poverty" has recently been highly criticized, and a few investigators have begun to focus on those patterns which may be adaptive within the school in a depressed environment, even if they are not totally adaptive within the school environment.(25)

The relationship between specific childrearing practices and academic achievement has been copiously studied. Concentrating particularly on mother-child interaction, investigators have identified maternal influences which may create such characteristics as language behavior, task orientation and value commitment in the disadvantaged child. Implicit in these studies is the assumption of a middle-class norm, and most studies compare interactions in disadvantaged families with those in more privileged households.(26) So far there has been little attempt to describe the variations in childrearing practices among lower-class or minority-group families, and there has been scant research on those elements in these families which lead to academic success.(27)

A neglected area in educational research has been the investigation of the relationship between health status and school performance. Data on the effects of poverty on health and nutrition are substantial, all showing that disadvantaged populations suffer from poorer health care, a greater proportion of premature deliveries, higher mortality rates, poorer nutrition, etc.(28) There is also some research indicating the possible effects of the health of the pregnant mother on the intellectual functioning of the developing child.(29) However, there is little data on the relationship between the individual's own health and nutritional condition and his cognitive development or academic performance in school. There is also little research showing the mechanisms by which poor health affects performance. Most investigators assume this to be the case, however, and conclude that poor health may result in lowered performance through impaired efficiency or reduced energy levels or, in more serious conditions, through impairment of the nervous system.(30)

Still concentrating on demographic characteristics, racial and economic segregation of a disadvantaged population as it relates to school performance is one of the most heavily researched areas.(31) Investigations have consistently led to the conclusion that low school achievement is associated with the concentration of low-income and minority group students in separate school situations (the one possible exception being Oriental students in segregated situations).(32) A small group of studies have focused on separating out the effects of economic from racial or ethnic isolation, and the predominating view has been that economic segregation is even more deleterious to school performance than is racial segregation. However, the point has often been made that it is impossible to draw strictly comparable socio-economic groups across racial or ethnic lines.(33)

Related to this research on economic and racial isolation have been those investigations which focus on the effects of desegregation on school achievement. Studies in this area take two forms: those which measure achievement before and after desegregation, and those which examine the relationship between the degree of ethnic or economic mix and the level of achievement. Research in the former group has arrived at the conclusion that differential responsibility to desegregation is based on such factors as the reasons for desegregation, students' expectations of how they are going to be evaluated in the integrated setting, and the degree of organization or disorganization in the integrated as compared to the segregated setting.(34) Studies in the latter group, which are usually based on larger populations than the former, show that desegregation is more likely to be associated with heightened achievement for the minority-group child when the receiving school population is predominantly white and middle-class.(35) However, caution is often expressed about applying these findings to smaller populations and individual cases because of the intervening variables, such as student expectations or school disorganization.(36)

An area of research which is crucial to the interpretation of any results on population characteristics is that of testing and measurement. Most of the effort in this area has been directed toward validation of the content and construction of existing standardized tests and the predictive value of test scores.(37) Research on testing and measurement of disadvantaged populations has been largely concerned with the relative predictability of specific tests for minority-group versus white students, the efficacy of traditional as opposed to culture-fair and other innovative tests, and the problems inherent in testing minority-group populations.(38) More recently, there has been an interest in factorial analyses of test data; the aim of this research is to identify specific patterns of functioning in different populations in order to understand variations in skills as well as deficits.(39) A small group of investigators has also begun to research the effects of intelligence and achievement tests on such variables as teacher attitudes, student expectations, and school administrative policy.(40)

PROGRAMS AND PRACTICES

In contrast to the rather well-designed and detailed research into the characteristics of disadvantaged groups, the description and evaluation of educational programs and practices for these children have generally been superficial. There has been little effort at matching treatment efforts with the nature and needs of the subject population. Programs are often designed on the basis of long-standing theoretical models or the special biases of researchers. Program evaluations stress little more than the fact or the magnitude of the intervention and a general assessment of the impact. What is lacking are detailed descriptions of the nature of the intervention, the interaction between the intervention and the learner, and the outcome of a particular treatment or intervention program when used with specific kinds of learners.

Research on programs and practices can be grouped into four types on the basis of the scope of the subject treated. Most prominent are studies which report on large-scale projects such as Head Start, Title I, More Effective Schools, Project Talent and Upward Bound. A second group of studies reports on specific programs and services in the schools. A third attempts to relate administrative and organizational change to student progress. Changes in attitudes and orientations of school personnel are the subject of the fourth type.

Large-scale projects run the gamut from preschool to college. The aim of these programs has been to provide intensive compensatory education — school readiness, remediation of lagging achievement levels, or supply of the necessary skills for success in higher education — to disadvantaged students. With the exception of preschool projects, where centers have developed experimental programs, most of the large-scale programs have been more intensive versions of standard curriculum and teaching methods.(41) The projects have been evaluated by pre- and post-treatment test scores and subjective evaluations of student progress; little research has focused on describing the exact nature of program input or on following the subjects' longitudinal development once the treatment is completed.(42)

Project evaluations in general indicate that compensatory education has failed. In those cases where positive findings are reported, it has been difficult to identify or separate treatment effects responsible for the result from Hawthorne effects (the impact of a changed situation itself) or from Rosenthal effects (the result of changed expectations). However, recent reviews of the research criticize evaluation methods and indicate that the tests used may be insensitive instruments for tapping whatever progress might be made.(43)

Evaluations of specific programs and services in the schools include studies of such elements as counseling programs, tutoring projects, special service personnel (bilingual teachers, reading specialists, paraprofessionals, etc.), curricular innovations, such as bilingual or ethnically-oriented studies and teacher-student developed materials, and changes in teaching techniques (individualized instruction, teaching machines, team teaching, etc.).(44) Here too, much of the intervention has been a continuation of traditional programs and services, and little effort has been given to matching the specific needs of the population with the intervention instituted. Only projects focusing on curriculum relevance and individualized instruction have been directed toward matching learner and the learning experience.(45) Adequate evaluations of these programs have also been scarce. Programs tend to introduce a number of services simultaneously, and it has been difficult to identify, even in successful programs, the element or elements which are most instrumental in causing change.(46)

Until recently, studies of administrative and organizational change in the schools have been directed primarily at desegregation. Research on desegregation in Southern school districts describes the politics and process of desegregation, including the implementation of federal guidelines and community resistance to change.(47) Literature on Northern desegregation deals with the same issues, but also describes the development and implementation of specific desegregation plans such as bussing and transfer programs, school zoning, or the creation of the middle school and education parks.(48) As reported earlier, findings on the effects of desegregation tend to show that the single most important school factor influencing academic achievement for black and other minority-group children (as well as low-income students) is that the classroom be made up predominately of white middle-class students.(49)

More recent organizational and administrative changes in the schools include experiments with homogeneous and heterogeneous groupings, changes in pupil-teacher ratio, and the implementation of parent and community involvement. Major research on ability groupings shows that it has no measurable effect on student achievement.(50) When homogeneous grouping causes defacto segregation, it may, in fact, lower the achievement of minority-group and low-income students.(51) Changes in pupil-teacher ratio have been studied by a number of investigators with differing viewpoints and, as might be expected, the conclusions reached vary according to the point of view of the researcher.(52) Since extensive parent and community involvement are still relatively new areas for investigation, there is no definitive work on this subject. However, a number of researchers have hypothesized that the influence of parent and community forces in the schools may provide a powerful force for instituting needed changes in both the children and the schools.(53) Several investigators have linked the "sense of fate control," which has been found necessary for school achievement, with parental involvement in the schools.(54) One major research project concludes that the only hope for narrowing the spatial, cultural and emotional gap between school personnel and school children is through introducing parents and other community members into the schools.(55)

There is a rapidly growing body of research which relates teacher attitudes and expectations to student performance. Studies in this area point to the debilitating effect of low teacher expectations.(56) A number of investigations have been aimed at identifying factors which form teacher attitudes and behavior.(57) So far, this research is inconclusive, but indications are that it is not social class background alone, as previously thought, which creates either positive or negative attitudes and behaviors toward disadvantaged children.(58) Without any clear indications of what causes teachers' negative attitudes toward low-income and minority-group children, a few studies have focused on the possibilities of changing teacher attitudes. Research in this area is difficult to interpret, since positive changes are usually measured by answers to a questionnaire(59) and thus indicate little more than the fact that teachers have learned more "acceptable" responses. It has been hypothesized that artificially changing teachers' expectations of student performance can create measurable change in student achievement; but data on this subject also remains inconclusive.(60)

The question of "equal educational opportunity," which for a long time has been dealt with merely as a concept holding a wide range of definitions, is beginning to be the focus of research attention. Studies show differences in such factors as school expenditures, teacher training and experience, teacher salaries, school facilities, teacher-pupil ratio, and access to outside resources, between schools in depressed and advantaged neighborhoods. Such factors have, in turn, been shown to be instrumental in forming a learning climate.(61) Finally, research indicates that even in schools with greatly expanded resources due to compensatory education programs, the learning environment in schools in depressed neighborhoods is far less conducive to achievement than in schools serving more affluent children.(62)

The very question of the vast amount of study of minority group populations raises serious research questions. It has recently been pointed out, for example, that the investigator's attitude and ethnic and social background may affect the research questions he poses, his methodology and data gathering techniques, and, ultimately his access to particular populations.(63) Although the relationship between the nature of the investigator and the nature of his research on minority populations has not been studied as yet, the findings of such research will supply a useful context for reexamining past investigations and for undertaking future research.

NOTES

1. Kennedy, W. A., Van De Riet, Vernon, and White, James C., Jr. *A Normative Sample of Intelligence and Achievement of Negro Elementary School Children in the Southeastern United States.* Chicago, Illinois: Society for Research in Child Development, Serial No. 90, 28 (6), 1963.

2. Jensen, Arthur R. "Social Class, Race, and Genetics: Implications for Education," *American Educational Research Association Journal*, 5: 1-42, 1968.

Jensen, Arthur R. "How Much Can We Boost IQ and Scholastic Achievement?" *Harvard Educational Review*, 39: 1-123, 1969. (ED 023 722)

Shuey, Audrey M. (ed.). *The Testing of Negro Intelligence.* 2nd edition. New York: Social Science Press, 1966.

3. Hunt, J. McVicker. *Intelligence and Experience.* New York: Ronald Press, 1961.

Hunt, J. McVicker. "Black Genes — White Environment," *Transaction*, 6:12-22, June 1969.

4. *IRCD Bulletin*, 5(4), Fall 1969. [See especially "Behavior-Genetic Analysis and Its Biosocial Consequences" by Jerry Hirsch (pp. 3-4; 16-20). This article also appears in the February, 1970 issue of *Seminars in Psychiatry*, Henry M. Stratton, Inc., publisher.]

5. Cleary, T. Anne, and Hilton, Thomas L. "An Investigation of Item Bias," *College Entrance Examination Board Research and Development Report 65-6, No. 12.* Princeton, N.J.: Educational Testing Service, 1966. (ED 011 267)

Cleary, T. Anne. "Test Bias: Validity of the Scholastic Aptitude Test for Negro and White Students in Integrated Colleges," *College Entrance Examination Board Research and Development Report 65-6, No. 18.* Princeton, N.J.: Educational Testing Service, 1966. (ED 018 200)

6. Stodolsky, Susan S., and Lesser, Gerald S. *Learning Patterns in the Disadvantaged.* New York: Yeshiva University, ERIC Information Retrieval Center on the Disadvantaged, 1967. (ED 012 291)

7. Bloom, Benjamin S. *Stability and Change in Human Characteristics.* New York: John Wiley, 1965.

8. Examples of this research are:

Schwebel, Milton. *Who Can Be Educated?* New York: Grove Press, 1968.

Bereiter, Carl, and Engelmann, Siegfried. *Teaching Disadvantaged Children in the Preschool.* Englewood Cliffs, N.J.: Prentice Hall, 1966.

Hurley, Rodger. *Poverty and Mental Retardation: A Causal Relationship.* New York: Vantage Books, 1969.

9. Skodak, M., and Skeels, H. M. "A Followup Study of Children in Adoptive Homes," *Journal of Genetic Psychology*, 66: 21-58, 1945.

10. Granger, R. L., et al. *The Impact of Head Start. An Evaluation of the Effects of Head Start on Children's Cognitive and Affective Development.* Vol. 1. Report to the U. S. Office of Economic Opportunity by the Westinghouse Learning Corp. and Ohio University, 1969.

11. Thorndike, Robert L. *Head Start Evaluation and Research Center Annual Report, September 1966-August 1967*. New York: Teachers College, Columbia University, 1967. (ED 020 781)

12. Smilansky, Sarah. "Promotion of Preschool, 'Culturally Deprived' Children Through Dramatic Play," *American Journal of Orthopsychiatry*, 35: 201, 1965.

13. Thorndike, E. L. *The Measurement of Intelligence*. New York: Teachers College, Columbia University, 1927.

14. Bloom, 1965.

15. Smilansky, Moshe. "Fighting Deprivation in the Promised Land," *Saturday Review*, 82: 85-86, 91, October 15, 1966.

16. Hawkridge David G., et al. *A Study of Selected Exemplary Programs for the Education of Disadvantaged Children: Part II, Final Report*. Palo Alto, Calif.: American Institutes for Research in the Behavioral Sciences, 1968. (See especially the evaluation of the New York City College Bound Program.) (ED 023 777)

Guerriero, Michael A. *The Benjamin Franklin High School Urban League Street Academies Program. Evaluation of ESEA Title I Projects in New York City, 1967-68*. New York: Center for Urban Education, 1968. (ED 034 000)

17. Leacock, Eleanor B. *Teaching and Learning in City Schools: A Comparative Study*. New York: Basic Books, 1969. (ED 033 989)

Jensen, Arthur R. "Cumulative Deficit in Compensatory Education," *Journal of School Psychology*, 4: 37-47, Spring 1966.

18. For a collection of this literature see:

Goldstein, Bernard. *Low Income Youth in Urban Areas, A Critical Review of the Literature*. New York: Holt, Rinehart and Winston, 1967. (The "Annotated References for Chapter One" (Family of Orientation), are especially relevant.)

19. Birch, Herbert G. *Health and the Education of the Socially Disadvantaged Children*. Presented at the Conference on "Bio-Social Factors in the Development and Learning of Disadvantaged Children," Syracuse, New York, April 1967. (ED 013 283)

Birch, Herbert G., and Gussow, Joan D. *The Disadvantaged Child — Health, Nutrition and School Failure*. New York: Harcourt Brace and World, 1970.

20. Goldstein, 1967.

21. A recent conference sponsored by the U. S. Office of Education addressed itself to the question "Do Teachers Make a Difference?" The papers which were presented which soon will be available as conference proceedings discuss this topic along with other teacher influences. The relevant papers are by: James Guthrie, Stephen Michelson, Eric Hanushek, Henry Levin, George Mayeske, and Alexander Mood.

22. U. S. Commission on Civil Rights. *Racial Isolation in the Public Schools*. Washington, D.C.: U. S. Government Printing Office, 1967. (Vol. I: ED 012 740: Vol. II: ED 015 959)

23. Goldstein, 1967.

24. Several examples are:

Moynihan, Daniel P., and Barton, Paul, *The Negro Family: The Case for National Action.* Washington, D.C.: U. S. Office of Policy Planning and Research, 1965.

Lewis, Oscar. *La Vida: A Puerto Rican Family in the Culture of Poverty – San Juan and New York.* New York: Random House, 1966.

Valentine, Charles A. *Culture and Poverty: Critique and Counter-Proposals.* Chicago, Ill.: University of Chicago Press, 1968. (ED 035 707) The latter, while covering the concept of the culture of poverty, is critical of its usage.

25. See for example:

Lewis, Hylan. "Culture, Class, and Family Life Among Low-Income Urban Negroes," in *Employment, Race, and Poverty.* New York: Harcourt, Brace and World, 1967.

Valentine, 1968.

26. The work of Robert Hess and his associates done at the Urban Child Study Center at the University of Chicago should be noted. A representative piece is:

Hess, Robert D., and Shipman, Virginia C. *Maternal Attitudes Toward the School and the Role of Pupil: Some Class Comparisons.* Paper presented at the 5th Work Conference on Curriculum and Teaching in Depressed Urban Areas, Teachers College, Columbia University, 1966.

27. An exception to this is: Davidson, Helen H., and Greenberg, Judith W. *Traits of School Achievers from a Deprived Background.* New York: City University of New York, City College, 1967. (ED 013 849)

28. For a comprehensive overview of a wide variety of studies in this area, see: Scrimpshaw, Nevin, and Gordon, John. *Malnutrition, Learning and Behavior.* Cambridge, Mass.: MIT Press, 1967.

29. The work of Lilienfeld and Pasamanick during the 1950's is still among the best concerning possible effects of various pregnancy experiences. Two of the best references include:

Pasamanick, Benjamin, and Lilienfeld, A. M. "Association of Maternal and Fetal Factors with the Development of Mental Deficiency, I: Abnormalities in the Prenatal and Perinatal Periods," *Journal of the American Medical Association*, 159: 155, 1955.

Lilienfeld, A. M., Pasamanick, B., and Rogers, Martha. "The Relationship Between Pregnancy Experiences and the Development of Certain Neuropsychiatric Disorders in Childhood," *American Journal of Public Health*, 45: 637-43, 1955.

30. No investigator has been more critical of the lack of research in this area than Birch, who recently published a comprehensive and incisive volume emphasizing which specific mechanisms actually affect performance. The book's particular strength is its inclusion of references to research which substantiates what has been assumed for some time. See: Birch, Herbert G., and Gussow, Joan D. *The Disadvantaged Child: Health, Nutrition and School Failure.* New York: Harcourt, Brace and World, 1970.

Cravioto, J., Delicardie, E. R., and Birch, H. G. "Nutrition, Growth and Neurointegrative Development: An Experimental and Ecologic Study," *Pediatrics*, 38: 319, 1966.

31. For the most complete review of the research in this area, see: St. John, Nancy H. *Minority Group Performance Under Various Conditions of School Ethnic and Economic Integration: A Review of Research.* New York: Teachers College, Columbia University, ERIC Clearinghouse on the Disadvantaged, 1968. (ED 021 945)

32. Coleman, James S., et al. *Equality of Educational Opportunity.* Washington, D.C.: U. S. Office of Education, 1966. (ED 012 275)

33. St. John, 1968.

34. Three sources offer a comprehensive discussion of these three factors.

Katz, Irwin. *Desegregation or Integration in Public Schools: The Policy Implications of Research.* New York: Teachers College, Columbia University, ERIC Information Retrieval Center on the Disadvantaged, 1967. (ED 015 974)

McPartland, James. *The Segregated Student in Desegregated Schools: Sources of Influence on Negro Secondary Students: Final Report.* Baltimore, Md.: Center for the Study of Social Organization of Schools, Johns Hopkins University, June 1968. (ED 021 944)

St. John, Nancy. *Minority Group Performance Under Various Conditions of School Ethnic and Economic Integration: A Review of Research.* New York: Yeshiva University, ERIC Information Retrieval Center on the Disadvantaged, 1968. (ED 021 945)

35. Coleman, et al., 1966.

36. St. John, 1968.

Weinberg, Meyer. *Desegregation Research: An Appraisal.* Bloomington, Indiana: Phi Delta Kappa, Commission on Education and Human Rights, 1968.

(Also see articles by Meyer Weinberg in *Integrated Education* from Volume 4 (6), 1966 to Volume 6 (6), 1968.)

37. For example: *Testimony of Dr. Roger T. Lennon as Expert Witness on Psychological Testing in the Case of Hobson, et al. vs. Hansen, et al. (Washington, D.C. Schools).* New York: Harcourt, Brace and World, 1966.

38. The Educational Testing Service, Princeton, N.J. has done much work in this area. See: Campbell, Joel. "Testing Culturally Different Groups," *College Entrance Examination Board Research and Development Report 63-4, No. 14.* Princeton, New Jersey: Educational Testing Service, 1964.

39. Stodolsky and Lesser, 1967.

Minuchin, Patricia. *Patterns and Correlates of Achievement in Elementary School Children.* New York: Bank Street College of Education, 1965.

40. Rosenthal, Robert, and Jacobson, Lenore. *Pygmalion in the Classroom: Teacher Expectation and Pupils' Intellectual Development.* New York: Holt, Rinehart and Winston, 1968.

41. A notable exception to this is the work Susan Gray and her associates have done at George Peabody College.

Gray, Susan W., and Klaus, Rupert A. "An Experimental Preschool Program for Culturally Deprived Children," *Child Development*, 36: 887-898, 1965.

Another exception is the Perry Preschool Project in Ypsilanti, Michigan. See: American Institute for Research in Behavioral Sciences, Palo Alto, California. *Perry Preschool Project, Ypsilanti, Michigan. One of a Series of Successful Compensatory Education Programs.* 1969.

42. References to pre-school projects which are exceptions to this generalization include:

Wolff, Max, and Stein, Annie. *Six Months Later, A Comparison of Children Who Had Head Start with Their Classmates in Kindergarten — A Case Study of Kindergartens in Four Public Elementary Schools, Study I.* New York: Yeshiva University, Ferkauf Graduate School, 1966. (ED 015 025)

Wolff, Max, and Stein, Annie. *Long Range Effects of Preschooling on Reading Achievement, Study III.* New York: Yeshiva University, Ferkauf Graduate School, 1966. (ED 015 027)

Klaus, Rupert, and Gray, Susan W. *The Early Training Project for Disadvantaged Children — A Report After Five Years* (Monograph), Vol. 33(4). Chicago, Illinois: Society for Research in Child Development, 1968. So far no one has studied longitudinal development after treatment at the primary, intermediate, secondary or college levels.

43. Scrimpshaw and Gordon, 1967. (See especially Part VIII, pp. 464-542.)

44. A cross-section of studies which discuss these elements include:

Channon, Gloria. "The More Effective Schools: An Evaluation," *Urban Review*, Vol. 2, February 1967. (ED 013 845)

Khanna, J. L. *Human Relations Training Program.* 1969. (ED 032 965)

Rigrodsky, Seymour. *Speech Therapy for Disadvantaged Pupils in Non-Public Schools: An Evaluation of the New York City Educational Project 1966-67.* New York: Center for Urban Education, Committee on Field Work and Evaluation, Sept. 1967. (ED 026 756)

Shaw, Merville C., and Rector, William. *Influencing the Learning Environment by Counseling With Teachers.* Monograph No. 6, July 1968. (ED 022 233)

American Institutes for Research in the Behavioral Sciences, Palo Alto, California. *Diagnostically Based Curriculum: A Compensatory Program; An Evaluation.* Washington, D.C.: Superintendent of Documents, U. S. Government Printing Office, 1969.

Jablonsky, Adelaide. *A Selected ERIC Bibliography on Individual Instruction, ERIC-IRCD Urban Disadvantaged Series No. 2.* New York: Teachers College, Columbia University, ERIC Information Retrieval Center on the Disadvantaged, January 1969. (ED 027 358)

45. Glasser, Robert. *The Education of Individuals.* Penn: Learning Research and Development Center, Univ. of Pittsburgh, 1966. (ED 014 785)

Glasser, Robert. *Objectives and Evaluation: An Individualized System.* Penn: Learning Research and Development Center, Univ. of Pittsburgh, 1967. (ED 015 844)

46. For example, in the Title I, E.S.E.A. project in Camden in 1966-67, a number of global variables including class size, teaching conditions, corrective reading, medical services, audio-visual programs and teachers aides were introduced simultaneously, preventing isolation and evaluation of those specific variables which actually had impact. See: Camden City Schools, New Jersey. *Title I: E.S.E.A., 1966-67, Projects of the Camden City Board of Education — Evaluative Report.* 1967. (ED 018 473)

47. Orfield, Gary. *The Reconstruction of Southern Education. The Schools and the 1964 Civil Rights Act.* New York: Wiley-Interscience, 1969.

48. Weinberg, Meyer. *Integrated Education: A Reader.* Beverly Hills, Calif.: Glencoe Press, 1968.

49. Coleman, et al., 1966.

50. Passow, A. Harry, Goldberg, Miriam, and Tannenbaum, A. J. *Education of the Disadvantaged: A Book of Readings.* New York: Holt, Rinehart and Winston, 1967.

51. Esposito, Dominick. *The Relationship Between Ability Grouping and Ethnic and Socioeconomic Separation of Children.* New York: Teachers College, Columbia University, ERIC Information Retrieval Center on the Disadvantaged (In Press).

52. For example, the Center for Urban Education did an evaluation of New York City's "More Effective Schools" program which criticized it.

Kravetz, Nathan, et al. *The More Effective Schools Program.* New York: Center for Urban Education, 1966.

The United Federation of Teachers responded with a criticism of the Center for Urban Education's report.

Schwager, Sidney. *An Analysis of the Evaluation of the More Effective Schools Program Conducted by the Center for Urban Education.* New York: United Federation of Teachers, 1967.

Hawkridge, 1968. (Hawkridge named "More Effective Schools" an exemplary compensatory program.)

53. For a recent and complete discussion see:

Lopate, C., Flaxman, E., Bynum, E., and Gordon, E. W. "Some Effects of Parent and Community Participation on Public Education," *Review of Educational Research*, February 1970. (ED 027 359)

54. Coleman, et al., 1966.

55. Leacock, Eleanor B. *Teaching and Learning in City Schools: A Comparative Study: Psychosocial Studies in Education.* New York: Basic Books, 1969.

56. Rosenthal, Robert, and Jacobson, Lenore. *Pygmalion in the Classroom: Teachers' Expectations and Pupils' Intellectual Development.* New York: Holt, Rinehart and Winston, 1968.

57. Look for the future publication entitled:

How Do Teachers Make a Difference? by the Division of Assessment and Coordination, Bureau of Educational Personnel Development, U. S. Office of Ed., Washington, D.C.

Two more references should also be helpful:

Webster, Staten W. (ed.). *The Disadvantaged Learner: Knowing, Understanding, Educating.* San Francisco, California: Chandler, 1966. (ED 013 266)

Flaxman, Erwin. *A Selected Bibliography on Teacher Attitudes: ERIC-IRCD Urban Disadvantaged Series No. 1.* New York, Teachers College, Columbia University, ERIC Clearinghouse on the Urban Disadvantaged, January 1969. (ED 027 357)

58. Webster, 1966.

59. Flaxman, 1969.

60. Rosenthal, and Jacobson, 1968.

61. Coleman, et al., 1966.

62. Leacock, Eddy, Weinstein and Fantini have contributed the most to this area. See:

Eddy, Elizabeth. *Walk the White Line: A Profile of Urban Education.* Garden City, New Jersey: Anchor Books, 1967.

Eddy, Elizabeth. *Urban Education and the Child of the Slum: Project True.* New York: Hunter College, Teachers and Resources for Urban Education, 1965.

Leacock, Eleanor. *Teaching and Learning in City Schools: A Comparative Study,* 1969.

Weinstein, Gerald, and Fantini, Mario. *Social Realities and the Urban School.* A Paper presented at the ASCD Conference in Atlantic City, New Jersey, March 10-13, 1968. (ED 023 733)

63. Miller, LaMar P., and Sommerfield, Donald A. *The Black and White of Educational Research.* Paper presented at the American Educational Research Association Convention, Minneapolis, Minnesota, March 2-6, 1970.

Hessler, Richard M., et al. *Research as a Process of Exchange.* Paper to be given at the "Advocacy and Objectivity and Exchange in Poverty Research" session of the Society for the Study of Social Problems, Washington, D.C., August 28, 1970.

chapter 6
research literature on desegregation

DESEGREGATION AND MINORITY GROUP PERFORMANCE

Nancy H. St. John

The 1954 Supreme Court desegregation decision was based on fine legal and moral argument, but on rather slim social science evidence (Deutscher and Chein, 1948; Clark, 1953). In view of the clear challenge to the caste system that the decision represented and the extent of the changes called for, it is singular that so few empirical tests of the dictum that segregation *per se* is harmful to children were undertaken in the decade that followed. Then came the Equality of Educational Opportunity Survey (Coleman, 1966). The magnitude of this study and its unexpected findings suggest that research on the education of minority children should be labeled "before Coleman" or "after Coleman." The insights afforded by the survey and its methodological limitations propel social scientists to more definitive research. To date no longitudinal studies with adequate samples and controls have been published, but reports on an increasing number of small-scale bussing experiments are becoming available. Pieced together, such bits of evidence help define the shape of the larger puzzle and identify what is known and what is not known.

This paper reviews Pre-Coleman, Coleman, and Post-Coleman empirical evidence on the relations of school racial composition to the academic performance of black children. The independent variable is called "racial composition" advisedly; neither scholars nor schoolmen agree on the definitions of *racial balance*, *desegregation*, *non-segregation*, or *integration*. Some use these words interchangeably, while others distinguish between them according to whether or not the school ethnic mix matches that of its community, whether or not a uni-racial school has become bi-racial, whether or not the process was planned, and whether or not the minority group is accepted into the social life of the school. I am interested in school racial mixture of any type, although I recognize that surrounding circumstances may condition its relationship to academic performance.

Many possible outcomes of schooling-creativity, curiosity, civic responsibility, moral judgment, artistic taste, human sensitivity — are important, but they typically go unmeasured in social research. Therefore, although the subject of this paper could be the relation of school racial composition to children's total intellectual, emotional and moral development, for the most part I review research in which achievement *test scores* were the criterion available.

CHOICE OF RESEARCH DESIGN

The experimental model is a convenient way of organizing the evidence I am interested in. To establish a causal relationship between classroom ethnic composition and academic performance, a researcher should employ the classic pre-test, post-test model with subjects randomly selected and assigned to experimental and control groups. Both groups are tested before the experimental group is subjected to the test condition (desegregation), all other conditions must remain the same for both groups, and later both groups are tested again. A greater change between Time 1 and Time 2 for the experimental than for the control group can presumably be attributed to the effect of desegregation (Stouffer, 1962; Campbell and Stanley, 1963; Pettigrew and Pajonas, 1964).

Such experimental research in the area of desegregation is very difficult to achieve. The random assignment to control and experimental conditions usually seems politically and morally questionable, and the loss of cases through migration or school leaving is apt to jeopardize the randomness of the sample. Therefore one finds frequent use of a longitudinal design without a control group, of a cross-sectional design without a Time 1 measurement, or of quasi-experiments with statistical rather than actual control of other variables, even though any correlation between key variables can not be taken as evidence of a causal relation between them.

Two rival independent variables, school quality and family background, are especially likely to contaminate research on the effect of ethnic segregation on the performance of children. In pre-Coleman Report days probably few people doubted that school quality varied with racial composition or that predominantly black schools were by and large inferior to predominantly white ones in physical plant, equipment, curricular offerings and teacher qualifications. Comparisons of Negro and white schools in the South (McCauley and Ball, 1969; Miller, 1960) or ghetto and non-ghetto schools in the North (Public Education Association, 1955; Conant, 1961; Sexton, 1961; Wolff, 1963; Katzman, 1966) certainly supported this conclusion. There have also been repeated reports that teachers in ghetto schools have low morale, a low opinion of their pupils, and an eagerness to transfer to more middle class (or white) settings (Becker, 1952; Gottlieb, 1964; Clark, 1965; Herriott and St. John, 1966). Coleman (1966) found many differences within regions between schools attended by majority and minority children, to the advantage of the former, though most of these were surprisingly slight. Critics of the Coleman Report argued that various methodological limitations of the study mask the true relation between race and school quality (Nichols, 1966; Bowles and Levin, 1968; Dyer, 1968). Thus, any superiority in the performance of integrated over segregated children could in part be due to a difference in school quality.

The issue of school equality is raised in a different form by the recent introduction of compensatory programs into most Northern city school systems. To the extent that such programs tend to remove former inequities and to equalize education across schools, they act as a control in studies comparing performance in segregated and integrated settings. To the extent that they go beyond equalization and offer *extra* services to minority group children — newer buildings, smaller classes, greater per pupil expenditure, better prepared teachers — they in theory make it more rather than less difficult to test the effect of ethnic composition *per se* (Gordon and Wilkerson, 1966; U. S. Commission on Civil Rights, 1967).

The second variable most likely to contaminate research on the effect of school desegregation on pupil performance is the social and economic level of home or neighborhood. Most researchers find that socioeconomic status (SES) predicts achievement for Negroes, though less well than for whites (for example, McGurk, 1953; Klineberg, 1963; Kennedy, Van de Riet and White, 1963; Pettigrew, 1964; Stodolsky and Lesser, 1967). In an attempt to isolate other measures of a child's home environment that would predict his school achievement better than the usual indices of SES, Peterson and Debord (1966) interviewed 11 year-old Negroes in a Southern city; they found a set of 11 home variables that had a multiple correlation of .82 with achievement scores. In a similar endeavor, Whiteman, Brown and Deutsch (1966) developed a Deprivation Index (measuring housing dilapidation, number of siblings, kindergarten attendance, educational aspiration of parent for the child, dinner conversation, and family cultural experiences) which contributed significantly to the verbal test performance of Negro children in New York. The Coleman (1966) and U. S. Commission on Civil Rights (1967) reports corroborated such evidence on the relationship between aspects of home background and the verbal achievement of minority group children. If school quality and the family background are positively related to the achievement of minority pupils and to their schools racial composition, it is crucial to control them in any study of the influence of ethnic composition.

LONGITUDINAL ONE-GROUP STUDIES

The merit of the longitudinal study is that selection bias is partly ruled out if the same subjects are tested before (or at the beginning of) a period of non-segregated schooling and again after some months or years in the desegregated situation. The weakness of such a design is that without a control group, there is no assurance that any observed effect is not due to the influence of previous testing, to normal maturation, to extraneous events, or especially to a change in the quality of schooling.

DESEGREGATION OF SCHOOL SYSTEMS

Two studies often referred to as evidence of the beneficial effect of the desegregation of a school system are Hansen's report on Washington, D.C. (1960) and Stallings's report on Louisville, Kentucky (1959). Hansen reported that in the five years following consolidation of the separate school systems in the District of Columbia, median city-wide achievement improved at all grade levels and in most subject areas. Unfortunately, for a number of reasons this finding is not evidence that desegregation was causally related to improved minority group performance. 1. No testing of black children was done before desegregation, and no separation of black and white scores was made after desegregation. 2. The scores of the same children were not traced through the years; instead successive third grade (etc.) classes were compared. 3. Actual racial composition of schools and classrooms was not considered, and the simultaneous establishment of the track system probably resulted in considerable classroom segregation in those schools that were technically desegregated. 4. With desegregation came major improvements in the quality of education — lowered teacher-pupil ratios, increased budget, more remedial services; these furnish plausible alternative explanations of the improved performance.

Schools in Louisville were desegregated by court order in 1956. Stallings (1959) reported that the academic achievement of Negro and white students was significantly higher after than before desegregation and that the Negro students made greater gains than the white students did. But again there is evidence that most schools remained segregated. The gains of black pupils were greatest when they remained with black teachers, i.e., in all-black schools (United States Commission on Civil Rights, 1962, p. 34). Stallings suggested that one factor may have been increased motivation resulting from legal desegregation.

DESEGREGATION OF INDIVIDUALS

In studies of the effect of Northern residence on the intelligence test scores of Negro children, the investigators regularly found that migrants from the South score higher in proportion to their length of residence in the North (Klineberg, 1953; Lee, 1951; Moriber, 1961). Unfortunately in these migration studies, the racial mix of the Northern schools was not reported and the effects of three variables are confounded: community with school desegregation and school desegregation with school quality. Researchers can more successfully test the unique effect of school desegregation when individuals enter a mixed school, especially if those individuals do not change residence to a mixed neighborhood.

A large longitudinal study of the impact of desegregation on pupil attitudes and performances is in process in Riverside, California. In the fall of 1965 the Riverside Board of Education decided to close three buildings and bus their Negro and Mexican-American pupils to other buildings in the system (Purl, 1967, 1969). Since *de factò* segregation was thereby eliminated, no control group will be available. To date the only progress reports indicate that two years of integration have had "not much effect" on achievement, but since neither social class nor other variables were controlled, even this conclusion seems unwarranted.

Katzenmeyer (1963) studied all pupils who entered the public kindergartens of 16 Jackson, Michigan schools in the year 1957 and 1958. The 192 Negro children, who thus represented the full socio-economic range in the city, were distributed among 11 integrated schools; one school was 66% black and the rest were below 40% black. Children were given the Lorge-Thorndike IQ test at the beginning of Kindergarten and second grade. The two-year gain for white children was 1.87 points, for Negro children 6.68 — a difference significant at the .001 level. It is regrettable for research purposes that no matched group of black children spent those years in segregated Jackson schools.

A recently completed evaluation of Project ABC, a scholarship program which brings disadvantaged high-school students to independent boarding schools, followed an entering class of 82 boys (70% Negro, 10% American Indian, 9% Puerto Rican, 2% Oriental, and 9% white) who entered 39 different schools in the Fall of 1965 (Wessman, 1969). Faculty reported scholastic gains for half the group, but test-retest showed no significant change on mean Otis IQ or Cooperative English Achievement tests.

Clark and Plotkin (1963) surveyed Negro students at integrated colleges. The sample consisted of the 509 students who returned questionnaires out of the 1519 who received aid or counseling from the National Scholarship and Service Fund, 1952-1956. College grades were found to be higher than could have been predicted on the basis of pre-college scholastic aptitude test scores. The net dropout rate of 10% was one-fourth the national rate and far below the rate for segregated Negro colleges. This study would have been strengthened by more random sampling, by post-tests and by the testing of a control group of similar students at segregated colleges, since it seems probable that many students who applied to the NSSFNS were especially able, motivated and likely to succeed wherever they enrolled. Even so, there would be no way of knowing whether any differences found were due to the integration or to the quality of the college experience. These criticisms, especially of the lack of control on other variables, apply not only to the Clark and Plotkin study but to all one-group "before and after" studies that have been reviewed here.

The major weakness of cross sectional studies, in which segregated and integrated subjects are compared without either group having been tested before the introduction of desegregation, is that there is no guarantee that the two groups were originally equivalent. Systematic differences are found by researchers who compare the characteristics of families living in integrated and segregated neighborhoods (Duncan and Duncan, 1957; Stetler, 1957; Hughes and Watts, 1964) or of families who do and do not volunteer for bussing experiments (Crockett, 1957; Luchterhand and Weller, 1965; Weinstein and Geisel, 1962). It is therefore quite likely that the integrated subjects are a selected group, in terms of social class and/or ability.

PRE-COLEMAN STUDIES

As early as 1930, Crowley studied Stanford Achievement Test scores of Negro fourth to sixth grade pupils in two segregated and four mixed schools in Cincinnati. Of 110 children equated on grade, age, and Stanford Binet IQ, half had experienced only segregated and half only integrated schools. The two groups were said to be comparable also on "Physical condition, family history and social status." No statistically significant differences were found on 11 of 13 achievement tests. Spelling and writing were the exceptions; differences in these skills favored mixed schools (Crowley, 1932).

Radin (1966) studied the black pupils of two neighboring elementary schools (45% and 100% Negro) in Ypsilanti, Michigan. The schools were said by Radin to be alike in financial support and curriculum and in the IQ and SES of pupils, but the original equivalence of pupils in the two schools was not satisfactorily demonstrated. No statistically significant differences were found in mean scores on IQ or Iowa Test of Basic Skills, though the direction of the difference was uniformly in favor of the integrated school. When the performance of very high or very low achievers was examined, however, the differences were in favor of the segregated school.

In a similar study of naturally segregated and non-segregated elementary school children in New York, Jessup (1967) compared a) Negro and Puerto Rican second and fifth graders in a traditional, middle-class school (75% white) with b) students in a comparable, low SES, project school (96% Negro and Puerto Rican) and with c) students in a new, Higher Horizons school (93% Negro). Since social class (measured by residential census tract data) was found to be so highly related to achievement, subsamples of 18 integrated and 80 segregated low SES children were compared on IQ, math and reading. This comparison revealed a distinct disadvantage for the segregated children, even for those in the Higher Horizon school with superior facilities and remedial services. The lowest SES children in the integrated school showed higher achievement than middle SES children in the segregated school. This study is handicapped by small sample size, inadequate control on individual SES, and lack of any "before" measurement.

In four recent dissertations, the investigators used roughly the same design. Meketon (1966) gave a battery of tests to Negro fifth and sixth graders in three schools in Kentucky: school A, *de facto* segregated; school B, peacefully integrated; and school C, integrated under "anxiety arousing circumstances." In schools A and B samples of children were matched on age, grade, sex, Otis Quick Scoring IQ and SES. In school C all children were included; though not matched with the other children they were reported to be generally similar in background but of somewhat higher IQ (on the California Test of Mental Maturity). Contrary to prediction children in school C had significantly higher scores than pupils in school A on the Digit Span Backward and Verbal Meaning Tests, and higher than school B pupils on these and a Space Ability Test. Unfortunately, the initial difference in IQ could explain the superior performance of school C pupils.

In a New York State community, Lockwood (1966) compared 217 sixth grade black students attending balanced and unbalanced (over 50% Negro) schools for two years or longer. Contemporaneous scores on Iowa Tests of Basic Skills and the California Test of Mental Maturity indicated that the students in the balanced schools were significantly higher at all IQ levels. When IQ was not controlled or when students had been less than two years in balanced schools, the differences were in the same direction but not statistically significant. The absence of control on individual SES and the evidence presented of higher mean SES in the balanced schools render the findings inconclusive. Samuels (1958) matched Indiana students on IQ and SES and found that at the first and second grade levels, Negroes in a segregated school had higher achievement scores, but in the third through sixth grades the achievement was higher in a racially mixed school.

The most statistically sophisticated study in this group is Matzen's (1965) correlational analysis of the fifth and seventh grade achievement scores of 1,065 Negro and white children in 39 segregated and integrated classrooms in one California community. Zero order correlations indicated that per cent of Negroes in the classroom was significantly and negatively related to Negro achievement, especially at the higher grade level (presumably because there was grouping by ability for seventh graders but not for fifth graders). However, when IQ and SES were controlled, second-order partial correlation showed the relationship to be no longer statistically significant.

Thus, of six recent cross-sectional comparisons of black children's performance in segregated and integrated elementary schools in six different communities and in five states, all found that without controls, achievement was higher in integrated schools. Several of the studies then controlled on IQ, but since they used a score more or less contemporaneous with that of achievement, they naturally found that the differences between segregated and desegregated children tended to disappear. IQ as well as achievement is malleable and the two tend to co-vary. A more valid procedure would be to test ability at the outset of pupils' careers in segregated or integrated settings. But none of these investigators did so. Moreover the controls on social class were rough. The suspicion remains, therefore, that self-selection may have biased their findings.

There have been a number of quasi-longitudinal cross-sectional studies in which investigators compared the secondary or college performance of students from segregated and integrated earlier schools. Wolff (1962) examined the high school records of black students in Plainfield, New Jersey; he found fewer dropouts, higher reading achievement, higher rank in the graduating class and higher enrollment in further education for the 20 graduates of an all-Negro school. No SES data and no significance tests on their differences were reported. Vane (1966) compared the high-school records of 52 black children from predominantly white schools in a large suburban community with those of 19 black children from an 89% Negro school. The average IQ was 100 for students from both types of school. She equated 17 pairs on IQ and SES and found no significant differences in achievement at any level. St. John (1962, 1964) reported that with SES controlled there was a non-significant trend toward higher high school test scores for those New Haven blacks who had attended more integrated elementary schools.

Johnson, Wyer and Gilbert (1967) tabulated first term grades of 121 Negro freshmen at one University of Illinois campus according to the racial composition of their Chicago high schools. A curvilinear relation was found; students from schools less than 50% or more than 90% black did better than those from schools 50-89% black. Further examinations indicated that students from one group of schools more than 90% black attained considerably higher grades than those from another group of schools of the same racial composition. The authors speculated that individual or school social class probably explained the difference, but they gave no data with which to test their assumption.

St. John and Smith (1969) analyzed the achievement of two-thirds of the black ninth graders in the city of Pittsburgh in 1966 (1388 pupils). When the effects of individual and neighborhood SES and sex had been removed through regression analysis, arithmetic achievement was significantly and negatively related to the average racial composition of a pupil's school in grades 1-9.

Thus, the balance of evidence of pre-Coleman cross-sectional studies is that, at the very least, integration had little negative effect on minority group performance and that it apparently had a positive effect, though it is hard to be sure, since other variables could account for the observed trends. (See Weinberg, 1968, for reports on other cross-sectional studies.)

COLEMAN AND COMMISSION REPORTS

In the Equality of Educational Opportunity Survey (EEOS), the investigators administered a series of achievement tests and questionnaires to more than 600,000 students in some 4,000 elementary and secondary schools (Coleman, 1966). Verbal ability scores showed more variation than other test scores and were selected as the chief measure of academic achievement.

Only a small part (10-20%) of the variance in achievement was found to be *between* rather than *within* schools (see Table 3.221.2 in Coleman et al., 1966).

For Negroes, up to 30% of the between-school variance was accounted for by differences in family background (see Table 2.221.2). With the effect of family background removed, school characteristics accounted for little of the remaining achievement variance, but of these, characteristics of fellow students accounted for more than other school attributes (see Table 3.23.1). For this review the most important findings of the report concerns the effect of racial segregation: when students' own background, characteristics of the school, and characteristics of the student body were controlled, school per cent white accounted for almost no verbal ability variance for Negroes (see Table 3.23.4).

The U. S. Commission on Civil Rights (1967) reanalyzed the Coleman data in tabular form; they concentrated on twelfth grade Negro students in the metropolitan Northeast and on ninth grade Negro students in eight regions. The analysis showed that classroom racial composition (in the previous year) made a difference in verbal achievement, beyond the social class of either the pupil or his fellow students or of teacher quality. (See Appendix Tables 4.1 to 8.12.) Moreover, the earlier the grades at which Negroes reported first having had white schoolmates, the higher their achievement. There are three probable reasons why classroom per cent white "last year" should be more related to achievement than school per cent "this year": 1. At the ninth grade many pupils move from segregated elementary schools to desegregated secondary schools. "Last year's" experience may be a proxy for eight years' experience and, therefore, more influential than a few weeks' experience "this year." (The EEOS tests were administered in September.); 2. Within desegregated schools, considerable segregation often results from the practice of assignment to classrooms on the basis of test scores: i.e., ability influences classroom per cent white. (It may also influence school per cent white but less strongly.); 3. Classroom per cent white influences ability and has a stronger effect than school per cent white. The authors of the Commission Report stressed this last point, but either of the other two may also be operative.

Further analysis of the EEOS data (McPartland, 1968) supported the Commission's conclusion on the relation between classroom composition and achievement. McPartland showed that school desegregation was associated with higher achievement for black pupils only if they were in predominantly white classrooms, but classroom desegregation was favorable irrespective of school per cent white. He claimed that the classroom racial composition effect was not entirely explained by selection into track or curriculum.

The evidence that the Equality of Educational Opportunity survey made available on the *extent* of ethnic segregation and academic retardation for minority group children is invaluable. The evidence of the *relation between* segregation and retardation is not completely convincing, since it is subject to a number of methodological criticisms: 1. The representativeness of the sample was compromised by the non-cooperation of a number of large cities. 2. The measures of social class are unconvincing. There is no measure of family income. The item measuring parental occupation proved uncodable. Eighteen per cent of the ninth graders left blank or did not know their parents' educational level. Other researchers have found that children tend to upgrade their parents' education or occupation on a precoded questionnaire (Colfax, 1967. St. John, 1969). Self-reports on items in the home may also be biased and in any case, only the quantity not the quality of these items was told. The reliability study conducted by Coleman's staff in two school districts in Tennessee found 64% to 100% agreement between children and their teachers depending on grade level and nature of item. It should be noted, however, that teachers' and children's responses were not necessarily independent and that blanks and *I don't know's* were counted as agreement, a questionable procedure. In short, it is difficult to have confidence that the effect of social class was entirely removed. 3. Part of the apparent effect of the background of fellow students may be due to unmeasured variation in a pupil's own background. Smith's (1969) reanalysis of the EEOS data indicated that two errors made in the original analyses led to underestimation of the effect of home background and an exaggeration of the effect of student characteristics. 4. The percentage of white schoolmates in the current year or of white classmates in the previous year may be less important than the per cent of white schoolmates or classmates over a number of years. Particularly at the ninth grade level *present* school racial experience is a poor estimate of *past* school racial experience. (See St. John and Smith, 1969). 5. A cross-sectional analysis with no estimates of original ability or of the original equivalence of segregated and nonsegregated students can not conclusively demonstrate a causal relation between segregation and achievement or attitude.

EXPERIMENTAL OR QUASI-EXPERIMENTAL (FOUR-CELLED) STUDIES

A few studies have employed an experimental or quasi-experimental model, in that they provide Time 1 and Time 2 measurement of segregated and desegregated children matched on key variables. Two dissertation studies in the border South are four-celled in this sense. Fortenberry (1959) studied the mean achievement gains made in three subject areas during eighth and ninth grades of black pupils of similar IQ who attended mixed and nonmixed classes in Oklahoma City. Those in mixed classes made greater gains in arithmetic and language, but less gain in reading than did segregated pupils. No controls on social class were reported. Anderson (1966) found that 75 black fourth, fifth and sixth graders in five Tennessee desegregated (8 to 33% Negro) schools achieved significantly higher scores on Metropolitan Achievement Tests than did 75 black students from three segregated schools. The segregated and desegregated schools were judged "equivalent with respect to tangible factors" and their pupils were matched on age, intactness of family, third grade IQ scores and second grade achievement. The younger the age at which children had entered the desegregation schools, the greater was the apparent benefit.

With increasing frequency in the last few years, school systems have issued reports of bussing experiments in which ghetto children are transported to predominantly white schools. In most cases the bussed children were tested before the program began and again one or two years thereafter, and their gains were compared with those of children who remained in segregated schools. The validity of the comparison as a test of the effect of racial composition on pupil performance hinges on 1. the equivalence of the bussed and non-bussed children at the outset, 2. the holding power of the two programs, and 3. the equality of schooling in every way except racial composition. Therefore, evaluation of bussing studies should note a) whether there is random assignment to experimental and control groups, or at least matching on key variables, b) whether there is mortality of cases through withdrawal from either program or failure to appear for tests, and c) whether children are bussed to another school in the same system or to schools in a presumably superior system.

New York state was the scene of a number of desegregation experiments and of the first five studies reviewed here. An early study of the effect of bussing in New Rochelle does not really belong in this grop of 4-celled studies since it lacks measurement of pre-desegregation achievement (Wolman, 1964). Except at the kindergarten level, no statistically significant differences were found between those who transferred to integrated, middle class schools and those who stayed in a *de facto* segregated school, perhaps because as another study indicated (Luchterhand and Weller, 1965) more lower class families elected to transfer. It is also reported that in the year of the study the segregated school had the benefit of extra services (Kaplan, 1962).

In 1964 the White Plains school board initiated a racial balance plan which involved closing one elementary school and bussing about 900 black pupils from two sending schools to six receiving schools (White Plains Board of Education, 1967). Participation was mandatory. A three-year study was made of the IQ and Stanford Reading and Arithmetic Test scores of 33 of these black pupils (who entered grade 3 in 1964) in predominantly white schools. Since segregated schools no longer existed in the city, the 33 were compared with 36 black pupils who in 1960 had entered the third grade in the segregated school. The newly desegregated children gained slightly more in paragraph meaning and arithmetic than the earlier central city children. However, in word meaning the segregated children gained more. The findings remain inconclusive due to a number of methodological limitations, especially the small number of students tested and the lack of a contemporaneous control group.

Another small program involved bussing 75 pupils from central Rochester to a suburb, West Irondiquoit (Rock et al., 1966, 1967, 1968). Each year from 1965 to 1967, kindergarten teachers selected a pool of above-average pupils from which fifty names were drawn and assigned randomly, half to the experimental and half to the control group. Parental objections resulted in some shifts, and testing mortality was high. In 13 of 27 comparisons on Metropolitan Achievement Tests over three years, there were significant differences between the bussed and non-bussed black children; in each instance the difference was in favor of the bussed children. It should be noted that the receiving schools were in a high quality school system.

Beker (1967) reported on an experiment in Syracuse in which 60 of the 125 Negro elementary children bussed in the year 1964-1965 to a predominantly white school (Experimental Group) were compared with 35 children whose parents requested transfer but for whom places were not available (Control Group 1) and with 36 children whose parents refused transfer (Control Group 2). After the first year there was no significant differences in achievement gain among the three groups. This contradicts the U. S. Commission's (1967) Report for Syracuse of greater gains for 24 bussed children in comparison with an unspecified number of non-bussed children who had the benefit of a compensatory program. The latter gain may have been a Hawthorne effect in the first year of the program. Nevertheless, the small numbers involved and the lack of any control of SES make the Syracuse findings quite inconclusive.

In Buffalo, New York in 1965, there was mandatory bussing of 560 Negro pupils from closed and overcrowded schools to predominantly white schools in the same city (Dressler, 1967). Of these, 54 in grade 3 were tested and compared with 60 in a sending school. The author did not specify how these were selected. Comparison on reading showed greater gain over the year for bussed students. No controls on SES or other variables and no significance tests were reported. A later report from Buffalo (Banks and DiPasquale, 1969) described a 1967-1968 study of 1200 fifth to seventh grade Negro pupils bussed from 6 segregated inner city schools to 22 integrated schools. Whole classes were selected for the transfer. Though there was no difference in control test scores, the main growth for the year for the integrated pupils was .83 and for the segregated pupils .56 (grade equivalence scores). There was, however, no assurance that the integrated children or those with available test scores did not have more favorable background or higher native ability than the segregated.

There are two sources of information on the results of a bussing experiment in Philadelphia. The U. S. Commission (1967) reported that bussed Negro children of the same social class and reading grade level as Negroes in segregated schools with compensatory education (EIP) had by the third grade surpassed EIP children and equaled students of slightly higher SES in non-EIP schools. Laird and Weeks (1966) may have referred to the same experiment; in any case they make more details available. Ninety-nine pupils in grades 4-6 were bussed from one segregated school to two integrated schools and compared with the 420 pupils who remained in the segregated school. The bussed pupils performed better on reading and arithmetic tests than their IQ's predicted, especially at the fourth and fifth grade levels. When a smaller sub-sample of control and experimental children were matched on grade, sex and IQ, the bussed children made significant gains only on reading.

The Berkeley, California experiment reported by the U. S. Commission on Civil Rights (1967, p. 131) for the 1965-1966 year is corroborated by an evaluation of the following year's bussing project (Jonsson, 1967). Two hundred and fifty Negro students transported from segregated low SES schools in the Flats to integrated middle-class schools in the Hills made higher average gains than in previous years and higher gains than non-bussed students receiving compensatory education. Though SES data were not available on individuals, the students bussed to Hill schools were presumably lower class, since they came from a lower-class area of Berkeley (Sullivan, 1968). However, the Negro children selected for bussing were those "who were predicted to adjust well emotionally and academically to the new school" and parental consent was required (Jonsson, 1966). In other words, the children bussed to the Hills might well have been initially superior to their neighbors who remained behind. (See also Wilson, 1963.)

Under the auspices of the Metropolitan Council for Educational Opportunity (METCO), over 700 Negro students from Boston are being bussed at their parents' request to schools in suburban communities. During the first year of the program pre- and post-Metropolitan Achievement Test scores, available for 66 children in grades 3-8 in three school systems, showed significant improvement on reading, word, and spelling tests, but not on arithmetic. No control group was possible, since the Boston school system did not supply records on its students (Archibald, 1967). In his recent evaluation of the same program, Walberg (1969) solved the control group problem in an ingenious fashion by using siblings of the bussed children matched as closely as possible to them on age. As Walberg pointed out, the design does not guarantee the equality of groups, since there may be bias in the family's choice of child to be bussed, but at least the family and neighborhood environments of siblings are similar. Further bias was introduced because only 47% of the 737 eligible METCO children and 25% of the 352 eligible siblings were tested in both October 1968 and May 1969. Except that METCO children gained significantly less on mathematics at grades 5-6, there were no significant differences in achievement between the two groups from grades 2-12. Neither sex, nor year in program (1-3), nor initial achievement level interacted with bussing status.

Project Concern, which involves bussing Central Hartford, Connecticut Negro and Puerto Rican students to several suburbs in the metropolitan area, was more carefully designed (Mahan, 1967, 1968). Intact classes were randomly selected from eight eligible (85% or more nonwhite) elementary schools in the low SES North End. All 300 children in these classes with an IQ of 80 or above were bussed, except 12 whose parents refused and a random 22 for whom no places were available. A control group of 305 children drawn from the same schools proved to be like the experimental group in grade distribution (K-5) but to have more girls. In the course of the two-year study, 25% of the experimental and 20% of the control group were lost through moves from the target area, dropping out of the project or missing tests. A unique feature of this project is that, by selecting whole classes, central city teachers were released to accompany the pupils to their new schools and supply extra remedial and guidance services. Since not all bussed students received this supportive team assistance, it was possible to compare bussed students with and without compensatory education in their segregated schools.

In his two-year evaluation the project director concluded that 1. "Youngsters placed in suburban classroom at grades K-3 have a significantly greater tendency to show growth in mental ability (WISC and Test of Primary Mental Abilities) than those remaining in inner city classrooms"; 2. In measures of school achievement differences in lower grades are significantly in favor of the experimental group, but in the upper grades in favor of the control group; 3. Suburban placement with special supportive assistance proved more effective than suburban placement without such assistance; and 4. "There is no evidence that special supportive assistance is an effective intervention within inner city schools."

The final bussing study reviewed here is the largest — the New York Open Enrollment Study (Fox, 1966, 1967; Fox et al., 1968). Since 1960 some 22,300 pupils have, on their parents' initiative, transferred from predominantly Negro and Puerto Rican "sending" schools to predominantly white "receiving" schools. Fox (1968, p. 27) concluded: "When children who entered O. E. in 1962 were matched in initial reading ability with children who remained in the sending school, data from the 1965-66 study indicated no difference between them in reading ability. The 1966-67 study found that unmatched, randomly selected samples of O. E. children were reading at higher levels than randomly selected samples of sending school children. These findings suggested to the investigator that the O. E. children did not reflect the full range of ability in the sending schools and that academically more able children entered the O. E. programs."

Investigators in five of the nine bussing studies here reviewed found greater gains for desegregated children than for segregated children, but the case for the beneficial effect of desegregation is marred by several methodological shortcomings. The numbers involved were not large, and (more serious) in all cases the number tested is considerably smaller than the number bussed. This alone would jeopardize the randomness of the sample, even if the experimental and control groups were randomly drawn from the same pool, but in no case is there assurance on this point. Staff selection or parental self-selection always played a part, even in Hartford, where assignment was most nearly random. Therefore, it is possible and likely that more favorable home background and "achievement press" explains the somewhat better performance of bussed pupils. In none of the studies was there a careful attempt to evaluate the equality of education in integrated and segregated classrooms. In the Boston, Rochester, and Hartford experiments there was the further complication of bussing out of a central school district into suburban districts where schools have benefits that ampler budgets provide. Therefore, there is no way of comparing the effects of the rival independent variables of school quality and school ethnic or economic composition. The short duration of most of the programs — too short to offset the stimulation or trauma of transfer — is another reason for concluding that the over-all effectiveness of desegregation via bussing programs has not yet been demonstrated and must await further evidence. (For more details on bussing experiments, see Matthai, 1968.)

Of all the studies on the relation of school ethnic composition to minority group performance, the one with the most adequate design was Alan Wilson's (1967) survey, reported in an appendix to the Civil Rights Commission Report. The sample was a stratified random sample of more than 4,000 junior and senior high school students in the San Francisco Bay area. The design is a cross-sectional comparison of verbal test scores, according to the racial and social class composition of neighborhoods and schools, but longitudinal control is introduced by the data on school racial and social class composition at each grade level and first grade individual mental maturity test scores. Wilson argued that controlling on these test scores equates children on the effects of genetic differences and preschool home environment, so changes can be attributed to new (school?) experiences and not to uncontrolled initial differences.

Although the sample is large (over 2,400 Negroes), analysis of the separate effects of neighborhood and school segregation or of racial and social class segregation is hampered for Negroes by the confounding of these variables, and the fact that few Negroes live in integrated neighborhoods. Nevertheless, Wilson showed by regression analysis that after controlling for variation in first grade IQ, the social class of the primary school had a signficant effect on sixth grade reading level and the social class of the intermediate school had a significant effect on eighth grade verbal reasoning scores. School racial composition, however, had no significant effect on achievement over and above school social class (pp. 180-84).

Other than the small size of the numbers in some of the cells, there are further limitations to this study. First grade scores were presumably available only for the most stable members of the sample, and its representatives may have been affected by attrition. Children were matched only by father's occupation and primary mental maturity scores; in other respects segregated and integrated children could have been quite different. Parental and school social class assignment based on the questionnaire replies of students are potentially inaccurate. No evidence is offered as to the equality of segregated and integrated schools in Richmond. But in spite of these quibbles, the study is impressive in design and quite convincing that in this community, at least, racial integration *per se* was not significantly related to the academic performance of Negroes.

CONCLUSION

The literature reviewed offered some evidence as to the relation between school racial composition and academic achievement, but much more evidence as to the difficulties of research in this area.

The "before and after" studies of the desegregation of school systems or individuals suggest that following desegregation, of whatever type or at whatever academic level, subjects generally perform no worse, and in most instances better. Those studies in which the same individuals were measured at Time 1 and Time 2 (Lee, 1951; Katzenmeyer, 1963; Wessman, 1969; and Clark and Plotkin, 1963) have thus largely ruled out the enduring characteristics of the subjects and factors in their past (SES, IQ) as explanation of the change. But interaction between desegregation and quality of schooling has not been ruled out as the explanation of the difference. In fact, desegregation in Washington, D.C. reportedly brought an upgrading of education and in Louisville gave a psychological boost to teachers. Such changes could well explain the gain in achievement in those cities and in situations involving more classroom desegregation.

The general finding of the pre-Coleman cross-sectional studies reviewed is that achievement levels are higher for desegregation than for segregated pupils. Several of these studies were so small-scale and statistically limited that researchers would have little confidence in the generalizability of their findings, if they were not in agreement with studies such as those by Matzen or St. John and Smith which with larger samples and better controls also found higher achievement for the desegregated. However, for all these studies the unresolved question is: Were the desegregated students a select group to start with?

The Coleman data are extensive and have been analyzed with statistical finesse. However, the attempt to draw conclusions from the data is handicapped by the cross-sectional design, the unconvincing measures of social class, the failure to separate the effects of neighborhood SES and of school quality, the imprecise and non-longitudinal measure of school ethnic composition. In spite of such limitations, the survey provides fairly convincing evidence for the existence of a powerful relation between social class integration and achievement. The evidence is less clear for a residual relation between racial integration and achievement. The effect appears to be small, but could be either exaggerated or masked by inadequate control of school quality and home background characteristics.

In theory, investigators using four-celled studies can avoid most of the weaknesses of both panel and cross-sectional research. But no investigation to date has been able to meet all the canons of pure or quasi-experimentation. The matching problem plagues all attempts to equate naturally segregated and non-segregated populations. Wilson (1967) achieved a *post facto* "before" measurement by controlling on primary grade mental maturity, but this procedure did not control on all variables and may have masked the effect of racial segregation.

If, in bussing studies, subjects could be randomly assigned to experimental and control groups, the matching problem would be avoided; but politics and parental preferences seem invariably to bias the selection. Further bias is introduced by differential subsequent dropout from experimental or control groups as some children leave town, leave the program or are not tested. The small number of children involved in most bussing experiments not only handicaps statistical tests of their effectiveness, but also may add to the Hawthorne effect for those involved. The stimulation or embarrassment of being a guinea pig or a newcomer is probably short-run and can be discounted if the experiment is of long enough duration. But the effect of riding a bus to a community other than one's own might be continuing and could only be controlled if students were bussed both to segregated and to integrated schools.

The laboratory experiments of Katz (1964, 1968) and the lessons he draws from them are very convincing as to the "threats" and "facilitations" involved in the process of desegregation. Though as yet unsupported by adequate field research, the most plausible hypothesis is that the relation between integration and achievement is a conditional one: the academic performance of minority group children will be higher in integrated than in equivalent segregated schools, providing they are supported by staff and accepted by peers. As evidence for the first condition there is the report from Hartford that bussed students who received staff support in their new schools showed greatest gains (Mahan, 1968). As evidence for the second condition, there is the findings of the U. S. Commission on Civil Rights (1967) on the importance of interracial friendship to achievement in an integrated setting. In this review, I have perforce ignored the growing and important literature on the relation of ethnic integration and self-concept on one side and of self-concept and achievement on the other. As Wilson (1967) and Pettigrew (1968) suggest, researchers must assume a very complicated, two-way process in which the three variables interact. Support by staff and acceptance by peers undoubtedly contribute to both.

In rapidly changing times the nature of variables and their interrelationship may change. This review has revealed rather inconclusive evidence of a relation between ethnic integration and achievement. But the research examined refers to the immediate or distant past. The meaning of integration may be changing, and the conditions under which it is implemented can be made different in the future. One good reason that there has been no adequate research to date on the effect of integration is that there have been no adequate real-life tests — no large-scale, long-run instances of top-quality schooling in segregated minority-group schools. Until our society tries such experiments, researchers will not be able to evaluate them.

BIBLIOGRAPHY

Anderson, Louis V. *The Effects of Desegregation on the Achievement and Personality Patterns of Negro Children.* Doctor's thesis. Nashville, Tenn.: George Peabody College for Teachers, Univ. Microfilm No. 66-11, 237; 1966. Abstract: *Dissertation Abstracts* 27: 1529A-30A, No. 6A; 1966.

Archibald, David K. *Report on Change in Academic Achievement for a Sample of Elementary School Children: Progress Report on METCO.* Roxbury, Mass.: METCO Education Program (178 Humboldt Ave.), 1967. (Mimeo.)

Banks, Ronald and Di Pasquale, Mary E. *A Study of the Educational Effectiveness of Integration.* Buffalo, N.Y.: Buffalo Public Schools, Jan. 1969.

Becker, Howard S. The Career of the Chicago Public School Teacher. *American Journal of Sociology* 57: 470-77; 1952.

Beker, Jerome. *Final Report: A Study of Integration in Racially Imbalanced Urban Public Schools.* Syracuse, N.Y.: Syracuse Univ. Youth Development Center, May 1967. (Mimeo.)

Bowles, Samuel and Levin, Henry. The Determinants of Scholastic Achievement: An Appraisal of Some Recent Evidence. *Journal of Human Resources* 3: 1-24; Winter 1968.

Campbell, Donald T. and Stanley, Julian C. Experimental and Quasi-Experimental Designs for Research on Teaching, *Handbook of Research on Teaching*. (Edited by N. L. Gage.) Chicago: Rand-McNally, 1963. Pp. 171-246.

Clark, Kenneth, B. Desegregation: An Appraisal of the Evidence. *Journal of Social Issues* 9: 1-76; 1953.

Clark, Kenneth B. *Dark Ghetto: Dilemmas of Social Power.* New York: Harper and Row, 1965.

Clark, Kenneth B. and Plotkin, Lawrence. *The Negro Student at Integrated Colleges.* New York: National Scholarship Service and Fund for Negro Students, 1963.

Coleman, James S. et al. *Equality of Educational Opportunity.* U. S. Dept. of Health, Education, and Welfare, Office of Education. Washington, D.C.: Superintendent of Documents, Government Printing Office, 1966.

Colfax, Allen. Pre-Coded versus Open Ended Items and Children's Reports of Father's Occupation. *Sociology of Education* 40: 96-98; 1967.

Conant, James B. *Slums and Suburbs: A Commentary on Schools in Metropolitan Areas.* New York: McGraw-Hill, 1961.

Crockett, Harry J. A Study of Some Factors Affecting the Decision of Negro High School Students to Enroll in Previously All-White High Schools in St. Louis, 1955. *Social Forces* 35: 351-56; 1957. Microfilm No. 181.

Crowley, Mary R. Cincinnati's Experiment in Negro Education: A Comparative Study of the Segregated and Mixed Schools. *Journal of Negro Education* 1: 25-33; 1932.

Deutscher, Max and Chein, Isidor. The Psychological Effects of Enforced Segregation: A Survey of Social Science Opinion. *Journal of Psychology* 26: 259-87; 1948.

Dressler, Frank J. *Study of Achievement in Reading of Pupils Transferred from Schools 15 and 37 to Peripheral Schools to Eliminate Overcrowding to Abandon an Obsolete School, and to Achieve a More Desirable Racial Balance in City Schools.* Buffalo, N.Y.: Board of Education, Division of Curriculum Evaluation and Development, Mar. 1967. (Mimeo.)

Duncan, Otis D. and Duncan, Beverly. *The Negro Population of Chicago.* Chicago: Univ. of Chicago Press, 1957.

Dyer, Henry S. School Factors and Equal Educational Opportunity. *Harvard Educational Review* 38: 38-56; 1968.

Fortenberry, James H. *The Achievement of Negro Pupils in Mixed and Non-Mixed Schools.* Doctor's thesis. Bloomington: Univ. of Ind., Univ. Microfilm No. 59-5492, 1959. Abstract: *Dissertation Abstracts* 20: 2643; 1960.

Fox, David J. *Free Choice Open Enrollment – Elementary Schools.* New York: Center for Urban Education, Aug. 31, 1966. (Mimeo.)

Fox, David J. *Evaluation of the New York City Title I Educational Projects 1966-1967: Expansion of the Free Choice Open Enrollment Program.* New York: Center for Urban Education, Sept. 1967. (Mimeo.)

Fox, David J. et al. *Services to Children in Open Enrollment Receiving Schools: Evaluation of ESEA Title I Projects in New York City, 1967-1968.* New York: Center for Urban Education, Nov. 1968. (Mimeo.)

Gordon, Edmund W. and Wilkerson, Doxey A. *Compensatory Education for the Disadvantaged: Programs and Practices Preschool through College.* New York: College Entrance Examination Board, 1966. Chapter 7, A Critique of Compensatory Education, pp. 156-89. ERIC: ED 011 274, MF $0.45; HC $12.36.

Gottlieb, David. Teaching and Students: The Views of Negro and White Teachers. *Sociology of Education* 37: 345-53; 1964.

Hansen, Carl F. The Scholastic Performances of Negro and White Pupils in the Integrated Public Schools of the District of Columbia. *Harvard Educational Review* 30: 216-36; 1960.

Herriott, Robert E. and St. John, Nancy H. *Social Class and the Urban School.* New York: John Wiley and Sons, 1966.

Hughes, Helen and Watts, Lewis G. Portrait of the Self-Integrator. *The Journal of Social Issues* 20: 103-15; 1964.

Jessup, Dorothy K. School Integration and Minority Group Achievement. *The Urban R's.* (Edited by Dentler, Mackler and Warshauer.) New York: Frederick Praeger, 1967.

Johnson, Norma J.; Wyer, Robert; and Gilbert, Neil. Quality Education and Integration: An Exploratory Study. *Phylon* 28, Fall 1967.

Johnson, Harold A. *Attitudes Towards Bussing and Integration Expressed by Berkeley Mothers, Teachers, and Children: A Summary of 1966 Survey Findings.* Berkeley, Calif.: Berkeley Unified School District. Nov. 1966. (Mimeo.)

Kaplan, John. *New Rochelle: Civil Rights U.S.A. Public Schools. Cities in the North and West: A Report to the United States Commission on Civil Rights.* Washington, D.C.: Superintendent of Documents, Government Printing Office, 1962.

Katzenmeyer, William Gilbert. *Social Interaction and Differences in Intelligence Test Performance of Negro and White Elementary School Pupils.* Doctor's thesis. Durham, N.C.: Duke Univ., Univ. Microfilm No. 63-2227, 1962. Abstract: *Dissertation Abstracts* 24: 1904-1905, No. 5; 1963.

Katz, Irwin. Review of Evidence Relating to Effects of Desegregation on the Intellectual Performance of Negroes. *American Psychologist* 19: 381-99; 1964.

Katz, Irwin. Academic Motivation and Equal Educational Opportunity. *Harvard Educational Review* 38: 57-65; 1968.

Katzman, Martin T. Distribution and Production in a Big City Elementary School System. *Yale Economic Essays,* No. 8. New Haven, Conn.: Yale Univ., Spring 1968. Pp. 201-56.

Kennedy, A.; Van De Riet, V.; and White, J. C. A Normative Sample of Intelligence and Achievement of Negro Elementary School Children in the Southeastern U. S. *Monographs of the Society for Research in Child Development* 28: 6; 1963.

Klineberg, Otto. *Negro Intelligence and Selective Migration.* New York: Columbia Univ. Press, 1935.

Klineberg, Otto. Negro-White Differences in Intelligence Test Performance: A New Look at an Old Problem. *American Psychologist* 18: 198-203; 1963.

Laird, Mary Alice and Weeks, Grace. *The Effects of Bussing on Achievement in Reading and Arithmetic in Three Philadelphia Schools.* Philadelphia: Board of Education, Division of Research, Dec. 1966. (Mimeo.)

Lee, Everett S. Negro Intelligence and Selective Migration: A Philadelphia Test of Klineberg's Hypothesis. *American Sociological Review* 16: 227-33; 1951.

Lockwood, Jane Durand. *An Examination of Scholastic Achievement, Attitudes and Home Background Factors of 6th Grade Negro Students in Balanced and Unbalanced Schools.* Doctor's thesis. Ann Arbor: Univ. of Mich., Univ. Microfilm No. 67-8303, 1966. Abstract: *Dissertation Abstracts* 28: 54A, 1967.

Luchterhand, Elmer and Weller, Leonard. Social Class and the Desegregation Movement: A Study of Parents' Decisions in a Negro Ghetto. *Social Problems* 13: 83-88; Summer 1965.

Mahan, Thomas W. *Project Concern: An Interim Report on an Educational Exploration.* Hartford, Conn.: Board of Education, Sept. 1967. (Mimeo.)

Mahan, Thomas W. *Project Concern – 1966-1968: A Report on the Effectiveness of Suburban School Placement for Inner-City Youth.* Hartford, Conn.: Board of Education, Aug. 1968.

Matthai, Robert Arthur. *The Academic Performance of Negro Students: An Analysis of the Research Findings from Several Bussing Programs.* Qualifying Paper. Cambridge, Mass.: Harvard Graduate School of Education, June 1968.

Matzen, Stanley Paul. *The Relationship between Racial Composition and Scholastic Achievement in Elementary School Classrooms.* Doctor's thesis. Stanford, Calif.: Stanford Univ., Univ. Microfilm No. 66-2518, 1965. Abstract: *Dissertation Abstracts* 26: 6475-76, No. 11; 1966.

McCauley, Patrick and Ball, Edward D. (editors). *Southern Schools: Progress and Problems.* Nashville, Tenn.: Southern Education Reporting Service, 1959.

McGurk, F. C. J. On White and Negro Test Performance and Socioeconomic Factors. *Journal of Abnormal and Social Psychology* 48: 448-50; 1953.

McPartland, James. *The Segregated Student in Desegregated Schools.* Final Report to the Center for the Study of Social Organization of Schools. Baltimore, Md.: Johns Hopkins Univ., June 1968.

Meketon, Betty Field. *The Effects of Integration Upon the Negro Child's Response to Various Tasks and Upon His Level of Self-Esteem.* Doctor's thesis. Lexington: Univ. of Ky., 1966.

Miller, Carroll L. Educational Opportunities and the Negro Child in the South. *Harvard Educational Review* 30: 195-208; 1960.

Moriber, Leonard. *School Functioning of Pupils Born in Other Areas and in New York City.* Publication No. 168. New York: Board of Education, May 1961.

Nichols, Robert C. Schools and the Disadvantaged. *Science* 154: 1312-14; 1966.

Peterson, R. A. and DeBord, L. *Educational Supportiveness of the Home and Academic Performance of Disadvantaged Boys. IMRID, Behavioral Science Monographs,* No. 3. Nashville, Tenn.: George Peabody College, 1966.

Pettigrew, Thomas F. Negro American Personality: Why Isn't More Known? *Journal of Social Issues* 20: 4-23; Apr. 1964.

Pettigrew, Thomas F. Race and Equal Educational Opportunity. *Harvard Educational Review* 38: 67-76; 1968.

Pettigrew, Thomas F. and Pajonas, Patricia J. Social Psychological Consideration of Racially Imbalanced Schools. Paper presented at New York Educational Dept. Conference, Mar. 1964. *Report of the Advisory Committee on Racial Imbalance and Education of the Massachusetts State Board of Education.* Boston, Mass.: Board of Education, Apr. 1965.

Public Education Association. *The Status of the Public School: Education of Negro and Puerto Rican Children in New York City.* New York: Public Education Assoc., Oct. 1955.

Purl, Mabel C. *The Effect of Integration on the Achievement of Elementary Pupils.* Riverside, Calif.: Dept. of Research and Evaluation, Riverside Unified Schools, Nov. 1967 and Mar. 1969.

Radin, Norma. *A Comparison of the Test Performance of Negro Students Attending All-Negro and Integrated Elementary Schools in One Community.* Ypsilanti, Mich.: Board of Education, Apr. 1966.

Rock, William C. et al. *An Interim Report on a Cooperative Program Between a City School District and a Sub-urban School District.* Rochester, N.Y.: Board of Education, July 20, 1966 and July 25, 1967. (Mimeo.)

Rock, William C. et al. *A Report on a Cooperative Program Between a City School District and a Suburban School District.* Rochester, N.Y.: Board of Education, June 28, 1968. (Mimeo.)

St. John, Nancy Hoyt. *The Relation of Racial Segregation in Early Schooling to the Level of Aspiration and Academic Achievement of Negro Students in a Northern High School.* Doctor's thesis. Cambridge, Mass.: Harvard Univ., 1962.

St. John, Nancy H. *Measuring the Social Class Background of School Children.* Cambridge, Mass.: Harvard Univ., School of Education, 1969. (Mimeo.)

St. John, Nancy Hoyt and Smith, Marshall S. *School Racial Composition, Aspiration and Achievement.* Cambridge, Mass.: School of Education, Harvard Univ., June 1969. (Mimeo.)

Samuels, Ivan G. *Desegregated Education and Differences in Academic Achievement.* Doctor's thesis. Bloomington: Ind. Univ., Univ. Microfilm No. 58-2934, 1958. Abstract: *Dissertation Abstracts* 19: 1293-94, No. 6; 1958.

Sexton, Patricia. *Education and Income: Inequalities of Education in Our Public Schools.* New York: Viking Press, 1961.

Smith, Marshall S. *A Replication of the EEOS Report's Regression Analysis.* Cambridge, Mass.: Harvard Univ., School of Education, 1969.

Stallings, Frank H. A Study of the Immediate Effects of Integration on Scholastic Achievement in the Louisville Public Schools. *Journal of Negro Education* 28: 439-44; 1959.

Stetler, Henry G. *Private Interracial Neighborhoods in Connecticut.* Hartford, Conn.: Commission on Civil Rights, 1957.

Stodolsky, Susan and Lesser, Gerald. Learning Patterns in the Disadvantaged. *Harvard Educational Review* 37: 546-93; 1967.

Stouffer, Samuel A. Some Observations on Study Design. *Social Research to Test Ideas.* Glencoe, Ill.: Free Press, 1962. Pp. 290-99.

Sullivan, Neil V. Discussion: Implementing Equal Educational Opportunity. *Harvard Educational Review* 38: 148-55; 1968.

United States Commission on Civil Rights. *Public Schools Southern States.* U. S. Dept. of Health, Education, and Welfare; Office of Education. Washington, D.C.: Superintendent of Documents, Government Printing Office, 1962.

United States Commission on Civil Rights. *Racial Isolation in the Public Schools.* U. S. Dept. of Health, Education, and Welfare; Office of Education. Washington, D.C.: Superintendent of Documents, Government Printing Office, 1967.

Vane, Julia R. Relation of Early School Achievement to High School Achievement when Race, Intelligence and Socioeconomic Factors are Equated. *Psychology in the Schools* 3: 124-29; 1966.

Walberg, Herbert J. *An Evaluation of an Urban-Suburban School Bussing Program: Student Achievement and Perception of Class Learning Environments.* Draft of Report to METCO. Roxbury, Mass.: METCO Education Program (178 Humboldt Ave.), July 1, 1969. (Mimeo.)

Weinberg, Meyer. *Desegregation Research: An Appraisal.* Bloomington, Ind.: Phi Delta Kappa, Summer 1968.

Weinstein, Eugene A. and Geisel, Paul N. Family Decision-Making over Desegregation. *Sociometry* 25: 21-29; 1962.

Wessman, Alden E. *Evaluation of Project ABC (A Better Chance): An Evaluation of Dartmouth College Independent Schools Scholarship Program for Disadvantaged High School Students.* U. S. Dept. of Health, Education and Welfare; Office of Education. Washington, D.C.: Superintendent of Documents, Government Printing Office, Apr. 1969.

Whiteman, Martin; Brown, Bert; and Deutsch, Martin. *Some Effects of Social Class and Race on Children's Language and Intellectual Abilities.* Presented at the Biennial Meeting of the Society for Research in Child Development, Minneapolis, Minn., Mar. 1965. New York: New York Medical College, Institute for Developmental Studies, Dept. of Psychiatry.

White Plains Public Schools. *A Three-Year Evaluation of the White Plains Racial Balance Plan.* White Plains, N.Y.: Board of Education; Oct. 16, 1967.

Wilson, Alan B. Social Stratification and Academic Achievement. *Education in*

Depressed Areas. (Edited by A. Harry Passow.) New York: Bureau of Publications, Teachers College, Columbia Univ., 1963.

Wilson, Alan B. Educational Consequences of Segregation in a California Community. *Racial Isolation in the Public Schools.* Vol. II. Washington, D.C.: U. S. Commission on Civil Rights, 1967. Pp. 165-206.

Wolff, Max. *Racial Imbalance in Plainfield Public Schools. Annex Special High School Study.* Plainfield, N. J.: Board of Education, July 1962. (Mimeo.)

Wolff, Max. Segregation in the Schools of Gary, Indiana. *Journal of Educational Sociology* 36: 251-61; 1963.

Wolman, T. G. Learning Effects of Integration in New Rochelle. *Integrated Education* 2: 30-31; Dec. 1964, Jan. 1965.

IV.
EXEMPLARY
EVALUATION
AND
RESEARCH
STUDIES

chapter 7
status studies

EQUALIZING EDUCATIONAL OPPORTUNITY
IN THE PUBLIC SCHOOL

Edmund W. Gordon

Future historians may well conclude that the civil rights movement of the 1950's and 1960's had a more telling impact on public education than on any other single aspect of our society. Not only did this struggle contribute to a mid-twentieth century renaissance in education in the United States, as noted by former U. S. Commissioner of Education Keppel, but its concern with further democratizing education led also to the design and conduct of one of our most important pieces of educational research.

Section 402 of the Civil Rights Act of 1964 directed the Commissioner of Education to conduct a survey and report to the President and Congress on "the lack of availability of equal educational opportunities for individuals by reason of race, color, religion or national origin" in public educational institutions at all levels in the United States. The resulting report, *Equality of Educational Opportunity*, often referred to as the Coleman Report after its senior author and one of the nation's ablest research methodologists, is the most extensive survey of the U. S. public school in the entire history of the institution.

The Coleman Report, nevertheless, has received considerable criticism. Reviewers have commented on the absence of a theoretical basis for the study. Others have criticized problems in design, problems in sampling, and debatable approaches to data analysis. Some of the findings and conclusions of the survey, as well, have been at variance with assumptions that previously were widely held. Many of these problems and suggested weaknesses, no doubt, are due to the time limit imposed upon the study. Under requirement of the law, it was planned, designed, and conducted in two years. Additionally, within that same time period, data were analyzed and a final report prepared and published. But in spite of these suggested shortcomings, the fact is that the Coleman survey has produced some valuable data related to the general problem area of equality of educational opportunity. Indeed, there are findings from that report which most reviewers feel would stand tests of reanalysis or reinvestigation should the study be replicated or its data subjected to further analysis.

The four principal questions asked of the analysis of data in the Coleman Report and the findings related to each are summarized below:

1. What is the extent of racial and ethnic group segregation in the public schools of the United States? The great majority of children in this country attend schools in which most of the students are members of the same ethnic group. The assignment of children to schools by ethnic group identification is the dominant practice particularly in the South and, to a large extent, in the metropolitan North, Midwest, and West. "More than 65% of all Negro pupils in the first grade attend schools that are between 90 and 100% Negro. And 87% at grade one and 66% at grade 12, attend schools that are 50% or more Negro. In the South most students attend schools that are 100% white or Negro." A similar pattern of segregation is reported for teachers of Negro and white pupils.

2. Are the schools attended by children in the United States equal in their facilities, programs, staff and pupil characteristics? Negro children are likely to attend schools which are inferior to those attended by white children. The quality of schools attended, however, varies by region. "For the nation as a whole white children attend elementary schools with a smaller average number of pupils per room (29) than do any of the minorities (30 to 33) . . . In the non-metropolitan North and West and Southwest . . . there is a smaller average number of pupils per room for Negroes than for whites." But for secondary schools in the metropolitan Midwest, the average for Negroes is 54 pupils per room as compared with 33 per room for whites. "Nationally, at the high school level the average white has one teacher for every 22 students and the average Negro has one teacher for every 26 students." Nationally, Negro students also have fewer of the facilities which are thought to be most associated with academic achievement. "They have less access to physics, chemistry, and language laboratories. There are fewer books per pupil in their libraries. Their textbooks are less often in sufficient supply." Just as minority groups tend to have less access to physical facilities that seem to be related to academic achievement, they also have less access to curricular and extracurricular programs that would seem to have such a relationship. Negro high school students are less likely to attend schools that are regionally accredited. Negro and Puerto Rican students have less access to college preparatory programs and accelerated courses. Puerto Rican pupils have less access to vocational curriculums. Moreover, the average Negro pupil attends a school where the average teacher quality

is inferior to that of the teacher of the average white child, where type of college, years of experience, salary, extent of travel, educational level of teacher's mother and teacher's vocabulary score are considered. Differences are also to be found in pupil characteristics. "The average Negro has fewer classmates whose mothers graduated from high school, his classmates tend to come from larger families, they are less often enrolled in college preparatory programs, and they have taken fewer courses in English, math, science and foreign language." Differences in school characteristics are considered to be small when considered in the context of national averages, however, for fuller appreciation, regional differences should also be considered. Coleman notes that "in cases where Negroes in the South receive unequal treatment, the significance in terms of actual numbers of individuals involved is very great, since 54% of the Negro population of school going age, or approximately 3,200,000 children, live in that region."

3. What are the achievement patterns of children of different backgrounds as measured by their performance on achievement tests? With the exception of pupils of Oriental family background, the average pupil from the minority groups studied scored distinctly lower at every level than the average white pupil. The minority group pupils' scores were as much as one standard deviation below the majority pupils' scores in the first grade. At the twelfth grade level, the scores of minority group pupils were even further below those of the majority group. Of additional significance is the fact that a constant difference in standard deviation over the various grades actually represents a mounting difference in grade level gap as the pupils move toward the twelfth grade. Consequently, schools seem to do little about an initial deficit which only increases as the minority pupils continue in school.

4. What relationships exist between pupil academic achievement and characteristics of the schools they attend? When differences in socioeconomic background factors for pupils are statistically controlled, differences between schools account for only a small fraction of differences in academic achievement. "The schools do differ, however, in their relation to the various racial and ethnic groups." White pupils seem to be less affected by the quality of their schools than minority group pupils. "The achievement of minority pupils depends more on the schools they attend than does the achievement of majority pupils." In the South, for example, 40 percent more of the achievement of Negro pupils is associated with the particular schools they attend than is the achievement of white pupils. With the exception of children from Oriental family backgrounds, this general result is true for all minority groups. Coleman suggests that this finding "indicates that it is for the most disadvantaged children that improvements in school quality will make the most difference in achievement." Although the relationship between school characteristics and pupil achievement is relatively modest, several of the characteristics on which predominantly Negro schools score low are among those which are related to pupil achievement. The existence of science laboratories in schools, for example, shows a small but

consistent relationship to achievement — Negroes attend schools with fewer of these facilities. Teacher quality shows an even stronger relationship to pupil achievement, and it increases with grade level. Additionally, its impact on achievement is greater for Negroes than for whites. On measures of verbal skill and educational background, two relatively potent teacher variables, teachers of minority group pupils scored lower than teachers of majority group pupils. Educational background and aspirations of fellow students are also strongly related to pupil achievement. This relationship is less significant for white pupils than for Negro pupils. Coleman found educational backgrounds and aspirations to be lower among pupils in schools Negroes attend than in schools where whites are in the majority. In addition to the school characteristics which were shown to be related to pupil achievement, Coleman found a pupil characteristic which appears to have a stronger relationship to achievement than all the school factors combined. The extent to which a pupil feels that he has control over his own destiny is strongly related to achievement. This feeling of potency is less prevalent among Negro students, but where it is present, "their achievement is higher than that of white pupils who lack that conviction." Coleman reports that "while this characteristic shows little relationship to most school factors, it is related for Negroes to the proportion of whites in the schools. Those Negroes in schools with a higher proportion of whites have a greater sense of control."

In trying to draw implications from these findings, it is important to consider that Coleman has produced summary statistics which describe certain conditions and correlational statistics which, in turn, describe relationships which may be causal or simply coincidental. Causation certainly cannot be inferred from the strength of the relationships reported. When combined with the problems some critics see in the study, we are advised to move with caution in using the Coleman findings to determine public policy. Such caution, however, need not preclude serious thought and considered action. As the major findings of the study are reviewed, empirical experience, logic, and facts provide a contest in which Coleman's conclusions may be interpreted.

There are some findings which common sense and clear observation leave us no choice but to accept. Public schools in the United States are segregated by ethnic group and socioeconomic status. Negro children are more likely to attend schools of poorer quality than white children. Academic achievement for minority group children (except Orientals) is inferior to that of majority group children. There simply is no question that these findings correspond to reality as we have experienced it; in the area of relationships between factors, nevertheless, there may be room for debate.

It seems clear, however, that for the development of the young person who comes to school without the advantage of being raised in a privileged or economically and socially secure white family what happens in the school is of great importance. The quality of his school's curriculum, the quality of his teachers, and the background of his fellow pupils are importantly related to the quality of his academic achievement. Additionally, his experience in the educational setting appears to influence his sense of power to control his destiny. As pointed out before, this attitudinal factor, even more than all school factors combined, has a significant relationship to quality of achievement and rate of development.

Now, in a sense, whether or not one wants to accept these conclusions and act upon them is not in question. The fact is that the political realities of the present period strongly reflect sensitivity to these conclusions. Indeed, the primary political struggles in public education today have to do with economic and ethnic integration and with improved quality of education as the prime vehicles for equalizing educational opportunity. Even the current demand for "black" schools and "black" control of schools for "black" children is but an expression of this struggle. The recently accelerated unionization of teachers and their efforts to improve salaries, working conditions, professional status, and quality of education are another part of the same struggle. It is only unfortunate that these two expressions have not always moved in concert.

A major strategic error in the recent strike in New York City was the teachers' failure to make adequate provisions for the education of poor children during the period of the strike. If Coleman is right about the contribution of school factors to minority pupil achievement and given the modest use of the public school by more privileged families in New York City, the teachers were really striking against working class, Negro, Puerto Rican, and poor children. Important and necessary as this strike may have been, this was the effect without the advantage of providing any major inconvenience to the city's power structure and the upper classes as was true in the New York City transit strike when employers were deprived of workers who depended on public transportation. Surely, it is to the credit of the statesmen and more tolerant in the Negro community that the historic ties between the Negro community and labor unions were not ruptured and that we are not now faced with a sharper cleavage between teachers and the spokesmen of the "black" community who deeply resented the unavailability of teachers to carry on even the concededly inadequate educational services the schools provide. The "black" community did not need Coleman to tell them that what happens in school can be important in the development of their children. This they knew, and they have come to expect much from the school.

The contradictions involved in the expectations of the "black" community for the schools and the schools' obviously low performance in the achievement of academic mastery in minority group children bring into focus the central problem in the Coleman study. The public school was created for the purpose of making certain levels of achievement independent of social origin. Its historic mission has been to enable youngsters whose families could not adequately provide for their private education to acquire the knowledge and skill necessary for full participation in a democratic society. Coleman asked of his data whether or not the schools do this equally well for children from all segments of the population and found the answer to be no. He also asked if the schools' treatment of children from minority backgrounds is equal and found the answer to be no. The inappropriateness of this second question became clearer when he asked why the inequality existed.

When Coleman attempted to establish relationships between factors which help us understand why we do not do equally well with children from a variety of backgrounds, he found that what children come to school with accounts for more of the variation in their achievement than any other factor. Now, if this is true, it suggests that schools should not be providing equal treatment to all children but that treatment should, in fact, be unequal. The schools need to design their programs to meet the special characteristics and needs of the many kinds of children served; and, if a democratizing function is to be adequately served, these special programs must be designed to eventually bring all children to, at least, some common achievement goals. The schools are not doing this, and, furthermore, Coleman did not design his study to get at the dimensions of this aspect of the problem.

School factors may have been found to be of relatively modest importance for all pupils not because what the schools can do is not crucial but because Coleman did not look at what the schools actually do. He looked at static and status variables; he did not look at process variables. Variations in facilities, offerings, and teacher qualifications may be of less importance than pupil-teacher interaction, teacher expectation, classroom climate, pupil-pupil interaction, and the types and demands of the learning experiences available. Within the context of static and status variables, the dimensions studied may be too narrow to pick up the differences. Variations in class size between 26 and 36 may be unimportant. Differences between 18 and 36 may be highly significant. Although information was collected from administrators concerning their schools, the nature and quality of school administration was not evaluated. Differences in administrative styles and relationships and school climate resulting from such differences were not identified in the study. Coleman's study did not treat school factors sensitively; rather it approached them with crude measures that identified gross and not subtle differences.

When the gross nature of the study is combined with the fact that tradition did not lead Coleman to study the extent to which special pupil characteristics were reflected in the adequacy or the inadequacy of the schools' offerings, it is clear that important as this report is it only begins to suggest the magnitude of the problem. Educational opportunity in the United States is not equal, but it is even more unequal than this landmark study indicates.

The Coleman survey, nevertheless, does provide some leads as to what may be required to make educational opportunity and achievement more equal. An important step toward providing for equality of educational opportunity would be economic or social class integration. Additional data from the Coleman Report and some reanalyses reported in *Racial Isolation in the Public Schools* also indicate that ethnic group integration will be an essential step in this process. Even if racial integration in the schools is not essential in and of itself, it will be required in the achievement of social class integration since the Negro middle class is not large enough to provide an appropriate mix. Significantly, the pool of middle-class Negro children is reduced by the fact that in some areas better than one-fourth of these children are in institutions other than the public school. Despite the general conclusion that school factors are relatively unimportant as determinants of achievement in the total school population, Coleman's data also seem to indicate that enriched curriculums, improved teacher quality, and other improvements in the schools which Negro students attend should make for increased achievement of poor and Negro children.

A program feature which emerges from the study, as well as from other sources, has to do with school organization. Just as Coleman omitted sensitive examination of dynamic aspects of school administration, he also did not look at patterns of parent and community participation in school policy making. It would not be unreasonable, however, to conclude that the important "locus of control" or "control over one's destiny" variable would be influenced by the child's perception of such power or influence in his parents or the adults in the group with which he identifies. The tradition in school administration of discouraging lay people, particularly poor or minority lay people, from participating in the determination of school policy will need to be sharply modified. These parents and community spokesmen may be a hidden resource which the depressed area schools have used inappropriately or not at all. Coleman reminds us that we were wrong about the educational aspirations and interests of minority groups. It also appears that we may have been wrong in excluding them from any meaningful voice in the direction of the schools their children attend.

These beginning efforts at equalizing educational opportunity will certainly not be adequate to the task. What is needed to make educational opportunity and achievement equal for all groups in our population must be the subject of extensive action and research programs. The Coleman study is a beginning, and from it flow many questions which should engage the attention of research investigators and social activists as well.

A BIBLIOGRAPHY ON THE COLEMAN REPORT

The following is a bibliography related to the Coleman Report, Coleman, James S.; and others. "Equality of educational opportunity." Washington, D.C.: U. S. Government Printing Office, 1966. 737p. Included are selected reviews and reactions to the Coleman Report and two extensive bibliograhpies which point to broader references relevant to the subject under discussion. These references do not include several papers presented at recent professional meetings.

REVIEWS AND REACTIONS

Albert, Ilene; and Sheldon, Pamela. "Equality of educational opportunity."

Educational Leadership, 24:281-287, December 1966. This review cites the major findings of the Coleman Report. It raises questions that are left unanswered by the report and points out instances where conclusions are drawn from insufficient evidence.

Bowles, Samuel; and Levin, Henry. "Equality of eductional equality – a critical appraisal." 1967, unpublished. (Authors' affiliations: Harvard University and Brookings Institution.) A rigorous examination of the Coleman Report in which the design of the study and some of its analyses are criticized. The authors are particularly concerned that policy decisions not be based upon this preliminary study of so critical an area.

Coleman, James. S. "Equal schools or equal students?" The Public Interest, 70-75, Summer 1966. The principal author of "Equality of Educational Opportunity" emphasizes the fact that the real need is for equally effective schools not equal school facilities. Included is what the author terms "a modest, yet radical proposal."

Dentler, Robert A. "Equality of educational opportunity – a special review." Urban Review, 1:27-29, December 1966. Questions that were adequately answered in the Coleman Report are indicated and areas that might be given strong consideration in future research are suggested. The major conclusion is that the report made an outstanding contribution to the study of American intergroup relations.

Jencks, Christopher. "Education: the racial gap; finds of James Coleman's study." New Republic, 155:21-26, October 1, 1966. The report is praised because it sought to study how school characteristics can affect the individual learner. Findings and conclusions of the report are discussed. The conclusion is that Federal intervention is needed to provide equality of educational opportunity.

Nichols, Robert C. "Schools and the disadvantaged." Science, 154:1312-1314, December 9, 1966. The background and findings of the Coleman Report are discussed. Two areas of critical comment concern analysis of data regarding the effects of desegregation on Negro achievement and analysis of data regarding differences in educational opportunity.

U. S. Commission on Civil Rights. "Racial isolation in the public schools." Washington, D.C.: U. S. Government Printing Office, 1967. (Volumes I and II.) The major finding of this report is that racial isolation, regardless of its source, is harmful to Negro pupils. The Commission states its concern that compensatory programs in racially isolated situations have not proven successful. Recommendations are presented.

The following papers, presented at the American Psychological Association Division 15 Symposium on Implications of Coleman Report on Equality of Educational Opportunity, September 3, 1967, are presently being prepared for publication.

Pettigrew, Thomas. "Race and equal educational opportunity." (Author's affiliation: Harvard University.)

Dyer, Henry S. "School factors, peer influence, and equal educational opportunity." (Author's affiliation: Educational Testing Service.)

Katz, Irwin. "Motivation and equal educational opportunity." (Author's affiliation: University of Michigan.)

Gordon, Edmund W. "Family, environment, and equal educational opportunity. (Author's affiliation: Yeshiva University.)

BIBLIOGRAPHIES

St. John, Nancy; and Smith, Nancy, eds. "Annotated bibliography on school racial mix and the self concept, aspirations, academic achievement and interracial attitudes and behavior of Negro children." Cambridge: Center for Research and Development on Educational Differences, Harvard University, 1967. 251 ref. (Monograph No. 3.) A selective bibliography which concentrates on the "effect on children of racial segregation, desegregation and integration in schools." It includes reports and reviews of empirical research, studies of Northern de facto segregation, research with Negro subjects, social and economic class and school variables.

Weinberg, Meyer, ed. "School integration: a comprehensive classified bibliography of 3,100 references." Chicago: Integrated Education Associates, 1967. This compilation is based on the entries in the twenty-eight issues of the "Integrated Education" magazine published since January 1963. There are sixteen sections, a few of which are historical, effects on children, community, law and government, role of the church, Spanish-Americans, American-Indians, and foreign. Not annotated.

RACIAL ISOLATION IN THE PUBLIC SCHOOLS

U. S. Commission on Civil Rights

The Supreme Court ruled in 1954 that governmentally enforced school segregation violated the 14th amendment and that separated educational facilities were inherently unequal.

The immediate impact of the Court's ruling was upon the Southern and border States that had compelled segregation in the public schools. The decision also heightened concern about the extent of school segregation throughout the Nation.

Now, 13 years after the Supreme Court's decision, the majority of American children continue to attend schools that are largely segregated. The U. S. Office of Education in its national survey, *Equality of Educational Opportunity*, found that when judged by the standard of segregation ". . . American public education remains largely unequal. . . ."

To define the extent of racial isolation in the public schools, the Commission collected data on the racial composition of schools in more than 100 city school systems throughout the Nation. The data revealed that racial isolation in the public schools is extensive and has increased since 1954. School segregation is most severe in the Nation's metropolitan areas where two-thirds of the country's Negro and white populations now live.

There are 1.6 million Negro children and 2.4 million white children enrolled in elementary schools in 75 representative cities studied by the Commission. Of the Negro children, 1.2 million (75 percent) attend schools where the student bodies are more than 90 percent Negro. Of the white children, 2 million (83 percent) are enrolled in schools where the student populations are more than 90 percent white. Nearly 9 of every 10 Negro children in these 75 cities attend elementary schools where the student bodies range from 50.5 to 100 percent Negro. The extent of student segregation was not necessarily dependent upon the size of the school system, the proportion of Negroes enrolled, or whether the cities were in the North or the South.

The growth of segregation has been rapid. A survey of 15 Northern school systems revealed that the Negro enrollment has increased by 154,000 pupils since 1950, and that 130,000 of these Negro pupils attended schools where the student bodies were more than 90 percent Negro.

In Southern and border cities the proportion of Negroes attending all-Negro elementary schools has decreased, yet the *number* of children attending racially isolated schools has increased.

CAUSES OF RACIAL ISOLATION

The population increase in the Nation's metropolitan areas — 40 million persons between 1940 and 1960 — has been accompanied by an increase in the separation of the races. By 1960, four of every five Negro school-age children in metropolitan areas lived in the central cities while nearly three of every five white children lived in the suburbs. As a result, a substantial number of major cities have elementary school enrollments that are more than half Negro.

Racial isolation in city schools is caused by many factors. Isolation is rooted in racial discrimination that has been sanctioned and even encouraged by government at all levels. It is perpetuated by the effects of past segregation; reinforced by demographic, fiscal, and educational changes taking place in urban areas; and it is compounded by the policies and practices of urban school systems.

The racial contrasts between city and suburb are paralleled by contrasts in economic and social status. Suburban school districts are acquiring increasing numbers of children from well-educated and relatively affluent families. Almost all of them are white. Children — many of them Negro — from families of relatively low income and educational attainment are left behind in the city.

The discriminatory practices of the housing industry have been key factors in confining the poor and nonwhite to the cities. The practices and policies of government at all levels have contributed to the separation of racial and economic groups in cities and suburbs. For years, the Federal Government's housing policy was openly discriminatory and largely attuned to the suburban housing needs of relatively affluent, white Americans. Even now, Federal housing policy is inadequate to reverse the trend toward racial isolation in metropolitan areas.

The authority of local governments to decide on building permits, inspection standards, and the location of sewer and water facilities has been used in some instances to discourage private builders from providing housing on a nondiscriminatory basis. The power of eminent domain and suburban zoning and land-use requirements have been devices used to keep Negroes from settling in all-white communities.

Racial zoning ordinances, although declared unconstitutional in 1917, were enforced in some communities as late as the 1950s. Although racially restrictive covenants have not been judicially enforceable since 1948, they still are used, and the housing patterns they helped create continue to exist.

Increasing disparities in wealth have reinforced the separation between city and suburban populations. Because education is supported primarily by local property taxes, the adequacy of educational services has depended upon the ability of individual communities to raise tax money for education.

Cities are facing increasing financial burdens and demands for social services. Cities which formerly surpassed suburbs in educational expenditures are losing fiscal capacity. Suburban communities surrounding many central cities are spending more per pupil than the core cities. This widening gap between educational services in the suburbs and cities helps induce middle-class white families to settle in the suburbs.

State education aid often fails to equalize the disparity between suburban and central city public schools, and recently enacted Federal aid programs also are often insufficient to reverse the trend. The Elementary and Secondary Education Act of 1965 has helped close the gap but has not eliminated it.

Because of the high degree of residential segregation, Negro and white children typically attend separate schools in the central cities.

Residential segregation in the central cities has resulted in part from past actions of State and local governments such as the enactment of racial zoning ordinances and the judicial enforcement of racially restrictive covenants and from past and present practices of the housing industry. Federal housing programs aimed at meeting the needs of lower income families have been confined to central cities and typically have intensified and perpetuated residential segregation.

Private and parochial school enrollments are an additional factor in the increasing racial isolation in city school systems. Far more children in the cities than in the suburbs attend private schools, and almost all of them are white. This situation intensifies the concentration of Negro children in city public schools.

Although school segregation was sanctioned by law and official policy in Southern cities until 1954, there is a legacy of governmentally sanctioned school segregation in the North as well. State statutes authorizing racially separate public schools were on the books in New York until 1938, in Indiana until 1949, and in New Mexico and Wyoming until 1954. Although not sanctioned by law in other States, separate schools were maintained for Negroes in some communities in New Jersey, Illinois, and Ohio, as late as the 1940s and 1950s. In some cities such as New Rochelle, N.Y., and Hillsboro, Ohio, the courts found that school district lines have been gerrymandered for the purpose of racial segregation.

Geographical zoning is the common method of determining school attendance and the neighborhood school is the predominant attendance unit. When these are imposed upon the existing pattern of residential segregation, racial isolation in the schools is the inevitable result. In addition, the day-to-day operating decisions and the policies of local school boards — in matters involving the location of new school facilities, transfer policies, methods of relieving overcrowded schools, and the determination of the boundary lines of attendance areas — often have reinforced racial separation. In many instances there were alternatives that would have reduced racial concentrations.

RESULTS OF RACIALLY ISOLATED EDUCATION

The results of education for all students are influenced by a number of factors, including the students' home backgrounds, the quality of education provided in the schools they attend, and the social class background of their classmates. For Negro students, the racial composition of the schools also is important. Racially isolated schools tend to lower Negro students' achievement and restrict their aspirations. By contrast, Negro children who attend predominantly white schools more often score higher on achievement tests, and develop higher aspirations.

The educational and economic circumstances of a child's family long have been recognized as factors which determine the benefits he derives from his education. Differences in childrens' social and economic backgrounds are strongly related to their achievement in school. The elementary student from a disadvantaged home typically has a lower verbal achievement level than that of a more advantaged student.

The social class level of a student's classmates is another factor that determines the benefits he derives from education. From the early grades through high school, a student is directly influenced by his schoolmates. A disadvantaged student in school with a majority of more advantaged students performs at a higher level than a disadvantaged student in school with a majority of disadvantaged students.

This has a special significance for Negro students. Since there are fewer middle-class Negroes, any remedy for social class isolation would entail substantial racial desegregation.

There also is a strong relationship between the attitudes and achievement of Negro students and the racial composition of the schools which they attend. Relatively disadvantaged Negro students perform better when they are in class with a majority of similarly disadvantaged white students than when they are in a class with a majority of equally disadvantaged Negroes. When more advantaged Negro students are in school with similarly advantaged whites they achieve better than those in school with similarly advantaged Negroes. When disadvantaged Negro students are in class with more advantaged whites, their average performance is improved by as much as two grade levels.

There are differences in the quality of education available to Negro and white students in the Nation's metropolitan areas. For example, schools attended by white children often have more library volumes per student, advanced courses, and fewer pupils per teacher than schools attended by Negro children.

Negro students are more likely than whites to have teachers with lower verbal achievement levels, to have substitute teachers, and to have teachers who are dissatisfied with their school assignment. Do these differences in school qualities account for the apparent effect of racial isolation?

The quality of teaching has an important influence on students' achievement. Yet, Negro students in majority-white schools with poorer teachers generally achieve better than similar Negro students in majority-Negro schools with better teachers.

Racially isolated schools are regarded by the community as inferior institutions. Teachers and students in racially isolated schools recognize the stigma of inferiority which is attached to their schools and this has a negative effect on their attitudes and achievement.

The time spent in a given kind of classroom setting has an impact on student attitudes and achievement. The longer Negro students are in racially isolated schools, the greater the negative impact. The longer Negro students are in desegregated schools, the higher their performance.

The cumulative effects of education extend to adult life and account in part for differences in income and occupation. Negro adults who attended desegregated schools are more likely to be holding white collar jobs and to be earning more than otherwise similarly situated Negroes who attended racially isolated schools.

Racial isolation in the schools also fosters attitudes and behavior that perpetuate isolation in other areas of American life. Negro adults who attended racially isolated schools are more likely to develop attitudes that further alienate them from whites. Negro adults who attended racially isolated schools are more likely to have lower self-esteem and to accept the assignment of inferior status.

Attendance by whites at racially isolated schools also tends to reinforce the very attitudes that assign inferior status to Negroes. White adults who attended all-white schools are more apt than other whites to regard Negro institutions as inferior and to resist measures designed to overcome discrimination against Negroes.

REMEDY

There is no general agreement among educators and concerned citizens on the best way to remedy the academic disadvantage of Negro school-children. School systems generally have taken one of two basic approaches: the institution of compensatory education programs in majority-Negro schools, or school desegregation. There has been controversy and disagreement over both approaches.

Compensatory education programs which seek to improve the quality of education for disadvantaged children are often predicated on the assumption that deficiencies in a child's background are the main deterrent to learning. Many educators believe that the environment of poverty, the lack of cultural stimulation in the home, and the lack of motivation to learn, account for a child's failure to achieve in school.

There are four basic types of programs which have been designed to correct these deficiencies. Remedial instruction provides extra work in academic skills; cultural enrichment programs provide children with experiences normally beyond their reach, such as trips to museums; some programs seek to raise the expectations of teachers and students to overcome negative attitudes which impede learning; and preschool programs seek to provide training in verbal skills and cultural enrichment so that disadvantaged children may enter school more nearly able to compete with advantaged children.

Compensatory programs most often are found in predominantly Negro schools. In 12 city school systems surveyed by the Commission, more than two-thirds of the elementary schools with compensatory programs were majority-Negro. Allocations to city schools under Title I of the 1965 Elementary and Secondary Education Act, the largest single source of funds for compensatory education programs, tend to reinforce this pattern.

The Commission reviewed some of the better known compensatory education programs in majority-Negro schools that have served as prototypes for many others. Without evaluating the intrinsic merits or effectiveness of compensatory education, the Commission weighed only the measurable results of such programs upon the academic performance of Negro children. Some major programs, particularly the preschool programs, could not be evaluated because they have been instituted too recently.

Compensatory education programs such as Higher Horizons in New York City, and others, sometimes showed initial improvement in the test scores during the first years. But the gains were not sustained, and when children in the programs were compared with similarly disadvantaged children who had received no compensatory education, the two groups showed no significant or consistent difference in academic achievement.

The performance of Negro students who participated in compensatory education programs in majority-Negro schools was compared with that of similarly situated Negro students attending majority-white schools not offering such programs. Programs were compared in Syracuse, N.Y., Berkeley, Calif., Seattle, Wash., and Philadelphia, Pa. The results of test scores showed that the Negro children attending majority-white schools made better progress than those who attended majority-Negro schools with the compensatory programs.

The Commission's analysis does not suggest that compensatory education is incapable of remedying the effects of poverty on the academic achievement of individual children. There is little question that school programs involving expenditures for cultural enrichment, better teaching, and other needed educational services can be helpful to disadvantaged children. However, the compensatory programs reviewed by the Commission appeared to suffer from the defect inherent in attempting to solve problems stemming in part from racial and social class isolation in schools which themselves were isolated by race and social class.

In reviewing efforts to remedy educational disadvantage through desegregation the Commission found that the effectiveness of any school desegregation technique depends in part upon 1. the Negro proportion of the school population, and 2. the size of the city. The greater the Negro proportion of the school population, the more extensive will be the changes necessary to accomplish desegregation. Cities with relatively small areas of high-density Negro populations may find it easier to desegregate by such devices as strategic site selection, redistricting, or the enlargement of attendance areas.

Using a variety of techniques, with the common element being the enlargement of attendance zones, a number of small communities have desegregated their schools.

Princeton, N.J., Greenburg, N.Y. and Coatesville, Pa. have completely desegregated their elementary schools by pairing, a device which involves merging the attendance areas of two or more schools serving the same grades. Once paired, each school serves different grade levels.

The central school technique has been employed by the school systems in Englewood, N.J., Teaneck, N.J., and Berkeley, Calif. Under this plan certain schools are used to serve all children of a single grade in the city and the school's student body becomes representative of the population of the entire city. Other cities have desegregated their schools by enlarging attendance zones through the closing of a racially imbalanced school and assigning its students to other school districts.

Even though much remains to be done to completely abolish racial isolation in some of these smaller cities, educators there reported that the desegregation plans in most instances appear to have won acceptance by parents and civic groups. No evidence was found in the cities studied that white parents had withdrawn their children from the schools in any significant numbers.

Open enrollment plans sometimes have been used in an effort to relieve racial imbalance. Experience in some cities has shown, however, that while some Negro families take advantage of such a plan, others do not. Also, open enrollment often does not result in significant desegregation because it often is limited by the number of seats available in underutilized white schools. Racial isolation fosters negative attitudes toward desegregation for Negroes as well as whites. Also, some Negro parents do not participate in open enrollment because they are reluctant to have their children assume the role of pioneers and also because they may resent being asked to assume the entire burden of school desegregation themselves. Open enrollment places the responsibility for desegregation on individual parents rather than on the coordinated efforts of school officials. Also, it does not improve racial balance at majority-Negro schools.

The strategic use of site selection as a device to relieve racial imbalance also has limitations. The construction of a school on the periphery of a Negro ghetto, for example, may not guarantee stable desegregation because it is these very areas which experience rapid racial turnover.

The Nation's larger cities have not been as successful in desegregating their schools. The obstacles to desegregation are greater, and some educators have pointed out that workable solutions can best be achieved on a metropolitan basis. Programs which place Negro youngsters from majority-Negro city schools in neighboring suburban schools have potential for relieving racial imbalance in the central city schools. Even though they presently involve only small numbers of Negro children, such programs are operating successfully in Rochester, N.Y., Boston, Mass., and Hartford, Conn.

The Commission found that when local and State school officials exerted vigorous leadership, desegregation was more successful. In addition, school officials reported that the maintenance and improvement of educational standards and the provision of remedial assistance were critical factors in effective school desegregation. School authorities also found that it was often important to take steps to avoid or reduce racial tensions in schools.

White parents often fear that their children will suffer educational harm as a result of desegregation. But the Commission found that the performance of white students in desegregated classes was no different from the performance of similar white students in all-white classes. Indeed, many school administrators in communities such as White Plains, N.Y., Teaneck, N.J., and Berkeley, Calif., reported that desegregation was desirable for both white and Negro students.

The Commission examined many promising plans for desegregating schools and improving the quality of education in the Nation's larger cities and metropolitan areas. The plans contemplate giving more attention to the individual needs of all students in schools which would serve broad segments of the community. All of the proposals incorporate the view that only a combination of school desegregation and improved educational quality can provide equality of educational opportunity in urban areas. The proposals studied by the Commission were based upon the view that the schools can be desegregated and the quality of education improved best if attendance zones are expanded and school resources are consolidated.

Proposals for supplementary centers or magnet schools would establish specialized educational programs either in existing schools or in new facilities. Such special schools would serve children from broad attendance areas. The students still would attend their neighborhood schools but would spend part of their time at the special schools. Plans of this type are being developed in Mt. Vernon, N.Y., Cleveland, Ohio, Philadelphia, Pa., and Los Angeles, Calif.

The education complex involves the grouping of existing schools, and consolidating their attendance zones, to serve a heterogeneous student population. Schools in the group would be close enough together to allow the sharing of more specialized personnel and facilities than is now possible. This type of plan has been developed for New York City.

The education park is similar to the education complex. An education park, however, would be a new facility, consolidating a range of grade levels on a single campus site. One education park plan, appropriate for smaller cities, would assemble on one campus all school facilities for all students in the city. Another, appropriate for larger cities, would assemble on a single campus all school facilities for a particular level, such as all middle schools or all secondary schools. Other plans for larger cities contemplate several parks of comparable size, each serving a segment of the city or metropolitan area. Cities which are developing plans for education parks include Syracuse, N.Y., East Orange, N.J., Berkeley, Calif., New York, N.Y., Pittsburgh, Pa., Albuquerque, N.M., and St. Paul, Minn.

Proposals to build such large schools have understandably raised questions about the impact of size upon educational quality.

Many educators say, however, that education parks will enable teachers to devote more time to the individual needs of children. They suggest, for example, there will be numerous possibilities for individualized instruction through nongraded classes and team teaching. The larger teaching staffs of education parks will provide more specialists and teachers with more diverse training and skills to meet the particular needs of a greater number of children. Education parks also will permit technological innovations such as computer aids which are not economical in smaller schools. Educators who have examined the quality of education as it concerns education parks agree that the parks may make possible new approaches to teaching and learning, thereby resulting in new, superior educational programs and methods of instruction that are not available now.

Far from imposing uniformity, properly planned education parks will afford special opportunities for teachers because there will be greater opportunities for interaction among teachers now isolated in small schools with colleagues with the same skills. Bringing together teachers with similar training might allow them more freedom in developing specialized subject matter skills. The education park also could provide a laboratory for student teachers where they would have the opportunity to observe a greater variety of teaching styles and ties with universities would facilitate inservice training for professional teachers.

A major capital investment obviously would be necessary for the construction of large new schools. Estimates vary, but a review of existing proposals suggests that the capital costs would range from an amount roughly equal to the cost of regular classrooms to about twice that amount.

The transportation of students to education parks and other new facilities is another matter of concern to educators and others. Yet it should be noted that more than 40 percent of the Nation's public school children ride buses to school. It is estimated that 15 to 30 percent of the public school enrollment in the Nation's largest cities already rides public transportation to school.

Thus, although many would argue that a wrong which we as a Nation have inflicted upon Negro children must be righted even if it required real sacrifice, it is not necessary to face this dilemma. The goals of providing equal educational opportunity for Negro Americans and quality education for all children are consistent and the measures which will produce both in many respects are identical. The only sacrifice required is that of our resources and energies in securing these goals.

ROLE OF THE LAW

The courts have indicated that purposeful school segregation is unconstitutional even where it is less than complete and even when it is accomplished by inaction rather than by action. The Supreme Court has not ruled on the issue of whether school segregation not resulting from purposeful discrimination by school authorities is unconstitutional. The lower Federal courts and the State courts are divided on the issue. The courts, however, have upheld State and local remedial measures against the contention of white parents that it is unconstitutional to take race into account in assigning students to schools.

Thus, the results of most judicial decisions to date has been to leave the question of remedying racial imbalance to the legislative and executive branches of the Federal and State Governments. Only a small number of States — Massachusetts, New York, New Jersey, and California — have taken steps to require school authorities to take corrective action.

Federal action therefore is necessary. Since appropriate remedies may require expenditures of substantial sums of money, particularly where school construction may be involved, Congress, with its power to appropriate funds and to provide Federal financial assistance, is far better equipped than the courts to provide effective relief.

There is no clear Federal statutory authority dictating the imposition of sanctions if the States or local school authorities fail to take corrective action. The Constitution, however, confers upon Congress the power to require the elimination of racial isolation in the public schools.

Section 1 of the 14th amendment prohibits any State from denying to any person within its jurisdiction equal protection of the laws. Section 5 gives

Congress the power to enforce the amendment by "appropriate legislation." Recent Supreme Court decisions make it clear that section 5 is an affirmative grant which authorizes Congress to determine what legislation is needed to further the aims of the amendment. The decisions also establish that Congress may legislate not only to correct denials of equal protection but also to forestall conditions which may pose a danger of such denial.

Whether or not racial isolation itself constitutes a denial of equal protection, Congress may secure equal educational opportunity by eliminating the conditions which render the education received by most Negroes inferior to that afforded most white children. Such conditions involve, in part, the harmful effects upon attitudes and achievement which racial and social class isolation have on Negro students. Corrective congressional action also may be seen as a means of enabling Negroes, who generally are poorer than whites, attend schools of lower quality and exercise less influence on school boards, to obtain educational facilities equal to those obtained by white persons.

There are ample grounds, moreover, for congressional determination that racial imbalance contravenes the equal protection clause. "State action" to which the 14th amendment speaks, is clearly involved since public officials select school sites, define attendance areas, and assign Negroes to schools in which they are racially isolated. The resulting harm to Negro children involves a denial of equal protection of the laws.

Although the holding in *Brown v. Board of Education* was confined to school segregation compelled or expressly permitted by law, the rationale of the *Brown* opinion was that "public education . . . where the State has undertaken to provide it, is a right which must be made available to all on equal terms," and that segregated education is unequal education. Just as segregation imposed by law was held in *Brown v. Board of Education* to create feelings of inferiority among Negro students affecting their motivation and ability to learn, so there is evidence that adventitious segregation is accompanied by a stigma which has comparable effects.

Congress may require the States to provide solutions which will involve the joint education of suburban and central city children — either through reorganization of school districts or cooperative arrangements among school districts — where racial isolation cannot be corrected within the limits of the central city. The equal protection clause speaks to the State, and school districts are creatures of the State. A State cannot avoid its constitutional obligation to afford its school children equal protection of the laws by pointing to the distribution of power between itself and its subdivisions — a distribution which the State itself has created. As a court once said in another contest: "If the rule were otherwise, the great guarantee of the equal protection clause would be meaningless."

In legislating to implement the 14th amendment, Congress need not limit itself to suspending offensive State legislation but, like the courts, may require States to take affirmative steps to secure equal rights. Inconsistent State statutes or constitutional provisions, of course, must yield to the lawful acts of Congress under the supremacy clause of the Constitution.

There is ample basis to conclude, therefore, that Congress can enact the laws necessary to eliminate racial isolation and to secure to Negroes equality of opportunity in the public schools.

CONCLUSION

The central truth which emerges from this report and from all of the Commission's investigations is simply this: Negro children suffer serious harm when their education takes place in public schools which are racially segregated, whatever the source of such segregation may be.

Negro children who attend predominantly Negro schools do not achieve as well as other children, Negro and white. Their aspirations are more restricted than those of other children and they do not have as much confidence that they can influence their own futures. When they become adults, they are less likely to participate in the mainstream of American society, and more likely to fear, dislike, and avoid white Americans. The conclusion drawn by the U. S. Supreme Court about the impact upon children of segregation compelled by law — that it "affects their hearts and minds in ways unlikely ever to be undone" — applies to segregation not compelled by law.

The major source of the harm which racial isolation inflicts upon Negro children is not difficult to discover. It lies in the attitudes which such segregation generates in children and the effect these attitudes have upon motivation to learn and achievement. Negro children believe that their schools are stigmatized and regarded as inferior by the community as a whole. Their belief is shared by their parents and by their teachers. And their belief is founded in fact.

Isolation of Negroes in the schools has a significance different from the meaning that religious or ethnic separation may have had for other minority groups because the history of Negroes in the United States has been different from the history of all other minority groups. Negroes in this country were first enslaved, later segregated by law, and now are segregated and discriminated against by a combination of governmental and private action. They do not reside today in ghettos as the result of an exercise of free choice and the attendance of their children in racially isolated schools is not an accident of fate wholly unconnected with deliberate segregation and other forms of discrimination. In the light of this history, the feelings of stigma generated in Negro children by attendance at racially isolated schools are realistic and cannot easily be overcome.

Many Americans have sensed the grave injustice that racial isolation inflicts upon Negro children. But the need for a remedy sufficient to meet the injustice perceived has been obscured by the existence of other factors that contribute to educational disadvantage.

Thus, it is said with truth that Negro children often are handicapped in school because they come from poor and ill-educated families. But the conclusion drawn by a few pessimistic educators that the school cannot be expected to deal with these deficits does injustice both to the children involved and to American education. For the very purpose of American public education from Jefferson's time to the present has been to help youngsters surmount the barriers of poverty and limited backgrounds to enable them to develop their talents and to participate fully in society. The tributes accorded to public education stem largely from the fact that it has served this role so successfully for so many Americans — Negroes as well as whites. This record affords ample grounds for hope that education can meet today's challenge of preparing Negro children to participate in American society. Counsels of despair will be in order only if, after having done everything to create the conditions for success, we have failed.

It also is said with truth that disadvantaged Negro youngsters are in need of special attention, smaller classes, a better quality of instruction, and teachers better prepared to understand and set high standards for them. But the suggestion that this is all that is needed finds little support in our experience to date with efforts to provide compensatory education. The weakest link in these efforts appears to be those programs which attempt to instill in a child feelings of personal worth and dignity in an environment in which he is surrounded by visible evidence which seems to deny his value as a person. This does not appear to be a problem which will yield easily to additional infusions of money. More funds clearly are required and investments in programs that will improve teaching and permit more attention to the individual needs of students undoubtedly will benefit many children. The evidence suggests, however, that the better services additional funds will provide will not be fully effective in a racially isolated environment, but only in a setting which supports the teacher's effort to help each child to understand that he is a valuable person who can succeed.

Finally, it is held often that the problem of educational disadvantage is one of class, not race. And it is true that an important key to providing good education for disadvantaged youngsters lies in affording them the opportunity to attend school with children who, by reason of their parents' education and income, have a genuine headstart. Children benefit from association in schools with others more advantaged than they and from a classroom environment which permits the establishment of high standards toward which they must strive. But, as a practical matter, the relatively small number of middle-class Negro children in the public schools means that it will be possible to provide social class integration only by providing racial integration. And even if social class integration could be accomplished without racial integration, the remedy would be partial and inadequate, for children would still be attending schools stigmatized because of race.

Thus, the complexity of the problem of educational disadvantage should not be allowed to obscure the central fact — that racial isolation is the heart of the matter and that enduring solutions will not be possible until we deal with it.

BARRIERS TO REMEDY

More fundamental perhaps than the difficulties of understanding the problem of racial isolation is the belief held by many Americans that solutions will require both change and sacrifice.

Change certainly will be required. As our cities have grown, increasing distances — physical and psychological — have separated the affluent majority from disadvantaged minorities. We have followed practices which exclude racial and economic minorities from large areas of the city and we have created structures, such as our method of financing education, which, by providing more attractive facilities with less tax effort, tend to attract the affluent to the very areas from which minorities are excluded. And the fact of racial and economical separation itself has generated attitudes which make integration increasingly difficult. The lines of separation are now well established, self-perpetuating, and very difficult to reverse.

Because of the difficulties of effecting change, it has been tempting to think in terms of remedies which will require a minimum of effort on the part of the schools and least disrupt the educational *status quo*. So it has been suggested that the problem of securing equal educational opportunity is really a problem of housing, and that if discrimination in housing can be eliminated it will be possible to desegregate the schools without changing existing school patterns. But such a solution would require vast changes in an area where resistance to change is most entrenched. Laws designed to secure an open market in housing are needed now, but the attitudes fostered in segregated schools and neighborhoods make it unlikely that such legislation will be fully effective for years. To make integrated education dependent upon open housing is to consign at least another generation of children to racially isolated schools and to lengthen the time that will be required to overcome housing discrimination.

Similarly, it has been suggested that if integration were to be sought only at the high school level, it would be accomplished with relative ease and without unduly disturbing existing attendance patterns. But the hard fact is that attitudes toward learning are formed during a child's early years, and it is in this period that the educational process has its greatest impact, positive or negative. Remedies that are not instituted until children reach high school are those least likely to be successful.

Thus, it appears that meaningful remedy will require an alteration of the *status quo*; but in a changing world, change is hardly to be resisted for its own sake, particularly when it is designed to create a more just society. A more substantial question for many white American parents is whether what is required to right a wrong this Nation has inflicted upon Negro children will impair the interests of their children.

It is relevant to begin such an inquiry by asking whether the racially isolated education most white children receive now causes them any injury. There is evidence in this report which suggests that children educated in all-white institutions are more likely than others to develop racial fears and prejudices based upon lack of contact and information. Although it cannot be documented in traditional ways, we believe that white children are deprived of something of value when they grow up in isolation from children of other races, when their self-esteem and assurance may rest in part upon false notions of racial superiority, when they are not prepared by their school experience to participate fully in a world rich in human diversity. These losses, although not as tangible as those which racial isolation inflicts upon Negro youngsters, are real enough to deserve the attention of parents concerned about their children's developments.

Unfortunately, they do not seem as real to many parents as the feared consequences of integration. The fears most frequently articulated are that integration will destroy the concept of neighborhood schools and will require busing of children over long distances. The values of neighborhood and proximity, of course, are relative. In today's world, all of us, adults and children, are residents of many neighborhoods and communities, large and small. We do not hesitate to bus our children long distances in rural areas, or, in cities, to private schools or to other schools offering special advantages. Thus, the issue is not whether small neighborhood schools are good or busing bad, *per se*, but whether the interests of our children will be served or impaired by particular proposals or solutions. Will our children be held back by being placed in classes with children of other, less advantaged backgrounds? Will the education provided at the end of a trip be as good as, or better than, the education our children presently receive?

Most often these issues have been debated in the context of the inner-city, in circumstances which have made it easy for fears to be magnified and exaggerated. The image conjured up in the minds of many parents has been one in which their children are cross-bused to ghetto schools and taught in classrooms populated by large numbers of disadvantaged children and lacking in essential services. Moreover, ethnic and class tensions have been aroused by proposals for partial solutions which appear to place more responsibilities upon less affluent whites than upon those who are better off.

The fundamental answer to these fears is that solutions sought must be those that will not only remedy injustice, but improve the quality of education for all children. The Commission has been convinced, both by practical demonstrations and by sound proposals, that such solutions are available.

While public attention has been focused upon the more dramatic controversies, many small cities and suburban communities in the Nation have quietly integrated their schools. By a variety of techniques these communities have achieved their goal by substituting community schools for those serving smaller neighborhoods. In most cases the issue has been approached calmly and compassionately, with a view toward improving the quality of education for all children. Steps have been taken to maintain and improve educational standards, to avoid the possibility of interracial frictions, and to provide remedial services for children who need them. And, in most cases, the conclusion has been that advantaged children have not suffered from educational exposure to others not as well off, and that the results have been of benefit to all children, white and Negro alike.

In larger cities, while efforts to achieve integration have been fragmentary and in many cases more recent, the results generally have been the same. The most recent efforts, admittedly embryonic, involving cooperation between suburban and city school districts in metropolitan areas have met with favorable reactions from those involved. Negro parents have reported that the values of better education have not been diminished by the bus trips necessary to obtain it. White parents have reported that their children have benefited from the experience. And administrators and teachers have described the educational results as positive.

Fears of the unknown, therefore, are being refuted by practical experience. Efforts to achieve integration by establishing schools serving a wider community clearly will be more difficult and costly in large cities than in smaller cities and suburban communities, but there is every indication that they will yield beneficial results.

Equally as important, the establishment of schools serving larger student populations is consistent with what leading educators believe is necessary to improve the quality of education for all Americans. Education which meets the needs of a technological society requires costly equipment which cannot be provided economically in schools which serve small numbers of students. Further, educators have concluded that larger facilities will provide more scope for innovation and individual initiative in the development of curriculum and teaching techniques. Efforts to stimulate such initiative in small school units have been frustrated by lack of available resources.

At the same time, educators have concluded that in larger facilities techniques would be available to teachers which would permit them to give more attention to the individual needs of children. It has been pointed out, for example, that the present rigid system of classifying and teaching students by grades, with the limited options of promoting or keeping a child back, does not permit the full development of each individual child's abilities. The availability of more flexible classroom space would make possible the utilization of nongraded classes and team teaching in ways which would allow for greater attention to the individual needs and capabilities of students. Although the development of computer technology is at a very early stage, there is evidence to suggest that it, too, may become a valuable aid to teachers in meeting the needs of individual children. Thus, the development of new schools serving larger populations would make possible the use of techniques and instruments that would improve the quality of education for all students. They hold forth the promise that means can be devised to assure that the advancement of a child is not held back by the capabilities of any of his classmates — advantaged or disadvantaged.

Thus, although many would argue that a wrong which we as a Nation have inflicted upon Negro children must be righted even if it required real sacrifice, it is not necessary to face this dilemma. The goals of providing equal educational opportunity for Negro Americans and quality of education for all children are consistent and the measures which will produce both in many respects are identical. The only sacrifice required is that of our resources and energies in securing these goals.

The Commission has approached the question of remedy with the belief that it would be unwise, if not impossible, to prescribe uniform solutions for the Nation. We believe that there is an evil which must be corrected. We believe that the Federal Government has the authority, the responsibility, and the means to assure that it is corrected. We have satisfied ourselves that remedies are available which will provide better education for all American children and we believe that there are people in all sections of the Nation with enough wisdom and ingenuity to devise solutions appropriate to the particular needs of each area. The remaining question is whether this Nation retains the will to secure equal justice and to build a better society for all citizens. The Commission issues this report in the knowledge that this Nation has dedicated itself to great tasks before, and with the faith that it is prepared to do so again.

RECOMMENDATIONS

This report describes conditions that result in injustices to children and require immediate attention and action. The responsibility for corrective action rests with government at all levels and with citizens and organizations through-out the Nation. We must commit ourselves as a Nation to the establishment of equal educational opportunity of high quality for all children. As an important means of fulfilling this national goal, the Commission recommends that the President and the Congress give immediate and urgent consideration to new legislation for the purpose of removing present racial imbalances from our public schools, thus to eliminate the dire effects of racial isolation which this report describes, and at long last, providing real equality of educational opportunity by integrating presently deprived American children of all races into a totally improved public educational system.

Without attempting to outline needed legislation in great detail, our study of the problem convinces the Commission that new legislation must embody the following essential principles:

1. Congress should establish a uniform standard providing for the elimination of racial isolation in the schools. Since large numbers of Negro children suffer harmful effects that are attributable in part to the racial composition of schools they attend, legislation should provide for the elimination of schools in which such harm generally occurs. No standard of general applicability will fit every case precisely; some schools with a large proportion of Negro students may not in fact produce harmful effects while others with a smaller proportion may

be in schools in which students are disadvantaged because of their race. But the alternative to establishing such a standard is to require a time-consuming and ineffective effort to determine on a case-by-case basis the schools in which harm occurs. As it has in analogous situations, Congress should deal with this problem by establishing reasonable and practical standards which will correct the injustice without intruding unnecessarily into areas where no corrective action is needed.

In prescribing a reasonable standard, there is much to commend the criterion already adopted by the legislature in Massachusetts and the Commissioner of Education of New York, defining as racially imbalanced, schools in which Negro pupils constitute more than 50 percent of the total enrollment. It was found in the report that when Negro students in schools with more than 50 percent Negro enrollment were compared with similarly situated Negro students in schools with a majority-white enrollment, there were significant differences in attitude and performance. It is the schools that have a majority-Negro enrollment that tend to be regarded and treated by the community as segregated and inferior schools. Although there are many factors involved, the racial composition of schools that are majority-Negro in enrollment tends to be less stable than that of majority-white schools and to be subject to more rapid change.

Similar argument might be advanced for a standard which would deviate slightly from a 50 percent criterion, but a standard set significantly higher would not be adequate to deal with the problem and probably would not result in lasting solutions.

2. Congress should vest in each of the 50 States responsibility for meeting the standard it establishes and should allow the States maximum flexibility in devising appropriate remedies. It also should provide financial and technical assistance to the States in planning such remedies. It would be unwise for the Federal Government to attempt to prescribe any single solution or set of solutions for the entire Nation. There is a broad range of techniques which are capable of achieving education of high quality in integrated public schools. Each State should be free to adopt solutions best suited to the particular needs of its individual communities.

At the same time it is clear that the responsibility should be placed upon the States rather than the individual school districts. The States, and not individual communities alone, have the capacity to develop and implement plans adequate to the objective. The States have assumed the responsibility for providing public education for all of their citizens and for establishing the basic conditions under which it is offered. Responsibility for achieving the goal of high-quality integrated education can and should be placed upon the States under terms which afford broad scope for local initiative. But in many jurisdictions, particularly the major cities, solutions are not possible without the cooperation of neighboring communities. The States possess the authority and the means for securing cooperation, by consolidating or reorganizing school districts or by providing for appropriate joint arrangements between school districts. To help the States in devising appropriate remedies, the Federal Government should provide technical and financial assistance.

3. The legislation should include programs of substantial financial assistance to provide for construction of new facilities and improvement in the quality of education in all schools. In many cases, particularly in the major cities, integrating the public schools will require the construction of new facilities designed both to serve a larger student population and to be accessible to all children in the area to be served. Substantial Federal assistance is needed to supplement the resources of States and localities in building new schools of this kind and providing higher quality education for all children. Federal assistance also can be helpful in encouraging cooperative arrangements between States which provide education services to the same metropolitan area and between separate school districts in a metropolitan area. In addition, Federal financial assistance now available under programs such as said for mass transportation and community facilities should be utilized in ways which will advance the goal of integration.

Regardless of whether the achievement of integration requires new facilities, Federal financial assistance is needed for programs to improve the quality of education. States and localities should have broad discretion to develop programs best suited to their needs. Programs that are among the most promising involve steps — such as the reduction of pupil-teacher ratios, the establishment of ungraded classes and team teaching, and the introduction of specialized remedial instruction — which enable teachers to give more attention to the individual needs of children. Funds also could be used for purposes such as assisting the training of teachers, developing new educational techniques, and improving curriculum.

4. Congress should provide for adequate time in which to accomplish the objectives of the legislation. It is clear that equal opportunity in education cannot be achieved overnight. Particularly in the large cities where problems of providing equal educational opportunity have seemed so intractable, time will be necessary for such matters as educational and physical planning, assembling and acquiring land, and building new facilities. However, since the problem is urgent a prompt start must be made toward finding solutions, progress must be continuous and substantial, and there must be some assurance that the job will be completed as quickly as possible. The time has come to put less emphasis on "deliberate" and more on "speed."

The goals of equal educational opportunity and equal housing opportunity are inseparable. Progress toward the achievement of one goal necessarily will facilitate achievement of the other. Failure to make progress toward the achievement of either goal will handicap efforts to achieve the other. The Commission recommends, therefore, that the President and Congress give consideration to legislation which will:

5. Prohibit discrimination in the sale or rental of housing, and

6. Expand programs of Federal assistance designed to increase the supply of

housing throughout metropolitan areas within the means of low- and moderate-income families. Additional funds should be provided for programs such as the rent supplement program and FHA 221(d)(3), and these two programs should be amended to permit private enterprise to participate in them free from the special veto power now held by local governments under present Federal statutes.

In addition, the Commission recommends that the Department of Housing and Urban Development:

7. Require as a condition for approval of applications for low- and moderate-income housing projects that the sites will be selected and the projects planned in a nondiscriminatory manner that will contribute to reducing residential racial concentrations and eliminating racial isolation in the schools.

8. Require as a condition for approval of urban renewal projects that relocation will be planned in a nondiscriminatory manner that will contribute to reducing residential racial concentrations and eliminating racial isolation in the schools.

SUPPLEMENTARY STATEMENT

The worsening crisis in our cities is essentially a human crisis. This is a truth we tend to forget because the crisis is so often expressed in abstractions — dwindling tax revenues, housing trends, unemployment rates, statistics on air pollution, or crime and delinquency. Even in this report, which deals with a most fundamental aspect of our current urban dilemma — the crisis in public education — we have had to describe what has been happening in terms of achievement scores, graphs, and figures. But it must never be forgotten that what we have really been looking at is the brutal and unnecessary damage to human lives.

For it is unnecessary at this point in a Nation as affluent as ours that hundreds of thousands of poor children, a disproportionate number of them Negro children, should be isolated in inadequately staffed and equipped slum schools — schools which the community has stigmatized as inferior. And, at the same time, on the other side of the Great Divide which we have too long permitted in public education, the advantaged children — most of them white — attend schools in the suburbs and outlying residential sections of our cities which have a disproportionate share of the best teachers, which offer the most advanced curricula and facilities, and which provide individualized attention of a kind and quality seldom available to the minority poor.

Segregation is a term at which many northerners wince, but for generations of poor Negroes in the North, segregation has been a reality which has hardly been mitigated by legalistic distinctions between *de facto* and *de jure*. Neither the presence of nondiscrimination statutes nor the absence of overtly discriminatory laws has been very effective so far in erasing the barriers between Negro and white, advantaged and disadvantaged, educated and miseducated. Only if this is understood can we also understand why today there are Negro Americans who are saying, in effect: Since we seem to be tending toward public school systems offering a superior quality of education in middle-class and white schools and inferior quality in schools for poor Negro children, why not accept the separation as inevitable and concentrate on attemting to provide superior education in the schools attended by the Negro poor? This question is likely to have a more convincing ring than it otherwise would have because it comes at a time when education is only one of several pressing priorities which command the country's attention, and when there is doubt about the strength of this Nation's commitment to the social changes which simple justice and our national principles demand. To the extent that the civil rights movement of the past several years has produced an impatience with the *status quo*, and upsurge of self-esteem, and a new assertion of dignity and identity among Negro citizens, it is healthy and long overdue. However, there is little that is healthy and much that is potentially self-defeating in the emotionalism and racial bias that seem to motivate a small but vocal minority among those who now argue for "separate-but-equal" school systems.

It is certainly true that in the past a good many Negroes have emerged from segregated schools to earn advanced degrees, to acquire comfortable incomes, and to register achievements which are too seldom recorded in the books with which most American schoolchildren are supplied. But the fact that the barriers imposed by segregation have been overcome by some of the more talented, the more determined, and the more fortunate, would hardly seem to recommend it to thousands of disadvantaged youngsters for whom segregation has already demonstrated its capacity to cripple rather than to challenge. Quite aside from being poor democracy, it would seem to be poor economy, and criminally poor educational policy, to continue to isolate disadvantaged children by race and class when it is the interaction with advantaged children which appears to be the single most effective factor in narrowing the learning gap.

Let us be clear on the issues. The question is not whether in theory or in the abstract Negro schools can be as good as white schools. In a society free from prejudice in which Negroes were full and equal participants, the answer would clearly be "Yes." But we are forced, rather, to ask the harder question, whether in our present society, where Negroes are a minority which has been discriminated against, Negro children can prepare themselves to participate effectively in society if they grow up and go to school in isolation from the majority group. We must also ask whether we can cure the disease of prejudice and prepare all children for life in a multiracial world if white children grow up and go to school in isolation from Negroes.

We are convinced that a great deal more, not less, integration is the wisest course to follow if we are really concerned about the future of American children of all races and classes. As the principal value-bearing institution which at one time or another touches everyone in our society, the school is crucial in determining what kind of country this is to be. If in the future the adults in our society who make decisions about who gets a job, who lives down the block, or the essential worth of another person are to be less likely to make these decisions on the basis of race or class, the present cycle must be broken in classrooms which provide better education than ever, and in which children of diverse backgrounds can come to know one another. None of the financial costs or the administrative adjustments necessary to bring about integrated quality education will be as costly to the quality of American life in the long run as the continuation of our present educational policies and practices. For we are now on a collision course which may produce within our borders two alienated and unequal nations confronting each other across a widening gulf created by a dual educational system based upon income and race. Our present school crisis is a human crisis, engendered and sustained in large part by the actions, the apathy, or the shortsightedness of public officials and private individuals. It can be resolved only by the commitment, the creative energies, and the combined resources of concerned Americans at every level of public and private life.

Commissioner Hesburgh concurs in this statement.

—Commissioner Frankie M. Freeman

SUPPLEMENTARY STATEMENT

Because of the national importance of the educational situation described in this report and the large number of students in private elementary and secondary educational institutions, it would seem most important to me, speaking as an individual member of this Commission, that those involved in all of the private elementary and secondary educational endeavors in this country study the full implications of this report and consider most seriously what their institutions might contribute to the ultimate solution of this pressing problem.

—Commissioner Theodore M. Hesburgh

chapter 8
experimental studies

REVIEW OF EVIDENCE RELATING TO EFFECTS OF DESEGREGATION ON THE INTELLECTUAL PERFORMANCE OF NEGROES

Irwin Katz

This is a review of evidence regarding the effects of educational desegregation on the scholastic achievement of Negroes. It focuses on the problem of identifying the important situational determinants of Negro performance in the racially mixed classroom. Only a few studies have dealt directly with this problem, so that much of the evidence to be surveyed is only inferential. Included are the following: reports on the academic progress of Negro children attending integrated schools, evidence on aspects of the minority child's experience in desegregation that presumably affect his motivation to learn, relevant research on the behavioral effects of psychological stress, and, finally, a series of experiments on Negro productivity in biracial settings.

Negro Americans. In this paper the term "Negro Americans" refers to a minority segment of the national population that is more or less distinguishable on the basis of skin color, hair texture, etc., and that occupies a subordinate position in American culture. The extent of subordination varies in different regions and localities, but usually includes some degree of restriction on educational and economic opportunities, as well as social exclusion by whites and an attribution by whites of intellectual inferiority. While the term "race" will be used for convenience, no meaning is intended other than that of distinctiveness of appearance and commonality of experience; the issue of whether there are consequential differences in the genetic endowment of

Negroes and whites will not be considered. Thus the present discussion should be more or less applicable to any American minority group whose status is similar to that of Negroes.

Desegregation. Educational desegregation is a politico-legal concept referring to the elimination of racial separation within school systems. As such it embraces a great variety of transitional situations having diverse effects upon the scholastic performance of Negro children. The meaning of desegregation has been broadened in recent years to include the reduction of racial clustering due to factors other than legal discrimination — i.e., de facto segregation. A number of recent court decisions in the North have ruled that "racial imbalance" in a school (a predominance of minority-group children) constitutes de facto segregation (United States Commission on Civil Rights, 1962a, 1962b). Also described as de facto segregation by various social scientists are the racially homogeneous classes often found in schools where children are grouped according to ability (Deutsch, 1963; Dodson, 1962; Tumin, 1963).

The present concern is mainly with instances of desegregation that are marked by a substantial increase in the proportion of white peers, or both white peers and adult authorities, in the immediate environment of the Negro student. (In the South integration with white classmates is usually also the occasion of initial contacts with white teachers, while in the North the proportion of white teachers may be high even in schools where Negro students predominate.) Almost invariably in this type of desegregation experience the minority group child is confronted with higher educational standards than prevail in segregated Negro schools (United States Commission on Civil Rights, 1962a, 1962b). Both aspects of the Negro's experience — change in the racial environment and exposure to relatively high academic standards — are likely to have important influences on his scholastic motivation.

DETERMINANTS OF NEGRO PERFORMANCE IN DESEGREGATION

Social threat. Social threat refers to a class of social stimulus events that tend to elicit anxious expectations that others will inflict harm or pain. One may assume that novel types of contact with white strangers possess a social-threat component for members of a subordinated minority group. The degree of threat should be a direct function of (a) the amount of evidence of white hostility (or the extent to which evidence of white friendliness is lacking) and (b) the amount of power possessed by whites in the contact situation, as shown by their numerical predominance, control of authority positions, etc. It seems likely that Negro children would be under some degree of social threat in a newly integrated classroom. Mere indifference on the part of white peers may frustrate their needs for companionship and approval, resulting in lowered self-esteem and the arousal of impulses to escape or aggress. In more extreme instances, verbal harassment and even physical hazing may elicit strong fear responses. These external threats are likely to distract the minority child from the task at hand, to the detriment of performance.

In addition, psychological theory suggests that the Negro's own covert reactions to social threat would constitute an important source of intellectual impairment. In discussing the effect of psychological stress on the learning of skills, Deese (1962) mentions distraction by the internal stimuli of autonomic activation, as well as disruption of task responses by neuromuscular and other components of the stress reaction. Mandler and Sarason (1962) and others call attention to the disruptive role of task-irrelevant defensive responses against anxiety. Spence (1958) and Taylor (1963) propose that anxiety, conceptualized as drive, increases intratask response competition. And according to Easterbrook (1959), emotion lowers efficiency on complex tasks by narrowing the range of cue utilization. Also relevant is Bovard's (1959) hypothesis of a specific psychological mechanism to account for the apparent lowering of the stress threshold under conditions of social isolation.

Another way in which social threat may impair performance is by causing Negro children to abandon efforts to excel in order not to arouse further resentment and hostility in white competitors. That is, the latter may possess what French and Raven (1960) refer to as "coercive power." When academic success is expected to instigate white reprisals, then any stimulus which arouses the motive to achieve should also generate anxiety, and defensive avoidance of such stimuli should be learned. This response pattern would not be wholly nonadaptive in a situation where a small number of Negro students stood relatively powerless against a prejudiced white majority — if one assumes that evidence of Negro intellectual competence might have an ego-deflating effect on these white students. The Group for the Advancement of Psychiatry (1957) has put the matter this way:

> A feeling of superior worth may be gained merely from the existence of a downgraded group. This leads to an unrealistic and unadaptive kind of self-appraisal based on invidious comparison rather than on solid personal growth and achievement . . . [p. 10].

Finally with regard to possible social threat emanating from a white teacher — given the prestige of the adult authority, any expression by a white teacher of dislike or devaluation, whether through harsh, indifferent, or patronizing behavior, should tend to have unfavorable effects on Negro performance similar to those just described, and perhaps of even greater intensity.

Social facilitation. When the minority newcomer in a desegregated school is accepted socially by his white classmates, his scholastic motivation should be influenced favorably. It was noted earlier that achievement standards tend to be higher in previously all-white schools than in Negro schools. From studies based on white subjects, it is apparent that individuals are responsive to the standards of those with whom they desire to associate (reviewed by Bass, 1961; French & Raven, 1960; Thibaut & Kelly, 1959). That Negro children want friendship with white age mates was shown by Horowitz (1936), Radke, Sutherland, and Rosenberg (1950), and Yarrow (1958). Another study, by Criswell (1939), suggests that Negro children in racially mixed classrooms accept white prestige but increasingly withdraw into their own group as a response to white rejection. Thus, if their desire for acceptance is not inhibited or destroyed by sustained unfriendliness from white children, Negro pupils should tend to adopt the scholastic norms of the high-status majority group. Experimental support for this supposition comes from Dittes and Kelley (1956), who found with white college students that private as well as public adherence to the attitudinal standards of a group were highest among persons who had experienced a fairly high degree of acceptance from the group, with a possibility of gaining even fuller acceptance, while those who received a low degree of acceptance showed little genuine adherence to group norms.

Friendliness and approval on the part of white teachers should be beneficial to Negro motivation by increasing the incentive strength of scholastic success. Assuming that white teachers have more prestige for the minority child than do Negro teachers, the prospect of winning their approval should be more attractive. Hence, when such approval can be expected as a reward for good performance, motivation should be favorably influenced.

Probability of success. When the minority child is placed in a school that has substantially higher scholastic standards than he knew previously, he may become discouraged and not try to succeed. This common sense proposition is derivable from Atkinson's (1958a) theory of the motivational determinants of risk taking and performance. For individuals in whom the tendency to approach success is stronger than the tendency to avoid failure, task motivation is assumed to be a joint function of the subjective probability of achieving success and the incentive value of success. From a postulated inverse relationship between the latter two variables (assuming external influences on incentive strength are held constant) he derives a hypothesis that the strength of motivation is at a maximum when the probability of success is .50, and diminishes as this probability approaches zero or unity. The hypothesis is supported by findings on arithmetic performance of white college students (Atkinson, 1958b), and white elementary-school children (Murstein & Collier, 1962), as well as on digit-symbol performance of white high-school students (Rosen, 1961). (In these studies, the effect occurred regardless of whether subjects had scored relatively high or low on a projective personality measure of the motive to approach success.) It follows that if the Negro newcomer perceives the standards of excellence in a desegregated school as being substantially higher than those he encountered previously, so that the likelihood of his attaining them seems low, his scholastic motivation will decline.

Failure threat. Failure threat is a class of stimulus events in an achievement situation which tend to elicit anxious expectations of harm or pain as a consequence of failure. High probability of failure does not by itself constitute failure threat — it is necessary also that the failure have a social meaning. Thus in

Atkinson's formulation, the negative incentive strength of failure varies inversely with the subjective probability of failure, so that fear of failure is most strongly aroused when the probability of failure is at an intermediate level. This leads to the paradoxical prediction that as the probability of failure increases beyond .50, fear of failure declines. The paradox is resolved when one recognizes that Atkinson's model deals only with that component of incentive strength that is determined by the apparent difficulty of the task. Sarason, Davidson, Lighthall, Waite, and Ruebush (1960) call attention to the important influence of anticipated disapproval by parents and teachers on the negative valence of failure. (While their primary interest is in test anxiety as a personality variable, their discussion seems applicable to the present problem of identifying situational determinants of fear of failure.) Presumably, the child's belief that his failure to meet prevailing standards of achievement will bring adult disapproval is relatively unaffected by his own perception of the difficulty of a given task. Hence, fear of disapproval should increase as it becomes more probable – i.e., as the subjective probability of failure increases. Sarason and his associates suggest that a high expectancy of failure arouses strong unconscious hostility against the adults from whom negative evaluation is foreseen. The hostility is turned inward against the self in the form of self-derogatory attitudes, which strengthen the expectation of failure and the desire to escape the situation. Distraction by these and other components of emotional conflict may cause a decrement in the child's performance.

ACADEMIC ACHIEVEMENT OF NEGROES IN DESEGREGATED SCHOOLS

There is a dearth of unequivocal information about Negro performance in desegregated schools. A number of factors have contributed to this situation.

1. Many desegregated school systems have a policy of racial non-classification, so that separate data for Negroes and whites are not available.

2. Where total elimination of legal segregation has occurred, it has usually been accompanied by vigorous efforts to raise educational standards in *all* schools; hence the effects of desegregation per se are confounded with the effects of improved teaching and facilities.

3. In several Southern states only small numbers of highly selected Negro pupils have been admitted to previously all-white schools, and since before-after comparisons of achievement are not usually presented, reports of "satisfactory" adjustment by these Negro children shed little light on the question of relative performance.

Taking the published information for what it is worth, most of it presents a favorable picture of Negro academic adjustment in racially mixed settings. Stallings (1959) has reported on the results of achievement testing in the Louisville school system in 1955-56, the year prior to total elimination of legal segregation, and again 2 years later. Gains were found in the median scores of all pupils for the grades tested, with Negroes showing greater improvement than whites. The report gave no indication of whether the gains for Negroes were related to amount of actual change in the racial composition of schools. Indeed, Stallings stated, "The gains were greater where Negro pupils remained by choice with Negro teachers." A later survey on Louisville by Knowles (1962) indicated that Negro teachers had not been assigned to classrooms having white students during the period covered by Stallings' research. This means that the best Negro gains observed by Stallings were made by children who *remained in segregated classrooms*, and can only be attributed to factors *other* than desegregation, such as a general improvement in educational standards.

In both Washington and Baltimore, where legal segregation was totally abolished in 1954, the United States Commission on Civil Rights found "some evidence that the scholastic achievement of Negroes in such schools has improved, and no evidence of a resultant reduction in the achievement of white students [*Southern School News*, 1960]." A detailed account of academic progress in the Washington schools since 1954 has been given by Hansen (1960). The results of a city-wide testing program begun in 1955 indicated year-to-year gains in achievement on every academic subject tested at every grade level where the tests were given. The data were not broken down by race. As in the case of Louisville, it seems reasonable to attribute these gains primarily to an ambitious program of educational improvement rather than to racial mixing. For several years the Washington schools have had a steadily increasing predominance of Negro pupils (over 76% in 1960); this, combined with a four-track system of homogeneous ability grouping which has the effect of concentrating Negroes in the lower tracks, has resulted in a minimal desegregation experience for the majority of Negro children.

Little relevant data have been published on other Southern states where desegregation has been initiated. In 1960, 12 administrators of desegregated school systems testified at a Federal hearing on whether integration had damaged academic standards (United States Commission on Civil Rights, 1960). They unanimously replied in the negative, but only one official (from Louisville) mentioned gains in the achievement of Negro pupils. Reports of widespread academic failure on the part of desegregated Negro children are rare. Among those that have appeared recently is one by Day (1962) on Chapel Hill, North Carolina. Referring to a total of about 45 Negroes in predominantly white schools, he stated that the experience of 2 years of desegregation has shown "a disturbing portion of Negro children attending desergregated schools have failed to keep pace with their white classmates. . . . The question remains as to how to raise the achievement of Negro pupils disadvantaged by their home background and lack of motivation [p. 78]." Wyatt (1962) quoted the Superintendent of Schools in Nashville, Tennessee, as stating there was substantially more difficulty with Negro students entering desegregated situations in the upper grades. The official ascribed most of the difficulties to problems of social adjustment, although the cumulative effect of the generally lower achievement in the Negro schools was credited with some responsibility for the situation.

The academic achievement of Negro graduates of segregated Southern high schools who attended integrated colleges has been reviewed by the National Scholarship Service and Fund for Negro Students (NSSFNS, 1963). In a period of 15 years, NSSFNS helped over 9,000 Negro students to enroll in interracial colleges, situated mostly in the North. The report stated:

> Tabulations of the academic progress of former NSSFNS counselees and scholarship holders show that 5.6% of these students had a scholastic average of A or A−; 50.3% B+, B, or B−; 32.4% C+, C, or C−; and .7% D or below. Not listing grades were 11%. Fewer than 5% withdrew from college for any reason. This record of college success of an educationally and economically underprivileged group is far above the national average, which shows an over 40% incidence of dropouts from all causes [p. 9].

It should be noted that these students were carefully selected by NSSFNS for their academic qualifications. Nonetheless, the NSSFNS experience demonstrates that qualified Southern Negro youth can function effectively in predominantly white colleges of good quality. Later, there will be mention of additional material on these students which suggests that academic success was associated with social acceptance on the campus.

CONDITIONS DETRIMENTAL TO NEGROES' PERFORMANCE

It was proposed that the achievement motivation of Negro children in desegregation may be strongly influenced by the social behavior of their white classmates and teachers (social threat and facilitation), by their level of expectancy with regard to academic success (probability of success), and by their perception of the social consequences of failure (failure threat). In this section, evidence about conditions of desegregation that are assumed to have unfavorable effects will be considered. The focusing on negative factors is not meant to suggest that conditions favorable to Negro performance are lacking in present-day situations of desegregation, but rather that the former have received more attention from social scientists — apparently because they are more salient.

The rationale for assuming that social rejection is detrimental to the minority child's academic behavior has already been discussed. To what extent are Negroes rejected by white classmates? It is clear that this varies greatly from one community to another. The bulk of early studies on the racial attitudes of white school children in the North indicated that from an early age they expressed strong preference for their own racial group (e.g., Criswell, 1939; Horowitz, 1936; Radke et al., 1950; Radke, Trager, & Davis, 1949). Two examples of desegregation that was highly stressful for Negro children have been described by a psychiatrist, Coles (1963). He writes of the first Negroes to enter white schools in Atlanta and New Orleans:

When they are in school they may experience rejection, isolation, or insult. They live under what physicians would consider to be highly stressful circumstances ... [p. 4].

During a school year one can see among these children all of the medical and psychiatric responses to fear and anxiety. One child may lose his appetite, another may become sarcastic and have nightmares. Lethargy may develop, or excessive studying may mark the apprehension common to both. At the same time one sees responses of earnest and effective work. . . . Each child's case history would describe a balance of defenses against emotional pain, and some exhaustion under it, as well as behavior which shows an attempt to challenge and surmount it [p. 5].

Out of 13 original students who were studied during the first 2 years of integration, and 47 who became involved in integration 1 year later and were studied during the second year, "only one child has really succumbed to emotional illness." Coles does not present a systematic analysis of the various specific sources of fear and anxiety, but he suggests that worries about school work were of less importance than reactions to the prejudice of white children. Nor does he present adequate information about academic success, merely noting that very few learning difficulties "were insurmountable."

Severe stress due to social rejection has been experienced also by Negro students at various newly desegregated colleges and universities in the South. For example, several months after entering the University of Mississippi as its first Negro student, during which time he was often in considerable physical danger, James Meredith emphasized that rejection and social isolation were the most difficult features of his experience. He referred to himself as "the most segregated Negro in the world" despite his enrolment at the University. "Through it all," he said, "the most intolerable thing has been the campaign of ostracising me [*Southern School News*, 1963]."

Two Negro students who initiated integration at the University of Georgia experienced rejection and isolation during their entire 2-year enrolment (Trillin, 1964).

As Hamilton [Holmes] began his final ten-week quarter at Georgia, he had never eaten in a University dining hall, studied in the library, used the gymnasium, or entered the snack bar. He had no white friends outside the classroom. No white student had ever visited him and he had never visited one of them [p. 83].

The other student, Charlayne Hunter, eventually entered into friendly relationships with several white classmates, and was generally in the company of other students when walking to and from classes or eating on campus. However, she remained totally ostracized in the dormitory where she occupied a room by herself. She suffered from stomach trouble off and on during her entire stay at the University. Both Negroes have since graduated, Holmes with a distinguished academic record. Charlayne Hunter is now married to a white Southerner who was a fellow student at the University.

Desegregation under more favorable conditions has been investigated by Yarrow (1958). Comparable groups of Negro and white children of both sexes were observed in segregated and desegregated summer camps during 2-week sessions. The campers were from low-income families in Southern and Border states. The biracial camps had integrated adult staffs that were highly motivated to "make desegregation work." It was found that the behavior of children in segregated and integrated groups was quite similar. An initial tendency for both white and Negro children to prefer white friends lessened during the 2-week period studied. Satisfaction with the camp experience, as indicated by the percentage of children who expressed a desire that the camp session be extended, was somewhat higher in the desegregated camps. However, there were also indications of social conflict and emotional tension associated with the integration process. In older groups (ages 12 and 13) white children initially directed almost twice as much aggression toward Negro cabin mates as toward white age peers. At the beginning of contact 29% of all actions by white campers toward Negroes were hostile. On the other hand, Negro children of all ages aggressed more against one another than against whites. Overt manifestations of white prejudice tended to diminish during the 2-week period. Nonetheless, tension symptoms appeared in almost twice as many children in desegregated as in segregated groups (71% compared with 38%). Frequencies were the same for Negroes and whites. But Negro children in desegregation were more likely to manifest covert or internalized signs of distress (enuresis, fears, nightmares, withdrawal, physical symptoms) than those that were more overt (fighting, generally disruptive behavior, obscene language, complaining). Of the Negro campers showing tension, 85% showed reactions of the covert type. For the white children showing tension, neither covert nor overt responses predominated. That Negroes were particularly fearful of white disapproval is suggested by their oversensitiveness in desegregation to aggressive and dominative behavior in other Negroes, and their denial of such impulses in themselves. Both reactions are further evidence of a tendency to conceal tensions in the presence of whites.

Regarding the relevance of this study to school integration, it should be noted that the total period of interracial contacts was brief, but peer interactions were probably more intimate and intense than the usual classroom contacts. A generally favorable picture of race relations in Southern integrated schools is presented in a recent article by a journalist, Tanner (1964):

> On the social side, younger white and Negro children attending desegre- gated classes seem to accept each other better than the older ones. Negro and white youngsters can be seen playing together on the slides and swings of almost any desegregated Southern elementary school's play-

ground. At Nasvhille's Buena Vista Elementary School, Negro boys have won two of the three positions of captain on the school's safety patrol. And in Birmingham, often called the most segregated U. S. city, a Negro boy was chosen vice president of a sixth grade class that was desegregated last fall.

Even in desegregated high schools, some Negroes win quick social acceptance. When a lone Negro was admitted to the 10th grade of one high school in a small Texas town, he was elected vice president of the class his first day. A Negro also has become president of Oklahoma City's integrated Central High School student council.

One investigation has shown that experiences of social acceptance are associated with academic success. In the earlier-mentioned NSSFNS program of placing qualified Negro graduates of Southern high schools in Northern integrated colleges, it was found that those who participated in extracurricular activities, dated, and had a satisfactory number of friends got better marks than those who did not (NSSFNS, 1960). Though this finding is merely correlational, it is consistent with the proposition that acceptance by white peers is beneficial to the achievement motivation of Negro students.

It was suggested that low expectation of success is an important detrimental factor in the performance of minority children attending integrated schools. The evidence is strong that Negro students have feelings of intellectual inferiority which arise from an awareness of actual differences in racial achievement, or from irrational acceptance of the white group's stereotype of Negroes.

Inadequacy of previous training. The low quality of segregated Negro education is well documented. Plaut (1957) has summarized the overall situation:

> Negroes, furthermore, have long been aware that most of their schools in the South, and often the *de facto* segregated schools in the North, are rundown, poorly staffed, and short-handed. Second- and third-rate schooling for Negroes leaves them without the ability to compete with white students and robs them of the initiative to compete. Even the 1955 Speaker of the Georgia House of Representatives admitted recently that "Negro education in Georgia is a disgrace. What the Negro child gets in the sixth grade, the white child gets in the third" [p. 5].

A few specific instances of educational disparity at the grade-school level will be cited. Findley (1956) found in testing for achievement in the Atlanta schools that from 40% to 60% of white pupils met the standards set by the top 50% of a national sample on the different tests; but only 2% to 10% of Negro pupils met this standard on the various tests. In Tennessee, according to Wyatt (1962) Negro students averaged 1½ to 2 years behind grade level when transferred to biracial schools in the upper grades. In earlier grades, transfers performed satisfactorily. The same report described the status of Negro and white teachers in a Tennessee urban area. Only 49% of 901 academically qualified Negro teachers passed the National Teachers Examination; among white teachers, more than 97% of 783 qualified teachers passed the test. The Tennessee survey showed that the academic retardation of the segregated Negro elementary-school pupil is progressive.

The situation in northern Virginia was summarized by Mearns (1962) in a report written for the United States Commission on Civil Rights:

> The Negroes themselves have recognized that the achievement gap exists, but the only obvious reaction among most Negroes is reluctance to transfer to white schools. The question is raised as to whether Negroes really obtain a better education in desegregated schools where they must compete with better prepared, highly motivated white students. Frustration and failure engulf the ill-prepared Negro pupils . . . [pp. 209-210].

Other data indicate that the racial gap in achievement continues to widen through high school and college. Roberts (1963) pointed out that less than 3% of Negro graduates of segregated high schools would meet the standards of nonsegregated colleges. Roberts estimated that not more than 10 to 15% of Negro American college youth were capable of exceeding the threshold-level score on the American Council on Education test that was recommended by the President's Commission (100 on the 1947 edition).

Even in the urban North, where schools are legally integrated, the education afforded Negroes tends to be inadequate. Deutsch (1960), for example, found that in time samples of classroom activity, from 50% to 80% of all classroom time in New York City elementary schools with predominantly Negro, lower-class children was "devoted to disciplining and various essentially non-academic tasks." By comparison, only 30% of classroom time was given over to such activities in elementary schools attended mainly by white children of roughly similar economic status.

The foregoing material indicates that when grade-a-year plans of desegregation are adopted, it is obviously desirable from an educational standpoint to begin integration at the lowest grade and work upward. However, many Southern school systems are on grade-a-year plans of reverse order, with integration starting in the twelfth grade and proceeding down.

Unrealistic inferiority feelings. Apparently, the Negro child's feeling of intellectual inferiority is based not only on reality experience, but reflects an emotional accommodation to the demeaning role in American culture that has been imposed upon his racial group by the dominant white majority. The Group for the Advancement of Psychiatry (1957) has summarized the observations of numerous investigators of Negro personality:

> Wherever segregation occurs, one group, in this instance the Negroes,

always suffers from inferior social status. The damaging effects of this are reflected in unrealistic inferiority feelings, a sense of humiliation, and constriction of potentialities for self-development. This often results in a pattern of self-hatred and rejection of one's own group, sometimes expressed by antisocial behavior toward one's own group or the dominant group. These attitudes seriously affect the levels of aspiration, the capacity to learn, and the capacity to relate in interpersonal situations [p. 10].

Two experiments with Negro male college students suggest the marked extent to which loss of confidence when competing with whites can override reality. Preston and Bayton (1941) found that when students at a Negro college were told that their own scores on intellectual tasks were the same as the average scores of white students, they tended to set their goal levels lower on the next few trials than they did when told that their scores equalled those of other Negro students. The results can be interpreted on the basis of Atkinson's (1958a) theory of goal-setting behavior. Assuming that the Negro subject's motive to succeed tended to be stronger than his motive to avoid failure, he should have set his goal where the probability of success was .50. When a given level of performance was said to represent the white norm its apparent difficulty became greater than when it was supposed to represent the Negro norm, hence the goal level at which the expectancy of success was .50 tended to be lower immediately following the announcement of these norms. In an investigation of small biracial work terms at a Northern university, Katz and Benjamin (1960) observed that Negro students who had actually scored as well as their white teammates on various intellectual tasks afterwards rated their own performance as inferior. Here knowledge of white performance levels apparently influenced the Negro subjects' cognitions of their own *actual* performance, rather than just their estimations of *future* performance.

In an experiment suggested by Whyte's (1943) observations of status influence in a white street-corner gang, Harvey (1953) had members of white high-school cliques take turns on a dart-throwing task. After several practice trials, the boys openly estimated their own and their companions' future performance. Guesses were directly related to social rank in the group. Only boys of lowest rank showed a tendency to *under*estimate own performance. Moreover, they were expected by those of middle and high status to perform more poorly than they actually did. It should be noted that it is unclear from Harvey's results whether rank influenced perception of own ability or merely what one was willing to say in front of higher-ranking clique mates who had coercive power (French & Raven, 1960) to keep those of lesser rank "in their place."

EXPERIMENTS ON STRESS AND PERFORMANCE

Earlier some situational factors were described that presumably are detrimental to Negro academic achievement: social threat, low expectancy of success, and failure threat. Also, evidence was presented (some of it inferential) of their occurrence in actual situations of racial integration. A good deal of experimentation having to do with the influence of these factors on verbal and motor performance has been stimulated by the concept of psychological stress. Applezweig and Moeller (1957) proposed a definition of stress which focuses on the condition of the individual: Stress occurs when a motive or need is strongly aroused and the organism is unable to respond in such a way as to reduce its motivation. Deese (1962) finds it more useful to define stress as a class of stimulus events that elicit a set of correlated responses, among which are feelings of discomfort. He points out that the effects of stress on performance are specific to particular components of the performance under consideration — i.e., responses to stress may be either compatible or incompatible with the responses required in a given task.

Early studies of stress and performance did not employ the type of analytic comparison of stress responses and dimensions of ability in specific skills that Deese suggests. The general trend of findings on verbal performance (reviewed by Lazarus, Deese, & Osler, 1952) has been that stress impairs efficiency on relatively complex and difficult tasks, while on simple tasks stress has sometimes been shown to improve performance. The types of stress that have been used in experiments include failure feedback or threat of failure, exposure to highly difficult tasks (often under time pressure), annoying or painful stimulation such as electric shock, distraction such as flashing lights or noises, disapproval or disparagement.

Many investigations have employed stress inductions that apparently aroused fear of failure. For example, using 9-year-old boys, Lantz (1945) observed an impairment of Stanford-Binet scores following a failure experience, but no such effect after a successful experience. An examination by Lantz of the differential effects of this failure experience upon the various subtests indicated that tasks requiring visual or rote memory were not affected, while those involving reasoning or thinking suffered a decrement. In other studies that were reviewed by Lazarus, Deese, and Osler failure stress produced decrements in scores on the following verbal-symbolic tasks: learning and recall of nonsense syllables, digit-symbol substitution, arithmetic, recognition of briefly exposed sentences, sentence formation, and digit span. Similar effects were obtained on various types of perceptual-motor performance (e.g., card sorting, reaction time).

Turning to some representative studies of stress not directly involving failure, Barker, Dembo, and Lewin (1941) observed regression in the mental age of nursery-school children, as measured by the constructiveness of their play, when the children were frustrated by being denied access to attractive toys. Stress associated with the blocking of hostile impulses against an instigating agent (a teacher who arbitrarily disregarded the expressed desire of students) was found by Goldman, Horwitz, and Lee (1954) to impair performance on three tasks: retention of learned material, digit span, and problem solving. Laird (1923) reported loss of body steadiness in college students who were "razzed" by future fraternity brothers while working on simple motor tasks. Klein (1957) found that a strong task-irrelevant drive (thirst) caused a reduction in the accuracy of visual size judgments; and Callaway and Thompson (1953) obtained a similar effect when their subjects were required to hold one foot in a bucket of ice water.

During the past decade much research has been done on the role of personality factors in reactions to stress, with particular focus on the role of individual differences in chronic anxiety as measured by Taylor's Manifest Anxiety scale and Mandler and Sarason's Test Anxiety Questionnaire. A lengthy review of this work would fall outside the scope of this paper, inasmuch as the primary concern here is with *situational* factors that affect Negro performance. Yet it is of interest to note the general pattern of experimental results. Greater decrements due to stress are found in the performance of high-anxious individuals than in the performance of subjects lower in the anxiety-score distribution. These studies have been reviewed by Sarason (1960) and Taylor (1963).

Speculating about underlying physiological processes in stress, Bovard (1959) places the organizing center of bodily-emotional responses to stress in the posterior and medial hypothalamus. Of particular interest are his hypotheses that (a) activity in the anterior hypothalamus tends to inhibit or dampen posterior activity, and (b) excitation in the anterior hypothalamus is produced by certain types of social stimuli. *Thus an organism's vulnerability to stress depends upon the nature of its social environment.* Bovard reviewed studies which suggest that the presence of companions or members of the same species has a supportive effect under stress. At the human level it has been observed that separation from the family and evacuation from London was more stressful for London children than enduring the bombings with their family (Titmuss, 1950). Mandlebaum (1952) and Marshall (1951) dealt with the importance of social contact among soldiers in resisting battle stress. Research at Boston Psychopathic Hospital (1955) has shown that lysergic acid diethylamide (LSD) taken in a group situation results in less anxiety and inappropriate behavior than when taken individually. Schachter (1959) reported that fear, as well as hunger, increased the affiliative tendency in college students; and Wrightsman (1960) found that being with others in a similar plight was anxiety reducing for students who were first-born or only children.

Similar phenomena have been observed at the animal level. Liddell (1950) found that the presence or absence of the mother goat determined whether young goats would develop an experimental neurosis in a conditioning situation. In experiments with rats, animals tested together under stressful conditions gave less fear response (Davitz & Mason, 1955) and had less resultant ulceration (Conger, Sawrey, & Turrell, 1957) than animals tested alone. Similarly, monkeys showed fewer fear responses in a strange situation when another monkey was present (Mason, 1960). Monkeys raised in total isolation from age peers were deficient in normal defensive responses to environmental threat (Harlow & Harlow, 1962).

If Bovard's theory is correct, the extreme social isolation that is often experienced by Negroes in predominantly white environments would weaken their resistance to other stress conditions, such as might arise from the inherent difficulty of academic work, time pressure, financial problems, etc.

Various theories have been invoked to account for the tendency of stress to reduce efficiency on complex tasks, but to facilitate performance, or have no effect, on simple tasks. Sarason and others (Child, 1954; Mandler & Sarason, 1952; Sarason et al., 1960) have dealt primarily with the effects of individual differences in vulnerability to failure stress. They emphasize the interference that occurs when expectation of failure generates anxiety which, in turn, acts as an internal stimulus for defensive, task-irrelevant responses. Similarly, Deese (1962) mentions task interference from responses to the internal stimuli of stress-induced autonomic activity.

Some writers have concerned themselves with the effect of drive on specific characteristics of task-relevant behavior. Thus Easterbrook (1959) postulates an inverse relationship between drive level and the range of cue utilization. Complex tasks require a relatively broad awareness of cues for optimal efficiency, whereas simple tasks by definition require apprehension of only a few cues for successful responding. Hence, when drive is very high (as in stress), relevant cues will be missed on hard tasks, but more closely attended to on easy tasks. Hullian theory, as developed with respect to anxiety drive and learning by Spence, Taylor, and others, deals with the energizing effect of drive on task responses. As strength of drive increases the number of habitual response tendencies that can be elicited in a given task increases also. When activation is strong (as in stress) intratask response competition is heightened. The theory is supported by the results of experiments in which high and low scorers on Taylor's Manifest Anxiety scale were required to learn competitional and noncompetitional paired-word lists (reviewed by Spence, 1958; Taylor, 1963). Thus Easterbrook and the Hullians have each dealt with a particular component of a great number of tasks, and have tried to predict either favorable or detrimental effects of stress from the presence or absence of this component.

Discussing the effects of stress on perceptual-motor skills, Deese (1963) points out the need for systematic analysis of (a) the characteristics of motor arousal under stress, in relation to (b) the dimensions of psychomotor abilities that are requisite for various task performances. Both Deese and Spence (1958) mention that a fundamental weakness of present thinking about the effects of stress on *verbal* learning is that not enough dimensions of verbal skills have yet been explored to know what kinds of effects to look for.

Summarizing this section, there is a considerable amount of experimental evidence that types of stress which may be present in desegregation (as varieties of social threat and failure threat) impair certain kinds of verbal and perceptual-motor learning. However, there does not exist at present any comprehensive system of variables for predicting the specific effects of different conditions of stress on the Negro child's performance of various academic tasks.

EXPERIMENTS ON NEGRO PERFORMANCE IN BIRACIAL SITUATIONS

In recent years this author and his associates have been engaged in a series of experiments on the intellectual productivity of Negro male college students in situations involving white peers and/or white authority figures. The general aim of the research is the identification of underlying psychological factors that have either favorable or detrimental effects on Negro efficiency. In connection with the interpretation of the results that are now to be presented there evolved the set of postulated situational determinants of performance that were discussed in an earlier section of this paper.

In two exploratory studies, conducted at a Northern university (Katz & Benjamin, 1960; Katz, Goldston, & Benjamin, 1958), various cognitive and motor tasks were assigned to groups composed of two Negro students and two white students. Initially the men were total strangers. They worked together in several sessions for a total of 12½ hours. In general, it was found that Negroes displayed marked social inhibition and subordination to white partners. When teams were engaged in cooperative problem solving, Negro subjects made fewer proposals than did whites, and tended to accept the latter's contributions uncritically. On all tasks combined, Negroes made fewer remarks than did whites, and spoke more to whites, proportionately, than to one another. White men, on the other hand, spoke more to one another, proportionately, than to the Negroes. These behaviors occurred even when group members could expect a monetary bonus for good teamwork, and were informed that their abilities were higher than those of subjects in other teams. Moreover, in the second experiment Negro and white partners were matched on intelligence, and were even made to display equal ability on certain group tasks (by means of secret manipulation of tasks). Yet on a terminal questionnaire Negroes ranked whites higher on intellectual performance, preferred one another as future work companions, and expressed less satisfaction with the group experience than did whites.

The findings on Negro behavior may have been a result of (a) social threat (i.e., Negroes were fearful of instigating white hostility through greater assertiveness), (b) low task motivation in confrontation with white achievement standards (as derived earlier from Atkinson's model), or (c) failure threat (high expectancy of failure combined with anxious anticipation of disapproval and rejection by white peers and the white experimenter). The experimental data provide no basis on which to reject any of these factors as irrelevant.

In the next experiment, Katz and Cohen (1962) attempted to modify Negro behavior toward white partners in the direction of greater assertiveness and autonomy. It was predicted that (a) when Negroes were compelled to achieve on a task that was performed cooperatively with a white peer, they would subsequently display an increased amount of achieving behavior on another shared task of different content, and (b) Negro subjects who were not compelled to achieve on the first task would show an opposite tendency. Negro-white student dyads at a Northern university engaged in cooperative solving of problems adapted from the Raven Progressive Matrices. Some of the problems were made easy, to insure that both participants would perceive the correct answer. On other problems the subjects unknowingly received different information, so that one person had an insoluble version. Each subject had the easy version half the time. On every problem partners had to agree on a single team answer, after which the experimenter announced the correct solution. Before and after the problem-solving experience a disguised measure of social influence between the two men was obtained on a task which required group estimates of certain quantitative characteristics of briefly exposed photographs (e.g., the number of paratroopers in the sky).

In a control condition, the rules of the problem-solving situation did not require that each person openly propose an answer to every problem. It was found that Negroes tended to accept passively the suggestions of their white companions *even when they held the easy version and the teammate had to be in error*. Regarding intellectual efficiency, the private responses of Negroes, which they wrote down before each discussion began, showed *more errors than were made on the same problems at an earlier, individual testing session*. White subjects, on the other hand, made *fewer* private errors than they had made previously. As a consequence of the problem-solving experience in the control condition, Negroes showed increased social compliance on the picture estimations.

In an "assertion-training" condition the men were given their answer sheets from the previous session when they had worked alone. On every problem the two partners were required to read aloud their previous answers before negotiating a team reply. Thus, Negro subjects had the experience of openly announcing correct solutions in about half of all instances of disagreement (both men read off approximately the same number of correct answers). In the subsequent interactions over picture estimation there was an *increase* in the amount of influence Negroes had over the white partner. Further, Negro subjects were now inclined to accept the other person's influence only to the extent that he had displayed superior accuracy on previous pictures.

Thus, unless *forced* to express opinions at variance with those of a white peer, Negro students tended to suppress their own ideas in deference to the other person, and to show increased compliance on another task. But when they were *forced* to act independently on one task, they achieved greater autonomy in the second situation. The responses of white subjects on a postexperimental questionnaire indicate there may have been some hostility aroused against Negro partners who displayed intellectual competence. After working in the assertion-training condition whites tended to downgrade the Negro's performance and to accept him less as a future co-worker. However, since there were no all-white control groups, it is not known whether these reactions of white subjects were specifically interracial.

The results suggest that Negro submissiveness with the white companion was an effect primarily of social threat, and that probability of success was a relatively unimportant factor. As already mentioned, in both the assertion-training and control condition disagreement was experimentally arranged on almost all problems, with random alternation between partners in the assignment of easy and insoluble versions (on a few items *both* men had either easy or hard versions). Also, after each team decision the experimenter announced the correct answer (fictitious when both men had hard items) so that subjects could check the accuracy of their own private response and of the solution the partner had openly proposed. While there was a stable tendency in control teams for whites to make slightly fewer private errors than Negroes (all partners had been matched on pretest scores), it is doubtful that the average race difference of about two private errors on 49 items could have been discriminated by the average Negro subject. Hence the relative accuracy of own and partner's solutions was much the same for Negro subjects in the two experimental conditions, and the only difference between conditions was that in assertion training the Negro subject was forced to *disagree openly* with the partner. The disinhibiting effect of this experience on the Negro subject's behavior on another task seems attributable to a reduction in anxiety about instigating white hostility.

In the next experiment, Katz and Greenbaum (1963) examined more directly the influence of threat on Negro verbal performance by systematically varying the level of threat in different racial environments. Individual Negro students at a predominantly Negro college in the Suth were given a digit-symbol substitution task in the presence of two strangers who were both either white or Negro — an adult administrator and a confederate who pretended to be another student working on the same task. In order to minimize the amount of uncontrolled threat implicit in the white condition, there was no social interaction between the Negro subject and his white peer, and the task was described as a research instrument of no evaluative significance.

In addition to the variation of racial environment, the students were exposed to a condition of either high or low threat. Since the purpose of the threat variation was to determine whether individual Negroes were more vulnerable to debilitative effects of stress when they were alone with whites than when they were with other Negroes, it seemed desirable to use a threat stimulus that would not lead to intentional suppression of responses, by changing the social meaning of the task situation. The experiments used an announcement that severe electric shock (high-threat condition) or mild electric shock (low-threat condition) would be administered to the subject and the co-worker at random times during the task. No shocks were actually delivered.

The results indicated that Negro students' scores on the digit-symbol task depended upon the particular combination of stress and racial-environment conditions under which they worked. When only mild shock was threatened they performed better in the presence of whites than of other Negroes. But when told to expect strong shock their efficiency in the Negro condition improved, while in the white condition it went down. Apparently, the prospect of successful competition against a white peer, and of approval from a white authority figure, had greater incentive strength than the corresponding prospect in the all-Negro situation. This is reasonable on the assumption that the whites (particularly the experimenter) had higher prestige for the subject than their Negro counterparts. Since in all experimental conditions the instructions for the task played down its intellectual significance, Negro subjects in the white-environment-low-shock threat condition would not have experienced strong failure threat. Hence, they could respond to the stronger incentive strength of success in the white condition.

There are a number of ways of looking at the effects of shock threat. First, if Negro subjects cared more about performing well in the white condition they would have been more fearful lest the strong shock disrupt their task responses (failure threat). The expected stimulus would thus become more salient and distracting. An upward spiral of debilitation could then be set in motion as distraction and fear made the task seem more difficult, and this in turn aroused further emotion. Subjects in the Negro environment, on the other hand, had a relatively relaxed attitude toward the task in the low-threat condition (*too* relaxed for good performance). Hence they would not have been fearful of possible decrements due to shock, but perhaps just enough concerned to work harder than before. Also relevant to these data is Bovard's earlier-mentioned notion that the ability to withstand stress is strengthened by the presence of familiar social stimuli that have nurturant associations (in this case other Negroes).

The Hullian conception of the energizing effect of drive is also applicable: Efficiency declined in the white condition because the subject's initial stimulation in this racial environment, in combination with the additional stimulation of the strong shock threat, produced a total drive strength that exceeded the optimum for the assigned task. In the Negro condition, initial stimulation was relatively low, so that the increment in arousal due to strong threat brought the total drive level closer to the optimum than it had been under mild threat.

In a follow-up on the preceding experiment, Katz, Roberts, and Robinson (in press) investigated the effects of three factors on Negro students' efficiency; the race of the task administrator, the difficulty of the task, and the evaluative significance of the task. All subjects were students at a Southern Negro college. Half of them were tested individually by a Negro adult and the other half were tested by a white adult. In addition, one-third of the total sample worked on a relatively easy digit-symbol code, one-third were given a code of medium difficulty, and one-third had to do a relatively hare code. In order to attach a relatively nonthreatening significance to the situation, the task was described as a research instrument for studying eye-hand coordination, a nonintellectual characteristic. Unlike the Katz and Greenbaum experiment, there was no experimental confederate who posed as a second subject. The findings were consistent with results obtained in the low-threat condition of the earlier study — Negro subjects worked more efficiently when tested by a white adult than when tested by a Negro adult. However, the favorable influence of the white administrator was apparent only on the most difficult of the three tasks. On the two easier codes there were no statistically reliable differences in achievement associated with the skin color of the experimenters. Apparently the easier tasks were too simple to reflect the differences in motivation.

Then two additional groups of Negro students were tested by the same Negro and white administrators on the most difficult task only. But instead of being told that the task measured eye-hand coordination, it was presented to these subjects as a test of intelligence. Now the subjects did not attain higher scores in the presence of a white experimenter; rather, the effect of the IQ instructions was to slightly elevate performance with a Negro tester and to lower scores markedly in the white-tester group, so that the means for both testers were at about the same level. Thus in this experiment, making the most difficult task relevant to intellectual ability had effects not unlike those of strong threat in the previous study by Katz and Greenbaum. On the assumption that intellectual instructions were more highly motivating than the motor-test instructions, one can again apply the motor-test interpretation that motivation in the IQ-test—white-administrator treatment was excessive.

More directly relevant is Atkinson's (1958a) conception of motivation as a joint function of the subjective probability and incentive value of success, which was discussed earlier. Assuming again that a white experimenter has higher prestige for the Negro student than does a Negro experimenter, the prospect of eliciting the white person's approval would be more attractive. It follows that when the likelihood of winning approval by scoring well is equally high whether the tester is Negro or white, the subject will work harder for the white person. Thus in this experiment Negro students performed better with a white adult than with a Negro adult when the task was supposed to assess an ability which Negroes are not stereotyped as lacking (eye-hand coordination). Presenting the task as an intelligence test ought to have raised the incentive value of achievement in both racial conditions, with perhaps an even greater increment occurring when the experimenter was white (since *intellectual* approval by a white adult might be uniquely gratifying to the Negro students' self-esteem).

But suppose that on the intellectual task the Negro subject saw very little likelihood of meeting the white experimenter's standard of excellence. Unless the incentive strength of success increased enough to counterbalance the drop in subjective probability, Atkinson's model would predict a reduction in task motivation. As an additional source of impairment in this situation, low expectancy of success could have aroused fear of earning the white tester's *dis*approval (failure threat).

Turning now to the situation where the tester is Negro, there is no reason to assume that the subject's expectation of success would be markedly lower when the task was described as intellectual than when it was presented as a motor test. In both instances the racial identity of the tester would tend to suggest to the subject that he was to be compared with other Negroes. Accordingly, performance with the Negro tester ought to go up under IQ instructions. The fact that it rose only slightly in our experiment may be ascribed to the subject's unclarity about the tester's frame of reference for evaluating his score. That is, he was not actually informed whether he would be compared with norms for Negro students only, or with norms for *all* college students. The next study deals directly with this issue.

Katz, Epps, and Axelson (1964) investigated the effects on Negro students' digit-symbol performance of being told that they would be compared intellectually with other Negro students, or with white students. Hard and easy versions of the digit-symbol task were administered to different groups of students at a Southern Negro college under three different instructions: no test, scholastic aptitude test with own college norms, and scholastic aptitude test with national (i.e., predominantly white) college norms. Scores in all three conditions were reliably different from one another, with highest achievement occurring in the Negro-norms condition, intermediate achievement in the white-norms condition, and lowest achievement when no comparison was expected. These differences tended to be larger on the hard task than on the easy one.

Again referring to Atkinson's model, Negro performance was lowest in the no-test condition because of low incentive, while the difference between the two test conditions was due to higher subjective probability of success (closer to .50) when Negro subjects believed they were competing with members of their own race than when they expected to be compared with whites.

White students from a nearby state university were tested under comparable instructions on the hard task only. It was found that scores of the two norms groups — i.e., own college and national — did not differ, and *both* groups were more efficient than subjects in the no-comparison condition.

Future research can determine the usefulness of this application of Atkinson's theory for understanding Negro behavior in integrated schools. For example, the present formulation predicts that if the subjective probability of success were held constant, Negro subjects would perform *better* on certain types of intellectual test when the administrator was white than when he was Negro, or when they were competing with white peers rather than with Negro peers.

In a recent pilot study (unpublished), done in preparation for a larger experiment, students at a Southern Negro college were individually given a digit-symbol task by a white administrator under two conditions of probability of success. All subjects performed an initial trial under instructions that the task measured intelligence. Upon completing the first trial, every subject was informed that his final score would be compared with racially integrated norms. Half of all the subjects were told, in addition, that on the basis of their first-trial scores there was a statistical probability of about 60% that their final scores would exceed the mean for their age group. Then a second trial was administered to everyone. It was found that subjects who were given the probability information performed better on the second trial than those who were not. This preliminary investigation gives further weight to the suggestion that the perceived probability of success is an important determinant of Negro reactions to competition with whites.

Another line of investigation has to do with the appraisal of Negro subjects' emotional reactions to various test situations. In connection with the earlier discussion of failure threat, reference was made to the research of Sarason and his associates (Sarason, 1960; Sarason et al., 1960) on emotional factors in the test-taking behavior of white school children. In their view, the child who chronically experiences anxiety when tested is reacting with strong unconscious hostility to the adult tester, who he believes will in some way pass judgment on his adequacy. The hostility is not openly expressed, but instead is turned inward against the self in the form of self-derogatory attitudes, which strengthen the child's expectation of failure and his desire to escape the situation. Thus he is distracted from the task before him by his fear of failure and his impulse to escape.

Sarason has not as yet presented direct evidence that situations of adult evaluation arouse hostility in highly test-anxious children. However, in clinical studies by Lit (1956), Kimball (1952), and Harris (1961), difficulty in expressing aggression openly was found to be associated with scholastic underachievement. Rosenwald (1961) found that students who were relatively unwilling to give aggressive responses on a projective test showed greater impairment in solving anagrams after a hostility induction than did students who showed less inhibition of aggression on the projective test. Mention has been made of a study by Goldman, Horwitz, and Lee (1954), which demonstrated an association between the degree to which strong hostility against an instigator was denied expression and the amount of disruption of intellectual functioning.

These studies are pertinent to the problem of Negro children's learning efficiency in integrated classrooms, because these children often have to suppress strong hostility. It was seen that Yarrow (1958) found a much higher incidence of covert symptoms of emotional disturbance in Negro children than in white children at a desegregated summer camp. White children, it will be recalled, aggressed openly against their Negro cabin mates, but the latter did not respond in kind. Rather, they tended to deny aggressive impulses in themselves and to show heightened alertness to aggressive behavior in other Negro children. Another investigator who has reported stronger trends toward denial of hostile impulses in Negro children than in white children is Karon (1958), who examined individual personality by means of a projective technique, the Picture Arrangement Test.

It was suggested earlier that when the administrator of an intellectual test is white, or when comparison with white peers is anticipated, Negro subjects tend to become fearful of failure. Anticipation of failure would tend to generate feelings of victimization and covert hostility against the white tester. Since hostility against white authorities is dangerous, the hostile impulse would be strongly inhibited. Katz, Robinson, Epps, and Waly (in press) undertook to find out whether suppression of hostile responses occurs when a white adult makes Negro students take an intelligence test. Negro male students at a segregated high school in the South were given a test of aggression disguised as a concept-formation test. It consisted of 58 four-word items, with instructions to "circle the word that does not belong with the others." In half of the items one word had aggressive meaning, one word was nonaggressive, and two words were ambiguous. Hence the subject could choose either a hostile or a neutral concept. Two equivalent forms of the test were administered on successive days. On the first day it was given informally to all subjects by a Negro teacher. The following day the entire sample was divided into four groups, each of which was tested by either a white or a Negro adult stranger, with instructions that described the task as either an intelligence test or a research instrument.

The results show that when neutral instructions were used on the second day, average scores in both the white-tester and Negro-tester groups were the same as on the pretest. But in the intelligence-test condition, hostility scores *increased* over the previous day when the experimenter was a Negro, and they *decreased* when the experimenter was a white. The authors' interpretation is that both administrators instigated hostile impulses in the subjects when they announced that the task would be used to evaluate intelligence; when the adult authority was a Negro person, students revealed their annoyance by responding to the aggressive connotations of ambiguous words, but when the adult was a white person, the need to deny hostile feelings resulted in avoidance of aggressive word meanings. (The "denial" interpretation is of course inferential, since the results merely show that hostility scores in the white-adult—IQ-test condition went down; there was no *direct* evidence of increased emotional conflict in this condition.)

Assuming that these findings actually reflect variations in ability to express hostile impulses under different testing conditions, they furnish an interesting clue as to the nature of emotional processes attendant upon the disruption of Negro students' performance in the white-adult—IQ-test condition of an earlier experiment (Katz, Roberts, & Robinson).

SUMMARY

This paper brings together evidence relating to the effect of school desegregation on the academic performance of young Negroes. Negro Americans are defined as a subordinated minority group, and the focus of attention is on their adjustment in schools where white age peers and teachers predominate. In situations of this type there appear to be a variety of favorable and detrimental influences on Negro performance.

Low probability of success — where there is marked discrepancy in the educational standards of Negro and white schools, or where feelings of inferiority are acquired by Negro children outside the school, minority-group newcomers in integrated classrooms are likely to have a low expectancy of academic success; consequently, their achievement motivation should be low. *Social threat* — given the prestige and power of the white majority group, rejection of Negro students by white classmates or teachers should tend to elicit emotional responses (fear, anger, and humiliation) that are detrimental to intellectual functioning. *Failure threat* — when academic failure entails disapproval by significant others (parents, teachers, and perhaps also classmates), low expectancy of success should elicit emotional responses that are detrimental to performance.

On the other hand, *acceptance* of Negroes by white peers and adults should have a *social facilitation* effect upon their ability to learn, by motivating them to adhere to white standards of academic performance; anticipation that high performance will win white approval should endow scholastic success with *high-incentive value.*

Reports on the academic progress of Negro children in desegregated schools are on the whole inadequate for drawing any conclusions about the effects of biracial environments upon Negro performance. However, other types of evidence indicate that any or all of the situational factors mentioned above may be operative in specific instances. Research on psychological stress generally supports the assumption that social threat and failure threat are detrimental to complex learning.

Experiments on Negro male college students by the author and his associates have shown that in work teams composed of Negro and white students of similar intellectual ability, Negroes are passively compliant, rate their own performance as inferior even when it is not, and express less satisfaction with the team experiences than do their white companions. These results are seen as due to social threat and/or failure threat. Later studies have sought to identify specific situational determinants of Negro behavior in biracial settings.

Forcing Negro subjects into attempts to influence nonhostile white partners in problem solving had the effect of increasing their ascendancy on another task with the same white partner, apparently mainly through reduction of their fear of instigating hostility.

Experimentally creating a verbal-task situation that was low in both social threat and failure threat resulted in better performance by Negroes in the presence of whites than in the presence of other Negroes, suggesting that the incentive value of success was greater in the white environment. But when threat of strong electric shock was introduced, the white setting became less favorable to performance than the Negro one. Thus *vulnerability* to stress was greater in the white condition even though it was not apparent until a strong explicit threat was introduced.

The evaluative significance of a verbal task (e.g. whether it was described as a perceptual-motor test or an intellectual test) interacted with race of the tester in determining Negro performance, in a manner consistent with the notions that (a) the incentive value of success was higher with a white tester than with a Negro tester, and (b) the probability of success was lower with a white tester than with a Negro tester only when the task was defined intellectually.

Anticipated intellectual comparison with Negro peers was found to produce a higher level of verbal performance than anticipated comparison with white peers, in accordance with the assumption that the subjective probability of success was lower when the expected comparison was with whites. Also, performance was facilitated when a white tester raised the subject's expectancy of attaining a white standard of performance by giving him suitable "information" about his score on a previous trial.

Finally, suppression of hostile impulses appeared to occur in Negro students who were tested by a white adult, but not in those who were tested by a Negro adult.

Further research is needed to clarify the effects of the various situational factors mentioned above on the cognitive functioning of Negroes in biracial settings. However, it is possible even now to point out some implications for educational practice of the findings that have been reviewed.

IMPLICATIONS FOR EDUCATIONAL PRACTICE

The foregoing is relevant to a number of recent suggestions by social scientists on ways to foster movement toward equal education for all children (e.g., Klopf & Laster, 1963):

1. Educational standards of Negro schools should be raised to the level of white schools, so that minority-group children who transfer to previously all-white schools will have a reasonable chance of succeeding academically. This means, among other things, that the quality of training received by Negro teachers and the criteria used in selecting them for jobs must be raised to white levels, and racial integration of school faculties must be carried out.

2. Programs should be instituted for contacting parents and helping them to understand what they can do to prepare children for schooling, and to foster achievement once children are in school.

3. There should be in-service training of teachers and other personnel in newly integrated schools to develop awareness of the emotional needs of children in biracial situations. The training should include the imparting of techniques for helping children get acquainted with one another.

4. The widely accepted practice of assigning children to homogeneous ability groups (the "track" system) should either be abandoned entirely or modified to afford maximum opportunity for periodic re-evaluation of potentiality. Ability grouping tends inevitably to freeze

teachers' expectations as well as children's own self-images, hence it is particularly dangerous to intellectual development in the early grades.

5. Where grade-a-year plans of desegregation are adopted, the process should begin at the lowest grades, where Negro children have the smallest educational handicap and where unfavorable racial attitudes are least strongly learned.

REFERENCES

Applezweig, M. H., & Moeller, G. The role of motivation in psychological stress. *Off. Naval Res. tech. Rep.*, 1957, No. 3.

Atkinson, J. W. Motivational determinants of risk taking behavior. In J. W. Atkinson (Ed.), *Motives in fantasy, action, and society.* New York: Van Nostrand, 1958. Pp. 322-340. (a)

Atkinson, J. W. Towards experimental analysis of human motives in terms of motives, expectancies, and incentives. In J. W. Atkinson (Ed.), *Motives in fantasy, action, and society.* New York: Van Nostrand, 1958. Pp. 288-305. (b)

Barker, R., Dembo, Tamara, & Lewin, K. Frustration and regression: An experiment with young children. *U. Ia. Stud. Child Welf.*, 1941, 18, No. 1.

Bass, B. M. Conformity, deviation, and a general theory of interpersonal behavior. In I. A. Berg & B. M. Bass (Eds.), *Conformity and deviation.* New York: Harper, 1961. Pp. 38-100.

Boston Psychopathic Hospital. Experimental psychoses. *Scient. American*, 1955, 192(6), 34-39.

Bovard, E. W. The effects of social stimuli on the response to stress. *Psychol. Rev.*, 1959, 66, 267-277.

Callaway, E., & Thompson, S. V. Sympathetic activity and perception. *Psychosom. Med.*, 1953, 15, 443-455.

Child, I. L. Personality. In C. P. Stone & Q. McNemar (Eds.), *Annual Review of Psychology.* Stanford, Calif.: Annual Reviews, 1954. Pp. 149-170.

Coles, R. *The Desegregation of southern schools: A psychiatric study.* New York: Anti-Defamation League, 1963.

Conger, J. J., Sawrey, W. L., & Turrell, E. S. An experimental investigation of the role of social experience in the production of gastric ulcers in hooded rats. *Amer. Psychologist*, 1957, 12, 410. (Abstract)

Criswell, Joan H. A sociometric study of race cleavage in the classroom. *Arch. Psychol.*, N.Y., 1939, No. 235.

Davitz, J. R., & Mason, D. J. Socially facilitated reduction of a fear response in rats. *J. comp. physiol. Psychol.*, 1955, 48, 149-151.

Day, R. E. Part 2, North Carolina. In United States Commission on Civil Rights, *Civil Rights U.S.A. — public schools, Southern states.* Washington, D.C.: United States Government Printing Office, 1962. Pp. 57-104.

Deese, J. Skilled performance and conditions of stress. In R. Glaser (Ed.),

Training research and education. Pittsburgh: Univer. Pittsburgh Press, 1962. Pp. 199-222.

Deutsch, M. Minority group and class status as related to social and personality factors in scholastic achievement. *Soc. Appl. Anthropol. Monogr.*, 1960, No. 2.

Deutsch, M. Dimensions of the school's role in the problems of integration. In G. J. Klopf & I. A. Laster (Eds.), *Integrating the urban school.* New York: Teachers College, Columbia University, Bureau of Publications, 1963. Pp. 29-44.

Dittes, J. E., & Kelley, H. H. Effects of different conditions of acceptance upon conformity to group norms. *J. abnorm. soc. Psychol.*, 1956, 53, 100-107.

Dodson, D. Statement read at *Conference before the United States Commission on Civil Rights: Fourth annual education conference on problems of segregation and desegregation of public schools.* Washington, D.C.: United States Commission on Civil Rights, 1962. Pp. 137-141.

Easterbrook, J. A. The effect of emotion on cue utilization and the organization of behavior. *Psychol. Rev.*, 1959, 66, 183-201.

Findley, W. G. *Learning and teaching in Atlanta public schools.* Princeton, N. J.: Educational Testing Service, 1956.

French, J. R. P., Jr., & Raven, B. The bases of social power. In D. Cartwright & A. Zander (Eds.), *Group dynamics.* (2nd ed.) Evanston, Ill.: Row Peterson, 1960. Pp. 607-623.

Goldman, M., Horwitz, M., & Lee, F. J. Alternative classroom standards concerning management of hostility and effects on student learning. *Off. Naval Res. tech. Rep.*, 1954.

Group for the Advancement of Psychiatry. *Psychiatric aspects of school desegregation.* New York: GAP, 1957.

Hansen, C. F. The scholastic performances of Negro and white pupils in the integrated public schools of the District of Columbia. *Harvard educ. Rev.*, 1960, 30, 216-236.

Harlow, H. F., & Harlow, Margaret K. Social deprivation in monkeys. *Scient. American*, 1962, 207(5), 136-146.

Harris, I. *Emotional blocks to learning.* Glencoe, Ill.: Free Press, 1961.

Harvey, O. J. An experimental approach to the study of status relations in informal groups. *Amer. sociol. Rev.*, 1953, 18, 357-367.

Horowitz, E. The development of attitudes toward the Negro. *Arch. Psychol. N.Y.*, 1936, No. 194.

Karon, B. P. *The Negro personality: A rigorous investigation of the effects of culture.* New York: Springer, 1958.

Katz, I., & Benjamin, L. Effects of white authoritarianism in biracial work groups. *J. abnorm. soc. Psychol.*, 1960, 61, 448-456.

Katz, I., & Cohen, M. The effects of training Negroes upon cooperative problem solving in biracial teams. *J. abnorm. soc. Psychol.*, 1962, 64, 319-325.

Katz, I., Epps, E. G., & Axelson, L. J. Effect upon Negro digit-symbol performance of anticipated comparison with whites and with other Negroes. *J. abnorm. soc. Psychol.*, 1964, 69, in press.

Katz, I., Goldston, Judith, & Benjamin, L. Behavior and productivity in biracial work groups. *Hum. Relat.*, 1958, 11, 123-141.

Katz, I., & Greenbaum, C. Effects of anxiety, threat, and racial environment on task performance of Negro college students. *J. abnorm. soc. Psychol.*, 1963, 66, 562-567.

Katz, I., Roberts, S. O., & Robinson, J. M. Effects of difficulty, race of administrator, and instructions on Negro digit-symbol performance. *J. abnorm. soc. Psychol.*, in press.

Katz, I., Robinson, J. M., Epps, E. G., & Waly, Patricia. Effects of race of experimenter and test vs. neutral instructions on expression of hostility in Negro boys. *J. soc. Issues*, in press.

Kimball, Barbara. Sentence-completion technique in a study of scholastic underachievement. *J. consult. Psychol.*, 1952, 16, 353-358.

Klein, G. S. Need and regulation. In M. R. Jones (Ed.), *Nebraska symposium on motivation: 1957.* Lincoln: Univer. Nebraska Press, 1957. Pp. 224-274.

Klopf, G. J., & Laster, I. A. (Eds.) *Integrating the urban school.* New York: Teachers College, Columbia University, Bureau of Publications, 1963.

Knowles, L. W. Part 1, Kentucky. In United States Commission on Civil Rights, *Civil Rights U.S.A. – public schools, Southern states.* Washington, D.C.: United States Government Printing Office, 1962. Pp. 19-56.

Laird, D. A. Changes in motor control and individual variations under the influence of "razzing." *J. exp. Psychol.*, 1923, 6, 236-246.

Lantz, Beatrice. Some dynamic aspects of success and failure. *Psychol. Monogr.*, 1945, 59 (1, Whole No. 271).

Lazarus, R. S., Deese, J., & Osler, Sonia F. The effects of psychological stress upon performance. *Psychol. Bull.*, 1952, 49, 293-317.

Liddell, H. Some specific factors that modify tolerance for environmental stress. In H. G. Wolff, S. G. Wolf, Jr., & C. C. Hare (Eds.), *Life stress and bodily disease.* Baltimore: Williams & Wilkins, 1950. Pp. 155-171.

Lit, J. Formal and content factors of projective tests in relation to academic achievement. *Dissert. Abstr.*, 1956, 16, 1505-1506. (Order No. 16,311)

Mandlebaum, D. G. *Soldier groups and Negro soldiers.* Berkeley: Univer. California Press, 1952.

Mandler, G., & Sarason, S. B. A study of anxiety and learning. *J. abnorm. soc. Psychol.*, 1952, 47, 166-173.

Marshall, S. L. A. *Men against fire.* Washington, D.C.: Combat Forces Press, 1951.

Mason, W. A. Socially mediated reduction in emotional responses of young rhesus monkeys. *J. abnorm. soc. Psychol.*, 1960, 60, 100-104.

Mearns, E. A., Jr. Part 4, Virginia. In United States Commission on Civil Rights, *Civil Rights U.S.A. – public schools, Southern states.* Washington, D.C.: United States Government Printing Office, 1962. Pp. 155-217.

Murstein, B. I., & Collier, H. L. The role of the TAT in the measurement of achievement as a function of expectancy. *J. proj. Tech.*, 1962, 26, 96-101.
National Scholarship Service and Fund for Negro Students. *Annual report 1959-1960.* New York: NSSFNS, 1960.
National Scholarship Service and Fund for Negro Students. *Annual report 1962-1963.* New York: NSSFNS, 1963.
Plaut, R. L. *Blueprint for talent searching.* New York: National Scholarship Service and Fund for Negro Students, 1957.
Preston, M. G., & Bayton, J. A. Differential effect of a social variable upon three levels of aspiration. *J. exp. Psychol.*, 1941, 29, 351-369.
Radke, Marian, Sutherland, Jean, & Rosenberg, Pearl. Racial attitudes of children. *Sociometry*, 1950, 13, 154-171.
Radke, Marian, Trager, Helen G., & Davis, Hadassah. Social perceptions and attitudes of children. *Genet. psychol. Monogr.*, 1949, 40, 327-447.
Roberts, S. O. Test performance in relation to ethnic group and social class. Report, 1963, Fisk University, Nashville. (Mimeo)
Rosen, M. Valence, expectancy, and dissonance reduction in the prediction of goal striving. *Dissert. Abstr.*, 1961, 21, 3846. (Order No. 61-2062)
Rosenwald, G. The assessment of anxiety in psychological experiments. *J. abnorm. soc. Psychol.*, 1961, 63, 666-673.
Sarason, I. G. Empirical findings and theoretical problems in the use of anxiety scales. *Psychol. Bull.*, 1960, 57, 403-415.
Sarason, S. B., Davidson, K. S., Lighthall, F. F., Waite, R. R., & Ruebush, B. K. *Anxiety in elementary school children.* New York: Wiley, 1960.
Schachter, S. *The psychology of affiliation.* Stanford: Stanford Univ. Press, 1959.
Southern School News. Untitled. *Sth. sch. News*, 1960 (Aug.), 7, 6 (Cols. 1-2).
Southern School News. Untitled *Sth. sch. News*, 1963 (Apr.), 9, 11 (Col. 2).
Spence, K. W. A theory of emotionally based drive (D) and its relation to performance in simple learning situations. *Amer. Psychologist*, 1958, 13, 131-141.
Stallings, F. H. A study of the immediate effects of integration on scholastic achievement in the Louisville Public Schools. *J. Negro Educ.*, 1959, 28, 439-444.
Tanner, J. C. Integration in action. *Wall Street J.*, January 26, 1964, 64, 1.
Taylor, Janet A. Drive theory and manifest anxiety. In Martha T. Mednick & S. A. Mednick (Eds.), *Reseach in personality.* New York: Holt, Rinehart & Winston, 1963. Pp. 205-222.
Thibaut, J., & Kelley, H. H. *The social psychology of groups.* New York: Wiley, 1959.
Titmuss, R. M. *Problems of social policy.* London, England: His Majesty's Stationery Office & Longmans, Green, 1950.
Trillin, C. *An education in Georgia.* New York: Viking Press, 1964.
Tumin, M. The process of integration. In G. J. Klopf & I. A. Laster (Eds.),

Integrating the urban school. New York: Teachers College, Columbia University, Bureau of Publications, 1963. Pp. 13-28.

United States Commission on Civil Rights. *Second annual conference on education, Gatlinburg, Tenn.* Washington, D.C.: United States Government Printing Office, 1960.

United States Commission on Civil Rights. *Civil Rights U.S.A. – public schools, cities in the North and West.* Washington, D.C.: United States Government Printing Office, 1962. (a)

United States Commission on Civil Rights. *Civil Rights U.S.A. – public schools, Southern states.* Washington, D.C.: United States Government Printing Office, 1962. (b)

Whyte, W. F. *Street corner society; the social structure of an Italian slum.* Chicago: Univer. Chicago Press, 1943.

Wrightsman, L. S., Jr. Effects of waiting with others on changes in level of felt anxiety. *J. abnorm. soc. Psychol.,* 1960, 61, 216-222.

Wyatt, E. Part 3, Tennessee. In United States Commission on Civil Rights, *Civil Rights U.S.A. – public schools, Southern states.* Washington, D.C.: United States Government Printing Office, 1962. Pp. 105-130.

Yarrow, Marian R. (Issue Ed.) Interpersonal dynamics in a desegregation process. *J. soc. Issues,* 1958, 14 (1, entire issue).

PATTERNS OF PERCEPTUAL, LANGUAGE, AND INTELLECTIVE PERFORMANCE IN CHILDREN OF LOW SOCIOECONOMIC STATUS

Cynthia P. Deutsch
Linda Zener Solomon

It has recently been suggested (Havighurst, 1970) that approximately 15% of North American society can be characterized as "socially disadvantaged." This "underclass" of society is economically impoverished and has a high rate of unemployment. Moreover, there is every indication that currently this lower class does not have the skills to enter the opportunity structure of the society, and therefore tends to remain an "underclass." Failure to achieve in the school system can be seen as both a cause and an effect of this class membership. This failure has been documented by studies indicating that there is a high rate of reading disabilities among children from disadvantaged backgrounds (e.g. Deutsch, 1965; Feldmann and Weiner, 1966), and that such children are more likely than others to fail in school and to leave at an early stage (e.g. Harlem

Youth Opportunities, 1964).

THE DEFICITS OF DISADVANTAGED CHILDREN

The sources of the school failure of disadvantaged children are multiple and complex, and relate to the school organization and the broader society. The children from poor backgrounds have often not developed perceptual and cognitive skills which are commensurate with the demands of the school's middle-class-based curriculum. For instance, studies by Deutsch and Brown (1964) and Deutsch (1965) have indicated that disadvantaged children typically score in the low range on standard verbal intelligence tests. Bernstein (1960; 1961; 1962), using English families, has reported that middle socioeconomic status (SES) families use both "restricted" and "elaborated" language codes, whereas lower SES families use "restricted" language codes only. The restricted code is characterized by shorter sentences, less complex syntax, fewer modifiers and the like. Textbook language, generally, is elaborated code language. Studies carried out at the Institute for Developmental Studies (John, 1963; Deutsch et al., 1964; Cherry, 1965; Deutsch, 1965; Whiteman and Deutsch, 1967; Whiteman, Brown, and Deutsch, 1967) have indicated that disadvantaged children enter school with lower scores than their more advantaged peers on vocabulary, labeling, fluency and verbal explanation tests. Furthermore, studies at this Institute (1963; 1964; 1965) have indicated that the language test discrepancies between middle and lower class children increase with age. More specific analysis of language deficit has been made using the Illinois Test of Psycholinguistic Abilities. (See the Method section for a description of this test.) Bateman (1968) characterized the ITPA profile of the young disadvantaged black child as one of high auditory-vocal sequential performance (i.e. rote memory for digits), with weaker performance in the auditory-vocal automatic (i.e. grammar) area. Klaus (1965) and Weaver and Weaver (1967) obtained similar results. Finally, studies with two tests of auditory discrimination, the Wepman Test of Auditory Discrimination, and the Boston University Speech Sound Discrimination Test (Clark and Richards, 1966, and McArdle, 1965 respectively) have found lower performance for children in a lower social class. While the tests may have some bias against persons accustomed to a particular English dialect, it is also probable that ability to use and understand "middle-class" English is necessary for success in the present school system.

A number of the skill areas discussed above has been shown to be related to school-related and achievement measures. Lower ability levels in these skill areas tend to be correlated with a variety of school performance problems. For instance, low ITPA language age scores and low scores in the automatic-sequential area (the rote and automatic skills) tend to characterize children with reading disabilities (e.g. Raglund, 1964; Kass, 1966). Also, several studies have shown that poor auditory discrimination, as measured by the Wepman, as well as other tests, is typical of children with poor reading achievement. Results have been most clear with studies using children in grades 1, 2 and 3 (Katz and Deutsch, 1963; Thompson, 1963; Christine and Christine, 1964; Harrington and Durrell, 1965), while there is some indication that the relationship does not hold for children at the intermediate grade level (Reynolds, 1953; Templin, 1954; Katz and Deutsch, 1963).

PURPOSE OF THE PRESENT STUDY

The Institute for Developmental Studies (IDS) conducted an intervention enrichment program which sought to change the school organization, atmosphere and curriculum for disadvantaged children, as well as to build the skills found to be weak in children from low SES backgrounds. The present study undertook to compare test results for children taking part in this cognitively oriented program with results for children not taking part in the program. Through this comparison, it was hoped to increase information on the interrelationship of effects of intervention programs. Such information is essential for assessment of the potential of enrichment programs for counteracting the disadvantaged syndrome; and assessment of diagnostic uses of such tests for suiting enrichment programs to the needs of disadvantaged children.

METHOD

Subjects: Seventy-six lower socioeconomic status, black children living in the Harlem, New York area were employed as subjects. The experimental group (N = 40) was composed of children who attended the IDS cognitively-oriented enrichment program from prekindergarten through the third grade. The control group (N = 36) was composed of children who attended the same schools as the experimental group, but who began school at the kindergarten level and were enrolled in the regular New York City school curriculum.(1)

The control group had been constituted at the same time as the experimental group, and assignment of children to group was done on a random basis from a pool of children who all met the minimal screening criteria employed.(2) The present study began at the time the subjects were in the first grade.

Procedure: During their first-grade year and again during their second-grade year, subjects were evaluated for various aspects of language ability, perceptual functioning, intelligence and school achievement. When the subjects were in the third grade, only tests of language ability and perceptual discrimination were administered.

Test Administration and Description: Subjects were evaluated by trained examiners in rooms on the school premises set aside for this purpose. The tests were grouped into batteries designed to limit each testing session to under one hour. Specifically, the tests and method of testing(3) were as follows:

For linguistic abilities, the Illinois Test of Psycholinguistic Abilities (1961) and the IDS Verbal Identification Test were given. The ITPA was administered at the first-, second- and third-grade levels. Each of the 9 ITPA subtests has been designed to measure a specific psycholinguistic ability, varying in 3 dimensions: level of organization, psycholinguistic process, and channel of communication. Level of Organization refers to the functional complexity of the organism. The *representational* level of organization is required to mediate activities which involve meaning or significance of linguistic symbols. The *automatic-sequential* level of organization is required to mediate activities which involve retention of linguistic symbol sequences and the execution of automatic habit-chains. Psycholinguistic Process refers to the set of habits required for normal language usage. *Decoding* habits are required to obtain meaning from visual or auditory linguistic stimuli; *encoding* habits required for expression in words or gestures, and *association* habits required to manipulate linguistic symbols internally. Channel of Communication refers to the sensory motor paths over which the linguistic symbols are received and responded to. Channels of communication are divided into mode of reception (*auditory* or *visual*) and mode of response (*motor* or *vocal*). Both a total language age score, and a profile of all the subtest scores were obtained in this study.

The IDS Verbal Identification Test was given at the first- and second-grade levels. The subject is shown simple line drawings depicting either an action, or a collection of objects, and is asked to say what he sees in the picture. He is shown the pictures a second time, and asked to give the one word best describing each picture. The following scores were obtained in this study: object enumeration score: number of items identified correctly on those stimulus cards best described by a noun; action enumeration score: the number of items identified correctly on those stimulus cards best described by a verb; object gestalt score: a measure of the ability to describe a scene with a single word when the scene is best described by a noun; and action gestalt score: a measure of the ability to describe a scene with a single word when the scene is best described by a verb.

For perceptual data, the Wepman Auditory Discrimination Test, Form 1, was given at the first-, second- and third-grade levels. The test evaluates ability to perceive fine differences between pairs of similar-sounding English words. For the present study, the word pairs were pre-recorded on tape to insure standardization of procedure and to avoid contamination by the varied speech characteristics of different examiners. Earphones were used for each subject, who was instructed to listen carefully, and to indicate whether the two words in each pair were the same or different. In addition to the total score, two subscores were obtained: the number of correct responses when the word pairs were different in the initial phoneme (e.g. pat; cat) and, the number of correct responses when the word pairs were different in the final phoneme (e.g. bat; bad).

For School Achievement Data, the Gates Primary Reading Test, Type PPR (Paragraph Reading) was administered to the subjects in groups of approximately six, at the end of the first and the second grades. The test measures ability to comprehend material read silently and independently. The subject is asked to read a series of paragraphs of graded difficulty, and to complete a task, such as marking the appropriate picture. Two scores were obtained; the number of correct responses, and the number of items answered within the time limit of 20 minutes.

The Stern Reading Test was given at the first-grade level. The test was devised at IDS to measure the reading achievement of children receiving instruction based on the Stern Reading materials. The experimental group had been given this training, while the control group had received the standard, first-grade reading program. While the subject's task was made as similar as possible to that in the Gates PR Test, the two tests were necessarily very different due to the differences in the two teaching methods. Again, scores of number correct and number answered were obtained.

To measure intelligence, the Stanford-Binet Intelligence Scale, an individual test of intellectual ability, Form L-M, was administered to the subjects in the *summer* previous to the first-grade year. IQ scores were obtained. The Peabody Picture Vocabulary Test (PPVT), a second individual test, was administered in the *fall* of the first-grade year. The PPVT is a standardized, multiple-choice recognition vocabulary test. The child is given a word and required to select its referent by choosing the appropriate picture from a set of four pictures. According to standardized procedures, the raw score is the number of correct responses, and the unpresented items below the basal point are assumed to be correct. IQ scores were obtained. The Lorge-Thorndike Intelligence Test, Level 1, Form A, Primary Battery, a non-verbal group test of abstract intelligence, was administered in the *spring* of the first-grade year, and Level 2, Form A, Primary Battery in the spring of the second-grade year. This is one of the few tests that has a standardization population consisting of persons on varying socioeconomic levels. IQ scores were obtained.

IDS PROGRAM

Since it was hypothesized that participation in the IDS program would be instrumental in differentiating experimental from control group performance on the above tests, a brief description of the program is included here, although it is impossible to do it justice in several paragraphs. Briefly, important organizational aspects of the program included two adults in each classroom, continuing in-service training of supervisory and teaching staff, and maximal involvement of parents in the program. In terms of classroom environment, a major purpose of the two early years in particular was to provide order for the child. The child was asked to meet a world in which he could be both self-reliant and successful, independence and self-esteem being two of the continuing aims of the IDS program. As an example, materials in each area of the classroom were arranged by function, a well as size, shape or color, and placed on low shelves in clear, plastic boxes. The shelves were not crowded, and the arrangement of materials was a clear one, so that the children might independently take and return materials to the appropriate places. This allowed the children to spend time in supervised individual activities, as well as to learn and practice a number of concepts when starting or finishing a new activity.

In terms of subject matter, four major areas were language and communication, perceptual training, number skills and science, and self-concept building (e.g. by dramatic play). The general approach to curriculum was an attempt to teach basic skills in an ordered development, and an attempt to encourage independent thought and action. Several examples of the language training techniques developed by IDS personnel seem particularly relevant to effects demonstrated in the present study. As one example, the Listening Center consisted of a tape recorder and several sets of earphones in a partitioned area of the classroom. There, a child was able to independently play tapes, record or listen to his own voice, or listen to stories recorded by his own teacher, including hearing questions and having the opportunity to answer them. At more advanced levels, programmed lessons in various areas of the curriculum were available. Another example is a series of games in the traditional Lotto format. The boards had pictures on them, and the pictures were matched, in some specific way, to the cards accompanying each game. The teacher or caller (who often was one of the children) held up a card, and asked who had it; depending on the level of development, the child with a match might be required to raise his hand, to describe the nature of the match, or to perform some other related task. The types of matches required varied, ranging from simple object recognition to understanding prepositional phrases. A third example is the Language Master which enabled recording of both the teacher's voice and child's voice (so that the child might compare the two), and, at the same time, viewing of a laminated card with space for pictures and symbols. Thus, it promoted the integration of auditory and visual stimuli, sounds and symbols.

RESULTS

With the exception of the ITPA and the Wepman, data from each subtest at each testing period were analysed in separate 2 x 2 x 2 analyses of variance, variables being treatment, sex, and school. (The children attended classes in two different schools.) The ITPA and Wepman data were analysed in separate 2 x 2 x 2 x 3 repeated measures analyses of variance, with variables being treatment, sex, school, and time of testing (grade 1, 2, or 3).

The complete outline of results of these and other analyses is available (C. Deutsch, 1971); however, it seems most appropriate to limit the present report to a discussion of the differences between the experimental group and the control group. Treatment (subject group) represents not only the main focus of the study, but also the variable for which input can to some extent be specified, and cause-effect relations be suggested.

The mean scores relevant to the treatment main effect for all analyses are shown in Table 1.

In summary, the experimental group was significantly superior to the control group for the following:

Test	Time of Test	p value
IDS Verbal Identification Test		
Object Enumeration	grade 1	.05
Action Enumeration	grade 1	.05
Stern Reading Test*:		
Total correct	grade 1	.01
Stanford-Binet IQ Test	grade 1: beginning	.001
Wepman Auditory Discrimination Test:		
Final Phoneme	Repeated measures analysis	.01
Total Score	Repeated measures analysis	.05
ITPA:		
Total Score	Repeated measures analysis	.01
Visual Decoding(4)	ditto	.01
Visual-Motor Association	ditto	.05
Auditory-Vocal Association	ditto	.05
Motor Encoding(5)	ditto	.05
Vocal Encoding(6)	ditto	.05
Auditory-vocal Automatic	ditto	.05

The control group was superior to the experimental group for the following:
Gates Reading Test:*

Number answered	grade 2	.05

*It should be noted that the Experimental Group was taught the Stern Reading Program, while the Control Group had the standard New York City curriculum. Thus each of the two reading tests was appropriate for only one of the groups and the pattern of significant differences on the reading tests was anticipated.

DISCUSSION

In order to validate the choice of sample here, it is important to note that the control children resemble the picture of disadvantaged children previously reported in the literature, and presented in the introduction. For instance, in terms of IQ scores, the control group means, both for the Stanford-Binet (92.5) and for the Lorge-Thorndike (92.6 and 89.5 for the first and second grades) did not reach 100 (cf. Deutsch, 1965). Also, the mean ITPA profile for the control children exhibits a definite peak in auditory-vocal sequential, the test of digit memory, and clear dips in auditory-vocal automatic, the test of grammatical usage, and auditory-vocal association, the analogies test (cf. Klaus, 1965; Bateman, 1968).

Before turning to the comparison of control with experimental children, it should be noted that the test items used were not part of the IDS curriculum. In the case of the ITPA, the test was in fact not available when the program was begun. Also, it should be reiterated that the experimental and control children

Table 1

Mean Scores of Experimental and Control Groups
for Each Year on Each Measure

Measure	Experimental (N = 40)			Control (N = 36)		
	Year 1	Year 2	Year 3	Year 1	Year 2	Year 3
IDS Verbal Ident. object enumeration	44.32	44.64		41.42	43.11	
IDS Verbal Ident. action enumeration	27.58	26.65		26.08	26.60	
IDS Verbal Ident. object gestalt	21.85	28.35		21.69	26.72	
IDS Verbal Ident. action gestalt	21.07	27.48		21.19	24.64	
Gates Reading total correct	8.00	16.75		8.33	16.53	
Gates Reading total answered	18.45	23.05		19.78	25.19	
Lorge-Thorndike IQ	97.19	93.15		93.31	89.66	
Stanford-Binet IQ	103.88			92.42		
Peabody Picture Vocab.	93.15			86.06		
Stern Reading total correct	16.27			12.22		
Stern Reading number answered	24.55			22.89		
Wepman:						
Total Score	22.05	25.87	26.53	19.53	24.22	25.56
Initial phoneme	10.33	11.00	11.27	9.69	10.89	11.11
Final phoneme	8.95	11.42	11.72	7.00	10.08	11.03
ITPA:						
Total score	-.44	-.48	-.30	-.90	-1.08	-1.26
Aud. decoding	-.59	-.96	-.23	- -.84	-.88	-.68
Visual decoding	+.04	-.18	-.33	-.20	-.55	-.76
Visual-motor assoc.	+.08	-.23	-.11	-.21	-.73	-.48
Aud.-vocal assoc.	-.35	-.61	-.45	-.88	-.83	-1.14
Motor encoding	-.68	-.07	+.23	-.77	-.77	-.49
Vocal encoding	-.18	+.57	-.02	-.17	-.34	-.36
Aud.-vocal seq.	+.38	+.35	+.45	+.17	+.27	+.05
Visual-motor seq.	-.31	-.71	-.52	-.28	-.72	-.92
Aud.-vocal automatic	-.82	-.49	-.20	-1.18	-.89	-.92

were equivalent in terms of the various criteria of eligibility for the IDS program. Assignment to either experimental or control group was random, and was done at the beginning of the prekindergarten year. Both groups, then, would be expected to show the same trends of performance on social class-sensitive measures, and thus there was a strong force *against* obtaining treatment differences in this study.

Despite this force against obtaining differences, the experimental group was performed significantly better than the control group on a number of measures. At first grade level, they attained higher scores on the Stanford-Binet IQ test, Stern test (total correct) and the IDS Verbal Identification test (object enumeration and action enumeration). At all testing periods (repeated measures analysis), they scored higher on some ITPA (total score; visual decoding; visual-motor association; auditory-vocal association; motor encoding; vocal encoding; auditory-vocal automatic) and Wepman subtest scores (total score, final phoneme). The control group scored significantly better than the experimental group only on the "number of items answered" score of the Gates Reading Test.

Assessment of effects of the IDS program can be made under three rubrics: basic skills; intellectual ability; achievement.

BASIC SKILLS

Considering the results in terms of basic skills, there is clear evidence that the IDS program effected a change in the psycholinguistic abilities of the experimental children. Looking first at the IDS Verbal Identification Test, the experimental group performed significantly better than the control on two of the vocabulary measures. With regard to the more differentiated ITPA, the experimental group performed significantly better than the control in total language age, and this difference increased over the three years of testing. On the associative subtests involving conceptual tasks (auditory-visual association; visual-motor association), the experimental group performed significantly better than the control group. They also showed superiority on the tests of grammatical knowledge (auditory-vocal automatic), and ability to express oneself (motor and vocal encoding). Finally, on the test of conceptual matching (visual decoding), experimental subjects in at least one school appeared to achieve higher scores than the control. Apart from an overall rise in performance, it is interesting to note the indication of a pattern or profile change for the experimental group. One would expect "dips" for black, disadvantaged children on the auditory-vocal automatic and auditory-vocal association subtests, since one test reflects knowledge of standard grammar, and the other comparison to normative responses, and this type of pattern is reported by Bateman (1968) for this group. However, on these two tests, the experimental children scored significantly better than the controls. On the other hand, on the one test which usually shows a peak for black, disadvantaged children, auditory-vocal sequential, neither group was significantly different from the other. Thus, the expected pattern of ITPA performance was somewhat attenuated for the IDS children.

Further considering basic skills, on the Wepman Test of Auditory Discrimination, the experimental children performed significantly better than the control group both in total score and in ability to discriminate two spoken words differing only in final phoneme. Difficulty in discriminating final phonemes is typical of ghetto children, probably as a result of their dialect and its lack of articulation of ends of words. As with the ITPA results, there is an indication here that the IDS program effected a change in an otherwise expected pattern. Moreover, since the changes are in the direction of ability to deal with middle class and elaborated speech, they might well be beneficial to future school learning.

INTELLECTUAL ABILITY

Considering the results in terms of general intelligence test performance, the two nonverbal tests of intelligence did not yield a significant difference between control and experimental children (although the experimental group did average 4 points above the controls in Lorge-Thorndike IQ). However, on the Stanford-Binet, the individually administered, highly verbal test of intelligence, the experimental group averaged 103.8, and did score significantly better than the controls, who averaged 92.4. This test was given in the summer prior to the first grade, when the experimental group had experienced two years of enriched schooling (the nursery and kindergarten years), and the controls one year of regular New York City schooling (kindergarten). As with the results on the basic skills tests, the significant results on this test point to the beneficial effect of the IDS program on performance involving verbal skills.

ACHIEVEMENT MEASURES

The aim of the IDS program was not only change in expected deficits, but long-term effects on school performance. The curriculum was based on the notion that certain skills underlie and facilitate mastery of the reading, writing and arithmetic taught in the public schools. As cited in the introduction, there is evidence that auditory discrimination is related to reading failure in the early grades (Katz and Deutsch, 1963; Thompson, 1963; Christine and Christine, 1964, etc.), and that ITPA deficits, particularly at the automatic-sequential level, are related to reading failure (e.g. Raglund, 1964; Kass, 1966). Furthermore, one might suggest close relationships between language facility and thought; logically, increased vocabulary should enhance development of concepts and mediation; ability on the "representational" level, should be related to complex problem-solving. Hopefully, then, the experimental children achieved a foundation enabling them to avoid the usual pattern of early school failure for disadvantaged children.

The question of effect on future learning was beyond the scope of this study. However, two achievement measures were given in the early years. On one, the Stern test devised at IDS, the experimental children scored significantly better than the controls; on the other, the Gates, they did not. This result was to be expected; the experimental children performed significantly better on the test assessing the reading curriculum that was provided only for them; there were no significant differences between the groups on the test assessing progress on the more usual reading program. While no clear conclusions can be drawn, the fact that the experimental group did not do poorly on the standard reading tests speaks well for the potential generalizability of the enrichment experiences.

THE EFFECT OF ENRICHMENT

The design of this study does not allow one to claim exact cause-effect relationships in trying to pinpoint the source of the Institute's enrichment effect. However, there are some logical inferences which may be made. As indicated in the procedure section, the program concentrated on cognitive skills, rather than simply activity or emotional fulfillment. Building perceptual and language skills formed an important aim of the curriculum, and the tests showing clear superiority of experimental children over control children were in these areas. As an example of the possible effect of certain teaching techniques, the Language Master provided experience in listening to clear, grammatically-correct speech, understanding it, and verbally responding to it. The child was provided with immediate feedback, and was able to compare his own speech with that of the teacher. Such training might have been a determinant of performance on the Wepman final phoneme test, and the auditory-vocal automatic subtest of the ITPA, since both of these tests are biased against the child unfamiliar with middle-class dialect and grammar. As a further example, the language lotto games provided experience in listening to instructions, giving instructions, and consideration of concepts and relationships. Such training might have been a determinant of performance on the representational tests of the ITPA, and some part of the Stanford-Binet, since all of these tests require conceptual skills.

Apart from the effect of the particular enrichment program involved in this study, it is most interesting to be able to find in these results a refutation of several parts of the Jensen (1969) thesis. First, there is positive evidence here that an enrichment program can be effective. Second, this effect is at least as evident on "conceptual" skills (e.g. the analogies test of the ITPA) as it is on very "concrete" skills (e.g. enumeration and digit span). The over-all impression to be gained from this study is one of the potential both of disadvantaged children and of enrichment programs.

NOTES

(1) A small number of subjects moved to other New York City schools during the period of the study; these children were located and evaluated in their new schools.

(2) The screening criteria were: that the child be English-speaking; without serious physical or emotional disability; in the low SES classification (as defined by the IDS SES scale); and of appropriate age. It was also required at the beginning that the parent be prepared to assume responsibility for seeing that

the child got to school.

(3) It should be noted that the Kendler Concept Formation Techniques, IDS Drum Test, and Columbia Mental Maturity Scale have been omitted from this list; it was decided to drop them from the analysis for reasons of unreliability and lack of validity for this sample.

(4) A significant Treatment x School interaction was also obtained; the experimental group appears to be superior to the control group at one school only.

(5) A significant Treatment x Year interaction was also obtained; however, the level achieved at the third year appears to be higher for the experimental group than for the control group.

(6) A significant Treatment x Year interaction was also obtained; however, the level achieved at the third year appears to be higher for the experimental group than for the control group.

REFERENCES

Bateman, B.D. *Interpretation of the 1961 Illinois Test of Psycholinguistic Abilities*. Seattle: Special Child Publications: 1968.

Bereiter, C., & Engelmann, S. *Teaching disadvantaged children in the preschool*. Englewood Cliffs, New Jersey: Prentice-Hall, 1966.

Bernstein, B. Language and social class. *British Journal of Sociology*, 1960, 11, 271-276.

Bernstein, B. Social class and linguistic development: A theory of social learning. In A. H. Halsey, J. Floud, & C. A. Anderson, (Eds.) *Education, economy, and society*. New York: Free Press of Glencoe, 1961.

Bernstein, B. Social Class, linguistic codes and grammatical elements. *Language and Speech*, 1962, 5, 221-240.

Carter, J. L. The effect of a group language stimulation program upon Negro culturally disadvantaged first graders. *Dissertation Abstracts*, 1967, 27(9-A), 2870.

Charry, E. Children's comprehension of teacher and peer-speech. *Child Development*, 1965, 36, 467-480.

Christine, D., & Christine, C. The relationship of auditory discrimination to articulatory defects and reading retardation. *Elementary School Journal*, 1964, 65, 97-100.

Clark, A., & Richards, C. Auditory discrimination among economically disadvantaged and non-disadvantaged pre-school children. *Exceptional Children*, 1966, 33, 259-262.

Deutsch, C. Patterns of perceptual, language and intellective performance in children with cognitive deficits. Final Report to Office of Education, February, 1971.

Deutsch, M. The disadvantaged child and the learning process. In H. Passow (Ed.) *Education in depressed areas*. New York: Bureau of Publications, Teachers College, Columbia University, 1963. Pp. 163-172.

Deutsch, M. The role of social class in language development and cognition. *American Journal of Orthopsychiatry*, 1965, 35, 78-88.

Deutsch, M., & Brown, B. Social influences in Negro-white intelligence differences. *Journal of Social Issues*, 1964, 20, 24-35.

Deutsch, M., Maliver, A., Brown, B., & Cherry-Peisach, E. Communication of information in the elementary school classroom. Unpublished report, Cooperative Project No. 908, Office of Education, U. S. Department of Health, Education, and Welfare, 1964.

Feldmann, S., & Deutsch, C. P. A study of the effectiveness of training for retarded readers in the auditory perceptual skills underlying reading. Unpublished report, Office of Education, U. S. Department of Health, Education, and Welfare, June 1966.

Feldmann, S., & Weiner, M. A fourth validation of a reading prognosis test for children of varying socioeconomic status. *Educational and Psychological Measurement*, 1966, 26, 463-470.

Harlem Youth Opportunities Unlimited, Inc. *Youth in the ghetto: A study of the consequences of powerlessness and a blueprint for change.* New York: HARYOU, Inc., 1964.

Harrington, M. J., Durrell, D. Mental maturity versus perception abilities in primary reading. *Journal of Educational Psychology*, 1965, 46, 375-380.

Havighurst, R. J. Minority subcultures and the Law of Effect. *American Psychologist*, 1970, 25, 313-322.

Jensen, A. R. How much can we boost IQ and scholastic achievement? *Harvard Educational Review*, 1969, 39, 1-123.

John, V. P. The intellectual development of slum children: Some preliminary findings. *American Journal of Orthopsychiatry*, 1963, 5, 813-822.

Karnes, M. B., Hodgins, A. S., Stoneburner, R. L., Studley, W. M., & Teska, J. A. Effects of a highly structured program of language development on intellectual functioning and psycholinguistic development of culturally disadvantaged three-year-olds. *Journal of Special Education*, 1968, 2, 405-412.

Kass, C. E. Psycholinguistic disabilities of children with reading problems. *Exceptional Children*, 1966, 32, 533-539.

Katz, P. A., & Deutsch, M. Visual and auditory efficiency and its relationship to reading in children. Unpublished report, Cooperative Research Project No. 1099, Office of Education. U. S. Department of Health, Education, and Welfare, 1963.

Klaus, R. A. The Murfreesboro Project: Cognitive approaches to culturally disadvantaged children. *Selected convention papers, 43rd Annual CEC Convention.* Washington, D.C.: Council for Exceptional Children, 1965, 249-255.

McArdle, M. Auditory discrimination in preschool children. Unpublished report, University of Tennessee, August 1965.

Raglund, C. G. The performance of educable mentally handicapped students of differing reading ability on the ITPA. Unpublished report, University of

Virginia, 1964.

Reynolds, M. C. A study of the relationships between auditory characteristics and specific silent reading abilities. *Journal of Educational Research*, 1953, 46, 439-449.

Tannenbaum, A. J. An early intervention program that failed. Mobilization for Youth, New York City, (mimeo), January 26, 1966.

Templin, M. C. Phonic knowledge and its relation to the spelling and reading achievement of fourth grade pupils. *Journal of Educational Research*, 1954, 47, 441-454.

Thompson, B. B. A longitudinal study of auditory discrimination. *Journal of Educational Research*, 1963, 56, 376-378.

Weaver, S. J., & Weaver, A. Psycholinguistic abilities of culturally deprived Negro children. *American Journal of Mental Deficiency*, 1967, 72, 190-197.

Whiteman, M., Brown, B. R., & Deutsch, M. Some effects of social class and race on children's language and intellectual abilities. In M. Deutsch and associates (Eds.) *The disadvantaged child*. New York: Basic Books, 1967.

Whiteman, M., & Deutsch, M. Social disadvantage as related to intellective and language development. In M. Deutsch et al., *The disadvantaged child*. New York: Basic Books, 1967. Pp. 337-356.

chapter 9
survey studies

INTEGRATION AND ETHNIC STUDIES
IN ELEMENTARY AND SECONDARDY SCHOOLS

LaMar P. Miller

Two references are useful in placing ethnic studies in its proper context. In the early 1930's the late Black scholar, William E. B. DuBois(1) undertook the task of setting down an accurate record of Black participation in the reconstruction of the nation. His research led to the discovery of the distortion of interpretation and omission of fact perpetuated in historical and sociological studies by the most influential historians of the era such as Burgess and Dunning. According to DuBois, these historians were more concerned in making an apology for the unreconstructed Southern life style than rewriting an accurate account of United States history. Their interpretations were based on theories of white superiority and included numerous statements supporting the stereotypes of Blacks as ignorant, shiftless, and child-like. In short, DuBois outlines the kinds of distortion of history that have dominated the teaching of social sciences up to recent years.

DuBois cited the emergence of demands on school boards of such communities as Buffalo, and Mt. Vernon, New York, thereby placing an element of the present study into proper context as it related to the original impetus for Black or ethnic studies. The failure of the Buffalo Board of Education to follow mandates for integration set down by the State Department of Education and the demonstrations mounted by Black students in Mt. Vernon because of inadequate bus service, narcotics in the schools, the lack of courses in Negro history and the inadequacies of the counseling service are also treated in this work.

Further examination of the curricula and text book materials from 1935 to the 1960's in New York, shows little in the way of increased inclusion of factual, objective material in history text books in general use in public schools that would tend to offset the misinformation set down as standard fare by the Burgess-Dunning schools of historical rewrites and their successors. The background of "ethnic studies" then, is tainted with the misapplications of historical scholarship, aided and abetted by the racist theories of the Lothrop Staddard – Wm. Graham Sumner, – G. Stanley Hall-Herbert Spencer schools of thought.

While none of these various vehicles of racist theory and sentiment are in current vogue, nor are they rarely acknowledged, the persistence of their influence in educational theory and practice is seen in the resistance towards a thorough airing of the factors in history that contributed so greatly towards the present conditions in urban centers and rural areas for black and white citizens.

The second reference related to the context of this study concerns the lag between the period May 1954 and May 1968. Another Black scholar, Sociologist St. Clair Drake,(2) traced the development of black protest in the educational arena from 1964 when the first hot summer demonstrations and rebellions began in earnest in the black ghettos, to the student demonstrations and demands for more attention to the study of Afro-Americans on the college and high school levels after the prolonged fight over the passage of the Civil Rights bills of 1968. The murder of Dr. Martin Luther King, Jr. signalled the rise in student demands. Student demonstrations in Mt. Vernon, Lackawanna, Rochester, Hartsdale, New York City and other communities in New York State heralded the establishment of commissions to study and devise courses in black studies during the summer of 1968 and 1969.

It was obvious that the preceding facts were crucial to our understanding of the problem. We were struck with the possibility that the inception of courses in ethnic studies was, in the main, a response to pressures generated by students and parents of black or other minority group origin, rather than the results of long-term planning or committment initiated by local school boards or administrations. Moreover, precedents set by programs of Black, Spanish-speaking, or Jewish studies on the campuses of colleges and universities had not been extensively used as models for comprehensive inclusion of materials on ethnic studies in the general or special public schools. Even a cursory examination of the literature suggested to us that the implementation of ethnic studies in public school systems and the institution of related courses appeared to have been the exception rather than the rule. The implications drawn from DuBois and Drake's work clearly points to the need for consideration of the state of historical and sociological writing as it has affected the climate in which any examination of ethnic groups can be undertaken.

The research reported here was taken from a larger investigation on Ethnic Studies in Elementary and Secondary Schools(3) conducted for the New York

State Commission on the Quality, Cost and Financing of Elementary and Secondary Education. The study was designed to investigate on different levels several facits of ethnic modification on the curriculum of selected public schools throughout the State of New York. The Commission whose work is well known as the Fleischmann Report(4) was committed to the idea that the creation of educational opportunity in which every child's aspirations are checked, only by his or her individual limitations, must become a reality. Thus the Commission had as one of its main concerns equality of educational opportunity. Since the goals of the Fleischmann Commission were commensurate with our own, we concluded that our investigative effort ought to center on integration and approaches to ethnic studies in elementary and secondary schools.

Most experts in the field agree that with respect to ethnic studies school systems have faced new questions and troubling issues. They are faced with the question of educational significance and role in a changing social fabric. Debate and controversy regarding what this role should be can be heard from many quarters. In particular, the necessity for scrutinizing the curriculum in terms of the needs of a pluralistic society has become a key issue. Some, accepting the basic structure of American society argue that the function of education is to preserve the cultural heritage, especially the western culture. They stress the traditional notion of culture, that is the transmission of culture means man's capacity to learn, to organize learning in symbolic forms, and to communicate this learning as knowledge to other members of the species. Others reject this perspective and express a different hope based on the existence of a variety of ethnic minority groups. They feel that our society is enriched, often unknowingly, by its multi-ethnic characteristic. They believe that to focus only on man's capacity to learn too narrowly defines the concept of culture. Beyond this they question an orientation that so identifies the aspiration of various ethnic minority groups with those of the general society that the possibility of playing a unique role is lost.

Despite the considerable differences in philosophy and in judgment of society represented by these points of view, there is common concern that the educational system has contributed to negative racial and ethnic attitudes of a very serious nature. Moreover, there is a general agreement that desegregation cannot be considered on the basis of sociological reasons alone, but must be dealt with in terms of the nature and characteristics of specific teaching-learning situations. The problem then is not just that of desegregation, but the broader view of integration of school programs as a means through which pupils learn to overcome the detrimental effects of class structure.

Major social forces which have begun to reflect themselves in the program of the schools are identified as the growth of new knowledge, the growth of population, the growth of the economy, the influence of mass media, the short work week with its resultant increase in time for leisure pursuits, the changing relationship among nations, and the increasing urbanization of our population. Each of these influence who is to be taught, what is to be taught and how it is to be taught. Unfortunately, the concept of ethnic diversity has not had such emphasis in our schools.

As a result of the preceding analysis of the problem it was evident that there was a need to delineate those factors currently operating in school systems so that we can encourage or discourage choices. While many shortcomings in our curriculum are obvious to scholars, schoolmen, and members of ethnic groups, specific questions have not been raised and problem areas are left not well understood. We know very little for example about what school districts are actually doing about ethnic modification of the curriculum not to mention school by school attempts in New York State, or about what needs to be done to adjust the ethnic balance for study by all children and youth in our schools. What kinds of course offerings with specific relevance to a given ethnic group are or should be included in a school program? What criteria should be applied to the selection of instructional materials for ethnic and multi-ethnic education? What sources of evaluation are there that help screen out shoddy and the opportunistic approaches? These were among the questions which we attempted to answer in the larger study. In this report, however, we will confine our remarks specifically to the problem we raised earlier on the relationship between integration and the approaches to ethnic studies.

Before turning to a discussion of our methodologies and our results, it is important to spell out what we mean by the term "ethnic." The term "ethnic" has been used to refer to a variety of groups and people. It is recognized that there exists in the United States today a plethora of ethnic groups and that the differences that exist among these ethnic groups are great. To study the many groups that fit the definition of ethnic in the generic sense and then to multiply this by the diversity that exists within each group is beyond the scope of this investigation.

Ethnic often refers to groups whose members share a unique social and cultural heritage passed on from one generation to the next. Ethnic group is often used in the generic sense to cover racial, religious or nationality groups in the United States who assume to possess certain traits, real or affective, distinctive from those of the larger population. Above all else, members of such groups feel a sense of identity and an interdependence of faith with those who share the custom of the ethnic tradition.

In America members of some ethnic groups or their forebearers may have come from the same country, as in the case of Italian and Irish Americans. Their group is often referred to as nationalities. Some ethnic group members, however, like Jews are conjoined by common traditions and experiences which transcend political boundaries. They are frequently known as a "people." In a heterogeneous society the intensity of ethnic identity or ethnicity is apt to be determined by the attitude of the members of the dominant group in the society. This attitude in turn is often dependent upon how closely one ethnic group approximates the culture of a dominant society. Acceptance may mean stronger bonds of ethnic identity as in the case of Scottish and German immigrants to America while rejection and subordination as in the case of Black Americans today may mean bonds of ethnic identity.

Since there was no term, unfortunately in the English language which could be applied philosophically to all ethnic groups, sociologists as far back as 1932 adopted the term "minority" in a related context. Thus, the term minority has also come to be used to refer to those groups whose members share certain racial or ethnic similarities which are considered to be different from those of the majority group. While it is not the purpose of this study to debate the issue of what the term ethnic means, it is important that the term be precisely defined. For the purpose of this investigation, the term refers to non-white minority groups such as Black, Puerto Rican, American Indian, Oriental and Mexican American.

We should also comment briefly on the definition of "curriculum" as used in the study in its broad sense as well as in its narrower application to the study of content within the structure of the school system. Traditionally, the meaning of curriculum has been to encompass all of the impressions and experiences of the child both within and outside of the school building while under the supervision of the school staff. This belief has been modified to incorporate an emphasis on the physical and emotional needs of the child as a part of his experiences. The curriculum of the school, therefore, has been viewed in two phases. First, the school must help its students to be physically and attitudinally prepared for learning and second, it must provide the opportunity to learn through appropriate utilization of the necessary ingredients of environment, materials, and experiences. It is this latter definition of curriculum that provides a framework for the inclusion of ethnic studies. More specifically, curriculum can and should be viewed, at least in part, as providing experiences that foster the concept of pluralism. It is this view that is commensurate with the purpose of this investigation.

METHOD AND DESIGN OF THE STUDY

As we indicated earlier, this report was taken from a larger study in which one aspect of the design was based on a discriptive analysis of ethnic studies programs in a stratified random sample of 100 schools throughout the state. The data for that analysis was collected by means of an interview questionnaire. The research reported here is based on a shorter version of the interview questionnaire and was designed to identify such major factors as population to be served, available instructional resources, total and minority group student enrollment and total professional and minority staff.

In addition, a special check list describing ethnic studies programs was developed as a part of the mailed questionnaire. Eight approaches to the presentation of ethnic studies in the public schools were identified. The principal investigator, in concert with the project staff, categorized these approaches as either strong or weak programs. The categorization of the approaches as weak or strong programs was based on the premise that past omissions and distortions of the history and contributions of ethnic groups required both integration into the regular curriculum as well as courses aimed at specific teaching about ethnic groups.

Six approaches were designated as weak and two were designated as strong. Those approaches which were designated as weak were: 1. A district program conducted outside your school sponsored by funds from Federal, State or other sources, 2. An informal approach outside the regular curriculum including assemblies, ethnic clubs, etc., 3. Provision for ethnic instructional resources and materials such as books and films, with no specific focus on program, 4. A shared learning program with other school(s) that has a predominance of ethnic students, 5. A team teaching approach to at least one course that involves some combination of disciplines such as Black History, art, music, etc., and 6. Integration of ethnic studies into regular or traditional courses in the curriculum. It was also considered that any combinations of these six approaches used by a school was still indicative of a weak program.

The two approaches which were designated as strong were: 7. A series of courses aimed at specific teaching about an ethnic group, 8. A combination of items 6 and 7. Similarly, it was considered that any combination of approaches used by a school that included approaches 7 and 8 was indicative of a strong program. Since we had considerable experience through our process of interviewing 100 schools in the other part of our design or our study, we felt justified in identifying weak programs as those who claim only the integration of ethnic studies into regular or traditional courses in the Curriculum. In general schools who make this claim are hard-pressed to provide evidence of any real effort to integrate the curriculum other than the use materials found in textbooks.

Using the enrollment data in the *Survey of Enrollment, Staff and Student Housing,*(5) published by the University of the State of New York the percentage of total state student enrollment was computed for each county in order to determine the appropriate proportion of the sample schools to be selected from each county. The appropriate proportion were derived and schools were randomly selected. The ratio of elementary to high schools in most districts in the State as reported by the enrollment survey is 2 to 1 or 3 to 1. The distribution of schools that responded is a close approximation of these ratios. Moreover, for the purposes of this study the various school districts were categorized demographically as urban, suburban or rural. Since the urban areas had the largest proportion of total state, student enrollment with corresponding proportions in suburban and rural areas, the largest number of schools included in the sample were from urban areas with a lesser number from suburban and rural areas.

Of the 400 schools to which we sent questionnaires, 278 replied. Of the 278 schools, 207 or 75 percent of the questionnaires were completed by the principal of the school. The rest of the questionnaires were completed by a department chairman or curriculum specialist, the assistant principal, or a

Table I
Demographical Type

	No. of Schools	Percent
Urban	135	49
Suburban	81	29
Rural	62	22
Total	278	100

teacher with 13, 10, and 2 percent respectively. Forty-one percent of the schools that responded were Elementary Schools; 23 percent were Junior High Schools; and 28 percent were High Schools. The remaining 9 percent were Kindergarten through 12th grade and 7th through 12th grade schools inclusive.

Table II
Questionnaire Respondent

	No. of Schools	Percent
Principal	207	75
Assistant Principal	28	10
Teacher	7	2
Other (Department chairmen, Curriculum specialists, etc.)	36	13
Total	278	100

Table III
Level of School

	No. of Schools	Percent
Elementary Schools	113	41
Junior High Schools	62	23
High Schools	77	28
Kindergarten – 12	19	7
Seven – 12	7	2
Total	278	100

RESULTS

As shown in Table IV, the total student enrollment of the 278 schools is

389,578 with a mean student enrollment of 1406.42 per school. The total minority group student enrollment is 144,699 with a mean minority group student enrollment of 522.27 per school. However, an examination of the professional staff of these schools presents a somewhat different picture. The total professional staff of the schools is 22,801 with a mean staff of 82.3 per school, and the total minority group staff members is 1781 with a mean of 6.43 per school. There are 4909 professional staff members specifically involved in ethnic studies programs with a mean of 17.72 per school. Of the total number of professional staff members involved in ethnic studies programs, 932 are members of a minority group with a mean of 3.36 per school. In other words, while 37.5 percent of the total student body is composed of minority group members, only 7.8 percent of the total professional staff are minority group members. Furthermore, in the crucial area of ethnic studies programs where it is of vital importance to have adequate role models, only 18.9 percent of the professional staff is composed of minority group members.

Table IV
School Population Distribution

Student	Total	Mean
Total Enrollment	389,578	1406.42
Minority group enrollment	144,669	522.27
Professional		
Staff members	22,801	82.31
Minority group staff members	1,781	6.43
Ethnic studies staff members	4,909	17.72
Minority group ethnic studies staff members	932	3.36

In analyzing our results we determined that 2/3 of the schools that responded had weak ethnic studies programs as defined in this investigation. Only 70 of the 270 schools that responded appeared to have strong ethnic studies programs. Two schools replied they had no ethnic studies programs and 17 schools used various combinations of approaches.

Since we had collected the data on the number of minority students in the schools we wondered if relationships existed between the number of minority group students in the schools and their approach to ethnic studies programs. From the data obtained by questionnaires, the percentage of non-white student enrollment was computed for each school. A one way analysis of variance was computed to determine the degree of difference between the strengths and weakness of ethnic studies programs and the percentage of non-white student enrollment. The results of the analysis of variance revealed that the sample of 87 schools with strong programs has a mean of 51.0 percent of non-white student enrollment and the sample of 189 schools with weak programs has a mean of 25.8 percent of non-white enrollment. The difference between the sample means is 25.2 percent; that is, the schools with strong programs had 25.2 percent more non-white student enrollment than the schools with weak programs. Although some of this difference between the means may have occurred by chance, there is a 95 percent probability that the difference between the mean percentage of non-white students enrollments in schools with strong ethnic studies programs and the mean percentage of non-white student enrollment in schools with weak ethnic studies programs is at least 15.67 percent and at most 34.75 percent. Furthermore, there is a 90 percent probability that the difference between the mean percentage is at least 17.2 percent and at most 33.3 percent.

These findings strongly support our early suspicion that the higher the percentage of non-white student enrollment the more likely it is that the school has a strong ethnic studies program, and conversely, the lower the percentage of non-white student enrollment the more likely it is that the school has a weak ethnic studies program. We do not know that an increase in non-white student enrollment will result in a strong ethnic studies program, nor do we know that a strong ethnic studies program will lead to an increase in the enrollment of non-white students. However, we can state with a high degree of confidence that a positive relationship exists now between the amount of integration and the strengths of ethnic studies programs.

We also wanted to know what relationship, if any, existed between the level of the schools included in the sample and the type of approach used for ethnic studies programs. Therefore, a Chi-square contingency coefficient was computed using level of school as one variable and approach to ethnic studies as the other variable. Since only one school of the total sample indicated that it utilized approach number one (i.e., a district program conducted outside your school sponsored by funds from Federal, State or other sources), this approach was omitted. The 17 schools that had miscellaneous combinations of approaches were also omitted as being insignificant for this computation. In all cases, any rows or columns with zero frequencies were ignored in the computations of the Chi-square coefficients. Our results indicated that there was a significant relationship between these two variables.

Moreover, according to our findings most of the strong ethnic studies programs are found in high schools; that is 39 out of 71 high schools reported having strong programs. The lowest number of strong ethnic programs are found in the junior high schools with the elementary schools having slightly more. While 17 of the 105 elementary schools in this sample reported having strong programs, only 8 of the 58 junior high schools had similar reports.

Another factor of ethnic studies programs that we were concerned with was whether or not these programs are required as a part of the public school curriculum or are merely offered as electives. A Chi-square contingency coefficient was computed and was found to be significant at the .01 level of

Table V

Relationship of Level of School and Approach to Ethnic Studies

Approach	Level of School					Totals
	Elem.	J.H.S.	H.S.	K-12	7-12	
2. An informal approach outside the regular curriculum including assemblies, ethnic clubs, etc.	4	3	2	0	1	10
3. Provision for ethnic instructional resources and materials such as books and films, with no specific focus on program.	15	9	3	0	0	27
4. A shared learning program with another school(s) that has a predominance of ethnic students.	2	1	0	0	0	3
5. A team teaching approach to at least one course that involves some combination of disciplines such as Black History, art, music, etc.	0	2	1	1	0	4
6. Integration of ethnic studies into regular or traditional courses in the curriculum.	55	27	22	13	3	120
7. A series of courses aimed at specific teaching about an ethnic group.	2	1	3	0	0	6
8. A combination of approaches 6 and 7.	15	7	36	3	3	64
9. A combination of approaches 2 and 6.	2	0	0	0	0	2
10. A combination of approaches 3 and 6.	10	8	4	2	0	24
Total	105	58	71	19	7	260

$x^2 = 61.852$
df = 32
x^2 is significant at the .01 level of confidence.

confidence. Interestingly enough, a higher percentage of elementary schools surveyed had ethnic studies as a required part of the program than did junior and senior high schools. The lowest percentage of schools that required ethnic studies was at the high school level. Insofar as elementary schools are concerned, this finding was not too surprising when one recalls that it was at the elementary level where we found the largest percentage of weak programs. One might well speculate about the value of requiring students to participate in weak programs. Similarly, one might wonder why more schools with strong programs do not require them as a part of the regular curriculum. A further breakdown with respect to the required ethnic studies programs was made according to demographical type. Separate Chi-square contingencies were computed for schools located in urban, suburban and rural areas and in all cases the Chi-square coefficient were found to be significant at the .01 level. The pattern here was consistent with our earlier results, with the strongest relationship in schools located in urban areas.

DISCUSSION

The data presented in this report clearly indicate that integrated schools are more likely to have strong ethnic studies programs and that schools that are not integrated are likely to have either weak programs or no focus at all on ethnic minority groups. Regarding the quality of schooling there are at least two distinct but related points to be made from these observations. First, if we accept the notion that the study of ethnic groups enhances the curriculum then it follows that integrating our schools can improve the quality of education. And second that while bringing students of different backgrounds together in the classroom is important, it is equally important to provide for the integration of curriculum.

Indeed we might well consider that unless we provide for an integrated curriculum, children will be deprived of the opportunity to work with truth. Schools must be dedicated to the dissemination of knowledge, and through their very nature they must be able to see the world as it really is and not as any individual or group would like it to be. This means finding out what the experiences of ethnic minority groups have been and making available this knowledge to all students.

Our investigation also supports the fact that school systems continue to reflect staffing patterns based on the cumulative accretions of discriminatory patterns inherent in the relative absence of opportunity for and encouragement of members of ethnic minorities to enter public school systems over the years. The relative lack of minority group teachers and the virtual absence of minority group administrators and heads of departments means that the minority group child must develop his sense of a balanced view and his analysis of ethnic group histories through the administration and program designs of whites. Moreover, the relative absence of role models for children, especially in departmental, planning and administrative areas may alter the development of incentives for students to reach the upper levels of their potential for achievement.

The findings have implications for education in general and for individual schools in particular. In New York, for example, there are more than a thousand schools that are one hundred percent white. Our data indicate that it is unlikely that these schools will have programs which will reflect the diversity of our population. It is even more unlikely that these schools will have integrated staffs. Schools in general have taken at best, a token approach to ethnic modification of the curriculum in New York and we suspect that this situation prevails throughout the nation.

Although the thrust of this study has been propelled by the necessity for inclusion and planning for ethnic studies in the curriculum, it is a revision of the philosophy of education which is the essence of the report. It seems logical and appropriate that a pluralistic nation ought to have schools that have a pluralistic curriculum based on a philosophy that emphasizes cultural distinctiveness not assimilation. The concept of the melting pot is not an appropriate guide for new educational directions. It suggests that differences that exist among Americans of varying background can be ignored. It implies a cultural monologue rather than a cultural dialogue. True integration is based on differences rather than sameness.

The blends and patterns of education which should obscure former educational deficiencies in favor of a system of education that respects the life styles of Blacks and other ethnic groups clearly necessitates creative leadership. The committment to such patterns followed by decisive action rather than polemics should be the greatest concern for educational leaders. The goal of education must be to preserve the ethnic identity of Black, Indian, Chinese, Japanese, Puerto Rican, and Mexican American children through a curriculum that emphasizes the value of cultural diversity.

The pressures that have led to those ethnic studies programs that are operative can only mean a healthy development for education. However, in dealing with almost any difficult problem that is straited by sharp emotional conflict there is a time when it is easy to stop asking questions, to relax the pressure, and to live with compromise. We may be in or approaching that stage with the question of developing ethnic studies programs in the public schools. If a respite takes place, it will be unfortunate because this relaxation often extends to a permanent truce. As in all areas of study and in academic disciplines the search for legitimate purposes and effective content must continue. At this point in 1973 we still know very little about what can and ought to be done in the way of designing and developing ethnic studies programs. And we are unlikely to learn much more if we allow our interest to subside as soon as the clamor subsides.

NOTES

(1) William E. B. DuBois, *Black Reconstruction in America, 1860-1890* (New York: Harcourt Brace and Co. 1935) pp. 237-241 - 265 - 277.

(2) St. Clair Drake, "The Patterns of International Conflict in 1968 in Black America" in *The Year of Awakening*, Romero, Patricia, (Washington D.C. United Publishing Corporation 1968).

(3) LaMar P. Miller, *"Ethnic Studies in Elementary and Secondary Schools"* Institute of Afro-American Affairs, New York University, August 1971.

(4) *The Fleischmann Report*, Vol. 1 (New York: The Viking Press, Inc., 1973).

BIBLIOGRAPHY

Ablon, Joan and Reid, Joseph W. Jr., *An Experimental High School Project in Cultural Diversity*, School of Criminology, University of California, Berkeley, Cal. (May 1966).

A Bibliography of Multi-Ethnic Textbooks and Supplementary Materials, The National Education Association, 1201 Sixteenth Street, N.W., Washington, D.C. 20036.

An Index to Multi-Ethnic Teaching Materials and Teachers Resources, The National Education Association, 1201 Sixteenth Street, N.W., Washington, D.C. 20036.

Banks, James A., *Teaching the Black Experience*, Belmont, Cal., Fearon Publishers, 1970.

Berrol, Selma C., "The Schools of New York in Transition, 1898-1914," *The Urban Review*, Vol. 1, No. 5, (December 1966).

"Black Studies in Education," *The Journal of Negro Education*, Vol. XXIX, No. 3, (Summer 1970).

Black Studies in Schools. Washington, D.C. National Public Relations Association, 1970.

Books for Schools and the Treatment of Minorities: Hearings before the Ad Hoc Subcommittee on De Facto School Segregation of the Committee on Education and Labor, House of Representatives, 89th Congress, 2nd Session.

Boyer, James B., "Materials for Black Learners," *Educational Leadership*, XXVIII (November 1970).

Brooks, Charlotte, ed., *The Outnumbered: Stories, Essays and Poems about Minority Groups by America's Leading Writers*, New York, Dell Publishing Co., Inc. (Laurel-Leaf Library), 1967.

Bruner, Jerome S., *The Process of Education*, Cambridge, Mass., Harvard University Press, 1960.

Clark, Kenneth B., *Prejudice and Your Child*, Boston, American Book Company, 1963.

Cordasco, Francesco and Bucchioni, Eugene, *Puerto Rican Children in Mainland Schools: A Source Book for Teachers*, New York, Scarecrow Press, 1968.

————, and Hillson, Maurie, and Bullock, Henry A., *The School in the Social Order: A Sociological Introduction to Educational Understanding*, Scranton, International Textbook Company, 1969.

Cramer, M. Richard, Bowerman, Charles E. and Campbell, Earnest Q. *Social Factors in Educational Achievement and Aspirations Among Negro Adolescents*, 2 vols., Chapel Hill, North Carolina, Institute for Research in Social Science, 1966.

Cuban, Larry, "Black History, Negro History and White Folk," *Saturday Review*, LI (September 21, 1968).

Deutsch, Martin P., *Minority Group and Class Status as Related to Social and Personality Factors in Scholastic Achievement*, Ithaca, New York, Society for Applied Anthropology, 1960.

Dubois, William E. B., *Black Reconstruction in America 1860-1890*, New York, Harcourt Brace and Company, 1935.

Dunfee, Maxine, *Ethnic Modification of the Curriculum*, Washington, D.C., Association for Supervision and Curriculum Development, NEA, 1970.

Fenton, Edwin, "Crispus Attucks Is Not Enough: The Social Studies and Black Americans," *Social Education*, XXXIII (April 1969).

Forbes, Jack D., *Afro-Americans in the Far West: A Handbook for Educators*, Berkeley, Far West Laboratory for Educational Research and Development, 1967.

————. *Mexican-American: A Handbook for Educators*, Berkeley, Far West Laboratory for Educational Research and Development, 1967.

————. *Native Americans of California and Nevada: A Handbook*, Berkeley, Far West Laboratory for Educational Research and Development, 1967.

————. *The Education of the Culturally Different: A Multi-Cultural Approach*, Berkeley, Far West Laboratory for Educational Research and Development, 1967.

Friedman, Marjorie S., "Public School: Melting Pot or What?" *Teachers College Record*, January 1969.

Gibson, John S. and Kvaraceus, William C., *The Development of Instructional Materials Pertaining to Race and Culture in America*, Medford, Mass., *Lincoln Filene Center for Citizenship and Public Affairs*, 1966.

Grambs, Jean Dresden, *Intergroup Education: Methods and Materials*, Englewood Cliffs, N.J., Prentice-Hall, Inc. 1968.

Handlin, Oscar, *The Newcomers: Negroes and Puerto Ricans in a Changing Metropolis*, Garden City, New York, Anchor Books, Doubleday and Co., Inc., 1962.

Harlan, Louis R., "Tell It Like It Was: Suggestions on Black History," *Social Education*, XXXIII (April 1969).

Harrison, Charles H., "Black History and the Schools," *Education News*, October 21, 1968.

Howard, John R., ed., *Awakening Minorities: American Indians, Mexican Americans, Puerto Ricans,* Aldine Publishing Company, Trans-action Book 18.

Kane, Michael B., *Minorities in Textbooks: A Study of Their Treatment in Social Studies Texts,* Chicago, Quadrangle Books, 1970.

Katz, William Loren, *Teachers' Guide to American Negro History,* Chicago, Quadrangle Books, 1968.

Koblitz, Minnie, *The Negro in Schoolroom Literature: Resource Materials for the Teacher of Kindergarten through the Sixth Grade,* New York, Center for Urban Education, 1967.

Larrick, Nancy, "The All-White World of Children's Books," *Saturday Review,* XVIII (September 11, 1965).

Levine, Stuart and Lurie, Nancy O., eds., *The American Indian Today,* Baltimore, Penguin Books, 1970.

Lewis, Oscar, *La Vida: A Puerto Rican Family in the Culture of Poverty, San Juan and New York,* New York, Random House, 1966.

Miel, Alice, and Kiester, Jr., Edwin, "The Shortchanged Children," *New York Times Magazine,* April 1967.

Miller, LaMar P., "Materials for Multi-Ethnic Learners," *Educational Leadership,* XXVIII (November 1970).

————. "Revitalizing An Urban School," *The New Campus,* Association for Field Services in Teacher Education, Vol. XXIII, Spring 1970.

————. "Black Studies: A Pedagogical Device for a Pluralistic Society," *New York University Education Quarterly,* Winter 1971.

People Make Other People Important: A Human Relations Guide for Classroom Teachers, The Department of Public Instruction, Lansing, Michigan (Bulletin No. 2150).

Porter, Judith D. R., *Racial Concept Formation in Pre-School Children,* Ithaca, Cornell University Press, 1961.

Programs, Services, Materials of the New York State Education Department for Black and Puerto Rican Studies, The Multi-Ethnic Task Force, The University of the State of New York, The State Education Department, Albany, New York.

"Racial/Ethnic Distribution of Public School Students and Staff in New York State 1969-70," The University of the State of New York, The State Education Department, Information Center on Education.

Romero, Patricia, *In Black America, The Year of Awakening,* Washington, D.C. United Publishing Company, The Association of Negro Life and History 1968.

Sexton, Patricia Cayo, *Spanish Harlem: An Anatomy of Poverty,* New York, Harper Colophon Books, Harper and Row, 1965.

Silberman, Charles E., *Crisis in Black and White,* New York, Vintage Books, Random House, 1964.

————. *Crisis in the Classroom,* New York, Random House, 1970.

Sloan, Irving, *The Negro in Modern American History Textbooks*, Washington, D.C., American Federation of Teachers, AFL-CIO, 1968.

Steiner, Stan, *La Raza: The Mexican-Americans*, New York, Harper Colophon Books, Harper and Row, 1969.

Stirling, Matthew W., *Indians of the Americas*, Washington, D.C., The National Geographic Society, 1955.

Suggested Readings in the Literature of Africa, China, India, Japan, New York, Bureau of Curriculum Development, Board of Education, 1968.

Teaching About Minorities in Classroom Situations, New York, Bureau of Curriculum Development, Board of Education, 1968.

Working with Pupils of Puerto Rican Background: A Guidance Manual, New York, Bureau of Curriculum Development, Board of Education, 1966.

CORRELATES OF ACADEMIC ACHIEVEMENT AMONG NORTHERN AND SOUTHERN URBAN NEGRO STUDENTS

Edgar G. Epps

Katz (1964) has argued that personality and social factors interact to interfere with Negro students' ability to realize their academic potential. In his article in this issue, Katz poses the following questions for researchers: (a) Are there socioeconomic status differences in personality? (b) Are these differences related to differences in achievement? (c) Are these traits products of early family experiences?

This paper reports results of a survey of high school students attending inner-city schools in a large northern city and in a large southern city in order to identify some personality factors which are predictive of the Negro student's capacity to utilize his intellectual potential to achieve academically.

The research reported here is more adequate for answering Katz' first two questions than for the last. Some inferences about early experiences will be drawn, but no direct test of the hypothesis about early experiences will be attempted. It is assumed that social position determines values, and values in turn influence behavior. The behavior in question (parental socialization practices) acts to determine (in part) personality characteristics of students. Thus, a student's achievement behavior (performance) is a reflection of the interaction between social position, socialization experiences, and genetic endowment. We would, therefore, expect family status to be positively related both to achievement behavior and to achievement related personality characteristics. However, it is the end product of socialization — manifest personality characteristics and attitudes — that is thought to be most directly related to academic achievement.

The aspect of personality that is most clearly related to academic achievement is motivation. According to Atkinson (1964), the tendency to strive for success is the result of the combined positive and negative effects of *hope of success, fear of failure, perceived probability of success, and the incentive value of the task goal.* This paper will focus on some measures which appear to be related to the theory of achievement motivation. These self-report measures are not meant to be identical to the TAT based measure usually associated with *n* Achievement. They were selected for their potential utility in predicting academic achievement as well as for their assumed theoretical relevance for a theory of motivation for academic achievement.

Recent research by a number of authors has tended to find a communality of content in areas peripherally related to the theory of achievement motivation. Smith (1968) has brought much of this material together in the formulation of a provisional view of "the competent self." According to Smith, favorable self-evaluation is accompanied by an array of knowledge, skills, habits, and abilities that are required to translate hopeful expectations and active orientations into effective behavior. Smith also points out the relatedness of the sense of competence to power, respect, and opportunity. Thus, social background (social status and ethnic origin) influences the extent to which an individual's self-perception includes a sense of control over his own destiny. In the present usage, this is the "perceived probability of success" dimension of the *n* Achievement model.

This paper will be concerned primarily with three aspects of Atkinson's model of achievement motivation. These are fear of failure, perceived probability of success, and incentive value of success, all of which involve elements of self-perception. For this reason, considerable attention will be given to self-esteem. For example, low self-esteem may be symptomatic of both fear of failure tendencies and of perceived low probability of success in a valued domain. The major hypothesis to be tested is that *favorable self-perceptions are positively related to achievement behavior.* Favorable self-perceptions should be positively related to *n* Achievement, but are not considered synonymous with *n* Achievement. These self-perceptions are, however, thought to be more strongly related to academic achievement than to *n* Achievement. (This hypothesis is not tested in this paper.)

The self-perceptions being investigated here may be referred to as a "competence syndrome." This competence syndrome may be said to include elements of (a) ability, (b) favorable self-perception, (c) optimism about opportunities for success, and (d) achievement values (incentive). The independent variable in this study is family social status. Self-perception, perception of opportunities for success, and achievement values are viewed as intervening variables, and verbal ability, school grades, and amount of expected future education are seen as dependent variables.

Respondents were students attending four schools in a large northern city and four schools in a large southern city. Our aim was to select schools which differed in the proportion of middle-class students included in their enrollments. The original plan also called for sampling two biracial and two racially segregated schools in each city. We were able to conform to this plan in the northern city, but could obtain no students from biracial schools in the south. Sampling within each school was random within limits of school cooperation. Our northern sample consists of 400 Negro males and 566 Negro females (white students are not considered in this analysis). There were 721 males and 851 females in the southern sample. Students in grades 9-12 were included in two northern schools and all southern schools. The two biracial northern schools contained only students in grades 10-12, and the proportion of 9th grade students attending the remaining northern schools was smaller than the proportion of 9th graders in the southern schools. Thus, our northern and southern samples are not directly comparable. However, each may be said to contain students with a wide range of measured ability and social characteristics. Table 1 presents the descriptive statistics.

TABLE 1

Mean Scale Scores by Sex and Region

Sex and Regional Group

Variable Name	Northern Males (N = 400)		Southern Males (N = 721)		Northern Females (N = 566)		Southern Females (N = 851)	
	$\bar{X}$	S.D.	$\bar{X}$	S.D.	$\bar{X}$	S.D.	$\bar{X}$	S.D.
Self-Concept of Ability	34.3	6.0	33.6	5.5	34.2	6.1	34.2	5.3
Perception of Limited Opportunities	12.4	3.9	14.1	4.2	11.9	3.6	13.3	4.4
Test Anxiety	11.5	4.6	12.4	4.6	13.1	4.8	14.3	5.0
Self-Esteem	16.9	2.3	16.5	2.7	16.7	2.3	16.8	2.3
Conformity	14.0	4.1	15.7	4.2	13.5	4.4	15.1	4.5
Vocabulary Score	19.2	7.3	14.2	7.1	19.5	6.6	16.1	7.1
Amount of Expected Future Education	4.7	1.4	4.4	1.5	4.6	1.4	4.5	1.5
Father's Occupation	3.4	1.8	3.1	1.8	3.2	1.8	3.0	1.9
Mother's Education	4.2	1.5	3.8	1.4	4.0	1.5	3.6	1.4
Grade Point Average	2.7	.6	2.7	.8	3.0	.7	3.1	.8

When northern and southern students are compared, average socioeconomic status is a little higher in the North. There is some variation in student's average social status among schools within each city. Students also vary in average verbal ability scores, usually in the direction of higher mean scores in the more middle-class schools. Experimental analysis indicated that the direction of relationship among variables was usually the same for students in all schools, therefore, students are classified by region and sex only (northern males, northern females, southern males, and southern females). While not directly comparable, these groups are considered appropriate for a correlational analysis in which the focus is on the relationship between variables rather than on North-South differences.

DATA COLLECTION

Vocabulary tests and questionnaires were administered to groups of students in school auditoriums or classrooms by the author and members of the research staff during the fall of 1966. All data except grades are based on these self-report instruments. Most of the instruments used have been described elsewhere, as indicated by the references cited when an instrument is described.

ABILITY

The measure of ability used in this study is an expanded version (60 items) of the vocabulary test used by Miner (1957). This instrument was used because no common measure of tested achievement or ability was available for the two school systems from which our students were drawn. The test was administered with a three minute time limit. Scores on the vocabulary test ranged from 0 to 50. Test-retest correlation coefficients with the same instrument readministered (after a 3 to 4 month interval) to 377 Negro and white males and 431 Negro and white females were .84 and .82 respectively. Means for the first administration (retest sample) were 18.42 for males and 19.00 for females. Retest means were 20.12 for males and 21.41 for females. Scores used in this analysis are based on the first testing. Scores on the vocabulary test are correlated with other ability measures at a fairly high level. For southern students, product moment correlation coefficients involving vocabulary scores and Otis IQ scores were .66 for females and .73 for males. Correlation coefficients computed for vocabulary scores and scores on an achievement test (SCAT) for northern students were .64 for females and .67 for males (white students' correlation coefficients were .76 and .65 for females and males respectively for SCAT vs. vocabulary score).

In order to measure *school achievement*, students' grades in English, social studies, arithmetic, and science were obtained from school records. Grades for as many semesters of high school work as were available for each student were used in computing grade point averages. Scores were converted to a five point scale.

SELF-PERCEPTION

Two measures of positive self-perception are included in this analysis. The first scale in this category is called a *self-concept of ability scale* (Brookover *et al.*, 1962, 1965, 1967). The original version of this scale consisted of eight items with five response categories. Factor analysis of 56 items including the items of the self-concept of ability scale resulted in adding two items to the scale. One item asked students "How do your parents feel about the grades you get in school?" Four choices of response were allowed ranging from "very well satisfied" to "dissatisfied." The other new item stated that "A person like me has a pretty good chance of going to college." Choices (four) ranged from "strongly agree" to "strongly disagree." The combination of items resulted in a scale with a possible range of 10 to 48. The correlation between the two versions of the scale is .96 for the total sample of 2,826 Negro and white students.

A *general self-esteem scale* based on Rosenberg's work (1965) was also included in this study. Factor analysis of Rosenberg's original items (included in a pool of 56 items) yielded a *positive self-esteem scale* of five items. The possible range of scores was from 5 to 20. (The new scale vs. original scale correlation coefficient is .66.)

Three measures of negative self-perception are analyzed here. A short version of the Test Anxiety Questionnaire (Mandler and Sarason, 1952) was used to measure *fear of failure*. The version used here included five items. This version correlated .93 with a thirteen item version of the Test Anxiety Questionnaire. Little predictive value was lost by reducing the number of items in the scale. The thirteen item version is correlated with vocabulary score at a modest level ($-.24$) as is the shortened scale ($-.19$) for the total sample of 2,826 white and Negro students of both sexes. Scores can range from 5 to 25.

The fourth scale measures a *passive-conforming orientation* toward the world. This is a factor-analytically derived scale based on two sets of items. Two items were taken from the achievement values scale used by Rosen (1956). These are identified as items measuring "Present-Future Orientation" and "Passivistic-Activistic Orientation" in the work cited. The remaining three items in the scale are Feagin's (1965) conformity scale.(1) For convenience the scale used in this analysis is referred to as the *conformity scale*. The maximum score possible on this scale is 23, the minimum score is 5. The revised scale correlates .84 with the original conformity scale. The correlation between this scale and the internal vs. external control scale (Rotter, 1966) is $-.27$ for 924 northern and southern Negro males and $-.34$ for 1263 northern and southern Negro females.

OPPORTUNITIES FOR SUCCESS

Students' perceptions of limited opportunities for success were measured by a scale based on a 13 item "awareness of limited opportunities scale" (Landis and Scarpitti, 1965). It includes items such as "My family can't afford to give me the opportunities that most kids have." Four responses ranging from "strongly agree" to "strongly disagree" were allowed for each item. The correlation between the short version of this scale and the longer version is .89. The scale included seven items which permitted a range of scores from 7 to 28.

Students were asked how far they would like to go in school if they could go as far as they desired. They were also asked how far they actually expected to go in school. The latter item was used as a seven point scale to measure *expected level of future education.* This measure is considered to be more realistic than the "aspiration" item or a similar item asking students what they expect to be their future occupation. It is used here as a measure of the incentive value of academic success.

Socioeconomic status was determined by using either father's occupation as reported by students or mother's education as reported by students as single indicators of family status. No attempt was made to measure "social class," but a simple ranking of status levels on an objective index was desired. The single indicators serve this purpose. Therefore, father's occupation is used as a seven point socioeconomic status indicator, while mother's education is used as an eight point socioeconomic indicator. For multiple and partial correlation analyses, father's occupation is used to measure socioeconomic status for northern males, and mother's education is the socioeconomic measure for other students. This procedure is based on the zero order correlation between these measures(2) and vocabulary score (see Table 4, part b).

RESULTS

Because ten variables are involved in this study, results are presented in terms of correlation coefficients. The zero-order correlation matrix for males and females, northern and southern samples combined, is presented in Table 2. It can be seen that most of the variables are interrelated at a statistically significant level although none of the correlation coefficients is large enough to indicate that any variable can be substituted for another. For both sexes, self-concept of ability and self-esteem are negatively related to perception of limited opportunities, test anxiety, and conformity. In exploring the relation of the variables to socioeconomic status (SES) and achievement, correlation coefficients for northern and southern males and females will be examined separately. These are presented in Table 3.

SOCIOECONOMIC STATUS AND ACHIEVEMENT

Data in Table 3 indicate that there is not a very strong relationship between SES (socioeconomic status) and school grades among these students. SES is significantly correlated with grades only among southern females ($r = .21$). However, SES is related to vocabulary score in a positive direction for all four groups of students. The correlation coefficients are small (.18 to .25), but significant beyond the .001 level of significance. The relationship is a little stronger for females than for males in both the North and the South, but the sex difference is greater in the South. SES is more strongly related to amount of expected future education than to any other variable in this study. This finding supports common sense expectations since the decision to attend college is often influenced by financial considerations. Results of a partial correlation analysis which controlled for all other variables indicated that the partial correlation

TABLE 2

Interrelations of all Variables for Males and for Females, North and South Combined*

Variable Name	1	2	3	4	5	6	7	8	9	10
1. Self-Concept of Ability		-.26	-.25	-.38	-.24	.33	.50	.46	.14	.15
2. Perception of Limited Opportunities	-.17		.27	-.22	.18	-.38	-.13	-.36	-.15	-.24
3. Test Anxiety	-.19	.35		-.14	-.10	-.23	.19	-.15	-.06	-.04
4. Self-Esteem	.35	-.28	-.18		.37	.17	-.37	.23	.05	.03
5. Conformity	-.14	.37	.16	-.14		-.46	.48	-.30	-.06	-.21
6. Vocabulary Score	.30	-.39	-.22	-.03	.37		-.37	.36	.12	.26
7. Grades in School	.45	-.26	-.18	.18	-.28	-.38		.37	.26	.26
8. Expected Future Level of Education	.45	-.30	-.14	.18	-.28	.37	.38		.21	.33
9. Father's Occupation	.09	-.15	-.03	.02	-.09	.19	.02	.21		.27
10. Mother's Education	.06	-.22	-.04	-.01	-.16	.20	.06	.22	.30	

*Correlation coefficients above the diagonal represent girls. Coefficients below the diagonal represent males. For both, correlation coefficients of .09 or larger are significant beyond the .05 level of confidence. The number of cases involved in the computation of each correlation coefficient varies due to missing data on one or both variables. The minimum number of cases for girls is 914, while for boys the minimum is 695.

TABLE 3

Correlation of Socioeconomic Status with Personality and Achievement
by Sex and by Region[a]

Correlation with SES by Sex and Region

Variable Name	Northern Males (N = 400)	Southern Males (N = 721)	Northern Females (N = 566)	Southern Females (N = 851)
Self-Concept of Ability	.10*	.09**	.16***	.14***
Perception of Limited Opportunities	-.17***	-.21***	-.23***	-.23***
Test Anxiety	.00	-.05	.05	-.08**
Self-Esteem	.08	-.07	.03	.03
Conformity	-.07[b]	-.15***	-.22***	-.18***
Vocabulary Score	.21***	.18***	.25***	.24***
Grade Point Average	.01	.08*	.06	.21***
Amount of Expected Future Education	.19***	.23***	.30***	.34***

$*p < .10$
$**p < .05$
$***p < .01$

[a] The SES indicator is mother's education for all groups except northern males for whom father's occupation is the SES measure. This procedure yields the largest correlation coefficients when SES is correlated with verbal ability. The number of cases in each comparison varies slightly due to missing data for one or both variables.

[b] This variable correlated $-.12$ $(p < .05)$ with mother's education for northern males.

TABLE 4

Zero Order Correlation Between Each Independent Variable and Grades,
Vocabulary Score, and Expected Education by Sex and Region

	Northern Males (N = 400)[a]	Southern Males (N = 721)[a]	Northern Females (N = 566)[a]	Southern Females (N = 851)[a]
a. *Grades as Dependent Variable*				
Self-Concept of Ability	.50	.43	.60	.44
Perception of Limited Opportunities	-.11	-.32	-.14	-.39

	Northern Males (N = 400)[a]	Southern Males (N = 721)[a]	Northern Females (N = 566)[a]	Southern Females (N = 851)[a]
Test Anxiety	-.13	-.20	-.15	-.14
Self-Esteem	.26	.26	.24	.15
Conformity	-.25	-.25	-.39	-.39
Vocabulary Score	.34	.49	.42	.57
Amount of Expected				
Future Education	.38	.38	.36	.38
Father's Occupation	.01	.03	.07	.07
Mother's Education	.03	.08	.06	.21

b. *Vocabulary Score as Dependent Variable*

Self-Concept of Ability	.33	.27	.36	.32
Perception of Limited				
Opportunities	-.21	-.43	-.23	-.43
Test Anxiety	-.20	-.21	-.19	-.22
Self-Esteem	.32	.34	.19	.18
Conformity	-.32	-.37	-.41	-.46
Grade Point Average	.34	.49	.42	.57
Amount of Expected				
Future Education	.36	.35	.37	.36
Father's Occupation	.21	.14	.10	.12
Mother's Education	.13	.18	.25	.24

c. *Expected Education as Dependent Variable*

Self-Concept of Ability	.56	.38	.53	.42
Perception of Limited				
Opportunities	-.24	-.31	-.28	-.40
Test Anxiety	-.21	-.10	-.13	-.15
Self-Esteem	.21	.16	.24	.22
Conformity	-.36	-.21	-.34	-.28
Vocabulary Score	.36	.35	.37	.36
Grade Point Average	.38	.38	.36	.38
Father's Occupation	.19	.21	.21	.21
Mother's Education	.17	.23	.30	.34

[a] The number of cases on which these correlation coefficients are based varies due to missing data for some students on several variables. For northern males, coefficients of .11 and .15 are needed for $p < .05$ and $p < .01$; for southern females, coefficients of .09 and .12 are needed for $p < .05$ and $p < .01$. The minimum number of cases in each group is: northern males, 305; southern males, 476; northern females, 424; southern females, 566.

TABLE 5

Partial Correlation Between Each Independent Variable and Grades,
Vocabulary Score, and Expected Education (Controlling for
Effects of Other Independent Variables) by Sex and Region

Variable Name	Northern Males (N = 400)[a]	Southern Males (N = 721)[a]	Northern Females (N = 566)[a]	Southern Females (N = 851)[a]
a. *Grades as Dependent Variable*				
Self-Concept of Ability	.32	.28	.46	.29
Perception of Limited Opportunities	.05	-.08	.08	-.12
Test Anxiety	.01	-.04	.06	.09
Self-Esteem	.02	.03	-.02	-.06
Conformity	-.12	.06	-.22	-.14
Vocabulary Score	.17	.30	.23	.37
Socioeconomic Status[b]	-.09	-.07	-.13	.03
Amount of Expected Future Education	.08	.15	.01	.07
b. *Vocabulary Score as Dependent Variable*				
Self-Concept of Ability	.00	.00	.00	.01
Perception of Limited Opportunities	.00	-.16	-.02	-.15
Test Anxiety	-.10	-.01	-.12	-.08
Self-Esteem	.20	.24	.03	.06
Conformity	-.18	-.25	-.22	-.25
Grade Point Average	.17	.30	.23	.37
Socioeconomic Status[b]	.17	.11	.16	.07
Amount of Expected Future Education	.13	.11	.12	.07
c. *Expected Future Education as Dependent Variable*				
Self-Concept of Ability	.44	.26	.34	.25
Perception of Limited Opportunities	-.06	-.15	-.09	-.19
Test Anxiety	-.05	.07	.03	.03
Self-Esteem	-.13	-.02	.01	.07
Conformity	-.23	-.04	-.10	-.06
Vocabulary Score	.13	.11	.12	.07
Socioeconomic Status[b]	.13	.16	.19	.25
Grade Point Average	.08	.15	.01	.07

[a] The number of cases on which these correlation coefficients are based varies due to missing data for some students on several variables. For northern males, coefficients of .11 and .15 are needed for $p < .05$ and $p < .01$ respectively; for southern males and northern females, coefficients of .10 and .13 are needed for $p < .05$ and $p < .01$; for southern females, coefficients of .09

and .12 are needed for $p < .05$ and $p < .01$. The minimum number of cases in each group is: northern males, 305; southern males, 476; northern females, 424; southern females, 566.

[b] Father's occupation is the SES measure for northern boys; mother's education is the SES measure for all other groups. This procedure yields the largest zero-order correlation between SES and vocabulary score for each group.

between SES and vocabulary score is significant for all groups except southern females, and the partial correlation between SES and expected education is significant for all four groups (see Table 5, part c).

SOCIOECONOMIC STATUS AND PERSONALITY CHARACTERISTICS

Table 3 also shows correlations of SES with personality variables. SES is significantly and positively related to self-concept of ability, but the correlation coefficients are very small. The negative correlation of SES with perception of limited opportunities and conformity is slightly higher. As one would expect, students with low family status are more likely than those with high family status to feel that their opportunities for occupational and educational success are limited. They are also more likely to adopt a passive conforming approach to life. Only one significant relationship is found between text anxiety and SES. None is found between self-esteem and SES.

PERSONALITY CHARACTERISTICS AND ACHIEVEMENT

In presenting results of this portion of the analysis, grades, verbal ability, and amount of expected future education are each treated separately as dependent variables. The zero-order correlation coefficients for grades are presented in Table 4 (part a). Self-concept of ability and self-esteem are positively correlated with grade point average. As expected, perception of limited opportunities and conformity are negatively related to grades. Although some correlation coefficients are quite small, most of the relationships are statistically significant; this is due essentially to the large size of the sample.

It is apparent that self-concept of ability is the strongest personality correlate of grades. For northern students, this variable is more highly correlated with grades than vocabulary score. While the relationship of self-concept of ability to grades is strong in the South, it is not as good a predictor of grades as vocabulary score. Next to self-concept of ability and vocabulary score, amount of expected future education is the variable most consistently related to grades among the four groups of students.

Sex and regional differences in the strength of associations between the remaining personality characteristics and grades are evident. Perception of limited opportunities is more strongly related to grades in the southern sample than in the northern sample, while conformity is more strongly related to grades of females than of males. Test anxiety is not strongly related to grades in this population.

Since most of the variables examined in this study are interrelated, partial correlation coefficients were computed to determine how much each variable independently contributes to the prediction of academic achievement. The partial correlation coefficients provide a statistical estimate of the contribution of each variable when the influence of all other variables is statistically controlled.

It is quite clear from the partial correlation coefficients in Table 5 (part a) that self-concept of ability and vocabulary score account for most of the explained variation in grades. The partial correlation between self-concept of ability and grades is significant for all groups except southern males. Expected education is not significantly related to grades when the effects of other variables are removed except among southern males. The partial correlation between SES and grades is negative in three of the sex and regional samples, but reaches significance only among northern females. In summing up the results of this analysis, it is apparent that the correlation of most of these variables with grades is based on their intercorrelation with other variables. Most of the relationship between grades and perception of limited opportunities, self-esteem, expected education, and test anxiety, is probably explainable in terms of their relatively high correlation with either vocabulary score or self-concept of ability or both.

The combined effects of several variables is indicated by the technique of multiple correlation. The combination of variables in Table 5 (part a) resulted in the following multiple correlation coefficients with grades as the dependent variable: northern boys, .55; southern boys, .61; northern girls, .67; and southern girls, .66. Thus, these variables are least effective for predicting academic achievement among northern boys and most effective for predicting academic achievement among northern and southern girls.

PERSONALITY CHARACTERISTICS AND VOCABULARY SCORE

Table 4 (part b) shows the zero-order correlations of personality variables with vocabulary score. The conformity scale is the most consistent personality correlate of vocabulary score across the four samples. Grade point average and amount of expected education are also strongly related to vocabulary score in all four samples. The remaining scales are differentially predictive by sex or region.

The partial correlation results for vocabulary score (Table 5, part b) indicate that, with other variables controlled, conformity is still a strong correlate of vocabulary score in each of the four groups. It is the only personality variable with a consistently significant partial correlation coefficient. Some interesting sex and regional variations are evident when we look at other variables. For example, perception of limited opportunities is significantly related to vocabulary score among southern students, but is not significant for northern students. The regional difference in the effect of test anxiety is in the opposite direction. Self-esteem is significantly related to vocabulary scores of male students, but is not related to the scores of female students.

When the combined effect of this set of variables is examined, regional differences in their effectiveness are quite apparent. With vocabulary score as the dependent variable, the respective multiple correlation coefficients are: northern males, .53; southern males, .64; northern females, .56; and southern females, .66. Vocabulary scores of southern students are predicted more effectively than those of northern students.

CORRELATES OF AMOUNT OF EXPECTED EDUCATION

In the treatment of grades and vocabulary score, amount of expected education was discussed as an independent variable. In Table 4 (part c), it is treated as a dependent variable. As pointed out earlier, SES is more strongly related to this aspect of academic achievement than to either vocabulary score or grades. The two achievement measures, grades and vocabulary score, are about equally correlated with amount of expected education in all four groups. For northern students of both sexes, self-concept of ability is by far the most effective correlate of amount of expected education. Among southern students, self-concept of ability is only a little more highly correlated with expected education than grades and vocabulary score.

Data in Table 5 (part c) show that the partial correlation between self-concept of ability and amount of expected education is considerably larger than the partial correlation of any other personality variable with amount of expected education. This pattern is found in all four groups. Socioeconomic status is the only other variable which is significantly related to expected education in each sample. Vocabulary score is significantly related to expected education in all groups except southern females. Test anxiety is not significantly related to this variable. The relationship of the remaining variables to expected education varies by sex or region.

The combined effect of these variables for predicting educational expectations varies by region. The amount of expected future education is predicted more effectively among northern males (multiple correlation coefficient = .65,) and northern females (multiple correlation coefficient = .60) than among southern males and females (multiple correlation coefficients = .53 and .58 respectively) by this combination of variables.

IN CONCLUSION . . .

Socioeconomic status was found to be negligibly related to student grades for northern males, southern males, and northern females. Only for southern females is SES significantly related to grades. SES is significantly related to vocabulary score and amount of expected education for all four groups of students, but the relationship between SES and expected education is stronger than that between SES and vocabulary score. SES is not strongly related to the personality-attitude variables examined in this study, although some statistically significant relationships are present. Results indicate that SES is very weakly related to test anxiety and self-esteem (positive self regard), but is more strongly related to perception of limited opportunities and conformity (negatively). Low family status is associated with high perceived limitations on opportunities and a passive conforming approach to life.

Results of zero-order and partial correlation analyses indicate that intercorrelation among variables explains some of the correlation between personality variables, vocabulary score, grades, and amount of expected education. With grades as the dependent variable, only self-concept of ability and vocabulary test score are significant correlates in all four samples when other variables are controlled. Self-concept of ability is not related to vocabulary score when other variables are controlled, but conformity is a strong correlate of vocabulary score in each sex and regional sample. Sex and regional differences in relative effectiveness of other variables for predicting vocabulary score were quite prevalent. Self-concept of ability and socioeconomic status are the most consistent correlates of amount of expected future education.

SELF-CONCEPT OF ABILITY AND CONFORMITY

The principle value of this paper has been the identification of two variables, self-concept of ability and conformity, which appear to have considerable value as non-ability predictors of academic achievement among northern and southern Negro students. The pioneer work of Brookover and his associates (1962, 1965, 1967) in developing the self-concept of ability scale deserves recognition. They have pointed out in a recent report (1967) that it is in precisely those schools where the greatest obstacles to achievement are present (those with high academic standards) that the self-concept of ability scale is most effective. The fact that the correlation of self-concept of ability and grades is higher among northern students than among southern students in this study supports this contention. Brookover *et al.* (1965, 1967) have also demonstrated that self-concept of ability is modifiable and that changes in self-concept of ability are related to changes in academic achievement.

The "conformity" variable used in this study is perceived as a measure of a control similar to alienation. It is a negative correlate of sense of control. The finding that conformity is more strongly related to verbal ability than to grades, but self-concept of ability is more strongly related to grades than to verbal ability raises a question about one of the results of the Coleman study (1966). Coleman found that sense of control explained more of the variance in academic achievement than academic self-concept. If a different measure of academic achievement had been employed, he might have found academic self-concept to be more important than his measure of sense of control for predicting academic achievement of Negro students. Two measures of academic achievement were used here because no good rationale could be found for selecting one in preference to the other.

Although correlational studies do not result in the determination of direction of causation, additional studies of this type are needed to help identify the factors associated with academic achievement. Effective experimental studies must be based on a knowledge of the relevance of variables for the behavior in question. Many significant experimental studies turn out to be irrelevant for predicting academic achievement under uncontrolled conditions. It would appear that researchers should start with variables of known relevance before going on to experimental analyses in a search for causes. The results of this study suggest that empirical validation of predictive instruments for specific populations of students is a necessity for researchers.

NOTES

(1) The two Rosen (1956) items are: (a) When a man is born, the success he's going to have is already in the cards, so he might as well accept it and not fight it; and (b) Nowadays, with world conditions the way they are, the wise person lives for today and lets tomorrow take care of itself. These items used the following alternatives: strongly agree; agree somewhat; disagree somewhat; strongly disagree.

The three Feagin (1965) items are: (a) It is more important to be loyal and conform to your own group than to try to cooperate with other groups; (b) To be successful, a group's members must act and think alike; and (c) When almost everyone agrees on something, there is little reason to oppose it. Responses for these items were: strongly agree; agree; undecided; disagree; strongly disagree.

(2) The rationale for using a different measure of socioeconomic status for northern boys than for the other group is based on the desire of the author to allow family social status to explain as much of the variation in academic achievement in each group as possible. Therefore, when choosing between father's occupation and mother's education, the indicator which yielded the higher zero-order correlation with vocabulary score was selected for inclusion in the partial correlation matrix.

REFERENCES

Atkinson, J. W. *An Introduction to Motivation.* Princeton, N. J.: D. Van Nostrand, 1964.

Brookover, W., Paterson, Ann, and Thomas, S. Self-concept of ability and school achievement: final report of cooperative research project number 845.

Michigan State University, 1962.

Brookover, W., Le Pere, Jean M., Hamacheck, Thomas, S., and Erickson, Edsel. Self-concept of ability and school achievement, II: final report of cooperative research project number 1636. Michigan State University, 1965.

Brookover, W., Erickson, E., and Joiner, L. M. Self-concept of ability and school achievement, III: final report of cooperative research project number 2831. Michigan State University, 1967.

Coleman, J., Campbell, E., Hobson, Carol, McPartland, J., Mood, A., Weinfield, F., and York, R. *Equality of Educational Opportunity.* Washington, D.C.: U. S. Government Printing Office, 1966.

Feagin, J. Prejudice, orthodoxy and the social situation. *Social Forces,* 1965, 44, 46-56.

Katz, I. Review of evidence relating to effects of desegregation on the intellectual performance of Negroes. *American Psychologist* 1964, 19, 381-399.

Landis, J., and Scarpitti, F. Perceptions regarding value orientation and legitimate opportunity: delinquents and non-delinquents. *Social Forces,* 1965, 44, 83-91.

Mandler, G., and Sarason, S. B. A study of anxiety and learning. *Journal of Abnormal and Social Psychology,* 1952, 47, 166-173.

Miner, J., *Intelligence in the United States.* New York: Springer Publishing Company, 1957.

Rosen, B. C. The achievement syndrome: a psychocultural dimension of social stratification. *American Sociological Review,* 1956, 21, 203-211.

Rosenberg, M. *Society and the Adolescent Self-Image.* Princeton: Princeton University Press, 1965.

Rotter, J. B. Generalized expectancies for internal versus external control of reinforcement. *Psychological Monographs.* 1966, 80, No. 1, (Whole No. 609).

Smith, M. B. Competence and socialization. In J. A. Clausen (Ed.), *Socialization and Society.* New York: Little Brown, 1968.

chapter 10
evaluative research studies

COMPARATIVE STUDY OF THREE PRESCHOOL CURRICULA

David P. Weikart

Recent efforts through massive Federal and State programs to improve the intellectual and academic performance of disadvantaged children through compensatory education projects have met with only limited success. Both professionals and parents are gradually becoming aware of this fact, with disquieting results. Professionals are openly pessimistic and are often ready to reduce support for programs and limit their own involvement. Parents of disadvantaged children are increasingly aggressive in their demands for action. They are determined that someone is going to assume the blame for years of waste of human potential while ivory tower theorists wrestled with minutia and the education "establishment" promoted its own interests. And the worst is yet to come as the details of compensatory education's limited successes become more widely known.

Professional educators and psychologists are expressing in public observations and conclusions limited to private conversations several years ago. Jencks (1968), writing in the New York Times Magazine about the outcome of any compensatory or remedial program, said: "Unfortunately, none of these programs has proved consistently successful over any significant period." This indictment has been verified by a group of researchers from the American Research Institute reviewing compensatory programs covering preschool through 12th grade for the period 1963 to 1968 for the U. S. Office of Education. Hawkridge, Chalupsky, and Roberts (1968) found only 21 compensatory educational programs which met a criterion of improved intellectual or academic functioning in a total sample of over 1000 such projects nominated for the study from throughout the country.

Parents of all minority groups are becoming increasingly outspoken in their criticism of the schools. Recently in Harlem a parent at a Follow Through advisory committee meeting asked when the experimental project was going to teach her kindergarten youngster his ABC's. Strongly supported by the other parents with vigorous head nodding and comments of "you tell it" and "that's right," the mother proceeded to read off the school in which her children had failed to learn and to place the blame on the teachers, the curriculum, and the administration. This parent had no concern for the theoretical basis of curriculum development; she wanted education for her child now. She was especially bitter about the implication common in professional circles that her children had failed because she had failed as a parent. Such parents seem to be convinced that shifting the blame for learning failure upon the school and teachers will miraculously produce a reformed institution providing adequate education relevant to and respectful of their children.

While there is developing a consensus that compensatory education is limited in its potential for ameliorating the educational deficits found in disadvantaged children, it is inconceivable that these efforts should be abandoned. The social pressure created by the poor, especially in the cities, is simply too great, and social conscience demands further effort. It is essential, then, that we examine those programs which are successful to find, if possible, key elements that can be employed to improve the potential for success.

Most compensatory education efforts have focused on curriculum reform, especially on making educational content relevant to the interests of the youngsters. The project reported in this paper started as a curriculum comparison study. As a research project, other components such as program operation and staff model were held as constant as possible. While the various curricula proved to be necessary elements, the outcome of the project strongly suggests that other components are of critical importance. In order to examine this finding in some detail, a description of the project will be presented, followed by a presentation and discussion of the results.

Since 1962, research projects throughout the country have attempted to determine whether or not preschool intervention with three and four year olds makes a difference in later school performance. Various projects following several theoretical models have now either reported initial findings or filed final reports (Deutsch, 1968; Klaus and Gray, 1968; Weikart, 1967; Curtis and Berzonsky, 1967; Hodges, McCandless, and Spicker, 1967; Karnes, Teska, and Hodgins, 1969; Di Lorenzo and Salter, 1968). While the cumulative results of these projects offer little to cheer about, the basic conclusion is that the more structured or task-oriented the program, the greater the gains in immediate intellectual competence and, where follow up data are available, academic achievement. While further development of specifically programmed curriculum styles and assessment of various intervention methods against "no treatment" control groups is essential, investigation of the relative effectiveness of curriculum models now available is of equal importance. The preschool field has reached a point at which several theoretically divergent curricula may be pulled together in a controlled study to determine their relative impact upon the cognitive, social-emotional, and academic growth of the disadvantaged child.

Although several such comparative studies are underway, little information is available. Karnes (1969) has reported the most extensive data. She found that two specially designed cognitive programs (the Bereiter-Engelmann Language Training project and the Karnes curriculum based on the Illinois Test of Psycholinguistic Abilities) were more effective in promoting intellectual growth than was a traditional nursery school program. Dickie (1968) reports on the effectiveness of three methods of language instruction in preschool and finds no differences in the effects of unstructured vs. structured methods of instruction. The training was limited to 20 minutes each day with no instructional carry-over into the 2½ hour total program. Di Lorenzo and Salter (1968) report better success with structured programs of the Bereiter-Engelmann type than with unstructured traditional preschool programs. The study was not designed to explore the impact of differing curricula, and the finding is incidental to the total evaluation of their large research project. Much more information is needed to evaluate the relative impact of various curricula upon the development of disadvantaged children.

The Ypsilanti Preschool Curriculum Demonstration Project was established in the fall of 1967 to document and evaluate three curricula thought to have remedial potential for the disadvantaged: (a) A *unit-based curriculum* emphasizing the social-emotional development goals of the traditional nursery school programs. The hallmarks of this curriculum are introduction of themes and material to acquaint the child with the wider environment, close attention to the individual social and emotional needs of each child, and a considerable degree of permissiveness in classroom operation (Sears and Dowley, 1963). (b) A *cognitively oriented curriculum* developed over the last five years by the Ypsilanti Perry Preschool Project (Weikart, 1967). This is a carefully structured program specifically designed for use with disadvantaged children who are functionally retarded. The curriculum is based on methods of "verbal bombardment," socio-dramatic play, and certain principles derived from Piaget's theory of intellectual development. (c) A *language training curriculum* emphasizing learning of academic skills. This curriculum was developed by Bereiter and Engelmann (1966) at the University of Illinois. It is a task-oriented curriculum employing many techniques from foreign-language training and includes the teaching of arithmetic and reading. While this program was specifically developed for disadvantaged children, it has not been tried out on functionally retarded youngsters. The project employs the most recent material published for this program.

The children for the curriculum study are drawn from the total available three and four year old population of functionally retarded disadvantaged children in the Ypsilanti school district. The contrast group is one of the five no-treatment control groups employed in the five year Perry Preschool Project. All treatment groups are balanced by measured intelligence, sex, and race. Two teachers are assigned to each curriculum model after they have had an opportunity to express a preference. They teach class for half a day and then conduct a teaching session in the home of each of their children for 90 minutes every other week. The home teaching phase of the curriculum is executed in the same curriculum style as the classroom program the child attends.

Essential to the demonstration aspect of the project is that all three programs have clearly defined week-by-week goals. The curriculum implementation follows a carefully planned daily program designed by the teachers themselves to achieve the goals of each curriculum. This provision for teacher involvement is a crucial aspect of the overall project.

RESULTS

Results of the project are available from the first year of operation. The replication of the study is now underway, and the data from the second year,

Table 1
Stanford-Binet Scores
Wave 5

	Unit (N-8)		Cognitive (N-11)		Language (N-8)		Contrast (N-14)		F-ratio
	M	SD	M	SD	M	SD	M	SD	
Pre-test	76.4	4.55	75.3	6.06	73.9	5.33	80.8	2.90	
Post-test	94.1	2.42	98.6	12.82	98.2	9.43	84.1	9.70	
Change	17.6		23.4		24.4		3.8		11.3857*

* p .01

Table 2
Stanford-Binet Scores
Wave 6

	Unit (N-8)		Cognitive (N-4)		Language (N-8)		Contrast (N-14)		F-ratio
	M	SD	M	SD	M	SD	M	SD	
Pre-test	73.6	6.93	82.7	5.26	84.4	3.12	80.8	2.90	
Post-test	101.1	7.08	110.7	12.34	114.6	6.14	81.2	10.10	
Change	27.5		28.0		30.2		0.4		25.3940*

* p .01

along with follow up information on the first year, will be available in the fall of 1969. The data now available are based on intelligence tests scores, social-emotional and general development ratings by teachers, and systematic class-room observations.

Intelligence tests. Data from intelligence tests indicate the immediate impact of the programs upon the general level of functioning of the children involved. Scores are in no way considered to be indicative of either innate ability or potential capacity. Standardized intelligence tests are easily available indicators of effective programming, and for the population under study here, help to predict later social adjustment in school and academic achievement (Weikart, 1967).

Tables 1 and 2 present the information from the Stanford-Binet, Form LM, as a pre-test, post-test, and change scores. Both Wave 5 and Wave 6 change scores are significantly different across groups when the contrast groups are included in the analysis. However, with the contrast groups removed, no significant differences are found among treatment groups. The three year olds in the program of Wave 6 have almost identical I.Q. gains with a narrow range of 27.5 to 30.2 points gained. The four year olds in Wave 5 show a range of 17.6 to 24.4 points gained. Three year olds seem to typically record greater gains than four year olds, reflecting the type of items on the Stanford-Binet, the greater malleability of this age group in situations producing change, or the impact of large mental age changes on a limited chronological age base. The essential point of the table,

Table 3

Wave 5 (4 year olds) Leiter International Performance Scale
and Peabody Picture Vocabulary Test Post-test Scores

	Unit (N-7)		Cognitive (N-11)		Language (N-7)		F-ratio	p
	M	SD	M	SD	M	SD		
Leiter	96.0	6.07	93.9	11.10	89.8	9.97	<1	NS
Peabody	94.7	19.65	84.0	20.46	77.3	13.80	<1	NS

Table 4

Wave 6 (3 year olds) Leiter International Performance Scale
and Peabody Picture Vocabulary Test Post-test Scores

	Unit (N-8)		Cognitive (N-4)		Language (N-8)		F-ratio	p
	M	SD	M	SD	M	SD		
Leiter	103.2	19.77	112.7	0.83	110.6	7.79	<1	NS
Peabody	78.0	7.61	84.7	9.30	88.4	9.45	1.3656	NS

however, is that all groups gained equally. Indeed, at the three year old level almost identical gains were obtained by children in each of the three programs.

Waves 0, 1, 2, 3, and 4 were part of the original Ypsilanti Perry Preschool Project which started in the fall of 1962. Each curriculum group of Wave 5 (4 year olds) and Wave 6 (3 year olds) attended one school together. Wave 5 Cognitive program children had completed two years of preschool at the post-testing. The pre-test scores for all children are from the first Stanford-Binet administration, and the post-test scores are from the most recent testing (June, 1968). The contrast group is Wave 3 control group of the Perry preschool project taken at ages 3 and 4, and is typical of no treatment controls throughout the five years of that study.

Tables 3 and 4 present post-test scores for the three curriculum treatment groups on the Leiter International Performance Scale and Peabody Picture Vocabulary Test. Again, all three treatment groups obtained scores that are not significantly different. The results do not show any predictable pattern. The Leiter is in the expected direction for the Wave 5 children. The Unit and the Cognitive programs, being more manipulative and object experience oriented, have the higher scores. However, the pattern is not repeated with Wave 6 children. Then too, the Peabody is clearly in the expected direction for Wave 6 with the Language Training children obtaining higher scores. The reverse is true, however, of Wave 5 children. In general, the Stanford-Binet gives the highest estimate of the child's functional level. The essential point is that there are no significant differences in intelligence test scores for the children in the three treatment groups, and the gains are unusually large.

Classroom teacher ratings. The teachers in each program were asked to rate all children in their program on two scales: Pupil Behavior Inventory and the Ypsilanti Rating Scale. These instruments reflect such factors as independence, academic competence, emotional adjustment, socio-emotional state, etc. These ratings were completed by each team of teachers for their own class; as such they are not independent indicators of the actual behavior, etc., of the children. When these data are analyzed according to curricula, there are no significant differences. The children in each of the three programs are seen by their teachers as being much the same in spite of differentiated program focus fostering potentially differentiated modes of adjustment. In addition, it is also important to note that the teachers in all three programs rated children who showed academic competence as emotionally adjusted ($4 = .67$, $p < .01$).

Classroom Observations. A recent paper by Seifert (1969) reports on the observations of classroom behavior in the Cognitive and Language Training programs (the Unit program was not observed) using the OScAR method. Observing group teaching sessions and employing total statements per minute, verbal feedback by teacher, amount of pupil-initiated interaction, amount of direct teacher management of pupil, and amount of affect expressed by teacher, Seifert found only total statements per minute as a significant difference between the two programs. The language program apparently does not operate differently, just more intensely.

Thus, in analyzing data from intelligence tests, teacher ratings, and classroom observations, no statistically significant differences are found among the programs. The gains recorded in intelligence tests are unusually high. While long-term follow-up data on school achievement, social adjustment, and eventual disposition of I.Q. level are not available at this time, data from the five year Perry Preschool Project indicate that children who show early and rapid intellectual growth as a result of preschool intervention also show later social adjustment and academic achievement.

These results are unexpected. While there is no special merit in finding no differences among treatment groups, these results, obtained in a compensatory education project with disadvantaged children, raise two critical questions: 1) Why are the intelligence test change scores so large; that is, why are I.Q. gains far above those usually reported in the literature? and 2) Why are there no differences in impact among curricula?

It must be stated that these programs really *are* different in their apparent or symptomatic operation. As part of the evaluation program a wide range of outside critics are brought to Ypsilanti to appraise the program. Among these consultants have been E. Kuno Beller, Marion Blank, Courtney Cazden, Joseph Glick, Lawrence Kohlberg, and Todd Risley. These critics find the programs different in theoretical commitment and differentiated in application. The Unit and Cognitive curricula are more similar to each other in classroom operation than either is to the Language Training program. The observations of these critics along with the systematic data collected from the approximately 850 visitors who have spent one to five days at the demonstration center in the last year clearly indicate that the programs appear to operate differently. Thus, even though the results of the programs are the same, when children are measured on general tests, it may be assumed that the operation is actually different for each.

Why are the change scores so large? The answer to this question is difficult and would seem to revolve around the selection of the curricula, staff model for program implementation, and the method of project operation.

Curriculum. Each of the three classroom units had a clear commitment to a specific theoretical curriculum model. This use of a model provided a framework that set limits for classroom operation and provided a challenge to the teachers. For example, the Cognitive program, derived in part from Piagetian theory, was intellectually challenging and suggestive of specific teaching methodologies. The same was true of the other two curricula to some degree. A framework also helped the teacher select appropriate activities, match program with desired outcome, and fit total classroom operation into a scheme directed at producing specific end products. However, it must again be noted that, at least among the three curricula studied here, the outcomes seem to be the same. The condition of no curriculum, typical of many preschools, was not tested.

Staff Model. A research and demonstration project produces a fairly specialized environment for staff operation. Since this particular project was aimed at the study of relative curriculum impact, the way the staff operated was kept uniform in all three programs. Some of the factors directly contributing to the unusually good results are:

1. *Planning.* All teachers had to prepare lesson plans at least a week in advance based upon the specific goals of the theoretical framework for their program. These plans proved to be a daily struggle demanding much thought and preparation, and they were available to visitors viewing the demonstration and to supervisors and consultants working with the teachers. The planning forced specific attention on the use of time in the classroom and the particular goals for each unit of operation. It provided opportunity for a constant review of curriculum effectiveness.

2. *Team teaching.* Two teachers were assigned to each classroom unit for teaching in and operation of one of the program models. Both teachers taught all the time, necessitating a constant effort to develop activities and to solve problems within the theoretical framework of the particular model they were employing. The team relationship permitted focus and support on classroom problems.

3. *Commitment.* In order to meet the expectations of the project and to be effective in the classroom, the teachers had to spend time over and above regular teaching time to stay ahead of the demands. Lunch hours, after school, "break times," etc., were often employed to prepare lessons, write reports, and meet with various staff members and visitors. This type of involvement came from a firm commitment to the program. It also meant that the program operated in each classroom was a direct expression of the individual teachers.

4. *Supervision.* Each team of teachers was supervised by an experienced teacher who worked with them to provide focus and to "referee" problems within the team. Rather than smoothing over problems, the supervisor worked with the teachers to help them face the issues and to work out a solution within the theoretical framework of their particular curriculum model. The supervisor also provided inservice training for the teachers within their curriculum model. While not authoritarian in operation, the supervisor was clearly responsible for helping the teachers keep to the instructional problems at hand.

5. *Respect for individual.* The project was operated as a group of professionals working to produce information. While this group operation ideal often broke down, the project attempted to keep all staff members in communication. It was interaction that gave the staff members an actual part in the development of the total project. It also kept the project "honest" by forcing all involved to consider all aspects of decisions.

6. *Project operation.* Several things that characterized the project operation would be expected to have impact on the quality of the results.

Involvement of the mother. Each of the three curricula included home teaching as part of the program in order to actively involve the mother in the process of education. While group meetings were held about once a month and some preschool observations were scheduled, the primary focus with parents was the educational activities in the home. The mothers responded well to these visits and increased their participation throughout the period of preschool attendance by their youngsters. The staff felt home teaching provided powerful supportive action for the child's growth.

Focus on the child. In order to prepare for the 90 minute home teaching session, the teacher would direct her attention to the particular problems of the child before the visit. Upon returning from the home the teacher would write a report on the visit documenting her observations. The home teaching sessions, therefore, provided an unusual opportunity for the teacher to focus upon the learning problems of each child. This knowledge was carried over into the classroom instructional program.

Focus on education. The project did not have professional staff other than teachers and research personnel. The project did not offer social work services, health services, referrals to clinics, agencies, etc. The teachers and the project families saw the teacher's role as clearly educational in nature. This single-purpose approach is practical in Southeastern Michigan where the services of the many agencies are readily available.

Language. Essential to the operation of all three curricula was the heavy use of language in the classroom with the students. While the method of language training varied greatly, in all the classes language was used extensively by the adults and was encouraged in the children.

Why are there no differences in impact among curricula? This question is difficult to answer because the results are much better than expected. Generally, projects of this nature detain similar results among intervention styles because none of the methods are very effective. This was not the case with this project. Among the many factors that may have contributed, three seem most crucial:

1. *The staff model and program operation are constant.* In the original design, the curricula were varied and the staff model and program operation were kept constant. From the initial data collected in this study, then, it is apparent that the choice of a curriculum framework is only of minor importance as long as *one* is selected that permits the intensive operation suggested by the staff model and program operation requirements.

2. *The curricula are equivalent.* The project data suggest that children may profit intellectually from any structured curriculum that is based on a wide range of experiences. In almost the sense that Chomsky uses in talking about the development of linguistic competence, a child has the potential to develop cognitive skills and good educational habits if he is presented with a situation which requires their expression. Kohlberg (1968) concluded that a child needs broad general forms of active experience for successful development of adequate cognitive abilities. He commented that a variety of specific types of stimulation are more or less functionally equivalent for cognitive development. These three curricula, as diverse as they appear to be, apparently are equivalent.

3. *The staff expectations for the children are high.* Much has been said recently about the "Rosenthal" effect and the impact of motivational changes on preschool outcomes when assessed by standard tests. Certainly a portion of

these gains has been produced by these factors. For example, Zigler (1968) identified a change of about six to ten I.Q. points as a product of improved motivation. Rosenthal has reported impressive gains in test performance by children in early grades labeled as "bright" for teachers by outside researchers. While these factors contributed to the size of the gains reported here, it is assumed that they were operating equally in all programs and that such gains were only a portion of the total.

CONCLUSIONS

The basic implication of these findings is that a shift in focus is necessary for both preschool education and compensatory education. The heavy emphasis on curriculum development, while important, has greatly overshadowed the need for careful attention to both the staff model and the program operation employed by a project. Either the mechanical application of a specific curriculum or the busy concern with administrative procedure that any program operation entails will doom a project to failure.

For preschool operation these findings mean that a staff is free to develop or employ any active curriculum that is believed to match the needs of the children so long as that curriculum provides an adequate vehicle for staff expression and program operation. The arguments about the relative effectiveness of the various approaches to preschool education are irrelevant. Then too, waiting for *the* curriculum for disadvantaged children to be developed so that early education programs can be effective is pointless. The process of creating and the creative application of *a* curriculum, not the particular curriculum selected or developed, is what is essential to success.

In addition, program operation must include careful attention to three areas. First, the program must include opportunity for the teacher to intensively think about each child in the project. Teachers apparently treat the educational development of young children more effectively if they evolve an intimate knowledge of how a child learns and responds through their own direct experience with that child. Second, the project must provide a way to include mothers in the educational process. This is not so much a transfer of information or experience to the mother as an attempt to create an atmosphere of support for intellectual growth in the home. Third, the staff model employed must allow opportunity for each individual to be creatively involved in the total operation. While administrative direction and good curriculum selection are important in obtaining program success, staff involvement is crucial. In an almost romantic sense, the human involvement of concerned teachers and staff is the key element in program success.

Featherstone, in a recent article, comments on the British Infant Schools:

> But the danger I'm most anxious to avoid is leaving the impression that one can single out a few elements of a good school and turn them into a

formula to impose on teachers and children in other schools. There is no single lever to pull, or technical solution. What we can do is work toward an idea of the kind of learning we wish to promote. That, among other things, is a matter of choosing what we value. (1969)

Our data agree with Featherstone's observation that there is no single lever to pull and certainly no technical solution. Compensatory education can reach the child through a range of programs appropriate to him. To be effective, however, it is necessary that the programs be organized and operated in such a manner as to allow the full utilization of human insight and commitment.

REFERENCES

Bereiter, C. and Engelmann, S. *Teaching disadvantaged children in the preschool.* Englewood Cliffs, N. J.: Prentice-Hall, 1966.

Curits, C. A., and Berzonsky, M. D. Preschool and primary education project. Council for Human Services Commonwealth of Pennsylvania, Harrisburg, Pa., 1967.

Deutsch, M. Interim progress report, part II. Institute for Developmental Studies, New York University, New York, 1968.

Dickie, J. P. Effectiveness of structured and unstructured (traditional) methods of language training. In Brottman, M. A. (Ed.) Language remediation for the disadvantaged preschool child. *Monographs of the Society for Research in Child Development.* No. 124, 1968, 62-79.

Di Lorenzo, L. T. and Salter, R. An evaluative study of prekindergarten programs for educationally disadvantaged children. *Exceptional Children,* 1968, 35, 111-119.

Featherstone, J. Why so few good schools? *New Republic,* January 4, 1969, 18-21.

Hawkridge, D. G., Chalupsky, A. B., and Roberts, A. O. A study of selected exemplary programs for the education of disadvantaged children. United States Department of Health, Education, and Welfare, 1968.

Hodges, W. L., McCandless, B. R., and Spicker, H. H. The development and evaluation of a diagnostically based curriculum for preschool psychosocially deprived children. United States Department of Health, Education, and Welfare, 1967.

Jencks, C. An alternative to endless school crisis – private schools for black children. *The New York Times Magazine,* November 3, 1968.

Karnes, M. B., Teska, J. A., and Hodgins, A. S. A longitudinal study of disadvantaged children who participated in three different preschool programs. Paper presented at the annual meeting of the American Educational Research Association, Los Angeles, California, 1969.

Klaus, R. A. and Gray, S. W. The early training project for disadvantaged children: a report after five years. *Monographs of the Society for Research in Child Development*, No. 120, 1968.

Kohlberg, L. Early education: a cognitive-developmental view. *Child Development*, 1968, 39, 1013-1062.

Sears, P. S. and Dowley, E. M. Research on teaching in the nursery school. In Gage, N. S. (Ed.) *Handbook of research on teaching*. Chicago: Rand McNally, 1963, 811-864.

Weikart, D. P. (Ed.) *Preschool intervention: preliminary report of the Perry Preschool Project*. Ann Arbor, Michigan: Campus Publishers, 1967.

Zigler, E. and Butterfield, E. C. Motivational aspects of change in I.Q. test performance of culturally deprived nursery school children. *Child Development*, 1968, 39, 1-14.

EVALUATING COMPENSATORY EDUCATION: A CASE STUDY

Philip K. Jensen, James M. O'Kane,
David Graybeal and Robert W. Friedrichs

Providing enrichment opportunities for lower-income children has increasingly become an integral part of urban educational programs. Compensatory education projects presently number in the thousands, and each year hundreds of new approaches and applications are reported in the literature (for a partial listing and substantive discussion of such programs, see Wilkerson, 1965; also see Gordon and Wilkerson, 1966; Miller and Woock, 1970: 220-261). Generally, these programs assume that innovative curricula, nontraditional teaching methods, cultural enrichment projects, inner-city reading materials, and the like *should* have a positive impact on objective academic achievement. Such an assumption has provided the basis for both massive public funding and private foundation support for elementary and secondary education. In most of these instances, there has been minimal questioning of the presumed cause-effect relation between these compensatory programs and positive academic achievement.

Yet, for all the concern, there have been comparatively few studies which satisfactorily test the outcome of such programs. When they have been evaluated, the results are often meager, and opinions based on them contradictory simply because the methodologies are, at best, suspect. Thus, Arthur Jensen (1969), for example, suggests that compensatory education has been a failure, while Hunt (1969) feels that it has never really been fully implemented. Miller and Woock (1970) also attempted an evaluation of the area; yet due to the paucity of substantive data, they included only three major programs in their assessment (Headstart, New York's More Effective Schools Program, and the Quincy Illinois Project). The evaluation of Headstart by the Westinghouse Learning Corporation (1969) has produced findings which seriously question the effectiveness of this program.

It is, then, understandable that the Coleman report (Coleman et al., 1966) has evoked surprise and controversy in the educational community. Although the report was not specifically concerned with compensatory education, it did indicate that for both minority and white children, curriculum differences, school facilities, teacher experience, and teacher resources have little impact on academic achievement, as measured by verbal ability test scores. The two major factors contributing to achievement were the social class background of the student and the social class composition of the school. This at least suggests that the heavy expenditures involved in compensatory programs may have been misplaced in light of the actual sources of educational failure.

However, the Coleman report has come under attack from numerous sources. Bowles (1968) has criticized some aspects of its use of multiple regression analysis, as have Cain and Watts (1970). Dyer (1968) has taken issue with the use of verbal ability scores as a measure of school achievement.

On the other hand, Moynihan (1968) has defended the report and has criticized various "establishments" for trying to ignore its findings. Even Coleman's critics note that their criticisms do not necessarily destroy either the impact or the tone of his findings. Bowles (1968:95) writes,

> were we merely to raise the quality of the teaching resources devoted to the education of Negroes to the level currently devoted to whites, we would significantly improve Negro achievement. Nevertheless, we would reduce the gap in Negro and white verbal achievement at grade 12 by only a little more than a quarter.

A telling criticism of compensatory education is found in the work of Elsbery (1969). Citing reading achievement scores, he concludes that no demonstrable gains have been achieved through the provision of compensatory programs. He notes that, more often than not, the child is manipulated rather than educated in these programs. In this same vein, Dentler (1969) suggests that the programs that have been designed to develop reading competency and which have been funded under conditions similar to Title I auspieces are of indeterminate educational value.

It seems apparent that the argument over the relative success or failure of compensatory education is far from settled. There is *little* consensus regarding the effectiveness of various programs as presently constituted and *no* consensus relative to their future continuance, reform, or abandonment. Even the political impact of evaluating such programs has been rasied (Weiss, 1970). Much of this uncertainty arises from the absence of concrete data evaluating such programs;

not too surprisingly, the confusion largely stems from the fact that few people know, with any degree of certitude, *what* has actually been accomplished in these programs.

In the analysis that follows, the authors have addressed themselves to some aspects of this problem. Each has been engaged in a team effort to evaluate the still operating Newark-Victoria Plan over the first full five years (1966-1970) of its existence. Annual evaluations of the project's operations have involved not only subjective factors (interviews with teachers, staff, administrators) but have also utilized such "hard" data as could be obtained. The present analysis will concentrate on the latter.

THE NEWARK-VICTORIA PLAN

The plan has been funded by the Victoria Foundation in conjunction with the Newark, New Jersey, Board of Education. Specifically, one public elementary school in Newark's Central Ward — the Cleveland School — had been selected as the focus of a massive attack on educational deprivation. The Cleveland School might be described as a "typical" lower-income urban school. It is located in Newark's Central Ward (the focal point of the urban disorders of 1967), and its student population is over 99% nonwhite. All the social and educational indices point to an overwhelmingly lower-income population. In short, the Cleveland School is a good example of the so-called "inner-city school." During an approximately six-year period, the Victoria Foundation has invested roughly $1,000,000 beyond the school's regular budget in an attempt to enrich the students' educational experience. The Newark Board of Education likewise allocated additional funds beyond the usual amount for other comparable inner-city schools, as Victoria phased out some of the areas of the program. In substance, then, the program has been well funded, and monies have been available for experimentally innovative programs. The plan has thus enjoyed considerable financial and moral support from both the Victoria Foundation and the Board of Education.

The overall approach used by the staff in the Cleveland School might be described as similar to that of other compensatory programs. In addition to the traditional educational methods employed, a vast array of innovative services and techniques have been introduced, some of which will be described below.

The planning of the project has been largely in the hands of the teachers: new curriculum policy and decisions are usually controlled by the teachers themselves, in conjunction with the school's administration and the project staff. Teachers are given wide latitude in the use of new methods and materials, and grade-level workshops have been sponsored as a means of infusing new ideas and eliminating archaic and irrelevant materials.

The plan has supplemented the regular teaching staff with a developing staff of *project teachers* in such areas as science, speech, remedial and developmental reading, mathematics, language arts, and music. These project teachers were viewed as specialists who worked with the regular teacher in implementing the learning process. A *helping teacher*, whose function has been to assist the younger, less experienced teachers in their teaching roles was also introduced. The plan conducted a program of instruction for the substitute teachers at the Cleveland School, helping them prepare for certification and to upgrade their training. In summary, the program has provided for enriched and remedial instruction in nearly all major curricular areas.

Besides the experimental use of new teaching roles, the plan invested a substantial effort in curriculum changes. A prekindergarten program was initiated, and an increasingly heavy emphasis was placed on reading ability throughout all the grades. Various approaches were used, including the *Bank Street Readers*, the Frostig approach, and a set of materials titled *Hear, See and Read* developed in the school by one of the Cleveland teachers. Over the years, the curriculum has been continually examined and refurbished with new programs and emphases. Also, toward the end of the period, students were given practice standardized tests to orient them to test-taking.

The library of the school was greatly expanded and presently triples its original capacity of roughly one thousand books. A full-time librarian was made available to oversee the library and assist the children. Comprehensive health services, both medical and dental, were also provided.

Special efforts were made to enlarge the cultural horizons of the children. Field trips, an after-school club program, an Afro-American program, school assemblies dealing with Black history, and the like were all provided by the plan with the intention of building the self-esteem and cultural identity of the children.

Finally, the plan involved an unusually comprehensive set of sociopsychological services for the children and their families. A Social Service Center was established with five full-time professional social workers who provide casework services for the children in need of them. In addition, parent groups have been initiated to encourage parental involvement. A school psychologist also has been engaged, and together the social workers and psychologist have provided sociopsychological services far beyond those available to non-plan schools. These were supplemented at the staff level by a three-day "human relations session" during which personal and racial tensions were encouraged to surface in order to be handled responsibly. After an initial period during which turnover was high, largely as a result of promotions to supervisory positions in other compensatory education projects, the staffing has been fairly stable, permitting the growth of an integrated program.

In substance, then, the Newark-Victoria Plan can only be described as comprehensive in scope and imaginatively diversified in its operation. Its uniqueness rests on three attributes: first, it has been in operation for over six years; second, the teachers essentially control the curricula of the program; third, the plan has been backed up with substantial sociopsychological professional services. It has functioned with ample funding, creative leadership, and the active support of both the local community and Newark's Board of Education. It has incorporated numerous innovative features of other programs and has in turn served as a model for more recent projects. It has been unified by a highly trained staff who have attempted to reverse the usual downtrend in lower-income urban education. This saturation of one school with some, if not most, of the best compensatory approaches should, if the usual explanations of compensatory education are correct, effect some real changes in the students' academic performances.

From a vast amount of anecdotal material gathered over the plan's duration (interviews with teachers, administrators, social workers, and so on), the authors discovered that there was a great deal of enthusiasm, particularly in the earlier years of the program. Most of the individuals interviewed were highly positive toward the new efforts, and most felt that changes had taken place. Yet in light of the frequent discrepancies between opinions and measurable accomplishments in educational data, little confidence should be placed in this type of result. The main weight of the evaluation was placed on empirical data collected to ascertain the spceific effects of the plan. What follows then constitutes a summary picture of these data.

METHODOLOGY

In order to assess such effects, experimental and control groups were established for the 1966-1967 school year and for each subsequent year. The actual testing was done in October of each year. Hence, the data are always a year old. Consequently, for the six years of the project, the authors are utilizing five years of empirical data. In the Cleveland School, the entire third and sixth grades were used. These grades were chosen because there is a comprehensive, citywide testing program for the third and sixth grades in Newark. Hence, there would be comparable scores across all the schools in the Newark system. For control groups, two schools similar to the Cleveland School were selected. The student population of these schools was similar to that of the experimental school in size, geographical residence, racial composition, socioeconomic variables, IQ scores, and reading levels. The control groups for any given data analysis were selected from their third and sixth grades. Thus, in each year's analysis, the possible control groups contained approximately twice the number of subjects as the experimental group.

In the data presented below (Tables 1 to 3), a number of different variables are analyzed. The overall pattern used was an examination of the means for reading, absences, and intelligence comparing the full experimental and control groups to the city norms. Next, in an effort to further clarify the data, selected subgroups were subjected to a factorial analysis of variance of their reading scores and absence records. The independent variables used in these analyses were sex, high versus low intelligence, and project or nonproject membership.

Yet a major difficulty remained. Since the research analysis entailed basically the examination of standardized test scores (IQ and reading ability level), there was no way to control the possible effects of such cultural problems as inappropriate norms, or restricted range of variables such as IQ in this population, which might limit the proportion of true to error variance in the data. Thus as Dyer (1968) has noted, the positive effects of the program might be masked by measurement problems for all the children, both experimental and control, on standardized tests. Another possibility which also remained was that the children were learning something *other* than the variables being tested.

To minimize these pitfalls, the authors decided to examine the academic success of junior high school students who had been exposed to the Newark-Victoria Plan at the Cleveland School. The junior high school was chosen which was attended by the largest number of Cleveland's graduates. This school also draws heavily from the graduates of four other elementary schools in the area. In addition, its students are grouped homogeneously on the basis of IQ and reading ability. Plan students from Cleveland are present and more or less evenly distributed in all classes from lowest to highest ability.

The experimental group was thus composed of all the students from the Cleveland School. The control subjects were from other schools not having a similarly developed compensatory program. In choosing them, the next two names on each class roll following a Cleveland student were selected as controls.

These groups were then compared, not on the basis of standardized test data, but rather in terms of the semester grades they achieved. Thus, their actual academic performance was used as the criterion variable. Again, if effects from the plan were present and they did not emerge in the standardized data, they might surface in the actual records of performance. This comparison of grades presents a method of avoiding the social class bias noted as a possible problem in standardizing testing.

It should be mentioned that the junior high school teachers did not know which students in their classes had been from the plan and which students were from typical schools. The authors interviewed teachers and discovered no bias resulting from elementary school attended was operative in terms of teachers' attitudes.

Over the five years for which grades were analyzed, it was possible to investigate the effect of the experimental group subject's length of exposure to the project at the Cleveland School.

In a general repetition of the analyses of the hard data at the Cleveland School, the overall comparisons of means were supplemented by an analysis of variance on selected samples using sex, ability levels, and project membership in elementary school as factors.

RESULTS

Our discussion of the results falls into three main areas. The first section deals with the data on reading scores, intelligence tests, and absences compiled while the children were enrolled in the Cleveland School and thus members of the ongoing program. The second part deals with the achievement of children who graduated from the Newark-Victoria Plan at the Cleveland School and are in their first year of junior high school. The third presents a suggestion on what may actually be happening as a result of the plan.

THE EVALUATION AT THE CLEVELAND SCHOOL

Every year in the early fall, the school system in Newark conducts a series of tests on all third- and sixth-grade students. The tests used include the 1963 edition of the Stanford Reading Tests, the Metropolitan Reading Tests, and the Kahlman-Anderson sixth and seventh editions. These tests are used to measure reading and intelligence, for a variety of educational, counseling and administrative purposes.

These tests formed the basis for an examination of measurable gains resulting from the Newark-Victoria Plan. The Cleveland students were compared to their counterparts from the two control schools both as a group, utilizing a simple comparison of means and also in selected samples using an analysis of variance design.

Table 1 compares the experimental and control groups on reading level. The scores are expressed as months above or below the city norms to facilitate comparisons which would otherwise be confused by shifts in the tests used and by major cultural changes affecting the city as a whole.

TABLE 1

Average Reading Scores Shown as Months
Above or Below City Norms(a)

	1965-1966	1966-1967	1967-1968	1968-1969	1969-1970
Third Grade					
Cleveland	−3	−2	−1	−2	0
Control	2½	½	0	0	2
Sixth Grade					
Cleveland	0	−2	−2	−6	− ½
Control	−4	−1½	−2	−1	−1

(a) The standard error for third-grade scores is roughly half a month at third-grade levels and about a month at sixth-grade levels.

The first year shown, 1965-1966, is based on tests given in October 1965. The scores reflect about one month of full operation of the plan and may be thought of as a baseline for the later comparisons. Thus 1966-1967 scores show a full year of program effects, and 1969-1970 scores have been influenced by four years of operation. The majority of the students included in the 1969-1970 third grade had spent their entire academic lives under the Newark-Victoria Plan.

Particular attention should be paid to the cohort of students who were in third grade in 1965-1966 and sixth grade in 1968-1969, since they represent an anomaly. They are markedly below their controls in reading, a situation that did not exist either in the preceding or following cohorts. This cohort will appear again below and in the junior high school data.

Overall there is no evidence of a shift favoring the Cleveland students, which implies that the plan did little to raise their level of reading.

Table 2 shows a similar pattern for intelligence test scores. Once again, the Cleveland and control students follow each other along the years, neither gaining nor losing in any fixed pattern. Again, the implication is that the plan did little to change the average IQ scores of the Cleveland subjects.

TABLE 2

Average IQ Scores Shown as Points
Above or Below City Norms(a)

	1965-1966	1966-1967	1967-1968	1968-1969	1969-1970
Third Grade					
Cleveland	−1	−6	−2	−2	−2
Controls	−1	−1	0	0	−3
Sixth Grade					
Cleveland	−5	−1	−3	−2	−2
Controls	−3½	−2½	−2	−1	−2

(a) The standard error for any of these scores may be considered approximately 1 point.

An attempt to gain additional information was made by running an analysis of variance on samples of the test scores. Table 3 presents a breakdown on the variation in the reading scores with level of intelligence (high versus low, defined as above or below the mean for Cleveland and the control schools), sex, plan membership (Cleveland or control), grade level (third versus sixth grade), and year (1966-1967, 1967-1968, and 1968-1969), taken as factors. These three years were chosen simply because ample data for these years were available. While a complex design of this type poses problems for an accurate evaluation of

TABLE 3
Analysis of Variance of Reading Scores Received
by Sample Third- and Sixth-Grade Children
from Cleveland and Control Schools

Source of Variation	Sums of Squares	Degrees of Freedom	Mean Squares	F-Ratios
A (intelligence)	13885.209	1	13885.209	178.724(b)
B (sex)	417.384	1	417.384	5.372(a)
AB	21.301	1	21.301	—
C (Cleveland versus control schools)	2378.251	1	2378.251	30.612(b)
AC	251.126	1	251.126	3.232
BC	4.959	1	4.959	—
ABC	49.959	1	49.959	—
D (3rd versus 6th grade)	84543.844	1	84543.844	1088.206(b)
AD	1502.501	1	1502.501	19.339(b)
BD	.459	1	.459	—
ABD	73.151	1	73.151	—
CD	466.209	1	466.209	6.001(a)
ACD	635.376	1	635.376	8.178(b)
BCD	151.209	1	151.209	1.946
ABCD	1.751	1	1.751	—
E (year)	670.352	2	335.176	4.314(a)
AE	288.356	2	144.178	1.856
BE	607.881	2	303.941	3.912(a)
ABE	108.777	2	54.389	—
CE	3091.264	2	1545.632	19.895(b)
ACE	750.952	2	375.476	4.833(b)
BCE	105.994	2	52.997	—
ABCE	5.856	2	2.928	—
DE	297.231	2	148.616	1.913
ADE	3.077	2	1.539	—
BDE	124.619	2	62.309	—
ABDE	202.390	2	101.195	1.303
CDE	1066.919	2	533.459	6.866(b)
ACDE	799.464	2	399.732	5.145(b)
BCDE	111.506	2	55.753	—
ABCDE	127.727	2	63.864	—
Error	70854.000	912	77.691	—
Total	182599.054	959		

(a) $p < .05$.
(b) $p < .01$.

significance levels and interpretation of multiple interactions, the F ratios obtained serve as a good summary of the comparative strength of effects. The total number of subjects in the sample was 960, half from Cleveland and one-quarter from each of the two control schools. While a full discussion of all effects and a presentation of the related means would be inappropriate to this paper, some consideration of the results, particularly those involving the Cleveland school (c), serves to verify the position that there was no direct profit from attending Cleveland. In fact, the data suggests that with the additional statistical control over sex, intelligence, and grade level, the comparative position of the Cleveland students deteriorates.

The fact that high-intelligence students read better than low (A), or that third graders are somewhat poorer readers than sixth graders (D) is not surprising. The point which is most interesting is that the strong effect for membership in the Cleveland program (C) results from the Cleveland students averaging three months *below* their controls in reading. While part of this deficit is attributable to the odd cohort noted before, the general message is clear. The Cleveland students do *not* outperform their controls on standardized reading tests. In fact, the opposite has occurred — the controls have outdistanced the Cleveland subjects.

The interaction between plan and year (CE) again points up the odd cohort's unusually large deficit. The girls are predictably more than a month ahead of the boys in level (B). While the remaining cluster of effects is apparently due to a variety of differences involving particular years and grades, it is worth noting that six of the eight largest interactions, including the one noted above, involve program membership.

A similar anslysis of variance, run on the absence data from the same three years, shows no difference between program and control students in overall attendance. However, there was a significant effect (F = 10.431) in the interaction of grade level with plan. Specifically, Cleveland third graders missed two more days of class than their counterparts, while the sixth-grade students missed three less.

In summary then: (a) the averages in intelligence and reading for the entire classes both at the third-grade and at the sixth-grade levels show no advantage for the Cleveland students over their controls; (b) the factorial analyses of reading scores and absence records over three years show no evidence of any superiority for program members, but do suggest somewhat different patterns within the experimental and control groups.

THE EVALUATION AT THE JUNIOR HIGH SCHOOL

Each year, as pointed out earlier in this paper, when the students from Cleveland and the other feeder schools reach junior high school, they are assigned to homogeneous classes. These are formed on the basis of the students' previous academic record and standardized test scores. Students in the low-numbered classes are those persons judged most capable. Those in groups with high numbers are those of whom the least is expected. This structure permits an unusually valid control group to be constructed. When possible, two students from other schools were chosen for each former Cleveland student in a given group. The resulting controls were matched not only in overall academic ability as reflected by test scores and previous work, but also in terms of teachers and daily class experiences during the seventh grade. While the number of Cleveland and control students varied from ability group to ability group and from year to year, the overall distribution of the two samples was always closely matched.

Grade point averages based on A equals 4, B equals 3, down to F equals 0 were computed for major courses. Table 4 shows the averages for all students in the experimental and control groups.

TABLE 4

Typical Grade Point Averages in Seventh Grade
at Junior High School (a)

Year	Cleveland	Controls	Difference
1965-1966	2.01	1.94	.07
1966-1967	1.86	1.82	.04
1967-1968	1.82	1.54	.28
1968-1969	1.95	1.62	.33
1969-1970	1.92	1.77	.15

(a) N varied between 85 and 100 for the Cleveland groups and between 160 and 190 for the controls. The respective standard errors of the means vary from about .08 to .05.

As before, the 1965-1966 year serves as a baseline with little or no effect expected from the program; 1969-1970 shows students who spent up to four full years at Cleveland. The first year of added educational advantages produced no effect, but students who spent two or more years under the plan clearly outperformed their controls.

A complication is added to the interpretation since the 1969-1970 group of Cleveland students are the previously noted odd cohort. Whether the effect of the plan has crested or not is difficult to determine. What is clear is that students who were *lower* on reading tests a year earlier received *higher* grades than would be expected.

In examining this table, no attempt should be made to compare the grades from year to year, since these fluctuated considerably during the five-year period for reasons largely irrelevant to this study. The central point is the size of the advantages obtained by plan students over their respective controls.

The students from the 1967-1968 and 1969-1970 seventh grades were followed into eighth grade to measure the durability of the noted gains. The advantage of the former group drops from .28 in seventh grade to .02 in eighth grade. The latter group dropped back from .33 to .23. Since the curriculum diversifies sharply at the ninth-grade level, it is impossible to trace the gains further with the same level of control. In individual subject areas where tracing was possible, the remaining advantage was dissipated in the third year. Whether the gains will eventually prove durable remains to be seen, but the evidence suggests that the advantage of the plan for children diminishes with each additional year in junior high school.

An analysis of variance based on a randomly selected sample and using grade point averages over the five years is shown in Table 5. The four factors are ability level (defined as those students in the third of the classes with the highest academic potential and those in the third with the lowest academic potential), sex, plan membership (ex-Cleveland students and their controls), and year (1965-1966 through 1969-1970). The number of students used was 480.

In variables A and B, the ratios result from the fact that high-ability students outscore low-ability ones by .43 and that girls outscore boys by .40, again hardly surprising findings.

In examining the effect of the plan (C), the advantage of the Cleveland group amounts to .22, producing an F which is significant beyond the 1% level. This is of particular interest, since the data included the two early years and the last year of the plan — years which could have masked the effects of the program.

An analysis of variance of a similar structure was run on absence data for the same students. There was no indication of a difference between plan and control students either in the main effects or the interactions.

In summary, although absence records show no differences between the experimental and control subjects, there is a definite advantage for Cleveland students, demonstrated in the overall means and the related analysis of variance when academic grade received is used as the criterion.

A SUGGESTION ON WHAT IS HAPPENING

What conclusions can be based on these two sets of data? The situation presented is one in which, using standardized tests of reading and intelligence or using absence records, no evidence was discovered which showed gains for the Cleveland program. However, using academic grades, it was possible to demonstrate a real, albeit small, profit in a follow-up study of the former plan students in attendance at the local junior high school. Apparently the advantages came in areas *other* than those tapped by the standardized measures.

If a breakdown by course of study over the last three years is performed, we find a .37 grade point advantage for project students in social studies; the next highest is .32 in English; and the third is .23 in reading. Science with .22, and mathematics with .07 complete the list of major subjects. In each of these last

TABLE 5

Analysis of Variance of Grades Received by Sample
Cleveland and Control Students in the
Seventh Grade at the Junior High School

Source of Variation	Sums of Squares	Degrees of Freedom	Mean Squares	F-Ratios
A (ability level)	39.465	1	39.465	58.294(a)
B (sex)	19.226	1	19.226	28.441(a)
AB	.058	1	.058	—
C (Cleveland versus control schools)	5.648	1	5.648	8.355(a)
AC	.004	1	.004	—
BC	1.412	1	1.412	2.089
ABC	.881	1	.881	1.305
D (year)	5.233	4	1.308	1.935
AD	1.259	4	.315	—
BD	3.249	4	.812	1.201
ABD	3.369	4	.842	1.246
CD	.943	4	.236	—
ACD	3.463	4	.866	1.281
BCD	.290	4	.072	—
ABCD	.368	4	.092	—
Error	297.468	440	.676	—
Total	382.336	479	—	—

(a) $p < .01$.

areas (science and mathematics), Cleveland has operated a specific program using a specialized project teacher. In the two courses with the most direct relationship to reading — English and reading — the differential gains are greater than in those with special programs which were aimed directly at producing improvements.

An evaluation of a similar but somewhat less extensive program (Jensen et al., 1968) had previously suggested that larger gains were to be found for males than for females in compensatory programs of this type.

One way of combining the idea of gains in academic achievement (without increases in standardized test results) with the larger gains being recorded by the normally academically weaker male is to suggest that the gains may be largely due to improved *social* adjustment to the school situation. This adjustment could be related to improvements in motivation or interest, or in specific skills involving classroom behavior. It might be suggested that the better students in any group should have already made satisfactory adjustments which would consequently mean that the largest gains would be on the part of the weaker students. If this is realistic, then it is reasonable to expect a similar advantage to show up for low-ability students, as well as for the male students.

To test this suggestion, the data for the last three years, during which the project effects have been demonstrable, were reexamined. The differences between Cleveland and control means were calculated based on all the students in the high- and low-ability groups. Table 6 shows these mean advantages over the appropriate control groups broken down by sex and year.

TABLE 6

Mean Advantages in Grade Point Average of
High- and Low-Ability Cleveland Students over Their Controls(a)

	1967-1968		1968-1969		1969-1970	
	Female	Male	Female	Male	Female	Male
High ability	.38	.42	.15	.06	−.23	.03
Low ability	.21	.25	.23	.47	.13	.34

(a) The number in the various cells average 16 for the program students and 34 for the controls. The standard error for the various means are on the order of .10 to .15.

In five of the six possible comparisons, the males profited more than the females, while, in four of the six cases, students of low ability have shown a greater advantage over their controls than high-ability students. In combination, the suggestion that the traditionally weaker academic group should show the greatest gain is borne out in nine of twelve cases (p < .08).

The case for this hypothesis is further strengthened if we follow the weaker groups' gains across the three years to note the effect of longer periods of plan exposure. If we combine the ability groups, the pattern of the results shows that the advantage of the males over their controls when contrasted to the advantage of the females over their controls increases between 1967-1968 and 1969-1970 from .04 to .07 to over .23. Likewise collapsing the data for sex shows the low-ability groups starting with .17 *less* of an advantage the first year, improving to .24 *more* the second year, and reaching .33 *more* by the last year!

The reason this effect does not appear in Table 5 is probably to be found in the considerably smaller numbers of cases in each group and the masking effect of the first two years before the results of the plan became apparent.

This line of reasoning on the effects of this type of compensatory education program does *not* suggest that there can be no gains in specific subject areas or in areas measurable on standardized tests. It *does* suggest that there may be gains in areas other than these and that these other gains may well be the major ones in the types of general compensatory programs which have largely been used in recent years.

The question remains as to whether gains on the order of an increase in grade point average of less than .35 (approximately one-third of a letter grade) are sufficient to warrant the effort, time, money, and dedication that have gone into this program. The problem is complicated by the probability that the largest gains are being registered by those students least likely to continue their education beyond high school. Similarly, there is little evidence on the question of whether or how well adjustment to school generalizes to the larger world. Still another issue is found in the fact that the durability of gains must be shown if they are to have value at more than the immediate level of the child's adjustment in school. Finally the priorities to be assigned to different outcomes such as increasing the child's satisfaction with school, improved academic achievements, and the like must be clarified.

SUMMARY AND CONCLUSIONS

This analysis has attempted to assess the impact of a long-range compensatory education program in Newark, New Jersey. Using an array of data from a five-year period and a variety of statistical devices, the authors have found no observable gains in reading level, school attendance, or IQ scores as the result of a five-year analysis of the Newark-Victoria Plan. The experimental subjects who were exposed to the extensive academic programs show little or no gain over their non-plan controls. In certain instances, they actually did more poorly than their controls.

If the analysis had been limited to these data, the plan would necessarily have been judged a failure. However, the use of standardized tests as a sole criterion of improvement is suspect. Therefore, the authors decided to follow the plan children into junior high school to see how they compared with children not exposed to programs as extensive as those of the plan. In this analysis, the major criteria were the actual grades received in courses of study.

In this stage of the evaluation, the plan students markedly outperformed their non-plan controls. Since the teachers were unaware of which students had been exposed to the plan, it is fair to assume that the observed differences are real and are not effects of teacher selection, self-fulfilling prophecies, or the like. The identifiable effects of the Newark-Victoria Plan, to date, appear to lie mainly in the area of academic achievement, but not in those facets measured by standardized tests.

In further analyzing the data, the authors recalled that, in another compensatory education project at the junior high school level, the male children outgained their female counterparts. Combining this observation with the overall finding that the plan children do not perform significantly better in academic areas than their non-plan controls, the authors hypothesized that what the plan children learn are not *academic skills*, but rather *social adjustment skills* involving the incorporation of the cues for successful classroom behavior (e.g., deference to teachers, discipline, orderliness, and so on). In pursuing this hypothesis, authors speculated that, in the Cleveland data, the males should show greater improvement than the females in grades and that, further, if the line of reasoning were correct, the lower-ability children would outperform their higher-ability counterparts, when compared to the appropriate control groups.

In re-analyzing the data, the authors found substantial verification of their hypothesis, since the greatest comparative gains were indeed recorded by the male and low-ability groups.

In summary then, four basic suggestions have been presented:

1. The investment in a fully developed compensatory program such as the one described has little or no impact on reading ability or IQ score.

2. It is possible to produce academic gains in such a program, even though these gains may not be demonstrated through traditional standardized test procedures. In this program, the gains were apparent in the follow-up analysis of junior high school course grades.

3. While these gains are desirable and important, they can only be described as modest, since they represent roughly a movement of one-third grade difference between plan and non-plan children (e.g., C+ as opposed to C).

4. The main thrust of the program may have been in the area of the development and internalization of social adjustment skills. Hence, the largest gains in such programs will be made in the lowest groups (e.g., low-ability male students) rather than the highest groups, as commonly expected.

It is worth noting that these findings indirectly substantiate some of the more controversial findings of the Coleman report. Coleman et al. (1966), indicated that school resources contribute little to academic achievement, as indicated through standardized measures. This analysis has similarly shown that the investment in up-to-date compensatory educational techniques registers little or no gain vis-a-vis reading level and IQ. In addition, Coleman indicated that differences in educational facilities would affect poorer students more than it would better students. This analysis indirectly supports this finding since, in the Newark-Victoria Plan, those who gained most were those normally judged as least likely to succeed academically. Overall, this study suggests answers to certain questions while posing numerous new ones.

REFERENCES

Bowles, S. (1968) "Toward equality of educational opportunity?" Harvard Educational Rev. 38: 89-99.

Cain, G. and H. Watts (1970) "Problems in making policy inference from the Coleman Report." Amer. Soc. Rev. 35, 2: 228-242.

Coleman, J. S. et al. (1966) Equality of Educational Opportunity. Washington, D.C.: Department of Health, Education and Welfare.

Dentler, R. (1969) "Urban eyewash: a review of 'Title I, year II.'" Urban Rev. 3: 32 ff.

Dyer, H. (1968) "School factors and equal educational opportunity." Harvard Educational Rev. 38: 38-56.

Elsbery, J. W. (1969) "Educational reform: changing the premise." Urban Rev. 3: 4 ff.

Friedrichs, R. W., D. Graybeal, and P. K. Jensen (1968) The Newark Plan at West Kinney Junior High School: An Evaluation. Newark, N. J.: Board of Education.

———— and J. M. O'Kane (1970) The 1970 Report of the Status of the Newark, New Jersey Board of Education — Victoria Foundation Plan. Newark, N. J.: Victoria Foundation.

Gordon, E. W. and D. Wilkerson (1966) Compensatory Education for the Disadvantaged. New York: College Entrance Examination Board.

Hunt, J. M. (1969) "Has compensatory education failed? Has it been attempted?" Harvard Educational Rev. 39: 278-300.

Jensen, A. R. (1969) "How much can we boost IQ and scholastic achievement?" Harvard Educational Rev. 39: 1-123.

Miller, H. and R. Woock (1970) Social Foundations of Urban Education. Hinsdale, Ill.: Dryden.

Moynihan, D. P. (1968) "Sources of resistance to the Coleman Report." Harvard Educational Rev. 38: 23-35.

Westinghouse Learning Corporation (1969) "An evaluation of the effects of Head Start experience on children's cognitive and affective development." Preliminary draft, Ohio University, April.

Weiss, C. H. (1970) "The politicization of evaluation research." J. of Social Issues 26, 4: 57-68.

Wilkerson, D. (1965) "Programs and practices in compensatory education for disadvantaged children." Rev. of Educational Research 35 (December): 426-440.

COMPENSATORY EDUCATION: EVALUATION IN PERSPECTIVE

Edmund W. Gordon

In the mid 1960's the federal government began its large-scale intervention in the development and education of poor children. At the time, a preeminent educational research scientist — one of the most distinguished in the nation — reportedly declined to participate in an evaluation of the government's premier effort. Further clarification of activities and aspirations was necessary, this scholar contended, before criteria could be set and evaluation could occur. His pessimistic view did not deter an army of able, as well as not so able, investigators from rushing to evaluate the impact of Head Start and other programs of compensatory education. This is not to condemn them for their courage, or perhaps even their opportunism or recklessness. The author of this article marched along in the front ranks and even barked out a few of the orders for what proved to be rather futile skirmishes. However, it appears that the pessimistic prophet was by no means wrong — simply unheeded.

During the past five years, more than $10 billion has been invested in the education of poor and minority group members and at least $75 million has been spent on evaluations and special research projects. Despite this enormous expenditure, we are still not able to make definitive statements concerning the value of compensatory education. Even those of us who have been the most enthusiastic advocates of the need for such efforts have to concede that evidence of the value of our efforts is modest, if it exists at all. Some critics are far more harsh in their condemnation of the endeavor. A few have predictably asserted that compensatory education has not worked because it was practiced on a population which is genetically inferior and, hence, incapable of adequate response.

The sparsity of evidence in support of compensatory education may have little to do with its value. Some studies indicate that considerable slippage occurs between the designation of a program as compensatory and the actual imple- mentation of compensating elements in a child's education. As in the case of ethnic integration in public schools, it may be incorrect to conclude that the programs have not worked when in most instances they have not been tried. Yet, it is probably correct that some compensatory education is not very effective. The traditional use of drill and repetition in remedial education is not likely to improve achievement for disadvantaged children. Similarly, increasing guidance contacts from one to two or three per year or even providing more intensive personal counseling as a solitary treatment seems to make little difference. Reducing class size without changing what teachers do seems unimportant, and, similarly, modest increments in available materials have hardly brought about radical improvements. But these and other observations are impressions, partially supported by data, but generally inconclusive. There are few intensive, qualita- tive and systematic evaluations of compensatory education. Hard data are needed; solid research studies are required as a basis for policy decisions. We have instead an abundance of indefinite, conflicting and confusing studies. The value of compensatory education may be obfuscated, in part, because the practice of evaluative educational research is poor.

The weaknesses in the application of evaluative research to compensatory education partially stem from the complex political and economic circumstances under which these programs were initiated and developed. From their inception, programs involved large expenditures — often made for other than purely experimental educational reasons. Foundations, local and federal governments channeled more than $10 billion into the education of poor and minority group children. Some of the foundation efforts unfortunately seemed also to reflect a desire to establish organizational leadership, a domain of action, or a model program which would be identified with the foundation. The federal programs that succeeded the work of the foundations were subject to a different set of pressures, mainly political concerns. Federal programs were in part responses to the rising demand for a social revolution, for the improvement of human rights, and for the increased development of underprivileged populations. For a while, it seemed more important, politically to act, to be identified with the effort to do something, than to act wisely. There was little time for planning. With large sums of money being spent, and with political objectives clearly the motive, "pork barreling" and politically determined distribution of funds naturally developed. To maintain some semblance of responsible government, the executive branch began to press for evaluation data — to prove favored programs successful and to provide the basis for reducing or eliminating unpopular activities. Initially the legislature was not greatly concerned with evaluation. Rather, the executive branch initiated the evaluation of the impact of compensatory education.

In this context, it is easy to see that large expenditures hastily appropriated for new programs, political pressures for change and a piece of the action, and the demand for immediate proof of impact have complicated the evaluation of the effectiveness of these programs. Evans (Office of Education) and Schiller (Office of Economic Opportunity) discuss the pressures they were under while designing and implementing Head Start:

> Unfortunately, the political process is not orderly, scheduled, or rational. Crests of public and congressional support for social action programs often swell quickly and with little anticipation. Once legislation is enacted, the pressures on administrators for swift program implementation are intense. In these circumstances — which are the rule rather than the exception — pleas that the program should be implemented carefully, along the lines of a true experiment with random assignment of subjects so that we can confidently evaluate the program's effectiveness, are bound to be ignored.

The results of such conditions were program and research designs based upon well intended but precipitous decisions. Often when evaluations were attempted after the fact, it was discovered that the original design had been inadequate.

In addition, as Caro observes, the clients of such programs can present a sensitive and difficult situation for the evaluative research. He continues:

> Even though evaluative researchers may firmly believe that their efforts contribute ultimately to the cause of the poor, minority activists may confront them with great hostility . . . Preoccupied with the immediate,

tangible, dramatic, and personal, the minority activist is likely to be impatient with the evaluator's concern with the future abstract concepts, orderly procedures, and impersonal forces.

Quite apart from the problems related to the conditions under which programs were initiated and conducted are the problems of evaluative research in general. Here one often finds a low level of expertise and inadequately developed methods. The best educational research scientists often choose to work with basic problems in areas such as child development, learning, linguistics, rather than with evaluative research. Evaluative and field research have only recently gained in respect and demand among educators and the public. Consequently, high demand has been suddenly created in a field with insufficient expertise. Although many good research scientists were drawn into evaluation, they could not readily transfer their research competence to the new situation. Indeed, given their experience in controlled laboratory settings, the problems of evaluative and field research may have been more difficult for them than for some less experienced investigators.

In the conduct of evaluative research, one can distinguish three approaches or three levels of concern. The first attempts to discover whether or not a particular intervention program is effective: Are developmental and learning processes accelerated following the application of a particular teaching method, curriculum, etc.? The second level of concern is comparative: Is the particular intervention more effective than other known methods? The third level is explanatory: What is the nature of the relationship between specific intervention methods and specific associated changes in behavior? Most evaluative research has been directed at the first two levels of concern. The third level, however, is the most important. By answering questions on this level, one can establish a rational basis for action and begin to specify treatments in relation to known characteristics of the children to be served. At the third level the distinction between basic research and evaluative research collapses. The questions posed demand a quality of design which is appropriate to basic research but which can also serve the purposes of evaluation. Unfortunately, evaluative research of this quality has seldom been applied to compensatory education.

All of these approaches are made more complex by technical operational problems. The more compensatory education programs approach laboratory experimental conditions, the more one can discover what, how and why certain educational treatments alter educational underdevelopment. Yet, numerous obstacles stand in the way of establishing the necessary degree of precision and control in isolating variables and discovering the effectiveness of specific treatments.

One such obstacle involves difficulties in the utilization of an adequate method for selecting subjects. As Campbell and Erlebacher point out, "experimental" subjects are often not selected on a random basis. While the "control" group is selected to closely match the experimental group according to various indices, the control group is too often different from the experimental group in crucial aspects, however small a degree. Without random selection of subjects, the results of a program may reflect differences in the development of two populations — differences which are unrelated to the experimental treatment in question. In addition, matching procedures may produce regression artifacts. As for analysis of covariance and partial correlation, such biases may occur both where pretest scores are available and in after-the-fact studies. Campbell and Erlebacher propose true experiments in which randomization of subjects will avoid difficulties that previous quasi-experimental designs have encountered. However, parental objections, coupled with political pressures, have made large-scale application of random assignment of subjects impossible. Controlled comparative studies of this sort are often resisted by communities who will not accept arbitrary selection of subjects for experimentation when everyone wants the benefit of special treatment.

Another difficulty in establishing comparable experimental and control groups can be attributed to the influence of what has been called the radiation effect. Even if the two groups are initially "comparable," the effect of experimentation on the experimental subjects is radiated onto their families, siblings and eventually onto the control subjects if there is any contact, direct or indirect, between these several groups. Susan Grey (1966) reported the confounding impact of preschool on the experimental children's families and even on other members of the community in which they lived. Reporting on the Early Training Project, Grey found that at the end of each school year the controls caught up to the gains made during the summer by the experimental group. However, another control group in a town 60 miles away did not show such gains. In addition, untreated younger brothers and sisters of experimental subjects were observed to make unusual progress, no doubt as a result of the influence of the program on their parents or siblings (Kohlberg, 1966). Obviously, control subjects should be selected in a manner such that they can in no way be affected by the experimental treatment. However, this condition is increasingly difficult to maintain in large-scale field studies and demonstration projects.

In addition, investigators have discovered other effects that are associated with an intervention program — efforts which again are not direct results of the treatment itself. Rosenthal reported that a teacher's expectations can have an important influence on the performance of students. Shephard reported a similar experience in the early stages of his work in St. Louis. Where the teacher's expectation of the child's performance is high, the child is likely to show high achievement. Where expectations are low, achievement tends to be low. Consequently, in any compensatory education program, the expectations of the subjects' teachers may influence their subsequent performance. The Hawthorne effect, in which the mere fact of experimentation or altered learning conditions may cause a temporary change in performance, unrelated to the specific intervention method applied, can also color the results. In the evaluation of compensatory education, such interferences have not been identified or controlled for; hence the real consequences of the various treatments cannot be determined from these studies.

There are still more problems referrable to evaluative research design which confuse, distort or limit the initial data as well as subsequent findings. Most evaluations of compensatory education studies depend excessively on static variables and quantitative measures to the neglect of the process variables and the qualitative analysis of behavior, circumstances and conditions. This dependence on quantitative measures of status to the neglect of qualitative study of process not only opens these works to questions related to the validity of the measurement instruments; it also ignores the growing appreciation of situational and transactional factors as determinants of function. Compensatory education programs under study include and affect a wide variety of independent and dependent variables which are insufficiently accounted for in the more narrowly designed evaluation studies that have dominated the field to date.

This rather static approach to assessment has led investigators to view pupil characteristics which differ from some presumed norm as negative, as well as to consider any correlation between these negative characteristics and learning dysfunction as support for a deficits theory of intervention. In practice this has meant that researchers see all differences between the target populations and the standard group as deficits to be overcome rather than characteristics to be utilized and developed.

Relationships between stereotypical and fairly static input and output variables (usually isolated in pairs) are investigated; no attention is paid to the complex dialectic relationships between patterns of dependent variables and patterns of independent variables, many of which may be idiosyncratic to individuals and situations. These inadequate attempts at the assessment and treatment of pupil characteristics are often accompanied by an even less adequate appraisal of program variables. In practically all of the so-called national impact studies and most of the evaluation of specific programs little or no attention is paid to the fact that intervention treatment is uneven and control of that treatment almost nonexistent. When national impact data are pooled we could easily have results which show no effect, if the effect of specified programs with positive impact is cancelled out by other programs with no positive effect. Even more serious is the apparent disregard of our growing conviction that individual pupils respond differentially to treatments. When mean changes in status are used as the indices to outcome, again we may have negative responders cancelling positive responders to indicate no effect-even though the treatment may be highly effective for specific individuals under specific circumstances.

Several possible explanations have been advanced to illustrate how these confusing data can be interpreted to demonstrate the programs' ineffectiveness. The most extreme is the theory that the subjects involved are simply genetically inferior and not able to be brought up to hoped-for standards. Those who have attempted to advance such hypotheses have been blasted from all sides for the extremely questionable nature of their scientific "support," as well, of course, as for the dubious social value of advancing such theories at this point in the society's development, when they cannot be adequately proven.

However, whatever the range of possible interpretations of apparently discouraging data, what cannot be ignored is that far too many children from economically or ethnically disadvantaged groups are failing to master the traditional learning tasks of schooling. The problem is not only tragic, but staggeringly complex. Perhaps the most important response to the discouraging data presented by many evaluation reports, after allowing for many of the research problems already discussed, is a rigorous examination of the suitability of what is actually taking place in the schools.

Public schools as social institutions have never had to assume responsibility for their failures. Only recently have observers begun to view and describe objectively some of the horrors that are perpetrated in the name of public education. We must come to grips with the problem of the utterly stultifying atmosphere of many classrooms, with the way in which rote learning and repetition discourage *real* learning; and we must also realize that discipline for discipline's sake serves the purpose of creating artificial order, but at the same time produces dull automatons instead of eager students, or turns the inmates of public schools against education, to their lifelong detriment.

Even where extraordinary programs of compensatory education have brought about some beneficial results, larger social factors may negate these results in the long run. Outside the classroom, disadvantaged children confront a society that is hostile to their healthy development. Learning in structured situations may be irrelevant in the context of their life outside the school. There is some evidence to suggest that ethnic, economic, or social integration does have beneficial effects on children whose background results in such school problems. Achievement levels have been shown to rise after desegregation in many schools, although the exact interplay of reactions leading to this result has not been conclusively determined. For example, improved teacher morale or other improved conditions brought about by the process of desegregation may result in an overall increase in the quality of education throughout the system. Other evidence points to the conclusion that integration on a social status group basis has beneficial effects for disadvantaged children when the majority of their peers in the school are from higher status groups. Even these results, however, are not sufficiently conclusive to provide a legitimate basis for large-scale generalizations. The problem is further complicated by the new renaissance in cultural nationalism among ethnic minorities, a movement which affects any assumptions to be made about ethnic integration and education. In a society which has alternately pushed ethnic separation or ethnic amalgamation and which has never truly accepted cultural and ethnic pluralism, blacks, chicanos, Puerto Ricans, and native Americans are insisting that the traditional public school is guilty not only of intellectual and social but also of cultural genocide for their children. There are class and caste conflicts to which insufficient attention has been given in the organization and delivery of educational services. If cultural and ethnic identification are important components of the learning experience, to ignore or demean them is poor education, at best. Even if these factors are sufficiently taken into account in the school, we are far from any guarantees that the society will honor such values outside the classroom. It is not at all clear that intensive, short-term in-school treatment can counter the negative, external forces working upon disadvantaged populations.

The schools face a difficult challenge if they are to make learning an exciting and stimulating experience, relevant and effective, for all their students from all cultural and social backgrounds. However, even meeting these criteria will not be enough. Educators still face the problem of matching the developmental patterns, learning styles and temperamental traits of individual learners to the educational experiences to which they are exposed. Many researchers have concentrated on differences in level of intellectual function, a concern reflected in the heavy emphasis on intelligence testing and the placement, even "track-ing," of pupils based on these tests. This tradition has emphasized quantitative measurement, classification, and prediction to the neglect of qualitative measure-ment, description and prescription. These latter processes are clearly essential to the effective teaching of children who come to the schools with characteristics different from those of both their teachers and the other children to whom most teachers are accustomed. Research data indicate wide variations in patterns of intellectual and social function across and within sub-populations. Variations in function within privileged groups may be less important because of a variety of environmental factors which support adequate development and learning; how-ever, among disadvantaged populations — where traditional forms of environ-mental support may be absent — attention to differential learning patterns may be crucial to adequate development. Understanding the role of one set of behaviors as facilitators of more comprehensive behaviors is at the heart of differential analysis of learner characteristics and differential design of learning experiences. Schooling for disadvantaged children — indeed, for all children in our schools — comes nowhere near meeting these implied criteria. Assessment technology has not seriously engaged the problem. Curriculum specialists are just beginning to face the task, in some of their work in individually prescribed learning.

The problems of social disadvantage in the society at large, and the failure of the schools to mold their practices to cultural differences and individual learning styles are not the only obstacles to successful compensatory education. Social disadvantagement gives rise to a variety of harmful health and nutritional problems which militate against healthy development and adequate utilization of educational opportunities. It is becoming increasingly recognized that low income results in poor health care and frequent malnutrition; these disadvan-tages are related to high risks for the pregnant mother and fetus, and for the child after birth, in terms of mortality or maldevelopment. Poor health conditions may result in either a direct impairment of the nervous system or an indirect interference with the learning process by a low level of energy or high level of distractability. Such health-related conditions probably have a crucial effect on school and general social adjustment. It has now been shown that impaired health or organic dysfunction can influence school attendance, learning efficiency, developmental rate as well as personality development. Clearly, adequacy of health status and adequacy of health care in our society are influenced by adequacy of income. Thus poverty results in a number of conditions directly referrable to school success and to development in general.

Despite the many problems in the design, implementation and evaluation of compensatory education programs and the equivocal status of much of the evaluation effort, we are nonetheless constantly called upon to make judgments and policy decisions based upon the experiences so far. There are useful insights to be drawn from these experiences:

1. The search for the best or the generic treatment is clearly a futile search. Problems of human development and learning are so complex and conditions of life so varied that the chances of finding a curriculum which is universally superior are quite modest. In well designed and conducted studies comparing different approaches to early childhood education, differences in curriculum orientation seemed less important than the following factors: systematic planning, clear objectives, intensity of treatment, attention to individual needs and learning patterns, opportunities for individual and small group interaction, support in the home environment for the learning experiences provided at school and the presence of personnel committed to the pedagogical procedures prescribed. It seems that as these conditions are approached, no matter what the content or method, personal development and content mastery are advanced. Hard data in support of these conclusions are scarce since few studies have been designed to be particularly sensitive to this constellation of variables. Nonetheless logical and impressionistic evidence mounts in support of the validity of these observations.

2. Although the concept of individual differences has been with us for a long time, individualization is underrepresented in programs of treatment and evaluation of programs. Confusing interpretation of evaluation data may occur because of this neglect and the counter-tendency to generalize too freely. In a few longitudinal studies where impact on individuals (or on youngsters identified as having been exposed to known treatments over time) has been investigated, emerging achievement patterns are encouraging. There appear to be insufficient studies of highly sophisticated programs of individually prescribed learning experiences to draw definitive conclusions. Yet some of the more generalized individually prescribed instructional programs do seem to be widening the range of achievement among pupils so exposed. These generalized IPI programs are probably not the answer even though they represent an advance in educational technology. The true matching of pace, content and conditions of learning to the specific characteristics of each learner is not yet a part of even our highly

experimental work. Insufficient progress in the qualitative analysis of learning behavior may be partially responsible for this situation. Such analysis is clearly prerequisite to any serious effort at achieving sophistication in the individualization of instruction and learning.

3. The absence of broader representation and utilization of the social sciences in the evaluation of compensatory education has contributed to the neglect of social psychological, social and political factors in these programs. Yet as important as the strictly pedagogical problems are, the politics of education delivery systems, the social psychology and political economy of education and the sociology of knowledge and learning share the stage with pedagogy in accounting for the success or failure of compensatory education. Whether we are considering the role of pupils in directing their own learning or the roles of parents and community in directing school policy, the influence of involvement, participation, commitment and values is so critical as to render much of our evaluation and our treatment useless unless we give these factors greater consideration. In the very inadequate studies of several informal schooling situations (storefront academies and the adult education programs of groups like the Black Panthers, Black Muslims, Young Lords, etc.) the blending of control, participation, politics, values and demonstrated change in opportunity structure begin to appear as important factors in educational rehabilitation. Unfortunately, the research and evaluation data that we have are not sufficient to erect guidelines or to draw firm conclusions but again impression and logic suggest that we should look to these concerns in our programs and evaluation.

chapter 11
comparative research studies

SOCIOCULTURAL FACTORS IN LABELING MENTAL RETARDATES

Jane R. Mercer

Field surveys,(1) studies using informants,(2) and educational surveys(3) consistently show a disproportionately large number of persons from ethnic minorities among those labeled as retarded by clinical measures. Such dispropor- tions are especially noticeable in school populations. For example, the ethnic survey conducted annually since 1966 by the California State Department of Education has consistently shown rates of placement for Mexican-American and Negro children in special education classes that were two to three times higher per 1,000 than rates for children from English-speaking, Caucasian homes, hereafter called *Anglos.*(4)

In the epidemiology of mental retardation which we conducted in Riverside, California, disproportions by socioeconomic level and ethnic group appeared in the case register of retardates labeled by community organizations. Forty-one percent of the 812 persons on the case register who were nominated as retarded by 241 formal organizations in the community were living on census blocks for which the median value of housing was under $10,720.(5) Only 22.7 percent of the general population of the community lived on such blocks. Disproportions were even greater for those labeled by the public schools. Fifty-three percent of the retardates labeled by the public schools lived on blocks with a median housing value of under $10,720.

Anglos, who comprise 82 percent of the population of the community, made up only 54 percent of the labeled retardates. Mexican-Americans, who comprised only 9.5 percent of the community population, contributed 32 percent to the register of labeled retardates, three times more than would be expected from their proportion in the population. Negroes, who constituted 7 percent of the population of the community, contributed 11 percent to the register of labeled retardates. Ethnic disproportions were especially marked in the public schools. Only 37 percent of the labeled retardates in special education classes were Anglo children while 45 percent were Mexican-American and 16 percent were Negro. When socioeconomic differences were controlled by comparing only low-status Anglos with low-status Mexican-Americans and Negroes, disproportions for Negroes were eliminated but Anglos were still significantly underrepresented and Mexican-Americans significantly overrepresented among the labeled retardates.

Why are there disproportionately large numbers of persons from low socioeconomic status and from ethnic minority backgrounds among those persons labeled as mentally retarded?

TWO EXPLANATORY FRAMEWORKS

The clinical perspective. Persons who view mental retardation from a clinical, medical perspective tend to explain socioeconomic and ethnic differences in rates for labeled retardation in biological terms. They tend to view mental retardation as individual pathology which exists regardless of whether it has been diagnosed. Using either a pathological-medical model or a statistical model for identifying symptoms of subnormality, they see mental retardation as a characteristic of the individual which transcends any particular social or cultural system. They believe that mental retardation can be discovered and diagnosed by the trained professional using the medical and psychological measures at his disposal. Within the framework of the clinical perspective, there are two types of explanations which are commonly given for disproportionately high rates of labeled retardation among the socioeconomically disadvantaged and ethnic minorities.

One school of thought, Zigler calls exponents of this school defect theorists, contends that all retardates suffer from specific physiological and cognitive defects over and above their slower rate of development. They argue that failure to detect the exact nature of the defect in those cases which appear to have no physiological defects is probably due to the relatively primitive nature of present diagnostic techniques. The overrepresentation of lower status persons results from the lower level of prenatal and postnatal care given to children reared in socioeconomically disadvantaged circumstances. Such children are exposed to a greater risk of organic damage because of poor diet, less adequate medical care, and other health hazards which are more prevalent in such environments than in more advantaged homes.(6) Because a large percentage of ethnic minority families in American society are socioeconomically disadvantaged, rates of defect tend to be higher for ethnic minorities. Considerable research evidence has accumulated to support this argument and differential exposure to biological hazards undoubtedly does account for some of the differences between groups.(7)

A second explanatory framework is that of the genetic theorists. They are prone to view higher rates among the disadvantaged and among ethnic minorities as the result of the polygenic distribution of the curve of intelligence in the population. They theorize that familial deficiencies in intelligence place those with lower intelligence at a competitive disadvantage which produces downward social mobility. Consequently, the families of the genetically retarded tend to gravitate to lower socioeconomic levels over several generations. The predominance of mental retardation among lower socioeconomic levels is explained as the result of the downward drift from higher social statuses. Such persons fall, genetically, in the lowest portion of the polygenic distribution of intelligence. Their performance is as much a part of the normal distribution of intelligence as the performance of persons who score in the upper ranges of the normal curve.

Research on sociocultural factors in mental retardation conducted from a clinical perspective tends to investigate hypotheses generated either by the defect theorists or the genetic theorists.

Social system perspective. The social system perspective defines mental retardation as an achieved social status which some persons hold in some social systems. The role of retardate consists of the behavior expected of persons occupying the status of mental retardate. It is possible to study how a person achieves the status of mental retardate just as it is possible to study how a person achieves the status of doctor, banker, or engineer. Within the social system perspective, the overrepresentation of socioeconomically disadvantaged persons and persons from ethnic minorities in the devalued status of mental retardate can be studied as a status assignment phenomenon similar to other comparable social processes. From this perspective, the research question becomes, "Why are persons from lower socioeconomic statuses and/or ethnic minorities more likely to be assigned the status of mental retardate by formal organizations in the community than persons from higher socioeconomic statuses and/or the Anglo majority?"(8)

This paper, written from a social system perspective, explores two general hypotheses: 1. the high rate of assignment of persons from lower socioeconomic status and/or ethnic minorities to the status of mental retardate is related to an interaction between sociocultural factors and the clinical referral and labeling process which makes persons from these backgrounds more vulnerable to the labeling process than persons from the Anglo middle-class majority, and 2. that high rates of assignment of lower status and/or ethnic minorities is related to interaction between sociocultural factors and the nature of clinical measurement instruments. Each hypothesis will be explored separately.

SOCIOCULTURAL FACTORS AND THE LABELING PROCESS

In the data files of the Riverside epidemiology of mental retardation, we have information on three different groups of labeled retardates in the City of Riverside, California. One data file contains information on persons who were nominated as mental retardates by formal organizations in the community. The other two files contain information on persons labeled by the public schools. Each of these data files was used to test the hypothesis that persons from lower socioeconomic levels and/or ethnic minorities are more vulnerable to the clinical labeling process.

There were 361 Anglos, 221 Mexican-Americans, and 79 Negroes nominated as mental retardates by those formal organizations in Riverside which employed psychologists or medical professionals to make diagnoses of mental retardation. We have called them the clinical organizations because they were staffed by professionals trained in the clinical tradition who presumably used standard clinical procedures in making evaluations. The persons on the clinical case register were those who had been assigned the status of mental retardate as a result of decisions made by these clinically trained professionals who selected, evaluated, and labeled clients in many different social organizations. It is not possible to know, in retrospect, exactly what factors were weighed in each case. However, we can gain some insight into the overall labeling process by a careful study of the end result of these interlocking, multiple decisions.

If labeled retardates from low-status homes and ethnic minorities are less clinically subnormal or less physically disabled than persons labeled as retarded from high-status homes and the Anglo majority, this difference would support the hypothesis that the former are more vulnerable to being labeled and that higher vulnerability tends to inflate rates for labeled retardation among low-status and minority groups. There are two questions to be answered. Do persons labeled as retardates from low-status homes and from ethnic minorities deviate as far from the statistical average on clinical measures as those from high-status homes and the Anglo majority? Are persons from low social status and ethnic minorities who are assigned to the status of mental retardate less physically disabled than high-status persons or persons from the Anglo majority?

Approximately 90 percent of the files of persons nominated by clinical organizations included direct or indirect information on six major trends of physical disabilities: speech, ambulation, hearing, arm-hand use in self care, vision, and seizures. Disability ratings using file information could not be based strictly on medical definitions because of the restricted nature of information in most dossiers, but it was possible to make global ratings for arm-hand use, speech, vision, ambulation, and hearing using four-point rating scales ranging from no difficulty to extreme difficulty. If a person was reported as having "no difficulty," he received a score of 0; "some difficulty," a score of 1; "much difficulty," a score of 2; and "extreme difficulty," a score of 3. If no seizures were mentioned, he received a 0 on that item. If seizures had occurred in the past but were no longer present or their infrequency was not given, he received a score of 1. If he currently had seizures less than once a year, or a few times a year, he received a score of 2. If he currently had seizures once a month or more, he received a score of 3. An individual received 0 if there was no mention of an illness, accident, or operation involving the central nervous system; and a score of 1 for each involvement mentioned. An individual's physical disability index score was the sum of his ratings on these items. Theoretically, scores could range from 0 through 21, however, actual scores ranged between 0 and 13.

Table 1 presents the mean IQ and the mean number of physical disabilities, by social status and by ethnic group, for the persons on the clinical case register. Median value of housing on the census block was used as the measure of socioeconomic status for analyzing the clinical case register. There were 365 of the persons on the clinical case register who were living on blocks for which the housing was valued at $10,750 or less and 323 living on blocks valued above that figure. There were no significant differences in mean IQ between socioeconomic levels as measured by housing value nor between the three ethnic groups. Low-status persons had a mean IQ of 63.6 and high-status persons a mean of 63.0. The average Anglo on the clinical case register had an IQ of 61.5, the average Mexican-American had a mean IQ of 64.3, and the average Negro had a mean IQ of 61.2.

Low-status persons and those from ethnic minorities were found to be significantly less physically disabled. High-status labeled retardates had significantly more physical disabilities, mean 2.1, than low-status labeled retardates, mean 1.2 ($p < .001$). Anglos had an average disability score of 2.2 while that for Mexican-Americans was 1.0 and for Negroes .8 ($p < .001$). Only 32 percent of the labeled Anglos had no disabilities while 61 percent of the labeled Mexican-Americans, and 71 percent of the labeled Negroes were without reported physical disabilities. Ethnic differences persisted when social status was controlled, although they were slightly reduced ($p < .001$).

However, there was a pattern in the distribution of IQ's within ethnic group, not shown in Table 1, which is worthy of note. Anglos had a higher percentage of persons with very low and very high IQ's, while the scores for Mexican-Americans and Negroes were concentrated in the middle ranges, IQ's between 40 and 79 ($X^2 = 44.6$, 8df, $p < .001$). This pattern persisted even when social status was held constant. Labeled retardates with IQ's above 80 were not only more likely to be Anglo but had more physical disabilities and were significantly more likely to have been nominated by a medical professional. Apparently, the medical doctor, using a medical pathological diagnostic model, diagnoses some physically disabled referrals as mentally retarded on the basis of physical anomalies when, in fact, they have IQ's which are in the normal range statistically. This produces a disproportionate number of disabled Anglos with high IQ's on the clinical case register because almost no Mexican-Americans or Negroes were nominated from medical sources. Most Mexican-American and Negro labeled retardates were normal-bodied and were labeled by the schools rather than their family doctor. Because the school used a strictly statistical rather than medical definition of normal, there were very few persons labeled as mental retardates by the school who had an IQ over 80. Consequently, labeled

TABLE 1

Mean IQ and Mean Number of Physical Disabilities for Persons Holding the Status of Mental Retardate in the Community by Socioeconomic Status and Ethnic Group

	Socioeconomic Status			Ethnic Group			
	Low Status Housing Under $10,750 (N=365)	High Status Housing Over $10,750 (N=323)	Significance Level(a)	Anglo (N=361)	Mexican-American (N=221)	Negro (N=79)	Significance Level(a)
Clinical Case Register							
Mean IQ	63.6	63.0	NS	61.5	64.3	61.2	NS
Mean Physical Disabilities	1.2	2.1	<.001	2.2	1.0	.8	<.001
	SES Index 0.29(b) (N=162)	SES Index 30+ (N=93)					
Educable Mental Retardates				(N=144)	(N=63)	(N=61)	
Mean IQ	70.0	68.9	NS	68.8	71.4	69.3	NS
Mean Physical Disabilities(c)	1.3	1.6	NS	1.8	.9	1.0	<.001(c)
Mean Adaptive Behavior Failures(b)	9.5	9.8	NS	10.3	9.9	7.2	<.001(c)

(a) One-way analysis of variance was used for ethnic comparisons and a test for socioeconomic comparisons.

(b) Duncan Socioeconomic Index for head of household's occupation was used. There were 13 cases for whom occupation of household could not be coded.

(c) The mean number of Physical Disabilities for the general population of the community 6-15 years of age was .2 and the mean Adaptive Behavior Failures was 2.7 on these scales.

retardation is more closely tied to the statistical model of normal and to performance on an IQ test for Mexican-Americans and Negroes than for Anglos. Simply comparing mean IQ's obscures these complexities. Physical disabilities appear to be the intervening variable. Anglos labeled as mentally retarded had more physical disabilities, hence, were more visibly different from the general population.

The comparison of the clinical characteristics of persons from different social statuses and ethnic groups nominated for the clinical case register supports the hypothesis that there is an interaction between sociocultural factors and the labeling process. Labeled low-status persons were less physically disabled than labeled high-status persons. Labeled Mexican-Americans and Negroes were less physically disabled than labeled Anglos. Overall, their mean IQ's were similar to the mean for Anglos but labeled Anglos had significantly more physical disabilities and were, presumably, more visibly different than either Mexican-American or Negro labeled retardates. This finding tends to support the hypothesis that less physically disabled members of minorities are labeled as retarded while labeled Anglos are more visibly different.

During the academic year 1969-70, the Pupil Personnel Departments of the Riverside and Alvord Unified School Districts re-evaluated all 268 children in their classes for the educable mentally retarded.(9) Students ranged from 7 through 19 years of age. Fifty-four percent were Anglos, 23 percent were Mexican-Americans, and 23 percent were Negroes. Approximately 80 percent of the children in these school districts were Anglos, 13 percent were Mexican-American, and 7 percent Negro. Thus, Mexican-American and Negro children were overrepresented and Anglo children underrepresented among those holding the status of mental retardate in the public school. Seventy-seven percent of the children in classes for the educable mentally retarded were from homes in which the head of household had a blue-collar job and 60.4 percent were from homes in which the head of household had a job rated between 0 and 29 on the Duncan Socioeconomic Index.(10)

A school psychologist retested each child using the Wechsler Intelligence Scale for Children. Interviewers, employed by the research project, interviewed the parents of each child. Interviewer and parent were matched for ethnic group and a Spanish version of the interview was used when the parent preferred being interviewed in Spanish. Information on the adaptive behavior and physical disabilities of each child and the sociocultural characteristics of his family were secured. The Adaptive Behavior and Physical Disability Scales used in this study were those developed for the field survey of the Riverside epidemiology.(11) The Adaptive Behavior Scales are age-graded measures which contain questions about the child's social-role performance in his family, neighborhood, community, and school. During the interview, the interviewer also secured information about the child's physical disabilities, any illnesses involving the central nervous system, and whether he had ever had seizures. Both the Adaptive Behavior and Physical Disability Scales were scored by counting the number of items failed by each child.

Table 1 presents the mean IQ, the mean number of physical disabilities, and the mean number of adaptive behavior failures for those labeled educable mental retardates by social status and ethnic group. As with the clinical case register, differences between the mean IQ's of the children of differing socioeconomic statuses and ethnic groups could be accounted for by chance. Differences in physical disabilities by socioeconomic status could also be accounted for by chance but this finding did not hold true for ethnic group. The average Anglo child failed 1.8 items on the Physical Disability Scales while the average Mexican-American labeled retardate had .9 physical disabilities and the average Negro had one physical disability (p < .001). When social status was held constant, ethnic differences persisted but were slightly reduced. The findings for adaptive behavior were identical to those for physical disability. Differences by socioeconomic status could be accounted for by chance but ethnic differences were statistically significant. The average Anglo labeled retardate in these school districts had 10.3 adaptive behavior failures compared to 9.9 for Mexican-American and 7.2 for Negro retardates (p < .001).

The mean number of physical disabilities for a representative sample of the general population of the community 6 through 15 years of age in the field survey of the epidemiology (N = 1875) was .2, and the mean number of adaptive failures was 2.7. Both averages are significantly less than the average number of failures for the labeled children. Thus, children labeled as educable mental retardates by the public schools in these two school districts were significantly more physically disabled and had more adaptive behavior failures than children in the general population; but, within the labeled population, Anglos had significantly more physical disabilities and more adaptive behavior failures than Mexican-Americans and Negroes. Findings from the study of children holding the status of educable mental retardate in the public schools paralleled those for the clinical case register. Even though these were two completely different populations of labeled mental retardates, the average IQ's of persons in the three ethnic groups were, essentially, identical, but persons from ethnic minorities had fewer physical disabilities and adaptive behavior failures.

The labeling process in the public schools was investigated by studying the characteristics of all 1,234 children referred, for any reason, to the Pupil Personnel Department of the Riverside Unified School District during a single school year.(12) Approximately 31 percent of the children were referred as possible candidates for classes for the gifted; 30 percent were referred primarily because of behavior and disciplinary problems; 20 percent were referred because of academic difficulty with no mention of special education; and 8 percent were referred specifically for evaluation and possible placement in special education classes for the mentally retarded. At the time of the study, approximately 81 percent of the children of the school district were Anglo, 11 percent Mexican-American, and 8 percent Negro. Thirty-six percent lived on census blocks for which the housing was valued below $12,000.(13) The distribution by social status and by ethnic group of all the children referred to the Pupil Personnel

Department was almost identical to the distributions in the school district itself. Low-status and/or minority children were not referred at a higher rate than their percentage in the population nor were they tested by the psychologist at a higher rate.

TABLE 2

Ethnic Characteristics of a Cohort of Children at Various
Stages in the Labeling Process in the Public Schools

Ethnic Group	Tested by Psychologist (N=865) Percentage	Found Eligible for Placement – IQ 79 (N=134) Percentage	Recommended for Placement (N=81) Percentage	Placed in Status of MR (N=71) Percentage
Anglo	82.9	47.4	37.9	32.1
Mexican-American	7.6	32.7	40.9	45.3
Negro	9.5	19.8	21.2	22.6
Median Value Under $12,000	38.8	70.7	72.7	74.6

Table 2 presents the ethnic characteristics of the 865 children who were tested by a psychologist from the 1,234 children in the original cohort referred for pscyhological evaluation; 82.9 percent were Anglo, 7.6 percent Mexican-American, and 9.5 percent were Negro. These percentages closely approximate the ethnic distribution of the school population. Among the children tested, there were 134 children who received an IQ of 79 or below. They were eligible for placement in a special education class on the basis of their test performance. It was at this stage in the referral process that the ethnic percentages shifted dramatically. Only 47.4 percent of the children failing the test were Anglo while 32.7 percent were Mexican-American and 19.8 percent were Negro. In other words, there were four times more Mexican-American children among those who failed the test than would be expected from their percentage in the population tested. There were twice as many Negro children as would be expected, and only about half as many Anglo children.

Although the IQ test was the major factor producing ethnic disproportions, the differential vulnerability of Mexican-American and Negro children to the labeling process persisted into the next two stages of the labeling. Eighty-one of the 134 children eligible for placement in classes for the mentally retarded were recommended by the psychologist for placement. Only 37.9 percent of those recommended for placement were Anglo while 40.9 percent were Mexican-American and 21.2 percent were Negro. Thus, there were disproportionately more of the eligible Mexican-American and Negro children recommended for placement and disproportionately fewer of the eligible Anglo children recommended for placement by the psychologist.

There were 71 children who were actually placed in the status of mental retardate in this school district. The ethnic distribution for the children who were placed is even more disproportionate than that for the children recommended for placement or children found eligible for placement. Less than a third of the children who achieved the status of mental retardate in this particular year were Anglos while 45.3 percent were Mexican-American and 22.6 percent were Negro. Six times more Mexican-American children and two and a half times more Negro children were placed than would be expected from their proportion in the school district population. Children from ethnic minority groups were not only failing IQ tests at a higher rate but selective factors operating in the labeling process resulted in disproportionately more minority children being recommended and placed in the status of mental retardate from among those who were eligible for placement.

The same pattern also appeared for socioeconomic status as measured by the value of housing on the block on which each child lived. About 39 percent of the children tested by the psychologists came from homes located on blocks with a median housing value of under $12,000 but 70.7 percent of those failing the IQ test came from homes on such blocks. The percentage increased for the final two stages of the labeling process, so that, ultimately, three-fourths of the children placed in the status of mental retardate in the year of the referral study were from homes located in blocks with low housing values.

The analysis of the characteristics of labeled retardates on the clinical case register, of labeled retardates in the program for educable mental retardates in the public schools, and of children referred for physical evaluation in the public schools all showed a similar pattern. Persons from low socioeconomic level and ethnic minority groups were more vulnerable to the labeling process. Those who were labeled from ethnic minority groups had significantly fewer physical disabilities than their Anglo counterparts and had fewer adaptive behavior failures. Persons from minority groups assigned the status of mental retardate were not only less deviant physically and behaviorally than Anglo labeled retardates, but the anslysis of the labeling process in the public schools indicated that children from minority groups were more likely to be recommended for placement and placed in the status of mental retardate than Anglo children once they failed an IQ test. An identical pattern was found for children from low socioeconomic levels. This interaction between referral and labeling processes and the sociocultural characteristics of the person being evaluated could account for some of the socioeconomic and ethnic differences in prevalence rates found in studies of labeled retardation.

INTERACTION BETWEEN SOCIOCULTURAL FACTORS AND CLINICAL MEASURES

The second hypothesis to be explored in this paper is that overrepresentation of persons from ethnic minorities in the status of mental retardate may be related to interaction between sociocultural factors and clinical measures. Because the primary clinical measure used in the diagnosis of mental retardation is an intelligence test, the discussion will concentrate on this particular clinical measure.

In the field survey which was conducted in Riverside, a representative sample of persons living in that city was selected for study. As part of the survey, intelligence measures were secured on a subsample of 556 Anglos, 100 Mexican-Americans, and 47 Negroes from 7 months through 49 years of age. In order to determine the amount of the variance in IQ accounted for by ethnic group and socioeconomic status, a regression analysis was computed using IQ as the dependent variable and ethnic group (dichotomized Anglo vs Mexican-American and Negro) and socioeconomic status (dichotomized Duncan Socioeconomic Index score of occupation of head of the household 0-29 vs 30 or higher) as the independent variables. Table 3 presents the findings from that analysis.

TABLE 3

Correlations Between Ethnic Groups, Socioeconomic Status, and IQ
in the Riverside Field Survey

Children	Adults	Entire Sample (N=703)	
	7 Mos.–15 Yrs.	16-49 Yrs.	7 Mos.–49 Yrs.
	Percentage Variance	Percentage Variance	Percentage Variance
Ethnic Group Only	r = .45 20.3	r = .62 38.4	r = .53 28.1
SES Only	r = .27 7.3	r = .40 16.0	r = .33 10.9
Ethnic Group Plus SES	R = .46 21.2	R = .65 42.3	R = .55 30.3

For children 7 months through 15 years of age, ethnic group alone was correlated .45 with IQ, accounting for 20.3 percent of the variance in IQ. The correlation was higher for adults 16-49 years of age, .62, accounting for 38.4 percent of the variance in IQ. When all ages were combined, the correlation was .53, accounting for 28.1 percent of the variance in IQ. All correlations are significant beyond the .001 level of significance.

Socioeconomic status, alone, was not as highly predictive of IQ as ethnic group. It accounted for only 7.3 percent of the variance in the IQ's of children, 16 percent of the variance in the IQ's of adults, and 10.9 percent of the variance in the IQ's for the entire sample.

When ethnic group and socioeconomic status were both used in a stepwise multiple regression to predict IQ, the correlation was only slightly higher than for ethnic group alone. This indicates that knowledge of socioeconomic status adds relatively little predictability beyond ethnic group because most of the variance accounted for by socioeconomic status is shared with ethnic group. The most important finding, however, is that between 20 percent and 40 percent of the variance in IQ of the persons in this sample could be accounted for by ethnic group alone, depending upon the age of the persons being studied. Sociocultural factors were more highly correlated with IQ for adults than children.

In order to determine how much of the variance in IQ within each ethnic group could be accounted for by sociocultural factors, the sociocultural characteristics of the families of the persons in the sample were used as independent variables and a regression analysis was done for each ethnic group separately. Each sociocultural characteristic was dichotomized so that one category corresponded to the community mode on that characteristic and the other category was nonmodal. All sociocultural variables described characteristics of the family or family members and were not characteristics of the person himself, except as we infer that he may have acquired certain characteristics because of the environment in which he lives.

TABLE 4

Correlations Between Family Background Characteristics and IQ

	R	Variance Accounted for
		Percentage
Mexican-American (N=100)	.61	37.2
Negro (N=47)	.52	27.0
Anglos (N=556)	.31	9.6
All Ethnic Groups (N=703)	.50	25.0

The first set of data in Table 4 presents the findings for Mexican-Americans. Eighteen sociocultural characteristics of the family were correlated .61 with IQ. They accounted for 37.2 percent of the variance in the measured intelligence of this group of Mexican-Americans (p < .01). The six sociocultural characteristics which best predicted high IQ were: living in a household in which the head of household had a white-collar position; living in a family with five or fewer members; living in a family in which the Duncan socioeconomic index score for the head of household's occupation was 30 or higher; living in a family in which the head of household was reared in an urban environment; living in a family in which the head of household was reared in the United States; and living in a family in which the head of household was male. These six variables, combined, produced a multiple correlation coefficient of .57 and accounted for 32.5 percent of the variance in IQ.

The multiple correlation coefficient for the small number of Negroes in the sample, .52, did not quite reach the .05 level of significance. However, the pattern of relationships is similar to that for Mexican-Americans. The variables studied were identical to those used in the analysis of Mexican-Americans except that an item on use of English in the home was omitted. For Negroes, living in a family in which the spouse of the head of household was reared in a nonsouthern state was the best single predictor. The five other family variables which, together, predicted the most variance were: male head of household; head of household having a white-collar job; a family consisting of biological parents and their children; a family living in a home they own or are buying; and a family in which the spouse of the head of household has had an eighth grade education or more.

The multiple correlation coefficient for Anglos was .31 ($p < .01$), accounting for 9.6 percent of the variance in IQ. Independent variables used in the regression analysis were identical to those used for Negroes except that segregated vs desegregated minority neighborhood was omitted for Anglos because all Anglos lived in nonminority neighborhoods. For Anglos, two socioeconomic variables were among the six best predictors: living in a household in which the socioeconomic index score of the head of household's occupation was 30 or higher and a household in which the head of household had a white-collar occupation. Anglos with higher IQ's also tended to come from nuclear families that had not been broken by divorce or separation; families in which the spouse of the head of household had been reared in an urban environment and had had a high school education or more.

When all three ethnic groups were combined, sociocultural characteristics of the family backgrounds were correlated .50 with IQ, accounting for 25 percent of the variance.

It is clear from the preceding analysis that the correlation between sociocultural factors and standard measures of intelligence are significant. Ethnic group, alone, accounted for 28 percent of the variance in IQ's between Anglos, Mexican-Americans, and Negroes in this particular sample, while socioeconomic status, alone, accounted for only 10.9 percent of the variance. The two, together, accounted for 30.3 percent of the variance. Studying each ethnic group, separately, we found that more than 25 percent of the variance in IQ's within the Mexican-American and Negro populations could be accounted for by characteristics of the individual's family background. However, family background characteristics accounted for only 9.6 percent of the variance in Anglo IQ's. The relatively small amount of the variability in the IQ's of the Anglos in this sample which could be accounted for by family background characteristics may be due, in part, to the homogeneity of the Anglo population of Riverside, which is mainly middle- and upper-middle class in status.

It is not possible with our data to compare the clinical and social system perspectives, directly, as explanatory frameworks for interpreting higher rates of labeled mental retardation among ethnic minorities. Undoubtedly, medical care is poorer and health hazards greater among the economically and educationally disadvantaged. To the extent that ethnic minorities are economically and educationally disadvantaged, we would expect higher rates of organic damage and higher rates of mental retardation among them. However, this argument does not explain why rates for labeled retardation among ethnic minorities are three to five times higher than those for Anglos, even when socioeconomic status is held constant? Neither does it explain, if there is more biological damage among persons from lower socioeconomic levels and ethnic minorities, why labeled retardates from lower socioeconomic levels and ethnic minorities have fewer physical disabilities reported in organizational records and by parents than persons from higher socioeconomic levels and the Anglo majority?

Genetic theorists would argue that the biological differences are genetic and not manifest in visible physical disabilities and that downward drift of the genetically inferior accounts for differentials by socioeconomic level. If one assumes relatively equal access to the opportunity structure for all Anglos, the downward drift hypothesis could have some validity when applied to the Anglo population. However, that hypothesis cannot explain the surplus of Mexican-Americans and Negroes among the labeled retarded. They have never had equal access to the opportunity structure of American society nor have they ever held higher social statuses from which the poorly endowed could drift downward.

We have proposed a third hypothesis — that differential vulnerability to the labeling process may account for a large part of the unexplained difference in rates for labeled retardation. We have seen that persons from ethnic minorities who are labeled as retarded have fewer physical disabilities and fewer adaptive behavior failures than labeled retardates from the Anglo majority. Clinical measures, such as the standard intelligence test, are correlated with sociocultural characteristics so that persons from nonmodal sociocultural backgrounds are systematically handicapped. In these circumstances, higher rates of labeled mental retardation for ethnic minorities and persons from socioculturally nonmodal backgrounds are inevitable. However, these higher rates may have little or no relationship to the biological or genetic characteristics of the persons being labeled. Instead, they may be the result of the culture-bound perspective with which clinical measures are being interpreted.

It is time to analyze more carefully the assumptions of the clinical perspective and to assess critically whether these assumptions are warranted in identifying mentally retarded persons in America's multi-cultural society. A diagnostic nomenclature and evaluation system which treats persons from diverse cultural backgrounds as if they were culturally homogeneous cannot provide an adequate framework for comprehending the complexities of a pluralistic world.

What is needed is an evaluation system that is as multifaceted as American society. One way this goal could be achieved is by developing pluralistic norms for clinical measures. With such norms, an individual's performance could be evaluated in relation to the distribution of scores of others who have had comparable opportunities to learn the cognitive and verbal skills measured by the test. Only if a person rates as subnormal in the distribution of scores for his own sociocultural group would he be regarded as subnormal. However, such pluralistic norms could not be developed for an entire ethnic group because there is little homogeneity within ethnic group. We have seen that 27 percent to 37 percent of the variance in IQ within ethnic group can be accounted for by sociocultural factors. There are individuals in each ethnic group who come from socioculturally modal backgrounds. For them, standard norms based on the modal population of the United States are appropriate. For those from nonmodal backgrounds, the standard norms are not appropriate.

One possibility is to classify each person within ethnic group by the sociocultural modality of his family background using those sociocultural characteristics most highly correlated with clinical measures for his ethnic group as the basis for classification. Norms could then be developed for each category of sociocultural modality. The *meaning* of a particular clinical score could then be evaluated against two normative frameworks:

1. The person's position relative to the standard norms for the test would indicate where he stands in relationship to the general population of the United States. For a child, this score would indicate his probability of succeeding in American public schools as now constituted. For an adult, this score would indicate his probability of participating fully in the mainstream of American life.

2. The person's location on the norms for his own sociocultural modality group would reveal the amount of knowledge he has acquired about the language and culture of the dominant society compared to others who have had comparable opportunities to learn. This comparison would provide insight into his potential for learning, if he were given further opportunities to acquire the knowledge and skills needed to participate fully in American life. In other words, the person's placement on the standard norms would indicate how far he has to go to participate in American urban, industrial society. His placement on the sociocultural norms appropriate for his sociocultural background would indicate the probability that he will get there, if given adequate educational experiences.

NOTES

(1) J. F. Jastak, H. M. MacPhee, and M. Whiteman, *Mental Retardation: Its Nature and Incidence* (Newark, Delaware, 1963); P. Lemkau, C. Tietze, and M. Cooper, "Mental-hygiene Problems in an Urban District," *Mental Hygiene*, XXV (January 1941), 624-646; W. P. Richardson, A. C. Higgins, and R. G. Ames, *The Handicapped Children of Alamance County, North Carolina: A Medical and Sociological Study.* (Wilmington, 1965).

(2) R. G. Ferguson, *A Study of the Problem of Mental Retardation in the City of Philadelphia*, Report of the Philadelphia Commission on the Mentally Retarded (Philadelphia, 1956); E. Gruenberg, *A Special Census of Suspected Referred Mental Retardation in Onondaga County*, Technical Report of the Mental Health Unit (New York, 1955).

(3) G. Brockopp, "The Significance of Selected Variables on the Prevalence of Suspected-mental Retardates in the Public Schools of Indiana," unpublished dissertation, Indiana University (Bloomington, 1958); F. A. Mullen and M. M. Nee, "Distribution of Mental Retardation in an Urban School Population," *American Journal of Mental Deficiency*, LVI (April 1952), 777-790.

(4) *Racial and Ethnic Survey of California Public Schools*, Part I: Distribution of Pupils, Fall, 1966, 1967, (Sacramento, 1967).

(5) *U. S. Censuses of Population and Housing: 1960*, Final Report PHC (1)-135, Census Tracts, San Bernardino-Riverside-Ontario, California, Standard Metropolitan Statistical Area, (Washington, 1962).

(6) E. Zigler, "Familial Mental Retardation: A Continuing Dilemma," *Science*, CLV (January 1967), 292-298.

(7) B. Pasamanick and H. Knobloch, "The Contributions of Some Organic Factors to School Retardation in Negro Children," *Journal of Negro Education*, XXVII (Winter 1958), 4-9.

(8) Jane R. Mercer, "The Epidemiology of Mental Retardation in an American City," presentation for the Staff Development Conference of the President's Committee on Mental Retardation," AIRLIE Conference Center, June 4-5, 1970; ————, "The Meaning of Mental Retardation," forthcoming in Richard Koch and James Dobson, eds., *The Mentally Retarded Living in the Community*, (Seattle, 1970); ————, "Sociological Perspectives on Mild Mental Retardation," in H. C. Haywood, ed., *Socio-Cultural Aspects of Mental Retardation: Proceedings of the Peabody-NIMH Conference* (New York, 1970); ————, "Institutionalized Anglocentrism: Labeling Mental Retardates in the Public Schools," forthcoming in Peter Orleans and Eilliam Russel, Jr., eds., *Race, Change, and Urban Society* (New York, 1971); ————, "Who Is Normal? Two Perspectives on Mild Mental Retardation," in E. G. Jaco, ed., *Patients, Physicians, and Illness*, 2nd ed. (Glencoe, 1971, in press).

(9) I wish to thank Albert Marley, of the Riverside Unified School District, and Robert W. Hocker and J. Martin Koeppel, of the Alvord School District, and their staffs for their support, advice, and cooperation in collecting the data for this analysis. I also wish to thank Rosa McGrath and Lillian Redmond who served as interviewers in the reevaluation study.

(10) A. J. Reiss, Jr., *Occupations and Social Status* (Glencoe, 1961).

(11) Mercer, *The Eligibles and the Labeled.*

(12) I wish to thank the following persons in the Riverside Unified School District who made this study possible: Superintendent Bruce Miller; Richard Robbins, director of pupil personnel; Donald Ashurst, director of special education.

(13) *U. S. Censuses of Population and Housing: 1960.*

EXCERPTS FROM "COMPARATIVE PSYCHOLOGICAL STUDIES OF NEGROES AND WHITES IN THE UNITED STATES: 1959-1965"

Ralph Mason Dreger and
Kent S. Miller

In this section the sequence is related generally to the chronological age of subjects compared. Assuming that school achievement depends in part upon prior experiences in the preschool years, Gray and her associates at Peabody (Gray, 1964, 1965; Gray & Klaus, 1964) have been studying lower socio-economic Negro preschool children for a number of years. Gray's qualitative observations are important as considerations in making educational and/or intellectual comparisons. She contends that the *culturally deprived* child receives a smaller gross amount of reinforcement, as the mother spends more time coping with rather than shaping her child's behavior; that the child gets more reinforcement from his peers and his own sensations than from adults; that consquently he receives less verbal reinforcement than the more culturally fortunate child; that he is rewarded more for inhibitory than exploratory behavior; and that the verbal reinforcement that takes place is more a diffuse type than precisely focussing on the adequacy of the child's performance.

Further, Gray indicated that children in her study are children of *the poor.* The mothers devote all their energies to subsistence activities. The family structure is diffuse and frequently lacking in the presence of a wage earning male. Child care by grandmothers, aunts, and others is intended to maximize behavior expectations which make it easy for the child-caring adult. In terms of cognitive development, in contrast to what Piaget has found when the child reaches the "What's that" stage, no one is there to answer and tell him what *that* is, and to delight in the child's new discovery. In line with John's expectations as suggested previously, the child learns concrete properties of objects but not their interrelations and symbolic representations. Such a child receives early independence training, not in such ways as to give rise to an achievement motivation, but primarily in terms of caring for his physical needs.

School-related materials are virtually lacking in the home of the culturally deprived child.

> No one reads, no one writes, or draws pictures, no one cuts and pastes. Most of all, no one interacts with the child in the use of such materials. No one reads to him, draws a picture for him, or admires the picture he has drawn. Perhaps this lack of interaction is why television seems to have so little effect in such homes. Almost every one of our children has a television set in his home, usually on from morning till night, but we can discern no positive effects of its presence [Gray, 1964, p. 5].

Gray's observations lead her to the conclusion that in its turn the school perpetuates the distance between the child's world and his achievement. Reinforcement in school is for maximizing of appearances for neatness and attractiveness, and especially for "manners" and docility, none of which is especially relevant to academic achievement. In presenting its demands on the child, the school also fails to match what the child has in storage with what it expects him to input. Because teachers and schools have to keep up appearances, as it were, they place materials in the child's hands which are beyond his comprehension.

Particularly for the deprived Negro child, the problem of identity and self-esteem are made exceedingly difficult.

> Unless you have looked at it in this particular light, you would hardly believe in the overpowering impact of the WASP world that the child encounters in his school materials — the world of the white, Anglo-Saxon Protestant. No wonder that the child, who finds his pre-primers and primers full of golden haired boys and girls, with business-suited and brief-cased fathers, happy housewife mothers, and cocker spaniels, begins to believe that something is wrong with his brown skin, his father-absent home, and his yellow pup. Health charts, safety posters, magazines, and all his library books, as well as his textbooks, when they depict children, show fat, chubby little WASPS. Of course, everyone loves everyone in the primer world, and nobody fails, and everybody gets birthday presents. . . . Such books are none too realistic for the middle-class child, but for the deprived child, and particularly the Negro child, these books are tragic in their implications of who is important, who is worthwhile and therefore, by contrast, who is worthless and unimportant [Gray, 1964, p. 7].

Hess (1964a, 1964b) has independently discovered similar comparative lack of preparation for middle-class schooling in the lower of the socioeconomic classes among the 160 Negro mothers and their 4-year-old children whom he has studied in Chicago.

In the project under Gray's direction an attempt was made to change attitudes toward achievement, particularly achievement motivation, persistence and ability to delay gratification, and interest in school-related activities. An attempt was also made to manipulate the variable of parental attitude toward achievement and to raise the parental educational aspiration level. The final concern was with aptitudes for achievement, particularly perceptual and cognitive development and language. Although at this point the results in school achievement have not been reported, by the first grade experimental and control groups already had diverged in measured intelligence and language development, and preschool screening tests indicated that the experimental children were conspicuously better than the controls, approximating non-deprived children in the school which the children are attending.

Shuey suggests that examiner bias may have something to do with the significant differences between experimental and control groups on Gray's intellectual measures. Probably she is correct, although Gray exercises precautions in this respect; the gain of nine IQ points for the first treatment group probably would not be entirely the result of examiner bias.

In view of the interest in recent years in teaching 3-year-old children to read, a study by Fowler (1965) should be mentioned. Three-year-old twins and triplets from both Negro and white groups were given training in reading. Generally, the ability to learn to read at this age was about the same for the two groups. However, the numbers are too small for any definitive conclusions.

Summarizing more than a dozen studies, Pasamanick and Knobloch (1958) concluded that both socioeconomic factors and neurological factors are responsible for educational retardation. They assert that nutritional factors seem to be implicated in complications surrounding pregnancy and in prematurity, factors which presumably are directly related to socioeconomic status.

Whatever the relative contributions of innate differences and preschool experiences are to school experiences, Lepper (1965) employed ingenious means for getting at science-related concepts based on Piaget's notions of conservation of continuous and discontinuous substances, number, length, and area. The general conclusion to which Lepper comes is that there were Negro-white differences on experientially based conservations, but not on conservations more innately determined; that is, the Fs for number, length, and area revealed significant differences between Negroes and whites, with whites high, but did not show such differences for continuous substance and discontinuous substance. Once more the objection should be raised that with only one (white) examiner, no subject-examiner interaction effect could be tested. One might also add that relatively small numbers are involved in the comparisons that were made.

Two studies concerning school achievement mentioned by Shuey, but also included here because of one of the author's conclusions, are those by Osborne (1960, 1961). In three testings with California tests, in sixth, eighth, and tenth grades, 1,815 white and 446 Negro children achieved greater overlapping in the earlier than in the later grades, although in each case differences favored white children. In the other study, with 1,388 white and 723 Negro students equated for mental and chronological ages by the analysis of covariance, the adjusted F for the reading portion of the California tests was 180.06 and for arithmetic was 145.19, highly significant results in favor of white students.

Osborne's conclusions from his two studies can be combined. Because Negro teachers had more years of preparation and higher salaries, the implication is that Negro students had better teaching than white students. Cultural deprivation, Osborne holds, could be the explanation for differences on the reading test, but not for those on the arithmetic test. A regression effect was noted, in that the brightest of both groups went down and the dullest went up. On the basis of his results, Osborne feels that forcing integration would be harmful to both groups. We have reservations and questions about each of Osborne's conclusions, but rather than detail these questions, we present other research in the same general area.

Opposite results to those of Osborne were reported by Semler and Iscoe (1963) in a study of about 275 white and Negro children in public and private schools and kindergartens of Austin, Texas. The authors concluded that while learning ability as measured by a paired-associates task may be different in the two groups at 5- and 6-year levels, it is not at 8- and 9-year age levels. They also considered that a difference may have resulted from the fact that the younger Negro children were from a more deprived socioeconomic group, whereas the older Negro students came from a good school. They believe that their findings of no overall race differences in learning ability should not be minimized and that educators should exercise caution in inferring learning ability from measured intellectual level (WISC) only. We agree with the authors that replication of this study is necessary on methodological grounds.

Under the aegis of the National Merit Scholarship Corporation, a National Achievement Scholarship Program (NASP) was instituted to identify outstanding Negro high school students and give them financial aid to attend college (Roberts & Nichols, 1966). The nation's high schools were asked to nominate their outstanding Negro seniors. From these seniors, by means of two siftings, a group of 224 scholars was selected. Although other aspects of the characteristics of these scholars are of import, at this point only the following need to be mentioned. The percentage of students nominated and those surviving the sifting process was distributed in the geographic areas of the country about as one would expect from the proportions of Negro student populations in the various areas. However, 61.8% of the nominees were girls (a significant difference from the proportion of girls in the nonwhite high school population) suggesting what has been recognized elsewhere that the American Negro female has relative advantages over the male in comparison to the white culture. With other talented students the NASP scholars and finalists tend to be firstborn in their families. The parents of the total group of nominees did not have significantly higher educational level than parents of a representative sample of college students in general.

Significantly, more books were found in the homes of the NASP scholars and finalists than in the homes of high school seniors participating in PROJECT TALENT. Schools with high concentrations of Negroes were more likely to have sent nominations of students who became finalists, but the actual number of nominees was probably not any greater than one would expect in terms of the proportion of Negroes in a high school. Although only 5% of the scholars reached the 99th percentile on the National Merit Scholarship Qualifying Test, the median of the NASP scholars on the NMSQT was about at the 93rd percentile.

How these students will perform in college has not yet been revealed. As Roberts and Nichols (1966) wrote before the end of the first college year of these students:

Promising students have been identified, but they have been given difficult assignments. Many students with no traditional intellectual achievement in their backgrounds have entered the most prestigious academic communities, where Negroes have rarely been before. How will they perform? What are the characteristics of those who can succeed in this task? Answers to these questions await further follow-ups [Roberts & Nichols, 1966, pp. 42-43].

It will be indeed interesting to find out how these students achieve against some of the best competition in the country.

COLLEGE YEARS

On the college level, a comparison of three Negro colleges and three non-Negro colleges in the Georgia University system (Biaggio & Stanley, 1964) revealed that the Scholastic Aptitude Test predicted subsequent college grades just as well for both Negro and white students. When the coefficients for the Negro group were corrected for attenuation, the SAT predicted better for the Negro group. Without such a correction a better prediction was made for the non-Negro females than for Negro females, while no difference was found for the males.

Several large scale surveys and/or investigations have produced educational comparisons. The first is a summary of reading investigations among three Negro colleges covering a period from 1940 to 1954 by Boykin (1958) who discovered that for the 3,686 students across these years different types of reading tests yielded mean grade levels with a range of 9.2 to 12.1. For individuals, reading level ranged from fifth grade to that of college senior. The next (Dailey, 1964), a study in PROJECT TALENT with 450,000 9th to 12th graders in 1,353 schools, investigated the relation between the Information Total Test and education and occupation one or more years out of high school. Educational attainment was found to be highly related to the eventual occupational status. Of primary interest is the fact that the schools with a percentage of Negroes up to about 20% show up approximately at the median level.on the ITT. With an increasing percentage of Negroes, a steady drop in ITT scores occurs. It is significant that not only do the Southeast and Southwest contribute schools with 100% Negro constituencies, but also the Plains states, the Great Lakes region, and the Mideast provide such schools.

In discussing the progress of the Negro in higher education from 1950 to 1960, Doddy (1963) shows that a steady increase in the ratio of Negroes to whites completing 1 to 3 and 4 or more years of college, respectively, has occurred. In 1940 the ratio was 3.10 white over Negro; in 1950 2.60; and in 1960 2.11 for completion of 1 to 3 years. For 4 years of college only, the corresponding ratios are 3.79, 3.00, and 2.31. All of which means that even in

1960 the proportion of whites completing the respective amounts of education was well over twice that of Negroes. Further, Doddy indicates that, although in the general population the excess of males over females in colleges and universities in 1960 was of the order of a ratio of 1.7, in 104 Negro institutions investigated, women outnumbered men with a percentage of 54.3. The author claims that this pattern will perpetuate the unfortunate Negro family organization.

One sidelight casting considerable illumination on the quality of education Negroes have obtained in Southern institutions is given prominence by Doddy. Until the mid-1950s, the Southern Association of Colleges and Secondary Schools had a separate list of Negro colleges and did not hold them to the same standards as white colleges or admit them to membership. By 1957, by changing to a program of raising standards, 15 senior and 3 junior colleges were admitted to membership, leaving 43 senior and 2 junior colleges not approved, although several have been admitted since then. The national government provided funds directly and also through NDEA, NSF, and other agencies, or the colleges could not have become accredited. Doddy suggests that the Negro college in the future may serve only a remedial function to overcome the effects of segregation.

SCHOOLS AND TEACHERS

Since quality of schools seems to have some effect upon educational achievement, and possibly on intellectual level as measured by standard intelligence tests, some attention should be paid to the characteristics of Southern schools which have until relatively recently been notoriously discriminatory in relation to white and Negro. Weyl (1960), partly on the basis of the famous Bulletin No. 39 on Negro education put out by the Department of the Interior Bureau of Education and partly on the statistics of state school systems, reports that in 1912 the estimated per capita expenditure for Negro education in the South was $1.71 as compared to the figure of $15.00 for the education of whites. In 1930 the ratio of expenditure ranged from 2 to 1 to 4 to 1. Johnson (1941) reported that in 1937-38 Alabama spent $49.37 for its white student and $14.75 for its Negro student for current expense, interest, and capital outlay. In 1952, representatively, Alabama spent 60% as much on Negro children per capita as for white children, and North Carolina, the best among the Southern states in this regard, spent 80% of the white child's per capita for the Negro child.

That there are still many inequities is evident to anyone who has intimate knowledge of Negro and white schools in the South. These inequities are epitomized by the remark of a Negro student who had gone from a segregated school to a desegregated school in the community in which one of the reviewers live (Baton Rouge, Louisiana), "We have books and laboratory equipment there!"

Although other comparisons can be found in the literature, the one by

Greene (1962) is a fairly careful representative study. Greene investigated the characteristics of white and Negro teachers in a large Southeastern school system by comparing both records and test scores. He indicated the following factors as significant or not at the .01 level or better for T or chi-square tests. Not significant at this level were age, number of siblings, number of progeny, number of high schools attended, number of years in the school system, number of years of teaching experience, number of hours of absence, number of months of leave, and number of professional memberships reported. Significant at the .01 level, for Negro teachers higher than whites, were the number of years of college training, the yearly salary, the number of higher level teacher certificates, the reported number of nonprofessional memberships, the reported number of professional magazines read, the reported number of nonprofessional magazines read, the number of separations or divorces, the amount of urban background, and membership in the Protestant church. Significant at the .01 level, for whites more than Negroes, were the number of years of legal residence in the state, the number of physical deviations from the norm, the socioeconomic status, the status of father's occupation, school grades completed by father and mother, the number of colleges attended, the number of years since the bachelor's degree, later birth order, longer residence in the state, being born outside the county of present residence, the principal's ratings of teacher competence, and the six individual scores of a validated teacher competence scale.

We are reminded by Greene's results of the British "who lose every battle except the last one." For the Negro teachers "win" and white teachers "lose" on almost every measure of teaching-related factors except principals' ratings of teacher competence and objective teaching competence as measured by Greene's test. If teaching effectiveness is related to these measures (and ordinarily one would expect the ratings by the Negro principals to be higher than actual effectiveness), it would seem that Negro teachers are paid more to accomplish less. But several things need to be noted. First, Negro teachers attended fewer colleges than did white teachers. They had more training within the state, which meant more training in Negro institutions, and they tended more to have resided in the same county as that in which they presently resided. In other words, in this tight, segregated system poor teaching in one generation led to poor students in the next generation, who in turn became poor teachers in the succeeding generation whose poor teaching led to poor students in the next succeeding generation.

EFFECTS OF DESEGREGATION

The effects of desegregating schools in the South and border states have been the subject of controversy. When objective studies have been made, the reports are generally favorable in terms of maintaining or raising educational achievement levels, although the evidence concerning other forms of reaction, especially emotional reaction, is not clear (Coles, 1963; Stinson, 1963).

One of the first school systems in the American South to be desegregated was that in Louisville, Kentucky. Stallings (1959) studied the records of the Louisville schools to determine the immediate effects of desegregation on scholastic achievement with what he considered to be relevant variables held constant. Gains of white children in the schools with or without substantial Negro percentages were over and above what would normally be expected. For Negro children there were similar gains in the second year. For the previous 9 years there had been no instance of similar gains among Negro children. Stallings does point out that the gains were greater for the Negro children who remained voluntarily with Negro teachers. He concludes that *Negro* motivation, at least, was increased by the desegregation process, leading to substantial achievement gains. Obviously, also, there was no deterioration of white achievement in the three grades under consideration. The fact that Negro children who remained voluntarily with Negro teachers made greater gains than those who moved over into formerly all white schools is open to equivocal interpretation.

The other major school system which desegregated voluntarily immediately following the 1954 decision of the Supreme Court banning forced segregation in the public schools was the Washington, D.C., public school system. A special committee, under Georgia Representative Davis of the House Committee on the District of Columbia, which investigated desegregation effects during the 1956-57 school year, concluded that desegregation had worked immense evils on the Washington public school system and its children in particular. Opponents of the committee maintained that these findings were biased and exaggerated (Muse, 1964).

As Superintendent of the Washington, D.C., schools almost since the beginning of the desegregation period, Hansen (1960a, 1960b, 1963) has reported on the results of desegregation in his school system. The record appears to be impressive in favor of the improvement of the school system since desegregation. Hansen insists that it is not primarily the result of desegregation itself, but the result of continuing efforts to improve factors affecting learning. Desegregation, which forced the city to look at its total school system rather than primarily at its white segment, served as a catalyst for a total reevaluation and redirection. A controversial four-track plan of educating children according to their measured abilities has resulted in gains in school achievement, as measured on individual pupils, which equal or exceed the national norms of expected growth. Contrary to fears expressed prior to the desegregation or by the Davis committee, the Honors groups in Tracks 1 and 2 were not held back, but instead appeared to gain under the present systems.

The somewhat roseate picture which Hansen presents has not been unchallenged (Weyl, 1960). However, unless better studies are done than that of McCown (1960) on which apparently Hansen based some of his conclusions, and unless the figures have been deliberately falsified or unconsciously selected to present a favorable picture, we should hesitate to reject Hansen's conclusions that, for whatever reasons, the desegregation of Washington's public schools has not resulted in the deterioration predicted by those who expected disastrous consequences.

In a conference of administrators of 17 desegregated school systems (Southern Regional Council, 1960) agreement was reached that generally desegregation had not lowered white achievement and it had raised Negro achievement, although as Superintendent Hansen indicated from Washington, the results were from a general overhauling of school systems more than from the desegregation itself. Since desegregation in the Deep South until relatively recently has been "token tokenism," the educational effects of desegregation in the hardcore segregated areas will have to await future research. Forces within both the Negro and white communities keep the desegregation process at a minimum (Pettigrew, 1965), so that reports of such research may come only after a considerably extended period of time. What will happen in the desegregation of Northern schools is also still questionable. Only the report by Wolman (1964) in which some favorable results were found in desegregating a Negro school in New Rochelle, New York, has come to our attention as an objective study.

EDUCATIONAL AND OCCUPATIONAL
ASPIRATIONS AND EXPECTATIONS

The Negro revolution of the 1960s and the federal government's concern with the lower socioeconomic classes have resulted in a series of studies measuring educational and occupational hopes and plans. Subjects have been studied from the third grade through high school, and from all sections of the country. The general approach has been to administer questionnaires to large groups, occasionally in conjunction with individual interviews.

As with the other areas being reviewed in this paper, generalizations are difficult to make. Sexton (1963) has accurately summarized the major problems: Frequently there is a failure to distinguish between aspirations and expectations; none of the studies are national in scope; in most instances there has been no attempt to quantify the intensity of aspiration. Nevertheless, some cautious generalizations are attempted here.

Earlier research had suggested that the expressed educational and occupational aspirations of Negroes were higher than those of whites. Recent work indicates that the aspirations of Negroes are high, but expectations are less, and with increasing age, reality factors become more significant. The Negro continues to stress education as the main route to occupational advancement but there is a realistic outlook in terms of job expectancies.

One of the most comprehensive studies to be reviewed is that of Bowerman and Campbell (1965). The subjects were 16,000 high school students in four Southern states, covering urban and rural areas. The investigators found that the overwhelming majority of both races say they plan to graduate from high school, but fewer than one-half of the Negroes are absolutely sure about carrying out these plans, as contrasted with two thirds of the whites. Negroes are as likely as whites to say that they definitely want to go to college. In general, the races are found to have very similar educational goals. The authors make the same statement in regard to the level of occupational aspirations and expectations, but there are differences in the kinds of jobs sought and expected. Both groups seek white-collar occupations; but Negroes are more likely to desire and expect blue collar or military jobs and less likely to be interested in farming. Consistent with earlier findings, Negro girls have a low interest in being housewives and they have higher educational hopes than do Negro boys.

Essentially the same findings are reported for a sample from three low-income rural counties in Florida (Youmans, Grigsby, & King, 1963). About half of both Negro and white youth planned to continue their education in some way after leaving high school, and equal proportions expected to go to college. Compared with Negro boys, about twice as many Negro girls actually entered college.

Florida Negroes see their greatest occupational opportunity as existing in the city, and approximately three-fourths of those questioned by Bowerman and Campbell (1965) in their four-state survey would prefer living outside of the South. These are the only two studies to be reported in this section which involved subjects from the deep South. Reports from other sections of the country generally support the trends mentioned above.

Reiss and Rhodes (1959) surveyed over 21,000 students in the Nashville area, about 15% of whom were Negro. They concluded that the Negro places a much greater emphasis upon education and is more achievement oriented than whites. The age, sex, IQ, and socioeconomic status position of the Negro was found to be of lesser influence on behavior than race position when comparison was made with white adolescents. Negro high school seniors in Kentucky set occupational goals similar to those of whites with the exception that the Negro female has higher expectations (Lott & Lott, 1963). The Negro girls concentrated their occupational expectations among the professions and totally rejected the role of housewife. Out of a total of 52 Negro female subjects not a single one wanted to be a housewife, as contrasted with 24% of the white girls. Sprey (1962) studied ninth graders and reported an ambitious pattern of aspiration and expectation among Negro girls, with a much greater percentage of Negro girls than boys actually enrolled in college preparatory programs. Study of ninth-grade students in New Jersey revealed that Negroes had uniformly high aspirations but planned lower than whites and were less certain about their plans (Stephensen, 1957). Stephensen's study has the merit of distinguishing between aspirations and plans; he was able to conclude that occupational aspiration does not seem to be affected by class, whereas plans and expectations are more definitely class based. Working with ninth- and twelfth-grade pupils in Kansas City, Gist and Bennett (1963) found that there were no significant differences in occupational aspirations, but Negroes had higher educational aspirations. In contrast to the Stephensen study, Gist and Bennett found no differences in plans for education.

Antonovsky and Lerner (1959) interviewed a sample of lower-class youths in New York and found that the Negroes generally had a higher level of aspiration. They suggest that among many of the Negro families the poor model provided by the father might raise aspirations by the child's choosing not to be like the father. An additional sample of New York children of a lower social class also reflected greater educational and occupational aspirations among the Negroes (Smith & Abramson, 1962).

The related factors of social class mentioned at several points in the previous discussion also seem to apply at younger ages. Sixth- through eighth-grade students of the lower classes have been found to plan below the middle classes in both educational and occupational areas, regardless of race (Holloway & Berreman, 1959). They also plan below the level to which they aspire.

One final study reflecting the high educational aspirations of Negroes deserves mention. Rosen (1959) studied 427 pairs of mothers and sons from four Northeastern states. Of the Negro mothers 83% said that they intended that their sons go to college, although these aspirations were not significantly different from those of Jews, Protestants, and Greeks. Of seven ethnic groups studied, the Negro mother's vocational aspirations for her son were lower than all but one group.

In addition to asking direct questions regarding aspirations, a number of investigators have been interested in measuring generalized achievement motivation. The most popular approach has been to employ some variation of the McClelland method. But regardless of the technique employed, it appears that Negroes are less achievement oriented than whites (Lott & Lott, 1963; Merbaum, 1962; Mingione, 1965; Rosen, 1959). Note the contrast between the results of direct questioning indicated above and those derived from more indirect methods. We found only one study in which a significant racial difference was not reported; and even then, on the basis of another measure, the whites were said to have a greater achievement-oriented value system (Smith & Abramson, 1962). These results appear to hold up even when intelligence and social class status are controlled, and when the examiners are of the same race as the subject. The sex differences frequently mentioned in previous paragraphs also seem to operate in this area with the Negro female's achievement motivation exceeding that of the Negro male. The research reviewed here is consistent with the empirical studies relating to prestige criteria. Glenn (1963a), in reviewing this literature, reports that for the Negro formal education is the most important determinant of prestige, whereas for whites occupation and income have been as important, if not more important.

Over the years education has been seen as the major route for advancement for Negroes, and Negro parents have held high aspirations for their children. Recent research continues to reveal high aspirations, but when concrete expectations and plans have been assessed, Negroes have been found to be much more pessimistic and realistic than whites. The expressed goals are similar for the two races but Negroes plan less and generally appear to be less achievement oriented. Once again, as with so many other areas of comparison, the probability of planning appears to be class linked.

It is important that racial comparisons be made by sex. With respect to both the occupational and educational areas, the Negro female has consistently higher aspirations, more achievement motivation, and she is more likely than the male to make plans and follow through with them. There are also differences among Negroes and whites in occupation preference. The most striking of these is Negro girls' almost total rejection of the role of housewife.

These conclusions have been based on large-scale studies from most regions of the country. In contrast with the work covered in our earlier review, most of the current reports are at least aware of the distinction between aspirations and expectations, although there have been few attempts to quantify their intensity. It will be interesting to observe changes in aspiration in view of the large-scale effort to modify the educational and occupational opportunities for Negroes.

REFERENCES

Antonovsky, A., & Lerner, M. J. Occupational aspirations of lower class Negro and white youth. *Social Problems*, 1959, 7, 132-138.

Biaggio, A., & Stanley, J. C. Prediction of freshman grades at southern state colleges. Paper presented at the meeting of the Ninth Interamerican Congress of Psychology, Miami Beach, December 1964.

Bowerman, C. E., & Campbell, E. Q. Aspiration of southern youth: A look at racial comparisons. *Transaction*, 1965, 2, 24.

Boykin, L. L. A summary of reading investigations among Negro colleges: 1940-1954. *Journal of Educational Research*, 1958, 51, 471-475.

Coles, R. *The desegregation of southern schools: A psychiatric study.* New York: Anti-Defamation League of B'nai B'rith, 1963.

Dailey, J. T. Education and emergence from poverty. *Journal of Marriage and the Family*, 1964, 26, 430-434.

Doddy, H. H. The progress of the Negro in higher education, 1950-1960. *Journal of Negro Education*, 1963 Yearbook, 32, 485-492.

Fowler, W. A study of process and method in three-year-old twins and triplets learning to read. *Genetic Psychology Monographs*, 1965, 72, 3-89.

Gist, N. P., & Bennett, W. S., Jr. Aspirations of Negro and white students. *Social Forces*, 1963, 42, 40-48.

Gray, S. W. Some implications of research on young culturally deprived children. In J. McV. Hunt (Chm.), Implications of research in cultural disadvantage for counseling psychology. Symposium presented at the American Psychological Association, Los Angeles, September 1964.

Gray, S. W. The cumulative effects of cultural deprivation: A sidelight on racial comparisons. In R. M. Dreger (Chm.), Recent research in the psychology of race. Symposium presented at the Southeastern Psychological Association, Atlanta, April 1965.

Gray, S. W., & Klaus, R. A. An experimental preschool program for culturally deprived children. Paper presented at the meeting of the American Association for the Advancement of Science, December 1964.

Greene, J. E., Sr. A comparison of certain characteristics of white and Negro teachers in a large southeastern school system. *Journal of Social Psychology*, 1962, 58, 383-391.

Hansen, C. F. Scholastic performance of Negro and white pupils in the integrated public schools of the District of Columbia. *Harvard Educational Review*, 1960, 37, 216-236. (a)

Hansen, C. F. *Addendum: A five-year report on desegregation in the Washington, D.C. schools.* New York: Anti-Defamation League of B'nai B'rith, 1960. (b)

Hansen, C. F. Scholastic performance of Negro and white pupils in the integrated public schools of the District of Columbia. *Journal of Educational Sociology*, 1963, 36, 287-291.

Hess, R. D. Educability and rehabilitation: The future of the welfare class. Paper presented at the meeting of the Thirtieth Groves Conference on Marriage and the Family, Knoxville, Tenn., April 15, 1964. (a)

Hess, R. D. Maternal teaching styles and the socialization of educability. In V. C. Shipman (Chm.), Socialization of attitudes toward learning in urban working-class families. Symposium presented at the American Psychological Association, Los Angeles, September 1964. (b)

Johnson, C. S. *Growing up in the Black Belt: Negro youth in the rural South.* Washington, D.C.: American Council on Education, 1941.

Lepper, R. E. A cross-cultural investigation of the relationship between the development of selected science-related concepts and social status and reading readiness of Negro and white first graders. Unpublished doctoral dissertation, Florida State University, 1965.

Lott, A. J., & Lott, B. E. *Negro and white youth: A psychological study in a border state community.* New York: Holt, Rinehart and Winston, 1963.

McCown, G. W. A critical evaluation of the Four Track curriculum program at the District of Columbia high schools with recommendations for improvements. Unpublished doctoral dissertation, University of Maryland, 1960.

Muse, B. *Ten years of prelude: The story of integration since the Supreme Court's 1954 decision.* New York: Viking Press, 1964.

Osborne, R. T. Racial differences in mental growth and school achievement: A longitudinal study. *Psychological Reports*, 1960, 7, 233-239.

Osborne, R. T. School achievement of white and Negro children of the same mental and chronological ages. *Mankind Quarterly*, 1961, 2, 26-29.

Pasamanick, B., & Knobloch, H. The contribution of some organic factors to school retardation in Negro children. *Journal of Negro Education*, 1958, 27, 4-9.

Pettigrew, T. F. Continuing barriers to desegregated education in the south. *Sociology of Education*, 1965, 38, 99-111.

Reiss, A. J., Jr., & Rhodes, A. L. Are educational norms and goals of conforming, truant, and delinquent adolescents influenced by group position in American society? *Journal of Negro Education*, 1959, 28, 252-267.

Roberts, R. J., & Nichols, R. C. Participants in the national achievement scholarship program for Negroes. Unpublished manuscript, National Merit Scholarship Corporation, Evanston, Ill., 1966.

Semler, I. J., & Iscoe, I. Comparative and developmental study of the learning abilities of Negro and white children under four conditions. *Journal of Educational Psychology*, 1963, 54, 38-44.

Sexton, P. Negro career expectation. *Merrill-Palmer Quarterly*, 1963, 9, 303-316.

Smith, H. P., & Abramson, M. Racial and family experience correlates of mobility aspiration. *Journal of Negro Education*, 1962, 31, 117-124.

Sprey, J. Sex differences in occupational choice patterns among Negro adolescents. *Social Problems*, 1962, 10, 11-23.

Stallings, F. H. A study of the immediate effects of integration on scholastic achievement in the Louisville public schools. *Journal of Negro Education*, 1959, 28, 439-444.

Stephensen, R. M. Mobility orientation and stratification of 1,000 ninth graders. *American Sociological Review*, 1957, 22, 204-212.

Stinson, H. N. The effects of desegregation on adjustment and values of Negro and white students. Unpublished doctoral dissertation, George Peabody College for Teachers, 1963.

Weyl, N. *The Negro in American civilization.* Washington, D.C.: Public Affairs Press, 1960.

Wolman, T. G. Some initial effects of integrated schooling on the reading achievement scores of transfer students in New Rochelle elementary schools. Paper presented at the meeting of the American Psychological Association, Los Angeles. September 1964.

Youmans, E. G., Grigsby, S. E., & King, H. C. After high school what? Cooperative Extension Service, University of Florida, 1963. (Mimeo)

chapter 12
descriptive research studies

THE COLLEGE READINESS PROGRAM: A PROGRAM FOR THIRD WORLD STUDENTS AT THE COLLEGE OF SAN MATEO, CALIFORNIA

Carol Lopate

In its heyday between 1966 and 1968, the College Readiness Program received the acclamation of being the finest program for students of color anywhere in the country. Through its active recruitment efforts, the minority enrollment on campus had jumped from 80 to nearly 800 within a two-and-a-half year period; counseling, tutoring, and a strong Program Center had reduced the dropout rate among "risk" students from 90 to 15 percent; leadership as well as student effort had created a sense of loyalty and a degree of morale rarely achieved in any facet of academic life. Yet, by the end of the fall 1968 semester, police had been called on campus, the directors of the College Readiness Program had been removed from their posts, and over half of the minority students in the Program had either been expelled or had themselves withdrawn from the college.

While it is impossible in any historical account to vouch for information gathered after the event, the many participants and observers in the San Mateo story tend to contradict each other less than simply to see what happened from different vantage points and thus give their attention and approval or disapproval to different issues. Community members, trustees, administration, faculty and students both in and outside the Program acknowledge its dramatic if frightening success, the inability of the college to incorporate it into the mainstream of academic life, the tightening of financial and political controls, and the resulting dissolution of the project and its replacement by a more containable program of compensatory education.

To understand what happened at the College of San Mateo, and what may happen in other junior colleges throughout the country as they attempt to provide programs for Third World students, it is necessary to place the college in the context of higher education, and in particular, of higher education in the State of California.

In the past twenty-five years, we in the United States have witnessed the dramatic growth of higher education. Education, and defense, have become the two most rapidly expanding industries in our country. The Council of Economic Advisors notes that education spending has been increasing ten and a half percent a year for the last decade while the total economic growth has been less than four percent a year.(1) According to Clark Kerr, "The production, distribution, and consumption of 'knowledge' in all its forms is said to account for 29 percent of the gross national product . . . and knowledge production is growing at about twice the rate of the rest of the economy."(2)

From most viewpoints, this dramatic growth has been considered a positive element in our nation's history. Since universal education has traditionally been linked with the possibility of a democracy, the chance for increased higher education for a greater number of individuals has been regarded as an opportunity to train more citizens for playing a vital role in American life. However, this disproportionate growth has not merely been the result of an idealism on the part of those in power which seeks to involve more individuals in the nation's wealth and decision-making. Rather, it has been a product of a changeover in our economy from one requiring large numbers of untrained workers to one demanding proportionately fewer workers, many of whom must now have technical-scientific training. It is estimated that by 1970, ninety percent of all workers will have a high school education,(3) and a significant proportion will be in jobs requiring advanced training. Whether or not this increased education is merely the result of more complicated job tasks is open to argument. A strong case can be made for the position that increased educational requirements serve the more important function of keeping youth out of an ever-constricting labor market and that in many jobs employees with less training perform equally well or better than their colleagues with more education.(4) Be that as it may, American colleges, and especially junior colleges, have increasingly taken on the role, not only of providing the liberal arts background necessary for "free choice," but, subsidized by public taxes, of relieving corporations of the need to train their own labor force while absorbing surplus manpower.

California, having one of the most inclusive publicly-supported higher education systems, provides an excellent case study for the political and social ramifications of higher education's new role as a tax-supported training ground for entrance into political and economic life in the United States. Prior to 1959, California state colleges were supposedly prepared to accommodate any student in the top seventy percent of his graduating class; various campuses of the University of California were to accommodate the top 33 percent. However, financing for the state educational institutions was, and still is, provided by a tax system in which business and industry bear only twenty percent of the burden while household units through property and sales tax bear eighty percent. As a result of this inability to tap the real sources of wealth in the state, 1959 found higher education in California suffering from a financial crisis. And, in the period between 1960 and 1975 full-time enrollment in the state institutions was expected to triple. In an attempt to solve the problem, the state legislators authorized the University of California Board of Regents and the State Board of Education to draw up a Master Plan for higher education. Under the direction of Clark Kerr, this group arrived at a plan which focused on eliminating "duplication of efforts" in the state colleges and the university. Unfortunately, however, this was done through quantitatively eliminating enrollments by raising academic standards in the four-year institutions and channeling those not qualified into two-year junior colleges to be financed chiefly by local rather than state taxes. (This, of course, meant an additional tax, decided on by the communities.) Admission to the University of California was now restricted to the top twelve percent of the high school graduating class, while admission to state colleges was narrowed to the top 33 percent. Junior colleges were theoretically open to any high school graduate or anyone over 18. Hence, the reputation that California's educational system was more inclusive than ever.(5) And the junior colleges did grow by leaps and bounds. However, the Master Plan was followed by a drop in minority enrollment on most public campuses. At San Francsco State, for example, which is in a city whose public schools are nearly seventy percent students of color, the implementation of the Master Plan was followed by a decline in black enrollment from 17 to 4 percent.

If a racial bias seems to be reflected in the Master Plan, a class bias is even more obvious. Shapiro and Barlow, in an article which reviews the relationship between education, on the one hand, and race and class, on the other, report:

> Nearly two thirds of the students in the junior colleges have parents whose yearly income is less than $10,000. For the state college, the figure is precisely one half. And for the University of California, two thirds of the students come from family income brackets of over $10,000 a year, and for a majority, the figure is closer to $12,000. But income brackets under $10,000 pay over half the state's taxes; at least half of these taxpayers are thirdworld, among them 3½ million chicanos, 1½ million blacks, Chinese, Japanese, Filipinos, and American Indians. Yet the state spends twice as much money on the average university student as on the average state college student, and three times as much on the average state college student as on the average junior college student.(6)

Although junior colleges are supposed to specialize in lower division education and to be equipped with facilities for salvaging "late bloomers," the state colleges receive more money both for teaching salaries and total instructional expenditure in their own lower divisions. Faculty workload, salaries, and fringe benefits all show a clear differential between junior colleges, state colleges, and the state university. State colleges and universities have considerably more money for financial aid than do the junior colleges.

San Mateo County, an upper-middle-class suburban area about ten miles outside of San Francisco, has had a junior college since 1922 when one opened in the city of San Mateo to serve thirty-five students. The present site of the College of San Mateo on top of a hill overlooking the county and the nearby bay was secured in 1958, and through a $5.9 million bond issue the complex of spacious modern white one-story buildings surrounded by parking lots was completed in 1963 to accommodate 5,000 students. Since the advent of the Master Plan, an additional $12.8 million bond issue has been voted to provide two more junior college campuses in San Mateo County, each accommodating 8,000 students, and to expand the College of San Mateo to serve the same number. Because of a shortage of funds for completing the two campuses, a third bond was voted on last year, but this time turned down by the voters. (Some attribute this rejection to the community's resistance to supporting what they considered the growing activism on campus; others simply regard it as the logical result of over-taxation.)

Until 1966, when the College Readiness Program brought in a sudden influx of students of color from East Palo Alto and other nearby ghettos, the College of San Mateo served a maximum of 80 non-white students in any one year. Thus, even the large numbers of technical jobs available in the county were closed to non-whites, as were, of course, the more prestigious and highly trained occupations. Equally important during the recent years of high draft rates, while college attendance kept large numbers of white males out of the service, black and Mexican American males had no such sanctuary to protect them from military service.

THE COLLEGE READINESS PROGRAM

Because the College Readiness Program was one of the earlier compensatory programs aimed at students of color, and because it sought to deviate even from those guidelines which had been established in the scattered projects already in existence, its leaders had little sense of the areas in which a program such as they envisioned would challenge the structure of the junior college, or how soon its goals would be considered threatening by the college administration. Seen from the viewpoint of more progressive members of the community, the story of the College Readiness Program is that of the struggle of a number of dedicated, dynamic personalities against a traditionalist system.

In the fall of 1965, the president of the College of San Mateo, Julio

Bortolazzi, delivered an opening address in which he asked that the faculty work towards recruiting more students of color into the college. Out of 300 faculty members, Jean Wirth, an English teacher, was the only volunteer. Miss Wirth had just returned from a leave of absence after six years of teaching at the college. During her leave she had worked with Mills College girls who were practicing teaching in Oakland. Having seen the kinds of experiences which black students had in the school system had made her acutely aware that in most cases students had simply been turned off of formal education and so, of course, did not respond to the new "opportunities" provided by the junior colleges.

During the 1965-66 school year, Miss Wirth worked with a Stanford project aimed at raising the achievement of disadvantaged college students. Through this program she became acquainted with the residents of East Palo Alto, the "target" black community, and an area which logically might also have fed into the College of San Mateo. Concurrently, she established a tutorial program in her own office in the English Department for the eighty black students who were at the college. At the time almost all of these students were in non-academic programs.

The College Readiness Program, with enthusiastic support from President Bortolazzi and a boost of $10,000 from the trustees, was officially begun in the summer of 1966. Because the East Palo Alto community, where most of the recruiting was done, had long ago decided that the College of San Mateo was a "white" institution, it was not easy to recruit students. Young people were approached in high schools, on street corners, in pool halls, and any other place a prospect might be found. Out of 150 interviewees, 39 young people – all but three of whom were black – finally agreed to come. Qualifications for admission into the program were unique: the candidate had to 1) be a person of color; 2) be poor; 3) have a high school grade average below C; 4) test badly; and 5) say in the first interview that he was not interested in going to college! The point of these qualifications was to reach those people who were always passed up in the traditional "compensatory education" programs, at times because they were considered "too high a risk," at other times because they lived beyond the vision of recruitment officers. As one might predict, most of these students had police records, and most were unemployed (and thus found the work-study pay of $1.50 an hour which the Program offered an adequately attractive incentive), although few expected to receive more than a summer's pay or a weird experience from the project.

It was the conviction of those organizing the program that the success of the students in it would depend on intensive personal relationships and an environment accepting of their past and present ways of living. The heart of the Program was the CRP Center, where Program students got together and relaxed from the tensions of acting "right" (or white) in the regular college classes. The Center was decorated by the students and contained posters of such men as Malcolm X, and Mao Tse-tung; listings of community activities were continually posted as were news items and activities involving Program students and their community. Inside the Center, students were encouraged to iron out complaints against teachers, administrators, or other officials; hold political discussions questioning any and all assumptions about the existing order of society; and, in general, work out their hostilities against the white, established world. Some have described the College Readiness Program as a "halfway house." This is apt in the sense that, while students were expected to conform to the behavior expected of them while on the college campus, inside the Center they were encouraged to live freely and express their preferred tastes and habits. However, the term also leads to the misconception that the world of the college was considered as an ideal, and "health" the total adjustment to it.

Educators speak glibly of raising the self-esteem of people of color. The College Readiness Program did not articulate this as a goal, since even the articulation of such a goal tends to imply condescension. Rather, students were considered — and consider themselves — worthwhile human beings who had been deprived of some of the necessary skills and deserved opportunities. The fact that a CRP student might only read at a fifth-grade level was not seen as a reason for limiting his educational or occupational goals; it was only viewed as a cause for acknowledging that hard work would have to follow.

From the start, Program students were given control over almost all phases of the College Readiness Program. This included recruitment, student and faculty selection, and retention, tutoring, counseling and general program policy-making.

Perhaps the only "non-negotiable" structure of the Program was the system of classes and tutoring which Program students had to follow for one semester, or until their grades reached a C average. Each student was given a tutor; there were two students per tutor. This ratio changed only once, during the second summer when the ratio was one-to-one. Beginning with the second year, tutors were divided into groups under the direction of tutor-supervisors, who in turn were responsible to counselors. Counselors assisted students in program planning, budgeting, and any of the many other problems which they might encounter. During the first summer a large proportion of the tutors and counselors were white activist students from the College of San Mateo, but this changed in successive semesters as CRP black and brown students moved up into these positions. As of the fall of 1968, the structure of the College Readiness Program looked as follows:

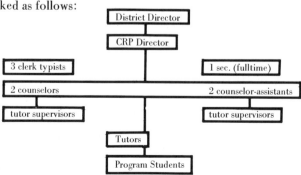

Each day during the summer, Program students attended one-and-a-half hours of a three-point academic course of their choosing (usually a subject in one of the social sciences, such as history, sociology, psychology or philosophy), a one-hour English class, one hour of counseling, an hour lunch break, and in the afternoon three hours of work for work study. After returning home at six for an hour dinner break, they were picked up again for three hours of tutoring.

Transportation to the College of San Mateo was a major problem. Most regular students, whether they live in the county or elsewhere, have their own cars. Public transportation to the college from East Palo Alto costs one dollar a day, takes more than an hour each way, and is extremely irregular. Thus, in order to make college attendance a viable alternative, a special bus had to be chartered to pick up Program students in East Palo Alto and surrounding neighborhoods and drive them to the college, returning them home again in the evening. For the first week of the summer 1966 program's existence, whenever a student had been negligent about meeting the bus in the morning, tutors went out in cars to pick them up. Once enrolled students realized they would end up at the college in any case, they made the buses and attendance was excellent throughout the summer. Although transportation is still not optimal, it continues to be taken care of through this daily bus system.

Before the summer session, and again before each of the following semesters, tutors and counselors were given a four-day in-training session at a retreat in the Napa Valley during which they were taught tutorial skills and helped to gain a general receptivity to the cultures of those students they would teach. In addition, tutors met every Monday afternoon throughout the summer from 1-5 and for one full day each weekend. They were also given readings and asked to attend various community activities. The training was extensive and a great deal of effort was also expended in ensuring that the tutors knew and trusted each other and solidified as a group. Thus, cohesiveness was reinforced at all levels in the College Readiness Program.

In contrast to the predicted high dropout rate, 36 of the 39 students completed the summer project. In the fall 34 returned as regular college students, although they were still part of the College Readiness Program. More surprising even than this high rate of return is that almost all of these 34 students arrived at registration with one or more friends. By the end of registration it was clear that 150 students of color had bought the idea of the College Readiness Program and wanted to enter Junior College at San Mateo.

THE GROWTH OF THE PROGRAM

From the fall of 1966 to the fall of 1968, the College Readiness Program remained basically the same in its philosophy and goals, although at times its unexpected growth put strains on existing staff, decreased the number of staff meetings, and lowered counselor-student or tutor-student ratios. By the fall of 1967, the program had expanded to include 256 students receiving tutorial and counseling help, 87 tutors (some of whom were also receiving such assistance), and another 200 students who, although not officially registered with the Program, were actively involved in CRP activities. An additional number of students of color had entered the College of San Mateo because of its new reputation of being receptive to them, but had not become involved in the College Readiness Program.(7)

This number had again increased significantly by the fall semester of 1968. At this time there were 400 students directly associated with the College Readiness Program and 298 indirectly associated with it. This included 395 students, 277 tutors, and 26 tutor supervisors. An additional 308 students, not registered at the college during the fall, had been enrolled in the Program at some time in the past.

Although the College Readiness Program had begun with a primarily black student body, it had expanded to serve a significant number of other students of color during the intervening two years. In the fall of 1968, 229 white students were in the Program, 90% of whom were serving as tutors. There were 85 brown students in the Program, most of whom were directly related to it. There were also 29 oriental students, half of whom were indirectly related to the Program, 8 American Indians, and 26 other non-white students in the College Readiness Program. However, black students numbered 302 and comprised 45% of all students in the Program; they also represented the largest proportion of students using program services on a drop-in basis and not assigned to counselors.

Sex and age ratios have remained approximately the same throughout the Program's duration. Of the fall 1968 enrollment, sixty percent were men and forty percent women. About four out of five students were single – the proportion being somewhat lower among students directly associated with the Program. Nearly 75 percent of all students associated with the Program were under 21 years of age. Financial assistance needs were most prevalent among the 200 students in the 21-or-older group.

In the fall of 1967, a year and a half after the Program's inception, an "Intergroup Relations Specialist," Robert Hoover, was hired to spend part time counseling, part time in relations with the minority community, and part time as assistant to the president. The events leading up to Hoover's appointment illustrate the ambivalence of the president, the college administration, and trustees to the goals of the Program. Miss Wirth had asked from the start for an Afro-American to serve as director of the Program, and her request had been supported by CRP students. The appointment of a white, middle-class woman must have seemed safer to college officials. The long-awaited decision to hire an Afro-American, when it came in the form of "Intergroup Relations Specialist," placed Robert Hoover second in title and pay to Miss Wirth. And even then, approval of Hoover, who had been endorsed by both Jean Wirth and Program students, was preceded by a request for a pool of 25 interviewees for the position, not an easy task but one which was rapidly fulfilled. However, despite the formal title, Hoover was unofficially considered the director by everyone in the College Readiness Program. When this position was finally made official in the fall of 1968, it was only because the new president, Dr. Ewigleben, wanted one person to be in charge; Hoover and Wirth would agree to a co-directorship but not to having only Miss Wirth in charge.

The background of Robert Hoover suggests all too easily that it was not lack of credentials nor extreme militance which had caused this reluctance to have him as head of the College Readiness Program. Hoover had received his degree from Pennsylvania State University and his teaching credentials from San Jose State College. At the time of his appointment to the College of San Mateo, Hoover was a trustee of the Ravenswood Elementary School District of Menlo Park and East Palo Alto and principal of the East Palo Alto Day School, a community-organized school which was providing supplementary elementary and secondary education on Wednesday evenings and Saturday mornings to students in the community. If Hoover was considered a threat by the College of San Mateo, he was viewed as a man of reason in his own community. One of his main reasons for even coming to the College of San Mateo was to help to educate his own people for leadership in their communities. Hoover was set on reversing the traditional route of black B.A.'s and Ph.D.'s out of their community.

To combat this outward flow of talent and resources, Hoover felt that it was essential to keep students in constant touch with their neighborhoods all the time they attended college. One of the more notable projects established under Robert Hoover while he was director of the College Readiness Program was one called the "Teen Project." This project ran in both the summer of 1967 and the summer of 1968 and consisted of a scheme whereby thirty College Readiness students tutored three hundred and fifty East Palo Alto high school students in the morning, who, in turn, taught preschoolers in the afternoon. Program students were also kept active in community issues. Their role as recruiters for the College Readiness Program gave them the additional link with high school age youth. Thus attendance at the College of San Mateo became for CRP students a well-integrated life of standard academic instruction, special cultural orientation programs, and community work. It was this combination which made the Program increasingly successful, from one point of view, but which seems to have made it frightening to the college and helped to make its position increasingly tenuous on campus.

THE ACADEMIC SUCCESS OF CRP STUDENTS

Projects such as the College Readiness Program have by definition two goals: 1) to increase the number of Third World students in the college, and 2) to ensure that, once admitted, these students will be given the necessary financial, emotional, and academic backing to succeed within the general framework of the college. While compensatory education programs have recently helped to highlight the need for changes in curriculum throughout the university, including a breakdown of the walls between the university and the surrounding community, most programs have run on the assumption that except for remedial courses their students would have to accept and succeed in the standard college curriculum. In fact, students have generally been wary of receiving non-standard curricula, and in such projects as SEEK, the lack of regular college credits for classes attended has led to protest by students. At the College of San Mateo, with the exception of reading labs and a number of "non-transferable" English courses used also by many non-academic students (and generally shunned by CRP students) the school did not offer any compensatory courses for this new group of students. Thus, though one may evaluate the Program using perhaps even more significant criteria such as increased political and social awareness or the development of the self, a review of the number of students who remained in the college and the grades they received is a good indicator of their success as judged by the more traditional college standards.

Although most educators within and outside the college have been openly enthusiastic about the academic achievement of CRP students, only one comprehensive study exists which documents college achievement by Program students. Completed in the fall of 1968 by Frank Pearce, Director of Research and the present Dean of Instruction at the College of San Mateo, the study covers the period of summer 1966 through the fall of 1967. The investigation was updated in greatly abbreviated form in December, 1968 to include the 1967-68 year; wherever possible, this more recent data is also included in the following summary. It should be kept in mind that the trend of the Program's results was upward, and that none of the data reported below takes into account the summer of 1968, or fall 1968 of the Program.

According to Pearce, by the fall 1967 semester, there had been a total of 256 students in the College Readiness Program, of whom 35 percent were no longer attending the day school at the time. Of those students who had withdrawn, fifteen had completed 60 credits (received the A.A. degree) or transferred to a four-year college, sixteen were attending the night school and so were no longer regular participants in the College Readiness Program, which consisted largely of day-time activities, and only 59 students or 23 percent of the total had dropped out of the Program and the college without having come to a normal academic termination. This percentage of actual dropouts is in sharp contrast to a rate of nearly ninety percent among non-white students before the onset of the Program(8) and an attrition rate of 75 percent among low achieving students in most junior colleges in California(9) and an (unofficial) attrition rate of 50 percent among regular students at the College of San Mateo.

Extensive case histories were kept of all CRP students, and a review of them indicates that even this attrition rate does not reflect academic difficulties of the students. Out of the 59 (i.e. 23 percent) who can be considered "dropouts," over one fourth left to go to work because of serious financial problems, nearly a fifth left because of "family problems" or "personal difficulties," eight percent were called into the armed forces, and 20 percent or only 15 students gave academic difficulties as their reasons for leaving. (The reasons for withdrawal of the remainder are not known). Pearce notes in his report that "... it would appear that the withdrawal rate could be reduced 23 to 17 percent simply by increasing the financial support for students."(10)

The College Readiness Program has made a point of seeking out those students who have been excluded from most college programs because of the exitless tunnel of the tracking system. Although under the directorship of Hoover and Wirth it was antithetical to the philosophy of the Program to select students on the basis of proven academic capabilities, Pearce looked at high school grades and standardized test scores to see if, *ex post facto*, these traditional indicators could be said to have any predictive value in determining which students would do well in the college. A review of the SCAT scores of the 256 students showed that approximately three-fourths had scored at or below the 25th percentile, and that their quantitative subtest scores tended to be higher than quantitative ones. Ten percent of the Program students scored in the 50th percentile or above on the SCAT. However, the Standard Deviation on the total SCAT for College Readiness students was 21.1, as compared with 12.1 for all College of San Mateo students. Pearce concludes that "the variance is so great that the reliability of the SCAT for Program students is practically non-existent."

Of the 87 tutors who had been part of the Program and were drawn largely from the same group of students, 57 percent made a total score at or above the 50th percentile, with 76 percent receiving at or above the 50th percentile on the verbal subtest and 39 percent making similar scores on the quantitative section.(12)

Comparing College Readiness students' SCAT scores with grade point averages in college, Pearce found that for those who scored at or above the 10th percentile on the SCAT verbal subtest, there was an 80 percent probability that they would earn less than a 2.0 grade point average. However, predictions were not made for other groups.(13)

Another common predictor of college achievement is high school grade averages. College Readiness students had earned a mean of 1.9 grade points on a 4-point scale in high school (some had not completed the full number of years); two-thirds had earned a high school GPA between 1.4 and 2.4. This is in comparison to a mean of 2.4 among those CRP students who had become tutors, and a similar mean grade point average among College of San Mateo students not in the Program. The cumulative grade-point average for College Readiness students at the College of San Mateo in 1967 was 1.6, measured on a 4-point system. The mean GPA for student tutors was 2.3.(14) In the fall of 1968 the median for CRP students was 1.99 and for tutors 2.44.(15)

A comparison of high school and college grades of Program students in the fall of 1967 showed a low correlation coefficient of .36. Among students with a 1.0 to 1.9 high school GPA, approximately one-half maintained the same average in college, one-fourth dropped and one-fourth increased their GPA. Forty-two percent of the students who had maintained a C average or above in high school were able to do the same in college, and 29 percent of the students who had earned less than a C average were able to earn a C average or better in college.(16)

Again, however, high school GPA's were more predictive of tutors' college achievement than they were for other Program students. "Among tutors with 1.0 to 1.9 GPA, it was found that approximately one-third showed no increase, while two-thirds advanced one cumulative grade point. Two-thirds of the tutors with 2.0 to 2.9 high school grade point average maintained the same college GPA, while 16% went down one cumulative grade point and 16% went up one cumulative grade point."(17)

More Program students reached the minimum "acceptable" level of C or better in the fall 1967 semester than in the summer 1967 semester. However, this was accomplished by a drop in the "good to outstanding" levels of B or better.

> . . . the grades of program students during both summers were approximately one-third A and B grades, 40% C grades during the first summer and 23% C grades during the second summer, and about 15-20% of the grades were F and W. During the subsequent fall semester, the proportion of A and B grades decreased by one-half, and the C and D grades tended to remain constant, but the number of F and W grades declined substantially during the following spring semester. During the subsequent fall semester 1967, the proportion of D or better grades tended to remain constant, the F grades increased, and the number of W grades decreased somewhat.(18)

Because of the large number of English classes, the small enrollment per class, and the fact that 95 percent of the College Readiness students took one form of English or another, Pearce isolated the grades earned by Program students in the various English classes offered by the college. Students scoring below the 25th percentile on the verbal subtest of the SCAT were usually placed in English 50A (a remedial course entitled "Fundamentals of Reading and Writing"); those who scored between the 26th and the 50th percentile were generally placed in English A (a remedial course entitled "Preparatory Composition"); and those who scored between the 51st and 75th percentile were placed in either the non-credit English A or in 1A ("Reading and Composition," a course offering transferable credits); and those scoring above the 75th percentile were placed in English 1A.

In general, CRP students received fewer A and B grades than the proportion of A and B grades earned by all College of San Mateo students. However, "the differences between Program students and all students in the percentage of C grades for classes in English A and 50A were insignificant."(19) Students serving as tutors received much higher English grades, irrespective of the classes they took. Fifteen percent had taken 50A, 49 percent English A, and 35 percent English 1A; combining grades received in these classes, approximately 70 percent of the tutors had received C grades or better in English.(20) Moreover, even tutors who scored in the low percentiles on the SCAT verbal subtest were as likely to receive an A grade as they were a B or C.(21) This may indicate the benefits to the tutors of having to instruct other students in English.

Until a special Reading Laboratory was organized in the summer of 1968 by two CRP-involved teachers, the regular Reading Laboratory was avoided by all but 20 percent of the CRP students. Of the small proportion taking the regular Reading Lab, results were insignificant in terms of total GPA earned. "The proportion of students who earned under 1.0 GPA and had taken the Reading Lab was three to ten times lower than the proportion of students who did not have the Reading Lab or failed to complete it." However, ". . . the Reading Laboratory experience clearly helps the student who is earning less than a 1.5 GPA to move closer to the 2.0 average, but the grade point averages of students who earned above 1.5 average cannot be clearly related to their participation in the Reading Laboratory."(22) Forty percent of those whose vocabulary and/or reading comprehension was less than an eighth grade level when they began the lab finished at the same level, and 60 percent advanced approximately one grade level.(23) Although there is no data on the results of the Program-organized Reading Laboratory, students were enthusiastic about it, claiming that they did learn how to read.

Pearce notes, as have others commenting on students in contemporary education programs, that CRP students tended to select social science majors. Almost all CRP students entered the liberal arts program. In 1967, less than three percent were in the vocational-technical areas, even if they had started there before entering the College Readiness Program. This percentage was slightly higher at the time of the December 1968 survey, however; at the time over six percent of the students had selected vocational-technical programs.(24)

This increase in the percentage of students entering non-academic programs, even though slight, indicates one of the main areas of tension surrounding the College Readiness Program. It may be that the few extra students choosing vocation-technical fields did so because of a clear sense of their abilities. On the other hand, there is a sense of increasing pressure from the college administration to channel College Readiness students into these non-academic areas. Whether this is partially due to a levelling philosophy which views no one group as deserving "better" than the other, or whether it is due to real pressures from outside groups such as the State Board of Education, which in turn is responding to industry, is hard to say. Certainly, it is true that as the junior colleges now stand one of their main functions is to provide the training grounds for industry. And, despite the Master Plan's promise of unlimited access to higher education, junior colleges cannot afford to become totally academic institutions. While it would not seem disastrous to the American economy to allow 500 or so students of color in a single college to enter academic fields, and might, in fact, even help to keep the labor supply in check, there has been a growing tendency to channel CRP students away from academic programs at the College of San Mateo. Many students expect that in the future CRP students will be actively counselled to choose one of the many vocational-technical areas of study.

FINANCIAL RESOURCES AND FINANCIAL AID

Junior colleges in California, as elsewhere, operate under a tighter budget than any other state institution of higher education. The College of San Mateo, which maintains the highest salary schedule of any junior college in the state, had an operating cost of $13,401,409 (not including capital gains expenditures) in 1968. Approximately 12,000 day and evening students were served by 295 equivalent full-time day teachers and 368 evening college faculty. The annual cost per unit of average daily attendance for 1967-68, without transportation or financial aid, was estimated at $634.67. Most of the college's financial resources come from district-raised funds, which support not only the College of San Mateo but also Canada Junior College and the still unopened Skyline Junior College.

The College Readiness Program at San Mateo is considered one of the least expensive remedial programs for Third World students anywhere in the country. However, the cost of the Program has nearly doubled each year and has consistently gone over even increased budgets. Full-year budgets have been mainly for staff and for the district's share of work-study programs. In 1966-67, $10,000 was budgeted and $29,851 spent for the Program. In 1967-68, the cost of the College Readiness Program was $53,300, as opposed to a budget of $33,430. In 1968-69, the expenditure was $103,638; and the budget request for 1969-70 is approximately $180,000. Budgets are based on a predicted cost of approximately $500 per Program student per year. Despite administrative resistance to the Program, administrative staff and trustees are adamant in stating that its operation has not been a financial drain on the college. This is because amounts over the budget seem to have been raised by the Program itself, and district sources have never had to be tapped.

Financial aid above and beyond work-study monies provided by the state comes through federal funds: National Defense Student Loans (NDSL), Federal Insured Student Loans (FISL), and Economic Opportunity Grants (EOG). Since EOG is a matching program, however, additional financial assistance is needed from the college's private resources.

In the summer of 1968, federal financial aid allocations in the state of California were cut by forty percent. When $150,000 of EOG matching monies were promised the College of San Mateo to be used for the 1968-69 academic year, CRP staff and students were anxious to start a fund-raising campaign. The trustees' delay in appointing a citizens' committee needed to seek private contributions — probably due partially to their desire not to have any fund-raising project compete with the bond issue needed for Canada and Skyline Colleges, and perhaps partially to their general antipathy to the Program — placed the financial aid resources of the college in serious trouble. The official reason given by the trustees for their delay was that they first had to conduct an audit into why funds had been used up during the summer. However, the audit, once completed, revealed no "misfeasance or malfeasance." At the same time, several changes were suggested in the emergency loan fund, and in order to keep closer track of funds a proposal called for all CRP mail to go through the Dean of Student Personnel's office, "checks removed and mail forwarded."

By December of 1968, when a citizens' committee was finally appointed, some 500 students had received $352,451 in financial aid (an average of less than $700), but 130 had been turned away for lack of funds and another 500 had had to drop out of school altogether because of financial difficulties. This 500 was, of course, made up almost totally of Third World students directly counselled by or affiliated with the College Readiness Program.

One of the most pronounced areas of contention between college administration and Program members has been the financial aid office. Both CRP personnel and administration have been increasingly mistrustful and dissatisfied about the manner in which existing financial resources have been allocated and used. With the rapid growth of the College Readiness Program, the financial aid office had become understaffed in addition to being underfunded. During the past year, there have been three changeovers in financial aid officers, only the last of whom is a person of color. Interestingly, the present officer, the first non-white to hold this position, is a Mexican-American who was hired on a trial basis during the summer of 1968 to complete a tripartite directorship with Robert Hoover and Jean Wirth, and who was given the job of financial aid officer after he did not "work out" with the students. Each changeover in financial aid staff has been accompanied by the perennial question of where and how the money has gone, at the same time as College Readiness students have felt increasingly that their financial needs have not been met.

It should be remembered that CRP students come from low income families, most are not being supported by the families, and a number — both married and unmarried — have families of their own to maintain. Part or full-time work on the side is difficult to find. Not only is work scarce in surrounding communities, particularly for non-whites, but the college is isolated from commercial and industrial centers, with public transportation undependable and expensive. Thus work-study grants, which simultaneously require a full credit load of 12½ units, scholarships and, to a lesser extent, loans, provide the only realistic means of enabling many of these students to attend college. The present financial aids officer estimates that as much as $2,400 may be needed to get one student through a year of college; this is in contrast to top assistance for white students, which has usually come to no more than $1,200.

Given these very real needs, it is still common opinion among the administration and trustees as well as the more conservative segment of the college community that College Readiness students have been out to drain the college's resources and have been quite adept at gaining far more than is their "rightful share." Unfortunately, this area of discussion is tinged with class values and racial prejudices which are fueled by a variety of situations. For example, in the past financial allotments were often given in the form of "emergency grants," which meant that a student could not expect a certain amount during the course of the academic year, but rather was left to his own resourcefulness in getting as much as possible out of the financial aid office. Under this system it is rumored that one or two students managed to accumulate as much as $5,000 in a year. This "emergency grants" system also helped to perpetuate the traditional generalization of the middle-class that low-income people cannot budget. The financial office staff spent much energy wondering how they might teach these students to use their money "wisely" so that they would not have to come continually for funds.

The Protestant Ethic also seems to have played an important part in the attitudes of the more conservative members of the college community toward the use of financial aid by Program students. A small number of black students had expensive cars, which, for those interested in finding fault, were parked conspicuously behind the CRP student center. It is said that a few students had been so blatant as to come openly to the financial aid officer for money for car payments. (It is an ironic truth that the College of San Mateo is surrounded by huge parking lots filled with all kinds of cars, from old Chevrolets to extravagant sports models, but, of course, these cars are not owned by "indigent" students.)

A discussion between the author and the president of the board of trustees of the college, Francis W. Pearson, revealed the following solution to the financial problems of College Readiness students. According to Mr. Pearson, who is an accountant, these students should attend the College of San Mateo for a few months, long enough to get vocational training. Then once they had a full-time job, if they still wanted to go to college for an academic degree, they could attend the night school. It was Mr. Pearson's contention, however, that academic and professional training were unrealistic expectations for these students. The unspoken correlate, one suspects, was that after a brief try at this fancy stuff they would realize where they belong.

Because of the obvious difficulties of the "emergency fund" system, and the assumption of the president and his colleagues that the most militant students were receiving the most financial aid, a new program of financial aids management has been instituted. According to the new system, all students needing financial aid and living away from home will receive $150 a month, while all students needing financial aid and living at home will receive $100 a month. While this system is more equitable from the disperser's point of view, it will probably result in serious difficulties among those receiving the funds. It is also questionable whether such a means of dispersing financial aid does not violate the individual "need" basis under which federal grants for financial assistance are supposed to be allocated.

THE COLLEGE READINESS PROGRAM AND THE COLLEGE

Before going on to an historical account of the particular events which led up to and were included in the dissolution of the original College Readiness Program, it should be useful to analyze the various sources of tension which existed between the Program and the College. One can attribute the violence on campus and the dissolution of the College Readiness Program as it was known to a number of causes, some structural, some economic, and some having to do with individual personalities. An examination of these causes is particularly interesting as it reveals that what may appear as "weak spots" in retrospect can also be sources of strength during a program's development. Generalizations and possible implications can be drawn from what happened at San Mateo and transferred to other college situations. Hopefully, they will be useful in preventing similar disasters.

1. For the College Readiness Program to have been what it was, it needed the loyalty and hard work of staff, students, and community members. Within the context of the college, however, three people can be said to have been the pivotal points in the Program: Jean Wirth, Robert Hoover, and Julio Bortolazzi. Jean Wirth acted as the "nutrient" of the Program; both before and after Hoover was made director, she gave the program a totality of her professional and personal self rarely found in academic circles. Her home was always open to students, a large proportion of her salary went to posting bail, paying legal fees, and paying for whatever else the students needed in order to stay in school. Robert Hoover brought to the Program an identifiable sense of purpose. Coming from their community, he linked students at each point to the goals and needs of their own people. President Bortolazzi provided the Program with a strong administrative backing. Although he was often ambivalent about the Program's goals, there was a sense of trust between him and Program individuals, and Robert Hoover and Jean Wirth felt that they could count on his support at crucial moments. With the dedication of these three extraordinarily strong individuals, the College Readiness Program maintained its dynamic growth despite apathy and even resistance on the part of more conservative members of the college and its community.

On the negative side, concentration of responsibility in the hands of these three people implied two possible sources of difficulty: 1) that without them at the helm the Program would probably not be able to continue, at least along the lines set by them; and 2) that significant individuals within the university and community were not as involved in the Program as they might have been with less dynamic leaders, and would therefore be less likely to offer support in times of need.

2. One important group not involved in the College Readiness Program was

the faculty senate. Although the faculty at the College of San Mateo remained out of touch with CRP activities, this was not due to its being a group inactive in decision-making. Rather, faculty participation at the College is effected through a strict committee system organized along such divisions as the Committee on Instruction, the Committee on Personnel, etc. Because the College Readiness Program did not fit into the spheres of any of the existing faculty committees (and no move was made by the president or CRP staff to introduce it into any one committee), the Program functioned outside of these democratic channels. This had the result of giving the Program far more freedom than it might have had had it been accountable to a faculty committee. On the other hand, it also resulted in the alienation of CSM faculty from the operation of the Program.

With the exception of a half dozen faculty members who were involved in tutoring or other activities, and two members of the administration who were sympathetic to and remained in close contact with the Program, there was virtually no communication between the College Readiness Program and the college at large.

3. Orientations and values within the College Readiness Program were at times antithetical to those of the college at large. This can be seen most clearly through two issues: the type of course work chosen by CRP students, and the socio-political orientation of the Program. Because many Program students had suffered from the tracking system and had had their fill of trade and industrial courses, they were justifiably suspicious of any such training offered by the college. Common experience with hiring policies of such industries as the airline companies in the area had convinced students that even aeronautic training did not lead to open-ended jobs. Courses which led to *no* jobs were in machine shops, tool and dye-making and drafting. But even worse than this failure to lead to jobs, vocational-technical departments at the College of San Mateo had long been known for their resistance to training students of color. Most resistant to accepting non-white students were the health-related courses — dental assisting and the 2-year nursing programs. It was said that instructors didn't like the students' appearance or language. The entrance requirements were always prohibitive, and if a student qualified through IQ or grades, she was often eliminated for "having the wrong attitude." Thus, in a college in which large numbers of middle-class white students focused on vocational-technical training, low-income minority students avoided such courses, and threw their energies to subjects leading towards transfer to another college and a B.A. degree.

The socio-political orientation of the College Readiness Program apparently did not cause any overt difficulty with non-Program individuals in and around the college until the fall of 1968. However, as student demands, sit-ins, and a strike set these students apart as a source of disruption, the attitude toward them as "revolutionaries" was extended to the community work they had been doing. At this time, such phrases as "revolution *or* education" (a common phrase of the president) became prominent, and it was felt by the more conservative members of the college and surrounding communities that Program students, particularly because of their poorer academic backgrounds, should not dilute their energies through "community action."

4. The lack of financial resources has been a threat to the Program from its inception, although it did not cause a crisis until last fall. The cutback in federal financial aid allocations in the state of California, on the one hand, and the failure of the two bond elections, on the other, put funds for the College Readiness Program in competition with other priorities of the district. Moreover, defeat of the second bond issue was partially blamed on the College Readiness Program by such groups as the board of trustees, who felt that these students had both "actively campaigned against the second bond," (supposedly because they objected to the building priorities to be given the money) and had made passage of the bill next to impossible simply through the "activist" reputation which they had given the college. Home owners in San Mateo county are taxed at a rate of 35c on every $100 of their owned property. Understandably, most feel strained by this tax and are particularly resistant to the idea of paying taxes to support any group which might pose a threat to their social and financial security.

5. A problem which has probably influenced all others is that of culture conflict, or, from another point of view, racism. The first sign of difficulty appeared quite early in the Program's history. In the fall of 1966, the College Readiness Program had been given temporary headquarters in the bomb shelter under the administration building. While the CRP Center was thus centrally located on campus, it was also next to the offices of building and grounds personnel and had the character — with its lively posters and informal atmosphere — of being an intruder amidst the more serious business of atomic protection and maintenance. Moreover, building and grounds personnel had to walk through the Center to get to their offices, which provided a continuing source of tension for both groups.

Around exam time of the first semester this tension reached a crisis. One of the secretaries had been in the habit of talking loudly about her fear of being raped each time before she entered the Center on her way to her own office, after which, according to Program people, she would walk provocatively past the group of CRP staff and students and then lock herself in her office. When a visitor came to see her boss one day, she would not open the door, believing the knock to be that of a CRP student. Finally, a student made a lewd remark about what she was doing inside. Hearing this, the girl opened the door in outrage. In the next few days a petition was circulated among secretaries of all departments in the college asking for the removal of the Program. According to CRP staff, signatures of the secretaries were largely consonant with the overt or covert views of their bosses. Equally interesting, however, is the fact that secretaries — an occupational group which very rarely organizes even for increased salaries — had gotten together on the issue of the College Readiness Program.

The result of this petition was the immediate transfer of the CRP Center from the administration building to much better quarters in the Student Center.

A large section of the cafeteria was walled off with two small offices created for the directors. However, the need for more space became clear later in the year when the Program had grown tremendously and there was hope of adding to the staff. In the fall of 1968, the Center was once again transferred, this time to the Horticulture Building on the outskirts of the campus. However, even here the Center and Program students were not entirely free from the critical eyes of the college, nor was their isolation conducive to the goal of integration verbalized by the college at a later period. There was much covert criticism of the decor, which was finally destroyed by policemen during their stay on campus. Student cars were watched with an eye to conspicuous consumption among black students. The view of the new president, Robert Ewigleben, that the Center was "hostile territory," is probably not unique to him, although he has never shown support for the Program. Considering that the Center had been relegated to this lonely outpost on campus and that a strong attempt had been made by participants to develop cohesiveness and dignity in the face of increasing adversity, this hostility may have existed — particularly in relation to official administrators. Most college students not involved in the Program as tutors, tutor-supervisors or counselors simply never entered the area. It was said that before the crisis few non-Program students knew more than that the College Readiness Program existed. This lack of communication between College Readiness and general students cannot be seen as due only to the Program's philosophy of developing a unity within itself. Students at the College of San Mateo, like those in most junior colleges, have tended to be apolitical; few have used the college for more than the expediency of gaining their trade or the credits necessary for transfer to a four-year college.

It was these, and perhaps other less identifiable, tensions between the College Readiness Program and the College of San Mateo which put the Program on shaky ground when the new president assumed his duties in the fall of 1968. However, these tensions in themselves might never have led to a crisis if a number of other coincidences had not intervened.

DISSOLUTION AND REORGANIZATION

The events of the fall of 1968 can be briefly summarized as: 1. the presentation of demands by Program students, 2. failure by the administration to act on any of the demands, 3. a series of violences perpetrated by students on and off campus, 4. the closing of the campus followed by its reopening under "full police protection," 5. the "reassignment" of Robert Hoover and Jean Wirth to other duties, off campus, and 6. the general deterioration and dissolution of the College Readiness Program as it had existed for two and a half years. However, even these events occurred after a series of other unfortunate incidents had taken place.

The first marked change in the status of the College Readiness Program occurred with the changeover of the presidency at the onset of the school year. It is not clear to what extent President Julio Bortolazzi's acceptance of the post of District Superintendent and President of San Joaquin Delta Junior College was motivated by a simple desire for a new setting. Bortolazzi had been president of San Mateo for twelve years, a substantial period for a president to stay at any one college, and it has been said that he did not realize that the Program would not be able to continue without him. On the other hand, the choice of the new president (made by the trustees and ratified by the faculty), indicates that an extremely different kind of president may have been wanted. This leads one to wonder to what extent President Bortolazzi's resignation from the College of San Mateo was prompted by the changing climate of the college community.

Whether or not one can regard Bortolazzi's withdrawal from the college scene as merely an unfortunate coincidence, the new president brought to the office a distinctly new manner of dealing with situations both on and off campus. President Ewigleben himself describes Bortolazzi as "the last of a dying breed," and sees himself as a "democrat," responsive to those around him, and also able to delegate power. It is important to note that there are a number of similarities in the philosophy and behavior of President Ewigleben and other college presidents who have assumed posts during the last two years of student activism.

To College Readiness staff and students, one of the first signs of change was the difficulty they encountered in trying to see the new president. President Bortolazzi's door had always been open to faculty and students; President Ewigleben often could not be reached, and scheduled meetings between him and Program staff or students were delayed numerous times before they occurred. Equally discouraging to communication, it was felt that, once in the meeting, the president could not be pinned down on any issue. Whereas President Bortolazzi had often said "no" but then had changed his mind, President Ewigleben remained aloof from all discussion or commitment. (This difficulty in receiving a direct statement of a position from the president has apparently not been restricted to Program individuals, but has been experienced by other student groups on campus, as well as community organizations.)

The lack of communication between the new president and CRP participants was exacerbated by a political change which occurred at the same time as he assumed office. Because of the opening of the Canada campus and the prospective opening of Skyline College, a new position of San Mateo Junior College District Superintendent, separate from that of the college president, was created. This separation of the presidency from the office of superintendent put a new distance between the college and the board of trustees. More important, although a superintendent had been elected, he was not able to assume the new post until December. In the meantime the three college presidents maintained the position on a rotating basis. Thus a good deal of President Ewigleben's energies during the first weeks of his new office and the new school year were consumed by district-level activities and problems. Finally, the expansion of the San Mateo Junior College system was accomplished through the use of several

College of San Mateo faculty and administration members who had been relatively supportive to the College Readiness Program. Their removal from the scene left disastrous breaks in the lines of communication from CRP members to administration and the board of trustees.

Amidst this dispersion of administrative leadership, the Program was suffering from a particularly serious crisis in staffing and funds. Four counselors had been requested to take care of the nearly 800 students now involved in the Program. These had been hired, but with the students' rejection of one of them (the man who became Financial Aids Director), and the president's refusal to replace him with someone more acceptable to them, two were left. Jean Wirth and Bob Hoover were given the task of helping with the counseling, training tutors, and teaching a course in guidance. In addition they had to run in-service training for faculty, meet daily with the administration on racial issues, give frequent talks in the community, and serve on a state-wide committee on the disadvantaged. Finally, while Hoover was to play a major role in the Urban Coalition, Miss Wirth was to make periodic trips to Washington and serve as consultant to other schools.

The cut in federal allocations to California meant drastic reductions in work-study payments and student loans. And the financial aids officer of the preceding year had been one of the College of San Mateo staff members to take a post in another college, so that CRP students were confronted by a new officer who knew little more than the fact that the college was short of funds. (Throughout the first months the trustees continued to delay appointing a Citizen's Committee to raise matching funds for the $150,000 from Washington.)

It was difficulties such as these which helped to give rise to the series of demands which Program students presented to the administration on October 11, 1968. And it was these same factors, centering largely around the changes in the lines of power in the San Mateo Junior College District, which continued to exacerbate tensions throughout the fall semester.

The most obvious additional impetus was the situation at San Francisco State. The two colleges lie some twenty miles apart, and there has been regular communication between Third World students in them since the beginning of the trouble at San Francisco State in 1967. The eleven demands presented at the College of San Mateo largely duplicate those presented at San Francisco. Although such a duplication can be attributed to similar pre-conditions equally well as to the simple fact of communication between students, the latter interpretation is the more popular among the large numbers of subscribers to the "conspiracy" or "outside agitator" theory.

Not surprisingly, College Readiness student demands centered around the three following issues: changes in the composition of the financial aids office and in the allocation of financial assistance; increased funds for tutors and counselors in the College Readiness Program; and a specific Third World curriculum open to Program as well as general students. These demands were reviewed by the administration as well as the faculty senate on October 16-18. However, despite senate recommendations to act on a number of the demands, nothing was done toward this end. Two months later, after the college had "blown up," the board of trustees emphasized to public sources that some of the demands would have involved infractions of state rules had they been met, others could not be met simply because of inadequate funds, while still others — such as the demand for a new area of studies — could not be decided on without approval from the State Board of Education. However, these objections were not expressed at the time.

The next overt move by the administration (backed by the board of trustees) was the suspension of Robert Hoover from his position as CRP director on November 1. The ostensible reason for this action was the fact that Hoover, in permitting an activist counselor to remain in the Program, had defied the order of the president, who had wanted the young man removed and had asked to be informed should this counselor "appear on campus." It should be remembered in this context that CRP guidelines gave Program staff and students total control over the hiring and firing of personnel. Moreover, the counselor was a volunteer, so that the hiring and firing was in no way part of the jurisdiction of the college. Hoover's response to the president had been that while he would not stand in the way of any action that the college might take, the counselor was serving the Program with dedication and that he could not remove him until Program members became dissatisfied with his services. The president's suspension of Hoover was rescinded three days later, largely due to a request by the governing council of the academic senate.

Relations between the administration, the trustees, and the College Readiness Program representatives continued to worsen throughout November as students dropped out because of the lack of financial aid. On November 28, someone set off a small bomb outside President Ewigleben's office, and a number of small fights broke out. Several students were suspended, a number expelled, and criminal charges brought against a few during the next weeks. The college existed in a state of high tension.

On December 11, the board of trustees ruled that out-of-district students would no longer be eligible for the College Readiness Program. This ruling in effect eliminated a group of Mexican-American students from San Francisco and oriental students from Oakland which the Program had planned to bring in. Funding for twenty native American students already recruited had been pretty much guaranteed from the Bureau of Indian Affairs and other groups. The new ruling meant that these students could not come, no matter what funding was provided. No one in the College Readiness Program had known about there being such a proposal or that it would go before the Board. Since Program members considered recruitment of minority students one of the main goals of the College Readiness Program, and were attempting to increase the number of students of two poorly represented minority groups through the move, they felt that it was their right to be consulted on such changes. On the other hand, the trustees responded that decisions regarding geographical boundaries to be served by the college were not in the domain of students and that they had had no obligation to inform the College Readiness Program of the change.

On December 12, a strike was called in support of the still unmet eleven demands and to protest the president's suspension and expulsion of over thirty students of color during the preceding weeks of tension. On the 13th a rally was called at noon by a CRP student and leader of the Black Student Union. Over 1,000 College of San Mateo students attended this rally, which ended in 150 students marching through the campus, breaking a number of windows in select buildings and injuring eight students and four faculty members. (Although the march made its way through the entire campus, the only buildings where damage occurred were those housing the vocational-technical sciences. In the vocational-technical buildings, occupants attempted to stop the marchers by force, while in the other buildings faculty and students made way for them to pass peacefully through.)

Not surprisingly, it has been said by individuals of all attitudes that the violence on the campus was instigated by outside agitators, largely from San Francisco State, who came to the rally armed with metal pipes and wooden canes. Out of some 500 activists on campus during the rally, police reports identify only ten College of San Mateo students in the actual scenes of violence. However, the point seems almost irrelevant in the light of the reprisals taken. Within half an hour, police had been called on campus and the college was shut down for the day. On the following Monday when it reopened, it was under the occupation of 300 police officers. Moreover, both Jean Wirth and Robert Hoover had been removed from their positions in the College Readiness Program and prohibited from entering the college campus. (Miss Wirth was later "reassigned" to a full-time job as an English teacher, which she refused. Hoover was given the job of Assistant District Planner of Minority Programs, a position which he recognized had only nominal power, but which he assumed for several months while waiting to enter his present post as full-time employee of Nairobe College.)

The occupation of the College of San Mateo by the police seems to have done more to destroy the College Readiness Program than any other type of "security" measure might have done. First, police established check points at the entrance to the college, and, although they did not bother white students, made searches of all cars carrying students of color. In this way, a number of arrests were made on the basis of old warrants which had never been served. Unpaid traffic violations, charges of possessing narcotics, or resisting arrests — these are part of the records of most young adults in urban ghettos, and the College of San Mateo had been aware of the arrest records of these students since the beginning of the College Readiness Program. However, on the recommendation of the CRP directors most students stayed away from campus. The fact that the remaining rooms of the Horticulture Building were given over for police headquarters, so that police were in and out of the Center all day, had also discouraged many from going to the college. In the next weeks the Dean of Student Services, a man with notable sympathy for the Program amidst an increasingly unsympathetic group of colleagues, was given the role of temporary director. But he maintained his directorship over only an occasional white tutor who came around to see what was happening. Without the leadership of Wirth and Hoover, morale was so low that it looked to all concerned as if there would never again be a College Readiness Program.

On the Friday before Christmas vacation, a general faculty convocation was called. At this meeting a motion was made and passed unanimously to the effect that the action taken by the president was necessary in view of the circumstances and that he was supported in his attempt to protect the campus. This motion was probably, at least in part, an emotional response to the three injured teachers attending the meeting and to the fourth who was still in the hospital with a scalp injury. But, despite unanimous support given to the president on the subject of police protection, the faculty stood divided in their attitudes toward the College Readiness Program. At most, a dozen faculty members had been involved in the Program in any manner during the two and a half years of its existence. Another 25-30 had been and continued to be sympathetic to its goals, while an equal number were violently against it. Amidst jeering and shouting, motions to support the Program were made, amended and rejected. Eventually one was passed stating that the faculty "support College Readiness Students." Thus, by omission, faculty disclaimed any support for the goals of the Program or for its leaders.

Fortunately, feeling for the students alone was strong enough to bring about a general liberalization of academic standards in the next months. Already during Christmas vacation, a number of faculty members began to attempt to assist students in recouping the academic losses caused by their absence from school. Make-up lectures and laboratory sessions were organized and tutorial help given. Students were personally called by their teachers and urged to take finals. Finally, in January, the faculty senate voted that the traditional attendance regulation be set aside and that, whenever possible, students be given credit for work completed before the middle of December. The college also extended the deadline on withdrawals from a class, in the attempt to eliminate F's which CRP students might otherwise have received.

Despite this liberalization of grading, hundreds of College Readiness students did not complete the fall semester or register for the spring term. In April of 1969, there were 130 students in the Program, and only a small number of students of color in the college at large. After the initial wave of dropouts by students who could not attend college without financial aid, attrition among CRP students did not let up, but continued to increase throughout the semester, reaching approximately 55 percent by the end of the term. The most obvious reason for this mass dropout was the conviction among the students that the College Readiness Program was dead. They felt that the college's desire to eliminate the Program as they knew it was made evident through the removal of the two directors who had encompassed its ideals and gave it their charismatic leadership. The attrition was furthered by the presence of police on campus and by the legal charges brought against the most prominent CRP student leaders.

If one can accuse the College Readiness Program of having been a radicalizing experience for its participants, one must also understand the degree to which the College of San Mateo has acted as a radicalizing agent. The College Readiness Program was established as part of an institution of higher education, and its leaders worked actively to keep students in the system. At times they were quite conscious that movement in this direction meant giving a shake to the parent institution; and within the course of the two years they began to feel that too great a proportion of their time was devoted toward educating the college, as opposed to their own students. However, it was the college, and not the Program leadership, which effectively removed students and staff from the confines of the established academic world. A number of CRP graduates are now active members of black student unions or brown student organizations on other campuses. But a still greater number, particularly among those students who had been in the Program less than a year, have retreated back into the uncontainable world of the ghetto where real revolutionaries are made. Having observed for themselves that a white college was not ready to accept them, they have moved one step further from believing in the ability of the United States to deliver the American dream.

EPILOGUE

In the spring of 1969, Dr. Frank Pearce, author of the study of academic achievement among CRP students, presented a plan to the faculty for revising the College Readiness Program. Known as the Pearce Plan, its main thrust is the integration of the Program into the general college life of San Mateo. Tutorial help is to be given to students of *all* colors, irrespective of ethnic identity, and an effort will be made to recruit white students into the Program. There is to be greater emphasis on the vocational-technical fields of study. The ethnic component of the Program is to be redirected into a new Ethnic Studies Division, which will include courses in Afro-American, Mexican-American, and Oriental-American histories open to all students in the college. Whether this pacific plan can be achieved as outlined is questionable. Despite the removal or withdrawal of most activist students of color from the campus, it is unlikely that the college can retreat to a position which permits education only within the traditional framework. Probably much will depend on what happens in other colleges all over the country, and particularly on the degree of opposition to change encountered by students.

In the meantime, the idea of a college program directed toward the needs of Third World students is very much alive. During the police occupation and in the weeks following the "reassignment" of Wirth and Hoover, a number of community groups such as the East Palo Alto Mothers for Equal Opportunity,

MAPA (The Mexican-American Political Association), the Mid-Peninsula Human Relations Commission, the Palo Alto-Stanford Democratic Club, and the Redwood Citizens Against Racism appeared at the college to protest the removal of Jean Wirth and Robert Hoover and to support the College Readiness Program. These groups, as groups, were never acknowledged by the administration and apparently had little effect on policy-making. But they have continued to support Hoover and Wirth outside the college. In the last few months they have worked together with Wirth, Hoover, and a number of College Readiness students and ex-students in planning a private college based on the principles of autonomy and liberation for people of color. The college, to be known as Nairobe, will be situated in East Palo Alto. Because of a shortage of funds, classes will be held in empty churches, schoolrooms and storefronts, and volunteer teachers will be drawn largely from Stanford, San Francisco State, and other nearby universities. The community itself will provide a training ground as well as teachers for the new college.

Nairobe will be open to any student who demonstrates his interest in being trained for leadership in minority and/or poor communities. It will extend the idea of student participation from recruitment, student and faculty selection and retention, tutoring and counselling, to curriculum development and overall policy-making for the functioning of the college within the community it is to serve. Perhaps the most striking form of student participation at Nairobe will be their service on the board of trustees. The board will consist of one-third community members, one-third faculty, and one-third students. Each of these three groups will have equal representation of black, brown, and yellow members.

Such an enterprise runs high risks. There are the problems of finances, of accreditation, of administrative know-how. Those involved in the new college are well aware of these problems. And they are also aware of the difficulties which any project centered around ethnic minorities will encounter. But the vision which enabled the College Readiness Program to grow as it did has been reinvested in this new project. One might now question whether any organization run on the boldness and dedication of two or three individuals can long survive; on the other hand, one might equally well ask whether an organization without such leadership is even worth undertaking.

NOTES

(1) John Rowntree and Margaret Rowntree, "Youth as Class: The Political Economy of Youth," *Our Generation Magazine*, Summer 1968.

(2) *Ibid.*

(3) Ernest H. Berg and Dayton Axtell, *Programs for Disadvantaged Students in the California Community Colleges*, Peralta Junior College District, 1968.

(4) Ivar Berg, "Rich Man's Qualifications for Poor Man's Jobs," *Transaction*, 6 (March 1969), 45-50.

(5) Bill Shapiro and Bill Barlow, "San Francisco State," *Leviathan*, 1 (1) (April 1969), 4-11.

(6) Robert Sommerskill, Speech made while President at San Francisco State, 1967.

(7) Shapiro and Barlow, "San Francisco State," 6.

(8) These and the following statistics are drawn from two reports: Frank C. Pearce, "A Study of Academic Success of College Readiness Students at the College of San Mateo," Office of Research, San Mateo Junior College District, 1968; and Frank C. Pearce, "A Profile of Students in the College Readiness Program at the College of San Mateo," Office of Research, San Mateo Junior College District, 1968-69.

(9) Berg and Axtell, *Op. cit.* p. 33.

(10) John E. Roueche, *Salvage, Redirection, or Custody: Remedial Education in the Community Junior College*, ERIC Clearinghouse for Junior College Information, American Association of Junior Colleges Monograph Series, 1968, p. 2.

(11) Pearce, "A Study of Academic Success," p. 8.

(12) *Ibid*, p. 10-11.

(13) *Ibid*, p. 11.

(14) *Ibid*, p. 15.

(15) *Ibid*, p. 12.

(16) Pearce, "A Profile of Students" p. 7.

(17) Pearce, "A Study of Academic Success," p. 14.

(18) *Ibid*, p. 15.

(19) *Ibid*, p. 21.

(20) *Ibid*, p. 24.

(21) *Ibid*, p. 25.

(22) *Ibid*, p. 26.

(23) *Ibid*, p. 28.

(24) *Ibid*, p. 28.

(25) Pearce, "A Profile of Students" p. 5.

INDIAN COMMUNITIES AND PROJECT HEAD START

Murray L. Wax
Rosalie H. Wax

Many of the programs aimed at assisting the American Indians have been misdirected because they assumed that Indians were homogeneous and that one Indian could speak for his fellows and so insure their participation and cooperation – that, in short, chiefs could commit their followers, that interpreters could clearly portray the attitudes of those ignorant of English, or that progressive "mixedbloods" could represent the interests of conservative "fullbloods." While the Office of Economic Opportunity programs of the present day are premised on involvement of the total community, in actuality they are failing to secure it inasmuch as they assume or allow the assumption that Indian tribal councils can speak for or accurately transmit the beliefs and feelings of Indian mothers, or that the acculturated "Uncle Tomahawk" in his clerical or bureaucratic guise can really represent the humble and impoverished as he participates in conferences or commissions, or that the clique or faction that controls the Indian community organization (and so monopolizes the available jobs) will consult the subordinated cliques in the design of a Head Start Program. The problem of gaining community participation is not diminished and is usually exaggerated when white persons or organizations benevolently interested in Indian affairs intervene on the assumption that they can accomplish the task better than the community can itself. In all these cases the Indian or non-Indian worthies in control believe or assert that they are meeting the requirement of community participation by holding a few community meetings *after* all the plans are securely frozen and by presenting to the handfuls that attend some sales talk on the merits of the program.

Before elaborating the above statements, we should like to emphasize that, as judged by *ordinary scholastic standards*, the Head Start programs we observed were with few exceptions highly successful. Especially when we consider the haste with which these programs were initiated and the meagre facilities and modestly trained personnel normally available to these impoverished areas, the results – as compared to conventional schools – were excellent. Moreover, in addition to the many benefits being enjoyed by children of preschool age, we should note that other individuals in the community were profiting by employment and that the community as a whole was better off because of the influx of goods and services. However, O.E.O. and its projects, such as Head Start, were designed to achieve more than the conventional and transient benefits of social welfare programs, and it is toward the achievement of these more ambitious goals that we have tailored the following discussion.

The homogeneous and harmonious Indian band has vanished (and may never have existed), and the contemporary community is as heterogeneous and divided as its larger urban counterparts. Even using such simple sociological criteria as religious affiliation and years of schooling achieved, the typical Indian band spans a surprisingly wide range. Among the Oglala Sioux of Pine Ridge are members of the Roman Catholic, Episcopalian, Latter Day Saints, Pentecostal, and Native American churches; the same people include persons who have completed but three grades of schooling as well as others who are college graduates. Even the range of income, or standard of living, is socially great, for as compared to the family that is destitute that which has some steady income and a snug cabin is comfortably situated, while the family where several members have federal employment is positively wealthy. Under these circumstances, the representation in a project of some part of the community does not imply understanding or acceptance by the population as a whole.

In the case of Head Start programs it is especially important to bear in mind that Indian communities maintain much of the aboriginal and pioneer division of labor by sex. The persons who are most knowledgable about young children and most influential in their guidance are women — mothers, grandmothers, aunts, whereas men usually have but a small role in regard to the younger children. Moreover, patterns of sociability follow the same division by gender, so that matrons discuss the upbringing of children with other women and seldom with manfolk. It is the women who are knowledgeable and responsible to the difficulties of the young at play, in the primary grades, or in Head Start programs, and it is they who must be significantly involved if the Head Start program is to become more than another of the multitude of programs designed by a federal bureaucracy and launched against the Indians. Yet the very style of federal operations and the exigencies of budgets of personnel and money make it difficult to involve any of the lowly in the planning, and among those least likely to be involved are the mothers and other womenfolk.

Yet, if community participation is essential for the success of many kinds of programs (such as Head Start), it can also be highly uncomfortable for the administrator. The interests and concerns initially voiced by the Indian parents may have little apparent relevance to those of the administrator, and the parental conception of the proper division of labor between themselves and the administrator is likely to be quite other than his. In particular, school administrators have complained to us that as Indian parents have become involved in school affairs, they have often insisted on reviewing in painful detail grievances arising from disciplinary cases and, even more troublesome, have sometimes complained about the "meanness" of teachers, whom the administrator has felt obliged to defend. With Head Start and similar programs, the initial interest displayed by the community had usually centered about jobs and related perquisites and has often eventuated in complaints of favoritism in hiring. Concerning these kinds of issues all that needs to be said is that they are signs of a healthy community: the arbitrariness of institutional power does need to be checked, even if the authority finds the restraint to be uncomfortable. In the matter of the patronage represented by jobs or the erection of community buildings, we have little counsel of a direct nature, except again to remark that the interest in partaking of the political and economic pie is healthy and sane. Moreover, given the scarcity of reservation employment and given the national shortage of fully-qualified teachers, we do feel impelled to offer the following suggestion: might it not be far better to advise Indian communities that they could (if they wished) plan their centers so as to reduce the number of qualified, professional teachers while diverting that money to increasing the number of the local staff who are partially qualified by having some college education. Team teaching seems peculiarly suited to the operations of a child development center, and the presence on the staff of so many local persons in responsible positions would be encouraging to educational aspirations.

COMMUNITY PARTICIPATION — TECHNIQUES

If the community is to interest itself more broadly in Head Start policy, then it needs to be encouraged; phrasing genuine alternatives — such as those concerned with the staffing of the centers — and setting them before the local folk, while allowing them some days and some privacy for debate and discussion, and then making sure that the voice of the majority is indeed heard and heeded, this surely is an effective way to enlarge community participation. Some cautions need to be added. We should, for example, point out that traditionalist Indians prefer to withdraw from a gathering rather than declare themselves publicly to be in the negative on an issue, and accordingly administrators should be extremely careful about taking the voice of the handful who may attend a meeting as representing the wishes of the absent Indian community. Moreover, following the opinions of the small but vocal minority who have attended may set a pattern of abstention by the majority from participation in the project. Some experienced Indian politicians are quite unscrupulous in their use of Robert's Rules of Order and can by this manipulation effectively exclude the remainder of the audience from voicing its wishes. Especially early in the program, it may be necessary to go to great lengths in polling sentiments in order to convince Indians that their voice is indeed important.

Once one is acquainted with the life of Indian communities, one can discern a surprising number of issues, usually decided in terms of the conventions of the greater society or by administrative fiat, that might better have been left to the community. Not only would community decision heighten the involvement of the parents in the Center activity but it is quite likely to facilitate some unexpected improvements in operation. Let us briefly outline some of the issues that have occurred to us as we inspected various Head Start centers.

1. What should be the schedule of sessions? Most Indian communities have a cycle of social and ceremonial activities, such as powwows, and these often conflict in their timing with the rigidity of the conventional teaching schedule. Administrators then complain about lack of parental concern about attendance, when the parents might with equal justice complain about the rigidity of scholastic schedules.

2. What should be the languages of instruction? In most of the communities we visited there were some persons who were interested in maintaining the native Indian language and who were inclined to favor the introduction and use of that language within the curriculum of the school and of the Head Start Centers. Usually, other persons were opposed or unsure about this proposal, since they regard the learning of English as a necessary skill for the securing of employment. Meanwhile, the educators themselves — to the extent that they knew of or had considered the issue — usually regarded it as out of the question

because of their own ignorance of the native language. Yet , as the Carnegie Cross-cultural Educational Project (University of Chicago) has demonstrated among the Cherokee, it is possible to introduce the native language within an otherwise conventional school curriculum, and the side benefits in involvement of conservative parents and pupils can be very significant. Accordingly, the question of the native language and its place within the program of Head Start activities is another issue that might well be raised for community decision.

3. What other native skills and crafts are worthy of incorporation within the curriculum of the Center is another issue. Having ourselves heard some excellent Indian singing and watched some wonderful Indian dancing and then shortly thereafter seen Center teachers leading their charges through dreary routines of music, we ourselves would be inclined to propose that the Centers enlist the assistance of Indian men in leading singing and dancing. And, in like vein, we would suggest that some attention be given to incorporating other Indian artistic expressions, such as the beadwork so beautifully being executed by Chippewa and Sioux. Again, these are issues to be decided by the community, but they need to be raised by those administering the program so that the local folk can perceive that there are matters to be discussed and weighed.

4. How should the local Head Start program be described and presented to the public? As we note in the cases of the projects at Rapid City and Red Shirt Table, much resentment was bred among the local folk by programs and newspaper stories which they felt to be degrading and untrue. That kind of publicity could well antagonize from participation in the program persons whom it would be valuable to have included. Yet, given the difficulty of controlling the kinds of stories the news media relate, all that can be done is to make sure that the accounts given the press by the administration of the local project do represent what the local folk wish to have said; and so again here is an issue to be brought to the community for discussion and decision.

INDIAN POVERTY – A PROBLEM FOR INDIAN COMMUNITIES

Since the passage of civil rights legislation, there has been a tendency to regard the Indians as simply an aggregate of poor people, lacking any distinct individuality. Administrators and welfare workers tend to assert that it is useless sentimentalism of anthropological mythology to talk in terms of "Indian cultures," when, so they insist, there is only "reservation culture," a species of the culture of poverty. Furthermore, they contend that granting recognition to Indians as specific communities runs the risk of violating civil rights legislation and the provisions of the U. S. Constitution. Now, disregarding the latter contention as being a better issue for debate among lawyers versed in the complexities of Indian treaties and Indian legislation, there is an important sense in which the contention of these critics is true – on the pragmatic level. For insofar as there is today an "Indian problem" it is the problem of Indian poverty, of little political power, and of low social status. The "Indian problem" is thus akin to the "Japanese problem" of the West Coast before the recent war, or to the "Negro problem" of the South before the recent civil rights struggles, or to the various ethnic problems that have characterized the eastern seaboard (the Irish, Italian, Jewish, Puerto-Rican problems, and so on). In all these cases, the spokesman for the dominant socio-political strata contended that the problem rested in the peculiar cultural practices of the subordinate minority, whereas the course of further development exposed the fact that the real problem was the lack of power and wealth of that minority. Once they had attained various forms of power and status within the broader society, these groups found that they did not have to apologize for or regard as a "problem" either their retaining of traditional practices or their instituting forms of community organization.

So far, then, we are in pragmatic agreement with those who criticize the emphasis on Indian culture in analyzing the "Indian problem." Indian *culture* is not the problem; but Indian *poverty* is a problem. However, where we differ with these administrators, welfare workers, and other critics is in assessing the significance of Indian culture and society for programs of Indian betterment. Insofar as any ethnic, religious, or minority group has raised itself above poverty and adapted itself to our urban society, it has required a collective effort and a collective struggle; it has not required a dissolution of social bonds with their fellows but rather the strengthening of these. By the same logic, Indians will require more and better social solidarity, rather than less, and if the example of other ethnic groups is any guide, then Indians will create this solidarity about what they perceive to be traditional Indian symbols and values.

The notion that Indians can be benefited by compulsorily "integrating" them into programs with local Whites is a delusion, and a very pernicious one, of the order of believing that — in the absence of the might of the federal government and of the militant civil rights organizations — Negroes in the Deep South would be benefited by compulsory integration into programs with local Whites. For in both cases the Whites would simply capture the organization to serve their own interests. Without effective organization to present his view-point, the Indian (and the Negro) will simply be subjected to further harassment by Whites who think they know what is best for him.

Many people born as Indians have assimilated into the society about them, and this disappearance is usually regarded as a "success" by the administrative or benevolent agency that may have conspired to assist this process. Yet, there is by now some evidence to indicate that the effort to assimilate Indians, to integrate them into the White community and to dissolve their identity via the acids of education and retraining, that this process may in fact be contributing far more to the creation of a deracinated proletariat — a faceless urban poor — people without identity or hope. If this is so, those who are interested in assisting Indians to rise from poverty might well desist from their bureaucratic warfare against Indian communities and instead encourage Indians to organize in the forms of their choice. The deracination of Indians into proletarians is concealed behind the enthusiasm for the occasional Indian who dissolves into the general urban middle class; besides, removing Indians from federal rolls is regarded as a positive accomplishment by those who administer the federal budget, and when these deracinated individuals appear among the urban poor, few are concerned about their ethnic history. On the other side, Indian communities suffer from the fact that the successful person — he who makes good in the general urban environment — is no longer defined as an Indian and no longer preserves any ties to the Indian community. Under these circumstances, Indian communities are robbed of persons who might be leaders, or intermediaries between the traditional folk and the greater society, or, at least, models of success.

The sociological literature is voluminous on the role of ethnic and religious minorities within the U. S. and it abundantly confirms the notion that for most persons adaptation to urban society was via collectivities, rather than as disparate individuals. Italians, Irish, Jews, Poles, and so on, each attempted to reconstitute within the urban environment a miniature of their village life within the old country. The notion of traditional Indian culture may be an anthropological myth, but an even grosser fallacy is the notion that Indians can rise above poverty and adapt to urban society by being deprived of their right to maintain an Indian society and a sense of Indian identity.

PINE RIDGE

In the past, Pine Ridge has been subjected to a multitude of federal and other plans for community betterment. While the overall target of these plans has seldom been realized, so that the large mass of Sioux has remained impoverished, the plans have had important effects. Generally, they have ameliorated conditions by providing some employment and related economic activity; and, as a more long-run effect, they have contributed toward diversifying the reservation population and increasing the social and economic distance between the more traditional "Country Indians" and those more urbanized "Mixedbloods" who have managed to secure a greater share of such benefits as steady employment. Most of this planning has occurred for, rather than by, the Indians who were the target population, and when Sioux have been brought into the discussion, it is the more urbanized types who have stepped forward and "spoken for the Indian." The Country Indians have not been consulted and have anyway been poorly informed, and the plans for the betterment of their communities have failed to raise them out of poverty.

As of our visit in July-August, the various Office of Economic Opportunity programs at Pine Ridge were following the familiar course outlined above, except for a change of agencies and actors. Design of projects and application for funds was being spearheaded by the Tribal Attorney, a person of energy, benevolent concern for the Indian, and marked political influence via the Association on American Indian Affairs. A Community Development Program had come into existence, whose direction had been turned over to a man who had resided in the area for many years and had been active on many organized programs for community welfare. The attitude of this director is symbolized by the fact that, despite his long residence in the community and his occupational status as liason man, he pointedly refrains from participating in the social life of the Indian folk and remains ignorant of Lakota, the language which constitutes the principal medium for political and social discourse among adult Country Indians. As is typical of the role which such men create for themselves on the reservation, he is hard-working, conscientious, and much concerned to import into Indian life the standards which he thinks of as distinguishing the national society. From his perspective, the less communicated to the local folk about community development programs, the better; because otherwise everyone would be hounding his office trying to secure perquisites and places on the payroll for their relatives. Besides, the task of "public relations" is conceived as belonging to another person, the Fifth Member of the Tribal Executive, an official who by the terms of the O.E.O. contracts is supposed to devote himself to acting as liason between the Community Development Program and "the tribe." In fact, however, the man currently holding the post of Fifth Member is overwhelmed by his other responsibilities as a member of the Executive, and also, feels ignorant of the O.E.O. programs and so reluctant to involve himself.

Meanwhile, the day-to-day operations of the Community Development Program, including the liason with the tribal government and the communication with the Indian public, have devolved upon a VISTA worker who has been recruited into playing the role of Assistant Director. Being White, young, and an outsider, she has been saddled with such hostility-provoking tasks as hiring and firing for the Neighborhood Youth Corps or of the aides for the Child Development Centers. Her genuine desire to assist the community is being exploited while the responsibilities of her position keep her locked in Pine Ridge town and the C.D.P. office. In time she is likely to suffer the fate of idealistic Bureau of Indian Affairs employees, who are similarly isolated from the social life of Country Indians and whose desire to "help them improve themselves" is continually frustrated by the resistance these folk offer to well-meant federal plans.

The same paternalistic pattern is visible in the program to establish child development centers (of a Head Start variety) throughout the reservation. The local folk have not been consulted, and planning and expediting had been turned over to outsiders. In particular, the overall educational design had been delegated to an educator located several hundred miles from Pine Ridge, and since he was not present when we made our brief visit, we can say nothing as to his qualifications or his knowledge of the Sioux and their reservation. Meanwhile, the day-to-day administration had been entrusted to a summer volunteer — a student from the East. No one in authority seemed aware that they were by these tactics effectively depriving the local folk of the opportunity to learn by participating in planning.

In sum, then, the Community Development Program at Pine Ridge has been replacing the paternalism of the B.I.A. with a new and less rigid paternalism. The new situation does offer the Sioux the possibility of a greater influence upon and involvement with the program, but it is not particularly easy for them to perceive that. Moreover, the non-Indians who have moved into positions of authority within the Program have so defined the terms of Indian participation as to rule out — as illegitimate and self-seeking — the initial stages by which any community spokesman would attempt to exert influence, namely those who were interested in the welfare of their local communities and only derivatively interested in the welfare of the Oglala Sioux as a people or tribe.

The town of Pine Ridge now contains a cogent and concrete example of the fruits of the more recent paternalism in the Felis Cohen Home for the Aged. The Home was dedicated with much ceremony and many eminent visitors about two years ago. Clearly these outsiders regarded the Home as being something good that had been done for the Indians. Yet, today, in a Home designed to shelter forty persons, there are about ten elders resident, and this is half of the maximum that ever resided there. Evidently, the Home does not appeal to older Indians. The upper caste of Pine Ridge — the B.I.A., P.H.S., and similar staff personnel — explain this in terms of the incompetence of the tribal government which has the responsibility for operating the Home; these critics mention that the food is bad, the building lacks air conditioning (for which it was designed), and so on. Yet a few minutes conversation with the impoverished Indians for whom the Home was intended reveals that the Home is intrinsically a white elephant, because it simply does not meet the needs or arouse the interests of the older Indians with traditional ways and responsibilities. The planning, designing, and functioning of the Home fell into the hands of committees well exemplified by the director of the Community Development Program — a congeries of Pine Ridge personnel who are determined to uplift the Indians but who are quite ignorant of and indifferent to Indian needs and interests, and who regard Indian desires as something to be surmounted and reformed instead of something to be responded to, encouraged, and developed. Meantime, the tribal government was and is reluctant to criticize any project which brings money into the area — better a useless Home for the Aged than no such project at all.

Since the administration of the Home is now in difficult straits, the Director has detailed one of the VISTA workers to its administration. For this young man, the consequence will most likely be that he will be so preoccupied that he will never meet any Indians (except in a paternalistic and bureaucratic role); he will think of himself as devoting his energies on behalf of the Indians when in fact he will be shoring up a project designed and operated without consultation or communication with those whom it is supposed to benefit.

Informal interviews were conducted with parents who lived in the western area of the reservation, including the communities known as "Oglala Junior," "Number Four," "Calico," and "Number Six." The conversations were designed to elicit information on the needs of preschool youngsters, the types of programs children wished to attend, and the possibilities of a program which would encompass both these young children and their mothers. In the first two of these communities (Oglala Jr. and Number Four) our presence and our focus on the upbringing of the young children tended immediately to elicit questions about Robert V. Dumont and the "Harvard-Radcliffe Summer School Project" he organized and directed during the summer of 1964. Parents wanted to know where Dumont was and they lamented that the Summer School was not being repeated as they had hoped and as he had said it would be in 1965.

While a graphic report of the Harvard-Radcliffe Project may be obtained from its director, (Robert V. Dumont, Harvard School of Education Cambridge, Mass.), a summary may be useful here. As a participant in the research leading to the monograph, FORMAL EDUCATION IN AN AMERICAN INDIAN COM- MUNITY, Dumont had lived for over a year in these western areas of Pine Ridge. Before he left, he had discussed educational needs with the local folk and their leaders, and he had planned a summer camp-school. When he returned in 1964, he brought two Harvard and two Radcliffe students and secured lodging for them with local Indian families. The community was able to provide primitive facilities for the camp, in the way of a large cabin that otherwise served them as community hall; and the Bureau of Indian Affairs provided some assistance in such matters as food.

Recalling this project a year later, parents stated that their children had attended regularly and eagerly, rising of their own wish early in the morning to prepare themselves for the camp vehicle, and then, on returning home, talking volubly of the activities of the day. Parents also stated that their children had learned much from the activities, e.g. songs, stories, and games. When asked about the 1965 summer school programs offered by the B.I.A., mothers claimed that their children had been far less eager to attend and that they had nothing to report on returning home. Again, in discussing the Harvard-Radcliffe Project, parents revealed that their children had liked the young people, and they talked fondly of their residence among them and of their attempts to learn "Indian ways," including singing and dancing.

So far as we were able to determine by indirect questions concerning programs for children of preprimary level, no parent in this area had the slightest inkling of the nature, intent, or existence of the child development centers scheduled to begin operation on the reservation within two months.

A diversity of projects aimed at Indian children has been underway during this and recent summers. Many religious associations have sent youthful volunteers to the reservation to work with the children or otherwise to perform useful labor in community service. The Episcopalians were operating a series of two-week day camps that they described as Bible schools, but since the camp was then located in Pine Ridge town, we did not take time to observe it. The Jewish project, which involved community service, was over, and responses to its youth were not favorable, they being considered "snobbish." When asked whether the structures built by the Jewish youth on this project were being used, Indian parents said, "they were just standing there," and seemed under the impression that these buildings "belonged to the Bureau or some other Office" and that they as members of the community had no right to use them. The Holy Rosary Mission of the Roman Catholics was operating an afternoon program in the Calico area, and we did observe it. It was staffed by a youthful nun and about ten volunteers in their mid-teens, these latter coming for two week periods from outside the Reservation and living in the Mission compound. Eighteen children, aged three to five, were present, most having been walked in by the volunteers. In addition four older Indian boys (early adolescents) watched soberly and intently from a distance; two of these had horses and occasionally demonstrated their own and their steeds' prowess with a short bareback canter. The emotional tone of the gathering was so pleasing that we stayed and participated for an hour in the simple games. Both Indian children and White youth were enjoying the interaction and learning from each other. The location of these activities was a primitive cabin that served as community hall for Calico.

We talked with leaders from each of the four communities mentioned above about programs for children in the preschool age. All were interested, and one asked us to come and explain the Head Start Program to his people; the same person talked at length about how programs tend to be centralized in the hands of B.I.A. or Tribal governmental personnel and so to be removed from community needs or interests. Another explained that community workers are coming to his area without sufficient preparation or insight for dealing with the existing tribal organizations and customs of his people. He saw himself as devoting many hours (without compensation) to serving as a "bridge" (his phrase) between the various community workers and the local folk (many of whose elders know little English and have a deep skepticism about outsiders).

Although all of these leaders were well informed or participating in tribal government, none had any prior knowledge of the Head Start Program. More surprising, none made any reference to the new preprimary program which is being funded by O.E.O. on the reservation and which is due to begin operation this fall. It is true that the programs will initially be established in the eastern and central areas of the reservation, but the ignorance as to the nature and extent of the program was an unfortunate symptom of the paternalism described in the first section.

Several of these leaders criticized the structure of the Community Development Program — and thereby the O.E.O. — on the grounds that nothing was being done for the adult men. It could be argued that by their concentration on the young these programs are contributing further to the erosion of authority and responsibility of the Indian man. With reservation employment limited, and with the welfare programs designed for mothers, young children, the aged, and the ill, it is the men who are rendered useless and impotent.

RAPID CITY

Judged by its own standards, which are the traditional standards of most educators and welfare workers, Project Head Start in Rapid City is not only good, it is excellent. The classes are small, (fifteen children or less), the facilities are pleasing and appropriate, there is abundant auxiliary personnel, the teachers are well trained and pleasant, and the atmosphere of each room is happy. The children are playing, learning, and developing. One of the eight teachers was very talented, although unaware of the real values in what she was doing.

If we criticize the Rapid City Project, it is because its very excellence is achieved on the basis of a colonial or White-Man's-Burden set of standards, and this is already apparent to some of the Indian mothers at whom the project is aimed. The Project is sufficiently well staffed and organized so that the absence of broad participation and support from the mothers of the Indian community is not going to make the impact it should upon these mothers, and in the long run it will not provide the Indian community with the necessary assistance for its folk to move upward out of poverty.

To the north of Rapid City is a shanty town known politely as the "Sioux Addition." The children who come to the Project from this area tend to be concentrated in a few families. It would be interesting to make a census of the area and determine the total number of eligible youngsters; no one seemed to know the figures. As a wild guess, we would hazard that the participating children number about twenty percent of the eligible. Some of the non-participation must be attributed to travel, as the Sioux are highly nomadic, especially in summer; and some must be attributed to the simple process of turnover, as families come to or leave Rapid City.

From one family, three children were attending and an older daughter was serving as an aide. This is a pattern we suggest be watched and encouraged. Sioux families and kin groups have a great loyalty, Sioux children tend to be very shy and are greatly encouraged in any novel situation by the presence of an older family member. Since traditional families tend to be highly responsive to the desires and fears of their children, increasing the number and presence of Sioux volunteers or paid assistants would pay dividends in recruitment of children. Moreover, we should not discount the impact on an adolescent Sioux girl of participating in a responsible educational position, such as is represented by being a Head Start volunteer. We regret that, while 7/12ths of the children were Sioux, only one of the aides was a Sioux girl. We would suggest that a greater effort be made to recruit aides and volunteers from the community being served. Finally on this point, we emphasize the factionality and rivalry within Sioux communities, which means that rather than seeking for "Indians," the administration of a Head Start Center should (to the extent possible) select as aides those Indian persons who are part of the familial or kin group of the children who are to participate.

When we asked Indian mothers how they learned of the Head Start Project, they mentioned a variety of sources, predominantly welfare workers. However, in the Sioux Addition, one young mother (whose only child was too young as yet for the Program) spontaneously referred to the story which had appeared in the RAPID CITY SUNDAY JOURNAL, July 11. This mother was impressively and articulately indignant about the article and so, too, was another Indian mother (not resident in the Sioux Addition). They saw the article as patronizing — as implying that their children were savages who had not learned to eat with knife and fork, and as being in a state of starved neglect akin to the children portrayed in CARE advertisements. While the second of these two mothers viewed the article with amused tolerance, judging Head Start by what it was doing for her youngsters, the other was considerably more hostile. Thus, the question may well be raised whether such publicity releases may not further alienate needy persons of pride and self-respect from the community agencies which are established to assist them. Bluntly, if Head Start programs are defined as designed for the children of savage, drunken, or irresponsible parents, many parents may choose to withhold their children from the program.

As already indicated, we were impressed by the operation of the Center, during a normal weekday morning. The facilities seemed excellent; the personnel skilled; and the atmosphere pleasant.

One teacher seemed especially gifted, as indicated by the following observations:

> The first class I saw was by far the best of three I visited. When I entered — children were on hands and knees being sheep and cows. All boys were sheep and all girls (ten boys, four girls) were cows. Went through rhythm story of Little Boy Blue with tremendous verve and enjoyment. One teacher and two helpers in this room.
>
> In this and later play activities in this room I was struck by a number of remarkable fine phenomena. First-teacher always let children set sex distinctions — all boys wanted to be sheep — fine — all girls mooed with zest — also no evidence at all of what the B.I.A. teachers call "competition." Everybody in this kind of game was to help make it go. Whole situation is much more helpful to learning verbal fluency in English than for Beginners in Bureau schools. Heard teacher say about paints which only four children could use — though several others wanted to paint: "We have to *share* everything — don't we." Most remarkable thing — I think I saw was use of telephone. Four little girls — two Indian — were sitting at a table in the side playing with dishes. On the table with dishes was a toy telephone. Teacher at other end of room picked up telephone — and pretended she was asking operator for Mrs. ———— (probably name of one of the Indian girls). A girl picked up the phone — and teacher asked for her party. Girl handed phone to another — who giggled and looked around helplessly. Other Indian girl said; "say hello — Gee you're dumb." So the little girl said hello. Somehow in conversation with

teacher — she blurted out invitation to teacher to come right over. So teacher came over, knocked, was offered coffee.

The whole performance — the use of English in genuine communication between pupils and between pupils and teacher — the remarkable, yet natural and quite practical practice in social expertise — the joyous and unselfconscious role playing were, to me, incredible, after what I witnessed two years ago in Beginner's level classes on the reservation.

Talked to teacher — who — though first rate — thought of telephone gimmick mainly as way to teach children to use the telephone. (!!!) Told me that at orientation school teachers had been told to expect that the Indian children would be dirty and have head lice — and would need to be cleaned up in school. But Indian children in her class came very clean. She had one little Sioux boy (looked fullblood) who knew no English. But now, suddenly, at meal one day, he had asked, picking up sandwich, "What's that?" He did this with all food now and was learning new words consistantly. (This boy played well with other children — very happy with a farmyard set — he built a fence around — though during Boy Blue game, he had stood in line — sucking index finger of one hand and holding his pecker with the other. Nobody paid any attention to this.) Number of times heard Indian children talking spontaneously in English to other children — but perhaps they don't know Lakota.

Next class — in which boys and girls were playing Musical Chairs — to Pop Goes the Weasel — the children were far more sedate and less expressive. Somehow Musical Chairs came out looking like some kind of orderly ritual — and White girl aide who played along with the little ones was fiercely competitive and saw to it that she stayed in game till last. After finished teacher said: "Wasn't that fun!" in insincere voice. Still children were not unhappy.

We offer three comments in the way of advice rather than criticism. First, to the extent that publicity about the Center can be guided, we suggest that due emphasis be given to the positive qualities of parents who send their children to Head Start Centers, and that some attention might be given to the particular or unique virtues of children coming from Indian or other ethnic communities. For example, the article in the RAPID CITY SUNDAY JOURNAL, July 11, 1965, mentioned the disposition of Indian children to take food home from the Center meal in order to share it with their family, but they portrayed this as a vice or archaism to be overcome; it could equally well have been appreciated as a virtue fantastic for children aged four to six.

Second, the Indians of Rapid City tend to be protected and administered by a federation of individuals, representing various welfare and interest associations, and organized together under the appelation of the "Mayor's Commission." This

Commission and its affiliated associations includes "professional Indians," who speak for "The Indian" during the course of urban planning. Needless to say, these individuals are unencumbered by ties which would require them to account for their stewardship to the Indians themselves. Undue reliance upon these individuals is a poor substitute for reaching out directly to the Indian families. Less planning should be done via these persons, and more direct contact should be made by such processes as home visits.

Third, in its recruitment of volunteers and auxiliary personnel, more effort should be made to recruit from the target communities.

RED SHIRT TABLE

The center operates under great technical and social difficulties. Isolated in the Badlands of South Dakota, lacking running water or a telephone, and connected to the greater society only by a system of dirt and gravel roads, a modern type Center is difficult to maintain. Preparing the school building for occupancy this summer required a week's arduous labor, cleaning and repairing, by the staff who had been recruited to operate the Center. Considerable effort is now being expended on such matters as hauling water, transporting provisions, and maintaining adequate standards of sanitation. These basic chores have been responsibly and devotedly handled by the staff of two professionals (Mrs. Speak and Mr. Mayberry) and two aides (Mrs. Yellow Horse and Mrs. TwoBulls), assisted by Mr. Speak.

The Indian community of Red Shirt Table recognizes the dedication of the professional staff and speaks highly of them and of the Center. However, the operation of the Center and the future of the program within the community have been gravely jeopardized by tension between the local folk and the missionary who is himself serving as director of the community development program (O.E.O.) and whose wife serves as treasurer. Unfortunately, this couple, the Tiffany's, were absent on the day of our visit and so we were not able to discuss and counsel with them; and, since the drive from Pine Ridge town to Red Shirt Table is arduous, we were reluctant to undertake it again without definite knowledge that they would have returned from their vacation.

Many Indian inhabitants of Red Shirt Table speak of the Tiffany's with considerable ire. In his role as missionary (Seventh Day Adventist), he has apparently criticized the mode of housing and living of the local community, and since many of these folk are proud of their lives and houses they feel resentful toward him. Moreover, they hold him personally responsible for the content of a television program which was recently produced and which illustrated the operation of Project Head Start with commentary and pictures of Red Shirt Table. We have not seen this telecast and so are unable to judge whether or not the criticisms by the Indians have an objective foundation. They complained that the telecast described their children as entering school knowing only Lakota and no English, when the facts are that English has long been the primary language of the Sioux households of Red Shirt Village. They complained also that the telecast portrayed their children as not knowing the use of table utensils and that it described their houses as "ramshackle." Now, to a person of urban and middle-class background, the cabins of the Sioux may indeed appear ramshackle, even though they have been standing for many years and have served to shelter many persons from the elements. Yet, the significant fact is that the local community has great pride in itself and in its children, and it is this pride which could constitute a lever for community betterment. Moreover, if the recipients of Head Start and other O.E.O. programs are continually described in negative terms, then those who are "poor but proud" — and this includes many of the Sioux — will simply refuse to participate. As one mother remarked, "We need your help but you don't have to degrade us!"

The unfortunate association between the O.E.O. publicity and the local missionary is testimony to the fundamental failure of the design of the Head Start Project at Red Shirt Table. Effectively the local community has not been involved and has not shared in the planning or responsibility for the Center. The news media came to the missionary for their orientation and did not deal with the community or its representatives, and accordingly the local folk attribute the inaccuracies of the telecast to the missionary. The students who have come this summer to the village to operate the Center are regarded favorably by the local community, but they have not sought to initiate a different relationship of responsibility between the Center and the parents and instead have allowed themselves to be guided by the local missionary. Given the isolation of the village and the small population (a dozen families), it would be quite feasible to so inform and so involve the local folk that quite a sensational demonstration project might develop. As it is now, many parents have withdrawn from participation or attendance at the Center or its activities.

The teachers at the Center indicated that a problem had arisen concerning the medical care of the children. They had arranged for a physician attached to the Public Health Service in the town of Pine Ridge to visit the community to examine the children. In the course of this visit, the medical team had inoculated the children against various diseases and the children had complained of these injections to their parents. In turn, the parents were now using the physician and nurse as "bogeymen," threatening the children that if they did not behave properly, they would be sent to the nurse and have needles stuck in them. The teachers thought this a deplorable and inconsiderate action on the part of the parents, which would instill into the children improper attitudes toward medical care. We pointed out that the folk of Red Shirt Table were likely quite uninformed about the nature and purposes of the inoculations and could only respond to these medical practices as being some other strange and painful tactic of the White intruders. Here, surely, was an instance when a public health worker should have preceded the visit of the medical team with a community meeting and explanation of what was to be done to the children. In any case, the staff had risen to the occasion by introducing into the curriculum materials on physicians and dentists, so as to prepare the children for future experiences and to explain to them the rationale behind whatever pain might be inflicted during the course of medical or dental treatment.

As in other centers, the professional staff seemed unaware of the difference of Indian children about aggressive physical contact with adults. We noted that at Red Shirt Table the teachers were enthusiastic participants in a game that involved much pushing and shoving and that they were quite oblivious of the problem of courtesy and respect that was thereby being posed to the children. While we did point out the nature of the problem to the staff and while we did suggest that, so far as concerns rough body contact, the children be directed against their fellows of the same age and sex, nonetheless we should add that the development of this kind of intercultural problem was not simply a negative quality but rather testimony to the intermingling and happy intimacy of staff and children at this Center.

All in all, it is our impression that Mrs. Speak and Mr. Mayberry were unusually adept and considerate in their interpersonal contact with the Indian children. Instruction, play, feeding, and washing were carried on in an atmosphere of soft-spoken gentleness to which the children responded very well and which, we are sure, the Indian parents would have approved. Indeed, all Indian parents interviewed indicated that they liked the teachers as persons, that the children liked them, and that, on the whole "the school is a good thing."

WHITE EARTH RESERVATION

The problems with Head Start and other O.E.O. projects in this area are those which might reasonably be anticipated when an inexperienced local government is suddenly given rather large sums of money and corresponding responsibilities. The incumbent leaders and executives usually do not have strong or clear views about the form, content, or goals of education. They tend to be poorly informed, cautious, and disposed to be guided by the letter of the law or the edict of bureaucrats. The income represented by the projects is highly valued and — as jobs — tends to be apportioned among the members (usually kindred) of the incumbent or dominant socio-political faction. Meanwhile, members of those factions not sharing the spoils gripe and drag their heels, but enough of them can usually discern some modest advantage to themselves in participating so that the programs do move along.

Since the incumbent or "leading" faction is prone to believe that the interpretation of experts is correct and necessary for the continuation of the grant, the design of the projects is left almost entirely in the hands of persons from outside the Indian community, e.g., school administrators, VISTA workers, bureaucrats. These designs are often far from ideal and conform neither to the needs of the community nor the aims of the Head Start Program. Understandably, members of the community who are attached to the dominant faction are not critical of the programs. When other folk, and especially members of the subordinate factions, suggest innovations or changes in design, their remarks tend to be categorically dismissed as springing from trouble-makers or jealous persons.

The following considerations are important as background to further and more detailed discussion. First, the resident population of the White Earth tribal group has decreased to about a third of what it was in 1950. At that time, the figures showed a resident population of over 9,000 persons; a recent census shows less than 2,500. Evidently, there has been a substantial out-migration; local people say that most of these Indians have moved to the Twin Cities, Chicago, and Milwaukee; they also say that many persons are nomadic, rather than migrants, and that they return to the White Earth area as often and as long as they can, (the evidence is also that these migrants are having grave social and economic difficulties in the urban environment.) Second, the White Earth Chippewa are highly acculturated. Their native language is now English, and very few engage in traditional ceremonial activities. There seems to be no group which can be classified as "fullblood" and against which another group can be denoted as "mixedblood" or as "breeds"; rather, the differences seem to be between those factions (or kindred) who have more wealth and power and those which have less. Third, while the White Earth Chippewa are poor, they did not to us appear in as desperate and desolated condition as some of the Sioux in the Dakotas. Our guess is that out-migration has so reduced the density of the region as to make life generally easier for those who remain; in that case, the problem of the impoverished Indian may in some part have been moved to urban settings. Fourth, the conflict and rivalry which in the large, Western reservations is phrased as Fullblood versus Mixedblood is here a rivalry between loosely associated aggregates of kindred. Not only have the self conscious tradition-alists just about vanished, but also those persons who are archetypically "mixedbloods" — extolling the Protestant ethos of diligence and thrift and denouncing the Indian ethos of generosity and leisure — these persons too seem few in numbers and relatively powerless.

There were three Head Start Centers on the White Earth reservation, namely, White Earth Village, Ponsford, and Nattahwaush. We visited the first two of these Centers. As a further organizational note, we remind the reader that White Earth is one of the organizational units or district of the consolidated (or federated) Minnesota Chippewa Tribe. Since the White Earth reservation is now "open" and numerous Whites own property and live in the area, we tend herein to speak of the White Earth tribal group rather than of the reservation.

Among the parents of the lower socio-political faction there was praise for the Head Start Project, tempered by a number of criticisms. They had not previously been asked for their criticisms, although some had spontaneously expressed them to the social worker associated with the Project.

Mrs. Pfeilsticker, the teacher in the Center in the White Earth Village is not well liked. During the regular school year, she teaches the first grade, and so she is well known. She has the reputation of being an over-strict disciplinarian, and one mother allowed her child to withdraw from the program when the child complained of corporal abuse by the teacher. The mother had not registered a complaint.

Some parents pointed out that it was difficult to keep pupils in school throughout the long school year. If pre-schoolers are to have a special summer program and then go with scarcely a break into the school term, they may fatigue even sooner, so their parents believe and worry. It is possible that some of the parental concern expressed here about a child turning sour over school was fear that the child would not be able to tolerate so long a dosage of this one teacher. One parent remarked spontaneously that preschool programs would be better if conducted during the normal school year, so the child would at least have the companionship of its relatives.

When asked what kind of program they would like for their children several parents referred in glowing terms to the program of the previous year conducted by students from the University of Minnesota. They found the students highly congenial, and their children had welcomed the program.

Some urban mothers find children a nuisance and welcome any reliable institutionalized arrangement for handling them. While this attitude was also shared by some of the better-off women we interviewed, the majority of these Chippewa liked having their young children about the house, especially when older children were present to share the burden of their care. Accordingly, they may send their children to a Head Start Center if they believe it to be in the best interests of the child, but they are likely to pull the child out at any reasonable excuse. Moreover, most of the mothers would prefer a scheduled system of activities, covering part but not all of the day for most of their children. And some opined that a whole day at school was too tiring for the youngsters.

Some parents who withheld their children entirely from the Head Start Program explained that "all summer and all winter was too much school;" children needed some time for play. Indeed, the pre-school class we observed at White Earth Village entailed much drudgery and very little play or creative activity.

We observed operations at two of the three Centers, White Earth Village and Ponsford. In both cases, the sessions were being held in schoolrooms, and in both cases activities tended to be highly structured by the teacher and organized mostly about the acquisition of scholastic skills (counting and reading-readiness). The activities at Ponsford were markedly superior to those at White Earth Village (and the teacher had a much better reputation) but in neither case did they compare with what we had observed at Little Eagle (Standing Rock), Red Shirt Table (Pine Ridge), or Rapid City. Too much of the time was being spent with the children seated in neat rows and engaged in mass routines; too much of the time was devoted to "idiot questions" to which a few children were responding, while the remainder silently twisted in their seats. Given this definition of what Head Start activities should be, the teachers were delegating little responsibility to their aides and were utilizing them mostly for supervision of handwashing and the playground period.

It would be too easy to blame the teachers for this perversion of Head Start objectives. Th fault more clearly lies with an administration which has been content to abstain from the project and allow the educators to organize a program on conventional scholastic principles — a kind of prep-school for the first grade.

Both teachers we talked to were socially isolated from the local Indian community. As one of them expressed it, "They have their life, and I have mine, and I think that's the way they prefer it." The speaker, a well-meaning soul, did not seem to feel that she could learn anything or enrich her own life by contact with the parents of the children she was presuming to instruct. The only persons who seemed to be making any home visits were the social workers, who were new to the area.

The teacher at Ponsford did ask for more assistance in obtaining materials pertinent to the ethnic culture and history of her pupils. As she explained, even in such a matter as pictures and illustrations, the subjects are invariably urban White children and so quite foreign to the interests and experiences of her charges. (We were not able to provide her with suggestions for material at the level of the primary and pre-primary grades. We believe that such material is available and that more is being developed, and we suggest that educators in schools serving Indians be provided with lists and — where possible — samples.)

The teacher in Ponsford also complained of a lack of suitable toys and equipment for her preschool children. To some degree this deficiency should be attributed to the difficulties in organizing and designing the local program, for so far as we could gather, the task of choosing and requisitioning supplies had been turned over to the VISTA workers, and they of course had little background for this responsibility.

So far as we could quickly reconstruct, the White Earth tribal group was propeled into Head Start and other programs through the good efforts of O.E.O. representatives, who pushed matters along with great speed and energy. Initially, it had been believed that the Head Start Project could be sponsored via the local school board, and one of the members of the board attended a conference at Bemidji where the philosophy and design of Child Development Centers was explained. Then, it was discovered that the project could not be sponsored by the school board and had to be picked up by the tribal government, and since control of these agencies was then in the hands of opposing political factions, the advice of the board member who had been at Bemidji was not heeded. (Shortly thereafter, the political revolution affected the school board, and the board member in question resigned.) Accordingly, the administration of Project Head Start passed into the hands of novices who were quite unprepared for these responsibilities, although eager to utilize the funds coming in.

The rivals of the dominant political faction in White Earth politics accuse them of operating a spoils system in which all the major jobs have been assigned to their kindred. This favoritism does seem to be true, although there is no evidence that the appointees are incompetent, and the likelihood is that, in general, the victorious faction includes the better educated of the White Earth population. On the other hand, it may be true that, considering their formal qualifications, the federally-supported salaries they are receiving may be unduly large.

A complaint was registered that $400 of Head Start funds had been appropriated for tours by the Center at White Earth Village, but that during the entire term of operation only one trip was made — and that to the neighboring city of Detroit Lakes where the children had had boat rides. Whether that sum of money was unspent or misused we do not know, but certainly the children in the Center at White Earth Village should have been participating in more and better designed tours.

Conversation with Mr. Goodwin, the director of the Community Develop-ment Program at White Earth and the person therefore with formal responsibil-ity for the Head Start Program, revealed his feelings that these programs had developed prior to his assumption of office and had remained outside of his control and concern. He expressed irritation at the consultant sent earlier by Head Start ("noseying around and criticising"). He also indicated that he wanted O.E.O. to instruct him in detail on the operation of Head Start and other projects. However, when we indicated to him certain of the failings of the present White Earth program (e.g. lack of community involvement), his response was not encouraging, and it may be that for him to consider guidance authoritative, it must come down the chain of command from Washington through regional, state, and tribal authorities.

From our conversations at White Earth and Red Lake, we infer that the officials of the State of Minnesota who deal with the Chippewa on matters of education or welfare are persons who are totally ignorant of Chippewa culture and society. They regard Indians as being socially and psychologically Whites who happen to bear red skins but who are poor and afflicted with the vices and weaknesses of the poor. This view is very convenient for bureaucrats but it happens to be grossly in error and there is a mountain of ethnographic literature which refutes it (see the writings of A. I. Hallowell, V. Barnouw, F. Miller, and others). As we have asserted; it is true that the Indian problem is one of relative poverty and lack of power, but we should add here that in designing educational programs for Indians it is extremely helpful to have some knowledge of their culture and personality. Indians, even Indian children, do relate differently to people than do, for example, Lutherans of Scandinavian extraction or Catholics of German extraction, and the educational format that works well with one group will not necessarily work equally well for the other. Insofar as educators persist in regarding Indian children as identical with non-Indians, they are failing their task as educators, because they are not starting where the child is, but where they themselves wish him to be.

All this is of more than ideological importance. Instruction about Head Start and other programs for children tends to be filtered through the regional and state offices. If these administrators are hostile to the matter of ethnic differences and reluctant to heed the comments of parents, then the best of federal plans will come to nought.

RED LAKE

In its organization, Red Lake is more akin to the western reservations of Pine Ridge and Standing Rock than to White Earth, as it has a substantial and unified land base which is controlled by a tribal government together with the B.I.A. While the school system is public and is administratively organized under the school board, the boundaries of the school district were drawn so as to coincide with the reservation lines, in a pattern which seems to have been desired both by the tribal officials and — so it is said — by the neighboring White parents who did not wish their children to mingle with the Indians. Within the reservation, then, are three systems of political and economic power: the tribal government; the agency offices of the B.I.A., and the school system. The P.H.S. hospital might constitute a fourth system, but in the present context it may be identified with the B.I.A. as federally controlled and civil service.

So far as concern most areas of educational policy, the school system is governed by the superintendent with the board acting as a rubber stamp. In part, this may be due to the novelty of the public system; also, to the inexperience of the Indian board members; but, in part, certainly, it is due to the complexity of a modern educational system in which funds accrue from a variety of sources under a variety of types of legislation. Be that as it may, the school board has been known to raise issues only concerning the handling of disciplinary cases (so challenging the principal of the high school). Neither the board nor any other agency has yet acted as a vehicle for transmitting complaints about unpopular teachers, let alone for raising issues of curriculum.

While the Head Start Program was attained through application by the tribal government, its organization and administration were quickly turned over to the officials of the school system, so that its executive head is the high school principal. This delegation of authroity and responsibility seems to be so complete that we, as newcomers, to the situation, found it bewildering. For example, Roger Jourdain, the chairman of the tribal government told us that he was strongly interested in the preservation of the Chippewa language and its inclusion in the school system. Since Jourdain and the council obtained and had control of the funds for the Head Start Program, we would have thought that they could have used this strategic position to push for any type of curriculum they desired. Yet, they did not, and we can only regard this reticence as further evidence of the timidity of tribal governments about innovating with federally sponsored programs; they regard the immediate benefits of the program as too great to jeopardize by offering any challenge to the conventional wisdom of the professionally qualified authority. On the other hand, Jourdain does believe that the Head Start Program has served to improve relationships between, on the one side, himself and the tribal council, and, on the other side, the school administration, and he contends that the latter group now listen with greater concern and respect to the former group and that consultation is now more frequent. If this is so, then Head Start has at Red Lake moved toward one of its major goals, even if the movement is more modest and covert than had been hoped for.

The Head Start Program was held in high regard by the parents. The best evidence being, nor merely their response to direct questions, but the report of a University of Minnesota undergraduate, who as a part of a course in field research had inherited the task of administering the Head Start questionnaire (CAP-HS Form 41 January, 1965) to parents (and who, finding this question-naire quite idiotic in reservation conditions, had elaborated a more congenial schedule of her own). This young lady found that when she called on homes driving a car borrowed from the B.I.A. (and so labeled), she had encountered suspicion and reserve, but that when she identified herself as associated with Head Start, this suspicion was replaced by a tolerant or friendly interest.

In the small, isolated, and traditionalistic village of Ponemah, word of the project had been spread via the councilman (who has a reputation as a knowledgable operator), and the enrollment of youngsters had been one hundred percent, although attendance had fluctuated. In the Red Lake-Redby area, information about the project had not been so well or sympathetically spread and enrollment had been slow, rising as the project went along and parents learned of its merits. We surmise that among other hinderances there was a failure to obtain the endorsement of the Catholic educators who operate the mission school to which many Indians send their children for primary education. Head Start was strongly identified with the public school system, being held in its buildings and staffed by its personnel, and parents intending to send their children to the mission school could well have regarded the Head Start Center as irrelevant.

The nature of the interest the Head Start Program has for Chippewa mothers and the relationship between those mothers and their children are nicely illustrated with the following fragments from an interview:

> *Respondent:* I really think it's a good thing (Program). She (her daughter) was kind of bashful, kind of a big baby. It was good for her just to be away (from home).
> *Interviewer:* How did you hear about the Program?
> *Respondent:* I got a letter from the Tribal Office. Then I went and found out about it from the school; I went and asked.
>
> I just liked the idea. I asked her (daughter) if she wanted to go. I explained what it would be like, and that there wouldn't be much time in between (vacation between Head Start and the beginning of school). But she wanted to go, and she likes it real well. She tells me what goes

on, but she's still kind of quiet.

Formally, all educators and administrators were well qualified and experienced. However, basically, most were quite uninformed as to the nature of the local Indian communities or the social and personal dynamics of the Indian pupils. Again, most seemed decent and pleasant persons who were interested in understanding their pupils better but who were allowing themselves to be entrapped by the structure of the school system. On the one hand, they were well pleased with a system which kept the Indian parents subservient and at a distance from the schools; while, on the other hand, they were discomfitted at their inability to reach or understand their pupils.

Two persons were in exceptional positions. The Head Start teacher in the isolated and traditional community of Ponemah was somewhat more free in her local situation and had been assisted in her wish to meet the local folk by an anthropologist (Mary Black) who had been working with the elders there. The other person, being the daughter-in-law of the tribal chairman, again had more access to the community although not to its more traditional or impoverished side.

The gross physical facilities (the public school buildings) were excellent. However, the equipment left something to be desired. In the haste to organize and establish the project, the ordering of special materials and playthings for the pupils had been turned over to VISTA workers and they had purchased such expensive and inappropriate items as dummy electric ranges, which were unfamiliar to most Indian families.

While there were extensive periods of free play in the gymnasium with equipment there, work in the Red Lake classrooms was under the supervision and direction of the teachers and tended to be overly organized and overly pedagogic. Nonetheless, the atmosphere was generally good, and the children seemed to be happy and developing.

The boys gave a bit the appearance of bantam cocks who, the minute the teacher's attention wandered from them, were ready to square off against each other in a test of strength. Fighting and the establishment of a pecking order is a normal and important feature of Indian peer society. Accordingly, there might be some reason to incorporate some sort of regulated mayhem, such as wrestling, within the school activities, providing the parents were consulted, approved, and agreed to help proctor the contests. At present, there is too much of a ladylike and genteel flavor about most Head Start activities in most centers.

FINAL NOTE ON THE CHIPPEWA: ADVISORY PERSONNEL

O. Meredith Wilson, President of the University of Minnesota, has recently organized a University Committee on American Indian Affairs. Wilson himself was Chairman of the Commission on the Rights, Liberties, and Responsibilities of the American Indian (funded by the Fund for the Republic) and so has an excellent knowledge of contemporary Indian affairs on the national scene. Minnesota's committee includes members of a variety of departments within the University, including anthropologists, sociologists, social workers, and others, and it is chaired by Matthew Stark, who is Coordinator of the Human Relations Program within the Office of the Dean of Students. Barbara Knudson, who is a member of that Committee and who is Director of the Institute for Community Services (formerly Institute for Delinquency Prevention) of the University, directed the organization of an Institute for Teachers of Indian Children, which was held August 30 - September 3, 1965, at Bemidji State College. She secured the coopeation of all the major agencies and organizations involved in Indian affairs in Minnesota, including the tribal governments, and the participants at the Institute included about ninety educators, administrators, tribal officials, etc.

During the course of our work among the Chippewa, we encountered the following anthropologists also engaged in field work: on the White Earth Reservation, James G. E. Smith of the University of Alabama (formerly of Moorhead State College, Minnesota); on the Red Lake Reservation, Frank C. Miller, Univesity of Minnesota and Mary Black, University of California (Berkeley). All three would be knowledgable about the Chippewa and could provide counsel to Head Start and the O.E.O.

V.
NEW
PERSPECTIVES
FOR
RESEARCH

chapter 13
future problems and research

CONDITIONS FAVORING MAJOR ADVANCES IN SOCIAL SCIENCE

Karl W. Deutsch, John Platt, Dieter Senghaas

The environmental group conditions for creative success in the social sciences are a frequent subject for debate. It is not generally realized how much information about these creative conditions can be obtained from a statistical analysis of creative instances. To examine this question, we made a list of some 62 leading achievements in the social sciences in this century (see Table 1). With this list we have tried to explore the following major groups of questions.

1. Which were the major achievemnets, or advances, or breakthroughs in the social sciences from 1900 to 1965? Are there publicly verifiable criteria by which they can be recognized? Can such advances be called cumulative in the sense proposed by J. B. Conant — that is, have successive advances been built upon earlier ones?

2. In what fields did such breakthroughs occur?

3. Did major advances relate mainly to theory, or to method, or to matters of substance? In what fields did such advances occur most often?

4. Are there any changes and trends over time in the incidence and characteristics of these breakthroughs?

5. Who accomplished such advances most often — individuals or teams?

6. What were the ages of the contributors at the time of their achievements? Did they have any special personality characteristics?

7. Were the results quantitative, explicitly or by implication?

Table 1. Basic innovations in social science, 1900-65. Abbreviations in column 1: An, anthropology; Ec, economics; Math, mathematics; Phil, philosophy, logic, and history of science; Pol, politics; Psy, psychology; Soc, sociology. In column 6, +N indicates a larger number of collaborators with a less crucial share in the work. Abbreviations in column 7: QFE, quantitative findings explicit; QPE, quantitative problems explicit; QPI, quantitative problems implicit; Non-Q, predominantly nonquantitative.

Contribution 1	Contributor 2	Time 3	Place 4	Type of support 5	No. of workers 6	Quantitative aspects 7	Years until impact 8
1. Theory and measurement of social inequalities (Ec)	V. Pareto / C. Gini	1900 / 1908	Lausanne, Swit. / Cagliari, It. / Padua, It. / Rome, It.	University chairs	1 + N	QFE	25
2. Sociology of bureaucracy, culture, and values (Soc)	M. Weber	1900-21	Freiburg, Ger. / Heidelberg, Ger. / Munich, Ger.	University chair with research support	1	QPI	20 ± 10
3. Theory of one-party organization and revolution (Pol)	V. I. Lenin	1900-17	Shushenskoe, Siberia / London, Eng. / Munich, Ger.	Underground party	1 + N	QPI	10 ± 5
4. Psychoanalysis and depth psychology (Psy)	S. Freud / C. G. Jung / A. Adler	1900-25 / 1910-30 / 1910-30	Vienna, Aus.	University institute of psychology	1 + N	Non-Q	30 ± 10
5. Correlation analysis and social theory (Math)	K. Pearson / F. Edgeworth / R. A. Fisher	1900-28 / 1900-30 / 1920-48	London, Eng. / Oxford, Eng. / Cambridge, Eng. / Harfenden, Eng.	University chairs	1 + N	QFE	25 ± 15
6. Gradual social transformation (Pol)	B. Webb / S. Webb / G. B. Shaw / H. G. Wells	1900-38	London, Eng.	Fabian society	4 + N	QPE	35 ± 5
7. Elite studies (Soc)	G. Mosca / V. Pareto / H. D. Lasswell	1900-23 / 1900-16 / 1936-52	Turin, It. / Lausanne, Swit. / Chicago, Ill.	University institutes	1 + N	QFE	40 ± 10
8. Unity of logic and mathematics (Phil)	B. Russell / A. N. Whitehead	1905-14	Cambridge, Eng.	University institute	2	QPE	30
9. Pragmatic and behavioral psychology (Psy)	J. Dewey / G. H. Mead / C. Cooley / W. I. Thomas	1905-25 / 1900-34 / 1900-30 / 1900-40	Ann Arbor, Mich. / Chicago, Ill. / Ann Arbor, Mich. / Chicago, Ill. / New York, N.Y.	University chairs	1	Non-Q	20 ± 10
10. Learning theory (Psy)	E. L. Thorndike / C. Hull et al.	1905-40 / 1929-40	New York, N.Y. / New Haven, Conn.	Teachers college, Institute of human relations	1 + N	QFE	20 ± 5
11. Intelligence tests (Psy)	A. Binet / L. Terman / C. Spearman	1905-11 / 1916-37 / 1904-27	Paris, Fr. / Stanford, Calif. / London, Eng.	Testing organizations	1 + N	QFE	15 ± 5
12. Role of innovations in socioeconomic change (Ec)	J. A. Schumpeter / W. F. Ogburn / A. P. Usher / J. Schmookler	1908-14 / 1946-50 / 1922-30 / 1924 / 1966	Vienna, Aus. / Cambridge, Mass. / New York, N.Y. / Cambridge, Mass. / Minneapolis, Minn.	University chair and research program	1 + N	QPI	40
13. Conditioned reflexes (Psy)	I. Pavlov	1910-30	Leningrad, U.S.S.R.	Imperial medico-surgical academy	1 + N	QPI	20 ± 10
14. Gestalt psychology (Psy)	M. Wertheimer / K. Koffka / W. Koehler	1912-32	Berlin, Ger.	University chairs	3 + N	Non-Q	25 ± 5
15. Sociometry and sociograms (Soc)	J. L. Moreno	1915 / 1934-43	Innsbruck, Aus.	University chair	1	QFE	10
16. Soviet type of one-party state (Pol)	V. I. Lenin et al.	1917-21	Leningrad, U.S.S.R.	Politburo	1 + N	QPI	5 ± 5
17. Large-scale nonviolent political action (Pol)	M. K. Gandhi	1918-34	Ahmedabad, India	Political movement and institute (ashram)	1 + N	Non-Q	15 ± 10

Contribution 1	Contributor 2	Time 3	Place 4	Type of support 5	No. of workers 6	Quantitative aspects 7	Years until impact 8
18. Central economic planning (Ec)	Q. Krassin G. Grinko	1920-26	Moscow, U.S.S.R.	Government institute	1 + N	QFE	7 ± 6
19. Social welfare function in politics and economics (Ec)	A. C. Pigou K. Arrow	1920-56 1951	London, Eng. Stanford, Calif.	University chairs	1 + N	QPE	40 ± 10
20. Logical empiricism and unity of science (Phil)	M. Schlick R. Carnap O. Neurath P. Frank L. Wittgenstein H. Reichenbach C. Morris	1921-38 1921 1936-50	Vienna, Aus. Cambridge, Eng. Berlin, Ger. Chicago, Ill. Cambridge, Mass.	Vienna circle and university chairs University chairs	3 + N	QPI	20 ± 5
21. Quantitative mathematical studies of war (Pol)	L. F. Richardson Q. Wright	1921-55 1936-66	London, Eng. Chicago, Ill.	University chair and research program	1 + N	QFE	25 ± 10
22. Projective tests (Psy)	H. Rorschach H. Murray	1923	Herisau, Swit. Cambridge, Mass.	Cantonal mental institute University chair	1	Non-Q	15 ± 5
23. Sociology of knowledge and science (Soc)	K. Mannheim R. K. Merton D. deS. Price	1923-33 1937 1950-60	Heidelberg, Ger. Frankfurt, Ger. Princeton, N.J. New Haven, Conn.	University chairs, institutes, and programs	1 + N	Non-Q	10
24. Quantitative political science and basic theory (Pol)	C. Merriam S. Rice H. Gosnell H. D. Lasswell	1925-36	Chicago, Ill.	University chairs	3 + N	QFE	15 ± 5
25. Functionalist anthropology and sociology (An)	A. R. Radcliffe-Brown B. Malinowski T. Parsons	1925 1925-45 1932-50	Cape Town, S. Afr. Sidney, Aus. Chicago, Ill. Oxford, Eng. London, Eng. Cambridge, Mass.	University chairs and travel grants	1 + N	Non-Q	20 ± 10
26. Ecosystem theory (Soc)	R. Park E. W. Burgess	1926-38	Chicago, Ill.	University chairs	2 + N	QFE	25 ± 5
27. Factor analysis (Math)	L. Thurstone	1926-48	Chicago, Ill.	University chair	1 + N	QFE	15 ± 10
28. Operational definitions (Phil)	P. W. Bridgman	1927-38	Cambridge, Mass.	University chair	1	QPI	15 ± 5
29. Structural linguistics (Math)	R. Jakobson and Prague circle N. Chomsky	1927-67 1957-	Brno, Czech. Cambridge, Mass. Cambridge, Mass.	University chairs and programs	1 + N	QPE	20 ± 10
30. Economic propensities, employment, and fiscal policy (Ec)	J. M. Keynes	1928-44	Cambridge, Eng.	University chair	1 + N	QFE	6 ± 4
31. Game theory (Math)	J. v. Neumann O. Morgenstern	1928-44 1944-58	Berlin, Ger. Princeton, N.J.	University chairs and institute	2 + N	QFE	10 ± 5
32. Peasant and guerrilla organization and government (Pol)	Mao Tse-tung	1929-49	Kiangsi, P. R. China Yenan, P. R. China Peking, P. R. China	Political movement	1 + N	QPI	15 ± 10
33. Community studies (Soc)	R. Lynd H. Lynd L. Warner C. Kluckhohn	1929-62 1941	New York, N.Y. Chicago, Ill.	University chairs	2	QFE	20 ± 5

Contribution 1	Contributor 2	Time 3	Place 4	Type of support 5	No. of workers 6	Quantitative aspects 7	Years until impact 8
34. Culture and personality and comparative child rearing (An)	R. Benedict, M. Mead, G. Gorer, A. Kardiner, J. Piaget, E. Erikson, J. Whiting, I. Child	1930, 1930, 1939, 1940–60, 1950, 1953	New York, N.Y.; Geneva, Swit.; Cambridge, Mass.; Cambridge, Mass.; New Haven, Conn.	University chairs, research projects, and travel grants	3 + N	Non-Q	20 ± 10
35. Economics of monopolistic competition (Ec)	E. H. Chamberlin, J. Robinson	1930–33	Cambridge, Mass.; Cambridge, Eng.	University chairs	1	QPE	10 ± 5
36. Authoritarian personality and family structure (Psy)	M. Horkheimer, H. Marcuse, E. Fromm, T. Adorno *et al.*, A. Mitscherlich	1930–32, 1950, 1962	Frankfurt, Ger.; Stanford, Calif.; Frankfurt, Ger.; Heidelberg, Ger.	Institute for social research and university	3 + N	QPI	20 ± 5
37. Large-scale sampling in social research (Math)	M. Hansen	1930–53	Washington, D.C.	Government office	N	QFE	5
38. Laboratory study of small groups (Psy)	K. Lewin, R. Lippitt, R. Likert, D. Cartwright	1932–36	Cambridge, Mass.	University and research institutes	1 + N	QPI	10 ± 5
39. National income accounting (Ec)	S. Kuznets, C. Clark, U.N. Statistical Office	1933–40, 1953	Philadelphia, Pa.; Cambridge, Eng.; Washington, D.C.; New York, N.Y.	Public research institutes and university chairs	1 + N	QFE	10 ± 5
40. General systems analysis (Phil)	L. v. Bertalanffy, N. Rashevsky, J. G. Miller, A. Rapoport, R. W. Gerard, K. Boulding	1936, 1956	Vienna, Aus.; Chicago, Ill.; Ann Arbor, Mich.	University research institutes	4 + N	QPI	15 ± 5
41. Attitude survey and opinion polling (Psy)	G. Gallup, H. Cantril, P. F. Lazarsfeld, A. Campbell	1936, 1937–52, 1940, 1942	Princeton, N.J.; New York, N.Y.; Ann Arbor, Mich.	University and research institutes, commercial organizations	3 + N	QFE	5
42. Input-out analysis (Ec)	W. Leontief	1936–53	Cambridge, Mass.	University chair	1 + N	QFE	15
43. Linear programming (Ec)	L. Kantorovich, J. B. Souto, G. B. Dantzig, R. Dorfman	1938–50, 1941, 1948, 1958	Leningrad, U.S.S.R.; Buenos Aires, Arg.; Washington, D.C.; Berkeley, Calif.	University research institutes and government office	1 + N	QFE	10 ± 5
44. Content analysis (Pol)	H. Lasswell, I. deS. Pool, B. Berelson, P. Stone	1938–56	Chicago, Ill.	University institute	2	QFE	10
45. Operant conditioning and learning; teaching machines (Psy)	B. F. Skinner	1961–66, 1938–58	Cambridge, Mass.; Bloomington, Ind.; Cambridge, Mass.	University chairs	1 + N	QPE	15
46. Statistical decision theory (Math)	A. Wald	1939–50	New York, N.Y.	University chair	1 + N	QPE	15 ± 5
47. Operations research and systems analysis (Math)	P. M. S. Blackett, P. Morse, R. Bellman	1941–50, 1941–58	London, Eng.; Cambridge, Mass.	Government research institutes	N	QPE	5
48. Scaling theory (Psy)	L. Guttman, C. Coombs	1941–54	Ithaca, N.Y.; Ann Arbor, Mich.	University chairs	3 + N	QFE	10 ± 5

Contribution 1	Contributor 2	Time 3	Place 4	Type of support 5	No. of workers 6	Quantitative aspects 7	Years until impact 8
49. Quantitative models of nationalism and integration (Pol)	K. Deutsch, B. Russett, R. L. Merritt	1942–67	Cambridge, Mass. New Haven, Conn.	University chairs	1 + N	QFE	20 ± 5
50. Theories of economic development (Ec)	P. Rosenstein-Rodan, R. Prebisch, R. Nurkse, W. A. Lewis, G. Myrdal, A. O. Hirschman, R. F. Harrod, E. Domar, H. Chenery	1943–58	London, Eng. Santiago, Chile New York, N.Y. Manchester, Eng. Stockholm, Swed. New Haven, Conn. Oxford, Eng. Baltimore, Md. Stanford, Calif.	Government offices, U.N. regional commission, university chairs	6 + N	QFE	10 ± 5
51. Computers (Math)	V. Bush, S. Caldwell, D. P. Eckert, J. W. Mauchly	1943–58	Cambridge, Mass. Philadelphia, Pa.	University and government research laboratories	N	QFE	10 ± 5
52. Multivariate analysis linked to social theory (Soc)	S. Stouffer, T. W. Anderson, P. Lazarsfeld	1944–54	Washington, D.C. Cambridge, Mass. New York, N.Y.	Government and university research institutes	3 + N	QFE	5
53. Information theory, cybernetics and feedback systems (Math)	C. Shannon, N. Wiener	1944–58	Cambridge, Mass. Orange, N.J.	University research institute and Bell Laboratories	2 + N	QFE	10 ± 5
54. Econometrics (Ec)	J. Tinbergen, P. Samuelson, E. Malinvaud	1935–40 1947 1964	The Hague, Neth. Cambridge, Mass. Paris, Fr.	Government institute and university chairs	1 + N	QFE	10 ± 5
55. Cognitive dynamics of science (Phil)	J. B. Conant, I. B. Cohen, T. Kuhn, D. deS. Price	1946–64	Cambridge, Mass. Berkeley, Calif. New Haven, Conn.	University chairs	3 + N	Non-Q	15
56. Computer simulation of economic systems (Ec)	L. Klein, G. Orcutt	1947–60	Philadelphia, Pa. Madison, Wis.	Research institutes	2 + N	QFE	5
57. Structuralism in anthropology and social science (An)	C. Levi-Strauss	1949–66	Paris, Fr.	Museum (government)	1 + N	QPI	15 ± 5
58. Hierarchical computerized decision models (Math)	H. Simon	1950–65	Pittsburgh, Pa.	University research institute	1 + N	QPE	10
59. Cost-benefit analysis (planned programming and budgeting) (Pol)	C. Hitch	1956–63	Santa Monica, Calif.	Government-related research institute	3 + N	QFE	7
60. Computer simulation of social and political systems (Pol)	W. McPhee, H. Simon, A. Newell, I. Pool, R. Abelson	1956–66 1958–64	Pittsburgh, Pa. Cambridge, Mass. New Haven, Conn.	University chairs and research institutes	2 + N	QPE	5 ± 3
61. Conflict theory and variable sum games (Psy)	A. Rapoport	1960–	Ann Arbor, Mich.	University research institute	1 + N	QFE	2
62. Stochastic models of social processes (Math)	J. S. Coleman	1965	Baltimore, Md.	University and research institute	1 + N	QFE	5

8. Did such breakthroughs require much capital? Manpower? Other resources?

9. Where were they accomplished? At what geographic locations? At what types of institutions? Under what social and political conditions?

10. Where did the ideas come from? Were most advances made primarily within existing disciplines, or were they mainly interdisciplinary in character?

11. Did the major advances have any close relation to social practice? Were they inspired or provoked by practical demands or conflicts? Were they applied to practice? If so, were they applied by or to individuals, small or middle-sized groups, or national governments and states?

12. How long was the delay between each major breakthrough and its first major impact on social science or social practice, or both?

Some of the evidence bearing on these questions is summarized in Table 1 in relation to the 62 achievements in the years 1900-65. The achievements themselves were selected on the basis of our personal judgment as to their importance for social science in this century. We also called upon the opinions and advice of a number of colleagues in other fields, and we checked each contribution against the relevant entries of the recent edition of *International Encyclopedia of the Social Sciences.*(1)

The full range of answers to our questions, including various kinds of statistical analyses, will be given elsewhere,(2) but some of the broad results of more general interest are summarized here. There are three principal findings from this study. 1. There *are* such things as social science achievements and social inventions, which are almost as clearly defined and as operational as technological achievements and inventions. 2. These achievements have commonly been the result of conscious and systematic research and development efforts by individuals or teams working on particular problems in a small number of interdisciplinary centers. 3. These achievements have had widespread acceptance or major social effects in surprisingly short times; median times are in the range of 10 to 15 years, a range comparable with the median times for widespread acceptance of major technological inventions.

CRITERIA FOR RECOGNIZING MAJOR ADVANCES

The major achievements or breakthroughs selected for this study were defined as having the following characteristics. First, they either had to involve a new perception of relationships or they had to result in new operations, including scientific operations. That is, they had to help people see something not perceived before, as represented by new discoveries (statements of the form "there is . . .") or new verifiable propositions (statements of the form "if . . . then . . ."); or else they had to create the possibility of doing something that had not been done before.

A second essential condition for any major contribution, whether of perceptions or of operations, was that it should have proved fruitful in producing a substantial impact that led to further knowledge. Impacts simply upon social practice were treated as interesting but nonessential.

We believe that the 62 contributions listed in Table 1 are among the most significant achievements in social science that satisfy these criteria in the years 1900-65. We should emphasize that there is no intent to use this list for any invidious bestowal of professional recognition and that other achievements might well be chosen by other critiera of significance or for other purposes.

We omitted purely technical achievements such as television, in spite of their great impact on society, in the belief that they have thus far not contributed to social science in the way, for instance, that computers have. We also omitted the more purely political and organizational achievements, such as the National Aeronautics and Space Administration (NASA), the Manhattan Project, the British National Health Service, the European Common Market, the Tennessee Valley Authority, credit cards, "think tanks," the great public and private foundations, the Peace Corps, and the partial Nuclear Test Ban Treaty, although all these have intellectual components that would justify their inclusion in a broader list. On the same grounds, we omitted such primarily practical innovations as Henry Ford's development of the assembly line; the time and motion studies by F. W. Taylor and his followers; the studies of human relations in industry by F. J. Roethlisberger and his associates; the development of such rural organizations as the *kibbutzim* in Israel and the *kolkhozy* in the Soviet Union; B. Ruml's invention of the "pay-as-you-go income tax"; the development of high-information teaching by J. Zacharias and associates; man-and-computer designs as developed by C. E. Shannon, R. Fano, and others; and the proposal for a guaranteed annual income, or a negative income tax, by J. Tobin, M. Friedman, and other economists. By contrast, the innovations by Lenin, Mao, Gandhi, and the Webbs were included because they were connected with explicit theories.

Several contributions seemed to us to constitute borderline cases. In social psychology, these include the frustration-aggression hypothesis by J. Dollard, N. Miller, and their collaborators (New Haven, Connecticut, 1940); the theory of cognitive dissonance developed by L. Festinger, R. Abelson, and others (Stanford, California, and New Haven, 1956-57); the development of cognitive anthropology by F. Lounsbury and others (New Haven, 1956-68); the concept and measurement of the semantic differential by C. Osgood, G. J. Suci, and P. H. Tannenbaum (Urbana, Illinois, 1957); and the concept and partial measurement of achievement motivation by D. E. McClelland (Middletown, Connecticut, 1953, and later Cambridge, Massachusetts, 1961). At the borderlines of psychology, we find the discovery of a wider range of mind-influencing drugs; the works of K. Lorenz and others on "imprinting" in young animals; the broader explorations in the chemistry of memory; and the work on the electric stimulation on brain centers directing larger sequences of behavior, by J. Delgado and others. None of these have been included in our present list, primarily because we were not sure that the impact of any of these contributions on broader areas of the social sciences has been as large and lasting, so far, as the impact of the contributions that we did include. A future tabulation may well have to include some or all of these present-day borderline cases. In any case, a comparison with our tables in this article will show that an inclusion of these borderline cases would have strengthened rather than weakened the trends indicated by our major findings.

Clearly, other individuals and other schools of thought would have a different ranking for particular achievements, but one would hope that within our chosen boundaries there would be a considerable amount of overlap within the academic community in evaluating the top 50 to 70 contributions in this century.

An inspection of our list shows that many of the later contributions were clearly building on the earlier ones, and that they resulted in clear increases in the powers of social scientists to recognize relationships and to carry out operations. Many of the advances had a substantial impact on the subsequent development of several social sciences and on social practice as well. Together these advances add up to unmistakable evidence of the cumulative growth of knowledge in the social sciences in the course of this century. Today, statements such as "we know no more about human psychology and politics than Aristotle did" mainly express the ignorance of those who utter them.

MAIN FIELDS OF ADVANCES

The assignment of major social science innovations to particular fields is indicated in column 1 of Table 1, and their distribution among fields is shown in column 1 of Table 2. Table 2 reveals the leading position of psychology, economics, and politics with 13, 12, and 11 major contributions, respectively. On the average, therefore, a major advance was made every 5 or 6 years in *each* of these three fields.

Several contributions that involve the applications of mathematical and statistical methods to these subject fields are included in these numbers; thus linear programming and the computer simulation of economic systems were each coded as contributions to economics.

There were 11 major contributions that were primarily mathematical or statistical in nature but that were coded in a separate category, even though they may have had applications in various substantive fields. Factor analysis and information theory are two examples of this category. Although these coding rules tend to underrepresent the number of major advances in social science methods, it still appears that a major advance in mathematical or statistical method was made on the average at least once every 6 years.

Substantive advances in sociology seemed to have occurred once per decade, and in anthropology about once every 20 years. These calculations somehow underrepresent, however, the actual rate of progress in these fields, particularly with regard to sociology. Several of the advances in social psychology, political

TABLE 2.

Major Social Science Contributions by Field and Focus,
1900 to 1965

Field	Total	Major contributions		Focus on theory		Focus on method		Focus on results	
	1900 to 1965	1900 to 1929	1930 to 1965	1900 to 1929	1930 to 1965	1900 to 1929	1930 to 1965	1900 to 1929	1930 to 1965
Psychology	13	7	6	6	3	6	6	6	6
Economics	12	5	7	4	5	4	6	5	7
Politics	11	7	4	7	2	2	4	4	4
Mathematical statistics	11	4	7	2	5	4	7	4	6
Sociology	7	6	1	4	1	5	1	6	1
Philosophy	5	3	2	3	2	2	2	0	1
Anthropology	3	1	2	1	2	0	2	1	2
Total	62	33	29	27	20	23	28	26	27

science, and even economics were almost as important for the progress of sociology as they were in their fields of origin.

Another five contributions resemble those in mathematics and statistics in that their primary impact was not in any substantive fields of social science. Since they were not primarily quantitative, however, we coded them in a separate category as philosophy, logic, and history of science. Russell and Whitehead's demonstration of the unity of logic and science, the work of the Vienna circle on the unity of science, and Kuhn's work on the role of paradigms in scientific revolutions are examples of such entries.

Important advances typically combine theory, methods, and results, rather than choosing one of these elements as a focus of interest. Our analysis of these factors is summarized in Table 2. Most often such advances have cut across at least two of these aspects of social science and have often crossed all three of them. In the light of these findings the long-standing quarrel about whether to emphasize theory, methodology, or empirical results seems ill-conceived and obsolete. All three seem to form part of one production cycle of knowledge, and substantial advances in any one of these three phases are likely to lead to advances in the other two.

TRENDS WITH TIME

Substantial social science advances at the level of importance examined here have been surprisingly frequent, averaging close to one advance per year. When we take into account the greater difficulty of estimating the full impact of social science contributions after 1950, which drastically reduces the number of such contributions in our count, it seems that this high frequency has remained at least undiminished since 1930. Social science investigators who need to keep informed in several disciplines thus face serious problems in the partial obsolescence of their information.

A more detailed analysis indicates that the distribution of advances shows a certain amount of clustering in time. Particular fields show "great periods" of 5 to 15 years during which substantial advances were frequent, and two such great periods, 1925-29 and 1940-44, are common to many fields. (If several promising contributions that we considered but did not include in our count should prove to be fundamental, then the decade 1955-65 may yet prove to have been another period of greatness.) Since great periods often last several years, whereas 10 to 15 years may be required for working out the implications of particular achievements or for applying them to practice (Table 1, column 8), it would seem rational to organize 10- or 15-year programs of support in any social science field after a few initial breakthroughs have occurred.

Individual researchers produced nearly two-thirds of all major advances over the entire 1960-65 period, but our study indicates that their share declined from about three-quarters of all contributions before 1930 to less than one-half thereafter (Table 1, column 6). Teams of social scientists, by contrast, increased their contributions from less than one-quarter before 1930 to more than one-half thereafter. Teams of social scientists seem likely to be the main source of major advances during the next decade, but individual social scientists operating in the traditional "great man" or "lone wolf" styles will continue to be a significant, though secondary, source of new ideas.

AGES OF THE CONTRIBUTORS

The ages of the contributors at the time they made their breakthroughs have also been examined. Details of the analysis will not be given here, but for the entire period 1900-65, the median age group among 160 contributors was between 35 and 39 years, with a mean of 37 years. The modal age group, with 40 contributors, was a little older, in the range of 40 to 44 years. Slightly more than 40 percent of all contributors were more than 40 years old at the time of their contribution, but only 6 percent were over 50 years. The psychologists tend to be somewhat younger, the sociologists and anthropologists somewhat older, than the contributors in the other fields.

Since 1930 the contributors tend to be younger, with the modal age moving to the 30 to 34 age group. However, this could be an artifact, due to our better knowledge of the earlier stages of more recent developments. It also seems that the youngest contributors are in the fields with the largest number of contributors. Conceivably some fields are intrinsically more difficult today and require more experience for any successes.

It is worth emphasizing that older scientists are necessarily less numerous in any rapidly growing field, as D. Price has noted.(3) Since the number of social scientists grew between 1900 and 1965 at a rate of about 5 percent per year, doubling every 14 years, the proportion of scientists in the age groups 20 to 34, 35 to 49, and 50 to 64 at any given time is roughly as 4:2:1. When the creativity curves are normalized to take account of these differences in numbers, the creativity of men over 50 for social science achievements of this sort is comparable to that of the men under 35, but the mode is still in the 35- to 49-year range.

Our findings on the ages of peak creativity in these fields are in fair agreement with those of H. C. Lehman for the fields of architecture, psychology, economics, and education theory.(4)

Our biographical information is uneven and incomplete, but it suggests that the key members of the post-1930 teams were not colorless cogs in an anonymous machine. Usually we find among them strong and highly individualistic personalities, with some of the strengths and weaknesses found in the personalities of artists. Often they have appeared to some of their contemporaries as "rude and overbearing men," impatient with disagreement and obtuseness and unwilling to suffer fools or critics gladly. The decisive difference from the past is that today these creative individuals nonetheless know how to work with other people, how to support others, and how to elicit their cooperation and support in turn. Indeed, a surprising number of them founded significant organizations or institutes to carry on their work.

Quantitative problems or findings (or both) characterized two-thirds of all advances, and five-sixths of those were made after 1930 (Table 1, column 7). Completely nonquantitative contributions — the recognition of new patterns without any clear implication of quantitative problems — were rare throughout the period and extremely rare since 1930. Nonetheless, they include such substantial contributions as psychoanalysis, Rorschach tests, and the work on personality and culture; thus, their potential for major contributions in the future should not be underrated. Certainly both types of scientific personalities, the quantifiers and the pattern-recognizers — the "counters" and the "poets" — will continue to be needed in the social sciences.

REQUIREMENTS IN CAPITAL, MANPOWER, AND TIME

The making and testing of any new discovery require some kind of investment in the form of capital equipment, manpower, or the principal investigator's time. Libraries represent relatively low capital requirements, per investigator, but special laboratories, computing facilities, and organizations for survey or implementation represent high capital requirements.

In manpower, the extremes are represented by a single scientist working at a desk, or by the need for large numbers of laboratory assistants, polltakers, or tabulating clerks. In time, some achievements may require relatively short periods of insight and working out, whereas others require years of the principal investigator's time and thought, as did Max Weber's historical and sociological studies or Freud's development of psychoanalysis. We have coded each contribution in terms of these three types of requirements and analyzed their distributions.

Of particular interest was the difference in high and low capital requirements for the quantitative and the nonquantitative contributions, as summarized in Table 3. Here we find that out of 26 high capital contributions during the entire period, 18 produced explicit quantitative findings, whereas out of 36 contributions with low capital requirements only 14 produced such explicit quantitative results. There was already a tendency toward higher capital requirements for quantitative work in the 1900-29 period, but it becomes considerably stronger after 1930 as high capital work has become more frequent.

TABLE 3.

Capital Requirements and Quantitative Results,
1900 to 1965.
"High" and "Low" Refer to the Level of Capital Required.

Type of result	1900 to 1929		1930 to 1965		1900 to 1965	
	High	Low	High	Low	High	Low
Nonquantitative results	1	6	0	2	1	8
Applications to quantitative problems explicit and/or implied	3	9	4	5	7	14
Quantitative findings explicit	4	10	14	4	18	14
Total	8	25	18	11	26	36

The perception of social science work as cheap — a notion that is widespread among laymen and some university administrators — seems based on the experiences before 1930, when only one-fourth of all major social science contributions required major amounts of capital. Since 1930 more than three-fifths of all contributions have required relatively large amounts of capital, particularly for survey research and large-scale tabulations (see Table 3), and this proportion seems likely to increase in the future. If explicit quantitative results are desired, the requirement for capital support becomes still stronger. Low-budget research, the work of lone individuals, or work on nonquantitative topics may play a smaller and smaller role. The industrial revolution in the production of knowledge has not only reached a large part of the natural sciences but has reached the social sciences as well.

An analysis of major social science contributions by location is difficult because many investigators moved during the course of their work and because many advances involved the work of several investigators with changing institutional affiliations. Also, our own greater familiarity with some countries, institutions, and fields of social science may have distorted our assignments of location. Nevertheless, some relationships in the data come out so strongly that it seems unlikely that they could have been produced by errors of this kind, and they raise some interesting questions about the conditions for creativity in the social sciences.

The results of the geographical analysis of the data in column 4 of Table 1 are shown in Tables 4 and 5. In this coding we have counted all locations where any of our 62 important advances appear to have been initiated, which gives a total of 101 locations. However, the continuation of an advance initiated elsewhere was not counted separately, even if the initiator had moved to the new location to carry on his work. Thus, the work of the Vienna circle in the philosophy of science was credited both to Vienna and Berlin (H. Reichenbach) but not to Chicago, where the work was continued after 1936.

Tables 4 and 5 show that in the period 1900-29 Europe produced three-fourths of the contributions, but after 1930 the United States produced more than three-fourths, even though our method of coding tended to favor the assignment of contributions to their first origins in Europe. (Of the American contributions in the second period, only five could be credited in the main to European-born Americans.)

Two countries, the United States and Britain, produced more than 50 percent of all major social science contributions in the 1900-29 period, and almost 90 percent in the 1930-65 period. After 1930 contributions made in the United States greatly exceeded those from the rest of the world.

Within countries, a very few capital cities or univesity centers accounted for the great majority of all contributions; other cities and university centers of comparable size contributed little or nothing (see Table 5). Of the British contributions, one-half or more came from London and one-third from Cambridge, but the social science contribution of Oxford was minor. In the United States, one-half of all contributions before 1930 came from Chicago (7 out of 12). For 1900-65 as a whole, three centers – Chicago, Cambridge, and New York – provided more than one-half of all American contributions, with Washington, Ann Arbor, and New Haven providing another one-quarter. Since these six centers represent only a small minority of American social scientists [20 percent in the 1968 edition of *American Men of Science*(5)], they evidently achieved an increase in effectiveness by an order of magnitude for the men working in these centers, with one-fifth of the scientists producing about three times as many contributions as the remaining four-fifths. By contrast, centers like Berkeley and Princeton, so eminent in other scientific fields, each initiated only one major social science contribution during these 65 years, and a metropolis like Los Angeles made no contribution at all.

These concentrations of social science achievements in particular countries and particular centers seem to be even more marked than the concentrations in modern physics and biology, and they do not seem directly related to any general factors such as increased war funding or science funding in the fields involved. We surmise that contributions to social science may be extremely sensitive to external economies, such as the presence of local subcultures with other first-rate investigators and facilities in other fields, as well as to an intellectual climate specifically favorable to social science in the country and in the local community.

More than three-quarters of all contributions were made under democratic regimes. The remnant were made under authoritarian regimes and under communist dictatorships. Anticommunist totalitarian dictatorships such as Italian Fascism, German National Socialism, and Japanese militarism produced no major social science contributions at all.

In institutional terms, universities have been the prime source of intellectual advances (Table 1, column 5), but in the later period it is the university and government interdisciplinary institutes and "think tanks" that have accounted for about two-thirds of all contributions, as shown in Table 6.

Interdisciplinary work has been a major intellectual source of contributions throughout the period; responsible for nearly one-half of all advances from 1900 to 1929, it produced nearly two-thirds of the total thereafter. This growing importance of interdisciplinary work reinforces our finding of the great importance of locating social science work at major intellectual centers, in proximity to many kinds of information and expertise from many disciplines. Locating a highly specialized social science enterprise at a small town or college, "far away from all distractions," seems, on the contrary, to be a very promising prescription for sterility.

RELATION TO SOCIAL PRACTICE, DEMANDS, AND CONFLICTS

Details will be omitted here, but our analysis indicates that practical demands or conflicts *stimulated* about three-fourths of all contributions between 1900 and 1965. In fact, as the years went on, their share rose from two-thirds before 1930 to more than four-fifths thereafter. The contributions of "ivory-tower" social scientists in the future seem apt to be minor indeed.

Major social science advances were *applied* to social practice in almost exactly the same proportion as they were stimulated by it, and they showed

Table 4. Geographic locations of major social science advances,

	By Continents			
	Europe	North America (U.S.A.)	Other	Total
1900-29	33	12	4	49
1930-65	11	41	0	52
1900-65	44	53	4	101

considerable practical importance. Applications were most frequent at the level of social groups. Applications to problems of individuals occurred in about one-quarter of the cases in both periods. Applications to national policy increased from about one-third before 1930 to about two-thirds thereafter.

Increasingly, however, the same social science contributions produced applications at more than one level of the social system. Applications to individuals and groups, to groups and states or to all three levels together rose from less than one-half of all advances before 1930 to more than two-thirds of all advances between 1930 and 1965.

On the record, major advances in social sciences have been highly usable in practice and increasingly more so in the recent past. In all likelihood, such advances will be still more usable in the years ahead, if we take the trouble to make them so.

TIME DELAY IN THE IMPACT OF MAJOR ADVANCES

Like all advances in any science, social science advances take time before they have any identifiable impact on a broader field of scientific activity or on the practical affairs of society. Our estimates of this delay for each of the advances on our list are given in the last column of Table 1.

For the period 1900-65 as a whole, the minimum delay of the impact for nearly three-quarters of the major advances was less than 10 years, the median delay was about 10 years, and the maximum delay was in the neighborhood of 15 years. These figures may understate the true length of the delay because for the recent period, as for any time-limited study, the achievements with longer delays are less likely to be recognized and are underrepresented. As a practical rule of thumb it may be safer, therefore, to expect the first major impact of a social science advance to be delayed by 10 to 15 years after its inception.

Nevertheless, the delays in the recent period seem to have been decreasing, as might be expected in a society with greatly increased higher education and faster communications networks. The most frequent median delay time dropped from between 11 and 20 years in the years 1900-29 to less than 10 years in the years 1930-65; and the most frequent maximum delay time declined from about 25 years before 1930 to about 15 years in the more recent period. If one wishes to

1900-65 (by continents and by countries in Europe).

| | | By Countries in Europe | | | | | | |
	England	Germany	Russia	Austria	France	Swit-zerland	Other	Total
1900-29	13	8	4	3	1	2	2	33
1930-65	4	2	1	1	1	0	2	11
1900-65	17	10	5	4	2	2	4	44

Table 5. Geographic locations of major social
science advances, 1900 to 1965 (by cities).

	1900 to 1929	1930 to 1965	1900 to 1965
England			
London	7	2	9
Cambridge	4	1	5
Oxford	2	0	2
Manchester	0	1	1
Total	13	4	17
Germany			
Berlin	3	1	4
Heidelberg	2	0	2
Frankfurt	1	1	2
Munich	1	0	1
Freiburg	1	0	1
Total	8	2	10
Austria			
Vienna	3	1	4
Russia			
Leningrad	2	1	3
Moscow	1	0	1
Shushenskoe, Siberia	1	0	1
Total	4	1	5
Others in Europe			
Paris	1	1	2
Turin	1	0	1
Lausanne	1	0	1
Herisau	1	0	1
Brno	1	0	1
Rotterdam	0	1	1
Stockholm	0	1	1
Total	5	3	8
United States			
Chicago	7	3	10
Cambridge	1	9	10
New York	2	5	7
Washington	0	5	5
Ann Arbor	1	3	4
New Haven	1	3	4
Ithaca	0	2	2
Pittsburgh	0	2	2
Philadelphia	0	2	2
Princeton	0	1	1
Orange	0	1	1
Baltimore	0	1	1
Madison	0	1	1
Bloomington	0	1	1
Berkeley	0	1	1
Santa Monica	0	1	1
Total	12	41	53

extrapolate from these data, one might surmise that the time lags of impact may be further shortened in the future. However, part of this decrease in the time delay may be due to the tendency of research institutions or governments today to support research that is expected to have an early impact on practical affairs, and it may not be characteristic of more fundamental contributions.

TABLE 6

Types of Institutions Where Major Social Science Advances
Were Initiated, 1900 to 1965.

Type	1900 to 1929	1930 to 1965	1900 to 1965
1. University chair or lectureship	19	10	29
2. Institute or project	6	12	18
3. Government research organization	2	7	9
4. Combined items 2 and 3	8	19	27
5. Nongovernmental political organization	5	0	5
6. Other	1	0	1
Total	33	29	62

These time data suggest the desirability of extending the support of fundamental social science research efforts in the form of 10- or 15-year programs at clearly favorable locations. This more sustained support might encounter political and bureaucratic difficulties, but it would seem to be the most promising strategy for making and consolidating advances like those described here in our basic understanding of social relationships and in our ability to solve pressing social problems.

The radical increase in natural science knowledge and in its application has produced a radical increase in the problems of coordination in all industrialized societies. To cope with this radical increase in urgent problems it seems essential to produce an early and large increase in social science knowledge and in its constructive applications. The evidence here suggests that the intellectual and organizational means for such an increase are at hand if we care to use them.

REFERENCES AND NOTES

(1) *International Encyclopedia of the Social Sciences*, D. L. Sills, Ed. (Macmillan, New York, 1968). 17 vols. For specific advice we are indebted to R. Dorfman, A. O. Hirschman, S. Kuznets, W. Leontief, G. Quarton, A. Rapoport, J. D. Singer, G. E. Swanson, and others. None of these, of course, should be saddled with responsibility for our present work.

(2) K. W. Deutsch, J. Platt, D. Senghaas, "Major Advances in Social Science Since 1900: An Analysis of Conditions and Effects of Creativity," in preparation.

(3) D. J. deS. Price, *Nature* 206, 233 (1965).

(4) H. C. Lehman, *Age and Achievement* (Princeton Univ. Press, Princeton, N. J., 1953), pp. 324-326.

(5) *American Men of Science: The Social and Behavioral Sciences* (Bowker, New York, ed. 11. 1968). 2 vols.

RECONSTRUCTION OF EDUCATIONAL RESEARCH

Lee S. Shulman

> If there are some subjects on which the results obtained have finally received the unanimous assent of all who have attended to the proof, and others which ... have never succeeded in establishing any considerable body of truths, so as to be beyond denial or doubt; it is by generalizing the methods successfully followed in the former enquiries, and adapting them to the latter, that we may hope to remove this blot on the face of science.
>
> John Stuart Mill

> Some of the major disasters of mankind have been produced by the narrowness of men with a good methodology.... To set limits to speculation is treason to the future.
>
> Alfred North Whitehead

Educational research has been tried and apparently it has failed. Or has it?

If the object of such research is the development of coherent and workable theories, researchers are nearly as far from that goal today as they are from controlling the weather. If the goal of educational research is significant improvement in the daily functioning of educational programs, I know of little evidence that researchers have made discernible strides in that direction. Which way then do they turn? To more of the same? Or to a pragmatic attack on highly specific educational problems, eschewing theory development as a goal? Or do they reexamine the basic paradigms and parameters of both education and research in order to seek new directions? In this paper, I argue that neither a slavish continuation of current practices nor a monolithic rejection of them is likely to solve the problems of educational research. Researchers must step back, to solve the problems of educational research. Researchers must step back, regain perspective and then identify clearly the most fruitful routes toward development of an empirically based discipline of education.

I begin this paper with a brief examination of the nature of education and the history of its relations with the behavioral sciences, especially psychology. Then I discuss certain characteristics of the instructional process and problems involved in its study. I conclude this paper with a review of potentially useful strategies of educational research and the institutional prerequisites for their successful implementation.

RETROSPECT: EDUCATION AND PSYCHOLOGY

Moving up the phylogenetic scale, one finds that the period of childhood characteristic of the different species increases in length. Moving from the less complex to the more complex organisms, the relative proportions of instinct to learning as forces influencing behavior rapidly change, until, with man, the role of learning is so central that the concept of instinct becomes nearly irrelevant. Even in the highly nativistic theory of language acquisition proposed by Chomsky (1965) and his followers (see Lenneberg, 1967), learning plays a control role in the development of specific linguistic performance. Thus, the major discontinuity between the human species and all others lies in what McNeil (1963) has called "systematic developmental retardation."

> Indeed, the helplessness of human young must at first have been an extraordinary hazard to survival. But this handicap had compensations, which in the long run, redounded in truly extraordinary fashion to the advantage of mankind. For it opened wide the gates to the possibility of cultural as against merely biological evolution. . . . Biologically considered, the interesting mark of humanity was systematic developmental retardation, making the human child infantile in comparison to the normal protohuman. But developmental retardation, of course, meant prolonged plasticity, so that learning could be lengthened. Thereby, the range of cultural as against mere biological evolution widened enormously; and humanity launched itself upon a biologically as well as historically extraordinary career. . . . By permitting, indeed compelling, men to instruct their children in the arts of life, the prolonged period of infancy and childhood made it possible for human communities to eventually raise themselves above the animal level from which they began.
>
> (McNeil, 1963; pp. 20,21)

Thus, the absence of instinct, the absence of prefabricated behavior patterns which program the organism at a very early stage in his development, provides man with his most human characteristics — his educability. This malleability acts as a two-edged sword, for with plasticity comes not only the potential for limitless growth, but also the danger of inestimable damage.

Recognizing that man's education and the scope of his educability are the most human things about him, it seems only appropriate that those disciplines which purport to study man and his nature should concentrate rather heavily upon studies of his schooling. American psychology at the beginning of this century did precisely that. The great men of that period of American psychology — William James, E. L. Thorndike, G. Stanley Hall, Robert Woodworth, John Dewey and others — were vitally interested in studies of the educational process. Such investigations lay at the heart of American psychological thinking during that time. However, influenced by Lloyd Morgan's (1894) Canon which effectively placed unobservable mental processes out of bounds for psychological study, the discipline of scientific psychology in America was slowly transformed from James's (1890) "Science of Mental Life" to Watson's (1913) "Science of Behavior." In that generally fruitful-antimentalistic revolution was discarded not only the bath water of Titchenerian introspectionism but also, tragically, the baby of experimental educational research. Despite Thorndike's continuing admonitions that the proper laboratory for the psychologist was the classroom and its proper subject was the pupil, the study of infrahuman species and their behavior came to dominate psychology. In many ways the efforts of the rat or primate-oriented psychologists contributed significantly to man's understanding of the natural world. It would be an overstatement to assert that the study of school learning disappeared completely from psychology. It would be even more misleading to deny that such studies were now peripheral to the developing tradition of American experimental psychology.

Ironically, Soviet psychology, though greatly influenced by the Pavlovian tradition, never abandoned studies of school learning as a major component of psychological research (Menchinskaya, 1969). Because of the political and social importance of education in the Marxist-Leninist tradition, Soviet psychological studies focused frequently on instruction as a variable of interest. Kilpatrick and Wirszup (1969) report that in a recent year 37.5% of all materials published in Soviet psychology was devoted to educational and child psychology.

The only area of educational psychological research in America which remained unscathed by this post-Watsonian revolution was that of the then still infant investigations of mental measurement. This tradition, growing out of the work of Galton, Spearman, Binet and Simon, J. M. Cattell, Terman and others, continued to flourish and received its greatest impetus from the success of mental testing during World War I. The emphasis of this movement was quantitative and descriptive. The objectives were the careful measurement and prediction of individual differences in human abilities. The schism between the respective *Weltanschauungen* of experimental psychology and mental measurement grew progressively wider, and it was not totally inappropriate that for many years educational psychology was identified with educational measurement. (For fuller discussion of the meaning and implication of this distinction, see Cronbach: 1957, 1967, see also Cattell: 1966b). It is only in the most recent period that these trends began to reverse. The two traditions with their respective and almost nonoverlapping methodologies are beginning to coalesce.

A good sign that a new field is becoming popular is the creation and proliferation of shorthand ways of exchanging fundamental concepts. *ATI* is already recognized by many educational researchers as the acronym for "aptitude-treatment interaction" (Cronbach and Snow, 1969), a research strategy characterized by the marriage of experimental and differential approaches. One of the major problems attendant on this marriage is the prosperity gap between the two principals. Whereas differential psychologists possess a wealth of methods for characterizing individual differences, the classification of environments, settings or treatments remains relatively primitive (Mitchell, 1969). "Aptitude-treatment interaction" will likely remain an empty phrase as long as aptitudes are measured by micrometer and environments are measured by divining rod.

In the next section I examine several aspects of environment as a factor in educational research: the problems of investigating the effects of environments, the kinds of variables that can be used to characterize environments and the relevance of environmental analysis to the methodology of educational experimentation.

THE STUDY OF ENVIRONMENTS

Social scientists are dramatically impotent in their ability to characterize environments. Generally, they do not even try. It should by now be a truism to point out that neither individuals nor groups can be adequately described without reference to some setting. Thus, for Dewey, the starting point of his discussions was always "some organism in some environment" (Dewey, 1938). Murray (1938) posited two equally important categories for his studies of personality: *needs* and *press*, i.e. person variables and environment variables. The language of education and the behavioral sciences is in great need of a set of terms for describing environments that is as articulated, specific and functional as those already possessed for characterizing individuals.

An example that is familiar to all educators is the continued use of such gross terms as "deprived" or "disadvantaged" to characterize the environments of many minority-group children. Labeling the setting as "disadvantaged," of course, communicates little that is meaningful about the characteristics of that environment. Educators seem unable to progress beyond such a simple dichotomy as "advantaged-disadvantaged." Reviewers and critics of research have long realized that even those few categories which attempt to describe environments, such as *social class*, have been remarkably ineffectual in pinpointing the educationally relevant differences in the backgrounds of individuals (Bloom, 1964; Karp and Sigel, 1965).

Imagine if the nutritionist, in his attempts to characterize the nutritional status of the diets of individuals, were to be limited to a distinction between "well-nourished" and "malnourished" individuals. One would be quite skeptical of the value of generalizations such as "malnourished individuals have a higher incidence of respiratory ailments than well-nourished," or "well-nourished subjects were observed to run significantly faster than malnourished subjects." Are educators pronouncements about all the differences between culturally-disadvantaged and culturally-advantaged children any more fruitful, And are the myriadic studies contrasting lower-class and middle-class youngsters of any great value? Such descriptive studies do not begin to suggest the necessary ingredients of experimental programs to change the conditions. Should one simply elevate all lower-class people to the middle-class? What could that possibly mean?

The nutritionist can describe the nutritional environment of individuals in terms of caloric content, relative proportions of carbohydrates, fats and protein, the presence or absence of quantities of vitamins and minerals, etc. (Eichenwald and Fry, 1969). Possessing such precise terms allows him to plan systematic tactics of modifying the nutritional status of individuals in terms of highly complex, yet manageable patterns. Attaining such a level of facility in character-izing the *educationally-relevant* facets of environments should be one of the major goals of educational research. Without such an understanding, researchers are clearly handicapped in any attempt to make intelligent comparisons among proposed educational programs, (such as Headstart models) for these programs are themselves planned environments.

A number of behavioral scientists have begun to study the characteristics of environments in a systematic fashion. Bloom's work (1964) is of special interest. Bloom reported many instances of great improvement in the effectiveness of academic prediction when measures of the intervening environments were taken into account in the prediction equations. He emphasized that researchers must replace the older, static terms for describing environments (e.g., social class) with dynamic, process variables (e.g., achievement press). As evidence for this assertion, he cited the research of Dave (1963) and Wolf (1964). Such process variables could well prove to have causal influences on the characteristics of interest. This would have to be demonstrated through techniques of cross-validation. The goal of all such predictive research should be, Bloom maintained, not the inexorable stamping of fates on helpless children, but the identification of the critical processes contributing to those fates. An understanding of the process variables most responsible for the ultimate status of individuals in some growth area can provide valuable guidance as researchers attempt to develop effective methods for modifying those processes and, hence, for destroying the accuracy of their predictions.

The work of Barker and his colleagues (1968) reflects a totally different set of strategies — those of ecological psychology — for studying the environment. Pace and Stern (1958) applied the tools of psychological measurement to the task of characterizing the essential differences among college environments. Henry (1963) used the methods of anthropological investigations to study the home and school as elements of culture. From his work came the compelling concept of the "hidden curriculum" in the middle-class home. Workers in the field of sociology have long been involved in studies of the environment. In a recent review, Cartwright (1968) examined the sociologists' approaches to the problems of "ecological variables." Mitchell (1969) discussed the characterization of environments for studies of peron-environment interactions in educational research. It is only through such environment-centered research that behavioral scientists can develop adequate terms to describe the educationally relevant attributes of the settings within which human learning occurs.

THE EXPERIMENTAL SETTING: ENVIRONMENT FOR RESEARCH

In addition to the need for increased activity in the characterization and measurement of general environments, educational researchers must devote attention to one particular kind of environment with which they work most frequently — the experimental setting, with special reference to the tasks they create for the study of human behavior.

Most formal education currently involves groups of children studying standard school subjects. It seems clear that the classical psychological theories of learning and motivation are not capable of explaining or guiding those school activities. The reason for this incapacity can be expressed in terms analogous to those used to explain the limitations of transfer-of-training. To the extent that research is conducted in a setting similar in its characteristics to the school situation, to that extent one will get reasonable extrapolations from it to the classroom milieu.

It should be no surprise that the history of behavioral science research in education is not particularly glorious. The differences between the human learning laboratory and the typical classroom are numerous. The differences between the animal learning laboratory and the classroom are far greater. Researchers have been all too quick to generalize even from the latter setting to classroom behavior. In discussing the inadequacy of psychoanalysis as a general personality theory, Bettelheim (1960) cited quite parallel conditions. He pointed out that psychoanalysis was doomed to failure as a general personality theory because all of its generalizations were extrapolations from that most restricted of experimental settings, the psychoanalytic couch. In the same manner, does it not seem presumptuous to expect that a learning theory based upon evidence from the T-maze, the pigeon's press-bar or the memory drum can effectively be used to guide the planning of that most complex of human endeavors, the typical classroom? This is not to deny the future relevance of "conclusion-oriented" inquiry (Cronbach and Suppes, 1969) to the conduct of schooling. The present gap between such studies and needed educational applications is simply too great. An intermediate level of investigation is needed to bridge that gap and create the basis for educational theory.

There is a danger in the overextension of this principle of judging the relevance of research settings by their congruence with actual school settings. One must not be trapped into always viewing the contemporary configuration in which pupils, teachers, and schools are found as the necessary setting to which experimental results must always transfer. There is no *ipso facto* reason to judge that the current status of schooling is the only possible or necessary way to organize education. The educational researcher must be prepared to introduce change, not only into the experimental treatment, but into his conception of the accepted forms of instruction as well.

Researchers are caught in a bind. To maximize the *internal validity* of experiments, they develop carefully monitored settings within which they can govern their research. This has long been recognized as a necessity, but it is likely that the experimental tradition in Ameica over-emphasized the importance of reliability and precision at the expense of the characteristics affecting that other factor of equal importance in the development of experimental settings, *external validity* (Campbell and Stanley, 1963; Wiggins, 1968). It is not sufficient that the individuals studied as a sample are truly representative of that human population to which the results of a particular experiment will be inferred. Researchers must also ascertain that the experimental conditions can serve as a sample from which to make inferences to a population of external conditions of interest. That is, researchers must also attempt to *maximize the similarity* between the conditions in which they study behavior and those other conditions, whatever they may be, to which researchers may ultimately wish to make inferences. The similarity should hold between the psychologically meaningful features of the settings, not merely between the manifest aspects of the two situations.

Brunswick (1956, p. 39) wrote that "proper sampling of situations and problems may in the end be more important than proper sampling of subjects, considering the fact that individuals are probably on the whole much more alike than are situations among one another." Bracht and Glass (1968) analyzed in detail some of the problems of external validity in educational research, distinguishing *population validity* from *ecological validity*. Their emphasis in the latter category, however, is typically on the features associated with the research context, rather than on the specific features of the experimental tasks themselves. There is no doubt that such factors as Hawthorne Effect, Experimenter Effect, Pretest or Posttest Sensitization are important sources of ecological invalidity. I would focus, however, on the problem of *task validity*. Are the actual mental operations or behaviors the subject is called upon to perform in the course of the experiment reasonably congruent with what takes place in the external domain of interest?

Psychological investigation of verbal learning, concept learning, and problem solving — which ought to be most useful to educators — is most culpable on these grounds. Within these three areas lie most of the objectives of formal education. An excellent example of lack of external validity comes from verbal learning research which is shackled to the ubiquitous memory drum or to its apparent heir, the tachistoscope-linked Carousel slide projector. If by external validity is meant the ability to infer the results of studies using a Lafayette memory drum to others using a drum by MTA, then little criticism can be leveled against verbal learning investigators. But if one sees the goals of such research more broadly, as Ebbinghaus, James and others among its earliest practitioners did, then the fruits of this scholarship must appear quite disappointing.

If there is a single unit of analysis which distinguishes this domain of research (as well as most of the concept learning and problem solving literature), it is the *trial* (Melton, 1963). By any means of analysis, the *trial* must stand as an experimentally created artifact, devoid of the barest semblance of external validity. It is remarkably convenient to organize and arrange sequentially the material for learning experiments in the form of trials, timed or untimed. Such arrangements yield nicely manageable data in the form of "trials to criterion," "average errors per trial," and the like. Even a large field of "metatrialosophy" can develop, which deals with the alternative ways of computing or plotting trial data and the complexities of trials by subjects designs. But where, in the actual world of human beings attempting to learn new material, attain novel concepts or solve unfamiliar problems does one find the external analogue of a trial? For example, those learning the vocabulary of a second language in a natural setting rarely seem to present themselves with a list of new words, limiting their practice to timed exposures in unchanging sequence. Most often they learn new words in the context of ongoing discourse, either explicitly asking for a definition or making a shrewd guess from contextual clues.

To deal with the discontinuity between the settings of research and of educational application, a common language or set of terms for characterizing both experimental educational settings and curricula is needed. Researchers must seriously strive to develop a means of analyzing the characteristics of both experimental and school settings into a complex of *distinctive features*, so the task validity of any particular experiment can be estimated in terms of the particular criterion setting to which inferences are being made. The distinctive features approach was originally developed by Jakobson and Halle (1956) in a study of phonetic systems in language and was initially applied to educational problems by Gibson (1968) in her studies of reading. Gibson and her associates developed a distinctive features analysis for the characteristics of letters or graphemes and demonstrated that they could use such an analysis to generate many fruitful hypotheses concerning problems in learning to discriminate among letters.

A distinctive features approach uses a minimum of categories in combinations to characterize sets of phenomena. Thus, by using only twelve facets, such as grave-acute, lax-diffuse or vocalic-non-vocalic in a variety of "bundles," Jakobson and Halle differentiated among all the phonemes of all languages. Hunt (1962) discussed a similar strategy for identifying the minimum necessary set of features for specifying a particular concept. Barton (1955) described the sociologists' attempts to define the characteristics of social "property space," an analogous problem.

I envisage ultimately a situation in which use of such a distinctive features approach would allow one to characterize the instructional settings to which a particular body of experimental research would most effectively be applicable. Conversely, one could begin with a curriculum of interest and use such an approach to identify critical experiments that might be conducted to examine particular features of the complex curricular *Gestalt*. By specifying the precise degree of overlap between the settings under investigation, the relevance of particular studies to particular applications could be judged more accurately.

Such research might also stimulate progress in related areas. Currently there exists a great deal of argument about the validity of aptitude and achievement tests for disadvantaged populations. These debates usually focus on whether schools in the inner-city ought to rid themselves of all forms of standardized testing. Similarly, the question of using standard entrance examinations for disadvantaged college applicants is of major contemporary importance (Kendrick & Thomas, 1970).

There is no uniform response to such concerns. Clearly, a monolithic judgment cannot be made on the validity of educational tests. Like experiments, tests have internal and external validity. When one assesses a test's *reliability*, he is measuring its internal validity. When he examines what the test maker calls *validity*, he is looking at what the experimenter calls external validity. And like the experiment, the external validity of a test must be judged on at least two bases: population and task validity.

It is possible for members of two subgroups to receive the same average score on a standardized test but for this score to be predictive of very different consequences for each group. Thus the similarity of scores may mask more fundamental underlying differences. The validity of a test score is not only contingent upon the correlation which scores on that test bear with some criterion in the general population. A generally valid test may be differentially valid for different subgroups within the general population. Thus, when questioning the validity of a particular test, one must always ask, "valid *for whom*," (population validity) as well as "valid *for what*?" (task validity).

In some cases, crossvalidation for new populations and settings will confirm the validity of measures that had been held suspect. Thus, Stanley and Porter (1967) demonstrated that the Scholastic Aptitude Test (SAT) was as valid a predictor of academic performance for black students in Southern Negro colleges as it was for white students. Conversely, Shulman (1968a) reported that among adolescents classified as mentally handicapped, the Stanford-Binet is valid as a predictor of vocational competence only for a white middle-class group but not for a black lower-class sample.

By combining both concepts of external test validity, one can generate a "validity matrix" for any test of interest. Such a matrix would cross populations and criteria, reporting the empirically demonstrated validity coefficients for the joint occurrence of a population with a particular set of distinctive features and categories of criterion tasks with their own sets of distinctive features. Whenever a new test is standardized or an old one is restandardized, educators should insist on a standardization design which will yield a validity matrix for that test, rather than a single, generally uninterpretable, validity coefficient. Such an approach would also be consistent with the orientation of the growing body of research on aptitude-treatment interactions in learning (Cronbach and Snow, 1969).

It should be apparent that effectively studying the distinctive features of any settings — experimental treatments, curricula or tests — requires a carefully developed body of research on the nature of environments *per se*.

The educational significance of environment has become a focus of scholarly attention in the light of the most recent reformulations of the nature-nurture issue (Jensen, 1969). Before I examine the problems of weaving the data on environments into the fabric of externally valid educational investigations, a brief analysis of the implications of the nature-nurture issue for the study of environments may be in order.

ENVIRONMENT AND HEREDITY

Stimulated by recent controversies, too many educators have assumed extreme positions with regard to the nature and sources of the environment's impact on the educability of the child. Some lean in the direction of treating young pupils as examples of the classical *tabula rasa*, the clean slate of epistemology, upon which anything they write with the stylus of instruction should cut deeply and without interference. Others insist that educators view most of variability among students in terms of inherited individual differences.

The clear and erroneous implication of the above polarity is that declaring a developing characteristic (such as intelligence) "environmental" testifies to its infinite plasticity while labeling it "inherited" stains it eternally as fixed and immutable.

The recent period has seen the emergence of a new body of literature dealing with such matters, punctuated by Jensen's (1969) provocative assertion that "compensatory education has been tried, and apparently it has failed." (For responses to Jensen's paper see especially Cronbach, 1969; Hunt, 1969; Light and Smith, 1969; and the issues of the *Harvard Educational Review* in which they appear.) Once the unfortunate, if inevitable, polemics and recriminations are eliminated, a number of fundamental misunderstandings remain which contribute greatly to the confusion on this issue. My argument in this section grows from the following propositions:

> 1. There are no grounds for asserting that when the variance in the development of a characteristic is not attributable mainly to heredity, that it is therefore *not* amenable to change via environmental intervention.
>
> 2. There are no grounds for asserting that when the variance in the development of a characteristic is attributable mainly to environment,

that it is therefore a relatively straightforward and simple task, given enough time and resources, to modify that characteristic via environmental intervention.

When an investigator has wished to demonstrate the effects of heredity on the development of a trait such as intelligence, he has generally looked to the data on heritability. Such demonstrations are many. The correlation between the IQs of monozygotic twins is much higher than between dizygotic twins, who are essentially not distinguishable from siblings. The correlation between the IQs of foster children and their natural mothers is always higher than it is with their foster mothers. Roberts (1952) demonstrated the strong effect of genetic factors in the analysis of data on the contrasting IQs of the siblings of the severely and mildly retarded. Such observations say nothing about the *changes* possible in measured intelligence. They assert only that a substantial portion of the *variability* of intelligence scores can be attributed to heredity.

Often the same studies are approached by those supporting a strong environmental hypothesis, and what appears to be an utterly contradictory conclusion is reached. They choose to ignore the correlational findings which the first group finds so seductive. Instead, they compare the mean IQs of twins raised in different environments, emphasizing how *different* the scores are from each other. They also take pains to show that correlations not withstanding, the actual IQs of foster children are generally more similar to those of the foster parents than they are to the natural mothers.

What is important here is that *both* conclusions are drawn reasonably from the data and both are tenable. High correlations can hold between two sets of scores while the mean values of the two sets are highly disparate. Although heredity appears to make a major contribution to the relative rank-ordering of intelligence scores with environment held constant, it is the degree of abundance or deprivation of the environment that seems to contribute most to the attained IQ *status* of individuals.

Much of the heat in the nature-nurture controversy is a function of the assumption that a nurtured characteristic is easily changed, while a "natured" one is stubbornly resistant to modifications. This is simply not the case.

Research is psychotherapy has found emotional disorders, most likely environmental in etiology, remarkably difficult to ameliorate. The cure-rate for infantile autism, which at least some theorists (Bettelheim, 1967) insist is learned, is depressingly low. Conversely, the effects of phenylketoneuria (PKU), an inhereted disorder, can be ameliorated by careful control of diet. Certain inherited hemalitic anemias, such as spherocytosis, are brought under control through chemotherapeutic or surgical procedures. No facile generalizations can be made concerning the relationship between the sources of variability underlying a trait and the changes that can be brought about in its attained status.

Finally, we must keep in mind the important differences between the data on IQ, a variable of primarily theoretical interest, and school achievement, a variable of great practical significance. All studies show school achievement with a significantly lower heritability than IQ (Jensen, 1969). School achievement also stabilizes later than IQ, thus remaining sensitive to environmental change for a longer period (Bloom, 1964).

Thus, an understanding of the ways environment influences human growth and functioning remains a critical domain of inquiry for the educator, whatever his position on nature, nurture and intelligence. Until the gene is as manipulable as the printed word, the educator's only tool will be the modifiable environment. It is the environment which he must manipulate in his studies and from which he fashions the settings of formal instruction.

The study of environments is only one aspect of the needed reconstruction of educational research. In the next section, I discuss a broader conception of desirable general directions for educational research strategy.

RECONSTRUCTION OF RESEARCH STRATEGY

Research in education will have to venture forth from the safe and sterile surrounding of the traditional laboratory and address itself to that most threatening of settings for the educational researcher, the classroom or its carefully created equivalent. Instead of viewing experimental treatments in terms of single variables, such as "phonetic" versus "whole-word" or "discovery" versus "rote," researchers must begin to contrast total educational approaches, e.g., curricula or their parts, whose components have been carefully selected and combined.

Cronbach (1966) advocated that an educational tactic be studied in its proper context. This context includes its place in a sequence of other tactics which have been combined because they are particularly suited to each other. In this sense, the concept of a set of experimental groups which are equivalent to each other in all matters *save one dimension* whose effect is being studied, all of which are in turn compared to some "control group," is probably an anachronism.

> A particular educational tactic is part of an instrumental system; a proper educational design calls upon that tactic at a certain point in the sequence, for a certain period of time, following and preceding certain other tactics. No conclusion can be drawn about the tactic considered by itself. . . .
>
> An educational procedure is a system in which the materials chosen and the rules governing what the teacher does should be in harmony with each other and with the pupil's qualities. If we want to compare the camel with the horse, we compare a good horse and a good camel; we don't take two camels and saw the hump off one of them. (Cronbach, 1966; Pp. 77, 84)

Because educational programs are far more complex than the present psychological theories which purport to explain the teaching-learning process, it might be in the long range interest of both psychological theory and education to ignore those theories for the moment and proceed along a relatively atheoretical path in the study of education. If educators but look around, they will see that in contrast to their theoretical impotence, they do not lack for ideas and even numerous successes in teaching of many things to a wide variety of children. In fact, were there not a fairly large proportion of successful teaching experiences with working class children, a strikingly large proportion of those currently active in educational research would not be there.

It is not my intent to collapse the distinction between research and evaluation, or between "conclusion-oriented" and "decision-oriented" inquiries (Cronbach and Suppes, 1969). I am advocating the pursuit of different types of conclusion-oriented inquiry aimed at creating theoretical formulations that can be useful in guiding educational thought.

In the following section I review a number of research strategies for education. I have not invented them for this paper, nor do I claim that they are totally unique or novel. Other workers in related domains (e.g., Thoresen, 1969), have independently arrived at a partially overlapping list of such recommendations. The strategies I recommended are generally not independent alternative approaches but can be seen to fit into a larger over-all strategy of research which I would call, after Schwab (1960), a "grand strategy" (Keislar and Shulman, 1966, p. 197).

EPIDEMIOLOGICAL STRATEGIES

The epidemiological strategy derives from the kinds of research often conducted in the public health field (Rogers, 1965; Sartwell, 1965). Often an epidemic will spread rapidly through an area, affecting some parts of the population and leaving others unscathed. An important question raised in such a situation is what distinguished those who were susceptible to infection from those who were left unharmed. Similarly, in studies of such social phenomena as delinquency (Glueck and Glueck, 1968), it appears that individuals may come from what is ostensibly a common environment, with some turning to crime and others turning to more socially acceptable activities.

Researchers are warranted in inferring that while, in either case, the two groups in question may appear to come from the same setting, there must be some significant differences between them. Although these two groups were not created experimentally, questions can be raised by identifying representative members of each of the two contrasting groups and by attempting to analyze back and discover all of the differences between them. From such analysis, hopefully would come working hypotheses about kinds of purposeful differences in treatments one might develop either to raise the probability of immunity or the development of socially acceptable behavior patterns in future individuals. These hypotheses could in turn be tested in long-range experimental programs.

It is apparent that similar kinds of epidemiological strategy can and do work in areas such as the study of effective and ineffective teachers, successful and unsuccessful readers, and many others. The important thing to recognize is that researchers do not confirm hypotheses in such a manner, but rather they generate them. Educators have for too long used only armchair or laboratory-based theories for generating hypotheses, or the residue of many years of intuitive experience, rather than systematically gathering careful descriptive data to generate working hypotheses. Such epidemiological strategies could be extremely useful as the early stages of a complex program of educational research. The critical attribute of such a strategy is examining in detail the background variables which distinguish effective from ineffective performers in a particular domain for the purpose of using such discriminators as the basis for creating experimental treatment or training programs.

"GRAMMARS OF BEHAVIOR" STRATEGIES

A second strategy for using descriptive research to develop a testable set of models for education comes from the work done by field linguists as they confront previously unexplored aspects of linguistic systems and attempt to write adequate grammars for them. When a linguist confronts the problem of writing a new grammar, he generally begins by collecting a large corpus of speech from selected informants who are designated *a priori* as "native speakers" of that language. It is then asserted that their capacity to *perform* the operations of speaking and hearing that language rest upon an underlying system of rules, of which they are generally not conscious, which constitute the grammatical *competence* of the speaker. The linguist's task, once he has collected his corpus of speech, is to subject the data to a series of careful analyses in order to discover and make explicit that underlying rule system, which is known as the *grammar* of the language (Chomsky, 1965). As in my earlier examples, such formulations must subsequently be confirmed through cross-validation.

Analogous processes have been used in psychology for generating rule systems for providing mathematical theorems (Newell, Shaw and Simon, 1958) and for interpreting protocols of the Minnesota Multiphasic Personality Inventory (Kleinmuntz, 1968). It appears that similar approaches could be developed for studying the processes of education. The strategy would involve initially identifying *criterial educators*, who, like the native speaker of the language in linguistic studies, are taken to represent some standard of excellence as practitioner of the educational arts. Careful descriptive protocols of the criterial educators' *verbal and non-verbal* behavior would then be gathered and, using behavioral equivalents of the linguistic rule discovery tactics, educational researchers would attempt to write a grammar of their teaching behaviors. This grammar would be a set of rules adequate to account for their functioning. I would hypothesize that once made explicit and cross-validated, such rules could be used to develop instructional procedures to help new students attain the critical performer's level of competence. Jenkins (1969) reported that he and his co-workers are attempting similar grammatical analyses of the behavior of children attempting to perform certain of the Piagetian tasks. My colleagues and I (Shulman, 1968b) are also working with such a model for the study of criterial performance among medical diagnosticians.

An important lesson to be learned from experience with this kind of strategy as used by psychologists is that one does not limit himself to observation of the overt physical behavior of the subject alone. The evidence from the studies of general mathematical problem solving by Newell, Shaw and Simon, of interpretation of the MMPI by Kleinmuntz, and of chess playing by De Groot (1965; 1966) has made it abundantly clear that psychology's long dormant interest in introspective data must be reawakened. The most effective protocols gathered by these investigators included reports of not only what the subjects did, but also what they said about what they were doing, while doing it. Although I recognize the admonitions concerning introspection raised recently by Hebb (1969), I must insist that the evil reputation which introspection has received is more a function of its misuse by such distinguished figures as Titchener, than it is a function of some intrinsic insufficiency of the approach itself.

SIMULATION IN RESEARCH

I indicated above the need to increase the task validity of experiments by maximizing the similarity between the features of the experimental tasks and those of the ultimate transfer settings to which the research findings were to be inferred. Techniques of *simulation* can be extremely useful in creating such research settings. Here simulation does not refer to the use of games in teaching (Boocock and Schild, 1968) nor to the use of computers to mimic men or systems (Kleinmuntz, 1968). An investigator using simulation attempts to create an artificial environment that resembles the actual environment of interest as closely as possible. However, careful control over every input into the simulation is maintained and elements of the situation can be experimentally manipulated as needed. Thus, the experimental simulation can serve as the ideal middle ground between the artificiality of the typical experimental laboratory and the totally uncontrolled research environment of the behavioral ecologist studying organisms in their natural habitats.

Simulation can be used to create settings for studying widely diverse phenomena in education (Twelker, 1969) as well as specific cognitive functions in realistic situations (Shulman, Loupe and Piper, 1968). Simulation approaches afford a means of taking the working hypotheses generated from the descriptive tactics of epidemiological or behavioral grammar studies and testing them at an intermediate level between the laboratory and the field.

MULTIVARIATE EXPERIMENTAL-LONGITUDINAL STRATEGIES

Most conceivable schooling situations will possess certain common characteristics: 1. They involve the attempt to modify or manipulate a setting (with or without teacher) to bring about desired changes in a learner; 2. They take place over relatively extended periods of time; 3. They involve the simultaneous input of multiple influences and the likely output of multiple consequences—some predicated, others not; and 4. They are characterized by variability of reaction to ostensibly common stimuli, that is, not all learners learn equally or react similarly to specific acts of teaching.

What is described above is a highly complex and variegated activity, involving students, subject-matter and sources of instruction in an educational setting. Any research which purports to deal systematically with phenomena at this level of complexity must itself reflect an appropriate level of complexity. The ideal research setting, to be congruent with the description of the educational setting offered above, must be 1. *experimental;* 2. *longitudinal;* 3. *multivariate* at the level of both independent and dependent variables, and consistent with that, 4. *differential,* in that the interactions of the experimental programs with the students' entering individual differences are treated not as error variance, but as data of major interest in the research.

In experimental-longitudinal studies the long-term effects of continuing educational programs are examined (Carroll, 1965). As he does with experiments in general, the researcher attempts to equate the groups of subjects at the beginning of the study either through simple or stratified randomization. These are unlike the typical experiment because the researcher looks at the cumulative effects of ongoing programs rather than at the one-shot effects of a single exposure to instruction. Hence, the educational program is something that continues for a duration of months or years. The evaluation of these programs also is continuous during the full course of the investigation, rather than limited to the program's termination. The criterion variables are chosen to cover as wide a range of relevant behaviors as possible. This longitudinal quality characterizes current studies of computer-managed instruction (Cooley and Glaser, 1969) and computer-assisted instruction (Atkinson, 1968). For this reason alone, these studies are likely to prove educationally relevant, whether or not computer hardware is ever seriously used in schools.

A number of tactics are possible within the general experimental-longitudinal framework. Instead of beginning the entire study at a single point in time, the researcher can stagger the onset of the program over a period of months or years, with different experimental groups entering the treatment phase at different stages. In a situation in which the entire population must receive a program for political or social reasons, but justification can be made for a gradual implementation, the groups beginning the program later can serve as functional controls until their turn comes (Campbell, 1969). Also, a staggered longitudinal design has a built-in replication mechanism in the groups who begin later. These groups can also serve as controls for the possible effect of historical variables on the research results. Finally, a staggered design provides the opportunity for systematic tinkering with programs in midstream without washing out the entire study. In this sense, the problems dealt with in this research strategy become similar to those encountered when evaluating on-going school programs (Provus, 1969; Brickell, 1969).

In general, such research can and should use the techniques of experimental studies whenever possible. For example, while randomization is often a major problem in dealing with the assignment of individual students to program components, it can often be more easily achieved if the unit of analysis is classrooms or schools. That is, it is sometimes easier to randomly assign classrooms or schools than it is to assign pupils (Campbell, 1969).

Testing the hypotheses in experimental-longitudinal designs need not, however, stand or fall on the availability of random assignment and formal control or comparison groups. Approaches to the employment of correlation or regression-based techniques for the assessment of change in non- or quasi-experimental settings are increasing in usefulness and availability (Campbell, 1963, 1967; Campbell, Ross and Glass, in press; Yee and Gage, 1968; Land, 1968).

Designs of the proposed experimental-longitudinal genre will be multivariate in their independent and dependent variables. Cronbach (1966) pointed out the need for a broad spectrum of outcome measures in research on learning by discovery. His recommendations hold equally well for research in other learning areas. Campbell (1969) made a similar point for quasi-experimental studies in the public policy domain.

Cattell (1966b) argued that behavioral science research, previously moribund and sterile, will make visible progress only when it shakes off the constraints of bivariate studies and begins to deal with a multivariate universe in a multivariate way. Naturally, Cattell believes that the multivariate experimental techniques reviewed in his imposing handbook (Cattell, 1966a) hold the methodological keys to conducting such investigations. It is a bit ironic that I recommend this family of techniques to my colleagues in education, since Cattell observes that many of these, such as factor analysis and multivariate analysis of variance, were initially employed for solving educational or psychometric research problems.

When conducting such studies, researchers must not ignore the teacher as an independent variable. Stephens (1967), in a compelling and disturbing review of research, argued that no systematic effects for curriculum or program are observable in fifty years of educational research. He concluded that what determines the effectiveness of a program is that variable generally ignored or ostensibly randomized away — the teacher. Instead of pretending that teachers are merely sources of error variance, researchers must use multivariate experimental designs which include teachers' educationally significant characteristics as factors. At the present time, unfortunately, researchers have no idea what those characteristics are. Epidemiological or behavioral grammar studies may be useful in identifying those features.

In summary, researchers have fallen into the habit of conducting educational research in the classical two-group experimental mode or in the simple correlation descriptive mode. Examination of the true state of educational problems reveals that such approaches are extremely short on educationally relevant external validity. The tools and settings exist, however, for significantly improving such research through use of multivariate experimental-longitudinal designs of many kinds.

REPLICATION

The time has arrived for educational researchers to divest themselves of the yoke of statical hypothesis testing and to assign the test of significance to its proper role. Tukey (1969, p. 85) observed that the use of statistical significance testing was never meant to serve as a substitute for replication:

> The modern test of significance, before which so many editors of psychological journals are reported to bow down, owes more to R. A. Fisher than to any other man. Yet Sir Ronald's standard of firm knowledge was not one very extremely significant result, but rather the ability to repeatedly get results significant at 5%.
>
> Repetition is the basis for judging variability and significance and confidence. Repetition of results, each significant, is the basis, according to Fisher, of scientific truth.

I would recommend the following general strategy for establishing the educational significance of an experiment: 1. Identify the *magnitude* of the treatment effect that will be considered significant in a particular study; ("To be meaningful, this tactic should lead to an increase of at least two reading levels within 6 months.") 2. Establish the *proportion* of subjects who must achieve the desired magnitude of change for the results to be considered significant. ("At least 60% of the pupils should achieve the meaningful level of change.") 3. Report the findings in terms of the proportion of subjects who actually do achieve the desired magnitude of change, as well as in terms of the usual measures of mean difference. Apply techniques analogous to statistical significance testing at this stage to answer questions of inferential stability. In such studies, these "tests" will resemble estimation procedures such as confidence intervals, much more than classical significance testing. 4. Employ a wide range of entering individual difference measures to provide a basis for generating subsequently verifiable hypotheses about the characteristics of those subjects who profit especially from the treatment, and those who do not. 5. Employ a broader range of criterion variables than would be suggested directly by the independent variable alone. The greatest value of a program could turn out to be in its effect on categories of change never considered in its initial development (Campbell, 1969; Schwab, in press). 6. Whatever the findings, *replicate* them.

Make replication as integral a part of the research designs as posttesting or data analysis. Researchers are so unused to conducting replications that many of their current conceptions of replication turn out, after critical scrutiny, to be disturbingly naive and simplistic. Cronbach's (1968) discussion of the problems of replicating findings on creativity and intelligence at different age levels illustrates these problems well.

CLOSING THE METHOD GAP

Cattell (1966a) observed that progress in science is almost always presaged by methodological innovations or breakthroughs. He cites as examples the telescope, microscope and factor analysis, among others. Although Kuhn (1962) would doubtless remind us of the frequency with which new paradigms are created through empirically stimulated *theoretical* rather than methodological reorientations, Cattell's point remains a compelling one. It also raises an important question.

The present era is one of significant methodological progress in the behavioral sciences and education. The development of new techniques, especially in the multivariate domain, proceeds at a rate which dazzles the non-specialist, even though in the eyes of the educational statistician most of the "new developments" are merely variations on a few major themes. Why then do researchers not observe the application of such techniques in the conduct of substantive research? If anything, the gap between the methodologist and substantive researcher in education has grown wider in the past decade. Why has not this undeniable progress in research techniques given birth to the badly needed end of educational research's Dark Age?

The microscope, telescope, and factor analysis were not created by men who considered themselves primarily to be methodologists. They were scholars confronted by compelling research problems for which their extant methods could provide no solutions. Hence, from substantive puzzlement grew methodological innovation. For all practical purposes, there were not two groups — the methodologists and the substantive researchers. There were only researchers, striving to develop methods appropriate to solve the key problems confronting their disciplines.

In the present era this has changed. Educationalists currently train "research design specialists" almost independently of "learning and development men." The disaffection is two-way. Not only do the methodologists tend to disdain the necessity of gaining understanding in the substantive domains; the substantive researchers react defensively by denying the importance of methodological advances and by leading a generalized retreat to Chi Square.

It is rather ironic that most medical schools require at least one year of college mathematics for their entering medical students, although the typical medical curriculum makes woefully little use of any mathematical expertise. Yet, those in educational research, a domain which is becoming increasingly mathematics-involved, generally require no mathematics prerequisites for graduate students in areas like educational psychology.

Educational research training programs and many institutional organizations perpetuate this method gap. Unless it is breached, educational researchers are not likely to become capable of conducting the kinds of externally valid experiments discussed earlier in this paper.

THE ORGANIZATION OF RESEARCH

The need for conducting educational research on a multivariate and longitudinal scale has been recognized by a number of scholars in education. These men suggested many specific strategies for dealing with the problems created by such research (Carroll, 1965; Thoresen, 1969; Baker, 1967). Studies of this magnitude are in vivid contrast to the type most often reinforced in academic circles. These latter studies are usually short, quick, and speedily analyzed. The experimental treatments can be administered in a matter of minutes or hours and the results are assessed immediately thereafter. They are as unlike the form of experiment I have been discussing as they are unlike anything that happens to children in real classrooms. Yet, on the grounds that the greater complexity of classroom activities constitutes no more than a concatenation of these more simple operations sequentially linked together to form a curriculum, the argument is made that such strategies of research are justified for educational investigations.

Researchers must recognize, however, that there is also a network of institutions which work to reinforce this approach to research. As long as the academic setting is one where the patterns of reinforcement are contingent upon the number of articles published by an investigator, rather than the relevance and quality of his investigations; as long as the educational researcher is encouraged to operate as an individual entrepreneur, rather than as part of a research team; as long as the overwhelming proportion of studies conducted in education are one-shot doctoral dissertations designed to collect the most data in the shortest time, educational researchers will continue to produce research which is of little value to developing educational theory. What is needed is more than a change in the way in which the next generation of researchers is trained. A revolution is needed both in the structure of the research enterprise and in the kinds of criteria utilized by administrators who judge the quality of academic performance and parcel out the subsequent monetary and status rewards.

Tukey (1969) made the observation that research in psychology continues to operate as if the individual Ph.D. thesis served as the prototype for scholarly efforts in the field. Education suffers from the same malady. Tukey commented, "Other sciences have faced the transition from the Ph.D. thesis that stood on its own feet to the PH.D. thesis that is part of a bigger entity. No Ph.D. builds his own cyclotron as part of his thesis. No Ph.D. orbits his own satellite to get his data" (Tukey, 1969; p. 88). He recommended increased cooperative efforts in psychological research, with PH.D. theses planned as part of broader general programs of research engaged in collectively by their thesis supervisors.

Education must echo Tukey's call for reorganization of the structure of the educational research enterprise, leaving behind the model of the individual entrepreneur and replacing it with the coordinated, institutionally-supported research team. (Are we now to hear cries against "socialized educational research"?) My experience with several R & D Centers suggests that too often these ostensibly team operations are merely fiscal umbrellas facilitating the same kinds of individual and independent investigation conducted unprofitably for years. Perhaps it should be no surprise that the research "rockets" launched individually so often abort.

SUMMING UP

Has educational research been tried? Has it failed? Surely a kind of educational research has been attempted without notable success. But from its often clumsy gropings (or its over-so-precise figure eights, carefully retracing well-worn patterns) have emerged general strategies and approaches that could show promise for the future.

Educators need not feel uniquely culpable because of the necessity to make dramatic shifts in their most basic tactics of investigation. Even the hitherto impregnable fortress of experimental psychology is currently being shaken by that most devastating of saboteurs — the critic from within. Such eminent experimentalists as James Jenkins (1968) and James Deese (1969) are challenging not only the usefulness of classical S-R behavior theory, but the very behavioral emphasis of psychology itself and the future fruitfulness to psychology of the traditional methods of experimentation. That both Deese and Jenkins were nominated in 1969 for the presidency of the Division of Experimental Psychology of the American Psychological Association makes the situation doubly ironic. In all of the behavioral sciences, well-worn paradigms are being called into question as accomplishment falls far short of promise (Cattell, 1969a). Educational researchers are simply sharing in the long overdue discomfort of their parent and sister disciplines.

The solutions to these difficulties will not arise from a mere reshuffling of the "in" research designs. The approaches employed for training the next generation of educational researchers must change radically. Even more important, the structure of the educational research establishment must be significantly modified to create the necessary conditions for research in education.

REFERENCES

Atkinson, R. C. Computerized instruction and the learning process. *American Psychologist*, 1968, 23, 225-239.

Baker, F. B. Experimental design considerations associated with large-scale research projects, in J. C. Stanley (Ed.), *Improving experimental design and statistical analysis*. Chicago, Ill.: Rand McNally, 1967.

Barker, R. L. *Ecological psychology*. Stanford, Calif.: Stanford University Press, 1968.

Barton, A. H. The concept of property-space in social research. In P. F. Lazarsfeld & M. Rosenberg (Eds.), *The language of social research*. New York: Free Press, 1955.

Bettelheim, B. *The informed heart*. Glencoe, Ill.: Free Press, 1960.

Bettelheim, B. *The empty fortress*. New York: Free Press, 1967.

Bloom, B. S. *Stability and change in human characteristics*. New York: John Wiley & Sons, 1964.

Boocock, S. S., & Schild, E. O. (Eds.) *Simulation games in learning*. Beverly Hills, Calif.: Sage Publications, 1968.

Bracht, G. H., & Glass, G. V. The external validity of experiments, *American Educational Research Journal*, 1968, 5, 437-474.

Brickell, H. M. Appraising the effects of innovations in local schools. In R. W. Tyler (Ed.), *Educational evaluation: New roles, new means*. Sixty-eighth Yearbook, National Society for the Study of Education. Chicago: University of Chicago Press, 1969.

Brunswick, E. *Perception and the representative design of psychological experiments*. Berkeley, Calif.: University of California Press, 1956.

Campbell, D. T. From description to experimentation: interpreting trends as quasi-experiments. In C. W. Harris (Ed.), *Problems in measuring change*. Madison, Wis: University of Wisconsin Press, 1963.

Campbell, D. T. Administrative experimentation, institutional records, and nonreactive measures. In J. C. Stanley (Ed.), *Improving experimental design and statistical analysis*. Chicago: Rand McNally, 1967.

Campbell, D. T. Reforms as experiments. *American Psychologist*, 1969, 24, 409-429.

Campbell, D. T., & Stanley, J. C. Experimental and quasi-experimental designs for research on teaching. In N. L. Gage (Ed.), *Handbook of research on teaching*. Chicago: Rand McNally, 1963.

Campbell, D. T.; Ross, H. L.; & Glass, G. V. British crackdown on drinking and driving: A successful legal reform. *American Behavioral Scientist*, in press.

Carroll, J. B. School learning over the long haul. In J. D. Krumboltz (Ed.), *Learning and the educational process*. Chicago: Rand McNally, 1965.

Cartwright, D. S. Ecological variables. In E. F. Borgatta & G. W. Bohrnstedt (Eds.), *Sociological methodology 1969*. San Francisco, Jossey-Bass, 1968.

Cattell, R. B. (Ed.), *Handbook of multivariate experimental psychology*. Chicago: Rand McNally, 1966. (a)

Cattell, R. B. Psychological theory and scientific method. In R. B. Cattell (Ed.), *Handbook of multivariate experimental psychology*. Chicago: Rand McNally, 1966. (b)

Chomsky, N. *Aspects of a theory of syntax.* Cambridge, Mass.: MIT Press, 1965.

Cooley, W. W., & Glaser, R. The computer and individualized instruction. *Science,* 1969, 166, 574-582.

Cronbach, L. J. The two disciplines of scientific psychology. *American Psychologist,* 1957, 21, 11.

Cronbach, L. J. The logic of experiments on discovery. In L. S. Shulman & E. R. Keislar (Eds.), *Learning by discovery: A critical appraisal.* Chicago: Rand McNally, 1966.

Cronbach, L. J. How can instruction be adapted to individual differences? In R. M. Gagné (Ed.), *Learning and individual differences.* Columbus, Ohio: Charles E. Merrill, 1967.

Cronbach, L. J. Heredity, environment, and educational policy. *Harvard Educational Review,* 1968, 39, 338-347.

Cronbach, L. J., & Snow, R. E. *Individual differences in learning ability as a function of instructional variables.* U. S. Department of Health, Education and Welfare, Office of Education, Contract No. OEC 4-6-061269-1217. Stanford, Calif.: Stanford University, March 1969.

Cronbach, L. J., & Suppes, P. (Eds.) *Research for tomorrow's schools: Disciplined inquiry for education.* London: Macmillan, 1969.

Dave, R. H. *The identification and measurement of environmental process variables that are related to educational achievement.* Unpublished doctoral dissertation, University of Chicago, 1963.

Deese, J. Behavior and fact. *American Psychologist,* 1969, 24, 515-522.

DeGroot, A. D. *Thought and choice in chess.* The Hague: Mouton, 1965.

DeGroot, A. D. Perception and memory versus thought: Some old ideas and recent findings. In B. Kleinmuntz (Ed.), *Problem solving: Research, method and theory.* John Wiley, 1966.

Dewey, J. *Logic: the theory of inquiry.* New York: Henry Holt, 1938.

Eichenwald, H. F., & Fry, P. C. Nutrition and learning. *Science,* 1969, 163, 644-648.

Gibson, E. J. Perceptual learning in educational situations. In R. M. Gagné and W. J. Gephart (Eds.), *Learning research and school subjects.* Itasca, Ill.: F. E. Peacock, 1968.

Glueck, S. & Glueck, E. *Delinquents and non-delinquents in perspective.* Cambridge, Mass.: Harvard University Press, 1968.

Hebb, D. O. The mind's eye. *Psychology Today,* 1969, 2(12), 54-57, 67-68.

Henry, J. *Culture against man.* New York: Random House, 1963.

Hunt, E. B. *Concept learning, an information processing problem.* New York: John Wiley, 1962. (Ch. 2, analysis of the problem.)

Hunt, J. McV. Has compensatory education failed? Has it been attempted? *Harvard Educational Review,* 1969, 39(2), 278-300.

James, W. *The principles of psychology.* Vol. I. New York: Henry Holt, 1890.

Jakobson, R., & Halle, M. *Fundamentals of language.* The Hague, Mouton, 1956.

Jenkins, J. J. The challenge to psychological theorists. In T. R. Dixon & D. L.

Morton (eds.), *Verbal behavior and general behavior theory.* Englewood Cliffs, N. J.: Prentice-Hall, 1968.

Jenkins, J. Language and thought. In J. Voss (Ed.), *Approaches to thought.* Columbus, Ohio: Merrill, 1969.

Jensen, A. R. How much can we boost IQ and scholastic achievement? *Harvard Educational Review,* 1969, 39, 1-23.

Karp, J. M., & Sigel, I. Psychoeducational appraisal of disadvantaged children. *Review of Educational Research,* 1965, 35, 401-412.

Keislar, E. R., & Shulman, L. S. The problem of discovery: conference in retrospect. In L. S. Shulman & E. R. Keislar (Eds.), *Learning by discovery: A critical appraisal.* Chicago: Rand McNally, 1966.

Kendrick, S. A., & Thomas, C. L. Transition from school to college. *Review of Educational Research,* 1970, 40, 151-179.

Kilpatrick, J., & Wirszup, I. *The learning of mathematical concepts: Soviet studies in the psychology of learning and teaching mathematics.* Chicago: University of Chicago, 1969.

Kleinmuntz, B. The processing of clinical information by man and machine. In B. Kleinmuntz (Ed.), *Formal representation of human judgment.* New York: John Wiley, 1968.

Kuhn, T. S. *The structure of scientific revolutions.* Chicago: University of Chicago Press, 1962.

Land, K. C. Principles of pathanalysis. In E. F. Borgatta & G. W. Bohrnstedt (Eds.), *Sociologial methodology 1969.* San Francisco: Jossey-Bass, 1968.

Lenneberg, E. H. *Biological foundations of language.* New York: John Wiley, 1967.

Light, R. J., & Smith, P. V. Social allocation models of intelligence: a methodological inquiry. *Harvard Educational Review,* 1969, 39, 484-510.

McNeil, W. *Rise of the west.* Chicago: University of Chicago Press, 1963.

Melton, A. W. Implications of short-term memory for a general theory of memory. *Journal of Verbal Learning and Verbal Behavior,* 1963, 2, 1-21.

Menchinskaya, N. A. Fifty years of soviet instructional psychology. In J. Kilpatrick & I. Wirszup (Eds.), *The learning of mathematical concepts: Soviet studies in the psychology of learning and teaching mathematics.* Vol. 1. Chicago: University of Chicago, 1969.

Mitchell, J. V. Education's challenge to psychology: The prediction of behavior from person-environment interactions. *Review of Educational Research,* 1969 39, 695-722.

Morgan, C. L. *Psychology for teachers.* London: Edward Arnold, 1894.

Murray, H. A. *Explorations in personality.* New York: Oxford University Press, 1938.

Newell, A.; Shaw, J. C.; & Simon, H. A. Elements of a theory of human problem solving. *Psychological Review,* 1958, 65, 151-166.

Pace, C. R., & Stern, G. G. An approach to the measurement of psychological characteristics of college environments. *Journal of Educational Psychology,* 1958, 49, 269-277.

Provus, M. Evaluation of ongoing programs in the public school system. In R. W. Tyler (Ed.), *Educational evaluation: New roles, new means.* Sixty-eighth Yearbook, National Society for the Study of Education. Chicago: University of Chicago Press, 1969.

Roberts, J. A. F. The genetics of mental deficiency. *Eugenics Review,* 1952, 44, 71-83.

Rogers, F. (Ed.) *Studies in epidemiology: Selected papers of Morris Greenberg, M.D.* New York: G. P. Putnam's Sons, 1965.

Sartwell, P. In K. F. Maxcy & M. Rosenau (Eds.), *Preventive medicine and public health.* (9th ed.) New York: Appleton-Century-Crofts, 1965.

Schwab, J. J. What do scientists do? *Behavioral Science,* 1960, 5, 1-27.

Schwab, J. J. Curriculum and the practical. *School Review,* in press.

Shulman, L. S. Negro-white differences in employability, self-concept, and related measures among adolescents classified as mentally handicapped. *Journal of Negro Education,* 1968, 37, 227-240. (a)

Shulman, L. S. Inquiry, computers and medical education. *Proceedings of the conference on the use of computers in medical education.* Oklahoma City: University of Oklahoma Medical Center, 1968, 48-52. (b)

Shulman, L. S.; Loupe, M. J.; & Piper, R. M. *Studies of the inquiry process.* Department of Health, Education and Welfare, Office of Education, Project No. 5-0597. East Lansing: Michigan State University, July 1968.

Stanley, J. C., & Porter, A. C. Correlation of scholastic aptitude test score with college grades for negroes versus whites. *Journal of Educational Measurement,* 1967, 4, 199-218.

Stephens, J. M. *The process of schooling, a psychological examination.* New York: Holt, Rinehart and Winston, 1967.

Thoresen, C. E. Relevance and research in counseling. *Review of Educational Research,* 1969, 39, 263-281.

Tukey, J. W. Analyzing data: Sanctification or detective work? *American Psychologist,* 1969, 24, 83-91.

Twelker, P. A. (Ed.), *Instructional simulation systems: An annotated bibliography.* Corvallis, Ore.: Continuing Education Publications, Oregon State University, 1969.

Watson, J. B. Psychology as the behaviorist views it. *Psychological Review,* 1913, 20, 158-177.

Wiggins, J. A. Hypothesis validity and experimental laboratory methods. In H. M. Blalock, Jr., & A. B. Blalock (Eds.), *Methodology in social research.* New York: McGraw-Hill, 1968.

Wolf, R. W. *The identification and measurement of environmental process variables related to intelligence.* Unpublished doctoral dissertation, University of Chicago, 1964.

Yee, A. H., & Gage, N. L. Techniques for estimating the source and direction of causal influence in panel data. *Psychological Bulletin,* 1968, 70, 115-126.

THE POLITICAL ECONOMICS
OF EFFECTIVE SCHOOLING

Edmund Gordon

Almost as serious as is the failure of our society to insure the optimal development of all its members, is the repeated effort at excusing the society and its institutions from responsibility for insuring such development. Over the years the arguments vary. At one time we are told that certain groups are incapable of learning, as was asserted when low status persons were denied education. At another period we are told that development and achievement are unequal because of factors in the personality of which we are unconscious and that introspective psychotherapeutic preoccupation is the solution. And at still another period we are told that the institutions responsible for schooling can do little, only radical changes in the society itself can make a difference. These assertions have two characteristics in common: 1. No one of them has ever been subjected to a definitive research investigation in which the hypothesis is tested (some of us think they are not researchable questions) and 2. All of them relieve the schools and to some extent the society of responsibility for doing anything. Clearly if certain people are incapable of learning or too sick to learn or cannot learn until utopia is achieved, why try to improve education or why invest large sums of money in the equalization of educational opportunity or why bother to give all our citizens equal access to these dysfunctional institutions.

As a professor of education, I want to discuss the meaning of some of the recent attempts to use educational and behavioral science data to support the assertion that schooling can make little difference in the efforts of low status people — Blacks, Chicanos, Native Americans, Puerto Ricans and poverty stricken whites — to achieve equality or a fair chance at survival. There are primarily two lines of argument which have been advanced.

1. It is asserted that some ethnic groups or races are genetically inferior to others and thus are incapable of benefitting from schooling to the same extent as are others. Among the scholars whose work has been used to support this position are Jensen, Herrnstein, Shockley and others.

2. It is asserted that schools make little difference and are not effective forces in changing the life chances of the pupils who pass through them. Among the scholars whose work has been used to support this position are Jencks, Coleman and very recently an international

group of scholars including my colleague, Robert Thorndike.

In the debate which has emerged around these two issues, considerable energy has been directed at attacking the individuals whose work has been used and some have even objected to the scientific study of the questions as being immoral or politically dangerous. I want to disassociate myself from any of the arguments directed at limiting free research inquiry and serious discussion of the issues. I believe that the pursuit of knowledge and discussion must be uncensored. I shall not use this platform to join the argument concerning the individuals or their motives, however, there are differences among these scholars and some can be clearly identified as more democratic and humane in their convictions than others. What is more important than how these scholars feel and what may be their motives is what the media try to tell us about the meaning of this work and what the society decides to do about the problems at which their work is directed.

It should be of particular significance that those scholarly or not so scholarly pronouncements which support the racist convictions prevalent in the society get a better press than those which do not. Those statements and findings which support our preference not to spend money on the poor or to help low status minorities are given prominance while findings which could lend support to more humanistic development intervention some how seem to be ignored.

For example, when Jensen's work was being published by the Harvard Educational Review and picked up by the press all across this country, there were already major works on the subject which had been ignored. About a year and a half prior to the attention given Jensen's speculations, Margaret Mead and several equally distinguished scholars published through the Columbia University Press, the proceedings of the American Association for the Advancement of Science Symposium on Science and the Concept Race. Neither the black press or the so called liberal white press ran major stories on that contribution to scientific understanding. Could that work have been ignored because it did not come to the popular conclusion that blacks are genetically inferior to whites? And why was that work not highlighted when the press picked up Jensen's work, even if Jensen was not a meticulous enough scholar to have included it and similar works in his own review of existing research on the subject.

Despite the attention that has now been given to the Jensen and Shockley positions, when Professor Kamin of Princeton University presented and published his masterful analysis of the issues and research related the heritability of intelligence and concluded that there is no evidence to support the assertion, little notice of this development was taken by the media. It appears that when our side scores a point they ignore it, but when the opposition "burps" they give it a headline. There are substantive problems however involved in the question that Jensen raises and the answers that he offers.

Having concluded that compensatory education and other attempts to improve the intellectual functioning of poor and minority group youngsters have been to no avail, Jensen uses this conclusion to get into a discussion of some issues with which he is preoccupied. These can be summarized in three areas: 1. determination of the relative contributions of genetic and environmental factors to the development of intellectual function, 2. possible inherent differences between racial groups in the quality and character of intellectual capacity, and 3. the possibility that these differences have important implications for the design of learning experiences and may provide a basis for explaining the failure of the schools to educate certain children.

The first of these issues, concerning the relative influences of heredity and environment on the development of intelligence, simply cannot be resolved. This, in part, accounts for the fact that it continues to be debated. The fact is that the technology of human genetic research does not permit definite study of the genetic constitution of human organisms. We have only in 1969 isolated a single gene — and that in a bacterium. If such technology were available, our attitudes toward research utilizing human subjects would not permit it. Such attitudes would at least preclude the inclusion of high-status groups in experimental, comparative studies. In addition, the economic, political, and military commitments of the society obviously do not permit the kinds of experimentation with controlled and improved environmental conditions necessary to the conduct of such studies.

Even if the question could be answered and even if it were definitively determined that a specific portion or aspect of human behavior and potential were fixed by heredity, as a humanist and as an educator, I would still have the commitment to, and the responsibility for, expanding and optimizing the influence of environmental interactions. This is what directed learning or education is all about. Educators cannot manipulate genes; we can control experience and aspects of our environments.

If and when we are able to speak intelligently about the portion of intellectual function attributable to heredity, it will only be under specific interactions or conditions. When we talk about intelligence, we are talking about phenotype, and phenotype by definition is a function of environmental interactions with genotype. It is my judgment that when and if we are able to separate genotype in human behavioral development, its function will only be determinable in relation to, or as it is expressed through, phenotype. And in that relation its function will be determinable only to the extent that the interaction is specified.

The rather pessimistic view of the plasticity of human potential in selected populations which is advanced by some investigators is in part a function of their limited view of the potential significance of interaction variance. As long as they view environmental interactions in "normal" or traditional terms, these investigators severely limit their perspective and hopelessly bias their results. They seem to dismiss the possibility that interaction can be, may be, and in some instances have been made significant in specified directions. For example,

Goldstein has noted that recent advances in medical science have brought under man's control several physical disorders which are clearly genetic in origin and which might, therefore, according to this limited view of the possibilities of environmental interaction, be regarded as irreversible because genetically "fixed." The discovery of insulin, the isolation of Vitamin D, and the uncovering and control of phenylketonuria, Goldstein (1969) explains:

> . . . are all those exceptional environmental changes which will make this interaction term significant. They indicate that environments everywhere are not merely supportive of hereditary potentialities, but can, at times, reverse deleterious effects. The great achievements of mankind lie in making that interaction term significant. Indeed it could almost be a maxim for schools of education, psychology, public health, and medicine: "Make that interaction significant" [p. 20]

The nature-nurture controversy, as Birch (1968) has indicated, is a false issue perpetuated largely through ignorance of advances in scientific research, particularly regarding developmental process. The confusion between the two concepts "genetic" and "determined" underlies much of the problem. That is, while all aspects of an organism may be thought of as 100 percent genetic, they are not 100 percent determined. Rather, phenotype expressions are the result of a continuous biochemical and physiological interaction of the gene complex, cytoplasm, internal milieu, and external environment throughout the life of the organism.

Birch gives us more detailed information about this interaction process. Developmental influence, he notes, begins to complicate research in behavioral genetics even before birth through the influence of the maternal environment. Thus, even at birth phenotypic expressions do not correlate one to one with genotype. Another source of complication arises through differences in rates of maturation and in the patterning of maturation times among separate traits, which may lead to alterations in the patterns of phenotypic expression which do not arise from genetic differences in that trait.

In addition, Birch has noted, studies in behavioral genetics suffer equally from the fact that behavioral analysis is still at a rudimentary stage. What emerges in most research is the end product of learning a maze, the end score differences in discrimination, or mean differences between groups in intelligence test scores, and so on, and there is almost no determination of the specific characteristics of the organism that are involved in the mastery of the presented problem. The classic study by Tyron (1940) of the selective breeding of "bright" and "dull" rats illustrates the problem. Analysis of Tyron's study by subsequent investigators suggested that what the rats had been selected for was not "intelligence" but responsiveness to visual or nonvisual cues and aspects of temperament. Searle (1949), for example, showed that when visual cures were used, Tyron's "dull" rats were in some circumstances more effective learners than his "bright" strain.

As Birch pointed out:

> If the data of behavioral genetics permit us to draw any conclusions with respect to learning ability it is that learning ability is by no means a unitary trait, and that in different organisms different patterns of responsiveness, of motivation, of emotionality, and of antecedent history contribute substantially to determining which subgrouping will learn most effectively under conditions of different instruction and task demand. It appears, therefore, that a sober judgment would lead us to conclude that differences in learning achievements, whether measured by intelligence tests or by school achievement in human beings, represent the products of different degrees of goodness of fit between the learner, the task, and, in particular, the instructional mode. Such conclusions have positive rather than pejorative implications for a consideration of differences in learning style and achievement in human social groupings [Birch, 1968, p. 56].

Jensen's treatment of the second question that he poses for consideration — the possibility of inherent differences between racial groups in intellectual capacity — is likewise open to criticism on many grounds. According to Fried (1968), the humanistic intentions of most investigators who have studied intelligence, ability, or achievement endowment among different races do not alter the fact that their studies have invariably been based on racial constructs that are destructive and antisocial in addition to being unscientific. In almost all studies the so-called racial background of individual respondents and respondent populations has been derived in ways that show no resemblance to means used by genetic specialists. In those few cases where any information is given about criteria of assortment, one usually finds that skin color has been the sole or dominant criterion, and that is measured by the eye. In other words, the actual genetic background of the subjects is uncontrolled. The classic study by Shuey (1966) on the testing of Negro intelligence illustrates the racist implications of investigations conceived in this mode. In fact, there is as yet no study on a so-called racial sample that adequately links intelligence potential ability, educability, or even achievement to a specifiable set of genetic coordinates associated with an aggregate larger than a familyline or perhaps lineage.

The most useful studies linking race and certain specified socially valued traits make no pretense of dealing with biogenetic race: rather, they openly work with categories of "social race." A case in point is the massive survey by Coleman (1966), "Equality of Educational Opportunity," which focused on psychological reactions of being identified and identifying oneself as a Negro in the United States. If race is to be treated as a sociocultural construct, it is important to get the individual's views on his own identification and the identification he applies to others. However, if race is to be treated on a biological construct, the lay individual's views of his own racial identity or that of anyone else are unqualified and immaterial.

These two concepts of race relate to another flaw in such research to date, most of which has given insufficient attention to the problem of control for economic condition and social-status variance, not to mention physical conditions and surroundings. Investigators conducting these studies seem to feel that they have controlled for socioeconomic variance when the two comparison groups are selected from comparable income or occupational levels. However, most students of economic and ethnic status concede that equal income for whites and blacks in the United States, or comparable occupational level, greatly camouflages differential patterns of cultural experience and social interaction. Unless one is also arguing that conditions of life have no impact on affective and cognitive development, these sources of variance cannot be ignored in equating groups.

Even when comparison groups are established on the basis of comparability of income and of life conditions within the generation being studied, the problems of intergenerational variance and its contribution to physical and behavioral development are ignored. If, for instance, one selects fifty middle-class white children in New York City and compares them with fifty middle-class black children, the likelihood is that the families of the white children will have been at the middle-class status level for a longer time. Then, when one considers the relationship between socioeconomic status and health and nutritional status, and the derivative relationship between health and nutritional status and the quality of fetal life and development, the ludicrous character of failure to control for such variation becomes obvious.

We have, then, in these efforts at studying behavioral differences in racial groups, problems that relate to the identification and specification of pure race as well as problems in control for variations in life conditions. These variations so greatly confound racial effects as to make their separation impossible of solution by those who have sought to investigate the problem thus far. We might conclude that to create the social conditions necessary to make such investigation scientifically accurate and possible would be very likely to actually eliminate the problem before it could be examined!

If these questions regarding intelligence, race, and genetics are so difficult, even impossible, of solution given present scientific skill, what is the relevance of the controversy? Of course, we cannot fail to see the possible racist implications of this kind of superficially supported assertion regarding ethnic inferiority. Broader social consequences threaten if we give prevalence to those theories that posit only a limited effectiveness for environmental interaction. My argument with those who hold this more narrow view is that, despite their claim to interest in the advancement of science, few of them support the kinds and magnitude of changes in social, economic, and political conditions which could make the interaction component more significant and their own research more possible. I cannot accept this stance since it is supportive of the status quo: it means business as usual; it means limited opportunity for black and poor people. It means that we invest too little effort in trying to make the interaction significant, while the majority tries to fix the blame on the victims or on nature for differences, underdevelopment, or school failures, all of which are largely imposed on lower-status persons by man's indifference to, or abuse of, his fellow man.

It is this problem that relates to the purposes and intent of the society or its principal spokesmen that I call to your attention. In a sense it is this issue that Jencks is concerned with but it tends to get lost in his effort to justify his conclusion on the basis of the reanalysis of sundry, secondary data. Jencks uses his analysis of the relationship between schooling and the achievement of economic equality to make the point that the two have little or no direct relationship in the aggregate, that is to say, for the totality of our population what happens in school does not significantly influence the way in which income is distributed in the society. It is this part of his statement which has received considerable attention and is used to support the position of those who would reduce expenditures on schooling or make reduced demands of education. But his basic message is different and more important. Jencks claims that public policy decisions have never been seriously focused on equalization of income or economic status, and concludes that "as long as egalitarians assume that public policy cannot contribute to economic equality directly, but must proceed by ingenious manipulations of marginal institutions like the schools, progress will remain glacial. If we want to move beyond this tradition," he argues, "we will have to establish political control over the economic institutions that shape our society." Now I cannot take issue with this conclusion. I do object to the fact that the portion of Jenck's pronouncement that serves the status quo has been publicized and the part that threatens this has been ignored. Also I have problems with the questions he has posed and the way he has arrived at his conclusions.

As an educator I am not as much concerned with the contribution that education makes to income distribution as I am to its contribution to development of competent, happy and socially useful individuals. When I wear my hat as political economist and political being I am very much concerned with equality of economic status or at least with the abolition of economic disadvantaged status. For a long time now I have known that the problem of economic inequality would not be solved through education in other than some individual cases. I argued that point in my paper "Some Theoretical and Practical Problems in Compensatory Education as an Antidote to Poverty" which is published in Allen's *Psychological Factors in Poverty*. But let us return to the problems of education and the value of schooling. The data of the several studies which Jencks and his associates have reanalyzed use intelligence and achievement test scores as their primary indicators of competence. None of these studies are concerned with happiness and social usefulness as outcome dimensions. Jencks acknowledges some of the limitations of intelligence and achievement testing and dismisses the affective domain with a four page chapter in which he concedes that he knows little about this area and has not given attention to it in his reanalysis. Now there are several problems here.

1. There is no question but that if we look at intelligence and achievement test scores for large numbers of pupils and try to relate them to the characteristics of schools as we usually measure them, we find little variation that can be attributed to the impact of school. This was one of the major findings from the Coleman study, "Equality of Educational Opportunity." However, even Jencks concedes that Coleman's findings and the other available data did not include assessments of teacher-pupil and pupil-pupil interaction. These and other interactions I call process variables which probably make for differences when status variables like number of books, age of building and expenditure per pupil do not. Additionally, since Jencks was looking for gross effects one of Coleman's findings probably seems less important to him. Coleman reported that for the most disadvantaged children and black children quality of school does make a difference in terms of achievement. In other words, differences in the quality and quantity of schooling in the U.S.A. seem to make little difference in your achievement scores unless you are poor or black. If you are both, it seems to me schooling might make a powerful difference in your scores and your life chances.

2. Many educators believe that teaching and learning transactions deeply involve the affective (emotional) domain — one's feelings, sense of happiness, satisfaction, purpose, belonging, etc. It is these variables which are hardest to measure and are usually omitted from these studies either as inputs or outcomes. In fact from the Coleman data we see that a little measure, crudely conducted, of sense of power or environmental control, was more powerfully associated with achievement than any other variable studied save family background. Jencks did not study the affective and process variables, as input or output of the schools.

3. There appears to be considerable confounding or contaminating of data in the kind of analyses Jencks has used to arrive at the conclusion that schooling makes little difference. He concludes for instance that if "all elementary schools were equally effective, cognitive inequality among sixth graders would decline less than 3 percent." Now the data upon which this estimate is arrived at are the same data that reflect the problems referred to in my previous two points. In addition, Jencks uses the term "equally effective." It would be interesting to know what direction his argument would take if we used my term *maximally effective.* Schooling as a part of the process by which we facilitate development in our children must — though it never has — define its goals in terms of maximal effectiveness. This involves us in the process of predicting not what will happen if the child and the school continue to function at their present levels, but what happens if we put the two in orbit and free them from the restraints which probably are limiting both.

We must remember that Jencks was not concerned with what schooling can do to develop people, he was particularly concerned with what schooling can do to increase and equalize economic status. These are related but quite different processes. It is to the process of human development and learning that I have devoted my professional career. An examination of some of the factors which may complicate those processes may help us to put into proper perspective the conflicting opinions we hear concerning the influence of schooling.

For almost twenty-five years, hanging near my desk has been a print of the beautiful Thomas Hart Benton drawing which he aptly titled "Instruction." This sensitive drawing of an old black man with his tattered books, papers, clothing and surroundings is shown working at the task of helping a young black child to learn. It symbolizes an endeavor to which a host of persons, before and after this simple soul, have devoted their efforts — some enthusiastically and with skill, others reluctantly and with incompetence. Would that the problems of teaching and learning were as simple as the spirit Benton captures in this drawing. Too many black children fail to master the traditional learning tasks of schooling. Too many Puerto Rican, Chicano and Native American (American Indian) children are failed in our schools. Children from minority groups and low income families are over represented among our schools' failures. Why?

The problems involved in the equalization of educational achievement patterns across economic and ethnic groups continue to defy solution. The attempts at describing, evaluating and interpreting these problems and the efforts directed at their solution are frequently confusing. Over the past several years a variety of special programs have been developed to improve the educational achievement of disadvantaged children. These programs have spanned a range from preschool through college; their special emphases have included special guidance services to experimental curriculums: they have grown from a few special efforts in the great cities to nation-wide, federally sponsored programs supported by the Office of Economic Opportunity and the Office of Education under the Elementary and Secondary Education Act. Thousands of special programs have been spawned. Ten billion and more dollars have been spent over the past several years. Yet despite all of this activity, there is little evidence to suggest that we have come close to solving the problems of educating large numbers of ethnic minority group and poor white children.

The relative lack of success of these efforts at upgrading academic achievement in the target populations has resulted in some criticizing of the educational services provided, but has also resulted in a renewal of old arguments in support of the explanation of differences in the level of intellectual function across ethnic groups based on alledged inferior genetic traits in lower status groups. Neither of the simplistic approaches to understanding the problems or fixing the blame for our failure to make school achievement independent of ethnic or social class is adequate.

The problems of educating black and other disadvantaged populations who have been accidentally or deliberately, but always, systematically deprived of the opportunity for optimal development is far more complex. The problem of equalizing educational achievement across groups with differential economic, political and social status may confront us with contradictions which defy resolution. Adequate understanding and appropriate planning for an attack upon these problems will require that attention be directed to several issues. Among these are: 1. the problems related to differential patterns of intellectual and social function as well as varying degrees of readiness in multivariant populations served by schools whose programs are too narrowly conceived and too inflexible to provide the variety of conditions for learning dictated by the characteristics of the children served; 2. the problems related to the conditions of children's bodies and the conditions of their lives which may render them incapable of optimal development and which may seriously interfere with adequate function; 3. the problems related to ethnic, cultural and political incongruencies between the schools and their staffs on the one hand, and the children and communities served on the other; and 4. the problems related to the public schools as social institutions which have never been required to assume responsibility for their failures and thus become accountable to the society and its specific members whom they serve.

DIFFERENTIAL CHARACTERISTICS AND DIFFERENTIAL TREATMENTS

Despite the long history in education of concern with meeting the special needs of individual children and the highly respected status of differential psychology as a field of study, schools have made little progress in achieving a match between the developmental patterns, learning styles and tempermental traits of learners and the educational experiences to which they are exposed. A great deal of attention has been given to differences in level of intellectual function. This is reflected in the heavy emphasis on intelligence testing and the placement, even "tracking" of pupils based on these tests. This tradition has emphasized quantitative measurement, classification and prediction to the neglect of qualitative measurement, description and prescription. These latter processes are clearly essential to the effective teaching of children who come to the schools with characteristics different from their teachers and the children with whom most teachers are accustomed. Our research data indicate wide variations in patterns of intellectual and social function across and within subpopulations. These variations in function within privileged populations may be less important because of a variety of environmental factors which support adequate development and learning. Among disadvantaged populations where traditional forms of environmental support may be absent, attention to differential learning patterns may be crucial to adequate development.

Some workers in the field have given considerable attention to differential patterns of language structure and usage. For example, importance has been attached to "black English" or the dialects of black peoples as possible contributing to low academic achievement. These indigenous language forms are viewed by some as obstacles to be overcome. Others view them as behavioral phenomena to be utilized in learning. Workers holding the former position stress the teaching of "standard English" or English as a second language. Those holding the latter view emphasize the adaptation of learning experiences and materials to the indigenous language of the child. The debate is probably not important except as it may reflect respect or lack of respect for the language behavior of the learner. What may be more important than the fact of language difference is the role that language behavior plays in the learning behavior of the specific child. To understand and utilize that relationship in the education of the child requires more than teaching him how to translate "black English" into standard English and requires more than making him a more proficient utilizer of the indigenous language. Understanding the role of one set of behaviors as facilitators of more comprehensive behaviors is at the heart of differential analysis of learner characteristics and differential design of learning experiences. Schooling for black children, indeed for all children in our schools, comes nowhere near to meeting these implied criteria. Assessment technology has not seriously engaged the problem. Curriculum specialists are just beginning to, in some of the work in individually prescribed learning.

LIFE CONDITIONS: HEALTH, NUTRITION AND LEARNING

Contemporary research provides evidence of a variety of behaviors and conditions which are encountered in children from economically disadvantaged backgrounds with sufficient frequency to justify the conclusion that they are either induced by, or nurtured by conditions of poverty. The excellent studies by Knobloch and Pasamanick of the relationships between health status and school adjustment in low-income Negro children in Baltimore, by Lashof of health status and services in Chicago's South Side, and by Birch of health status and related learning patterns in an entire age group of school children in Aberdeen, Scotland, also of the health status of children from indigent families in the Caribbean area, provide mounting evidence in support of the hypothesis that there exists a continuum of reproductive errors and developmental defects significantly influenced by level of income. According to this hypothesis the incidence of reproductive error or developmental defect occurs along a continuum in which the incidence of error or defect is greatest in the population for which medical, nutritional and child care are poorest and the incidence least where such care is best.

These studies point clearly to the facts that: 1. nutritional resources for the mother-to-be, the pregnant mother and fetus, and the child she bears are inadequate; 2. except for the Aberdeen population studied by Birch, representing a society in which health care is considered a right, not a privilege, and is available to all, medical care — prenatal, obstetrical and postnatal — is generally poor; 3. the incidence of subtle to more severe neurologic defects is relatively high in low-income children; 4. case finding, lacking systematic procedures, is hit or miss, leaving the child not only handicapped by the disorder but frequently with no official awareness that the condition exists; and 5. family resources and sophistication are insufficient to provide the remedial and/or compensatory supports which can spell the difference between handicap and competent function.

These health-related conditions are thought to have important implications for school and general social adjustment. We know that impaired health or organic dysfunction influences school attendance, learning efficiency, developmental rate, personality development, etc. Pasamanick attributes a substantial portion of the behavior disorders noted in this population to the high incidence of subtle neurologic disorders. Silver relates a variety of specific learning disabilities to mild to severe neurologic abnormalities in children. Lustman and Greenburg have noted the relationship between frequent or chronic illnesses and poor school achievement. Clearly, adequacy of health status and adequacy of health care in our society are influenced by adequacy of income, leading to the obvious conclusion that poverty results in a number of conditions directly referrable to health and indirectly to development in general, including educational development.

CULTURAL, ETHNIC AND POLITICAL INCONGRUENCIES

Ethnic and economic integration in education for a brief while appeared to be a possible solution to underachievement in lower status children. The data seem to indicate that academic achievement for black children improves when they are educated in middle-class and predominantly white schools. It is not at all clear that ethnic mix makes the difference. However, the evidence overwhelmingly supports an association between separation by economic group and school achievement with low economic status being associated with low school achievement. Consistently, poor children attending school in poor neighborhoods tend to show low level school achievement.

Before-and-after studies of desegregated schools have also tended to show that achievement levels rise with desegregation, although the exact interplay of reactions leading to this result has not yet been conclusively defined. For example, the process of desegregation may, by improving teacher morale or bringing about other changed conditions result in an over-all increase in the quality of education throughout the system. There have been a number of studies examining the possible relationship of integration (along racial or status group lines) and achievement, and the over-all results of these efforts appear to demonstrate that children from lower status groups attending schools where pupils from higher status families are in the majority attain improved achievement levels, with no significant lowering of achievement for the higher status group. However when children from higher status groups are in the minority in the school, there tends not to be an improvement in the achievement of the lower status group.

Although these findings are generally supported in mass data compiled from large-scale populations, studies of minority group performance under experimental conditions of ethnic mix suggest a need for caution in making similar observations for smaller populations and individual cases. From these findings it becomes clear that the impact of assigned status and perceived conditions of comparison (that is, the subjects' awareness of the norms against which their data will be evaluated) results in a quite varied pattern of performance on the part of the lower status group subjects. Thus, it may be dangerous to generalize that across-the-board economic ethnic and social class integration will automatically result in positive improvement for the lower status group.

To further complicate the picture a new renaissance in cultural nationalism among all disadvantaged ethnic minorities has brought into question our assumptions concerning ethnic integration and education. In a society which has alternately pushed ethnic separation or ethnic amalgamation and which has never truly accepted cultural and ethnic pluralism as its model, blacks, chicanos, Puerto Ricans and native Americans are insisting that the traditional public school is not only guilty of intellectual and social but cultural genocide for their children. For many members of these groups the problem in education for blacks is that they have been subjected to white education which they see as destructive to black people. When one views this argument in the context of the current stage in the development of craft unionism in education, the position cannot be ignored. The conditions and status of professional workers in education are justly the concern of their unions but blacks increasingly view the union concern as being in conflict with their concern for their children's development. That in New York City the workers are predominantly white makes it easy for the conflict to be viewed as ethnic in origin unless one looks at the situation in Washington, D.C., where Negroes are heavily represented in the educational staff, but some of the problems between professionals and clients are no less present.

There are class and caste conflicts to which insufficient attention has been given in the organization and delivery of educational services. If cultural and ethnic identification are important components of the learning experience, to ignore or demean them is poor education. If curriculum and delivery systems do not take these factors into account, inefficient learning may be the result. One would hope that black education by black educators is not the only solution, yet we are being pressed to no longer ignore it as a possible solution.

Would that the problems ended even there. It may well be that what has surfaced as cultural nationalism may be only the wave crest of a more important issue. Public schools as social institutions have never been required to assume responsibility for their failures. They, nonetheless, eagerly accept credit for the successes of their students. This may be related in part to the functions that schools serve in modern societies. The noted anthropologist, Anthony Wallace, has discussed the differential attention given to training in technique or skills education for morality, and the development of intellect in societies which are revolutionary, conservative or reactionary. For more than one hundred years the United States has been a conservative society — liberal in its traditions but essentially conservative in its functions. Some of us fear that that conservatism has given way to a reactionary stance. According to Wallace, the conservative society places highest emphasis on training in techniques and skills, with secondary attention to morality (correct behavior) and the least attention to the development of the intellect. Societies in the reactionary phase place greatest emphasis on morality (now defined as law and order) second emphasis on techniques and skills and only slight or no attention to the development of intellect. He sees society in its revolutionary phase as placing greatest emphasis on morality (humanistic concerns), with second-level interest on the development of intellect, and the least attention given to training in technique. Schools may not have developed a tradition of accountability because techniques and skills may be the least difficult of the learning tasks to master, if the conditions for learning are right. For large numbers of children who have progressed in the mastery of technique, their status in the society has facilitated technique mastery. For those who have not mastered the skills our society has been able to absorb them into low skill work and non-demanding life situations. But by the mid 20th century, entry into the labor force and participation in the affairs of the society increasingly requires skills and techniques mastery. Those who would move toward meaningful participation and the assertion of power are increasingly demanding that the schools be accountable not only for pupils' mastery of skills, but also for the nurturance of morality and the development of intellectuality. In fact with the rapidly increasing demand for adaptability and trainability in those who are to advance in the labor force, DuBois' concern with the liberating arts and sciences (the development of intellect) moves to the fore. Yet we must remember that the schools are at present instruments of a conservative (possibly reactionary) society, but blacks, other minority groups and poor people increasingly see revolution (radical change) as the only ultimate solution to the problems and conditions in which their lives are maintained. As such, their concern with schooling may more sharply focus on issues related to morality and intellectual development, broadly defined — concerns which the schools have never proved competent to meet. If circumstance has converted these concerns to educational needs, the schools then, in their present form, are ill prepared to educate these young people whose ideals and goals should be revolutionary, not conservative, and certainly not reactionary. But this does not mean that schooling cannot be effective in the development of young people. To insure that our schools effectively educate our children independent of economic, ethnic, or social background is the overriding challenge to modern education. To achieve this, it would appear that equality of educational opportunity must be viewed as a problem of inquiry and not simply a problem of politics and management. The complex issues related to environmental and genetic influences on educability, the almost endless problems intrinsic to population diversity and the confounding and conflicting problems of institution, learner, and teacher purposes require the attention of sophisticated practitioners and researchers. These specialists must better define the questions as well as their investigations which follow if we are to move the achievement of equality of educational opportunity from slogan to reality.

REFERENCES

Birch, H. Boldness and judgment in behavior genetics. In M. Mead, T. Dobhansky, E. Tobach, and R. E. Light (Eds.), *Science and the Concept of Race*, New York: Columbia University Press, 1968.

Birch, H. Research needs and opportunities in Latin America for studying deprivation in psychological development, PAHO, WHO Scientific Pub. #134, 77-84, 1966.

Coleman, J. et. al. *Equality of Educational Opportunity*, Washington: U. S. Government Printing Office, 1966.

Fried, M. H. The need to end the pseudoscientific investigation of race. In M. Mead, T. Dobhansky, E. Tobach, and R. E. Light (Eds.), *Science and the Concept of Race*, New York: Columbia University Press, 1968.

Goldstein, A. C. A flaw in Jensen's use of heritability data. *Bulletin of the Information Retrieval Center on the Disadvantaged*, 5(4), Fall 1969.

Gordon, E. Some theoretical and practical problems in compensatory education as an antedote to poverty. In V. L. Allen, *Psychological Factors in Poverty*, Chicago: Markham Publishing Co., 1970.

Jencks, C. et. al. *Inequality: A reassessment of the effect of family and schooling in America*, New York: Basic Books, 1972.

Pasamanick, B. and Knobloch, H. The contribution of some organic factors to school retardation in Negro children, *Journal of Negro Education*, 27: 4-9, Winter 1958.

Searle, L. U. The organization of hereditary maze-brightness and maze dullness, *Genetic Psychology Monographs*, 1949, 39, 279-325.

Shuey, A.M. *The Testing of Negro Intelligence*, 2nd ed., New York: Social Science Press, 1966.

Tyron, R. C. Genetic differences in maze-learning ability in rats. In G. M. Whipple (Ed.), *Intelligence: Its Nature and Nurture*, Part I, The 39th Yearbook of the National Society for the Study of Education, Bloomington, Ill., 1940.

Wallace, A. Schools in revolutionary and conservative societies. In E. M. Lloyd-Jones and N. Rosenau (Eds.) *Social and Cultural Foundations of Guidance*, New York: Holt, Rinehart, and Winston, 1968.

index